Newnes

SPANISH
DICTIONARY

NEWNES
SPANISH
DICTIONARY

NEWNES BOOKS

NEWNES·BOOKS

First published in 1976 by
The Hamlyn Publishing Group Limited
Published in 1983 by Newnes Books,
Michelin House, 81 Fulham Road,
London SW3 6RB

Reprinted 1992

ISBN 0 600 36565 4

Printed at Thomson Press (India) Ltd.
Faridabad (Haryana)

Foreword

This dictionary aims to give concise and accurate definitions of 24,000 of the most important words in use in the English and Spanish languages today.

A pronunciation system based on the International Phonetic Alphabet is used (see *Key to symbols used in pronunciation*), indicating the pronunciation of all headwords in both sections of the dictionary.

Modern technical, commercial, and informal usage is given particular attention, in preference to outmoded terms or other expressions not in common contemporary use. Definitions are numbered in order to distinguish senses, and abbreviations are used to indicate use in specific technical, scientific, or commercial fields (see *Abbreviations used in the Dictionary*). An additional feature is the inclusion of idiomatic expressions and phrases, so necessary for the understanding and use of the foreign language.

This dictionary, with its emphasis on modernity, together with its compact form and clear typeface, should prove indispensable in the home, at school, in the office, and abroad.

Abbreviations used in the Dictionary

adj	adjective	*indef art*	indefinite article	*pol*	politics
adv	adverb	*inf*	informal	*poss*	possessive
anat	anatomy	*infin*	infinitive	*pref*	prefix
arch	architecture	*interj*	interjection	*prep*	preposition
aux	auxiliary	*invar*	invariable	*pron*	pronoun
aviat	aviation	*lit*	literature	*rel*	religion
bot	botany	*m*	masculine	*s*	singular
cap	capital	*math*	mathematics	*sci*	science
comm	commerce	*med*	medical	*sl*	slang
conj	conjunction	*mil*	military	*tab*	taboo
cul	culinary	*min*	minerals	*Tdmk*	trademark
def art	definite article	*mod*	modal	*tech*	technical
derog	derogatory	*mot*	motoring	*Th*	theatre
dom	domestic	*mus*	music	*US*	United States
educ	education	*n*	noun	*v*	verb
fam	familiar	*naut*	nautical	*vi*	intransitive verb
fml	formal	*neg*	negative	*v imp*	impersonal verb
game	cards, chess, etc.	*neu*	neuter	*vr*	reflexive verb
gram	grammar	*pers*	person	*vt*	transitive verb
geog	geography	*phot*	photography	*zool*	zoology

Key to symbols used in pronunciation

English

Vowels

i:	meet	u	put	ai	fly
i	b*i*t	u:	shoot	au	how
e	get	ʌ	cut	ɔi	boy
æ	hat	ə	ago	iə	here
ɑ:	heart	ɔ:	sir	ɛə	air
ɔ	hot	ei	late	uə	poor
ɔ:	ought	ou	go		

Consonants

θ	thin
ð	then
ŋ	sing
j	yes
ʃ	ship
ʒ	measure
tʃ	chin
dʒ	gin

' indicates that the following syllable is stressed, as in *ago* (ə'gou).

, placed under an *n* or *l* indicates that the *n* or *l* is pronounced as a syllable, as in button ('bʌtn̩) and flannel ('flænl̩).

Spanish

Vowels

i	*i*sla	o	li*b*ro
e	m*e*sa	u	*u*no
a	*a*la		

Consonants

j	*y*a	θ	*z*orro
ʎ	e*ll*a	β	de*b*er
ɲ	se*ñ*or	ð	co*d*o
tʃ	*ch*ulo		

' indicates that the following syllable is stressed, as in *uno* ('uno).

The Spanish alphabet treats *CH*, *LL*, and *Ñ* as separate letters following *C*, *L*, and *N*. When these letters occur within a word, they will follow *-cz-*, *-lz-*, or *-nz-*, e.g. *saña* after *santuario*, *resollar* after *resolver*, etc.

Plurals of almost all Spanish nouns are regularly formed by the addition of *-s* or *-es*. The few irregular plurals are shown immediately after the part of speech, e.g. **rubí** . . . *nm, pl* **rubíes**. Nouns that do not change in the plural are marked as invariable, e.g. **tocadiscos** . . . *nm invar* record-player.

Feminine forms of nouns are not shown when they can be derived in a regular way from the masculine form. Both masculine and feminine forms are shown when different translations are required, e.g. *hijo* son, *hija* daughter. When the same word may be both an adjective and a noun, the gender of the noun is given only when it is fixed. Thus, **mamífero** . . . *adj,nm* (mammal) indicates that the word is an adjective or a masculine noun; **mellizo** . . . *adj,n* (twin) indicates that the word is an adjective or a masculine or feminine noun (*el mellizo, la melliza*).

Adverbs derived from adjectives are not shown unless the formation is irregular or unless a translation different from that of the adjective is required. Spanish adverbs are regularly formed by the addition of *-mente* to adjectives (*-mente* being added to the feminine form of the adjective if the adjective has both masculine and feminine endings), e.g. *fácil*, *fácilmente*, *rápido*, *rápidamente*.

A swung dash (~) before a change of part of speech indicates that the part of speech refers to the headword, not the preceding subentry shown in heavy type.

Radical-changing verbs, which change their stem vowels when these vowels are stressed, are immediately followed by an indication of the vowel change, e.g. **acertar (ie)**, **aprobar (ue)**, **despedir (i)**. These changes are summarized in Table I below.

Irregular verbs are followed by an asterisk in the headword list in both sections of the dictionary. Table II below summarizes spelling changes that affect a large number of verbs ending in *-cer*, *-cir*, *-ger*, etc. In Table III are listed major verbs whose irregularities are not covered in the other tables.

English irregular verbs

Infinitive	Past Tense	Past Participle	Infinitive	Past Tense	Past Participle
abide	abode or abided	abode or abided	draw	drew	drawn
			dream	dreamed or dreamt	dreamed or dreamt
arise	arose	arisen			
awake	awoke or awaked	awoke or awaked	drink	drank	drunk
			drive	drove	driven
be	was	been	dwell	dwelt	dwelt
bear[1]	bore	borne or born	eat	ate	eaten
beat	beat	beaten	fall	fell	fallen
become	became	become	feed	fed	fed
begin	began	begun	feel	felt	felt
bend	bent	bent	fight	fought	fought
bet	bet	bet	find	found	found
beware[2]			flee	fled	fled
bid	bid	bidden or bid	fling	flung	flung
bind	bound	bound	fly	flew	flown
bite	bit	bitten or bit	forbid	forbade or forbad	forbidden or forbid
bleed	bled	bled			
blow	blew	blown	forget	forgot	forgotten or forgot
break	broke	broken			
breed	bred	bred	forgive	forgave	forgiven
bring	brought	brought	forsake	forsook	forsaken
build	built	built	freeze	froze	frozen
burn	burnt or burned	burnt or burned	get	got	got
			give	gave	given
burst	burst	burst	go	went	gone
buy	bought	bought	grind	ground	ground
can	could		grow	grew	grown
cast	cast	cast	hang[3]	hung or hanged	hung or hanged
catch	caught	caught			
choose	chose	chosen	have	had	had
cling	clung	clung	hear	heard	heard
come	came	come	hide	hid	hidden or hid
cost	cost	cost	hit	hit	hit
creep	crept	crept	hold	held	held
crow	crowed or crew	crowed	hurt	hurt	hurt
cut	cut	cut	keep	kept	kept
deal	dealt	dealt	kneel	knelt	knelt
dig	dug or digged	dug or digged	knit	knitted or knit	knitted or knit
do	did	done	know	knew	known

Infinitive	Past Tense	Past Participle	Infinitive	Past Tense	Past Participle
lay	laid	laid	shear	sheared	sheared or shorn
lead	led	led			
lean	leant or leaned	leant or leaned	shed	shed	shed
leap	leapt or leaped	leapt or leaped	shine	shone	shone
learn	learnt or learned	learnt or learned	shoe	shod	shod
leave	left	left	shoot	shot	shot
lend	lent	lent	show	showed	shown
let	let	let	shrink	shrank or shrunk	shrunk or shrunken
lie	lay	lain			
light	lit or lighted	lit or lighted	shut	shut	shut
lose	lost	lost	sing	sang	sung
make	made	made	sink	sank	sunk
may	might		sit	sat	sat
mean	meant	meant	sleep	slept	slept
meet	met	met	slide	slid	slid
mow	mowed	mown	sling	slung	slung
must			slink	slunk	slunk
ought			slit	slit	slit
panic	panicked	panicked	smell	smelt or smelled	smelt or smelled
pay	paid	paid			
picnic	picnicked	picnicked	sow	sowed	sown or sowed
put	put	put	speak	spoke	spoken
quit	quitted or quit	quitted or quit	speed	sped or speeded	sped or speeded
read	read	read			
rid	rid or ridded	rid or ridded	spell	spelt or spelled	spelt or spelled
ride	rode	ridden	spend	spent	spent
ring	rang	rung	spill	spilt or spilled	spilt or spilled
rise	rose	risen	spin	spun	spun
run	ran	run	spit	spat or spit	spat or spit
saw	sawed	sawn or sawed	split	split	split
say	said	said	spread	spread	spread
see	saw	seen	spring	sprang	sprung
seek	sought	sought	stand	stood	stood
sell	sold	sold	steal	stole	stolen
send	sent	sent	stick	stuck	stuck
set	set	set	sting	stung	stung
sew	sewed	sewn or sewed	stink	stank or stunk	stunk
shake	shook	shaken	stride	strode	stridden
shall	should		strike	struck	struck

English irregular verbs

Infinitive	Past Tense	Past Participle	Infinitive	Past Tense	Past Participle
string	strung	strung	wake	woke	woken
strive	strove	striven	wear	wore	worn
swear	swore	sworn	weave	wove	woven *or* wove
sweep	swept	swept	weep	wept	wept
swell	swelled	swollen *or* swelled	will	would	
swim	swam	swum	win	won	won
swing	swung	swung	wind	wound	wound
take	took	taken	wring	wrung	wrung
teach	taught	taught	write	wrote	written
tear	tore	torn			
tell	told	told			
think	thought	thought			
throw	threw	thrown			
thrust	thrust	thrust			
traffic	trafficked	trafficked			
tread	trod	trodden *or* trod			

[1] when *bear* means *give birth to,* the past participle is always *born.*

[2] used only in the infinitive or as an imperative.

[3] the preferred form of the past tense and part participle when referring to death by hanging is *hanged.*

Table I

Infinitive	Change	Occurs in
acertar, atender	e to ie	1, 2, 3 s, 3 pl present indicative and present subjunctive
aprobar, mover	o to ue	1, 2, 3 s, 3 pl present indicative and present subjunctive
dormir	(1) o to ue	1, 2, 3 s, 3 pl present indicative and present subjunctive
	(2) o to u	1, 2 pl present subjunctive; 3 s, 3 pl preterite
pedir	e to i	1, 2, 3 s, 3 pl present indicative; present subjunctive; 3 s, 3 pl preterite
sentir	(1) e to ie	1, 2, 3 s, 3 pl present indicative and present subjunctive
	(2) e to i	1, 2 pl present subjunctive; 3 s, 3 pl preterite

Spanish verb tables

Table II

Infinitive ending in	Change	Occurs in
-car	c to qu before e	present subjunctive; 1 s preterite
-cer, -cir	(1) c to z before a,o (e.g. vencer, esparcir)	1 s present indicative; present subjunctive
	(2) c to zc before a,o	1 s present indicative; present subjunctive
-gar	g to gu before e	present subjunctive; 1 s preterite
-ger, -gir	g to j before a,o	1 s present indicative; present subjunctive
-guir	gu to g before a,o	1 s present indicative; present subjunctive
-llir, -ñir	omit i after ll or ñ	3 s, 3 pl preterite
-quir	qu to c before a,o	1 s present indicative; present subjunctive
-uir	i to y	1, 2, 3 s, 3 pl present indicative; present subjunctive; 3 s, 3 pl preterite
-zar	z to c before e	present subjunctive; 1 s preterite

Table III

Infinitive	Present Indicative (1,3 s)	Preterite (1 s)	Future	Past Participle
andar	ando, anda	anduve	andaré	andado
caber	quepo, cabe	cupe	cabré	cabido
caer	caigo, cae	caí	caeré	caído
dar	doy, da	di	daré	dado
decir	digo, dice	dije	diré	dicho
erguir	yergo, yergue	erguí	erguiré	erguido
errar	yerro, yerra	erré	erraré	errado
estar	estoy, está	estuve	estaré	estado
haber	he, ha	hube	habré	habido
hacer	hago, hace	hice	haré	hecho
ir	voy, va	fui	iré	ido
oír	oigo, oye	oí	oiré	oído
oler	huelo, huele	olí	oleré	olido
poder	puedo, puede	pude	podré	podido
poner	pongo, pone	puse	pondré	puesto
querer	quiero, quiere	quise	querré	querido
reducir	reduzco, reduce	reduje	reduciré	reducido
reír	río, ríe	reí	reiré	reído
saber	sé, sabe	supe	sabré	sabido
ser	soy, es	fui	seré	sido
tener	tengo, tiene	tuve	tendré	tenido
traer	traigo, trae	traje	traeré	traído
valer	valgo, vale	valí	valdré	valido
venir	vengo, viene	vine	vendré	venido
ver	veo, ve	vi	veré	visto

A

a (a) *prep* 1 to, at. 2 in, on. 3 by, by means of.

abad (a'βaδ) *nm* abbot. **abadesa** *nf* abbess. **abadía** *nf* abbey.

abajo (a'βaxo) *adv* below, down, downstairs. ¡**abajo**! *interj* down with! **de abajo** *adj* lower.

abalanzar (aβalan'θar) *vt* 1 balance. 2 hurl, throw. **abalanzarse** *vr* rush forward.

abandonar (aβando'nar) *vt* 1 desert, leave. 2 abandon. 3 give up. **abandonarse** 1 let oneself go. 2 give way to, yield to. **abandonado** *adj* 1 abandoned. 2 neglected. **abandono** *nm* 1 abandonment. 2 neglect.

abanicar (aβani'kar) *vt* fan. **abanico** *nm* fan.

abaratar (aβara'tar) *vt* lower the price, cheapen. *vi* become cheaper. **abaratamiento** *nm* reduction in price.

abarcar (aβar'kar) *vt* include, take in.

abarrotar (aβarro'tar) *vt* fill to capacity.

abastecer* (aβaste'θer) *vt* supply, provide. **abastecedor** *nm* supplier. **abastecimiento** *nm* supply. **abasto** *nm* provisions.

abatir (aβa'tir) *vt* 1 knock down, demolish. 2 humble. 3 prostrate. **abatido** *adj* depressed, low, prostrated. **abatimiento** *nm* 1 demolition. 2 depression.

abdicar (aβδi'kar) *vt,vi* abdicate.

abedul (aβe'δul) *nm* birch.

abeja (a'βexa) *nf* bee. **abejar** *nm* beehive. **abejorro** *nm* bumblebee.

aberración (aβerra'θjon) *nf* aberration.

abertura (aβer'tura) *nf* opening, hole.

abeto (a'βeto) *nm* 1 fir. 2 fir cone.

abierto (a'βjerto) *v* see **abrir**. *adj* 1 open. 2 honest, sincere.

abismo (a'βismo) *nm* abyss. **abismal** *adj* abysmal.

abjurar (aβxu'rar) *vt* forswear.

ablandar (aβlan'dar) *vt,vi* soften. **ablandarse** *vr* 1 moderate. 2 mellow. 3 relent.

abnegarse (ie) (aβne'garse) *vr* 1 deny oneself. 2 be unselfish.

abobado (aβo'βaδo) *adj* stupid, silly.

abochornar (aβotʃor'nar) *vt* 1 overheat. 2 shame, embarrass. **abochornarse** *vr* 1 blush. 2 get overheated.

abofetear (aβofete'ar) *vt* slap, hit.

abogar (aβo'gar) *vi* 1 plead. 2 advocate. **abogado** *nm* 1 lawyer. 2 solicitor.

abolengo (aβo'lengo) *nm* ancestry.

abolir (aβo'lir) *vt* abolish. **abolición** *nf* abolition.

abollar (aβo'ʎar) *vt* dent. **abolladura** *nf* dent.

abominar (aβomi'nar) *vt* abominate. **abominable** *adj* abominable. **abominación** *nf* abomination.

abonar (aβo'nar) *vt* 1 guarantee, stand surety for. 2 subscribe to. 3 fertilize (earth). **abonado** *adj* reliable, trustworthy. *nm* 1 subscriber. 2 season-ticket holder. **abono** *nm* 1 subscription. 2 guarantee. 3 fertilizer.

abordar (aβor'δar) *vt* board (a ship, etc.). *vi* come into port.

aborigen (aβo'rixen) *adj,n* Aborigine, Aboriginal.

aborrecer* (aβorre'θer) *vt* hate. **aborrecimiento** *nm* hatred.

abortar (aβor'tar) *vt,vi* abort. **aborto** *nm* 1 miscarriage, abortion. 2 failure.

abotonar (aβoto'nar) *vt* button up.

abovedado (aβoβe'δaδo) *adj* arched.

abrasar (aβra'sar) *vt* 1 burn. 2 parch, waste. **abrasarse** *vr* burn (with heat, passion, etc.). **abrasivo** *adj* abrasive.

abrazar (aβra'θar) *vt* embrace, hug. **abrazo** *nm* embrace.

abrelatas (aβre'latas) *nm invar* tin-opener.

abrevar (aβre'βar) *vt* water (an animal, land, etc.). **abrevadero** *nm* drinking trough.

abreviar (aβre'βjar) *vt* 1 shorten, abbreviate. 2 hurry. **abreviatura** *nf* abbreviation.

abrigar (aβri'gar) *vt* shelter, protect, cover. **abrigo** *nm* 1 overcoat. 2 shelter.

abril (a'βril) *nm* April.

abrillantar (aβriʎan'tar) vt polish, burnish.

abrir (a'βrir) vt 1 open. 2 reveal. 3 unfold.

abrochar (aβro'tʃar) vt 1 fasten. 2 button.

abrogar (aβro'gar) vt repeal. **abrogación** nf repeal.

abrumar (aβru'mar) vt 1 weigh down. 2 crush, overwhelm. **abrumarse** vr become foggy. **abrumador** adj 1 exhausting. 2 overwhelming.

abrupto (a'βrupto) adj 1 abrupt, steep. 2 rough.

absceso (aβs'θeso) nm abscess.

ábside ('aβside) nm apse.

absolución (aβsolu'θjon) nf 1 rel absolution. 2 pardon.

absoluto (aβso'luto) adj absolute, complete. **en absoluto** absolutely, by no means.

absolver (ue) (aβsol'βer) vt absolve, pardon, acquit.

absorber (aβsor'βer) vt absorb, soak up. **absorbente** adj absorbent. **absorción** nf absorption. **absorto** adj 1 absorbed, lost in thought. 2 amazed.

abstemio (aβs'temjo) adj abstemious.

abstenerse (aβste'nerse) vr abstain.

abstinencia (aβsti'nenθja) nf abstinence.

abstracto (aβ'strakto) adj abstract. **abstracción** nf abstraction.

abstraer (aβstra'er) vt abstract, remove. **abstraer de** do without, exclude. **abstraerse** vr be preoccupied. **abstraído** adj 1 withdrawn. 2 absent-minded.

absurdo (aβ'surdo) adj absurd.

abuelo (a'βwelo) nm grandfather. **abuela** nf grandmother.

abultar (aβul'tar) vt enlarge, swell. vi be bulky. **abultamiento** nm 1 swelling. 2 bulkiness.

abundar (aβun'dar) vi be plentiful, abound. **abundancia** nf abundance. **abundante** adj abundant.

aburrir (aβur'rir) vt 1 bore. 2 tire. **aburrido** adj boring, dull. **aburrimiento** nm boredom.

abusar (aβu'sar) vt 1 impose upon. 2 misuse. **abuso** nm 1 abuse. 2 imposition.

abyecto (a'βjekto) adj vile, abject.

acá (a'ka) adv 1 here. 2 now, at this time. **acá y allá** here and there.

acabar (aka'βar) vt finish, complete. vi 1 end. 2 die. **acabar de** have just.

academia (aka'ðemja) nf academy. **académico** adj academic.

acaecer* (akae'θer) vi happen.

acalorar (akalo'rar) vt 1 make warm. 2 excite, inflame. **acalorarse** vr become hot or heated.

acampar (akam'par) vi camp.

acantilado (akanti'laðo) adj 1 (of a cliff) steep. 2 rocky. nm cliff.

acaparar (akapa'rar) vt 1 monopolize. 2 hoard.

acariciar (akari'θjar) vt caress, stroke.

acarrear (akarre'ar) vt 1 transport. 2 cause (damage, harm). **acarreo** nm transport, haulage.

acaso (a'kaso) adv perhaps. nm chance. **por si acaso** just in case.

acatar (aka'tar) vt respect, revere. **acatamiento** nm respect.

acaudalar (akauða'lar) vt 1 hoard. 2 acquire. **acaudalado** adj well-off, wealthy.

acaudillar (akauði'ʎar) vt lead, command.

acceder (akθe'ðer) vi accede. **acceder a** agree to. **accesión** nf agreement.

acceso (ak'θeso) nm 1 entry, access. 2 med attack.

accidente (akθi'ðente) nm accident. **accidental** adj accidental.

acción (ak'θjon) nf action. **accionista** nm,f shareholder.

acebo (a'θeβo) nm holly.

acechar (aθe'tʃar) vt 1 spy on. 2 ambush. **acecho** nm 1 spying. 2 ambush.

aceite (a'θeite) nm 1 oil. 2 olive oil. **aceitoso** adj oily. **aceituna** nf olive.

acelerar (aθele'rar) vt accelerate. **acelerarse** vr hurry. **acelerador** nm accelerator.

acentuar (aθen'twar) vt 1 stress. 2 accentuate. **acento** nm accent.

aceptar (aθep'tar) vt accept. **aceptable** adj acceptable. **aceptación** nf acceptance.

acequia (a'θekja) nf irrigation ditch.

acera (a'θera) nf pavement.

acerbo (a'θerβo) adj 1 sharp, sour. 2 harsh.

acerca (a'θerka) prep **acerca de** about, concerning.

acercar (aθer'kar) vt bring near. **acercarse (a)** vr approach. **acercamiento** nm 1 approach. 2 reconciliation.

acero (a'θero) nm steel.

acérrimo (a'θerrimo) adj 1 very strong. 2 obstinate.

acertar (ie) (aθer'tar) vt 1 hit (target). 2 find. 3 succeed. vi be successful. **acertar a** happen to. **acertado** adj 1 correct. 2 well-aimed.

acertijo (aθer'tixo) nm riddle.

ácido ('aθiðo) adj,nm acid.

acierto (a'θjerto) nm 1 success. 2 knack. 3 good shot.

aclamar (akla'mar) vt applaud, acclaim.

aclarar (akla'rar) vt 1 clarify, explain. 2 rinse (clothes). vi clear. **aclaración** nf explanation.

aclimatizar (aklimati'θar) vt acclimatize

acné (ak'ne) nm acne.

acobardar (akoβar'ðar) vt intimidate, frighten.

acoger (ako'xer) vt 1 welcome. 2 accept. **acogerse** vr take refuge. **acogedor** adj 1 (of a room) friendly, welcoming. 2 cosy. **acogida** nf welcome.

acolchar (akol'tʃar) vt 1 quilt. 2 pad.

acólito (a'kolito) nm acolyte.

acometer (akome'ter) vt 1 attack. 2 attempt. 3 overcome. **acometida** nf attack.

acomodar (akomo'ðar) vt 1 adapt. 2 find room for. 3 arrange. vi suit. **acomodarse** vr 1 comply. 2 agree. **acomodación** nf 1 adaptation. 2 accommodation. **acomodado** adj 1 suitable, convenient. 2 wealthy.

acompañar (akompa'ɲar) vt accompany, escort. **acompañamiento** nm 1 accompaniment. 2 following **acompañante** nm 1 escort. 2 accompanist.

acondicionar (akondiθjo'nar) vt 1 prepare. 2 fix. **acondicionarse** vr condition oneself. **bien/mal acondicionado** adj in good/bad condition.

acongojar (akongo'xar) vt sadden.

aconsejar (akonse'xar) vt advise. **aconsejarse** vr seek advice.

acontecer* (akonte'θer) vi happen. **acontecimiento** nm event.

acoplar (ako'plar) vt join, couple. **acoplarse** vr make up, become friends again.

acordar (ue) (akor'ðar) vt 1 decide. 2 harmonize. 3 remind. vi agree. **acordarse** vr 1 agree. 2 remember. **acorde** adj agreed. nm mus chord.

acordeón (akorðe'on) nm accordion.

acordonar (akorðo'nar) vt cordon off.

acorralar (akorra'lar) vt round up (animals, etc.).

acortar (akor'tar) vt shorten. **acortarse** vr be very shy.

acosar (ako'sar) vt 1 persecute, pursue. 2 harass. **acoso** nm 1 pursuit. 2 persecution.

acostar (ue) (akos'tar) vt 1 lay down. 2 put to bed.

acostumbrar (akostum'brar) vt accustom. vi be in the habit. **acostumbrarse a** vr become used to. **acostumbrado** adj usual.

acotar (ako'tar) vt 1 mark out. 2 limit. 3 survey.

acre¹ ('akre) adj 1 bitter. 2 acrid, pungent.

acre² ('akre) nm acre.

acrecentar (ie) (akreθen'tar) vt increase. **acrecentamiento** nm 1 increase. 2 growth.

acreditar (akreði'tar) vt 1 do credit to. 2 prove. **acreditado** adj reputable.

acreedor (akree'ðor) nm creditor.

acribillar (akriβi'ʎar) vt 1 riddle with holes. 2 wound.

acróbata (a'kroβata) nm,f acrobat.

acta ('akta) nf 1 minutes (of a meeting, etc.). 2 record. 3 certificate.

actitud (akti'tuð) nf attitude.

activar (akti'βar) vt stimulate, make active.

actividad (aktiβi'ðað) nf activity, bustle. **activo** adj 1 active. 2 lively. nm comm assets.

acto ('akto) nm act, deed.

actor (ak'tor) nm actor.

actriz (ak'triθ) nf actress.

actual (ak'twal) adj present, actual. **actualidad** nf 1 present (time). 2 pl current affairs. **actualmente** adv really and truly.

actuar (ak'twar) vt operate, work. vi act, work. **actuación** nf Th performance. **actuario** nm law clerk.

acuarela (akwa'rela) nf watercolour.

acuario (a'kwario) nm aquarium.

acuático (a'kwatiko) adj aquatic.

acuciar (aku'θjar) vt incite, urge. **acucioso** adj keen.

acuclillarse (akukli'ʎarse) vr crouch, squat.

acudir (aku'ðir) vi attend, come to.

acueducto (akwe'ðukto) nm aqueduct.

acuerdo (a'kwerðo) nm agreement.

acumen (a'kumen) nm talent.

acumular (akumu'lar) vt collect, gather. **acumulación** nf accumulation. **acumulador** adj accumulative. nm storage battery.

acuñar (aku'ɲar) vt 1 mint, coin (money). 2 wedge.

acuoso (a'kwoso) adj aqueous, watery.

acurrucarse (akurru'karse) vr curl up, crouch, huddle.

acusar (aku'sar) vt 1 accuse, charge. 2 comm acknowledge. **acusación** nf accusation. **acusado** adj accused. nm law accused person, defendant.

acústico (a'kustiko) adj acoustic.

achacar (atʃa'kar) vt attribute.

achaque (a'tʃake) nm illness.

achicar (atʃi'kar) vt 1 make smaller. 2 belittle. 3 naut bale out. **achicarse** vr 1 get smaller. 2 humble oneself.

achicoria (atʃi'korja) nf chicory.

achicharrar (atʃitʃar'rar) vt 1 scorch, overheat. 2 inf annoy.

adalid (aða'lið) nm leader.

adaptar (aðap'tar) vt 1 adapt. 2 adjust. **adaptabilidad** nf adaptability. **adaptable** adj adaptable. **adaptación** nf adaptation.

adecuado (aðe'kwaðo) adj 1 adequate. 2 suitable.

adefesio (aðe'fesjo) nm 1 inf folly, nonsense. 2 ridiculous person or sight.

adelantar (aðelan'tar) vt 1 move forward, advance. 2 speed up. vi 1 progress. 2 (of a clock) be fast. 3 mot overtake. **adelantarse** vr go forward. **adelantado** adj advanced. **adelantamiento** nm advance. **adelante** adv forward(s), on. **de hoy en adelante** in future. **adelanto** nm advancement, progress.

adelgazar (aðelga'θar) vt make thin. vi grow thin or slim.

ademán (aðe'man) nm 1 gesture, motion. 2 pl manners.

además (aðe'mas) adv besides, furthermore. **además de** prep in addition to.

adentro (a'ðentro) adv within, inside.

adepto (a'ðepto) adj adept. nm follower.

aderezar (aðere'θar) vt 1 adorn. 2 prepare. 3 repair. **aderezo** nm 1 preparation. 2 seasoning, dressing.

adeudar (aðeu'ðar) vt owe (money, etc.). vi become indebted by marriage.

adherir (ie) (aðe'rir) vi adhere, stick. **adherirse a** vr stick, adhere to. **adherencia** nf adherence. **adhesión** nf 1 adhesion. 2 support. **adhesivo** adj sticky. nm adhesive.

adición (aði'θjon) nf addition. **adicional** adj extra.

adicionar (aðiθjo'nar) vt add.

adicto (a'ðikto) adj addicted. nm 1 supporter. 2 addict.

adiestrar (aðjes'trar) vt train, teach. **adiestrarse** vr practise.

adinerado (aðine'raðo) adj wealthy.

adiós (a'ðjos) interj,nm goodbye.

adivinar (aðiβi'nar) vt 1 prophesy, foretell. 2 guess. **adivinación** nf 1 prophecy, divination. 2 guesswork. **adivinanza** nf 1 riddle. 2 prophecy. 3 guess. **adivino** nm fortuneteller.

adjetivo (aðxe'tiβo) nm adjective.

adjudicar (aðxuði'kar) vt 1 award. 2 adjudicate.

adjuntar (aðxun'tar) vt attach, enclose. **adjunto** adj attached, enclosed. nm 1 addition. 2 enclosure.

administrar (aðminis'trar) vt control, administer. **administración** nf administration. **administrativo** adj administrative.

admirar (aðmi'rar) vt admire, respect. **admirarse de** vr be surprised at. **admirable** adj admirable. **admiración** nf admiration. **admirador** adj admiring. nm admirer.

admisible (aðmi'siβle) adj admissible, allowable. **admisión** nf 1 admission. 2 acceptance.

admitir (aðmi'tir) vt 1 admit. 2 accept, allow.

adobar (aðo'βar) vt 1 prepare, dress (food, etc.). 2 pickle.

adolecer* (aðole'θer) vi fall ill. **adolecer de** suffer from.

adolescencia (aðoles'θenθja) nf adolescence. **adolescente** adj,n adolescent.

adónde (a'ðonde) conj where. **¿adónde?** adv where?

adoptar (aðop'tar) vt adopt. **adopción** nf adoption. **adoptivo** adj adopted.

adorar (aðo'rar) vt adore. **adorable** adj adorable. **adoración** nf adoration.

adormecer* (aðorme'θer) vt send to sleep, lull. **adormecerse** vr go to sleep.

adornar (aðor'nar) vt adorn.

adquirir (ie) (aðki'rir) vt obtain, acquire.

adquisición (aðkisi'θjon) nf 1 acquisition. 2 purchase. **adquisitivo** adj acquisitive.

adrede (a'ðreðe) adv on purpose, intentionally.

adscribir (aðskri'βir) vt appoint, assign.

aduana (a'ðwana) nf customs. **aduanero** nm customs officer.

aducir* (aðu'θir) vt offer as proof.

adueñarse (aðwe'narse) vr take possession.

adular (aðu'lar) vt flatter. **adulación** nf flattery.

adulterar (aðulte'rar) vt adulterate. vi commit adultery. **adulterino** adj adulterous. **adulterio** nm adultery.

adulto (a'ðulto) adj,n adult.

adusto (a'ðusto) adj 1 (of a country or region) very hot. 2 grave. 3 stern.

advenedizo (aðβene'ðiθo) adj 1 foreign, strange. 2 upstart.

advenimiento (aðβeni'mjento) nm arrival, advent.

adverbio (að'βerβjo) nm adverb.

adversario (aðβer'sarjo) n adversary. **adversidad** nf adversity, misfortune. **adverso** adj 1 unfavourable. 2 opposite.

advertir (ie) (aðβer'tir) vt 1 notice. 2 warn, advise. **advertencia** nf 1 warning. 2 preface.

adyacente (aðja'θente) adj adjacent.

aéreo (a'ereo) adj aerial.

aerodinámica (aerodi'namika) nf aerodynamics.

aeronáutica (aero'nautika) nf aeronautics. **aeronáutico** adj aeronautical.

aeroplano (aero'plano) nm aeroplane.

aeropuerto (aero'pwerto) nm airport.

aerosol (aero'sol) nm aerosol.

afabilidad (afaβili'ðað) nf affability, friendliness. **afable** adj affable, pleasant.

afamado (afa'maðo) adj famous.

afán (a'fan) nm 1 effort. 2 anxiety. 3 eagerness.

afanar (afa'nar) vt 1 urge, press. 2 inf steal, pinch. **afanarse** vr 1 exert oneself. 2 work hard. **afanoso** adj 1 hectic. 2 hard.

afección (afek'θjon) nf 1 affection. 2 disease.

afectar (afek'tar) vt 1 affect. 2 pretend. 3 law encumber. **afectado** adj affected. **afectivo** adj affective. **afecto** nm 1 affection. 2 emotion. **afecto a 1** affectionate towards. 2 subject to. **afectuoso** adj affectionate.

afeitar (afei'tar) vt shave. **afeitarse** vr make up one's face. **afeite** nm cosmetics, make-up.

afeminado (afemi'naðo) adj effeminate.

aferrar (ie) (afer'rar) vt 1 seize. 2 moor. **aferrarse** vr 1 cling, stick. 2 naut anchor. **aferramiento** nm 1 seizing, capture. 2 naut mooring.

Afganistán (afganis'tan) nm Afghanistan. **afgano** adj,n Afghan.

afianzar (afjan'θar) vt 1 fasten. 2 support. 3 guarantee. **afianzarse** vr 1 steady oneself. 2 become strong.

afición (afi'θjon) nf 1 fondness. 2 inclination. 3 hobby. **la afición** the fans. **aficionado** adj 1 keen, interested. 2 amateur. nm 1 fan. 2 enthusiast.

aficionarse (afiθjo'narse) vr 1 take a liking for. 2 become a follower of.

afilar (afi'lar) vt 1 sharpen. 2 grind. **afilador** nm sharpener.

afiliarse (afi'ljarse) vr join, become a member.

afín (a'fin) adj 1 near to. 2 related. nm relation by marriage.

afinar (afi'nar) vt 1 polish, perfect. 2 mus tune.

afinidad (afini'ðað) nf 1 affinity. 2 relationship.

afirmar (afir'mar) vt 1 affirm, state. 2 make firm. **afirmarse** vr steady onself. **afirmativo** adj affirmative.

aflicción (aflik'θjon) nf affliction, grief.

afligir (afli'xir) vt 1 afflict. 2 sadden. **afligirse** vr grieve.

aflojar (aflo'xar) vt,vi loosen, slacken.

afluencia (aflu'enθja) nf 1 crowd. 2 fluency. 3 abundance. **afluente** nm geog tributary. adj 1 flowing. 2 fluent. 3 abundant.

afluir (aflu'ir) vi flow.

afónico (a'foniko) adj hoarse, voiceless.

aforrar (afor'rar) vt line (clothes, etc.). **aforrarse** vr wrap oneself up. **aforro** nm also **forro** lining (of clothes).

afortunado (afortu'naðo) adj lucky, happy.

afrenta (a'frenta) nf 1 insult. 2 disgrace. **afrentar** vt insult. **afrentarse** vr be ashamed.

África ('afrika) nf Africa. **África del Sur** South Africa. **africano** adj,n African.

afrontar (afron'tar) vt 1 confront. 2 bring face to face.

afuera (a'fwera) adv out(side). **afueras** nf pl suburbs, outskirts.

agacharse (aga't∫arse) vr stoop, crouch.

agalla (a'gaʎa) nf 1 zool gill. 2 pl tonsils. 3 pl inf cheek, guts.

agarrar (agar'rar) vt seize, clutch. vi take hold. **agarro** nm grasp, hold. **agarradero** nm handle.

agarrotar (agarro'tar) vt 1 tighten. 2 strangle. **agarrotarse** vr med become numb.

agasajar (agasa'xar) vt treat well, entertain. **agasajo** nm 1 present, gift. 2 convivial entertainment.

agazapar (agaθa'par) vt inf grab. **agazaparse** vr 1 crouch. 2 hide.

agencia (a'xenθja) nf 1 agency. 2 office. **agencia de turismo** or **viajes** travel agency. **agente** nm agent. **agente de bolsa** stockbroker. **agente de inmobiliario** estate agent.

agenda (a'xenda) nf notebook, diary.

ágil ('axil) adj agile. **agilidad** nf agility.

agitar (axi'tar) vt 1 wave. 2 stir up, excite. 3 shake. **agitación** nf 1 waving. 2 excitement. 3 movement. **agitado** adj 1 excited. 2 agitated.

aglomerar (aglome'rar) vt crowd together.

agobiar (ago'βjar) vt bow or bend down, weigh down. **agobio** nm weight, burden.

agolparse (agol'parse) vr rush or crowd together.

agonía (ago'nia) nf 1 agony. 2 torment.

agonizar (agoni'θar) vt inf bother, urge. vi be dying.

agosto (a'gosto) nm August.

agotar (ago'tar) vt 1 exhaust. 2 drain. **agotado** adj worn out. **agotador** adj exhausting. **agotamiento** nm exhaustion.

agraciar (agra'θjar) vt adorn.

agradar (agra'ðar) *vt,vi* please. **agradable** *adj* pleasant.

agradecer* (agraðe'θer) *vt* 1 thank. 2 be grateful for. **agradecido** *adj* grateful. **agradecimiento** *nf* gratitude.

agrado (a'graðo) *nm* 1 pleasure. 2 liking.

agrandar (agran'dar) *vt* make larger.

agravar (agra'βar) *vt* increase, make worse.

agraviar (agra'βjar) *vt* offend, insult. **agravio** *nm* 1 wrong. 2 offence.

agredir (agre'ðir) *vt* attack, assault.

agregado (agre'gaðo) *nm* 1 aggregate. 2 assistant.

agresión (agre'sjon) *nf* aggression. **agresivo** *adj* aggressive. **agresor** *nm* attacker.

agrícola (a'grikola) *adj* agricultural. **agricultor** *nm,f* farmer.

agricultura (agrikul'tura) *nf* agriculture.

agrietar (agrje'tar) *vt* 1 crack. 2 chap.

agrimensor (agrimen'sor) *nm* surveyor. **agrimensura** *nf* surveying.

agrio ('agrjo) *adj* 1 bitter, sour. 2 rough.

agrupar (agru'par) *vt* gather together. **agruparse** *vr* come together.

agua (a'gwa) *nf* water. **agua dulce** fresh water. **aguas abajo** downstream. **aguas arriba** upstream. **entre dos aguas** undecided, sitting on the fence.

aguacate (agwa'kate) *nm* avocado pear.

aguacero (agwa'θero) *nm* shower, downpour.

aguantar (agwan'tar) *vt* 1 tolerate, bear. 2 hold up. **aguante** *nm* tolerance, patience, fortitude.

aguar (a'gwar) *vt* 1 water down (wine, etc.). 2 spoil.

aguardar (agwar'ðar) *vt* 1 wait for. 2 expect.

aguardiente (agwar'ðjente) *nm* liquor.

aguarrás (agwar'ras) *nm invar* turpentine.

agudeza (agu'ðeθa) *nf* 1 sharpness. 2 keenness. 3 wit. **agudo** *adj* 1 sharp. 2 acute. 3 witty.

agüero (a'gwero) *nm* omen, sign.

aguijar (agi'xar) *vt* 1 goad. 2 urge, encourage. *vi* hurry.

aguijón (agi'xon) *nm* 1 goad. 2 sting.

águila ('agila) *nf* eagle.

aguinaldo (agi'naldo) *nm* Christmas present.

aguja (a'guxa) *nf* 1 needle. 2 hand (of a watch, etc.). 3 spire. 4 *pl* railway points.

agujero (agu'xero) *nm* hole.

aguzar (agu'θar) *vt* 1 sharpen. 2 encourage.

ahí (a'i) *adv* there. **de ahí** so, thus. **por ahí** over there, somewhere.

ahijada (ai'xaða) *nf* 1 goddaughter. 2 protégée. **ahijado** *nm* 1 godson. 2 protégé.

ahincar (ain'kar) *vt* urge. **ahincarse** *vr* hurry. **ahínco** *nm* effort.

ahogar (ao'gar) *vt* 1 drown. 2 suffocate. 3 stifle, repress. **ahogarse** *vr* drown.

ahora (a'ora) *adv* now. *conj* now then. **ahora mismo** at this very moment.

ahorcar (aor'kar) *vt* hang.

ahorrar (aor'rar) *vt* 1 save (money). 2 avoid (trouble). **ahorrativo** *adj* thrifty. **ahorro** *nm* economy, saving.

ahuecar (awe'kar) *vt* hollow.

ahumar (au'mar) *vt* 1 smoke (fish, etc.). 2 make smoky. *vi* give out smoke. **ahumarse** *vr* taste smoky.

ahuyentar (aujen'tar) *vt* 1 frighten off. 2 drive away. **ahuyentarse** *vr* flee.

aire ('aire) *nm* 1 air, atmosphere. 2 appearance. 3 jaunty bearing. 4 tune. **aire acondicionado** air conditioning. **airoso** *adj* 1 airy. 2 windy. 3 jaunty.

aislar (ai'slar) *vt* 1 isolate. 2 insulate. **aislación** *nf* insulation. **aislado** *adj* 1 isolated. 2 insulated. **aislamiento** *nm* 1 isolation. 2 insulation.

ajar (a'xar) *vt* crease, crumple.

ajedrez (axe'ðreθ) *nm* chess.

ajeno (a'xeno) *adj* 1 foreign, alien. 2 belonging to another.

ajo ('axo) *nm* 1 garlic. 2 *inf* shady business.

ajuar (a'xwar) *nm* dowry, trousseau.

ajustar (axus'tar) *vt* 1 adjust. 2 fit. 3 settle. **ajuste** *nm* 1 fitting. 2 adjustment.

ajusticiar (axusti'θjar) *vt* execute.

al (al) contraction of **a el**.

ala ('ala) *nf* 1 wing. 2 brim (of a hat).

alabar (ala'βar) *vt* praise. **alabarse** *vr* boast. **alabanza** *nf* praise.

alabastro (ala'βastro) *nm* alabaster.

alacena (ala'θena) *nf* larder.

alacrán (ala'kran) *nm* scorpion.

alacridad (alakri'ðað) *nf* alacrity, readiness.

alambicar (alambi'kar) *vt* 1 distil. 2 examine carefully. **alambique** *nm* still.

alambre (a'lambre) *nm* wire. **alambrada** *nf* barbed wire, wire fence.

alameda (ala'meða) *nf* 1 poplar grove. 2 tree-lined walk.

álamo ('alamo) *nm* poplar.

alarde (a'larðe) *nm* display, show. **alardeo** *nm* boasting.

alargar (alar'gar) *vt* 1 lengthen. 2 reach for,

hand. 3 make last. 4 stretch out. **alargarse** vr get longer.

alarido (ala'riðo) nm yell, shout.

alarmar (alar'mar) vt alarm. **alarma** nf alarm.

alba ('alβa) nf dawn.

albahaca (alβa'aka) nf basil.

albañil (alβa'ɲil) nm mason, bricklayer.

albaricoque (alβari'koke) nm apricot.

albatros (al'βatros) nm albatross.

albedrío (alβe'ðrio) nm 1 free will. 2 whim.

albergar (alβer'gar) vt 1 shelter. 2 lodge. **albergue** nm 1 shelter. 2 lodging. **albergue para jóvenes** or **albergue juvenil** youth hostel.

albor (albor) nm dawn.

albornoz (albor'noθ) nm bathrobe.

alborotar (alβoro'tar) vt disturb, excite. vi make a noise. **alborotarse** vr become excited. **alboroto** nm disturbance, row, uproar.

alborozar (alβoro'θar) vt gladden. **alborozarse** vr rejoice.

álbum ('alβum) nm album.

alcachofa (alka'tʃofa) nf artichoke.

alcahuete (alka'wete) nm 1 go-between. 2 procurer.

alcalde (al'kalde) nm mayor.

alcance (al'kanθe) nm 1 reach. 2 range, scope. 3 chase. 4 intelligence. **al alcance** within reach.

alcantarilla (alkanta'riʎa) nf sewer, drain.

alcanzar (alkan'θar) vt 1 reach. 2 catch up. 3 obtain. 4 hit. 5 live in the time of. vi reach.

alcázar (al'kaθar) nm 1 castle. 2 fortress. 3 naut quarterdeck.

alcoba (al'koβa) nf 1 bedroom. 2 alcove.

alcohol (alko'ol) nm alcohol. **alcohólico** adj,n alcoholic.

alcornoque (alkor'noke) nm 1 cork tree. 2 inf idiot.

aldaba (al'ðaβa) nf 1 doorknocker. 2 bolt.

aldea (al'dea) nf village.

aleación (alea'θjon) nf alloy.

alegar (ale'gar) vt allege, state. **alegato** nm 1 allegation. 2 law plea.

alegoría (alego'ria) nf allegory. **alegórico** adj allegorical.

alegrar (ale'grar) vt 1 make happy. 2 excite, stir up. **alegrarse** vr 1 be happy. 2 inf get tight.

alegre (a'legre) adj happy, cheerful. **alegría** nf happiness, joy.

alejar (ale'xar) vt remove, move away. **alejarse** vr move away. **alejamiento** nm removal.

Alemania (ale'manja) nf Germany. **alemán** adj,nm German. nm German (language).

alentar (ie) (alen'tar) vi breathe. vt encourage. **alentarse** vr be encouraged. **alentado** adj 1 brave. 2 haughty.

alerce (a'lerθe) nm larch.

alergia (aler'xia) nf allergy. **alérgico** adj allergic.

alero (a'lero) nm eaves.

alerta (a'lerta) nm alert. adj watchful. interj look out!

aleta (a'leta) nf 1 small wing. 2 zool fin.

aleve (a'leβe) adj treacherous. **alevosía** nf treachery. **alevoso** adj treacherous.

alfabeto (alfa'βeto) nm alphabet. **alfabeto morse** morse code. **alfabético** adj alphabetical.

alfarero (alfa'rero) nm potter. **alfarería** nf pottery.

alféizar (al'feiθar) nm window ledge.

alférez (al'fereθ) nm mil second lieutenant.

alfil (al'fil) nm game bishop.

alfiler (alfi'ler) nm 1 pin. 2 brooch.

alfombra (al'fombra) nf carpet.

alforja (al'forxa) nf 1 saddle bag. 2 rucksack.

alga ('alga) nf seaweed.

algarabía (algara'βia) nf 1 Arabic. 2 din, garbled noise.

algazara (alga'θara) nf hubbub, clamour.

álgebra ('alxebra) nf algebra.

álgido ('alxiðo) adj 1 icy cold. 2 culminating (point).

algo ('algo) pron something. adv rather, a bit.

algodón (algo'ðon) nm cotton. **algodón hidrófilo** cotton wool.

alguacil (algwa'θil) nm bailiff.

alguien (al'gjen) pron someone, somebody.

alguno (al'guno) adj some, any. pron 1 some. 2 someone, somebody. 3 pl a few, some.

alhaja (a'laxa) nf 1 jewel. 2 treasure.

alhelí (ale'li) nm wallflower.

aliar (ali'ar) vt ally. **aliado** adj allied. nm ally. **alianza** nf alliance.

alicates (ali'kates) nm pl pliers.

alienar (alje'nar) vt 1 law transfer property. 2 alienate. **alienación** nf alienation. **alienado** adj insane.

aliento (a'ljento) nm 1 breath. 2 spirit, courage.

aligerar (alixe'rar) vt 1 lighten. 2 shorten.

alimentar (alimen'tar) vt 1 feed. 2 encourage. **alimentación** nf feeding, food. **alimenticio** adj nourishing. **alimento** nm food.

aliñar (ali'nar) vt 1 adorn. 2 cul prepare, season. **aliño** nm cul condiment.

alinear (aline'ar) vt line up.

alisar (ali'θar) vt smooth down, polish. **alisador** nm 1 polisher (person). 2 smoothing tool.

alistar (alis'tar) vt 1 list. 2 mil enlist. 3 prepare.

aliviar (ali'βjar) vt 1 lighten, relieve. 2 quicken. **alivio** nm 1 relief. 2 ease.

alma ('alma) nf 1 soul, spirit. 2 person. **con el alma en la boca** scared to death.

almacén (alma'θen) nm 1 warehouse. 2 store, shop. 3 pl department store. **almacenaje** nm storage. **almacenista** nm wholesaler.

almanaque (alma'nake) nm almanac.

almeja (al'mexa) nf clam.

almendra (al'mendra) nf almond. **almendro** nm almond tree.

almiar (al'mjar) nm haystack.

almíbar (al'miβar) nm syrup.

almidón (almi'ðon) nm starch. **almidonar** vt starch.

almirante (almi'rante) nm admiral. **almirantazgo** nm admiralty.

almohada (almo'aða) nf pillow, cushion.

almorzar (ue) (almor'θar) vi lunch.

almuerzo (al'mwerθo) nm lunch, snack.

alojar (alo'xar) vt lodge. **alojarse** vr lodge, stay. **alojamiento** nm lodging(s).

alondra (a'londra) nf lark.

Alpes ('alpes) nm pl Alps.

alpinista (alpi'nista) nm,f sport mountaineer. **alpinismo** nm mountaineering.

alquilar (alki'lar) vt 1 rent. 2 let. 3 hire. **se alquila** to let, for hire. **alquiler** nm 1 letting. 2 hire. 3 rent.

alquimia (al'kimja) nf alchemy. **alquimista** nm alchemist.

alquitrán (alki'tran) nm tar. **alquitranado** adj tarred. nm tarmac.

alrededor (alreðe'ðor) adv around. **alrededor de** prep around, about. **alrededores** nm pl 1 surroundings. 2 outskirts.

altar (al'tar) nm altar.

altavoz (alta'βoθ) nm loudspeaker.

alterar (alte'rar) vt change, alter. **alterarse** vr 1 get upset. 2 get angry. **alteración** nf 1 alteration. 2 disturbance.

altercar (alter'kar) vi argue, quarrel.

alternar (alter'nar) vt,vi alternate. vi be sociable, get around. **alterno** adj alternate.

alternativa (alterna'tiβa) nf alternative, choice. **tomar la alternativa** go through a ceremony

to become a fully qualified bullfighter. **alternativo** adj 1 alternative. 2 alternate.

alteza (al'teθa) nf 1 height. 2 highness (title).

altibajos (alti'βaxos) nm pl ups and downs.

altisonante (altiso'nante) adj 1 pretentious. 2 pompous.

altitud (alti'tuð) nf 1 height. 2 geog altitude.

altivez (alti'βeθ) nf arrogance. **altivo** adj arrogant.

alto[1] ('alto) adj 1 high. 2 tall. 3 loud. adv 1 high (up). 2 loudly. nm 1 height. 2 hill. 3 upper floor (of a building). 4 mus alto. **las altas horas** the small hours. **altura** nf 1 height. 2 top.

alto[2] ('alto) nm, interj mil halt. **hacer alto** stop.

alubia (a'luβja) nf French bean, kidney bean.

alucinación (aluθina'θjon) nf hallucination.

alud (a'luð) nm avalanche.

aludir (alu'ðir) vi mention, refer.

alumbrar (alum'brar) vt illuminate, light up. vi 1 give light. 2 have a baby. **alumbrado** nm lighting. **alumbramiento** nm 1 lighting. 2 childbirth.

aluminio (alu'minjo) nm aluminium.

alumno (a'lumno) nm 1 pupil. 2 law ward.

alusión (alu'sjon) nf allusion.

alzar (al'θar) vt 1 raise, lift. 2 hoist. **alzarse** vr get up, rise. **alza** nf rise (in price, etc.). **alzada** nf 1 height (of a horse). 2 law appeal. **alzado** adj 1 raised. 2 (of a price) fixed. **alzamiento** nm raising, rise.

allá (a'ʎa) adv there. **más allá** further on, beyond.

allanar (aʎa'nar) vt 1 level, flatten. 2 smooth away (a difficulty, etc.). 3 break into (a house, etc.). **allanarse** vr 1 level off. 2 collapse. 3 submit, give way.

allegado (aʎe'gaðo) adj near, close. nm relative.

allegar (aʎe'gar) vt 1 gather. 2 draw near. **allegarse** vr approach, arrive.

allende (a'ʎende) adv beyond.

allí (a'ʎi) adv there. **por allí** over there, that way.

ama ('ama) nf mistress of the house.

amabilidad (amabili'ðað) nf kindness. **amable** adj kind. **amador** (ama'ðor) adj loving, fond of.

amaestrar (amaes'trar) vt 1 train. 2 tame.

amainar (amai'nar) vi lessen, moderate.

amalgamar (amalga'mar) vt 1 amalgamate. 2 mix. **amalgamación** nf amalgamation.

amanecer* (amane'θer) vi dawn. nm dawn, daybreak.

amansar (aman'sar) vt 1 tame. 2 appease.
amante (a'mante) nm lover. nf mistress. adj loving.
amapola (ama'pola) nf poppy.
amar (a'mar) vt love.
amargar (amar'gar) vt 1 embitter. 2 make sour. vi be or taste bitter. **amargo** adj 1 bitter. 2 tart. **amargor** nm also **amargura** nf bitterness.
amarillo (ama'riʎo) adj yellow.
amarrar (amar'rar) vt fasten, moor. **amarradero** nm moorings. **amarre** nm fastening.
amartillar (amarti'ʎar) vt hammer.
amasar (ama'sar) vt 1 knead. 2 prepare. **amasador** nm baker. **amasijo** nm 1 kneading. 2 mixture, hotchpotch. 3 plot, scheme.
ámbar ('ambar) nm amber.
ambición (ambi'θjon) nf ambition. **ambicioso** adj ambitious.
ambiente (am'bjente) nm 1 atmosphere. 2 environment. adj surrounding.
ambiguo (am'bigwo) adj ambiguous. **ambigüedad** nf ambiguity.
ámbito ('ambito) nm 1 boundary. 2 sphere, range.
ambos ('ambos) adj,pron both.
ambulancia (ambu'lanθja) nf ambulance.
ambulante (ambu'lante) adj itinerant, travelling.
amedrentar (ameðren'tar) vt frighten.
amenazar (amena'θar) vt,vi threaten. **amenaza** nf threat. **amenazador** adj threatening.
amenguar (amen'gwar) vt 1 lessen. 2 dishonour.
amenizar (ameni'θar) vt make pleasant.
ameno (a'meno) adj pleasant, agreeable.
América (a'merika) nf America. **América del Norte/Sur** North/South America. **América Latina** Latin America. **americano** adj,n American.
ametralladora (ametraʎa'ðora) nf machine gun.
amiba (a'miba) nf amoeba.
amígdala (a'migðala) nf tonsil. **amigdalitis** nf tonsillitis.
amigo (a'migo) nm 1 friend. 2 boyfriend. **amigo por correspondencia** nm penfriend. adj friendly.
amilanar (amila'nar) vt terrify, scare.
aminorar (amino'rar) vt lessen, reduce.
amistad (amis'tað) nf 1 friendship. 2 pl friends.
amnesia (am'nesia) nf amnesia. **amnesia temporal** nf med blackout.

amnistía (amnis'tia) nf amnesty.
amo ('amo) nm 1 master. 2 owner. 3 inf boss.
amodorrarse (amoðo'rarse) vr become drowsy.
amolar (ue) (amo'lar) vt 1 grind, sharpen. 2 annoy.
amoldar (amol'dar) vt 1 mould. 2 adapt.
amonestar (amones'tar) vt 1 warn. 2 advise. **amonestación** nf 1 warning. 2 marriage banns.
amontonar (amonto'nar) vt 1 pile up. 2 accumulate. **amontonamiento** nm accumulation, piling up.
amor (a'mor) nm 1 love. 2 lover.
amoral (amo'ral) adj amoral.
amordazar (amorða'θar) vt 1 muzzle. 2 gag.
amorfo (a'morfo) adj shapeless, amorphous.
amoroso (amo'roso) adj 1 loving. 2 gentle.
amortiguar (amorti'gwar) vt 1 soften. 2 deaden. 3 moderate. **amortiguador** nm shock absorber.
amortizar (amorti'θar) vt 1 amortize. 2 redeem, recover.
amotinar (amoti'nar) vt incite, stir up. **amotinarse** vr mutiny.
amparar (ampa'rar) vt 1 shelter. 2 protect. **ampararse** vr take shelter. **amparo** nm shelter, refuge.
ampliar (am'pljar) vt 1 enlarge, extend. 2 amplify. **ampliación** nf phot enlargement. **amplio** adj 1 wide. 2 roomy.
amplificar (amplifi'kar) vt amplify. **amplificador** nm amplifier.
ampolla (am'poʎa) nf 1 bubble. 2 med blister. 3 med phial.
amputar (ampu'tar) vt amputate. **amputación** nf amputation.
amueblar (amwe'βlar) vt furnish.
anacronismo nm anachronism.
anagrama (ana'grama) nm anagram.
anales (a'nales) nm pl annals.
analfabeto (analfa'βeto) adj illiterate. **analfabetismo** nm illiteracy.
análisis (a'nalisis) nm invar analysis. **analítico** adj analytic(al).
analizar (anali'θar) vt analyse. **analizador** nm analyst.
analogía (analo'xia) nf analogy.
ananás (ana'nas) nm pineapple.
anaquel (ana'kel) nm shelf.
anarquía (anar'kia) nf anarchy. **anarquista** nm, f anarchist.
anatomía (anato'mia) nf anatomy.
anca ('anka) nf rump, haunch.

anciano (an'θjano) adj old. nm old man. **ancianidad** nf old age.

ancla ('ankla) nf anchor. **anclar** vi drop anchor.

ancho ('antʃo) adj wide, broad. nm width. **a sus anchas** at one's ease. **anchura** nf 1 width. 2 freedom. **anchuroso** adj wide, spacious.

anchoa (an'tʃoa) nf anchovy.

andadas (an'daðas) nf pl tracks, trail. **volver a las andadas** go back to one's old ways.

Andalucía (andalu'θia) nf Andalusia. **andaluz** adj,n Andalusian.

andamio (an'damjo) nm 1 scaffold, platform. 2 scaffolding.

andar* (an'dar) vi 1 walk, move. 2 (of a machine, etc.) work, go. **¡anda!** go on! get along! **andar en 1** be engaged in. 2 tamper with. nm walk, gait.

andas ('andas) nf pl portable platform.

andén (an'den) nm railway platform.

Andorra (an'dorra) nf Andorra. **andorrano** adj,n Andorran.

andrajo (an'draxo) nm rag. **andrajoso** adj tattered, ragged.

anduve (an'duβe) v see **andar.**

anécdota (a'nekðota) nf anecdote.

anegar (ane'gar) vt 1 drown. 2 flood. **anegarse** vr be drowned. **anegación** nf 1 drowning. 2 flooding.

anejo (a'nexo) adj attached, joining.

anemia (a'nemja) nf anaemia. **anémico** adj anaemic.

anestésico (anes'tesiko) adj,nm anaesthetic. **anestesista** nm,f anaesthetist.

anexar (anek'sar) vt annex.

anfibio (an'fiβjo) adj amphibious. nm amphibian.

anfiteatro (anfite'atro) nm amphitheatre.

anfitrión (anfitri'on) nm host.

ángel ('anxel) nm angel. **angelical** adj also **angélico** adj angelic.

anglicano (angli'kano) adj,n Anglican.

angosto (an'gosto) adj narrow. **angostura** nf narrowness.

anguila (an'gila) nf eel.

ángulo ('angulo) nm 1 angle. 2 bend. **anguloso** adj angular.

angustiar (angus'tjar) vt 1 grieve. 2 distress. **angustia** nf anguish.

anhelar (ane'lar) vi 1 med pant, gasp. 2 be eager to. vt desire. **anhelo** nm desire.

anidar (ani'ðar) vi (of birds) nest. vt shelter.

anillo (a'niʎo) nm ring. **anillo de boda** wedding ring.

ánima ('anima) nf soul.

animal (ani'mal) nm animal, beast. adj animal.

animar (ani'mar) vt enliven, encourage. **animarse** vr cheer up. **animado** adj lively.

ánimo ('animo) nm 1 soul, spirit. 2 courage. 3 intention. **¡ánimo!** courage! come on!

animoso (ani'moso) adj lively, spirited, courageous.

aniquilar (aniki'lar) vt annihilate, destroy.

anís (a'nis) nm aniseed.

aniversario (aniβer'sarjo) nm anniversary.

ano ('ano) nm anus.

anoche (a'notʃe) adv last night.

anochecer* (anotʃe'θer) vi grow dark. nm nightfall.

anomalía (anoma'lia) nf anomaly.

anónimo (a'nonimo) adj anonymous. nm unknown person.

anormal (anor'mal) adj abnormal.

anotar (ano'tar) vt note down.

ansiar (an'sjar) vt long for, desire. **ansia** nf 1 anxiety. 2 desire. **ansiedad** nf worry, anxiety.

antagonismo (antago'nismo) nm antagonism. **antagonista** nm,f opponent.

antaño (an'taɲo) adv 1 last year. 2 formerly.

antártico (an'tartiko) adj Antarctic. nm Antarctic.

ante[1] ('ante) prep before, in the presence of.

ante[2] ('ante) nm suede.

anteayer (antea'jer) adv the day before yesterday.

antecedente (anteθe'ðente) nm antecedent. adj preceding.

antecesor (anteθe'sor) adj former. nm predecessor.

antelación (antela'θjon) nf precedence. **con antelación** in advance.

antemano (ante'mano) adv **de antemano** in advance, beforehand.

antena (an'tena) nf 1 antenna. 2 aerial.

antenatal (antena'tal) adj antenatal.

anteojo (ante'oxo) nm 1 small telescope. 2 pl spectacles, glasses.

antepasado (antepa'saðo) nm ancestor. adj previous.

antepecho (ante'petʃo) nm 1 parapet. 2 window sill.

anteponer* (antepo'ner) vt 1 put in front. 2 prefer.

anterior (ante'rjor) adj 1 former, preceding. 2 fore, front.

antes ('antes) *adv* **1** before, formerly. **2** rather, sooner. **antes de** *prep* before. **cuanto antes** as soon as possible.

antiaéreo (antja'ereo) *adj* anti-aircraft.

antibiótico (anti'bjotiko) *adj,nm* antibiotic.

anticiclón (antiθi'klon) *nm* anticyclone.

anticipar (antiθi'par) *vt* bring forward, advance. **anticiparse** *vr* **1** happen early. **2** anticipate. **anticipación** *nf* **1** anticipation. **2** foretaste. **anticipado** *adj* premature. **anticipo** *nm* **1** foretaste. **2** *comm* advance.

anticoncepcional (antikonθepθjo'nal) *adj* birth-control.

anticonceptivo (antikonθep'tivo) *adj,nm* contraceptive.

anticuado (an'tikwaðo) *adj* old-fashioned.

antídoto (an'tiðoto) *nm* antidote.

antiguo (an'tigwo) *adj* **1** old, ancient. **2** former. **3** senior. *nm pl* ancients. **antigüedad** *nf* **1** antiquity. **2** antique.

antílope (an'tilope) *nm* antelope.

Antillas (an'tiʎas) *nf pl* West Indies.

antipatía (antipa'tia) *nf* dislike. **antipático** *adj* disagreeable, unpleasant.

antisemítico (antise'mitiko) *adj* anti-Semitic.

antiséptico (anti'septiko) *adj,nm* antiseptic.

antisocial (antiso'θjal) *adj* antisocial.

antítesis (an'titesis) *nf invar* antithesis.

antojarse (anto'xarse) *vr* want, take a fancy to.

antojo (an'toxo) *nm* **1** whim. **2** *anat* birthmark. **3** *pl* cravings.

antología (antolo'xia) *nf* anthology.

antorcha (an'tortʃa) *nf* torch.

antro ('antro) *nm* **1** cave. **2** den.

antropófago (antro'pofago) *adj,nm* cannibal.

antropología (antropolo'xia) *nf* anthropology. **antropólogo** *nm* anthropologist.

anual (a'nwal) *adj* yearly, annual. **anualidad** *nm* annuity. **anuario** *nm* yearbook.

anublar (anu'βlar) *vt* **1** cloud over. **2** obscure. **anublarse** *vr* cloud over, darken.

anudar (anu'ðar) *vt* **1** knot. **2** join.

anular (anu'lar) *vt* cancel. **anulación** *nf* cancellation.

anunciar (anun'θjar) *vt* announce, proclaim. **anunciador** *nm* announcer. **anuncio** *nm* announcement, advertisement.

anzuelo (an'θwelo) *nm* **1** (fish) hook. **2** bait.

añadir (aɲa'ðir) *vt* add. **añadidura** *nf* addition.

añejo (a'ɲexo) *adj* very old.

añicos (a'ɲikos) *nm pl* bits, fragments.

año ('aɲo) *nm* year. **tener...años** be...years old.

añorar (aɲo'rar) *vt* long for. *vi* be homesick.

añoranza *nf* **1** homesickness, nostalgia. **2** longing.

apacentar (ie) (apaθen'tar) *vt* graze.

apacible (apa'θiβle) *adj* **1** gentle. **2** peaceful.

apaciguar (apaθi'gwar) *vt* pacify, calm.

apagar (apa'gar) *vt* **1** put out, extinguish. **2** switch off. **apagado** *adj* **1** extinguished. **2** dull, lifeless. **3** muffled. **apagón** *nm* blackout, power cut.

apalear (apale'ar) *vt* beat, thrash.

apañado (apa'ɲaðo) *adj* skilful, clever.

aparador (apara'ðor) *nm* sideboard.

aparato (apa'rato) *nm* **1** machine. **2** apparatus. **3** show, display. **aparatoso** *adj* showy.

aparecer* (apare'θer) *vi* appear. **aparecido** *nm* ghost.

aparejar (apare'xar) *vt* **1** prepare. **2** saddle (a horse). **aparejador** *nm* foreman. **aparejo** *nm* **1** preparation. **2** gear, equipment. **3** harness.

aparentar (aparen'tar) *vt* pretend, feign.

aparente (apa'rente) *adj* **1** apparent, seeming. **2** visible, evident.

aparición (apari'θjon) *nf* **1** appearance. **2** publication. **3** apparition.

apariencia (apari'enθja) *nf* **1** appearance, look(s). **2** probability.

apartado (apar'taðo) *adj* separated, distant. *nm* **1** post-office box. **2** spare room. **3** paragraph. **4** box number.

apartamento (aparta'mento) *nm* apartment, flat.

apartar (apar'tar) *vt* **1** separate. **2** remove. **apartarse** *vr* **1** separate. **2** move away. **apartamiento** *nm* **1** separation. **2** isolation. **aparte** *adv* aside, apart. *nm* **1** aside. **2** (new) paragraph. **aparte de** *prep* apart from.

apasionar (apasjo'nar) *vt* stir, rouse deeply. **apasionarse** *vr* get excited or worked up. **apasionado** *adj* **1** passionate. **2** enthusiastic. **apasionamiento** *nm* passion.

apatía (apa'tia) *nf* apathy. **apático** *adj* apathetic.

apear (ape'ar) *vt* get down. **apearse** *vr* dismount, get down.

apedrear (apeðre'ar) *vt* stone. *vi* hail. **apedreamiento** *nm* **1** stoning. **2** hail.

apelar (ape'lar) *vi* **1** *law* appeal. **apelación** *nf* appeal.

apellido (ape'ʎiðo) *nm* **1** surname. **2** nickname. **apellido de soltera** maiden name.

apenar (ape'nar) *vt* **1** grieve. **2** cause pain.

apenas (a'penas) *adv* scarcely, hardly.

apéndice (a'pendiθe) nm appendix. **apendicitis** nf appendicitis.

apercibir (aperθi'βir) vt 1 prepare. 2 warn. 3 notice, observe.

aperitivo (aperi'tiβo) nm aperitif.

apero (a'pero) nm 1 equipment. 2 tools.

apertura (aper'tura) nf opening.

apestar (apes'tar) vt 1 med infect. 2 inf annoy. vi stink.

apetecer* (apete'θer) vt long for. vi attract, have appeal. **apetecible** adj attractive.

apetito (ape'tito) nm 1 appetite. 2 desire.

ápice ('apiθe) nm apex, summit.

apiñar (api'ɲar) vt group together. **apiñarse** vr crowd together.

apio ('apjo) nm celery.

apisonadora (apisona'ðora) nm steam-roller.

apisonar (apiso'nar) vt roll (flat).

aplacar (apla'kar) vt placate, calm.

aplanar (apla'nar) vt flatten, make even.

aplastar (aplas'tar) vt crush, flatten.

aplaudir (aplau'ðir) vt applaud, clap. **aplauso** nm applause.

aplazar (apla'θar) vt 1 postpone. 2 summon (a meeting, etc.). **aplazamiento** nm 1 postponement. 2 summons.

aplicar (apli'kar) vt apply. **aplicarse** vr 1 be applicable. 2 apply oneself. **aplicación** nf application.

aplomo (a'plomo) nm self-possession, assurance.

apocar (apo'kar) vt make smaller, reduce.

apodar (apo'ðar) vt nickname. **apodo** nm nickname.

apoderar (apoðe'rar) vt authorize. **apoderarse de** vr take possession of.

apogeo (apo'xeo) nm peak, summit.

apolillarse (apoli'ʎarse) vr be moth-eaten.

apoplejía (apople'xia) nf apoplexy.

aportar (apor'tar) vt 1 bring, contribute. 2 cause.

aposentar (aposen'tar) vt lodge. **aposento** nm lodging.

apostar (ue) (apos'tar) vt,vi bet.

apóstol (a'postol) nm apostle.

apóstrofo (a'postrofo) nm gram apostrophe.

apoyar (apo'jar) vt support. **apoyar en vi** lean against, rest on. **apoyarse en** vr lean on, be supported by. **apoyo** nm support.

apreciar (apre'θjar) vt 1 appreciate. 2 value. **apreciación** nf appreciation, appraisal. **aprecio** nm 1 comm estimate. 2 esteem, appreciation.

aprehender (apreen'der) vt 1 seize. 2 understand. **aprehensible** adj understandable.

apremiar (apre'mjar) vt 1 urge, press. 2 force. **apremio** nm 1 pressure. 2 law summons.

aprender (apren'der) vt learn. **aprendiz** nm 1 novice. 2 apprentice. **aprendizaje** nm apprenticeship.

aprensión (apren'sjon) nf apprehension, nervousness. **aprensivo** adj 1 apprehensive, worried. 2 nervous.

apresar (apre'sar) vt seize, capture.

aprestar (apres'tar) vt 1 prepare. 2 size. **apresto** nm 1 preparation. 2 sizing.

apresurar (apresu'rar) vt hurry.

apretar (ie) (apre'tar) vt 1 tighten. 2 squeeze in. 3 worry, annoy. 4 grit (the teeth). vi 1 get worse. 2 be too tight. **apretarse** vr squeeze together. **apretado** adj 1 difficult, dangerous. 2 mean. ¡**aprieta!** interj nonsense!

aprieto (a'prjeto) nm 1 squeeze, press, crush. 2 difficulty.

aprisa (a'prisa) adv quickly.

aprisionar (aprisjo'nar) vt imprison.

aprobar (ue) (apro'βar) vt 1 approve. 2 pass (an exam). **aprobación** nf 1 approval. 2 pass (in an exam). **aprobado** adj approved. nm pass mark or certificate.

apropiar (apro'pjar) vt adapt, make suitable. **apropiarse** vr appropriate. **apropiado** adj appropriate, suitable.

aprovechar (aproβe'tʃar) vt profit by, use. vi 1 be useful. 2 progress. **aprovecharse** vr take advantage of, profit by, use. **aprovechado** adj 1 diligent. 2 economical. 3 unscrupulous. **aprovechamiento** nm use, exploitation.

aproximar (aproksi'mar) vt bring nearer. **aproximar a** vr approach. **aproximación** nf 1 approximation. 2 nearness. **aproximado** adj approximate.

aptitud (apti'tuð) nf aptitude. **apto** adj suitable, fitting.

apuesta (a'pwesta) nf bet.

apuntar (apun'tar) vt 1 point. 2 note. 3 sharpen. 4 Th prompt. vi begin to appear. **apuntado** adj pointed. **apunte** nm 1 note. 2 prompter. 3 cue.

apurar (apu'rar) vt 1 tech purify. 2 drain, drink up. 3 examine carefully. 4 annoy. **apurarse** vr worry. **apuro** nm 1 hardship. 2 difficulty.

aquejar (ake'xar) vt med afflict.

aquel, aquella (a'kel, a'keʎa) adj 1 that. 2 pl those. **aquél, aquélla** pron 1 that. 2 the one. 3 the former. 4 pl those. nm inf charm.

aquí (a'ki) adv here. **de aquí en adelante** from now on. **de aquí** hence. **por aquí** this way.

aquietar (akje'tar) vt quieten, calm.

aquilatar (akila'tar) vt test, examine closely.

Arabia (a'raβja) nf Arabia. **Arabia Saudita** Saudi Arabia. **árabe** adj Arab, Arabic. nm,f Arab. nm Arabic (language). **arábigo** adj Arab, Arabic.

arado (a'raðo) nm plough.

arancel (aran'θel) nm tax, tariff.

araña (a'raɲa) nf spider. **araña de luces** chandelier.

arañar (ara'ɲar) vt scratch. **arañazo** nm scratch.

arar (a'rar) vt plough.

arbitrar (arβi'trar) vt,vi 1 arbitrate, judge. 2 referee. **arbitraje** nm arbitration. **arbitrario** adj arbitrary.

arbitrio (ar'βitrjo) nm 1 free will. 2 means. 3 law decision. **4** pl taxes.

árbitro ('arβitro) nm referee, umpire.

árbol ('arβol) nm 1 tree. 2 shaft, axle. 3 naut mast. **árbol de Navidad** Christmas tree. **arboleda** nf grove.

arbusto (ar'βusto) nm bush.

arca ('arka) nf box, chest.

arcada (ar'kaða) nf 1 arcade. 2 pl nausea.

arcaico (ar'kaiko) adj archaic.

arce ('arθe) nm maple.

arcilla (ar'θiʎa) nf clay.

arco ('arko) nm 1 arch, archway. 2 arc. 3 bow. **arco iris** rainbow.

archiduque (artʃi'ðuke) nm archduke. **archiduquesa** nf archduchess.

archipiélago (artʃi'pjelago) nm archipelago.

archivo (ar'tʃiβo) nm archives, records.

arder (ar'ðer) vt,vi burn.

ardid (ar'ðið) nm trick, crafty plan.

ardiente (ar'ðjente) adj 1 burning. 2 ardent, passionate.

ardilla (ar'ðiʎa) nf squirrel.

ardor (ar'ðor) nm 1 ardour. 2 heat, warmth. **ardoroso** adj 1 hot. 2 fiery.

arduo ('arðwo) adj hard, arduous.

área ('area) nf area.

arena (a'rena) nf 1 sand. 2 arena. **arena movediza** quicksand. **arenal** nm sandy ground.

arengar (aren'gar) vt harangue.

arenque (a'renke) nm herring.

argamasa (arga'masa) nf 1 plaster. 2 mortar.

Argelia (ar'xelja) nf Algeria. **argelino** adj,n Algerian.

Argentina (arxen'tina) nf Argentina. **argentino** adj,n Argentinian.

argolla (ar'goʎa) nf 1 large metal ring. 2 doorknocker.

argüir* (ar'gwir) vt 1 deduce. 2 indicate. 3 reproach. vi argue.

argumento (argu'mento) nm 1 argument. 2 Th plot. **argumentador** adj argumentative.

aridez (ari'ðeθ) nf 1 dryness. 2 barrenness, sterility. **árido** adj dry, arid.

arisco (a'risko) adj 1 shy. 2 unsociable. 3 wild.

aristocracia (aristo'kraθja) nf aristocracy. **aristócrata** nm,f aristocrat. **aristocrático** adj aristocratic.

aritmética (arit'metika) nf arithmetic.

armar (ar'mar) vt 1 arm, equip. 2 prepare. 3 cause. **armarse** vr 1 arm oneself. 2 prepare oneself. **arma** nf 1 arm, weapon. **armada** nf 1 fleet. 2 navy. **armado** adj armed. **armadura** nf 1 armour. 2 framework. **armamento** nm armament.

armario (ar'marjo) nm 1 cupboard. 2 wardrobe.

armazón (arma'θon) nf 1 frame(work). 2 tech skeleton.

armisticio (armis'tiθjo) nm armistice.

armonía (armo'nia) nf harmony. **armónico** adj harmonic, harmonious. **armonioso** adj harmonious.

armónica (ar'monika) nf harmonica.

aro ('aro) nm 1 hoop. 2 ring. 3 rim.

arpa ('arpa) nf harp. **arpicordio** nm harpsichord.

arpón (ar'pon) nm harpoon.

arquear (arke'ar) vt arch, bend. **arqueo** nm bending, arching.

arqueología (arkeolo'xia) nf archaeology. **arqueológico** adj archaeological. **arqueólogo** nm archaeologist.

arquero (ar'kero) nm archer.

arquetipo (arke'tipo) nm archetype.

arquitectura (arkitek'tura) nf architecture. **arquitecto** nm architect.

arrabal (arra'βal) nm 1 suburb. 2 pl outskirts.

arraigar (arrai'gar) vi take root, become established.

arrancar (arran'kar) vt 1 pull up, extract. 2 tear or snatch away. vi start, set off.

arranque (ar'ranke) nm 1 jerk, wrench. 2 mech start. 3 outburst.

arrasar (arra'sar) vt 1 demolish, flatten. 2 fill to the top. vi (of weather) clear up.

arrastrar (arras'trar) vt 1 drag. 2 carry along. **arrastrarse** vr creep, crawl. **arrastre** nm 1 dragging. 2 haulage.

arrebatar

arrebatar (arreβaˈtar) *vt* 1 snatch. 2 charm. 3 move deeply. **arrebatarse** *vr* get carried away. **arrebatamiento** *nm* 1 seizure. 2 rapture. **arrebato** *nm* 1 fit of rage. 2 ecstasy.

arrebujarse (arreβuˈxarse) *vr* wrap oneself up.

arreciar (arreˈθjar) *vi* 1 grow worse. 2 increase in intensity. **arreciarse** *vr* grow stronger.

arrecife (arreˈθife) *nm* 1 reef. 2 causeway.

arreglar (arreˈglar) *vt* 1 arrange. 2 mend, put right. 3 smarten up, tidy. **arreglarse** *vr* 1 come to terms. 2 work out. **arreglo** *nm* 1 arrangement. 2 rule, order.

arremeter (arremeˈter) *vt,vi* attack.

arrendar (ie) (arrenˈdar) *vt* 1 let. 2 rent. **arrendador** *nm* 1 landlord. 2 tenant. **arrendamiento** *nm* 1 letting. 2 rent.

arreos (arˈreos) *nm pl* 1 trappings, adornment. 2 equipment.

arrepentirse (ie) (arrepenˈtirse) *vr* repent. **arrepentimiento** *nm* repentance.

arrestar (arresˈtar) *vt* arrest. **arresto** *nm* 1 arrest. 2 boldness.

arriba (arˈriβa) *adv* 1 above, overhead. 2 up, upwards. 3 upstairs. **de arriba abajo** from head to foot. **arriba de** *prep* above. **¡arriba!** *interj* long live! up with!

arribar (arriˈβar) *vi* arrive. **arribar a** reach.

arriendo (arˈrjendo) *nm* 1 letting. 2 rent.

arriesgar (arrjesˈgar) *vt* 1 risk. 2 endanger.

arrimar (arriˈmar) *vt* draw or bring near. **arrimarse** *vr* 1 come close. 2 lean on. **arrimo** *nm* support.

arrinconar (arrinkoˈnar) *vt* 1 lay aside. 2 corner. **arrinconarse** *vr* withdraw.

arrobamiento (arroβaˈmjento) *nm* rapture, trance.

arrodillarse (arroðiˈʎarse) *vr* kneel (down).

arrogancia (arroˈganθja) *nf* arrogance. **arrogante** *adj* arrogant, proud.

arrojar (arroˈxar) *vt* 1 throw. 2 give out, emit. **arrojarse** *vr* hurl oneself. **arrojo** *nm* daring.

arrollar (arroˈʎar) *vt* 1 roll (up). 2 sweep away. 3 overwhelm.

arropar (arroˈpar) *vt* 1 cover. 2 wrap up. 3 tuck up (in bed).

arrostrar (arrosˈtrar) *vt* confront, face up to.

arroyo (arˈrojo) *nm* 1 stream. 2 gutter.

arroz (arˈroθ) *nm* rice.

arrugar (arruˈgar) *vt* 1 wrinkle. 2 crease, crumple. **arruga** *nf* 1 wrinkle. 2 crease.

arruinar (arruiˈnar) *vt* spoil, ruin.

arrullar (arruˈʎar) *vt* lull to sleep. *vi* coo.

arrurruz (arrurˈruθ) *nm* arrowroot.

arsénico (arˈseniko) *nm* arsenic.

arte (ˈarte) *nm,f* 1 art. 2 craft, skill. 3 workmanship. **no tener arte ni parte en** have nothing at all to do with.

artefacto (arteˈfakto) *nm* 1 appliance. 2 artefact.

arteria (arteˈria) *nf* artery.

artesano (arteˈsano) *nm* craftsman. **artesanía** *nf* craftsmanship.

Ártico (ˈartiko) *nm* Arctic. **ártico** *adj* arctic.

articular (artikuˈlar) *vt* 1 articulate. 2 join up. **articulación** *nf* 1 articulation. 2 joint.

artículo (arˈtikulo) *nm* 1 article, report. 2 thing, commodity. 3 *pl* goods.

artificial (artifiˈθjal) *adj* artificial.

artificio (artiˈfiθjo) *nm* 1 art, craft. 2 appliance. 3 trick, cunning.

artillería (artiʎeˈria) *nf* artillery.

artimaña (artiˈmaɲa) *nf* trick, trap.

artista (arˈtista) *nm,f* artist. **artístico** *adj* artistic.

artritis (arˈtritis) *nf* arthritis.

arzobispo (arθoˈβispo) *nm* archbishop. **arzobispado** *nm* archbishopric.

as (as) *nm* ace.

asa (ˈasa) *nf* handle.

asado (aˈsaðo) *adj* roast(ed). **poco asado** underdone. *nm* roast (of meat). **asador** *nm* cul spit.

asalariado (asalaˈrjaðo) *adj* paid, wage-earning. *nm* wage-earner.

asaltar (asalˈtar) *vt* 1 attack, storm. 2 (of an idea) come suddenly. **asalto** *nm* 1 attack. 2 sport round.

asamblea (asamˈblea) *nf* assembly, meeting.

asar (aˈsar) *vt* 1 roast. 2 inf pester.

asbesto (asˈβesto) *nm* asbestos.

ascendencia (asθenˈdenθja) *nf* ancestry, origin.

ascender (ie) (asθenˈder) *vi* 1 ascend. 2 be promoted. *vt* promote. **ascendiente** *nm,f* ancestor. *nm* influence.

ascensión (asθenˈsjon) *nf* 1 ascent. 2 promotion. **ascenso** *nm* promotion.

ascensor (asθenˈsor) *nm* lift, elevator.

asco (ˈasko) *nm* 1 disgust. 2 loathing. **dar asco (a)** disgust, sicken.

ascua (ˈaskwa) *nf* ember. **estar en ascuas** be on tenterhooks.

asear (aseˈar) *vt* 1 adorn. 2 tidy, clean. **asearse** *vr* tidy oneself. **aseado** *adj* 1 smart. 2 tidy.

asechar (aseˈtʃar) *vt* ambush. **asechanza** *nf* trap.

asediar (ase'ðjar) vt 1 besiege. 2 pester, bother. **asedio** nm siege.

asegurar (asegu'rar) vt 1 secure, fasten. 2 guarantee. 3 affirm. 4 insure.

asemejarse (aseme'xarse) vr resemble, be alike.

asentar (ie) (asen'tar) vt 1 place. 2 seat. 3 establish. 4 note down. vi be suitable. **asentarse** vr sit down.

asentir (ie) (asen'tir) vi agree, assent. **asentimiento** nm assent.

aseo (a'seo) nm cleanliness, tidiness.

asequible (ase'kiβle) adj 1 obtainable. 2 reasonable.

aserrar (ie) (aser'rar) vt saw. **aserradero** nm sawmill. **aserrín** nm sawdust.

aserto (a'serto) nm assertion.

asesinar (asesi'nar) vt murder, assassinate. **asesinato** nm assassination, murder. **asesino** nm assassin, murderer.

asesorar (aseso'rar) vt advise.

asestar (ases'tar) vt 1 aim. 2 strike.

asfalto (as'falto) nm asphalt.

asfixiar (asfik'sjar) vt suffocate. **asfixia** nf suffocation.

así (a'si) adv so, thus, in this way. **así así** so-so. **así como** the same way as, just as. **así que** as soon as, immediately.

Asia (a'sia) nf Asia. **asiático** adj,nm Asian, Asiatic.

asidero (asi'ðero) nm 1 hold. 2 handle. 3 excuse.

asiduo (a'siðwo) adj regular, constant.

asiento (a'sjento) nm 1 seat, place. 2 site. 3 stability. 4 sediment. 5 buttocks.

asignar (asig'nar) vt assign. **asignación** nf 1 allocation. 2 portion. 3 salary.

asignatura (asigna'tura) nf educ subject.

asilo (a'silo) nm 1 asylum. 2 shelter. 3 home, institution.

asimilar (asimi'lar) vt assimilate. **asimilación** nf assimilation.

asimismo (asi'mismo) adv similarly, in the same way.

asir* (a'sir) vt seize, take hold of. vi take root. **asirse** vr take hold.

asistir (asis'tir) vt 1 serve, attend. 2 help, assist. vi be present, attend. **asistencia** nf 1 attendance, presence. 2 help. **asistenta** nf 1 char. 2 daily help. **asistente** nm assistant.

asma ('asma) nf asthma.

asno ('asno) nm donkey, ass.

asociar (aso'θjar) vt associate. **asociarse** vr join, associate oneself. **asociación** nf 1 association. 2 partnership. **asociado** adj associated. nm member.

asolar (aso'lar) vt lay waste, destroy.

asolear (asole'ar) vt put in the sun. **asolearse** vr sunbathe.

asomar (aso'mar) vt show. vi begin to show, appear.

asombrar (asom'brar) vt 1 astonish. 2 shade, darken. **asombro** nm 1 amazement. 2 wonder. **asombroso** adj amazing.

aspecto (as'pekto) nm 1 aspect. 2 appearance, look.

áspero ('aspero) adj 1 rough. 2 harsh. **aspereza** nf 1 roughness. 2 harshness.

aspersión (asper'θjon) nf sprinkling, spray.

aspirar (aspi'rar) vt breathe in. vi aspire. **aspirador de polvo** nm vacuum cleaner.

aspirina (aspi'rina) nf aspirin.

asqueroso (aske'roso) adj 1 disgusting. 2 awful.

asta ('asta) nf 1 spear. 2 shaft. 3 horn. **a media asta** at half mast.

asterisco (aste'risko) nm asterisk.

astil (as'til) nm 1 pole. 2 handle. **astilla** nf splinter.

astillero (asti'ʎero) nm shipyard.

astringir (astrin'xir) vt 1 constrict. 2 med bind. **astringente** adj,nm astringent.

astro ('astro) nm star.

astrología (astrolo'xia) nf astrology. **astrólogo** nm astrologer.

astronauta (astro'nauta) nm,f astronaut. **astronáutica** nf astronautics.

astronomía (astrono'mia) nf astronomy. **astronómico** adj astronomical. **astrónomo** nm astronomer.

astucia (as'tuθja) nf 1 cleverness. 2 cunning.

astuto (as'tuto) adj 1 clever. 2 crafty.

asumir (asu'mir) vt assume.

asunto (a'sunto) nm 1 subject, matter. 2 business. **asuntos a tratar** agenda.

asustar (asus'tar) vt frighten.

atacar (ata'kar) vt 1 attack. 2 fasten, attach. **atacador** adj attacking. n attacker.

atado (a'taðo) nm bundle, roll.

atajar (ata'xar) vt intercept, stop. vi take a short cut. **atajo** nm short cut.

ataque (a'take) nm attack. **ataque aéreo** air-raid. **ataque cardíaco** heart attack. **ataque fulminate** med stroke.

atar (a'tar) vt tie, lace.

atardecer* (atarde'θer) vi get dark. nm dusk.

15

atareado (atare'aðo) *adj* busy.

atascar (atas'kar) *vt* 1 stop (a leak, etc.). 2 block, clog up. **atascarse** *vr* get stuck. **atasco** *nm* obstruction.

ataúd (ata'uð) *nm* coffin.

ataviar (ata'βjar) *vt* adorn. **atavío** *nm* attire.

ateísmo (ate'ismo) *nm* atheism.

atención (aten'θjon) *nf* 1 attention. 2 kindness, courtesy. 3 *pl* courtesies.

atender (ie) (aten'der) *vt,vi* attend.

atenerse* (ate'nerse) *vr* **atenerse a 1** abide by. 2 rely on.

atento (a'tento) *adj* 1 attentive. 2 polite. **atento a** in view of.

atenuar (ate'nwar) *vt* lessen, diminish.

ateo (a'teo) *adj* atheistic. *nm* atheist.

aterrar[1] (ie) (ater'rar) *vt* demolish.

aterrar[2] (ater'rar) *vt* frighten.

aterrizar (aterri'θar) *vi* *aviat* land. **aterrizaje** *nm* landing.

aterrorizar (aterrori'θar) *vt* 1 terrify. 2 terrorize.

atesorar (ateso'rar) *vt* hoard.

atestar (ie) (ates'tar) *vt* 1 stuff, fill. 2 crowd.

atestiguar (atesti'gwar) *vt* testify.

ático (a'tiko) *nm* attic.

atisbar (atis'βar) *vt* spy on, watch.

atizar (ati'θar) *vt* 1 poke. 2 stir up, excite. 3 slap. **atizador** *nm* poker.

Atlántico (a'tlantiko) *nm* Atlantic.

atlas ('atlas) *nm* atlas.

atleta (a'tleta) *nm, f* athlete. **atlético** *adj* athletic. **atletismo** *nm* athletics.

atmósfera (at'mosfera) *nf* atmosphere. **mala atmósfera** atmospherics. **atmosférico** *adj* atmospheric.

atolondrar (atolon'drar) *vt* 1 bewilder. 2 amaze.

átomo ('atomo) *nm* atom. **atómico** *adj* atomic.

atónito (a'tonito) *adj* astonished.

atontado (aton'taðo) *adj* 1 bewildered. 2 *inf* silly.

atormentar (atormen'tar) *vt* 1 torment. 2 torture.

atornillar (atorni'ʎar) *vt* screw, fasten.

atracar (atra'kar) *vt* 1 hold up, attack. 2 moor. 3 stuff (with food). **atracarse** *vr* gorge oneself. **atraco** *nm* robbery.

atracción (atrak'θjon) *nf* 1 attraction, charm. 2 *pl Th* entertainment. **atractivo** *adj* attractive.

atraer* (atra'er) *vt* attract.

atrancar (atran'kar) *vt* bar (a door). *vi* stride along.

atrapar (atra'par) *vt* 1 trap. 2 seize.

atrás (a'tras) *adv* 1 behind. 2 past. 3 back,

backwards. **atraso** *nm* 1 delay. 2 backward ness.

atravesar (ie) (atraβe'sar) *vt* 1 cross, go through. 2 lay across.

atreverse (atre'βerse) *vr* dare, risk. **atrevido** *adj* bold, daring. **atrevimiento** *nm* boldness.

atribuir* (atriβu'ir) *vt* attribute. **atributo** *nm* attribute.

atrocidad (atroθi'ðað) *nf* atrocity.

atropellar (atrope'ʎar) *vt* 1 trample over, run over. 2 do hurriedly. **atropello** *nm* 1 outrage 2 accident.

atroz (a'troθ) *adj* atrocious, savage.

atún (a'tun) *nm* tunny.

aturdir (atur'ðir) *vt* 1 daze. 2 bewilder. **aturdido** *adj* bewildered, silly. **aturdimiento** *nm* daze, confusion.

audacia (au'ðaθja) *nf* audacity. **audaz** *adj* audacious, daring.

audible (au'ðiβle) *adj* audible.

audición (auði'θjon) *nf* 1 hearing. 2 audition.

audiencia (au'ðjenθja) *nf* audience.

audífono (au'ðifono) *nm* hearing aid.

audiovisual (audiovisu'al) *adj* audiovisual.

auge ('auxe) *nm* 1 peak, zenith. 2 increase

aula ('aula) *nf* 1 classroom. 2 lecture theatre **aula magna** assembly hall.

aullar (au'ʎar) *vi* howl. **aullido** *nm* howl.

aumentar (aumen'tar) *vt,vi* increase. **aumente** *nm* increase, rise.

aun (a'un) *adv* even. **aún** *adv* still, yet.

aún (a'un) *adv* still, yet.

aunar (au'nar) *vt* join.

aunque (a'unke) *conj* (al)though, even though.

áureo ('aureo) *adj* gold(en).

aureola (aure'ola) *nf* halo.

auricular (auriku'lar) *adj* of the ear. *nm* 1 little finger. 2 receiver. 3 *pl* headphones.

ausencia (au'senθja) *nf* absence. **ausente** *ad* absent. *nm,f* absentee.

auspicios (aus'piθjos) *nm pl* 1 auspices. 2 patronage, protection.

austero (aus'tero) *adj* austere, severe, harsh **austeridad** *nf* austerity.

Australia (aus'tralja) *nf* Australia. **australiano** *adj,nm* Australian.

Austria ('austrja) *nf* Austria. **austríaco** *adj,nm* Austrian.

auténtico (au'tentiko) *adj* authentic, real.

autístico (au'tistiko) *adj* autistic.

auto[1] ('auto) *nm* car.

auto[2] ('auto) *nm* 1 decree. 2 *law* sentence. 3 mystery play. 4 *pl* law proceedings.

autobiografía (autoβiograˈfia) nf autobiography. **autobiográfico** adj autobiographical.

autobús (autoˈbus) nm bus.

autocar (autoˈkar) nm mot coach.

autodisciplina (autodisθiˈplina) nf self-discipline.

autoescuela (autoesˈkwela) nf driving school.

autoexpresión (autoekspreˈsjon) nf self-expression.

autógrafo (auˈtografo) adj,nm autograph.

automático (autoˈmatiko) adj automatic.

automatización (automatiθaˈθjon) nf automation.

automóvil (autoˈmoβil) nm automobile, car. **automovilista** nm,f motorist.

autonomía (autonoˈmia) nf autonomy. **autónomo** adj autonomous.

autopista (autoˈpista) nf motorway.

autopsia (auˈtopsja) nf autopsy, post-mortem.

autor (auˈtor) nm 1 author. 2 creator.

autorizar (autoriˈθar) vt 1 authorize. 2 approve. **autoridad** nf 1 authority. 2 show, pomp. **autoritario** adj authoritarian.

autorretrato (autorreˈtrato) nm self-portrait.

autoservicio (autoserˈviθio) nm self-service restaurant.

autostop (autoˈstop) nm hitch-hiking. **hacer el autostop** hitch-hike. **autostopista** nm,f hitch-hiker.

auxiliar (auksiˈljar) vt help, assist. adj auxiliary. nm,f assistant. **auxilio** nm help.

avalancha (aβaˈlantʃa) nf avalanche.

avalorar (aβaloˈrar) vt estimate, appraise.

avance (aˈβanθe) nm 1 advance. 2 comm balance.

avanzar (aβanˈθar) vt advance. vi advance, go forward.

avaricia (aβaˈriθja) nf greed, miserliness. **avaricioso** adj greedy, miserly. **avaro** adj miserly, mean.

avasallar (aβasaˈʎar) vt dominate, subdue. **avasallarse** vr submit.

ave (ˈaβe) nf bird. **aves de corral** poultry.

avecinarse (aβeθiˈnarse) vr approach.

avellana (aβeˈʎana) nf hazelnut.

avena (aˈβena) nf oats.

avenencia (aβeˈnenθja) nf agreement.

avenida (aβeˈniða) nf avenue.

avenir* (aβeˈnir) vt bring together, reconcile. **avenirse** vr come to an agreement, be reconciled.

aventajado (aβentaˈxaðo) adj outstanding, exceptional.

aventura (aβenˈtura) nf 1 adventure. 2 risk. **aventurero** adj adventurous. nm adventurer.

avergonzar* (aβergonˈθar) vt 1 shame. 2 embarrass. **avergonzarse** vr be ashamed.

avería¹ (aβeˈria) nf aviary.

avería² (aβeˈria) nf 1 mech breakdown. 2 damage. **averiado** adj 1 damaged. 2 faulty.

averiguar (aβeriˈgwar) vt find out, ascertain. **averiguación** nf 1 discovery. 2 investigation.

avestruz (aβesˈtruθ) nm ostrich.

aviación (aβjaˈθjon) nf 1 aviation. 2 air force.

aviador (aβjaˈdor) nm airman, pilot.

ávido (ˈaβiðo) adj 1 avid, eager. 2 greedy. **avidez** nf 1 greed. 2 eagerness.

avinagrado (aβinaˈgraðo) adj sour, acid.

avión (aˈβjon) nm (aero)plane, aircraft. **avión a reacción** jet. **por avión** by airmail.

avisar (aβiˈsar) vt 1 inform. 2 advise. **aviso** (aˈβiso) nm 1 piece of information, tip. 2 advice.

avispa (aˈβispa) nf wasp.

avivar (aβiˈβar) vt 1 enliven, stimulate. 2 stoke. **avivarse** vr revive.

aya (ˈaja) nf child's nurse.

ayer (aˈjer) adv 1 yesterday. 2 in the past. nm 1 yesterday. 2 past.

ayo (ˈajo) nm tutor.

ayudar (ajuˈðar) vt help, assist. **ayuda** nf help, assistance. **ayudante** nm helper, assistant.

ayunar (ajuˈnar) vi fast. **ayuno** nm fast, fasting.

ayuntamiento (ajuntaˈmjento) nm 1 town council. 2 town hall. 3 sexual intercourse.

azada (aˈθaða) nf hoe.

azafata (aθaˈfata) nf aviat stewardess.

azafrán (aθaˈfran) nm cul saffron.

azahar (aθaˈar) nm orange blossom.

azar (aˈθar) nm 1 fate. 2 chance. **al azar** at random.

azogue (aˈθoge) nm mercury, quicksilver.

azorar (aθoˈrar) vt 1 alarm, upset. 2 embarrass.

azotar (aθoˈtar) vt whip, beat. **azote** nm 1 whip, lash. 2 scourge. 3 spank.

azotea (aθoˈtea) nf flat roof.

azúcar (aˈθukar) nm sugar. **azúcar fina** castor sugar. **azucarado** adj sweet, sugary.

azucena (aθuˈθena) nf lily.

azufre (aˈθufre) nm sulphur.

azul (aˈθul) adj,nm blue. **azul marino** navy blue.

azulejo (aθuˈlexo) nm tile.

B

baba ('baβa) nf saliva, spit. **babero** nm bib.
babor (ba'βor) nm naut port (side).
babosa (ba'βosa) nf slug.
bacalao (baka'lao) nm cod.
bacía (ba'θia) nf 1 basin. 2 shaving bowl.
bacteria (bak'teria) nf 1 germ. 2 pl bacteria.
bache ('batʃe) nm pothole.
bachiller (batʃi'ʎer) nm educ bachelor. **bachillerato** nm 1 final school examination, baccalaureate. 2 bachelor's degree.
bahía (ba'ia) nf geog bay.
bailar (bai'lar) vi dance. **baile** nm dance. **baile clásico** ballet.
bajar (ba'xar) vi fall, come down. vt lower, bring or take down. **baja** nf fall, drop. **bajada** nf 1 slope. 2 descent. **bajamar** nm low tide.
bajo ('baxo) adj 1 low. 2 small. 3 (of a person) short. adv below. prep under. **bajeza** nf 1 lowliness. 2 baseness.
bajón (ba'xon) nm 1 bassoon. 2 decline.
bala ('bala) nf 1 bullet. 2 bale.
balada (ba'laða) nf ballad.
balancear (balanθe'ar) vt,vi 1 balance. 2 rock, sway. **balance** nm 1 balance. 2 stocktaking. **balanceo** nm 1 balancing. 2 swaying. **balanza** nf scales.
balar (ba'lar) vi bleat.
balazo (ba'laθo) nm 1 shot. 2 wound.
balbucear (balβuθe'ar) vi stammer, stutter. **balbuceo** nm stammer.
balcón (bal'kon) nm balcony.
balde[1] ('balde) nm large bucket.
balde[2] ('balde) nm **de balde** free of charge. **en balde** in vain.
baldío (bal'dio) nm waste land. adj 1 wild. 2 barren.
baldosa (bal'dosa) nf flagstone, paving tile.
balística (ba'listika) nf ballistics. **balístico** adj ballistic.
balneario (balne'arjo) nm spa.
balón (ba'lon) nm 1 (foot)ball. 2 comm bale. **baloncesto** nm basketball. **balonvolea** nf volleyball.
balsa[1] ('balsa) nf raft.
balsa[2] ('balsa) nf pond.
bálsamo ('balsamo) nm balsam, comfort.
Báltico ('baltiko) nm Baltic.
ballena (ba'ʎena) nf whale.

ballesta (ba'ʎesta) nf crossbow. **ballestero** nm archer.
ballet (ba'le) nm ballet.
bambolear (bambole'ar) vi sway, reel.
bambú (bam'bu) nm bamboo.
banca ('banka) nf 1 bench. 2 comm banking.
bancarrota (banka'rota) nf bankruptcy. **hacer bancarrota** go bankrupt.
banco ('banko) nm 1 bench, seat. 2 bank.
banda ('banda) nf 1 band, strip. 2 gang, group. **bandada** nf flock.
bandeja (ban'dexa) nf tray.
bandera (ban'dera) nf 1 flag. 2 banner. 3 ensign. **banderilla** nf (bullfighting) dart. **banderillero** nm bullfighter who places the darts.
bandido (ban'diðo) nm bandit, outlaw.
bando ('bando) nm 1 proclamation. 2 faction, side.
bandolero (bandɔ'lero) nm bandit.
banjo ('banxo) nm banjo.
banquete (ban'kete) nm banquet, feast.
bañar (ba'ɲar) vt bathe. **bañarse** (ba'ɲarse) vr 1 have a bath. 2 swim. **bañador** nm bathing costume. **bañera** nf bathtub. **baño** nm bath.
bar (bar) nm bar, snack bar.
barajar (bara'xar) vt shuffle. **baraja** nf pack of cards.
barandilla (baran'diʎa) nf rail, railing.
barato (ba'rato) adj cheap. **baratija** nf 1 trinket. 2 trifle. 3 pl junk. **baratura** nf cheapness.
barba ('barβa) nf beard.
bárbaro ('barβaro) adj 1 barbarous, savage. 2 sl terrific, marvellous. nm barbarian. **barbaridad** nf 1 barbarity. 2 inf huge amount.
barbilla (bar'βiʎa) nf chin.
barbudo (bar'βuðo) adj bearded.
barca ('barka) nf small boat. **barca de pasaje** ferry boat.
Barcelona (barθe'lona) nf Barcelona. **barcelonés** adj of Barcelona. nm inhabitant of Barcelona.
barco ('barko) nm ship, boat.
barnizar (barni'θar) vt varnish. **barniz** nm 1 varnish. 2 gloss.
barómetro (ba'rometro) nm barometer.
barón (ba'ron) nm baron. **baronesa** nf baroness. **baronet** nm baronet.
barquillo (bar'kiʎo) nm 1 wafer. 2 cornet.
barra ('barra) nf 1 bar. 2 small loaf.
barraca (bar'raka) nf 1 hut. 2 cottage. 3 booth.
barranco (bar'ranko) nm ravine, gorge.

barrenar (barre'nar) *vt* drill, bore. **barrena** *nf* drill.

barrer (bar'rer) *vt* sweep.

barrera (bar'rera) *nf* barrier. **barrera de peaje** tollgate.

barricada (barri'kada) *nf* barricade.

barril (bar'ril) *nm* barrel.

barrio ('barrjo) *nm* district, quarter.

barro ('barro) *nm* mud. **barroso** *adj* muddy.

bártulos ('bartulos) *nm pl* belongings, gear.

barullo (ba'ruʎo) *nm* 1 confusion. 2 row.

basar (ba'sar) *vt* base, found. **basarse en** *vr* be based on. **base** *nf* base, foundation.

básico ('basiko) *adj* basic, fundamental.

bastante (bas'tante) *adj* enough. *adv* 1 enough, sufficiently. 2 fairly.

bastar (bas'tar) *vi* be enough, suffice.

bastardear (bastarðe'ar) *vi* degenerate. *vt* adulterate. **bastardilla** *nf* italics. **bastardo** *nm,adj* bastard.

bastidor (basti'ðor) *nm* frame. **entre bastidores** offstage.

basto ('basto) *adj* 1 rude. 2 coarse. *nm* pack saddle.

bastón (bas'ton) *nm* stick.

bastos ('bastos) *nm pl* game clubs.

basura (ba'sura) *nf* rubbish, litter. **basurero** *nm* dustman.

bata ('beta) *nf* 1 dressing-gown. 2 overall.

batalla (ba'taʎa) *nf* battle.

batea (ba'tea) *nf* 1 trough. 2 punt.

batería (bate'ria) *nf* 1 battery. 2 *mus* percussion instruments. **batería de cocina** kitchen utensils.

batir (ba'tir) *vt* 1 beat. 2 clap. 3 knock down. 4 defeat. 5 *cul* whisk. **batirse** *vr* fight. **batido** *nm* 1 batter. 2 milk shake. **batidor** *nm* whisk, beater. **batiente** *nm* frame (of door, etc.).

batuta (ba'tuta) *nf* baton. **llevar la batuta** be in control.

baúl (ba'ul) *nm* trunk.

bautizar (bauti'θar) *vt* baptize, christen. **bautismo** *nm* baptism, christening. **bautizo** *nm* christening party.

baya ('baja) *nf* berry.

bayeta (ba'jeta) *nf* 1 baize. 2 rag, cloth.

bayoneta (bajo'neta) *nf* bayonet.

baza ('baθa) *nf* game trick. **meter baza** interfere.

bazar (ba'θar) *nm* bazaar.

beato (be'ato) *adj* 1 pious, devout. 2 blessed.

beber (be'βer) *vt,vi* drink. **bebida** *nf* drink.

beca ('beka) *nf* grant, scholarship.

becerro (be'θerro) *nm* 1 bullock. 2 yearling.

bedel (be'ðel) *nm* warden, porter.

béisbol ('beisβol) *nm* baseball.

Belén (be'len) *nf* Bethlehem. **belén** *nm* 1 crib. 2 crèche. 3 confusion.

Bélgica ('belxika) *nf* Belgium. **belga** *adj,n* Belgian.

bellaco (be'ʎako) *adj* 1 cunning. 2 wicked. *nm* rogue.

belleza (be'ʎeθa) *nf* beauty. **bello** *adj* 1 beautiful. 2 fine.

bellota (be'ʎota) *nf* acorn.

bemol (be'mol) *nm mus* flat.

bendecir* (bende'θir) *vt* 1 bless. 2 praise. **bendición** *nf* blessing. **bendito** *adj* blessed, holy.

beneficiar (benefi'θjar) *vt,vi* profit, be of benefit (to). **beneficio** *nm* 1 benefit. 2 gain. **beneficioso** *adj* profitable, beneficial.

benemérito (bene'merito) *adj* worthy, honourable.

beneplácito (bene'plaθito) *nm* consent.

benevolencia (benevo'lenθia) *nf* kindness, benevolence. **benevolente** *adj* also **benévolo** kind, benevolent.

benignidad (benigni'dað) *nf* kindness. **benigno** *adj* 1 kind. 2 (of weather) mild.

beodo (be'oðo) *adj* drunk.

berberecho (berβe'retʃo) *nm* cockle.

berenjena (beren'xena) *nf* aubergine.

bermejo (ber'mexo) *adj* 1 bright red. 2 ginger.

berrear (berre'ar) *vi* bellow, howl. **berrido** *nm* bellow, howling.

berrinche (ber'rintʃe) *nm* tantrum.

berro ('berro) *nm* watercress.

berza ('berθa) *nf* cabbage.

besar (be'sar) *vt* kiss. **beso** *nm* kiss.

bestia ('bestja) *nf* 1 beast, animal. 2 stupid or ignorant person. *adj inf* foolish, stupid. **bestial** *adj* 1 bestial. 2 *inf* marvellous, great.

betún (be'tun) *nm* 1 shoe polish. 2 bitumen.

Biblia ('biβlia) *nf* Bible. **bíblico** *adj* Biblical.

bibliografía (biβliogra'fia) *nf* bibliography. **bibliográfico** *adj* bibliographic(al).

biblioteca (biβlio'teka) *nf* library. **bibliotecario** *nm* librarian.

bíceps ('biθeps) *nm invar* biceps.

bicicleta (biθi'kleta) *nf* bicycle.

bicho ('bitʃo) *nm* 1 insect. 2 small animal.

bien (bjen) *adv* 1 well, right. 2 quite, very. 3 easily. *nm* 1 good. 2 advantage. 3 gain. 4 *pl* property, possessions. **bien que** *conj* though, although.

bienal (bje'nal) *adj* biennial.

bienaventurado (bjenaβertu'raðo) *adj* 1 fortunate. 2 blessed.

bienestar (bjenes'tar) *nm* 1 comfort. 2 well-being.

bienhechor (bjene'tʃor) *nm* benefactor.

bienio ('bjenjo) *nm* period of two years.

bienvenida (bjenβe'niða) *nf* welcome. **dar la bienvenida a** *vt* welcome.

biftec (bif'tek) *nm* steak.

bifurcarse (bifur'karse) *vr* branch off, fork. **bifurcación** *nf* junction.

bigamia (bi'gamja) *nf* bigamy.

bigote (bi'gote) *nm* moustache.

bilingüe (bi'lingwe) *adj* bilingual.

billar (bi'ʎar) *nm* billiards.

billete (bi'ʎete) *nm* 1 ticket. 2 banknote. 3 letter. **billete de abono** season ticket. **billete de ida y vuelta** return ticket. **billete sencillo** single ticket. **sacar un billete** buy a ticket.

binóculo (bi'nokulo) *nm* binoculars.

biografía (biogra'fia) *nf* biography. **biográfico** *adj* biographical.

biología (biolo'xia) *nf* biology. **biológico** *adj* biological. **biólogo** *nm* biologist.

biombo ('bjombo) *nm* screen.

bióxido (bi'oksido) *nm* dioxide. **bióxido de carbono** carbon dioxide.

bisagra (bi'sagra) *nf* hinge.

bisiesto (bi'sjesto) *adj* **año bisiesto** *nm* leap year.

bisturí (bistu'ri) *nm* scalpel.

bizarría (biθar'ria) *nf* 1 gallantry, valour. 2 splendour, show. **bizarro** *adj* 1 brave. 2 splendid. 3 dashing.

bizcar (biθ'kar) *vi* squint. **bizco** *adj* cross-eyed.

bizcocho (biθ'kotʃo) *nm* small cake, biscuit.

blanco ('blanko) *adj* 1 white. 2 blank. *nm* 1 whiteness, white. 2 blank. 3 target. **blanca** *nf* minim. **blancura** *nf* whiteness. **dar en el blanco** be on target. **quedarse en blanco** not have a clue.

blandir (blan'dir) *vt,vi* wave.

blando ('blando) *adj* 1 soft. 2 gentle. 3 mild. **blandura** *nf* 1 softness. 2 tenderness.

blanquear (blanke'ar) *vt* 1 whiten, bleach. 2 whitewash. **blanqueo** *nm* bleaching.

blasfemar (blasfe'mar) *vi* blaspheme, swear. **blasfemia** *nf* blasphemy, oath.

blasón (bla'son) *nm* 1 coat of arms. 2 heraldry.

blindar (blin'dar) *vt* protect with armour. **blindado** *adj* armour-plated. **blindaje** *nm* armour.

bloquear (bloke'ar) *vt* block, obstruct. **bloque** *nm* 1 block. 2 blockage. 3 bloc. **bloqueo** *nm* blockade.

blusa ('blusa) *nf* 1 blouse. 2 overall.

bobada (bo'βaða) *nf* 1 nonsense. 2 foolishness. **bobería** *nf* stupidity. **bobo** *adj* foolish, silly. *nm* idiot.

bobina (bo'bina) *nf* reel.

boca ('boka) *nf* 1 mouth. 2 opening. **a la boca de** at the start of. **a boca de jarro** 1 without restraint. 2 at point-blank range. **boca abajo/ arriba** face down/up.

bocacalle (boka'kaʎe) *nf* entrance to a street.

bocadillo (boka'ðiʎo) *nm* sandwich. **bocado** *nm* 1 mouthful. 2 bite.

bocina (bo'θina) *nf* 1 trumpet. 2 *mot* horn.

bochorno (bo'tʃorno) *nm* hot and sultry weather. **¡qué bochorno!** what an embarrassment! **bochornoso** *adj* 1 sultry. 2 thundery. 3 embarrassing.

boda ('boða) *nf* wedding, marriage.

bodega (bo'ðega) *nf* 1 wine cellar. 2 storeroom. 3 bar.

bofetada (bofe'taða) *nf* 1 slap. 2 blow.

boga ('boga) *nf* vogue, fashion.

bohemio (bo'emjo) *adj,nm* 1 Bohemian. 2 gypsy.

boicotear (boikote'ar) *vt* boycott. **boicot** *nm* boycott.

boina ('boina) *nf* beret.

bola ('bola) *nf* 1 ball. 2 fib. **bola de nieve** snowball.

bolero (bo'lero) *nm* 1 type of dance. 2 short jacket.

boleto (bo'leto) *nf* 1 ticket. 2 pass. 3 document.

boletín *nm* bulletin. **boletín meteorológico** weather forecast. **boletín de noticias** news bulletin. **boletín de precios** price list.

bolígrafo (bo'ligrafo) *nm* ballpoint pen.

Bolivia (bo'liβja) *nf* Bolivia. **boliviano** *adj,n* Bolivian.

bolsa ('bolsa) *nf* 1 bag. 2 purse. **bolsa de agua** hot-water bottle. **bolsillo** *nm* pocket. **bolso** *nm* 1 handbag. 2 purse.

bollo ('boʎo) *nm* roll, bun.

bomba ('bomba) *nf* 1 pump. 2 bomb. **bomba de gasolina** petrol pump. **bomba de mano** grenade. **bomba nuclear** nuclear bomb.

bombardear (bombarðe'ar) *vt* bombard, shell. **bombardeo aéreo** *nm* bombardment, air-raid.

bombero (bom'bero) *nm* fireman.

bombilla (bom'biʎa) *nf* 1 light bulb. 2 globe. 3 glass tube.

bombo ('bombo) *adj* stunnned, surprised. *nm* 1 drum. 2 great praise.

bombón (bom'bon) *nm* 1 sweet, chocolate. 2 *inf* beauty (girl).

bondad (bon'daθ) *nf* 1 goodness. 2 kindness. **bondadoso** *adj* 1 kind. 2 warm-hearted.

bonito (bo'nito) *adj* pretty, nice.

bono ('bono) *nm* 1 bond. 2 certificate. 3 voucher.

boquerón (boke'ron) *nm* 1 opening, large hole. 2 a variety of anchovy. **boquete** *nm* gap, small hole.

boquiabierto (bokja'βjerto) *adj* gaping, open-mouthed.

boquilla (bo'kiʎa) *nf* 1 mouthpiece. 2 nozzle.

borboll(e)ar (borβoʎ'ar) *vi* bubble. **borbollón** *nm* 1 bubbling. 2 spluttering.

borbotar (borβo'tar) *vi* 1 bubble. 2 boil. **borbotón** *nm* 1 bubbling. 2 boiling.

bordar (bor'ðar) *vt* embroider. **bordado** *nm* embroidery.

bordear (borðe'ar) *vt* 1 edge round. 2 border. **borde** *nm* 1 border, edge. 2 rim.

bordillo (bor'ðiʎo) *nm* kerb.

bordo ('borðo) *nm* naut board. **a bordo** on board.

borra (borra) *nf* 1 thick wool. 2 nap. 3 stuffing.

borracho (bor'ratʃo) *adj,nm* drunk. **borrachera** *nf* 1 drunkenness. 2 drinking bout.

borrar (bor'rar) *vt* erase, rub out. **goma de borrar** *nf* rubber. **borrador** *nm* 1 rough copy. 2 scribbling pad.

borrasca (bor'raska) *nf* 1 thick wool. 2 nap. 3 stuffing. **borrascoso** *adj* stormy.

borrico (bor'riko) *nm* ass, donkey.

borrón (bor'ron) *nm* 1 stain, blot. **borroso** *adj* 1 stained. 2 smudged. 3 blurred.

bosque ('boske) *nm* wood, forest.

bosquejar (boske'xar) *vt* 1 sketch. 2 draft. **bosquejo** *nm* sketch, outline.

bostezar (boste'θar) *vi* yawn. **bostezo** *nm* yawn.

bota ('bota) *nf* 1 boot. 2 wineskin.

botánica (bo'tanika) *nf* botany. **botánico** *adj* botanical. **botanista** *nm,f* botanist.

botar (bo'tar) *vt* 1 throw. 2 bowl. *vi* bounce.

bote[1] ('bote) *nm* 1 blow, bump. 2 bounce.

bote[2] ('bote) *nm* 1 tin can. 2 jar.

bote[3] ('bote) *nm* boat.

botella (bo'teʎa) *nf* bottle.

botica (bo'tika) *nf* chemist's shop. **boticario** *nm* chemist.

botija (bo'tixa) *nf* round earthenware pot. **botijo** *nm* earthenware jug with spout.

botín (bo'tin) *nm* loot.

botón (bo'ton) *nm* 1 button. 2 switch, knob. 3 bud. **botón de camisa** stud. **botones** *nm* invar pageboy.

bóveda ('boβeða) *nf* 1 vault. 2 cave. 3 dome.

bovino (bo'βino) *adj* bovine.

boxear (bokse'ar) *vi* box. **boxeador** *nm* boxer. **boxeo** *nm* boxing.

boya ('boja) *nf* buoy. **boyante** *adj* buoyant.

bozal (bo'θal) *nm* muzzle.

bracero (bra'θero) *nm* 1 labourer. 2 helper.

braga ('braga) *nf* 1 hoist, sling. 2 *pl* breeches. 3 *pl* (woman's) underpants.

bramar (bra'mar) *vi* roar, bellow. **bramido** *nm* roar, bellow.

brasa ('brasa) *nf* glowing cinder. **brasero** *nm* brazier.

Brasil (bra'sil) *nm* Brazil. **brasileño** *adj,nm* Brazilian.

bravío (bra'βio) *adj* 1 savage. 2 wild.

bravo ('braβo) *adj* 1 brave, courageous. 2 fierce. *interj* well done! **bravura** *nf* 1 bravery. 2 ferocity.

brazada (bra'θaða) *nf* 1 arm movement. 2 stroke. **brazado** *nm* armful.

brazalete (braθa'lete) *nm* bracelet.

brazo ('braθo) *nm* 1 arm. 2 branch. **a brazo partido** with bare fists. **brazo derecho** right-hand man.

brea ('brea) *nf* pitch, tar.

brebaje (bre'βaxe) *nm* brew, potion.

brécoles ('brekoles) *nm pl* broccoli.

brecha ('bretʃa) *nf* breach, opening.

bregar (bre'gar) *vi* 1 struggle. 2 quarrel. **brega** *nf* fight.

Bretaña (bre'tana) *nf* Brittany. **bretón** *adj,nm* Breton.

breve ('breβe) *adj* brief, short. *nm* rel papal brief. *nf* mus breve. **en breve** soon, before long. **brevedad** *nf* brevity.

brezal (bre'θal) *nm* heath, moor **brezo** *nm* heather.

bribón (bri'βon) *adj* 1 lazy. 2 dishonest. *nm* scoundrel.

brida ('briða) *nf* 1 bridle. 2 rein.

brigada (bri'gaða) *nm* sergeant-major. *nf* brigade, squad.

brillar (bri'ʎar) *vi* 1 shine. 2 sparkle. **brillante** *adj* 1 shining, bright. 2 brilliant. **brillo** *nm* 1 brilliance, shine. 2 sparkle.

brincar (brin'kar) vi 1 jump. 2 skip, hop. **brinco** nm jump, leap.

brindar (brin'dar) vt offer. vi drink a person's health. **brindis** nm invar toast.

brío ('brio) nm spirit, go. **brioso** adj 1 lively, spirited. 2 vigorous.

brisa ('brisa) nf breeze.

británico (bri'taniko) adj,nm British.

brocha ('brotʃa) nf 1 brush. 2 paintbrush.

broche (brotʃe) nm 1 fastener, clip. 2 brooch.

broma ('broma) nf 1 joke. 2 fun, merriment. **broma pesada** practical joke. **en broma** as a joke. **bromista** nm,f joker, practical joker.

bromear (brome'ar) vi joke.

bronca ('bronka) nf 1 row. 2 fuss.

bronce ('bronθe) nm bronze. **bronceado** adj 1 bronzed. 2 tanned.

bronco ('bronko) adj 1 rough. 2 harsh.

bronquial (bronki'al) adj bronchial. **bronquitis** nm bronchitis.

broqueta (bro'keta) nf skewer.

brotar (bro'tar) vi 1 bud. 2 spring up. 3 appear. **brote** nm 1 bud, shoot. 2 outbreak. 3 rash.

bruja ('bruxa) nf witch. **brujo** nm wizard.

brújula ('bruxula) nf compass.

bruma ('bruma) nf mist. **brumoso** adj misty.

bruno ('bruno) adj dark brown.

bruñir (bru'ɲir) vt polish. **bruñido** adj 1 polished. 2 shiny. nm shine.

brusco ('brusko) adj 1 brusque, abrupt. 2 sharp.

Bruselas (bru'selas) nf Brussels.

brutal (bru'tal) adj brutal, savage. **brutalidad** nf brutality, cruelty. **bruto** adj 1 brute. 2 rough, coarse. nm brute. **en bruto** min 1 uncut. 2 crude.

buba ('buβa) nf tumour.

bucear (buθe'ar) vi dive. **buceo** nm diving.

bucle ('bukle) nm ringlet, curl.

buche ('butʃe) nm 1 zool crop. 2 stomach.

budismo (bu'ðismo) nm Buddhism. **budista** adj,n Buddhist.

buenaventura (bwenaβen'tura) nf 1 good luck. 2 fortune.

bueno ('bweno) adj also **buen** before nm s 1 good. 2 sound. 3 right. 4 proper, suitable. interj,conj 1 well. 2 all right. **a buenas** willingly. **buena voluntad** goodwill. ¡buenas! hello! **buenas noches** good night. **buenas tardes** good afternoon, good evening. **buenos días** good morning. **de buenas a primeras** 1 straightaway. 2 suddenly.

buey (bwej) nm ox.

búfalo ('bufalo) nm buffalo.

bufanda (bu'fanda) nf scarf.

bufar (bu'far) vi 1 spit. 2 snort.

buhardilla (bwar'ðiʎa) nf 1 attic. 2 skylight.

búho ('buo) nm 1 owl. 2 inf hermit.

buitre ('bwitre) nm vulture.

bujía (bu'xia) nf 1 candle. 2 sparking plug.

bula ('bula) nf rel papal bull.

bulbo ('bulβo) nm bulb.

Bulgaria (bul'garia) nf Bulgaria. **búlgaro** adj,nm Bulgarian. nm Bulgarian (language).

bulto ('bulto) nm 1 bulk, size. 2 bundle. 3 med lump. **a bulto** 1 carelessly. 2 roughly. **de bulto** important.

bulla ('buʎa) nf confusion, racket.

bullicio (bu'ʎiθjo) nm 1 bustle. 2 noise. **bullicioso** adj 1 noisy. 2 bustling.

bullir (bu'ʎir) vi 1 boil. 2 bustle. 3 bubble.

buñuelo (bu'ɲwelo) nm 1 bun. 2 doughnut. 3 fritter.

buque ('buke) nm ship, boat. **buque de vapor** steamship.

burbujear (burbuxe'ar) vi bubble. **burbuja** nf bubble.

burdel (bur'ðel) nm brothel.

burgués (bur'ges) adj bourgeois, middle class. **burguesía** nf middle class.

burlar (bur'lar) vt 1 trick. 2 cheat. **burlarse** vr joke. **burlarse de** mock. **burla** nf 1 jeer. 2 joke.

burocracia (buro'kraθja) nf bureaucracy. **burócrata** nm,f bureaucrat, public official. **burocrático** adj bureaucratic.

burro ('burro) nm donkey.

buscar (bus'kar) vt search, look for. **busca** nf search. **buscador** nm searcher. **en busca de** in search of.

búsqueda ('buskeða) nf search.

busto ('busto) nm bust.

butaca (bu'taka) nf 1 armchair. 2 seat.

buzo ('buθo) nm diver.

buzón (bu'θon) nm pillar-box, letterbox.

C

cabal (ka'βal) adj 1 exact. 2 perfect. 3 right.

cábala ('kaβala) nf 1 intrigue. 2 guess.

cabalgar (kaβal'gar) vt,vi ride. **cabalgada** nf troop of horses. **cabalgador** nm horserider.

caballa (ka'βaʎa) nf mackerel.

caballero (kaβa'ʎero) nm 1 horseman. 2

gentleman. **3** knight. **caballeresco** *adj* chivalrous.

caballete (kaβa'ʎete) *nm* **1** ridge. **2** easel. **3** furrow. **4** bridge (of the nose). **5** trestle.

caballo (ka'βaʎo) *nm* **1** horse. **2** horsepower. **3** knight. **4** *game* queen. **a caballo** on horseback. **caballo de balancín** rocking-horse. **caballo de carreras** racehorse. **caballo padre** stallion. **caballería** *nf* **1** horse, mount. **2** cavalry. **caballito** *nm* pony.

cabaña (ka'βaɲa) *nf* **1** cabin, hut. **2** flock.

cabaret (kaβa're) *nm* **1** cabaret. **2** nightclub.

cabás (ka'βas) *nm* satchel.

cabecear (kaβeθe'ar) *vi* **1** shake one's head in negation. **2** nod sleepily. **cabeceo** *nm* nodding. **cabecera** *nf* **1** head (of a table, etc.). **2** bedside. **3** title, heading.

cabecilla (kaβe'θiʎa) *nm,f* ringleader.

cabello (ka'βeʎo) *nm* hair. **cabelludo** *adj* hairy.

caber* (ka'βer) *vi* **1** fit, have enough room. **2** possible. **no cabe duda** there is no doubt.

cabestro (ka'βestro) *nm* halter.

cabeza (ka'βeθa) *nf* **1** head. **2** chief, leader. **3** top, summit. **cabeza de turco** scapegoat. **romperse la cabeza** rack one's brains. **cabezada** *nf* **1** blow on the head. **2** nod. **dar cabezadas** nod off to sleep. **cabezudo** *adj* big-headed.

cabida (ka'βiða) *nf* space, area.

cabildo (ka'βildo) *nm* **1** *rel* chapter. **2** town council.

cabina (ka'βina) *nf* cabin. **cabina de teléfono*** telephone kiosk.

cabizbajo (kaβiθ'βaxo) *adj* downhearted, dejected.

cable ('kaβle) *nm* cable, wire.

cablegrafiar (kaβleɣra'fjar) *vi* cable. **cablegrama** *nm* cable(gram).

cabo ('kaβo) *nm* **1** end. **2** handle. **3** stump, stub. **4** strand. **5** chief. **6** corporal. **7** *pl* bits and pieces, accessories. **al cabo de** at the end of. **llevar a cabo** carry out, finish.

cabra ('kaβra) *nf* nanny goat. **cabrero** *nm* goatherd.

cabria ('kaβrja) *nf* hoist, crane.

cacahuete (kaka'wete) *nm* peanut.

cacao (ka'kao) *nm* cocoa, cacao.

cacarear (kakare'ar) *vi* crow, cackle. *vt* boast about.

cacería (kaθe'ria) *nf* hunting, hunt.

cacerola (kaθe'rola) *nf* (sauce)pan, casserole.

cacique (ka'θike) *nm* **1** chief, local leader. **2** despot.

caco ('kako) *nm* **1** pickpocket, thief. **2** coward.

cacto ('kakto) *nm* cactus.

cacharrería (katʃarre'ria) *nf* crockery. **cacharro** *nm* **1** earthenware pot. **2** piece of junk.

cachete (ka'tʃete) *nm* **1** blow, slap. **2** cheek, plump cheek.

cachivache (katʃi'βatʃe) *nm* **1** kitchen pot. **2** worthless fellow. **3** useless article, junk.

cacho ('katʃo) *nm* small piece, crumb.

cachorro (ka'tʃorro) *nm* puppy, cub.

cada ('kaða) *adj invar* each, every.

cadáver (ka'ðaβer) *nm* body, corpse.

cadena (ka'ðena) *nf* **1** chain, link. **2** sequence, series.

cadencia (ka'ðenθja) *nf* cadence, rhythm.

cadera (ka'ðera) *nf anat* hip.

cadete (ka'ðete) *nm* cadet.

caducar (kaðu'kar) *vi* **1** become senile. **2** expire, go out of date. **caduco** *adj* **1** senile. **2** out of date, expired, invalid.

caer* (ka'er) *vi* **1** fall down, go down, collapse, drop. **2** (of clothes) suit, fit. **3** be located, lie. **caer en** or **sobre** fall upon. **caer en la cuenta** realize, understand.

café (ka'fe) *nm* **1** coffee. **2** cafe. **café con leche** white coffee. **café solo** black coffee.

cafeína (kafe'ina) *nf* caffeine.

cafetera (kafe'tera) *nf* coffee pot.

cafetería (kafete'ria) *nf* coffee bar, cafe.

caí (ka'i) *v see* **caer.**

caída (ka'iða) *nf* **1** fall, drop, downfall. **2** slope. **3** fold, hanging. **la caída del sol** sunset.

caigo (ka'igo) *v see* **caer.**

caimán (kai'man) *nm* alligator.

caja ('kaxa) *nf* **1** box, chest. **2** safe, cashbox, cash desk. **caja de ahorros** savings bank. **cajero** *nm* cashier. **cajetilla** *nf* packet (of cigarettes, etc.). **cajita** *nf* small box. **cajón** *nm* large box, crate.

cal (kal) *nm min* lime.

calabaza (kala'βaθa) *nf* pumpkin, gourd. **dar calabazas a 1** reject amorous proposals (of a man). **2** fail (a student in an exam).

calabozo (kala'βoθo) *nm* **1** prison cell. **2** dungeon.

calamar (kala'mar) *nm* squid.

calambre (ka'lambre) *nm* cramp.

calamidad (kalami'ðað) *nf* calamity, misfortune.

calar (ka'lar) *vt* **1** soak, go through. **2** penetrate. **3** *tech* do fretwork. **4** *inf* understand, size up. *vi* **1** (of water, etc.) soak in. **2** leak.

calavera (kala'βera) *nf* skull.

calcar (kal'kar) vt trace, copy. **calco** nm tracing.

calce ('kalθe) nm rim (of a wheel), tyre.

calceta (kal'θeta) nf 1 stocking. 2 fetter. **calcetero** nm hosier. **calcetín** nm sock.

calcinar (kalθi'nar) vt burn, blacken.

calcio ('kalθjo) nm calcium.

calcular (kalku'lar) vt calculate. **calculadora** nf computer, calculating machine.

cálculo ('kalkulo) nm 1 calculation, estimate. 2 med gallstone, stone.

calda ('kalda) nf 1 heating. 2 pl hot springs.

caldera (kal'dera) nf cauldron, boiling pan. **calderilla** nf coppers, small change.

caldo ('kaldo) nm 1 broth, soup. 2 gravy. 3 dressing, sauce. 4 pl comm oil, wine, vegetable juices.

calefacción (kalefak'θjon) nf heating. **calefacción central** central heating.

calendario (kalen'darjo) nm calendar.

calentar (ie) (kalen'tar) vt heat, warm. **calentarse** vr 1 warm oneself. 2 become heated or excited. **calentura** nf med fever.

calibrar (kali'βrar) vt measure, guage. **calibre** nm 1 gauge. 2 calibre. 3 diameter (of tube, etc.).

calidad (kali'ðað) nf 1 quality. 2 character. **en calidad de** in the capacity of.

cálido ('kaliðo) adj hot, warm.

caliente (ka'ljente) adj warm, hot, heated.

calificar (kalifi'kar) vt 1 qualify. 2 assess, judge. **calificación** nf 1 qualification. 2 class, assessment. **calificado** adj 1 qualified. 2 well-known.

cáliz ('kaliθ) nm chalice, cup.

calmar (kal'mar) vt calm, soothe. **calmarse** vr calm down. **calma** nf calm, peace. **calmante** adj soothing. nm sedative. **calmoso** adj calm, tranquil.

calor (ka'lor) nm 1 heat, warmth. 2 excitement.

caloría (kalo'ria) nf calorie.

caluroso (kalu'roso) adj 1 warm, hot. 2 excited, enthusiastic.

calvo ('kalβo) adj 1 bald. 2 bare, barren. **calvicie** nf baldness.

calzar (kal'θar) vt 1 put on (shoes). 2 wear (shoes). 3 wedge, block. **calza** nf 1 wedge. 2 stocking. 3 pl breeches. **calzada** nf 1 road, drive. **calzado** adj wearing shoes, shod. nm footwear.

calzón (kal'θon) nm shorts, pants. **calzón de baño** bathing trunks. **calzoncillos** nm pl underpants.

callar (ka'ʎar) vt,vi keep silent. **callarse** vr become quiet, stop talking. **callado** adj 1 quiet, reserved. 2 silent.

calle ('kaʎe) nf road, street. **abrir** or **hacer calle** clear the way. **callejón** nm alley, side street. **callejuela** nf side street, passage.

callo ('kaʎo) nm 1 med corn, callus. 2 pl cul tripe. **calloso** adj hard, callous.

cama ('kama) nf bed, bedstead. **cama de campaña/matrimonio/soltero** camp/double/ single bed.

camaleón (kamale'on) nm chameleon.

cámara ('kamara) nf 1 room, chamber, hall. 2 camera.

camarero (kama'rero) nm waiter, steward.

camarilla (kama'riʎa) nf 1 small room. 2 pol lobby. 3 clique.

camarín (kama'rin) nm 1 dressing room. 2 niche.

cambiar (kam'bjar) vt exchange, convert. vi alter, change. **cambiante** adj changing, variable. nm moneychanger. **cambio** nm 1 change, alteration. 2 exchange. **en cambio** on the other hand, instead.

camello (ka'meʎo) nm camel.

caminar (kami'nar) vi walk, travel. **caminante** nm traveller, walker. **camino** nm 1 road, path. 2 route, way. **ponerse en camino** set out.

camión (ka'mjon) nm lorry, wagon.

camisa (ka'misa) nf 1 shirt. 2 jacket, casing. 3 casing, wrapper. **dejar sin camisa** leave penniless. **camiseta** nf vest. **camisón** nm nightshirt.

campamento (kampa'mento) nm camp.

campana (kam'pana) nf 1 bell. 2 bell-shaped object. **campanada** nf 1 peal (of a bell). 2 scandal. **campanario** nm belfry, bell tower.

campante (kam'pante) adj 1 outstanding. 2 inf self-satisfied, proud.

campaña (kam'paɲa) nf 1 countryside. 2 campaign.

campeón (kampe'on) nm champion. **campeón de venta** bestseller.

campo ('kampo) nm 1 country(side). 2 field, ground. 3 camp. 4 sphere, range. **campesino** adj country, rustic. nm countryman, peasant. **compestre** adj rural, country.

can (kan) nm 1 dog. 2 trigger.

cana ('kana) nf white or grey hair.

Canadá (kana'ða) nm Canada. **canadiense** adj,n Canadian.

canal (ka'nal) *nm* 1 canal. 2 channel. 3 pipe, tube. **canalón** *nm* gutter, spout, drainpipe.

canalla (ka'naʎa) *nf* mob, rabble. *nm* swine, scoundrel.

canapé (kana'pe) *nm* 1 sofa, couch. 2 *cul* canapé.

Canarias (ka'narjas) *nf pl* Canaries. **canario** *adj* of the Canaries. *nm* inhabitant of the Canaries.

canario (ka'narjo) *nm* canary.

cancelar (kanθe'lar) *vt* cancel, wipe out. **cancelación** *nf* cancellation.

cáncer ('kanθer) *nm* 1 cancer. 2 *cap* Cancer.

canciller (kanθi'ʎer) *nm* chancellor.

canción (kan'θjon) *nf* song, lyric. **cancionero** *nm* song book.

candado (kan'daðo) *nm* padlock.

candela (kan'dela) *nf* candle. **candelero** *nm* candlestick, lamp.

candente (kan'dente) *adj* red-hot, burning.

candidato (kandi'ðato) *nm* candidate. **candidatura** *nf* candidature.

cándido (kandiðo) *adj* simple, innocent. **candidez** *nf* simplicity, innocence.

candil (kan'dil) *nm* oil lamp.

candor (kan'dor) *nm* sincerity, simplicity. **candoroso** *adj* sincere, open.

canela (ka'nela) *nf* cinnamon.

canelón (kane'lon) *nm* 1 spout, gutter. 2 icicle.

cangrejo (kan'grexo) *nm* crab.

canguro (kan'guro) *nm* kangaroo.

caníbal (ka'niβal) *adj,n* cannibal.

canilla (ka'niʎa) *nf* 1 *anat* shin. 2 *tech* bobbin. 3 tap, spout.

canjear (kanxe'ar) *vt* exchange, swap. **canje** *nm* exchange.

cano ('kano) *adj* 1 grey-haired. 2 ancient, venerable.

canoa (ka'noa) *nf* canoe.

canon (ka'non) *nm* 1 rule. 2 *rel* canon. 3 *mus* canon.

canónigo (ka'nonigo) *nm rel* canon. **canónico** *adj* canonical.

cansar (kan'sar) *vt* tire, weary. **cansado** *adj* 1 tired. 2 tiresome. **cansancio** *nm* fatigue.

cantar (kan'tar) *vt,vi* 1 sing, chant. 2 *inf* squeal, confess. *nm* 1 song. 2 singing.

cántara ('kantara) *nf* 1 large pitcher. 2 liquid measure.

cántaro ('kantaro) *nm* jug, pitcher. **llover a cántaros** rain cats and dogs

cantera (kan'tera) *nf* quarry. **cantería** *nf* 1 quarrying. 2 masonry. **cantero** *nm* 1 quarryman. 2 stonemason.

cantidad (kanti'ðað) *nf* quantity, portion.

cantimplora (kantim'plora) *nf* water bottle, canteen.

cantina (kan'tina) *nf* buffet, canteen.

canto[1] ('kanto) *nm* 1 singing. 2 song.

canto[2] ('kanto) *nm* 1 edge, border. 2 stone, pebble. **de canto** on edge, edgeways.

cantor (kan'tor) *nm* singer. *adj* singing.

caña ('kaɲa) *nf* 1 reed, stalk. 2 shin, bone. 3 beer glass, tumbler.

cañada (ka'ɲaða) *nf* ravine, glen.

cáñamo ('kaɲamo) *nm* hemp.

caño ('kaɲo) *nm* pipe, sewer. **cañería** *nf* piping, drain.

cañón (ka'ɲon) *nm* 1 tube, pipe, shaft. 2 gun, cannon. 3 barrel (of a gun, etc.). 4 canyon.

caoba (ka'oβa) *nf* mahogany.

caos ('kaos) *nm* chaos. **caótico** *adj* chaotic.

capa ('kapa) *nf* 1 cloak. 2 layer, coating.

capacidad (kapaθi'ðað) *nf* 1 capacity. 2 ability, talent.

capar (ka'par) *vt* 1 castrate. 2 reduce.

capataz (kapa'taθ) *nm* foreman.

capaz (ka'paθ) *adj* 1 large, roomy. 2 capable.

capellán (kape'ʎan) *nm* chaplain.

capilar (kapi'lar) *adj,nm* capillary.

capilla (ka'piʎa) *nf* chapel, choir.

capital (kapi'tal) *nm comm* capital. *nf* capital (city). *adj* capital, principal.

capitán (kapi'tan) *nm* captain, chief. **capitanear** *vt* lead.

capitular (kapitu'lar) *vi* 1 make an agreement. 2 *mil* surrender.

capítulo (ka'pitulo) *nm* 1 chapter (of a book, etc.). 2 meeting (of a council, etc.). 3 *rel* chapter.

capote (ka'pote) *nm* 1 long cloak. 2 *inf* scowl. 3 cape (of a bullfighter).

capricho (ka'pritʃo) *nm* whim, fancy. **caprichoso** *adj* capricious.

cápsula ('kapsula) *nf* cartridge case, capsule.

captar (kap'tar) *vt* 1 gain, attract. 2 get control over.

capturar (kaptu'rar) *vt* capture, arrest. **captura** *nf* capture, seizure.

capucha (ka'putʃa) *nf* 1 hood. 2 circumflex accent.

capuchina (kapu'tʃina) *nf* nasturtium.

capullo (ka'puʎo) *nm* 1 cocoon. 2 bud.

cara ('kara) *nf* 1 face. 2 appearance. 3 cheek, boldness. 4 outside, surface. **cara adelante/atrás** forwards/backwards. **cara o cruz** heads or tails. **hacer cara a** face up to.

carabina (kara'βina) nf rifle, carbine. **carabinero** nm rifleman.

caracol (kara'kol) nm 1 snail. 2 curl (of hair). 3 spiral.

carácter (ka'rakter) nm 1 character. 2 nature, type.

característico (karakte'ristiko) adj characteristic.

caramelo (kara'melo) nm toffee, sweet.

carátula (ka'ratula) nf theatre, stage.

caravana (kara'βana) nf 1 caravan. 2 group, band.

carbohidrato (karβoi'δrato) nm carbohydrate.

carbón (kar'βon) nm 1 coal. 2 carbon paper.

carbonero (karβo'nero) nm coalman. adj coal. **carbonería** nf coalyard.

carburador (karβura'δor) nm carburettor.

cárcel ('karθel) nf prison. **carcelero** nm jailer.

carcomer (karko'mer) vt eat away, undermine. **carcomerse** vr become worm-eaten, decay. **carcoma** nf 1 woodworm. 2 gnawing anxiety. **carcomido** adj worm-eaten, rotten.

cardar (kar'δar) vt tech card, comb. **carda** nf 1 tech card, carding. 2 inf reprimand.

cardenal (karδe'nal) nm 1 cardinal. 2 bruise.

cardíaco (kar'δiako) adj cardiac.

cardinal (karδi'nal) adj principal, cardinal.

cardo ('karδo) nm thistle.

carear (kare'ar) vt confront, compare. **carear a** face towards. **carearse** vr meet, come face to face.

carecer* (kare'θer) vi lack, need. **carecimiento** nm lack, need. **carencia** nf lack, shortage.

carestía (kares'tia) nf 1 scarcity. 2 famine. 3 high price or cost. .

careta (ka'reta) nf mask, veil. .

cargar (kar'gar) vt 1 load, burden. 2 charge. 3 inf annoy. vi 1 be loaded. 2 bear, shoulder a load. 3 lean, incline, turn. **cargarse (de)** vr 1 burden oneself (with). 2 be abundant (with). 3 (of sky) become dark. **carga** nf 1 load, burden. 2 charge. 3 loading. 4 duty, tax. **cargadero** nm loading bay. **cargador** nm 1 loader, stoker. 2 tech charger. **cargamento** nm load, cargo.

cargo ('kargo) nm 1 load, burden. 2 comm debit, charge. 3 role, duty. 4 accusation, charge. **estar a cargo de** be in charge.

cariarse (ka'rjarse) vr (of teeth) decay.

caribe (ka'riβe) adj,n Caribbean. (**Mar**) **Caribe** Caribbean (Sea).

caricatura (karika'tura) nf caricature.

caricia (ka'riθja) nf caress.

caridad (kari'δaδ) nf charity.

cariño (ka'riɲo) nm affection, love. **cariñoso** adj affectionate, tender.

caritativo (karita'tiβo) adj charitable.

cariz (ka'riθ) nm appearance, look.

carmesí (karme'si) adj,nm crimson.

carnal (kar'nal) adj of the flesh, carnal.

carnaval (karna'βal) nm carnival.

carne ('karne) nf flesh, meat.

carnicería (karniθe'ria) nf 1 butcher's (shop), slaughterhouse. 2 carnage, slaughter. **carnicero** adj 1 carnivorous. 2 cruel. nm butcher.

carnívoro (kar'niβoro) adj carnivorous.

caro ('karo) adj 1 dear, beloved. 2 expensive. adv dear(ly).

carpeta (kar'peta) nf file, folder. **dar carpetazo a** shelve, do nothing about.

carpintería (karpinte'ria) nf 1 carpentry. 2 carpenter's (shop). **carpintero** nm carpenter.

carrera (kar'rera) nf 1 run, race. 2 course, row (of bricks, etc.). 3 career, profession. 4 ladder (in stocking, etc.). 5 course (of study).

carretear (karrete'ar) vt cart, haul. **carreta** nf cart, wagon. **carrete** nm spool, reel.

carretera (karre'tera) nf road, highway.

carril (kar'ril) nm 1 rut, furrow. 2 lane, track, rail.

carro ('karro) nm 1 cart, car. 2 carriage (of a typewriter).

carroña (kar'rona) nf carrion.

carroza (kar'roθa) nf 1 coach, carriage. 2 float.

carta ('karta) nf 1 letter. 2 charter, document. 3 map. 4 card. **poner las cartas boca arriba** lay one's cards on the table.

cartel (kar'tel) nm placard, poster. **cartelera** nf hoarding, notice board.

cartera (kar'tera) nf 1 wallet. 2 briefcase. 3 ministerial post.

cartílago (kar'tilago) nm cartilage.

cartón (kar'ton) nm 1 cardboard. 2 box, carton. 3 cartoon.

cartucho (kar'tutʃo) nm 1 cartridge. 2 paper cone.

casa ('kasa) nf 1 house, home. 2 flat. 3 building. 4 firm, business. **casa y comida** board and lodging. **en casa** at home. **poner casa** set up house.

casar (ka'sar) vt 1 marry off, give in marriage. 2 pair, join. **casarse con** marry, get married. **casamiento** nm marriage.

cascabel (kaska'βel) nm 1 small bell. 2 inf scatterbrain.

cascada (kas'kaδa) nf cascade, waterfall.

cascar (kas'kar) vt 1 crack, split. 2 inf beat, wipe the floor with. vi inf chatter. **cascarse** vr 1 break. 2 inf break down in health.

cáscara ('kaskara) nf shell, peel, bark.

casco ('kasko) nm 1 helmet. 2 skull. 3 broken piece (of china, etc.). 4 cask, barrel. 5 hoof. 6 pl brains. **cascote** nm rubble.

caserío (kase'rio) nm 1 group of houses, settlement. 2 country house.

casero (ka'sero) adj of the house, domestic. nm 1 landlord. 2 caretaker.

casi ('kasi) adv almost.

casilla (ka'siʎa) nf 1 cabin, hut. 2 pigeonhole, section.

caso ('kaso) nm case, event, matter. **en tal caso** in such a case. **en todo caso** in any case. **hacer caso** a notice, heed.

caspa ('kaspa) nf dandruff, scab.

casta ('kasta) nf 1 race, caste. 2 kind, class.

castaña (kas'taɲa) nf 1 chestnut. 2 bun (in the hair). nm chestnut tree. **castaño** adj brown, chestnut-coloured.

castañuela (kasta'ɲwela) nf castanet.

castellano (kaste'ʎano) adj,nm Castilian, Spanish.

castidad (kasti'ðað) nf chastity.

castigar (kasti'gar) vt punish, chastise. **castigo** nm punishment.

Castilla (kas'tiʎa) nf Castile.

castillo (kas'tiʎo) nm castle.

castizo (kas'tiθo) adj 1 pure. 2 traditional, authentic. 3 purebred, racially pure.

casto ('kasto) adj chaste, pure.

castor (kas'tor) nm beaver.

castrar (kas'trar) 1 castrate. 2 prune.

castrense (kas'trense) adj military.

casual (ka'swal) adj accidental, chance. **casualidad** nf chance, accident. **por casualidad** by chance.

casucha (ka'sutʃa) nf hovel, slum.

cataclismo (kata'klismo) nm cataclysm.

catadura¹ (kata'ðura) nf tasting, sampling.

catadura² (kata'ðura) nf inf looks, face, mug.

catálogo (ka'talogo) nm catalogue.

Cataluña (kata'luɲa) nf Catalonia. **catalán** adj,nm Catalan, Catalonian. nm Catalan (language).

catar (ka'tar) vt 1 taste, try. 2 examine, see.

catarata (kata'rata) nf 1 waterfall. 2 med cataract.

catarro (ka'tarro) nm catarrh, common cold.

catástrofe (ka'tastrofe) nf catastrophe. **catastrófico** adj catastrophic.

catecismo (kate'θismo) nm catechism.

cátedra ('kateðra) nf 1 lectureship. 2 subject for study. 3 lecture room.

catedral (kate'ðral) nf cathedral.

categoría (katego'ria) nf category, class. **categórico** adj categorical, downright.

cátodo ('katoðo) nm cathode.

católico (ka'toliko) adj 1 (Roman) Catholic. 2 true, right. nm (Roman) Catholic.

catorce (ka'torθe) adj fourteen.

catre ('katre) nm cot, camp bed.

cauce (kau'θe) nm bed (of a river, etc.), ditch.

caución (kau'θjon) nf 1 caution. 2 security.

caucho ('kautʃo) nm rubber.

caudillo (kau'ðiʎo) nm chief, leader.

causar (kau'sar) vt cause, create. **causa** nf 1 cause, reason. 2 trial.

cautela (kau'tela) nf 1 wariness, caution. 2 cunning. **cauteloso** adj 1 cautious. 2 cunning.

cautivar (kauti'βar) vt 1 capture. 2 charm, captivate. **cautivo** nm captive.

cauto ('kauto) adj cautious, careful.

cavar (ka'βar) vt dig (over). vi (of a wound) go deeply. **cava** nf cultivation. **cavadura** nf excavation.

caverna (ka'βerna) nf cave, cavern. **cavernoso** adj cavernous, deep.

cavidad (kaβi'ðað) nf cavity.

cavilar (kaβi'lar) vt think deeply about. **caviloso** adj suspicious, brooding.

cayado (ka'jaðo) nm stick, crook.

cayó (ka'jo) v see **caer.**

cazar (ka'θar) vt 1 hunt, chase. 2 catch. 3 inf trick. **caza** nf. 1 hunting. 2 hunt. 3 game. **cazador** nm hunter.

cazo ('kaθo) nm ladle.

cazoleta (kaθo'leta) nf 1 small pan. 2 bowl (of a pipe). 3 guard (of a sword).

cazuela (ka'θwela) nf stewpot, casserole.

cebada (θe'βaða) nf barley. **cebadal** nm barley field.

cebar (θe'βar) vt 1 feed up, fatten. 2 prime, charge (a gun, etc.). vi (of a nail, etc.) go in. **cebarse** (en) vr 1 vent one's anger (on). 2 devote oneself (to). **cebo** nm 1 feed. 2 bait.

cebolla (θe'βoʎa) nf 1 onion. 2 bulb (of a flower). **cebollana** nf chive.

cebra ('θeβra) nf zebra.

cecear (θeθe'ar) vi lisp.

ceder (θe'ðer) vt give up, yield. vi 1 give in. 2 diminish, abate. 3 sag, give way.

cédula ('θeðula) nf document, certificate.

cegar (ie) (θe'gar) vt 1 make blind. 2 block, close up. vi become blind. **ceguedad** or **ceguera** nf blindness.

ceja ('θexa) nf 1 eyebrow. 2 rim, edging. 3 cloud cap. 4 mountain peak. **fruncir las cejas** knit one's brows. **quemarse las cejas** burn the midnight oil.

celar (θe'lar) vt watch over carefully, check on. **celada** nf 1 ambush. 2 helmet. **celador** nm watchman, attendant.

celda ('θelda) nf cell.

celebrar (θele'βrar) vt 1 celebrate. 2 hold, conduct (a meeting, etc.). 3 praise, welcome. vi rel say mass. **celebrarse** vr take place.

célebre ('θeleβre) adj 1 famous. 2 witty, amusing.

celebridad (θeleβri'ðað) nf 1 celebrity, fame. 2 celebration, festivity.

celeridad (θeleri'ðað) nf speed.

celeste (θe'leste) adj celestial, heavenly.

celibato (θeli'βato) nm 1 celibacy. 2 inf bachelor. **célibe** adj unmarried, single. nm,f unmarried person.

celo ('θelo) nm 1 zeal, enthusiasm. 2 zool rut, heat. 3 pl jealousy. **dar celos a** make jealous. **tener celos (de)** be jealous-(of). **celosía** nf 1 lattice. 2 jealousy. **celoso** adj 1 zealous. 2 jealous.

celta ('θelta) adj,n Celtic, Celt. nm Celtic (language).

célula ('θelula) nf bot, zool cell.

cementerio (θemen'terjo) nm cemetery.

cemento (θe'mento) nm cement.

cenar (θe'nar) vi have one's evening meal. vt have for supper, dine on. **cena** nf evening meal, supper.

cenefa (θe'nefa) nf edging, border.

cenicero (θeni'θero) nm ashtray.

ceniza (θe'niθa) nf ash, cinder.

censo ('θenso) nm 1 census. 2 leasehold, mortgage.

censurar (θensu'rar) vt 1 censure, criticize, blame. 2 pol censor. **censura** nf 1 criticism, blame. 2 censorship. **censurable** adj blameworthy.

centellear (θenteʎe'ar) vi flash, twinkle. **centella** nf spark, flash (of lightning, etc.). **centelleo** nm sparkle, flashing.

centena (θen'tena) nf hundred.

centenal (θente'nal) nm also **centenar** nm hundred. **a centenares** by the hundred(s). **centenario** adj,nm centenary.

centeno (θen'teno) nm rye.

centésimo (θen'tesimo) adj hundredth.

centigrado (θen'tigraðo) adj centigrade.

céntimo ('θentimo) adj hundredth. nm cent, hundredth part of a peseta.

centinela (θenti'nela) nm,f guard, sentry.

centrar (θen'trar) vt centre. **central** adj central. nf head office, headquarters. **centro** nm 1 centre, middle. 2 goal, objective.

centuria (θen'turja) nf century.

ceñir (i) (θe'nir) vt 1 surround, girdle. 2 shorten, abbreviate. **ceñirse** vr 1 put on. 2 limit oneself, tighten one's belt.

ceño ('θeno) nm frown. **fruncir el ceño** frown. **ceñudo** adj frowning.

cepa ('θepa) nf 1 stump, stock (of a vine, etc.). 2 origin, stock.

cepillar (θepi'ʎar) vt 1 brush. 2 plane down, smooth. **cepillo** nm 1 brush. 2 tech plane. **cepillo de dientes** toothbrush.

cera ('θera) nf wax.

cerámico (θe'ramiko) adj ceramic. **cerámica** nf ceramics, pottery.

cerca ('θerka) adv near. **cerca de 1** near to, close by. 2 almost, about. **cercanía** nf 1 nearness. 2 suburbs, outskirts. **cercano** adj near, approaching.

cercar (θer'kar) vt enclose, fence in. **cerca** nf wall, fence. **cercado** nm 1 enclosure. 2 fence.

cerco ('θerko) nm 1 ring, hoop. 2 enclosure, circle. 3 frame, casing.

Cerdeña (θer'ðeɲa) nf Sardinia.

cerdo ('θerðo) nm pig, pork.

cereal (θere'al) adj,nm cereal.

cerebro (θe'reβro) nm brain. **cerebral** adj cerebral, brain.

ceremonia (θere'monja) nf ceremony. **ceremonial** adj ceremonial. **ceremonioso** adj ceremonious, formal.

cereza (θe'reθa) nf cherry. **cerezal** nm cherry orchard. **cerezo** nm cherry tree.

cerilla (θe'riʎa) nf match.

cerner (ie) (θer'ner) vt 1 sieve, sift. 2 watch carefully. **cernerse** vr 1 hover, threaten. 2 waddle.

cero ('θero) nm nothing, zero.

cerrar (ie) (θer'rar) vt 1 close, shut. 2 block, obstruct. 3 stop, turn off. 4 enclose. 5 close, complete. vi 1 close, shut. 2 close in. **cerrarse** vr 1 close up. 2 cloud over. 3 stand firm, be determined. **cerrar con llave** lock, bolt. **cerrado** adj 1 closed. 2 obscure. 3

cloudy. **4** secretive, quiet. **cerradura** nf **1** locking, shutting. **2** bolt. **cerraja** nf lock, bolt.

cerril (θer'ril) adj rough, rocky.

cerro (θerro) nm **1** hill. **2** zool spine, neck.

cerrojo (θer'roxo) nm bolt, lock.

certeza (θer'teθa) nf certainty. **certidumbre** nf certainty, conviction.

certificar (θertifi'kar) vt certify, register. **certificado** adj certified, registered. nm **1** certificate. **2** registered letter.

cervato (θer'βato) nm fawn.

cerveza (θer'βeθa) nf beer. **cervecería** nf brewery.

cerviz (θer'βiθ) nf **1** nape of the neck. **2** cervix.

cesar (θe'sar) vt cease, stop. vi **1** cease, stop. **2** leave one's job, quit. **cesación** nf stoppage, cessation. **cesante** adj out of work.

césped (θespeð) nm lawn, grass.

cesta ('θesta) nf **1** basket, hamper. **2** racquet. **cesto** nm large basket.

cetro ('θetro) nm sceptre, power.

cía ('θia) nf hip bone.

cianuro (θja'nuro) nm cyanide.

cicatriz (θika'triθ) nf scar.

ciclo ('θiklo) nm cycle. **cíclico** adj cyclic(al).

ciclón (θi'klon) nm cyclone.

ciego ('θjego) adj blind. nm blind person.

cielo ('θjelo) nm **1** sky, heaven. **2** roof. **¡cielos!** interj heavens!

ciénaga ('θjenaga) nf marsh, swamp.

ciencia ('θjenθja) nf science. **científico** adj scientific. nm scientist.

cieno ('θjeno) nm mud. **cienoso** adj muddy.

ciento ('θjento) adj,nm also **cien** hundred. **centésimo** adj,nm hundredth.

cierre ('θjerre) nm **1** closing, shutting. **2** fastener, clasp.

cierto ('θjerto) adj **1** certain, sure. **2** a certain (person or thing). **por cierto** certainly.

ciervo ('θjerβo) nm stag, deer.

cierzo ('θjerθo) nm north wind.

cifra ('θifra) nf **1** number, figure. **2** amount. **3** code, cipher. **4** abbreviation.

cigarro (θi'garro) nm cigar. **cigarrillo** nm cigarette.

cigüeña (θi'gweɲa) nf stork.

cilindro (θi'lindro) nm cylinder. **cilíndrico** adj cylindrical.

cima ('θima) nf **1** top (of a tree, etc.). **2** summit (of a mountain, etc.).

cimentar (ie) (θimen'tar) vt lay the foundations, establish. **cimiento** nm foundation, basis.

cinc (θink) nm zinc.

cincel (θin'θel) nm chisel. **cincelador** nm sculptor, stone cutter.

cinco ('θinko) adj,nm five.

cincuenta (θin'kwenta) adj,nm fifty.

cinchar (θin'tʃar) vt secure a saddle on (a horse). **cincha** nf girth (of a saddle). **cincho** nm belt, iron hoop.

cine ('θine) nm cinema.

cínico ('θiniko) adj **1** cynical. **2** impudent. nm cynic.

cinta ('θinta) nf ribbon, tape, strip.

cintura (θin'tura) nf **1** waist. **2** belt, girdle. **cinturón** nm belt. **cinturón de seguridad** nm safety belt.

ciprés (θi'pres) nm cypress tree.

circo ('θirko) nm circus.

circuito (θir'kwito) nm circuit.

circulación (θirkula'θjon) nf **1** circulation. **2** traffic, movement.

circular (θirku'lar) vt pass round. vi circulate, move about. adj circular, round.

círculo ('θirkulo) nm circle, ring.

circuncidar (θirkunθi'ðar) vt circumcise. **circuncisión** nf circumcision. **circunciso** adj circumcised.

circunferencia (θirkunfe'renθja) nf circumference.

circunflejo (θirkun'flexo) nm circumflex.

circunscribir (θirkunskri'βir) vt circumscribe, limit.

circunstancia (θirkun'stanθja) nf circumstance. **circunstancial** adj circumstantial. **circunstante** adj surrounding. nm,f bystander, onlooker.

ciruela (θi'rwela) nf plum. **ciruelo** nm plum tree.

cirugía (θiru'xia) nf surgery. **cirujano** nm surgeon.

cisco ('θisko) nm **1** min slack. **2** inf hubbub, row.

cisma ('θisma) nm schism, disagreement.

cisterna (θis'terna) nf cistern, tank.

cita ('θita) nf **1** appointment, date. **2** quotation.

citar (θi'tar) vt **1** make an appointment. **2** quote. **3** law summon.

ciudad (θju'ðað) nf city, town. **ciudadano** adj city, civic. nm citizen, city dweller. **ciudadela** nf citadel.

cívico ('θiβiko) adj civic, patriotic.

civil (θi'βil) adj civil.

civilizar (θiβili'θar) vt civilize. **civilización** nf civilization.

cizalla (θi'θaʎa) *nf* 1 wire cutters, shears. 2 (metal) shavings, filings.

clamar (kla'mar) *vi,vt* cry out, clamour. *nm* cry, shout. **clamoroso** *adj* noisy, loud.

clandestino (klandes'tino) *adj* secret.

clara ('klara) *nf* 1 white (of an egg). 2 bald patch.

claraboya (klara'βoja) *nf* skylight.

clarear (klare'ar) *vt,vi* brighten, light up. **clarearse** *vr* 1 be transparent. 2 *inf* reveal secrets.

clarete (kla'rete) *nm* light red wine, rosé.

claridad (klari'ðað) *nf* 1 clarity, brightness. 2 *pl* home truths, nasty remarks.

clarificar (klarifi'kar) *vt* clarify, illuminate. **clarificación** *nf* clarification.

clarín (kla'rin) *nm* bugle.

clarinete (klari'nete) *nm* clarinet.

claro ('klaro) *adj* 1 clear, bright. 2 (of colours) light. 3 distinct, clear. *adv* clearly. *nm* 1 opening, gap. 2 skylight. **¡claro que sí!** of course! **poner en claro** explain, clarify.

clase ('klase) *nf* 1 class, type. 2 class, lesson. 3 classroom. **clase media** middle class.

clásico ('klasiko) *adj* classic(al). *nm* 1 classic. 2 classicist.

clasificar (klasifi'kar) *vt* classify, sort. **clasificación** *nf* classification.

claudicar (klauði'kar) *vi* 1 limp. 2 hesitate, back down.

claustro ('klaustro) *nm* 1 cloister. 2 council. 3 faculty.

claustrofobia (klaustro'foβja) *nf* claustrophobia.

cláusula ('klausula) *nf* clause.

clavar (kla'βar) *vt* 1 nail, knock in. 2 fix, fasten. 3 *inf* cheat. **clava** *nf* club, truncheon. **clavado** *adj* nailed, fixed. **clavija** *nf* peg, plug. **clavo** *nm* nail, stud. **dar en el clavo** hit the nail on the head.

clave ('klaβe) *nf* 1 key (to problem, etc.). 2 *mus* clef. *nm* harpsichord.

clavel (kla'βel) *nm* carnation.

clavícula (kla'βikula) *nf* collar bone.

clemencia (kle'menθja) *nf* mercy. **clemente** *adj* merciful.

clérigo ('klerigo) *nm* priest, clergyman. **clerical** *adj* clerical. **clero** *nm* clergy.

cliente ('kljente) *nm* client, customer. **clientela** *nf* clients, patients, clientèle.

clima ('klima) *nm* climate. **climático** *adj* climatic.

clínica ('klinika) *nf* clinic, nursing home. **clínico** *adj* clinical.

cloaca (klo'aka) *nf* sewer, drain.

cloro ('kloro) *nm* chlorine.

clorofila (kloro'fila) *nf* chlorophyll.

coacción (koak'θjon) *nf* coercion. **coactivo** *adj* coercive.

coagular (koagu'lar) *vt* coagulate, clot, congeal.

coartada (koar'taða) *nf* alibi.

coartar (koar'tar) *vt* restrict, limit.

cobarde (ko'βarðe) *adj* cowardly. *rim,f* coward. **cobardía** *nf* cowardice.

cobertizo (koβer'tiθo) *nm* shed.

cobijar (koβi'xar) *vt* cover, shelter. **cobijo** *nm* shelter.

cobrar (ko'βrar) *vt* 1 recover, regain. 2 charge, earn. 3 gain. *vi* collect one's salary, draw wages. **cobrarse** *vr med* recover.

cobre ('koβre) *nm* 1 copper. 2 *mus* brass.

cocer* (ko'θer) *vt,vi* cook. **cocido** *adj* cooked. *nm* stew.

cocinar (koθi'nar) *vt,vi* cook. **cocina** *nf* 1 kitchen. 2 cookery. **cocinero** *nm* cook.

coco ('koko) *nm* 1 coconut. 2 maggot, grub. 3 bogeyman. 4 *inf* face, mug.

coche ('kotʃe) *nm* 1 car. 2 coach, carriage. **coche-cama** *nm, pl* **coches-cama** sleeping car. **cochero** *nm* coachman.

cochino (ko'tʃino) *adj* dirty, rotten. *nm* pig, swine.

codear (koðe'ar) *vt,vi* elbow, nudge.

codeína (koðe'ina) *nf* codeine.

códice ('koðiθe) *nm* manuscript.

codiciar (koði'θjar) *vt* greatly desire, covet. **codicia** *nf* greed. **codicioso** *adj* greedy.

código ('koðigo) *nm* 1 code. 2 law, rules.

codo ('koðo) *nm* 1 elbow. 2 angle, bend. **hablar por los codos** talk a great deal, talk nineteen to the dozen.

codorniz (koðor'niθ) *nf* quail.

coerción (koer'θjon) *nf* coercion, restraint.

cofia ('kofja) *nf* white cap, coif.

cofradía (kofra'ðia) *nf* fraternity, association.

cofre ('kofre) *nm* chest.

coger (ko'xer) *vt* 1 seize, grasp. 2 take, catch. 3 obtain, get. *vi* fit, have room. **cogida** *nf* 1 gathering. 2 fruit harvest. 3 (in bullfighting) goring. **cogido** *nm* fold, crease.

cogote (ko'gote) *nm* nape of the neck.

cohete (ko'ete) *nm* rocket.

cohibir (koi'βir) *vt* check, restrain. **cohibirse** *vr* feel embarrassed or shy. **cohibición** *nf* restraint, inhibition. **cohibido** adj restricted, shy.

coincidencia (koinθi'ðenθja) nf coincidence. **coincidente** adj coincidental.

cojear (koxe'ar) vi 1 limp. 2 wobble. 3 inf go astray. **cojera** nf lameness. **cojo** adj 1 lame. 2 wobbly, shaky.

cojín (ko'xin) nm cushion.

cok (kok) nm coke.

col (kol) nf cabbage. **col de bruselas** Brussels sprout.

cola ('kola) nf 1 tail, end. 2 train (of a dress, etc.). 3 queue. 4 glue.

colaborar (kolaβo'rar) vi collaborate, help. **colaboración** nf collaboration.

colapso (ko'lapso) nm collapse, breakdown.

colar (ue) (ko'lar) vt 1 strain, filter. 2 bleach. vi go through. **colarse** vr 1 slip through, steal in. 2 slip up, make an error. **colada** nf washing. **coladero** nm colander, sieve.

colcha ('koltʃa) nf bedspread.

colchón (kol'tʃon) nm mattress.

colear (kole'ar) vi wag (a tail).

colección (kolek'θjon) nf collection. **colectivo** adj collective. **colectividad** nf whole, sum total, collectivity.

colega (ko'lega) nm colleague.

colegio (ko'lexjo) nm school, college. **colegial** adj school, college. nm schoolboy.

cólera ('kolera) nf anger. nm cholera. **colérico** adj angry.

coleta (ko'leta) nf 1 pigtail. 2 postscript.

colgar (ue) (kol'gar) vt,vi hang. **colgadero** nm hanger, peg. **colgadizo** adj hanging. **colgante** adj hanging. nm pendant.

coliflor (koli'flor) nf cauliflower.

colilla (ko'liʎa) nf butt, cigarette end.

colina (ko'lina) nf hill.

colindar (kolin'dar) vi be adjacent. **colindante** adj neighbouring.

colisión (koli'sjon) nf collision, crash.

colmar (kol'mar) vt 1 fill to the top, heap. 2 fulfill. **colmado** adj abundant, overflowing.

colmena (kol'mena) nf (bee)hive.

colmillo (kol'miʎo) nm tooth, fang, tusk.

colmo ('kolmo) nm highest point, limit.

colocar (kolo'kar) vt 1 place, put, arrange. 2 place in a job. **colocación** nm employment.

colonia (ko'lonja) nf colony.

Colonia (ko'lonja) nf Cologne. **agua de colonia** nf toilet water.

colonizar (koloni'θar) vt colonize. **colonia** nf colony. **colonización** nf colonization.

coloquio (ko'lokjo) nm conversation, talk.

color (ko'lor) nm 1 colour, colouring. 2 paint, dye. **coloración** nf coloration. **colorado** adj 1 coloured, esp. red. 2 (of a joke) obscene, blue.

colorar (kolo'rar) vt colour, dye.

colorear (kolore'ar) vt 1 colour, dye. 2 gloss over, whitewash, put in a favourable light. vi grow red. **colorete** nm rouge. **colorido** nm colour(ing). **colorín** nm 1 vivid colour. 2 linnet.

colosal (kolo'sal) adj colossal.

columna (ko'lumna) nf column, pillar.

columpiar (kolum'pjar) vt swing. **columpiarse** vr 1 sway. 2 waddle. **columpio** nm swing.

collar (ko'ʎar) nm necklace, collar.

comadre (ko'maðre) nf 1 godmother. 2 midwife. 3 go-between. 4 friend, neighbour.

comadreja (koma'ðrexa) nf weasel.

comadrona (koma'ðrona) nf midwife.

comandante (koman'dante) nm commander. **comandancia** nf command, headquarters.

comandita (koman'dita) nf sleeping partnership. **socio comanditario** nm sleeping partner.

comarca (ko'marka) nf region, district.

comba ('komba) nf 1 bend, curve. 2 skipping rope. **combadura** nf curve or camber (in a road, etc.).

combatir (komba'tir) vt attack, fight, struggle against. vi fight. **combate** nm combat, fight. **combatiente** nm combatant.

combinar (kombi'nar) vt combine, join. **combinación** nf 1 combination. 2 scheme, plan. 3 underskirt.

combustible (kombus'tible) adj combustible. nm fuel.

comedia (ko'meðja) nf comedy, play. **comediante** nm (comic) actor.

comedido (kome'ðiðo) adj moderate, courteous.

comedor (kome'ðor) nm dining room.

comendador (komenda'ðor) nm knight commander.

comentar (komen'tar) vt comment on, criticize. **comentario** nm commentary. **comentarista** nm commentator. **comento** nm comment.

comenzar (ie) (komen'θar) vt,vi begin, commence.

comer (ko'mer) vt 1 eat, feed, consume. 2 fade, corrode. vi eat, have a meal. **comerse** vr eat up, swallow.

comercio (ko'merθjo) nm 1 commerce, business. 2 dealings, intercourse. **comercial**

adj commercial. **comerciante** *nm* dealer, merchant.

comestible (komes'tiβle) *adj* edible. **comestibles** *nm pl* provisions, groceries.

cometa (ko'meta) *nf* kite. *nm* comet.

cometer (kome'ter) *vt* commit. **cometido** *nm* task, commitment.

cómico ('komiko) *adj* comic(al). *nm* comedian.

comida (ko'miða) *nf* 1 food. 2 meal, lunch.

comienzo (ko'mjenθo) *nm* beginning.

comillas (ko'miλas) *nf pl* inverted commas, quotation marks.

comino (ko'mino) *nm* cumin (seed).

comisaría (komisa'ria) *nf* police station, commissariat. **comisario** *nm* commissary, head of police.

comité (komi'te) *nm* committee.

comitiva (komi'tiβa) *nf* retinue, procession.

como ('komo) *adv* 1 like, as, in the same way. 2 about, approximately. *conj* 1 as, since. 2 if. **tan pronto como** as soon as.

cómo *adv* how, why, in what way. *interj* what, eh. **el por qué y el cómo** the why and the wherefore.

comodidad (komoði'ðað) *nf* comfort, convenience, advantage.

cómodo ('komoðo) *adj* comfortable, convenient.

compacto (kom'pakto) *adj* compact, dense.

compadecer* (kompaðe'θer) *vt* pity. **compadecerse (de)** *vr* sympathize (with).

compadre (kom'paðre) *nm* 1 godfather. 2 friend, pal.

compañero (kompa'ɲero) *nm* 1 companion, comrade, partner. 2 (one of a) pair. **compañía** *nf* company, society.

comparar (kompa'rar) *vt* compare. **comparación** *nf* comparison. **comparativo** *adj* comparative.

comparecer* (kompare'θer) *vi* appear in court.

compartimiento (komparti'mjento) *nm* 1 compartment. 2 division.

compartir (kompar'tir) *vt* share, divide.

compás (kom'pas) *nm* 1 rhythm, time. 2 *math* compass(es). 3 *naut* compass.

compatible (kompa'tiβle) *adj* compatible. **compatibilidad** *nf* compatibility.

compeler (kompe'ler) *vt* compel.

compendio (kom'pendjo) *nm* summary, compendium. **en compendio** briefly.

compensar (kompen'sar) *vt* compensate, balance. **compensación** *nf* compensation. **compensatorio** *adj* compensatory.

competir (i) (kompe'tir) *vi* compete, rival.

competencia *nf* 1 competition, rivalry. 2 competence. 3 field, province. **competente** *adj* appropriate, apt, adequate. **competición** *nf* contest. **competidor** *nm* competitor, rival.

compilar (kompi'lar) *vt* compile. **compilación** *nf* compilation.

compinche (kom'pintʃe) *nm f* pal, chum.

complacer* (kompla'θer) *vt* please, help. **complacerse** *vr* be pleased to. **complacencia** *nf* pleasure, willingness. **complaciente** *adj* helpful, pleasing.

complejo (kom'plexo) *adj,nm* complex.

complementario (komplemen'tarjo) *adj* complementary. **complemento** *nm* complement.

completar (komple'tar) *vt* complete. **completo** *adj* complete, full, perfect.

complicar (kompli'kar) *vt* complicate, muddle. **complicarse** *vr* become confused or complicated. **complicación** *nf* complication. **complicado** *adj* complicated, complex.

cómplice ('kompliθe) *nm,f* accomplice.

complicidad (kompliθi'ðað) *nf* complicity.

complot (kom'plot) *nm* plot, intrigue.

componer* (kompo'ner) *vt* 1 compose, make up. 2 repair. 3 prepare, arrange. 4 settle (a quarrel, etc.). **componerse** *vr* 1 dress up. 2 consist.

comportar (kompor'tar) *vt* tolerate, bear. **comportarse** *vr* behave. **comportamiento** *nm* behaviour. **comporte** *nm* 1 conduct. 2 bearing, carriage.

composición (komposi'θjon) *nf* 1 composition. 2 settlement (of a quarrel, etc.). 3 arrangement. **compositor** *nm* composer.

comprar (kom'prar) *vt* buy, bribe. **compra** *nf* buying, purchase. **ir de compras** go shopping. **comprador** *nm* shopper.

comprender (kompren'der) *vt,vi* 1 include, comprise. 2 understand. **comprensible** *adj* understandable. **comprensión** *nf* 1 inclusion. 2 understanding. **comprensivo** *adj* 1 inclusive. 2 understanding.

compresa (kom'presa) *nf* 1 compress. 2 sanitary towel. **compresión** *nf* compression.

comprimir (kompri'mir) *vt* squeeze, compress. **comprimirse** *vr* control oneself.

comprobar (ue) (kompro'βar) *vt* prove, check. **comprobación** *nf* proof, checking.

comprometer (komprome'ter) *vt* 1 compromise. 2 risk. **comprometerse** *vr* 1 compromise oneself. 2 undertake, promise. **comprometido** *adj* 1 embarrassing. 2 committed.

compromiso nm 1 commitment, obligation. 2 engagement, agreement. 3 awkward situation.

compuerta (kom'pwerta) nf floodgate, sluice, hatch.

computar (kompu'tar) vt calculate. **computador** nm computer.

comulgar (komul'gar) vt give communion. vi take communion.

común (ko'mun) adj common, general. nm 1 community. 2 toilet. **por lo común** generally. **comunal** adj communal.

comunicar (komuni'kar) vt 1 communicate, transmit. 2 (of two rooms, etc.) connect. **communicarse** vr 1 be in touch, correspond. 2 connect. **comunicación** nf 1 communication. 2 message.

comunidad (komuni'ðað) nf community.

comunión (komu'njon) nf communion.

comunismo (komu'nismo) nm communism. **comunista** adj,n communist.

con (kon) prep 1 with, by means of. 2 in the company of. 3 in spite of. 4 to, towards. **con que** conj 1 and so. 2 whereupon. **con tal que** provided that.

cóncavo ('konkaβo) adj concave. nm hollow.

concebir (i) (kon θe'βir) vt conceive, imagine. vi med conceive. **concebible** adj imaginable.

conceder (konθe'ðer) vt concede, grant.

concejo (kon'θexo) nm council. **concejal** nm councillor. **concejil** adj municipal.

concentrar (konθen'trar) vt concentrate. **concentración** nf concentration.

concepción (konθep'θjon) nf 1 conception, idea. 2 med conception.

concepto (kon'θepto) nm 1 idea, opinion. 2 heading.

concerniente (konθer'njente) adj concerning.

concertar (ie) (konθer'tar) vt,vi harmonize, agree.

conciencia (kon'θjenθja) nf 1 conscience, conscientiousness. 2 awareness. **concienzudo** adj conscientious.

concierto (kon'θjerto) nm 1 agreement. 2 mus concert, concerto.

conciliar (konθi'ljar) vt 1 reconcile. 2 gain. adj of a council. **concilio** nm 1 councillor. 2 council, assembly.

conciso (kon'θiso) adj concise.

concluir (konklu'ir) vt 1 conclude, finish. 2 deduce, decide. vi end, finish. **conclusión** nf conclusion.

concordar (ue) (konkor'ðar) vt,vi agree. **concordancia** nf agreement. **concorde** adj agreed.

concretar (konkre'tar) vt bring together, make concrete. **concretarse** vr 1 become definite. 2 confine oneself. **concreto** adj concrete, definite.

concubina (konku'βina) nf concubine.

concurrir (konkur'rir) vi 1 meet, come together. 2 contribute. 3 coincide. **concurrido** adj crowded.

concurso (kon'kurso) nm 1 contest, competition. 2 meeting. 3 help, cooperation.

concha ('kontʃa) nf shell.

condado (kon'daðo) nm county, earldom. **conde** nm earl.

condecorar (kondeko'rar) vt decorate (a person). **condecoración** nf decoration, medal.

condenar (konde'nar) vt 1 condemn, convict. 2 block up. **condenarse** vr blame oneself. **condenación** nf condemnation. **condenado** adj condemned.

condensar (konden'sar) vt condense. **condensador** nm condenser.

condescender* (kondesθen'der) vi 1 condescend. 2 comply, agree, consent. **condescendencia** nf acquiescence.

condición (kondi'θjon) nf 1 condition, nature. 2 position, rank. 3 condition, requirement.

condicionar (kondiθjo'nar) vt condition, determine. **condicionado** adj conditioned.

condimentar (kondimen'tar) vt season, flavour. **condimento** nm seasoning.

condiscípulo (kondis'θipulo) nm schoolfellow.

conducir* (kondu'θir) vt 1 transport. 2 guide. 3 conduct, direct. vi 1 mot drive. 2 be suitable. **conducirse** vr behave, conduct oneself. **conducción** nf 1 transportation. 2 guiding. 3 contracting of services. **conducción a la izquierda** left-hand drive.

conducta (kon'dukta) nf 1 management. 2 conduct, behaviour.

conducto (kon'dukto) nm 1 conduit. 2 pipe. **conductor** nm tech conductor.

conduje (kon'duxe) v see **conducir**.

conduzco (kon'duθko) v see **conducir**.

conectar (konek'tar) vt tech 1 connect. 2 switch on.

conejo (ko'nexo) nm rabbit. **conejillo de Indias** nm guinea pig.

conexión (konek'sjon) nf 1 tech connection, coupling. 2 relationship.

confabularse (kanfaβu'larse) vr scheme, plot.

confeccionar (konfekƟjo'nar) *vt* **1** make, prepare. **2** *med* concoct.

confederar (konfeðe'rar) *vt* confederate, ally. **confederarse** *vr* confederate. **confederación** *nf* confederation, confederacy.

conferenciar (konferen'Ɵjar) *vi* confer, consult. **conferencia** *nf* **1** meeting, conference. **2** lecture, talk. **3** trunk call. **conferencia cumbre** summit conference.

conferir (le) (konfe'rir) *vt* **1** confer, grant. **2** consult.

confesar (konfe'sar) *vt,vi* acknowledge, confess. **confesar de plano** confess everything. **confesarse** *vr* **1** confess. **2** *rel* make confession. **confesarse de sus pecados** confess one's sins. **confesión** *nf* confession. **confesional** *adj* confessional. **confesionario** *nm* confessional.

confiar (kon'fjar) *vi* have faith, trust. *vt* entrust. **confiar en** trust in. **confiar al azar** leave to chance. **confianza** *nf* **1** trust. **2** self-assurance. **3** familiarity.

confidencia (konfi'ðenƟja) *nf* secret or confidential information. **confidencial** *adj* confidential.

confidente (konfi'ðente) *nm,f* confidant.

configurar (konfigu'rar) *vt* fashion, dispose, shape. **configuración** *nf* configuration, shape.

confinar (konfi'nar) *vt* **1** confine. **2** exile, banish. **confinar con** border on. **confín** *adj* bordering. *nm* **1** border. **2** *pl* confines.

confirmar (konfir'mar) *vt* confirm, prove.

confiscar (konfis'kar) *vt* confiscate. **confiscación** *nf* confiscation.

confitar (konfi'tar) *vt* **1** coat with sugar. **2** preserve in syrup. **confite** *nm* sweet. **confitería** *nf* confectioner's factory or shop.

conflicto (kon'flikto) *nm* conflict.

confluir (konflu'ir) *vi* **1** run or flow together. **2** *inf* gather, meet.

conformar (konfor'mar) *vt* adjust, make agree. **conformar con** agree with. **conformarse** *vr* **1** conform. **2** resign oneself. **conforme** *adj* **1** alike. **2** in agreement. *nm* written endorsement at the bottom of a document. **conforme a** in accordance with. **todo queda conforme estaba** everything remains as it was.

confortar (konfor'tar) *vt* **1** encourage. **2** comfort. **confortable** *adj* **1** encouraging. **2** comforting. **conforte** *nm* **1** encouragement. **2** comfort.

confrontar (konfron'tar) *vt* **1** bring face to face. **2** compare. **confrontar con** *vi* **1** border on. **2**

confront. *vr* face up to, confront. **confrontación** *nf* **1** confrontation. **2** comparison.

confundir (konfun'dir) *vt* **1** mix up, confuse. **2** mistake. **confusión** *nf* confusion, perplexity. **confuso** *adj* **1** mixed up. **2** blurred, indistinct. **3** bewildered.

congelar (konxe'lar) *vt* **1** freeze. **2** congeal. **congelarse** *vr* **1** become frozen. **2** be frostbitten.

congestión (konxes'tjon) *nf* congestion. **congestionarse** *vr* become congested. **se le congestionó la cara** he got red in the face.

conglomerarse (konglome'rarse) *vr* bring together.

congoja (kon'goxa) *nf* distress.

congratular (kongratu'lar) *vt* congratulate. **congratularse** *vr* **1** congratulate oneself. **2** be glad. **congratulación** *nf* congratulation.

congregar (kongre'gar) *vi* congregate. **congregación** *nf* congregation.

congreso (kon'greso) *nm* *pol* conference, assembly.

cónico ('koniko) *adj* conical.

conjeturar (konxetu'rar) *vt* guess, conjecture. **conjetura** *nf* conjecture.

conjugar (konxu'gar) *vt* **1** bring together, combine. **2** *gram* conjugate. **conjugación** *nf* conjugation.

conjunto (kon'xunto) *adj* **1** joint. **2** joined. **3** allied, united. *nm* whole. **en conjunto** as a whole.

conjurar (konxu'rar) *vi* **1** ally oneself with another by oath. **2** conspire. *vt* **1** take an oath, swear in. **2** exorcise. **conjurarse** *vr* ally oneself by oath.

conmemorar (konmemo'rar) *vt* commemorate.

conmigo (kon'migo) *pron 1st pers s* with me, with myself.

conmoción (konmo'Ɵjon) *nf* **1** commotion, agitation. **2** upheaval, riot. **conmoción cerebral** cerebral concussion.

conmutar (konmu'tar) *vt* exchange.

cono ('kono) *nm* cone.

conocer* (kono'Ɵer) *vt* **1** know. **2** understand. **3** distinguish, recognize. **4** be acquainted with. **conocer de nombre** know by name. **conocerse** *vr* **1** be acquainted with. **2** understand oneself. **se conoce que** it is known that, it is clear that. **conocer de** or **en** know about. **conocer de** or **en una causa** try a case. **conocedor** *adj,nm* expert. **conocido** *adj* well-known. *nm* acquaintance. **conocimiento** *nm* **1** knowledge. **2** understanding. **3** *med* consciousness. **perder el conocimiento** lose consciousness.

conozco (ko'noθko) v see **conocer.**

conque ('konke) conj so, then. nm inf condition, terms.

conquistar (konkis'tar) vt 1 conquer. 2 gain the affection of, win over. **conquista** nf 1 conquest. 2 conquered person or object. **conquistador** adj conquering. nm 1 conqueror. 2 inf lady-killer.

consabido (konsa'βiðo) adj aforementioned.

consagrar (konsa'grar) vt 1 consecrate, declare sacred. 2 dedicate, devote.

consanguíneo (konsan'gineo) adj related by blood. **consanguinidad** nf blood relationship.

consciente (kons'θjente) adj conscious.

consecuencia (konse'kwenθja) nf 1 result, outcome. 2 importance. **en** or **por consecuencia** consequently. **ser de consecuencia** be of importance. **traer** or **tener consecuencia** have consequences.

consecuente (konse'kwente) adj 1 subsequent, following. 2 consequential.

consecutivo (konseku'tiβo) adj consecutive.

conseguir (konse'gir) vt attain, secure, bring about.

consejo (kon'sexo) nm 1 advice. 2 council. **consejo de guerra** court-martial. **consejero** nm 1 adviser. 2 member of a council.

consentir (ie) (konsen'tir) vt 1 permit, allow. 2 pamper. vi agree. **consentir en** consent to. **consentirse** vr begin to crack or give way. **consentido** adj 1 pampered, spoiled. 2 complaisant.

conserje (kon'serxe) nm doorkeeper.

conservar (konser'βar) vt 1 preserve, save. 2 conserve, maintain. **conservarse** vr 1 be kept, remain. 2 take good care of oneself. **conserva** nf 1 preserved food. 2 naut convey. **conservas alimenticias** tinned food. **conservación** nf preservation. **conservativo** adj preserving.

conservador (konserβa'ðor) adj 1 preserving. 2 pol conservative. n 1 keeper, curator. 2 pol conservative.

considerar (konsiðe'rar) vt 1 think about. 2 take into account. **considerable** adj 1 worthy of consideration. 2 of considerable size. **consideración** nf 1 consideration. 2 rel subject for meditation. **en consideración** under consideration. **ser de consideración** be important. **tener** or **guardar consideraciones** show consideration.

consignar (konsig'nar) vt 1 consign. 2 deposit for safe keeping. **consignación** nf consignment. **consigna** nf left-luggage office.

consigo (kon'sigo) pron 3rd pers s 1 with him. 2 with her. 3 with you. 4 with one, with oneself.

consiguiente (konsi'gjente) adj consequent.

consistir (konsis'tir) vi consist. **consistir en** consist of. **consistencia** nf consistency, firmness. **consistente** adj consistent.

consolar (ue) (konso'lar) vt console, comfort. **consolarse** vr be consoled. **consolación** nf consolation, comfort.

consonante (konso'nante) adj 1 rhyming. 2 harmonious. nm consonant.

consorcio (kon'sorθjo) nm comm partnership, consortium.

consorte (kon'sorte) nm,f 1 consort, associate. 2 spouse.

conspicuo (kons'pikwo) adj conspicuous, evident.

conspirar (konspi'rar) vi conspire, plot. **conspiración** nf conspiracy, plot.

constante (kon'stante) adj constant. **constancia** nf constancy.

constar (kons'tar) vi 1 be certain, be clear. 2 be recorded, be on record. **constar de** consist of. **constar en** be recorded in or on. **consta que es así** it's clear that it's so.

constiparse (konsti'parse) vr catch a cold. **constipación** nf med cold. **estar constipado** have a cold.

constituir (konstitu'ir) vt constitute, compose. **constitución** nf constitution.

construir (konstru'ir) vt 1 construct. **construcción** nf construction.

consuelo (kon'swelo) nm consolation, alleviation.

cónsul ('konsul) nm consul.

consultar (konsul'tar) vt,vi consult. **consulta** nf consultation.

consumado (konsu'maðo) adj 1 consummate. 2 complete.

consumir (konsu'mir) vt 1 consume, destroy. 2 eat up. **consumirse** vr be destroyed. **consumido** adj 1 consumed. 2 inf emaciated, wasted. **consumo** nm consumption.

contabilidad (kontaβili'ðað) nf 1 calculability. 2 accounting. **contable** nm accountant.

contacto (kon'takto) nm contact.

contado (kon'taðo) adj 1 counted. 2 few, limited. **de contado** immediately. **pago al contado** nm cash payment. **contador** nm 1 counter. 2 cashier, bookkeeper. 3 *tech* meter. **contador de aparcamiento** parking meter.

contagiar (konta'xjar) *vt* 1 transmit a contagious disease to. 2 pervert. **contagio** *nm* contagion, infection.

contaminar (kontami'nar) *vt* contaminate. **contaminación** *nf* contamination.

contar (ue) (kon'tar) *vt* 1 count. 2 relate, tell. **contar una historia** tell a story.

contemplar (kontem'plar) *vt* 1 contemplate.

contemporáneo (kontempo'raneo) *adj,nm* contemporary.

contender (ie) (konten'der) *vt* 1 contend, fight. 2 dispute, debate. **contendedor** *nm* contender.

contener (ie) (konte'ner) *vt* contain. **contención** *nf* 1 containment. 2 contest.

contentar (konten'tar) *vt* satisfy, make happy. **ser de buen contentar** be easy to please. **contento** *adj* content, satisfied.

contestar (kontes'tar) *vt* 1 reply to. 2 confirm, support. **contestar una carta** answer a letter. **contestable** 1 debatable. 2 answerable. **contestación** *nf* 1 reply. 2 debate.

contexto (kon'teksto) *nm* context.

contienda (kon'tjenda) *nf* 1 contest, fight. 2 dispute.

contigo (kon'tigo) *pron 2nd pers s fam* with you.

contiguo (kon'tigwo) *adj* contiguous, adjoining. **contigüidad** *nf* contiguity.

continente (konti'nente) *adj* continent. *nm* 1 container. 2 bearing, air. 3 continent. **continencia** *nf* continence.

contingente (kontin'xente) *adj* contingent, possible. **contingencia** *nm* contingency, possibility.

continuar (konti'nwar) *vt* continue. *vi* last, endure. **continuarse** *vr* extend oneself, be continued. **se continuará** to be continued. **continuación** *nf* continuation. **a continuación de** immediately after. **continuo** *adj* continuous.

contorno (kon'torno) *nm* 1 outline. 2 *inf* neighbourhood. **en contorno** all around.

contra ('kontra) *prep* 1 against. 2 facing, opposite. **contra viento y marea** against all odds. **en contra** in opposition.

contrabajo (kontra'βaxo) *nm mus* double bass.

contrabando (kontra'βando) *nm* 1 act of smuggling. 2 contraband.

contracción (kontrak'θjon) *nf* contraction.

contradecir* (kontraðe'θir) *vt* contradict. **con-**

tradicción *nf* contradiction. **contradictorio** *adj* contradictory.

contraer (kontra'er) *vt* contract.

contrafuerte (kontra'fwerte) *nm* buttress.

contrahacer (kontrae'θer) *vt* imitate.

contrahecho (kontra'etʃo) *adj* deformed.

contramaestre (kontrama'estre) *nm* 1 *naut* warrant officer. 2 foreman.

contrapesar (kontrape'sar) *vt* 1 counterbalance. 2 compensate for.

contrariar (kontra'rjar) *vt* oppose, contradict. **contrariedad** *nf* setback, misfortune. **contrario** *adj* 1 opposed. 2 harmful. *nm* 1 opponent. 2 adversary. **en contrario** in opposition. **por lo contrario** on the contrary.

contrarrestar (kontrarres'tar) *vt* 1 counteract, offset. 2 *sport* return (the ball).

contrasentido (kontrasen'tiðo) *nm* inconsistency, nonsense.

contrastar (kontras'tar) *vt* 1 resist, oppose. 2 stamp with a hallmark. *vi* contrast. **contraste** *nm* 1 opposition. 2 contrast. **marca de contraste** *nf* hallmark.

contrato (kon'trato) *nm* contract.

contravenir (ie) (kontraβe'nir) *vt* contravene.

contribuir (kontriβu'ir) *vt,vi* contribute. **contribución** *nf* 1 contribution. 2 tax.

controversia (kontro'βersja) *nf* controversy.

contumacia (kontu'maθja) *nf* 1 obstinate disobedience. 2 contempt of court.

convalecer* (konβale'θer) *vi* 1 convalesce, recover. **convalecencia** *nf* 1 convalescence. 2 convalescent hospital.

convencer* (konβen'θer) *vt* convince. **convencerse** *vr* be convinced.

convención (konβen'θjon) *nf* convention.

convenir (ie) (konβe'nir) *vt* agree, be agreed. **me conviene** it suits me. **convenible** *adj* compliant. **conveniencia** *nf* 1 usefulness. 2 advantage. **conveniente** *adj* 1 convenient. 2 conformable. **convenio** *nm* agreement, contract.

convento (kon'βento) *nm* convent.

converger (konβer'xer) *vi also* **convergir** 1 converge. 2 concur. **convergencia** *nf* convergence. **convergente** *adj* convergent.

conversar (konβer'sar) *vi* 1 converse, talk. 2 live with others. **conversar en** or **sobre** converse on. **conversador** *adj* sociable. **conversación** *nf* conversation.

convertir (ie) (konβer'tir) *vt* convert. **conversión** *nf* 1 conversion. 2 convergence.

convicción (konβik'θjon) *nf* belief, conviction.

convidar (konβi'ðar) vt invite. **convidar a uno con** treat someone to. **convite** nm invitation.

convincente (konβin'θente) adj convincing.

convivencia (konβi'βenθja) nf coexistence.

convocar (konβo'kar) vt convoke, call together.

convoy (kon'βoj) nm convoy.

conyugal (konju'gal) adj conjugal, matrimonial.

cónyuge ('konjuxe) nm,f spouse.

coñac (ko'ɲak) nm cognac, brandy.

cooperar (koope'rar) vi cooperate. **cooperación** nf cooperation. **cooperativa** nf cooperative.

coordinar (koorði'nar) vt coordinate.

copa ('kopa) nf glass. **tomarse unas copas** have a few drinks.

Copenhague (kope'nage) nf Copenhagen.

copete (ko'pete) nm 1 tuft or lock of hair. 2 crest, tuft of feathers. **de alto copete** aristocratic.

copia ('kopja) nf 1 abundance, plenty. 2 copy, transcript.

copiar (ko'pjar) vt transcribe, record. **copiador** adj copying. nm 1 copier. 2 copybook. **copiante** nm,f copyist.

copla ('kopla) nf 1 lit couplet. 2 stanza. **coplas de ciego** doggerel rhymes.

copo ('kopo) nm 1 spinning yarn. 2 snowflake.

coque ('koke) nm coke.

coraje (ko'raxe) nm 1 courage. 2 irritation.

coraza (ko'raθa) nf armour.

corazón (kora'θon) nm heart. **con el corazón en la mano** sincerely. **dar** or **decir el corazón** have a premonition.

corbata (kor'βata) nf necktie.

Córcega ('korθega) nf Corsica.

corchea (kor'tʃea) nf mus quaver.

corchete (kor'tʃete) nm hook and eye, clasp.

corcho ('kortʃo) nm cork.

cordel (kor'ðel) nm thin rope, string. **a cordel** in a straight line.

cordero (kor'ðero) nm lamb.

cordial (kor'ðjal) adj 1 invigorating. 2 affectionate. **cordialidad** nf 1 affection. 2 sincerity.

cordillera (korði'ʎera) nf chain of mountains.

cordón (kor'ðon) nm string. **cordón umbilical** umbilical cord.

Corea (ko'rea) nf Korea. **coreano** adj,n Korean. nm Korean (language).

coreografía (koreogra'fia) nf choreography.

corneta (kor'neta) nf bugle. **corneta de llaves** cornet.

cornudo (kor'nuðo) adj 1 horned. 2 cuckolded. nm cuckold.

coro ('koro) nm chorus.

coronar (koro'nar) vt crown. **corona** nf crown. **coronación** nf coronation.

coronel (koro'nel) nm colonel.

coronilla (koro'niʎa) n crown, top of the head.

corpóreo (kor'poreo) adj corporeal.

corral (kor'ral) nm farm yard.

correa (kor'rea) nf leather strap. **correa de ventilador** fan belt.

corrección (korrek'θjon) nf correction.

corredor (korre'ðor) nm 1 sport runner. 2 comm agent, broker. 3 corridor.

corregir (i) (korre'xir) vt correct. **corregirse** vr reform oneself.

correo (kor'reo) nm 1 courier. 2 post, mail. **correo urgente** special delivery.

correr (kor'rer) vi 1 run, flow. 2 go, pass. vt cover, travel over. **correrse** vr move.

corresponder (korrespon'der) vi 1 correspond. 2 be fitting, match, go with. 3 concern. 4 respond, reply. **a quien corresponda** to whom it may concern. **corresponderse** vr 1 correspond. 2 agree. 3 be fond of each other. **correspondencia** nf 1 correspondence, letters. 2 contact. 3 agreement. **corresponsal** nm newspaper correspondent.

corrida (kor'riða) nf running. **corrida de toros** bullfight.

corrido (kor'riðo) adj exceeding the specified weight.

corriente (kor'rjente) adj 1 running. 2 current. 3 everyday, standard. nf current, flow. **agua corriente** nf running water. **al corriente** up-to-date, informed.

corroborar (korroβo'rar) vt corroborate.

corroer (korro'er) vt corrode.

corromper (korrom'per) vt corrupt, rot. vi inf smell bad. **corromperse** vr go bad, become corrupted.

corrosión (korro'sjon) nf corrosion.

corrupción (korrup'θjon) nf 1 corruption. 2 stench.

cortar (kor'tar) vt cut. **cortarse** vr 1 cut oneself. 2 become embarrassed or tongue-tied. **cortante** adj cutting, sharp. **corte** nm 1 cutting edge. 2 act of cutting. 3 cut.

corte ('korte) nf royal court.

cortejar (korte'xar) vt court. **cortejo** nm 1 courtship. 2 entourage.

cortés (kor'tes) adj gracious, courteous.

cortesía (korte'sia) nf courtesy.

corteza (kor'teθa) *nf* rind.

cortijo (kor'tixo) *nm* 1 farm. 2 farmhouse.

cortina (kor'tina) *nf* curtain. **cortina de hierro** iron curtain. **cortina de humo** smokescreen.

corto ('korto) *adj* short. **corto de vista** short-sighted.

corvo ('korβo) *adj* curved.

cosa ('kosa) *nf* thing. **cosa de oír/ver** something worth listening to/seeing.

cosecha (ko'setʃa) *nf* harvest.

coser (ko'ser) *vt* sew. **coserse la boca** not speak a word.

cosquillas (kos'kiʎas) *nf* tickling, ticklishness.

costa ('kosta) *nf* coast.

costado (kos'taðo) *nm* 1 side. 2 *pl* lineage.

costar (ue) (kos'tar) *vi* cost. **costa** or **coste** *nf* cost.

costilla (kos'tiʎa) *nf* rib.

costra ('kostra) *nf* 1 crust. 2 *med* scab.

costumbre (kos'tumbre) *nf* custom, habit. **de costumbre** usual, usually.

costura (kos'tura) *nf* sewing.

cotejar (kote'xar) *vt* compare.

cotidiano (koti'ðjano) *adj* daily.

coto ('koto) *nm* 1 reserved hunting grounds. 2 landmark.

coyuntura (kojun'tura) *nf* 1 *anat* joint. 2 opportunity, occasion.

coz (koθ) *nf* 1 kick. 2 insult.

cráneo ('kraneo) *nm* skull.

crear (kre'ar) *vt* 1 create. 2 invent. 3 found. **creación** *nf* creation. **creador** *nm* creator.

crecer* (kre'θer) *vi* grow. **crecerse** *vr* 1 increase. 2 acquire greater confidence. **creces** *nf pl* increase. **con creces** *adv* amply. **crecido** *adj* numerous. **crecimiento** *nm* 1 growth. 2 increase in value.

credenciales (kreðen'θjales) *nf pl* credentials.

crédito ('kreðito) *nm* 1 credit. 2 belief. **carta de crédito** *nf* credit card.

credo ('kreðo) *nm* creed. **en un credo** in an instant.

crédulo ('kreðulo) *adj* credulous.

creer* (kre'er) *vt,vi* 1 believe. 2 think. **¡ya lo creo!** *interj* of course! **creíble** *adj* credible.

crema ('krema) *nf* 1 cream. 2 cream of society. *adj* 1 beige. 2 best.

crepúsculo (kre'puskulo) *nm* twilight.

crespo ('krespo) *adj* 1 crispy. 2 curly.

cresta ('kresta) *nf* crest.

creyente (kre'jente) *adj* believing. *nm,f* believer.

cría ('kria) *nf* 1 act of breeding. 2 young animal. 3 litter, brood.

criado ('krjaðo) *n* servant. *adj* brought up, bred. **bien criado** well-bred.

criar (kri'ar) *vt* 1 create. 2 breed. 3 suckle, nurse. **criar carnes** put on weight. **crianza** *nf* 1 breeding. 2 lactation. **criatura** *nf* 1 creature. 2 new-born baby.

cribar (kri'βar) *vt* screen, sift. **criba** *nm* screen, sieve.

crimen ('krimen) *nm* 1 serious crime. 2 wicked deed. **criminal** *adj,n* criminal.

cripta ('kripta) *nf* crypt.

crisálida (kri'saliða) *nf* 1 pupa. 2 cocoon.

crisantemo (krisan'temo) *nm* chrysanthemum.

crisis ('krisis) *nf invar* crisis.

crisol (kri'sol) *nm* crucible.

crispar (kris'par) *vt* 1 cause to twitch or contract. 2 irritate, annoy. **crisparse** *vr* twitch.

cristal (kris'tal) *nm* crystal, glass. **cristal hilado** fibre glass. **cristalería** *nf* 1 glassworks. 2 glassware. **cristalino** *adj* crystalline.

cristiano (kris'tjano) *adj* Christian. *n* 1 Christian. 2 person. **cristiandad** *nf* Christianity.

Cristo ('kristo) *nm* Christ.

criterio (kri'terjo) *nm* criterion.

criticar (kriti'kar) *vt* criticize. **crítica** *nf* criticism. **crítico** *adj* critical. *n* critic.

cromo ('kromo) *nm* chromium, chrome.

crónica ('kronika) *nf* 1 chronical. 2 news report.

cronista (kro'nista) *nm,f* chronicler.

cronología (kronolo'xia) *nf* chronology. **cronológico** *adj* chronological.

croquis ('krokis) *nm invar* rough draft, sketch.

cruce ('kruθe) *nm* crossing. **cruce a nivel** level crossing. **cruce de peatones** pedestrian crossing.

crucificar (kruθifi'kar) *vt* 1 crucify. 2 molest, torment. **crucifijo** *nm* crucifix. **crucifixión** *nf* crucifixion.

crudo ('kruðo) *adj* crude.

cruel (kru'el) *adj* cruel. **crueldad** *nf* cruelty.

cruento (kru'ento) *adj* bloody.

crujir (kru'xir) *vi* crackle. **crujido** *nm* crackling.

crustáceo (krus'taθeo) *nm* crustacean.

cruz (kruθ) *nf* cross. **en cruz** crosswise.

cruzar (kru'θar) *vt* 1 cross. 2 lay across. **cruzarse** *vr* 1 cross each other, intersect. 2 cross oneself, make the sign of the cross. **cruzarse de brazos** be idle. **cruzada** *nf* crusade. **cruzado** *adj* 1 crossed. 2 cross-bred. *nm* crusader.

cuaderno (kwa'ðerno) *nm* notebook.

cuadra ('kwaðra) *nf* stable.

cuadrado (kwa'ðraðo) *nm* square.

cuadragésimo (kwaðra'xesimo) *adj* fortieth.

cuadrante (kwa'ðrante) *adj* squaring. *nm* quadrant.

cuadrar (kwa'ðrar) *vt* square.

cuadro ('kwaðro) *nm* 1 square. 2 painting, picture. **en cuadro** square-shaped.

cuadrúpedo (kwa'ðrupeðo) *adj,nm* quadruped.

cuajar (kwa'xar) *vt* 1 congeal, thicken. 2 ornament excessively. *vi* become set or established. **cuajarse** *vr* 1 thicken. 2 fill with.

cual (kwal) *pron* 1 which. 2 he who. **a cual más** equally.

cualidad (kwali'ðað) *nf* quality.

cuan (kwan) *adv* how.

cuando ('kwando) *adv* when. **de cuando** or **de vez en cuando** from time to time. **¿de cuándo acá?** since when?

cuantía (kwan'tia) *nf* quantity.

cuanto ('kwanto) *adj* 1 as much as. 2 how much. **¿cuántos?** how many? **por cuanto** inasmuch as.

cuarenta (kwa'renta) *adj,nm* forty.

cuaresma (kwa'resma) *nf* Lent.

cuartear (kwarte'ar) *vt* quarter, cut up.

cuartel (kwar'tel) *nm* 1 quarter. 2 *mil* barracks.

cuatro ('kwatro) *adj,nm* four. **cuarto** *adj* fourth. *nm* 1 quarter. 2 room. **cuarto de baño** bathroom.

cuba ('kuβa) *nf* barrel. **estar hecho una cuba** be drunk.

Cuba ('kuβa) *nf* Cuba. **cubano** *adj,nm* Cuban.

cubículo (ku'βikulo) *nm* cubicle.

cubierta (ku'βjerta) *nf* 1 cover. 2 *naut* deck. 3 *mot* bonnet.

cubierto (ku'βjerto) *adj* covered. *nm* 1 place at a table. 2 set of knife, fork, and spoon. 3 meal. **a bajo cubierto** under cover. **precio del cubierto** cover charge.

cubo ('kuβo) *nm* bucket.

cubrir (ku'βrir) *vt* 1 cover. 2 protect. **cubrirse** *vr* 1 put on one's hat. 2 protect oneself against a risk.

cucaracha (kuka'ratʃa) *nf* cockroach.

cuclillas (ku'kliλas) *adv* in a squatting position, sitting on one's heels.

cuclillo (ku'kliλo) *nm* 1 cuckoo. 2 cuckold.

cuchara (ku'tʃara) *nf* spoon. **cucharada** *nf* spoonful. **cucharadita** *nf* teaspoonful. **cucharón** *nm* ladle.

cuchichear (kutʃitʃe'ar) *vi* whisper. **cuchicheo** *nm* 1 whisper. 2 whispering.

cuchilla (ku'tʃiλa) *nf* 1 large knife. 2 cutting

tool. **cuchillada** *nf* slash, knife wound. **cuchilla de afeitar** razor blade. **cuchillería** *nf* 1 cutlery shop. 2 cutlery. **cuchillo** *nm* knife.

cuello ('kweλo) *nm* 1 neck. 2 collar.

cuenca ('kwenka) *nf* 1 bowl. 2 eye socket. 3 *geog* basin.

cuenta ('kwenta) *nf* 1 count, calculation. 2 *comm* account, bill. 3 report. **a cuenta y riesgo de uno** at one's own risk.

cuento ('kwento) *nm* 1 tale, story. 2 *inf* exaggerated talk, fuss. 3 *pl* trouble.

cuerda ('kwerða) *nf* 1 cord. 2 chord.

cuerdo ('kwerðo) *adj* sane. *nm* sane person.

cuerno ('kwerno) *nm* horn.

cuero ('kwero) *nm* 1 hide, skin. 2 leather.

cuerpo ('kwerpo) *nm* body. **cuerpo estatal** public body. **cuerpo extraño** foreign body.

cuervo ('kwerβo) *nm* raven.

cuesta ('kwesta) *nf* sloping ground. **a cuestas** on one's back.

cuestión (kwes'tjon) *nf* 1 question, issue. 2 dispute, quarrel. **cuestionar** *vt* question, argue about. *vi* argue.

cueva ('kweβa) *nf* 1 cave. 2 cellar.

cuidado (kwi'ðaðo) *nm* 1 care, carefulness. 2 fear, worry. **¡cuidado!** *interj* beware!

cuidar (kwi'ðar) *vt* take care of, pay attention to. **cuidar de que** take care that. **no cuidarse de** take no notice of.

culebra (ku'leβra) *nf* snake.

culebrear (kuleβre'ar) *vi* wriggle, zigzag.

culo ('kulo) *nm* backside, bottom.

culpar (kul'par) *vt* blame, condemn. **culparse** *vr* take the blame. **culpa** *nf* 1 blame, fault. 2 guilt. **culpable** *adj* 1 guilty. 2 blameworthy. *nm,f* culprit.

cultivar (kulti'βar) *vt* 1 cultivate. 2 practise, improve. **cultivador** *nm* cultivator, grower. **cultivación** *nf* cultivation. **cultivo** *nm* 1 cultivation. 2 crop.

culto ('kulto) *adj* 1 cultivated. 2 cultured. *nm* cult. **rendir culto a** worship.

cultura (kul'tura) *nf* culture, learning.

cumbre ('kumbre) *nf* summit, peak.

cumpleaños (kumple'aɲos) *nm invar* birthday.

cumplir (kum'plir) *vt* fulfil, realize. **cumplir años** reach an age. ~ *vi* fulfil one's duties.

cúmulo ('kumulo) *nm* 1 heap, accumulation. 2 *sci* cumulus.

cuna ('kuna) *nf* 1 cradle. 2 place of origin, birthplace. 3 lineage, family.

cundir (kun'dir) *vi* spread, expand.

cuneta (ku'neta) *nf* ditch.

cuña ('kuɲa) nf wedge.

cuñado (ku'ɲaðo) nm brother-in-law.

cuño ('kuɲo) nm tech stamp, die-stamp.

cuota ('kwota) nf 1 quota. 2 dues. **cuota del gremio** union dues.

cupe ('kupe) v see **caber.**

cupón (ku'pon) nm coupon.

cura ('kura) nm priest. **cura párroco** parish priest.

curar (ku'rar) vi recover, get well. vt 1 treat, apply a remedy. 2 cure. **curarse** vr 1 recover, be cured. 2 take treatment (for a wound). **cura** nf cure, remedy. **curación** nf curing. **primera curación** first aid. **curado** adj 1 cured. 2 hardened, tanned.

curioso (kuri'oso) adj 1 curious. 2 neat, clean. 3 careful. n curious person. **curiosidad** nf curiosity.

cursar (kur'sar) vt 1 frequent. 2 send out, dispatch. 3 study.

cursi ('kursi) adj inf in bad taste, flashy, cheap. n flashy, pretentious person.

curso ('kurso) nm 1 course, direction. 2 educ year. **curso acelerado** crash course.

curtir (kur'tir) vt 1 tan. 2 harden. **curtirse** vr 1 harden. 2 become accustomed to. **curtido** adj tanned, hardened. nm tanning. **estar curtido en** 1 be skilled at. 2 be hardened to. **curtidor** nm tanner.

curva ('kurβa) nf curve.

curvo ('kurβo) adj curved.

cúspide ('kuspiðe) nf peak, summit.

custodiar (kusto'ðjar) vt 1 take care of. 2 guard. **custodia** nf custody. **custodio** nm custodian, guardian.

cutis ('kutis) nm invar human skin, complexion.

cuyo ('kujo) pron 1 whose. 2 of which, of whom.

CH

chabacano (tʃaβa'kano) adj in bad taste. **chabacanería** nf 1 vulgarity. 2 vulgar remark.

chafar (tʃa'far) vt 1 flatten. 2 crumple. 3 spoil, make a mess of. **chafar a uno** cut someone short.

chal (tʃal) nm shawl.

chalado (tʃa'laðo) adj inf crazy, dotty.

chalán (tʃa'lan) nm 1 dealer, seller. 2 horse dealer. 3 inf crafty businessman, shady dealer.

chaleco (tʃa'leko) nm waistcoat.

chambelán (tʃambe'lan) nm chamberlain.

champaña (tʃam'paɲa) nm champagne.

champú (tʃam'pu) nm shampoo.

chamuscar (tʃamus'kar) vt singe, scorch.

chancear (tʃanθe'ar) vi joke, make jokes about.

chanchullo (tʃan'tʃuʎo) nm inf crooked deal.

chantaje (tʃan'taxe) nm blackmail.

chanza ('tʃanθa) nf joke. **en** or **de chanza** in fun.

chapa ('tʃapa) nf sheet, plate.

chaparro (tʃa'parro) adj squat, short, and fat.

chapotear (tʃapote'ar) vt moisten (with sponge, etc.). vi splash. **chapoteo** nm 1 moistening. 2 splashing.

chapucero (tʃapu'θero) adj 1 rough, crude. 2 clumsy, amateurish. nm clumsy person.

chapuzar (tʃapu'θar) vt plunge into water.

charca ('tʃarka) nf pool. **charco** nm puddle.

charlar (tʃar'lar) vi chat, gossip. **charla** nf inf talk, chatter. **charlador** adj also **charlatán** talkative, chattering. n chatterbox. **charladuría** nf gossip, small talk.

charol (tʃa'rol) nm 1 varnish. 2 patent leather. **darse charol** brag.

charro ('tʃarro) adj 1 vulgar, coarse. 2 flashy, in bad taste.

chasco ('tʃasko) nm 1 prank, trick. 2 disappointment.

chasquear (tʃaske'ar) vt 1 disappoint. 2 trick, make a fool of.

chato ('tʃato) adj 1 flat-nosed. 2 blunt, flattened. nm small glass, glass (of wine).

chaval (tʃa'βal) nm inf lad, kid.

Checoslovaquia (tʃekoslo'βakja) nf Czechoslovakia. **checoslovaco** adj,n Czechoslovak. **checoslovaca** nm Czech (language).

cheque ('tʃeke) nm cheque. **cheque de viajero** traveller's cheque.

chicle ('tʃikle) nm chewing gum.

chico ('tʃiko) adj 1 small. 2 very young. nm 1 youngster, lad. 2 inf old chap.

chichón (tʃi'tʃon) nm lump, swelling.

chiflar (tʃi'flar) vi whistle, hiss. vt 1 mock in public. 2 inf drink, gulp down. **chiflarse** vr become crazy. **chifla** nf whistle. **chiflado** adj crazy. **chifle** nm whistle.

chile (tʃile) nm chili.

Chile ('tʃile) nm Chile. **chileno** adj,n also **chileño** Chilean.

chillar (tʃi'ʎar) vi shriek, howl, scream. **chillador** adj howling, shrieking. **chillería** nf 1 noisy row. 2 scolding. **chillido** nm scream.

chimenea (tʃime'nea) nf 1 chimney. 2 fireplace.

chimenea francesa fireplace with mantelpiece.

chimpancé (tʃimpan'θe) nm chimpanzee.

china ('tʃina) nf chinaware.

China ('tʃina) nf China. **chino** adj,n Chinese. nm Chinese (language).

chinche ('tʃintʃe) nf bedbug.

chingar (tʃin'gar) vt inf drink too much or too frequently. **chingarse** vr get drunk.

Chipre ('tʃipre) nf Cyprus. **chipriota** adj,n also **chipriote** Cypriot.

chiripa (tʃi'ripa) nf stroke of luck.

chirriar (tʃir'rjar) vi 1 creak. 2 chirp. **chirriadero** adj 1 creaking. 2 chirping. **chirrido** nm chirping.

chisme ('tʃisme) nm 1 contrivance, gadget. 2 piece of gossip.

chismoso (tʃis'moso) adj gossiping. nm gossip.

chispear (tʃispe'ar) vi 1 spark. 2 sparkle. 3 drizzle. **chispa** nf 1 spark. 2 sparkle. 3 small amount.

chisporrotear (tʃisporrote'ar) vi spark. **chisporroteo** nm inf sparking.

chistar (tʃis'tar) vi mumble, mutter. **no chistar** not say a word. **¡chist!** interj sh!

chiste ('tʃiste) nf joke.

chocar (tʃo'kar) vt shock, surprise. vi 1 shock, be surprising. 2 collide, crash.

chocolate (tʃoko'late) nm chocolate.

choque ('tʃoke) nm 1 jolt, crash. 2 shock. 3 dispute, conflict.

chorizo (tʃo'riθo) nm spicy pork sausage.

chorrear (tʃorre'ar) vi 1 gush, spurt. 2 drip. **chorreo** nm gushing, dripping. **chorro** nm gush.

choza ('tʃoθa) nf hovel, hut.

chubasco (tʃu'basko) nm 1 shower. 2 adversity, difficulties.

chuleta (tʃu'leta) nf cutlet, chop.

chulo ('tʃulo) adj 1 amusing. 2 proud. 3 bold, outspoken. nm amusing, easy-going person.

chunga (tʃunga) nf inf fun, joking. **chungar** vi tell jokes, banter.

chupar (tʃu'par) vt suck, absorb, take in. **chuparse** vr become lean.

churro (tʃurro) nm 1 cul fritter. 2 inf mess.

chusma ('tʃusma) nf rabble, riffraff.

D

dádiva ('daðiβa) nf present, gift.

dado ('daðo) nm game die. **dados falsos** loaded dice.

daga ('daga) nf dagger.

dama ('dama) nf 1 lady. 2 mistress, lover. 3 game queen. 4 pl game draughts.

damasco (da'masko) nm damask.

damnificar (damnifi'kar) vt harm, injure.

danés (da'nes) adj Danish. nm 1 Dane. 2 Danish (language).

Danubio (da'nuβjo) nm Danube.

danzar (dan'θar) vi,vt dance. **danza** nf dancing, dance. **danzante** nm dancer.

dañar (da'nar) vt damage, harm. **dañarse** vr get hurt. **dañoso** adj bad, harmful.

dar* (dar) vt give. **darse** vr 1 surrender. 2 exist, occur. 3 regard oneself. **dar a** look out on, overlook. **dar como** or **por** consider, regard. **dar con** 1 meet. 2 find, discover. **lo mismo da** it makes no difference. **darse cuenta** notice, realize.

dardo ('darðo) nm dart.

dársena ('darsena) nm inner harbour, dock.

data ('data) nf 1 date. 2 comm item.

dátil ('datil) nm bot date.

dato nm piece of information, fact.

de (de) prep 1 of. 2 from.

debajo (de'βaxo) adv underneath. **debajo de** prep underneath.

debatir (deβa'tir) vt debate, dispute. **debate** nm debate.

deber (de'βer) vt owe. vi must, ought. **deberse a** be due to, be on account of. ~nm 1 duty. 2 debt.

débil ('deβil) adj weak.

debilitar (deβili'tar) vt weaken. **debilidad** nf weakness.

débito ('deβito) nm debt, debit.

decadencia (deka'ðenθja) nf decadence, decline. **decadente** adj decadent, declining.

decaer* (deka'er) vi decline. **decaído** adj 1 declining. 2 sad. **decaído de ánimo** in low spirits. **decaimiento** nm decline.

decano (de'kano) nm dean.

decapitar (dekapi'tar) vt behead.

decena (de'θena) nf unit of ten.

decencia (de'θenθja) nf 1 decency. 2 cleanliness.

decenio (de'θenjo) nm decade.

decente (de'θente) *adj* **1** decent. **2** tidy, clean. **3** respectable.

decepción (deθep'θjon) *nf* disappointment. **decepcionar** *vt* disappoint.

decidir (deθi'ðir) *vt* **1** decide. **2** convince. **decidirse** *vr* make up one's mind.

décimo ('deθimo) *adj* tenth. **décima** *nf* tenth. **decimal** *adj,nm* decimal.

decimoctavo (deθimok'tavo) *adj* eighteenth.

decimocuarto (deθimo'kwarto) *adj* fourteenth.

decimonoveno (deθimono'βeno) *adj also* **decimonono** nineteenth.

decimoquinto (deθimo'kinto) *adj* fifteenth.

decimoséptimo (deθimo'septimo) *adj* seventeenth.

decimosexto (deθimo'seksto) *adj* sixteenth.

decimotercio (deθimo'terθjo) *adj* thirteenth.

decir (de'θir) *vt,vi* say, tell. **a decir verdad** truthfully. **¡diga!** hello (on the telephone).

decisión (deθi'sjon) *nf* **1** decision. **2** determination. **decisivo** *adj* decisive.

declamar (dekla'mar) *vi* speak out. *vt* declaim, recite. **declamación** *nf* declamation, recital.

declarar (dekla'rar) *vt* **1** declare, state. **2** *law* find. **declararse** *vr* **1** declare oneself, make one's opinion known. **2** propose to (a girl).

declinar (dekli'nar) *vi* decline, decay. *vt* **1** decline, refuse. **2** *gram* inflect. **declinación** *nf* **1** decline, falling off. **2** *gram* declension.

declive (de'kliβe) *nm* **1** slope, incline. **2** *comm* slump.

decorar (deko'rar) *vt* decorate, adorn. **decoración** *nf* decoration. **decorador** *nm* decorator. **decorativo** *adj* decorative.

decoro (de'koro) *nm* **1** respect. **2** propriety, decorum.

decrecer (dekre'θer) *vi* decrease.

decrépito (de'krepito) *adj* decrepit.

decretar (dekre'tar) *vt* decree. **decreto** *nm* decree.

dedal (de'ðal) *nm* thimble.

dédalo ('deðalo) *nm* maze.

dedicar (deði'kar) *vt* dedicate, devote.

dedillo (de'ðiʎo) *nm* little finger. **saber al dedillo** know perfectly.

dedo ('deðo) *nm* **1** finger, toe. **2** small amount, drop. **estar a dos dedos de** be within an ace of.

deducir (deðu'θir) *vt* deduce. **deducción** *nf* deduction. **deductivo** *adj* deductive.

defender (ie) (defen'der) *vt* defend. **defendido** *nm law* defendant. **defensa** *nf* defence.

defensa pasiva civil defence. **defensivo** *adj* defensive.

deferencia (defe'renθja) *nf* deference.

deferir (ie) (defe'rir) *vt law* refer, relegate. **deferir a** defer to.

deficiencia (defi'θjenθja) *nf* deficiency. **deficiente** *adj* deficient.

déficit ('defiθit) *nm, pl* **déficits** *or* **deficits** **1** deficit. **2** shortage.

definir (defi'nir) *vt* define. **definición** *nf* definition. **definido** *adj* definite. **definitivo** *adj* definitive. **en definitivo** finally, in short.

deformar (defor'mar) *vt* **1** disfigure. **2** distort. **deformarse** *vr* become deformed, get out of shape. **deformación** *nf* deformation. **deforme** *adj* deformed, abnormal.

defraudar (defrau'ðar) *vt* **1** cheat, deceive. **2** disappoint. **defraudar impuestos** evade taxes. **defraudación** *nf* deceit. **defraudador** *adj* fraudulent.

defunción (defun'θjon) *nf* death.

degenerar (dexene'rar) *vi* **1** degenerate. **2** decline, get worse.

degollar (ue) (dego'ʎar) *vt* **1** cut the throat. **2** *law* behead. **degollación** *nf* **1** throat-cutting. **2** beheading. **degolladero** *nm* **1** throttle. **2** slaughterhouse. **3** scaffold.

degradar (degra'ðar) *vt* degrade. **degradación** *nf* degradation. **degradante** *adj* degrading.

degustar (degus'tar) *vt* taste, sample.

dehesa (de'esa) *nf* pasture.

deidad (dei'ðað) *nf* deity.

deificar (deifi'kar) *vt* deify.

dejar (de'xar) *vt* **1** leave, forsake. **2** allow, let. **dejar de 1** stop, leave off. **2** fail to, neglect to. **dejarse** *vr* neglect oneself. **dejarse de 1** stop (doing something). **2** let oneself be (heard, deceived, persuaded, etc.).

del (del) contraction of **de el**.

delantal (delan'tal) *nm* apron.

delante (de'lante) *adv* ahead, in front. **delante de** in front of, before.

delatar (dela'tar) *vt* **1** denounce. **2** betray. **delator** *nm* informer.

delegar (dele'gar) *vt* delegate. **delegación** *nf* delegation. **delegado** *adj* delegated. *nm* delegate.

deleitar (delei'tar) *vt* delight. **deleitarse** *vr* be delighted. **deleite** *nm* delight.

deletrear (deletre'ar) *vt* **1** explain, spell out. **2** interpret.

deleznable (deleθ'naβle) *adj* **1** brittle. **2** frail, weak.

delfín (del'fin) nm dolphin.

delgado (del'gaðo) adj 1 thin, slender. 2 delicate. **delgadez** nf 1 thinness. 2 delicateness.

deliberar (deliβe'rar) vt 1 discuss, debate. **deliberación** nf deliberation.

delicado (deli'kaðo) adj 1 delicate. 2 dainty. **delicadez** nf 1 debility, weakness. **delicadeza** nf 1 delicacy. 2 refinement. 3 tactfulness.

delicia (de'liθja) nf delight. **delicioso** adj delightful.

delimitar (delimi'tar) vt delimit.

delincuencia (delin'kwenθja) nf delinquency. **delincuencia de menores** juvenile delinquency. **delincuente** adj,n criminal.

delinear (deline'ar) vt outline, draw lines around. **delineante** nm draughtsman.

delirar (deli'rar) vi be delirious, rave.

delito (de'lito) nm crime.

demacrarse (dema'krarse) vr waste away. **demacración** nf emaciation. **demacrado** adj emaciated.

demagogia (dema'goxja) nf demagogy.

demandar (deman'dar) vt 1 request. 2 ask, question. 3 law petition.

demarcar (demar'kar) vt demarcate. **demarcación** nf demarcation.

demás (de'mas) adj other, rest, remaining. pron **los demás, las demás** the others.

demasía (dema'sia) nf excess.

demasiado (dema'sjaðo) adj,adv too much.

demencia (de'menθja) nf insanity.

democracia (demo'kraθja) nf democracy. **demócrata** adj democratic. nm,f democrat. **democrático** adj democratic.

demoler* (demo'ler) vt demolish.

demonio (de'monjo) nm devil, demon.

demorar (demo'rar) vt delay. vi linger. **demora** nf delay, procrastination.

demostrar (ue) (demos'trar) vt 1 prove, demonstrate. **demostración** nf 1 demonstration. 2 proof.

denegar (ie) (dene'gar) vt refuse, deny. **denegación** nf refusal.

denigrar (deni'grar) vt debase, denigrate. **denigración** nf denigration.

denominar (denomi'nar) vt name, designate.

denotar (deno'tar) vt indicate, express.

denso ('denso) adj dense.

dentado (den'taðo) adj 1 having teeth. 2 toothed, jagged.

dental (den'tal) adj dental.

dentera (den'tera) nf 1 nervousness, jitters. 2 envy, jealousy.

dentífrico (den'tifriko) nm toothpaste, dentifrice. **pasta dentífrica** nf toothpaste.

dentista (den'tista) nm,f dentist.

dentro ('dentro) adv within, inside. **dentro de** inside.

denunciar (denun'θjar) vt 1 denounce, report. 2 accuse. **denuncia** nf 1 accusation. 2 report.

departamento (departa'mento) nm department.

depender (depen'der) vi depend. **dependencia** nf dependence, reliance.

deplorar (deplo'rar) vt regret, deplore.

deponer* (depo'ner) vt 1 lay down, lay aside. 2 depose. vi law give evidence.

deportar (depor'tar) vt deport. **deportación** nf deportation.

deporte (de'porte) nm sport. **deportista** adj sporting, sports. nm,f sportsman.

depositar (deposi'tar) vt deposit, put away.

depósito (de'posito) nm deposit.

depravar (depra'βar) vt corrupt. **depravación** nf corruption. **depravado** adj depraved, bad. nm depraved person.

depreciar (depre'θjar) vt lessen in value.

depresión (depre'sjon) nf 1 depression. 2 sunken place, hollow.

deprimir (depri'mir) vt 1 press down. 2 depress, sadden. **deprimido** adj depressing, saddening.

depurar (depu'rar) vt purify.

derecha (de'retʃa) nf 1 right hand. 2 pol right wing. **¡derecha!** mil right turn! **a la derecha** to the right.

derecho (de'retʃo) adj 1 right, right-hand. 2 straight, upright. 3 right, just. nm law.

derivar (deri'βar) vt derive. **derivación** nf derivation, origin.

derogar (dero'gar) vt repeal, abolish.

derramar (derra'mar) vt 1 spill. 2 scatter, spread. **derramarse** vr spill, overflow.

derretir* (derre'tir) vt melt. **derretido** adj 1 melted. 2 inf deeply in love.

derribar (derri'βar) vt 1 demolish, tear down. 2 knock down (a person). **derribo** nm demolition.

derrochar (derro'tʃar) vt squander. **derrochador** adj,nm spendthrift. **derroche** nm waste, extravagance.

derrotar (derro'tar) vt 1 defeat. 2 tear, (clothing). 3 ruin. **derrota** nf disaster, defeat. **derrotado** adj 1 defeated. 2 shabby.

derrumbar (derrum'bar) vt 1 hurl down. 2 knock down. **derrumbarse** vr 1 be flung down. 2 collapse, fall down.

desabotonar (desaβoto'nar) vt unbutton. vi bot bloom. **desabotonarse** vr come undone.

desabrigar (desaβri'gar) vt remove the clothing from. **desabrigado** adj 1 unclothed. 2 lightly dressed. **desabrigo** nm lack of clothing or protection.

desabrochar (desaβro'tʃar) vt unfasten, unbutton.

desacato (desa'kato) nm disrespect, contempt.

desacertar (ie) (desaθer'tar) vi be wrong, make a mistake. **desacierto** nm blunder.

desacomodar (desakomo'ðar) vt inconvenience, put out. **desacomodado** adj 1 badly off. 2 unemployed.

desaconsejar (desakonse'xar) vt advise or counsel against. **desaconsejado** adj ill-advised. nm imprudent person.

desacordar (ue) (desakor'ðar) vt put out of tune. **desacordarse** vr get out of tune. **desacorde** adj discordant.

desacostumbrar (desakostum'brar) vt **desacostumbrar** a break (someone) of a habit. **desacostumbrarse** vr break a habit.

desacreditar (desakreði'tar) vt discredit.

desacuerdo (desa'kwerðo) nm disagreement, discord.

desafecto (desa'fekto) adj disaffected, indifferent.

desafinar (desafi'nar) vi 1 be out of tune. 2 inf speak out of turn:

desafio (desa'fio) nm challenge.

desagradar (desagra'ðar) vt displease, upset, bother. **desagradarse** vr be unpleasant, be disagreeable. **desagradable** adj unpleasant, disagreeable. **desagradecido** adj ungrateful. **desagrado** nm displeasure.

desagraviar (desagra'βjar) vt make amends to, apologize to. **desagravio** nm righting of a wrong, amends.

desaguar (desa'gwar) vt drain. vi 1 drain away. 2 (of a river) empty into the sea. **desaguadero** nm drain.

desagüe (de'sagwe) nm 1 drainage. 2 drain.

desahogar (desao'gar) vt 1 relieve. 2 console. **desahogarse** vr 1 (of emotions) give free rein to. 2 make oneself comfortable, relax. **desahogado** adj 1 impudent. 2 comfortable. **desahogo** nm 1 ease, relief. 2 freedom. 3 impudence.

desahuciar (desau'θjar) vt 1 evict, throw out. 2 deprive of hope. **desahucio** nm eviction.

desairar (desai'rar) vt disregard, treat with contempt, snub. **desairado** adj 1 unattractive, shabby. 2 unsuccessful. **desaire** nm snub.

desajustar (desaxus'tar) vt disarrange. **desajustarse** vr 1 disagree. 2 get out of order. **desajuste** nm 1 disorder. 2 disagreement.

desalentar (ie) (desalen'tar) vt 1 make breathless, cause to gasp. 2 discourage. **desalentarse** vr become discouraged.

desaliño (desa'liɲo) nm 1 slovenliness, uncleanliness. 2 carelessness.

desalojar (desalo'xar) vt remove, eject. vi evacuate. **desalojamiento** nm evacuation.

desalquilar (desalki'lar) vt vacate, leave. **desalquilarse** vr become vacant. **desalquilado** adj vacant.

desamor (desa'mor) nm indifference.

desamparar (desampa'rar) vt abandon. **desamparado** adj helpless, abandoned. **desamparo** nm 1 desertion. 2 defencelessness.

desangrar (desan'grar) vt 1 bleed. 2 impoverish. **desangrarse** vr lose much blood.

desanimar (desani'mar) vt discourage. **desanimarse** vr become discouraged. **desánimo** nm 1 discouragement. 2 lifelessness.

desanudar (desanu'ðar) vt untie.

desapacible (desapa'θiβle) adj unpleasant.

desaparecer* (desapare'θer) vt hide. vi disappear. **desaparición** nf disappearance.

desapercibido (desaperθi'βiðo) adj unnoticed.

desapretar (ie) (desapre'tar) vt loosen.

desaprobar (ue) (desapro'βar) vt disapprove of.

desaprovechar (desaproβe'tʃar) vt misuse, waste. vi lose ground. **desaprovechado** adj unproductive.

desarmar (desar'mar) vt,vi disarm. **desarme** nm disarmament.

desarraigar (desarrai'gar) vt uproot. **desarraigado** adj rootless.

desarreglar (desarre'glar) vt disarrange, upset. **desarreglado** adj 1 disorderly. 2 out of order. **desarreglo** nm disorder.

desarrollar (desarro'ʎar) vt 1 unroll. 2 develop, grow. **desarrollo** nm development, unfolding.

desarrugar (desarru'gar) vt smooth out.

desasir (desa'sir) vt undo, loosen. **desasirse** vr 1 get clear of. 2 free oneself of.

desasosegar (ie) (desasose'gar) vt disturb. **desasosiego** nm uneasiness, disquiet.

desastre (de'sastre) nm disaster. **desastrado**

adj 1 unlucky. 2 ragged, shabby. **desastroso** *adj* disastrous.

desatar (desa'tar) *vt* unfasten, undo. **desatarse** *vr* become undone, break loose.

desatender (ie) (desaten'der) *vt* 1 pay no attention to. 2 ignore. **desatención** *nf* 1 inattention. 2 discourtesy. **desatentado** *adj* absent-minded. **desatento** *adj* discourteous.

desatinar (desati'nar) *vt* bewilder, confuse. *vi* 1 talk nonsense. 2 act foolishly. **desatino** *nm* 1 foolishness, silliness. 2 foolish act, blunder.

desavenir (ie) (desaβe'nir) *vt* cause disagreement between. **desavenirse con** disagree with. **desavenencia** *nf* disagreement, quarrel. **desavenido** *adj* contrary, opposing, on bad terms.

desaventajado (desaβenta'xaðo) *adj* 1 inferior. 2 unfavourable.

desayunar (desaju'nar) *vi* have breakfast. **desayuno** *nm* breakfast.

desazón (desa'θon) *nf* 1 lack of flavour. 2 discomfort. 3 uneasiness, annoyance. 4 itch. **desazonar** *vt* 1 remove the flavour from (food). 2 annoy, displease.

desbandarse (desβan'darse) *vr* 1 *mil* disband. 2 flee in disorder.

desbarajustar (desβaraxus'tar) *vt* confuse, throw into disorder. **desbarajuste** *nm* disorder, confusion.

desbaratar (desβara'tar) *vt* 1 spoil, ruin. 2 squander, waste. **desbaratarse** *vr* 1 get out of order. 2 lose one's temper, become unbalanced. **desbarate** *nm* 1 destruction. 2 waste.

desbordar (desβor'ðar) *vt* pass, exceed. *vi* overflow. **desbordarse** *vr* overflow.

descabezar (deskaβe'θar) *vt* 1 behead. 2 *inf* surmount.

descalabro (deska'laβro) *nm* extreme misfortune, defeat.

descalificar (deskalifi'kar) *vt* disqualify.

descalzar (deskal'θar) *vt* take off (the shoes). **descalzo** *adj* barefooted.

descamisado (deskami'saðo) *adj* very poor, destitute. *nm* ragamuffin.

descansar (deskan'sar) *vi* rest, take a break. *vt* 1 lean on, rest on. 2 help, aid. **descanso** *nm* 1 rest time, break. 2 relief.

descarado (deska'raðo) *adj* shameless, brazen.

descargar (deskar'gar) *vt,vi* 1 unload, empty. 2 unburden. 3 (of electricity) discharge. **descargarse** *vr* 1 unburden. 2 relinquish obliga-

tions. **descarga** *nf* unloading. **descargo** *nm* 1 unloading. 2 discharge of debt.

descargue (des'karge) *nm* unloading of goods.

descartar (deskar'tar) *vt* leave out, lay aside.

descender (ie) (desθen'der) *vi* 1 descend. 2 flow, run. *vt* bring down, lower. **descendencia** *nf* descent, lineage. **descendiente** *nm,f* descendant. **descenso** *nm* 1 descent. 2 fall, decline.

descentralizar (desθentrali'θar) *vt* decentralize.

descerrajar (desθerra'xar) *vt* force a lock, break open.

descifrar (desθi'frar) *vt* decipher.

descolgar (ue) (deskol'gar) *vt* lower, take down, get down.

descolorar (deskolo'rar) *vt* discolour.

descomedido (deskome'ðiðo) *adj* excessive, immoderate.

descomponer (ue) (deskompo'ner) *vt* 1 break down into parts. 2 decompose. 3 disturb, put out of order. **descomponerse** *vr* 1 decompose. 2 break down. **descomposición** *nf* decomposition. **descompuesto** *adj* 1 broken, faulty. 2 angry, discourteous.

desconcertar (ie) (deskonθer'tar) *vt* 1 put out of order, damage. 2 disconcert, embarrass. **desconcierto** *nm* disorder, confusion.

desconectar (deskonek'tar) *vt* disconnect.

desconfiar (deskon'fjar) *vi* 1 lack confidence. 2 be distrustful. **desconfiado** *adj* distrustful. **desconfianza** *nf* mistrust.

desconocer (deskono'θer) *vt* 1 not to know, be ignorant of. 2 fail to recognize, ignore. **desconocido** *adj* unknown.

desconsiderado (deskonsiðe'raðo) *adj* inconsiderate.

desconsolar (ue) (deskonso'lar) *vt* grieve, distress. **desconsuelo** *nm* grief.

descontar (ue) (deskon'tar) *vt* 1 deduct. 2 discount.

descontento (deskon'tento) *adj* dissatisfied.

descorazonar (deskoraθo'nar) *vt* discourage. **decorazonarse** *vr* become disheartened.

descorchar (deskor't∫ar) *vt* uncork (a bottle). **descorchador** *nm* corkscrew.

descortés (deskor'tes) *adj* discourteous. **descortesía** *nf* discourtesy.

descrédito (des'kreðito) *nm* discredit.

describir (deskri'βir) *vt* describe. **descripción** *nf* description. **descriptivo** *adj* descriptive.

descuajar (deskwa'xar) *vt* 1 liquefy. 2 discourage, dishearten. 3 pull out, uproot.

descubierto

descubierto (desku'βjerto) adj 1 exposed. 2 hatless.

descubrir (desku'βrir) vt 1 discover. 2 uncover. **descubridor** n discoverer. **descubrimiento** nm discovery.

descuento (des'kwento) nm discount.

descuidar (deskwi'ðar) vt 1 neglect, be careless about. 2 relieve from care. 3 divert the attention of. vi be careless. **¡descuida!** don't worry. **descuidado** adj 1 neglected. 2 negligent. **descuido** nm 1 neglect. 2 negligence.

desde (desðe) prep from. **desde luego** of course.

desdecir (desðe'θir) vi 1 be unworthy of. 2 not suit, clash. **desdecirse** vr retract, take back.

desdén (des'ðen) nm disdain, scorn. **al desdén** with studied neglect. **desdeñar** vt disdain, scorn.

desdicha (des'ðitʃa) nf 1 misfortune. 2 misery, unhappiness. **desdichado** adj unfortunate, wretched.

desdoblar (desðo'βlar) vt 1 unfold, spread out. 2 make two of, split.

desdorar (desðo'rar) vt tarnish.

desear (dese'ar) vt desire, want.

desecar (dese'kar) vt dry up.

desechar (dese'tʃar) vt scrap, cast aside.

desembalar (desemba'lar) vt unpack (goods).

desembarazar (desembara'θar) vt remove an impediment, clear the way. **desembarazarse** vr free oneself of. **desembarazado** adj unobstructed. **desembarazo** nm 1 disencumbrance. 2 ease.

desembarcar (desembar'kar) vt,vi land, put ashore.

desembocar (desembo'kar) vi flow, empty.

desembolsar (desembol'sar) vt pay out.

desembragar (desembra'gar) vt release, disengage. vi mot declutch.

desembrollar (desembro'ʎar) vt disentangle.

desempeñar (desempe'ɲar) vt 1 recover pawned or pledged property. 2 free from debt or obligation. 3 perform (a role, duty).

desempleo (desem'pleo) nm unemployment. **desempleado** adj unemployed.

desencantar (desenkan'tar) vt disillusion. **desencanto** nm disillusionment.

desenfado (desen'faðo) nm 1 ease, freedom, lack of inhibition. 2 disrespect.

desenfrenar (desenfre'nar) vt unbridle. **desenfrenarse** vr give oneself up to evil or vice. **desenfreno** nm unruliness, licentiousness.

desenganchar (desengan'tʃar) vt unfasten.

desengañar (desenga'ɲar) vt free from illusions, disabuse. **desengañarse** vr see things as they really are. **¡desengáñate!** don't deceive yourself! **desengañado** adj disillusioned. **desengaño** nm disillusionment.

desenlace (desen'laθe) nm end, outcome.

desenredar (desenre'ðar) vt 1 disentangle. 2 clear up confusion, straighten out. **desenredarse** vr get out of a jam. **desenredo** nm disentanglement.

desenrollar (desenro'ʎar) vt unroll.

desentenderse (ie) (desenten'derse) vr 1 pretend to have no interest in or knowledge of (something). 2 take no part in.

desenterrar (ie) (desenter'rar) vt 1 unearth. 2 recall.

desentonar (desento'nar) vi be out of tune.

desentrañar (desentra'ɲar) vt 1 disembowel. 2 puzzle out, unravel.

desenvainar (desenβai'nar) vt draw (a sword).

desenvoltura (desenβol'tura) nf 1 naturalness, ease, confidence. 2 brazenness.

desenvolver (ue) (desenβol'βer) vt 1 unroll. 2 evolve, develop.

deseo (de'seo) nm desire, want.

desequilibrar (desekili'βrar) vt put out of balance. **desequilibrarse** vr become mentally unbalanced. **desequilibrado** adj mentally unbalanced. **desequilibrio** nm lack of equilibrium.

desertar (deser'tar) vt,vi desert. **desertar el hogar** leave home. **deserción** nf desertion. **desértico** adj deserted. **desertor** nm deserter.

desesperar (desespe'rar) vi despair, have no hope. vt drive to despair. **desesperarse** vr be exasperated. **desesperación** nf despair.

desestimar (desesti'mar) vt undervalue.

desfachatez (desfatʃa'teθ) nf brazenness, impudence.

desfalcar (desfal'kar) vt embezzle.

desfallecer (desfaʎe'θer) vt weaken. vi 1 get weak. 2 faint. **desfallecer de ánimo** lose heart. **desfallecido** adj 1 weak. 2 faint. **desfallecimiento** nm 1 weakness. 2 faintness.

desfavorable (desfaβo'raβle) adj unfavourable.

desfigurar (desfigu'rar) vt disfigure, alter.

desfilar (desfi'lar) vi parade. **desfiladero** nm long narrow pass. **desfile** nm parade. **desfile de modelos** fashion show.

desgajar (desga'xar) vt 1 break off, tear off.

desganarse (desga'narse) vr 1 lose one's

appetite. **2** lose interest. **desgana** nf **1** loss of appetite. **2** reluctance, disinclination.

desgarrar (desgar'rar) vt **1** tear, rip. **2** break (the heart).

desgastar (desgas'tar) vt **1** wear away, erode. **2** corrode.

desgraciar (desgra'θjar) vt **1** displease. **2** ruin, spoil. **desgraciarse** vr be spoiled, be ruined. **desgracia** nf misfortune. **desgraciado** adj **1** unfortunate. **2** graceless.

deshabitado (desaβi'taðo) adj uninhabited.

deshacer* (desa'θer) vt undo. **deshacerse** vr **1** be undone or destroyed. **2** become impatient.

deshelar (ie) (dese'lar) vt thaw, melt.

desheredar (desere'ðar) vt disinherit.

deshidratar (desiðra'tar) vt dehydrate.

deshielo (de'sjelo) nm thawing, melting.

deshilar (desi'lar) vt **1** unravel. **2** (of meat) shred. **deshilarse** vr fray, become worn.

deshilvanado (desilβa'naðo) adj (of speech, writing, etc.) disjointed, disconnected.

deshinchar (desin'tʃar) vt **1** deflate. **2** reduce swelling. **deshincharse** vr **1** deflate. **2** lose one's vanity.

deshojar (deso'xar) vt **1** defoliate. **2** pull petals off a flower. **deshojarse** vr **1** defoliate. **2** (of flower) lose petals.

deshonesto (deso'nesto) adj dishonest.

deshonrar (deson'rar) vt dishonour. **deshonra** nf dishonour. **tener a deshonra** consider dishonourable. **deshonrable** adj shameless. **deshonroso** adj dishonourable.

deshora (de'sora) **a deshora** adv **1** at an inconvenient time. **2** at the wrong time.

deshuesar (deswe'sar) vt **1** bone (meat). **2** stone (fruit).

desidia (de'siðja) nf carelessness.

desierto (de'sjerto) adj deserted. nm desert.

designar (desig'nar) vt designate. **designación** nf designation. **designio** nm plan, design.

desigual (desi'gwal) adj unequal.

desilusión (desilu'sjon) nf disillusionment.

desilusionar (desilusjo'nar) vt disillusion. **desilusionarse** vr become disillusioned.

desinfectar (desinfek'tar) vt disinfect.

desinflar (desin'flar) vt deflate.

desinterés (desinte'res) nm disinterest.

desistir (desis'tir) vi desist.

desleal (desle'al) adj disloyal.

desligar (desli'gar) vt **1** untie. **2** unravel.

deslinde (des'linde) nm fixing of limits, delimitation.

deslizar (desli'θar) vi,vt slide, skid.

deslucido (deslu'θiðo) adj tarnished, dull.

deslumbrar (deslum'brar) vt dazzle.

desmán (des'man) nm excess, outrage.

desmandarse (desman'darse) vr **1** be insolent. **2** (of animals) break away from the group.

desmantelar (desmante'lar) vt dismantle.

desmayarse (desma'jarse) vr faint, pass out. **desmayado** adj (of colour) faint, pale. **desmayo** nm faintness, weakness.

desmedirse (i) (desme'ðirse) vr act insolently, forget oneself.

desmejorar (desmexo'rar) vt **1** weaken. **2** spoil, impair. **desmejorarse** vr **1** deteriorate. **2** go downhill.

desmembrar (desmem'brar) vt **1** dismember. **2** separate, divide.

desmentir (i) (desmen'tir) vt **1** refute, deny. **2** belie.

desmenuzar (desmenu'θar) vt break into small pieces.

desmesurado (desmesu'raðo) adj **1** disproportionate, excessive. **2** discourteous, insolent. nm discourteous, insolent person.

desmontar (desmon'tar) vt **1** clear, level (land, etc.). **2** dismantle. vi dismount.

desmoralizar (desmorali'θar) vt demoralize.

desmoronar (desmoro'nar) vt destroy little by little. **desmoronarse** vr crumble into pieces.

desnatar (desna'tar) vt **1** skim (milk). **2** take the choicest part of.

desnivel (desni'βel) nm **1** unevenness. **2** difference of level, drop.

desnudar (desnu'ðar) vt strip, lay bare. **desnudarse** vr undress. **desnudamente** adv clearly, plainly. **desnudez** nf nakedness. **desnudo** adj **1** naked. **2** destitute.

desobedecer* (desoβeðe'θer) vt,vi disobey. **desobediencia** nf disobedience, rebellion. **desobediente** adj disobedient.

desocupar (desoku'par) vt vacate. **desocuparse** vr give up a business or occupation. **desocupación** nf **1** leisure. **2** unemployment. **desocupado** adj **1** unoccupied. **2** unemployed.

desodorante (desoðo'rante) nm deodorant.

desolar (deso'lar) vt lay waste, destroy. **desolarse** vr grieve. **desolación** nf desolation. **desolador** adj grieving.

desorden (de'sorðen) nm disorder. **desordenado** adj disordered.

desorganizar (desorgani'θar) vt disorganize. **desorganización** nf disorganization.

desorientar (desorjen'tar) vt lead astray, confuse.

despabilado (despaβi'laðo) adj wide awake.

despacio (des'paθjo) adv slowly, gently.

despachar (despa'tʃar) vt 1 attend to, settle. 2 get done promptly.

despacho (des'patʃo) nm 1 comm office, shop. 2 promptness. 3 message, dispatch. 4 resourcefulness.

despachurrar (despatʃur'rar) vt 1 burst, crush, squash. 2 make a mess of (a report, an account, a story one is telling).

desparpajo (despar'paxo) nm ease of manner, self-confidence.

desparramar (desparra'mar) vt 1 scatter. 2 squander.

despavorido (despaβo'riðo) adj terrified.

despectivo (despek'tiβo) adj scornful, derogatory.

despechar (despe'tʃar) vt cause to despair. **despecharse** vr despair. **despecho** nm despair. **a despecho de** in spite of.

despedazar (despeða'θar) vt 1 tear to pieces. 2 (of the heart) break.

despedir (i) (despe'ðir) vt 1 see off, show out. 2 dismiss (an employee). **despedirse** vr 1 say goodbye. 2 leave one's work. **despedida** nf 1 farewell, leave-taking. 2 dismissal from a job.

despegar (despe'gar) vt 1 unstick, unglue. **despegarse** vr become detached. **despegarse con** not to go well with. **despegado** adj 1 detached. 2 indifferent, cold.

despegue (des'pege) nm takeoff.

despeinar (despei'nar) vt ruffle (the hair).

despejar (despe'xar) vt free from obstructions. **despejarse** vr 1 clear up. 2 acquire assurance. **despejado** adj 1 clear, open. 2 wide awake. 3 intelligent. **despejo** nm 1 brightness. 2 self-assurance.

despellejar (despeʎe'xar) vt 1 skin, flay. 2 criticize harshly.

despensa (des'pensa) nf 1 pantry, food store. 2 stock of food.

despeñadero (despeɲa'ðero) adj 1 cliff. 2 inf risky business.

desperdiciar (desperði'θjar) vt waste, throw away.

desperezarse (despere'θarse) vr stretch one's limbs.

despertar (ie) (desper'tar) vt awaken. **despertarse** vr wake up. **despertador** nm 1 alarm clock. 2 warning. **despertamiento** nm awakening. **despierto** adj 1 awake. 2 alert.

despiadado (despja'ðaðo) adj cruel, inhuman.

despilfarrar (despilfar'rar) vt squander.

despintar (despin'tar) vt 1 remove paint from. 2 change, distort.

despistar (despis'tar) vt 1 throw off the scent. 2 mislead, confuse. **despistado** adj 1 absent-minded. 2 confused, muddled.

desplazar (despla'θar) vt 1 (of water) displace. 2 take the place of, replace. vr travel. **desplazamiento** nm 1 naut displacement (of water). 2 journey.

desplegar (ie) (desple'gar) vt 1 unfold, spread. 2 deploy.

desplomarse (desplo'marse) vr collapse.

despojar (despo'xar) vt 1 deprive, take away. 2 dispossess. **despojarse** vr undress. **despojo** nm 1 plundering. 2 dispossession. 3 plunder. 4 pl leftovers, scrap, waste.

desposado (despo'saðo) adj newly wed.

desposeer (despose'er) vt dispossess. **desposeerse** vr give up possession of something.

déspota ('despota) nm despot. **despótico** adj tyrannical, lawless. **despotismo** nm despotism.

despreciar (despre'θjar) vt 1 look down on. 2 underestimate. 3 reject. **despreciarse de** not deign to. **despreciable** adj worthless. **desprecio** nm scorn, contempt.

desprender (despren'der) vt detach, separate.

desprestigiar (desprestixi'ar) vt discredit.

desprevenido (despreβe'niðo) adj unprepared.

desproporción (despropor'θjon) nf disproportion.

desprovisto (despro'βisto) adj lacking.

después (des'pwes) adv 1 after, later, afterwards. 2 since, since then. **después (de que** conj after.

desquiciar (deski'θjar) vt 1 unhinge. 2 disturb upset.

desquite (des'kite) nm 1 compensation. 2 revenge.

destacar (desta'kar) vt 1 mil detail, detach. 2 Art make stand out.

destajo (des'taxo) nm piecework.

destapar (desta'par) vt uncover, open. **destaparse** vr show one's true character.

destartalado (destarta'laðo) adj 1 (of a house etc.) rambling. 2 disorderly.

destello (des'teʎo) nm sparkling.

destemplar (destem'plar) vt 1 disturb the harmony of. 2 put out of tune. **destemplarse** vr 1 get out of tune. 2 lose one's temper. **destemplado** adj 1 out of tune. 2 disagreeable.

des·eñi· (deste'ñir) vt discolour. vi fade.
desterrar (ie) (dester'rar) vt 1 exile, banish. 2 dismiss. **desterrarse** vr go into exile. **destierro** nm 1 exile. 2 place of exile.
destilar (desti'lar) vi drip, ooze. vt 1 distil. 2 exude. **destilería** nf distillery.
destinar (desti'nar) vt 1 destine. 2 designate. **destino** nm 1 fate. 2 destination. 3 position, job. **dar destino a** find a use for. **destinario** nm addressee.
destituir (destitu'ir) vt 1 deprive of. 2 remove from office. **destitución** nf 1 dismissal. 2 removal.
destornillar (destorni'ʎar) vt unscrew. **destornillarse** vr 1 behave in a wild manner. 2 inf go crazy. **destornillado** adj 1 unscrewed. 2 inf crazy. **destornillador** nm screwdriver.
destreza (des'treθa) nf skill, ability.
destronar (destro'nar) vt 1 dethrone. 2 overthrow from power.
destrozar (destro'θar) vt break, smash. **destrozo** nm destruction. **causar destrozos en** create havoc in.
destruir (destru'ir) vt destroy. **destruirse** vr math cancel each other out. **destructor** adj destructive. nm naut destroyer.
desunir (desu'nir) vt 1 separate, detach. 2 cause a rift between.
desuso (de'suso) nm disuse.
desvalido (desβa'liðo) adj destitute, helpless.
desvalijar (desβali'xar) vt 1 steal the contents of. 2 rob, burgle.
desván (des'βan) nm attic.
desvanecer· (desβane'θer) vt make disappear. **desvanecerse** vr 1 vanish. 2 evaporate. **desvanecimiento** nm disappearance.
desvarío (desβa'rio) nm 1 raving, delirium. 2 whim.
desvelar (desβe'lar) vt keep awake. **desvelarse** vr 1 stay awake. 2 be watchful. **desvelo** nm 1 lack of sleep. 2 watchfulness. **gracias a sus desvelos** thanks to his efforts.
desventaja (desβen'taxa) nf disadvantage. **desventajoso** adj disadvantageous.
desventura (desβen'tura) nf unhappiness, misfortune. **desventurado** adj unfortunate. nm wretched person.
desvergonzado (desβergon'θaðo) adj shameless. **desvergüenza** nf shamelessness.
desviar (des'βjar) vt turn aside, divert. **desviarse** vr turn away, leave, branch off. **desvío** nm 1 deviation, turning away. 2 detour.
desvirtuar (desβir'twar) vt detract from, impair.

desvivirse (desβi'βirse) vr long for, be crazy about.
detallar (deta'ʎar) vt 1 list in detail. 2 comm sell retail. **detalle** nm 1 detail, item. 2 gesture. **al detalle** 1 in detail. 2 comm retail. **detalladamente** adv in detail. **detallista** nm,f retailer.
detective (detek'tiβe) nm,f detective.
detener (ie) (dete'ner) vt detain. **detenerse** vr linger, delay. **detención** nf 1 delay. 2 detention, arrest. **detenido** adj 1 thorough. 2 under arrest. **detenimiento** nm thoroughness.
detergente (deter'xente) adj,nm detergent.
deteriorar (deterjo'rar) vt damage, spoil. vi deteriorate.
determinar (determi'nar) vt determine. **determinarse** vr make up one's mind. **determinación** nf 1 decision. 2 determination.
detestar (detes'tar) vt detest, hate.
detonar (deto'nar) vi detonate.
detractar (detrak'tar) vt defame. **detracción** nf slander, defamation.
detraer· (detra'er) vt 1 take away, separate. 2 denigrate.
detrás (de'tras) adv behind, at the back. **detrás de** prep behind. **por detrás de uno** behind someone's back.
detrimento (detri'mento) nm damage, harm. **en detrimento de** to the detriment of.
deuda ('deuða) nf 1 debt. 2 fault, offence. **deudor** adj indebted. n debtor.
deudo ('deuðo) nm relative.
devanar (deβa'nar) vt wind, spin.
devastar (deβas'tar) vt lay waste. **devastación** nf devastation.
devengar (deβen'gar) vt earn (wages or interest).
devenir· (deβe'nir) vi become. **devenir en** change into. ~nm process of development, change.
devoción (deβo'θjon) nf devotion.
devolver (ue) (deβol'βer) vt return. **devolución** nf return, repayment.
devorar (deβo'rar) vt devour.
devoto (de'βoto) adj 1 devoted. 2 devout.
di (di) v see **dar**.
día ('dia) nm day. **¡buenos días!** good morning. **de día en día** from day to day. **todos los días** every day.
diablo ('djaβlo) nm devil. **diabólico** adj diabolical.
diafragma (dja'fragma) nm diaphragm.

diagnosticar (djagnosti'kar) vt diagnose. **diagnóstico** adj diagnostic. nm diagnosis.

diagrama (dja'grama) nm diagram.

dialecto (dja'lekto) nm dialect. **dialectal** also **dialéctico** adj dialect(al).

diálogo ('djalogo) nm dialogue.

diamante (dja'mante) nm diamond.

diámetro ('djametro) nm diameter.

diario ('djarjo) adj daily. nm 1 newspaper, daily. 2 diary. **diario dominical** Sunday paper. **de diario** for everyday use.

diarrea (djar'rea) nf diarrhoea.

dibujar (dißu'xar) vt draw, sketch. **dibujarse** vr be outlined. **dibujante** nm,f 1 draughtsman. 2 cartoonist. **dibujo** nm drawing. **dibujos animados** animated cartoon.

dicción (dik'θjon) nf 1 word. 2 diction.

diccionario (dikθjo'narjo) nm dictionary.

dice (di'θe) v see **decir**.

diciembre (di'θjembre) nm December.

dictado (dik'taðo) nm 1 title of honour. 2 dictation. 3 pl dictates. **escribir al dictado** take dictation.

dictador (dikta'ðor) n dictator. **dictadura** nf dictatorship.

dictamen (dik'tamen) nm judgment, opinion. **dictamen facultativo** medical report. **dictaminar** vi give an opinion, pass judgment.

dictar (dik'tar) vt 1 dictate. 2 pass (a judgment or decree).

dicha ('ditʃa) nf 1 happiness. 2 good luck. **dichoso** adj happy.

dicho ('ditʃo) v see **decir**. nm 1 statement. 2 saying, proverb. adj above-mentioned. **dicho y hecho** no sooner said than done.

diecinueve (dieθi'inweße) adj,nm nineteen.

dieciocho (dieθi'otʃo) adj,nm eighteen.

dieciséis (dieθi'seis) adj,nm sixteen.

diecisiete (dieθi'sjete) adj,nm seventeen.

diente ('djente) nm tooth.

diestra ('djestra) nf right hand.

diestro ('djestro) nm bullfighter. adj right, right-hand. **diestramente** adv 1 skilfully. 2 cunningly.

dieta ('djeta) nf diet.

diez ('dieθ) adj,nm ten.

diezmar (dieθ'mar) vt decimate.

difamar (difa'mar) vt slander, libel. **difamación** nf slander.

diferenciar (diferen'θjar) vt differentiate. vi differ. **diferenciarse** vr be different. **diferencia** nf difference. **a diferencia de** unlike. **diferente** adj different.

diferir (ie) (dife'rir) vt 1 defer. 2 extend; prolong.

difícil (di'fiθil) adj difficult. **dificultad** nf difficulty. **dificultar** vt make difficult.

difidencia (difi'ðenθja) nf lack of faith, distrust. **difidente** adj distrustful.

difundir (difun'dir) vt 1 diffuse. 2 spread, divulge (news).

difunto (di'funto) adj deceased. nm 1 deceased person. 2 corpse.

difusión (difu'sjon) nf 1 diffusion. 2 diffuseness. 3 spreading. **difuso** adj 1 diffuse. 2 wordy.

digerir (ie) (dixe'rir) vt digest. **digerible** adj digestible. **digestión** nf digestion.

dignarse (dig'narse) vr condescend, deign.

dignidad (digni'ðað) nf 1 dignity. 2 rank, office. **dignatario** nm dignitary. **digno** adj worthy.

digo ('digo) v see **decir**.

digresión (digre'sjon) nf digression.

dije ('dixe) v see **decir**.

dilación (dila'θjon) nf delay.

dilatar (dila'tar) vt 1 dilate, expand. 2 prolong, delay. **dilatarse** vr dilate.

diligencia (dili'xenθja) nf 1 diligence. 2 job, errand.

dilucidar (diluθi'ðar) vt clear up, explain.

diluir (dilu'ir) vt dilute.

diluvio (di'luβjo) nm deluge, flood.

dimanar (dima'nar) vi arise from.

dimensión (dimen'sjon) nf dimension.

diminutivo (diminu'tiβo) adj diminutive. **diminuto** adj 1 tiny. 2 defective.

dimitir (dimi'tir) vt give up office, resign. **dimisión** nf resignation (from office).

Dinamarca (dina'marka) nf Denmark. **dinamarqués** adj Danish. nm 1 Dane. 2 Danish (language).

dinamita (dina'mita) nf dynamite.

dínamo ('dinamo) nf dynamo.

dinastía (dinas'tia) nf dynasty.

dineral (dine'ral) nm large amount of money, fortune.

dinero (di'nero) nm money. **dinero suelto** small change.

dintel (din'tel) nm lintel.

dio ('dio) v see **dar**.

diócesi(s) (di'oθesi) nf, pl **diócesis** diocese.

dios (di'os) nm god. **diosa** nf goddess.

diploma (di'ploma) nf diploma.

diplomacia (diplo'maθja) nf diplomacy. **diplomático** adj diplomatic. nm diplomat.

diputado (dipu'taðo) nm representative, delegate.

dique ('dike) nm 1 dam. 2 dike.

dirección (direk'θjon) nf 1 direction. 2 guidance. 3 address.

directo (di'rekto) adj direct.

director (direk'tor) nm 1 director. 2 manager. 3 headmaster. 4 mus conductor. adj managing, controlling.

dirigir* (diri'xir) vt 1 direct. 2 mus conduct. **dirigirse** vr go to, head for.

discernir (ie) (disθer'nir) vt discern, distinguish.

disciplina (disθi'plina) nf discipline.

discípulo (dis'θipulo) nm student.

disco ('disko) nm 1 disk, disc. 2 gramophone record.

disconformidad (diskonformi'ðað) nf disagreement.

discontinuo (diskon'tinwo) adj discontinuous.

discordia (dis'korðja) nf discord, disagreement. **discordante** adj also **discorde** discordant.

discoteca (disko'teka) nf 1 record library. 2 discothèque.

discreción (diskre'θjon) nf discretion. **a discreción** optional, discretionary.

discrepancia (diskre'panθja) nf discrepancy.

discreto (dis'kreto) adj 1 discreet. 2 reasonable.

disculpar (diskul'par) vt excuse. **disculparse** vr apologize. **disculpa** nf excuse, apology.

discurrir (diskur'rir) vt invent, think up. vi 1 roam about. 2 flow.

discurso (dis'kurso) nm 1 discourse. 2 use of reason, mental powers. 3 passage (of time).

discusión (disku'sjon) nf 1 discussion. 2 argument.

discutir (disku'tir) vt 1 discuss. 2 debate. vi dispute, argue. **discutible** adj debatable.

disecar (dise'kar) vt 1 sketch. 2 stuff, mount (dead animals). **disección** nf dissection.

diseminar (disemi'nar) vt scatter.

disensión (disen'sjon) nf dissension.

disentería (disente'ria) nf dysentery.

diseñar (dise'ɲar) vt 1 sketch. 2 design. **diseñador** nm designer. **diseño** nm 1 sketch. 2 design.

disfrazar (disfra'θar) vt disguise. **disfraz** nm fancy dress, disguise.

disfrutar (disfru'tar) vt have the benefit of, enjoy oneself. **disfrute** nm enjoyment, use.

disgregar (disgre'gar) vt disintegrate, separate.

disgustar (disgus'tar) vt displease, annoy. **disgustarse** vr be displeased. **disgusto** nm 1 unpleasantness, trouble. 2 displeasure, annoyance. **a disgusto** unwillingly.

disimular (disimu'lar) vt hide, disguise. 2 excuse, overlook. **disimulable** adj excusable. **disimulo** nm 1 dissimulation. 2 tolerance. **con disimulo** slyly.

disipar (disi'par) vt dissipate. **disiparse** vr disappear. **disipación** nf dissipation. **disipado** adj dissipated.

dislocar (dislo'kar) vt dislocate.

disminuir (disminu'ir) vt,vi diminish, decrease. **disminución** nf decrease.

disolución (disolu'θjon) nf dissolution.

disolver (ue) (disol'βer) vt dissolve.

disonar (ue) (diso'nar) vi 1 be discordant. 2 disagree. **disono** adj discordant. **disonancia** nf dissonance. **disonante** adj dissonant, discordant.

disparar (dispa'rar) vt,vi shoot, fire, discharge. **dispararse** vr 1 rush off. 2 (of firearms) go off. **disparador** nm trigger.

disparatado (dispara'taðo) adj absurd. **disparate** nm absurdity.

disparidad (dispari'ðað) nf disparity.

dispensar (dispen'sar) vt 1 dispense. 2 excuse, pardon. **dispensa** nf dispensation, exemption. **¡dispénseme Usted!** I beg your pardon!

dispersar (disper'sar) vt disperse.

disponer* (dispo'ner) vt 1 dispose, arrange. 2 prepare. vi **disponer de** have. **disponerse a** get ready to, be about to. **disponibilidades** nf pl money on hand, resources. **disponible** adj available, on hand.

disposición (disposi'θjon) nf disposition. **última disposición** last will and testament.

dispuesto (dis'pwesto) adj arranged, disposed.

disputar (dispu'tar) vt dispute, contest. vi argue. **disputa** nf dispute. **sin disputa** beyond dispute. **disputable** adj debatable.

distancia (dis'tanθja) nf distance.

distinción (distin'θjon) nf distinction.

distinguir (distin'gir) vt distinguish.

distinto (dis'tinto) adj 1 different. 2 distinct.

distraer* (distra'er) vt 1 entertain, amuse. 2 distract. **distraerse** vr 1 amuse oneself. 2 be inattentive. **distracción** nf 1 amusement. 2 absent-mindedness. **distraído** adj 1 inattentive. 2 absent-minded.

distribuir* (distribu'ir) vt 1 distribute. 2 (of post) sort, deliver. **distribución** nf distribution. **distribuidor** nm 1 distributor. 2 dealer, agent. **distribuidor automático** vending machine.

distrito (dis'trito) nm district.

disturbio (dis'turβjo) nm disturbance.

disuadir (diswa'ðir) vt dissuade.

diurno (di'urno) adj day.

divagar (diβa'gar) vi 1 digress. 2 wander.

divergir (diβer'xir) vi 1 diverge. 2 differ, disagree. **divergencia** nf divergence. **divergente** adj divergent, opposed.

diversidad (diβersi'ðað) nf diversity. **diverso** adj 1 diverse. 2 different. 3 pl various.

diversión (diβersi'on) nf amusement.

divertir (ie) (diβer'tir) vt 1 entertain, amuse. 2 turn away, divert. **divertirse** vr have a good time. **divertido** adj amusing. **divertimiento** nm amusement.

dividir (diβi'ðir) vt divide.

divinidad (diβini'ðað) nf divinity. **divino** adj divine.

divisa (di'βisa) nf 1 badge, emblem. 2 pl comm foreign exchange. **control de divisas** nm exchange control.

divisar (diβi'sar) vt see at a distance, make out.

división (diβi'sjon) nf division.

divorciar (diβor'θjar) vt divorce. **divorciarse** vr get divorced. **divorcio** nm 1 divorce. 2 division.

divulgar (diβul'gar) vt spread, circulate. **divulgarse** vr be spread about. **divulgación** nf disclosure.

doblar (do'βlar) vt 1 double. 2 fold, turn.

doble ('doβle) adj 1 double. 2 insincere. nm double amount. **el doble** twice as much.

doce ('doθe) adj,nm twelve.

docena (do'θena) nm dozen.

docente (do'θente) adj educational. **personal docente** nm teaching staff.

dócil ('doθil) adj obedient, gentle. **docilidad** nf obedience.

doctor (dok'tor) nm doctor. **docto** adj learned. **doctorado** nm doctorate. **doctoral** adj doctoral.

doctrina (dok'trina) nf doctrine. **doctrinal** adj doctrinal.

documentar (dokumen'tar) vt document. **documentación** nf 1 documentation. 2 identification papers. **documento** nm document.

dogal (do'gal) nm halter.

dogma ('dogma) nf dogma. **dogmático** adj dogmatic. **dogmatismo** nm dogmatism.

doler (ue) (do'ler) vt,vi 1 hurt. 2 grieve. **dolerse de** vr feel pity or sorrow for. **dolencia** nf ailment.

dolor (do'lor) nm 1 pain. 2 grief.

domar (do'mar) vt tame. **doma** nf taming. **domable** adj tamable. **domador** nm tamer.

doméstico (do'mestiko) adj,nm domestic.

domiciliar (domiθi'ljar) vt house. **domiciliarse** vr establish oneself. **domicilio** nm home.

dominar (domi'nar) vt,vi dominate.

domingo (do'mingo) nm Sunday. **hacer domingo** take a day off.

dominio (do'minjo) nm dominion. **dominio público** public property.

dominó (domi'no) nm domino.

don[1] (don) nm courteous title equivalent to Mr, used before the Christian name.

don[2] (don) nm 1 present, gift. 2 aptitude, talent.

donación (dona'θjon) nf donation.

donaire (do'naire) nm 1 cleverness, wit. 2 elegance, grace.

donde ('donde) adv where.

doña ('dona) nf courteous title, used before a woman's Christian name.

dorar (do'rar) vt 1 gild, cover with gold. 2 cul brown lightly.

dormir (ue) (dor'mir) vi 1 sleep. 2 rest. vt put to sleep. **dormirse** vr go to sleep. **dormilón** nm one who sleeps a lot. **dormitorio** nm 1 bedroom. 2 dormitory.

dorso ('dorso) nm back. **dorsal** adj dorsal.

dos (dos) adj,nm two. **dos veces** twice. **las dos** two o'clock. **los dos** both.

dosis ('dosis) nf invar dose.

dotar (do'tar) vt endow. **dotación** nf 1 endowment. 2 personnel, staff. **dotado** adj gifted. **dote** nm,f 1 dowry. 2 pl endowments, talents.

doy ('doi) v see **dar**.

draga ('draga) nf dredge.

dragón (dra'gon) nm dragon.

drama ('drama) nm drama. **dramática** nf dramatic art or literature. **dramático** adj dramatic. nm 1 dramatist. 2 dramatic actor.

drenaje (dre'naxe) nm drainage.

droga ('droga) nf 1 drug. 2 chemical substance. **drogar** vt drug.

dromedario (drome'ðarjo) nm dromedary.

dual (dwal) adj dual.

ducado (du'kaðo) nm duchy.

dúctil ('duktil) adj ductile, malleable.

ducha ('dutʃa) nf shower (bath).

dudar (du'ðar) vt,vi doubt. **duda** nf doubt. **sin duda** doubtless. **dudoso** adj 1 doubtful, dubious. 2 hesitant.

duelo[1] ('dwelo) nm 1 sorrow. 2 mourning. **sin duelo** unrestrainedly.

duelo² ('dwelo) *nm* duel.

duende ('dwende) *nm* imp, elf.

dueño ('dweɲo) *nm* proprietor. **mi dueño** my love.

duermo (du'ermo) *v* see **dormir**.

dulce ('dulθe) *adj* 1 sweet. 2 (of water) fresh. *adv* 1 sweetly. 2 softly. *nm* sweet.

dulzura (dul'θura) *nf* 1 sweetness. 2 mildness.

duodécimo (duo'ðeθimo) *adj* twelfth.

duplicar (dupli'kar) *vt* duplicate. **duplicado** *adj,nm* duplicate.

duque ('duke) *nm* duke. **duquesa** *nf* duchess.

durar (du'rar) *vi* 1 endure, last. 2 (of clothes, etc.) wear well. **durabilidad** *nf* durability. **durable** *adj* durable. **duración** *nf* duration, period of time.

dureza (du'reθa) *nf* hardness. **dureza de oído** hardness of hearing.

durmiente (dur'mjente) *adj* sleeping.

durmió (dur'mjo) *v* see **dormir**.

duro ('duro) *adj* 1 hard. 2 tough. **duro de mollera** pigheaded. ~*nm* coin worth five pesetas.

E

e (e) *conj* (variant of **y** before words beginning with *i* or *hi*) and.

ebanista (eβa'nista) *nm* cabinet-maker.

ébano ('eβano) *nm* ebony.

ebrio ('eβrjo) *adj* drunk.

eclesiástico (ekle'sjastiko) *adj* ecclesiastical. *nm* priest.

eco ('eko) *nm* echo.

economía (ekono'mia) *nf* economy, economics. **hacer economías** economize. **económico** *adj* economic, financial, economical. **economista** *nm,f* economist. **economizar** *vt* save, economize on. *vi* save money, economize.

ecuador (ekwa'ðor) *nm* equator.

ecuestre (e'kwestre) *adj* equestrian.

echar (e'tʃar) *vt* 1 throw, cast, fling. 2 throw out, eject. 3 send forth, emit. 4 pour out. **echar a** start to. **echar cartas** deal cards. **echar hojas** sprout leaves. **echar la llave** turn the key. **echar una carta** post a letter. **echar de menos** miss someone or something. **echarse** *vr* lie down.

dad (e'ðað) *nf* age. **Edad media** Middle Ages.

dición (eði'θjon) *nf* edition, issue.

dicto (e'ðikto) *nm* edict.

edificar (eðifi'kar) *vt* 1 build, construct. 2 edify. **edificio** *nm* building.

editar (eði'tar) *vt* 1 publish. 2 edit. **editor** *nm* 1 publisher. 2 editor. **casa editorial** publishing house.

edredón (eðre'ðon) *nm* eiderdown.

educar (eðu'kar) *vt* 1 educate. 2 bring up. 3 train. **educación** *nf* 1 education. 2 good manners. **educacional** *adj* educational. **educado** *adj* well-mannered, polite.

efectivo (efek'tiβo) *adj* 1 effective. 2 actual, real. **en efectivo** in cash. **efecto** *nm* 1 effect. 2 result. 3 purpose, end. 4 *pl* effects, goods, assets. **efectos en cartera** holdings, shares.

efectuar (efek'twar) *vt* put into effect, carry out.

efervescencia (eferβes'θenθja) *nf* effervescence. **efervescente** *adj* effervescent, fizzy.

eficacia (efi'kaθja) *nf* 1 efficiency. 2 efficacy. **eficaz** *adj* 1 efficient. 2 effective.

eficiente (efi'θjente) *adj* efficient. **eficiencia** *nf* efficiency.

efigie (e'fixje) *nf* effigy.

efímero (e'fimero) *adj* ephemeral, fleeting.

efusión (efu'sjon) *nf* 1 effusion. 2 shedding (esp. of blood).

Egipto (e'xipto) *nm* Egypt. **egipcio** *adj,n* Egyptian.

egoísmo (ego'ismo) *nm* selfishness, egoism. **egoísta** *adj* selfish, egoistical. *nm* selfish person, egoist.

egregio (e'grexjo) *adj* distinguished, eminent.

eje ('exe) *nm* 1 axle. 2 axis. 3 central part, main idea.

ejecutar (exeku'tar) *vt* 1 execute, fulfil. 2 perform (music). **ejecución** *nf* execution, performance. **ejecutivo** *adj,nm* executive.

ejemplar (exem'plar) *adj* model. *nm* copy (of a book, etc.), specimen. **sin ejemplar** without precedent. **ejemplo** *nm* example. **dar ejemplo** set an example.

ejercer (exer'θer) *vt* 1 exercise, apply (influence). 2 practise. **ejercicio** *nm* 1 exercise. 2 practice.

ejército (e'xerθito) *nm* army.

el (el) *def art m* the.

él (el) *pron 3rd pers s* he, it.

elaborar (elaβo'rar) *vt* manufacture, produce. **elaboración** *nf* manufacture, production.

elástico (e'lastiko) *adj,nm* elastic. **elasticidad** *nf* 1 elasticity, springiness. 2 resilience.

elección (elek'θjon) *nf* 1 election. 2 choice,

option. **elector** n elector. **electorado** nm electorate. **electoral** adj electoral.

electricidad (elektriθi'ðað) nf electricity.

eléctrico (e'lektriko) adj electric, electrical.

electrizar (elektri'θar) vt electrify.

electrocutar (elektroku'tar) vt electrocute.

electrodo (elek'troðo) nm electrode.

electrónico (elek'troniko) adj electronic.

elefante (ele'fante) nm elephant.

elegancia (ele'ganθja) nf elegance, smartness. **elegante** adj smart, fashionable.

elegir (i) (ele'xir) vt choose, select, elect.

elemental (elemen'tal) adj elementary. **elemento** nm element.

elevar (ele'βar) vt 1 raise, elevate. 2 promote. **elevarse** vr rise, ascend.

eliminar (elimi'nar) vt eliminate.

elocución (eloku υjon) nf elocution.

elocuencia (elo'kwenθja) nf eloquence. **elocuente** adj eloquent.

elogiar (elo'xjar) vt praise. **elogio** nm praise. **elogioso** adj very favourable.

elucidar (eluθi'ðar) vt elucidate.

eludir (elu'ðir) vt elude. **elusivo** adj evasive.

ella ('eʎa) pron 3rd pers s she, it.

ello ('eʎo) pron s it. **ello es que** the fact is that. **ello dirá** time will tell.

emanar (ema'nar) vi emanate, originate from. **emanación** nf emanation.

emancipar (emanθi'par) emancipate. **emancipación** nf emancipation.

embajada (emba'xaða) nf 1 embassy. 2 errand. **embajador** n ambassador.

embalar (emba'lar) vt pack, make a parcel of, wrap.

embarazar (embara'θar) vt 1 make someone pregnant. 2 hinder, get in the way. **embarazada** adj pregnant. **embarazo** nm 1 pregnancy. 2 obstruction, obstacle. **embarazoso** adj cumbersome, awkward.

embarcar (embar'kar) vt put on board, ship. **embarcarse** vr embark, set sail. **embarco** nm embarkation.

embargar (embar'gar) vt 1 law seize, impound. 2 hinder, impede. 3 (of the senses) confuse, paralyse. **embargo** nm seizure, embargo.

embarque (em'barke) nm shipment, loading.

embarrar (embar'rar) vt 1 smear. 2 cover with mud.

embeber (embe'βer) vt 1 soak up, absorb. 2 insert. 3 (sewing) gather, take in. **embeberse** vr be absorbed or engrossed in.

embellecer* (embeʎe'θer) vt embellish.

embestir (i) (embes'tir) vt 1 assault. 2 charge, rush against. **embestida** nf 1 onslaught. 2 charge (of a wild animal).

emblema (em'blema) nm emblem.

embocar (embo'kar) vt put into the mouth. **embocadura** nf 1 narrows (of a river, etc.). 2 mouth (of a river). 3 taste, flavour (of wine).

embolsar (embol'sar) vt put into one's pocket.

emborrachar (emborra't far) vt make drunk, intoxicate. **emborracharse** vr get drunk.

emboscar (embos'kar) vt ambush. **emboscarse** vr lie in ambush. **emboscada** nf ambush.

embotar (embo'tar) vt 1 tin (food). 2 blunt, take the edge off.

embotellar (embote'ʎar) vt bottle. **embotellamiento** nm traffic jam. **embotellarse** vr mot get into a jam.

embozar (embo'θar) vt muffle, wrap up. **embozo** nm muffler.

embragar (embra'gar) vi mot let the clutch in. **embrague** nm mot clutch.

embriagarse (embrja'garse) vr get drunk.

embrollar (embro'ʎar) vt 1 complicate. 2 confuse. **embrollo** nm entanglement, tangle. **embrollarse** vr get into a muddle.

embrujar (embru'xar) vt bewitch.

embrutecer (embrute'θer) vt brutalize. **embrutecerse** vr become brutalized or depraved.

embudo (em'buðo) nm funnel.

embuste (em'buste) nm lie, fib. **embustería** nf 1 lying. 2 trickery. **embustero** nm 1 liar. 2 trickster. adj deceitful.

embutir (embu'tir) vt stuff, cram. **embutirse** stuff oneself (with food). **embutido** nm sausage.

emergencia (emer'xenθja) nf 1 emergence. 2 emergency.

emigrar (emi'grar) vi 1 emigrate. 2 migrate. **emigración** nf emigration. **emigrante** adj,n emigrant.

eminencia (emi'nenθja) nf 1 height, eminence. 2 prominence. **eminente** adj high, elevated, eminent.

emisario (emi'sarjo) nm emissary.

emitir (emi'tir) vt 1 emit, give off. 2 broadcast, transmit. **emisión** nf 1 programme, broadcast. 2 emission. **emisor** nm transmitter. **emisora** nf radio station.

emoción (emo'θjon) nf 1 emotion. 2 excitement, thrill. **emocionante** adj exciting, thrilling.

empachar (empa't far) vt 1 clog. 2 impede. 3 give indigestion to. med get indigestion.

empacho nm 1 obstacle. 2 embarrassment. 3 indigestion. **empachoso** adj (of food) indigestible.

empadronar (empaðro'nar) vt make a list of, register. **empadronamiento** nm census.

empalagar (empala'gar) vt 1 bore. 2 weary. vi pall. **empalagarse** become surfeited. **empalagoso** adj sickly, cloying.

empalizada (empali'θaða) nf 1 fence. 2 stockade.

empalmar (empal'mar) vt join, connect. **empalme** nm 1 joint. 2 junction (of railway lines, etc.).

empañar (empa'nar) vt blur, tarnish. **empañarse** vr get misty, cloud over. **empañado** adj blurred, misty.

empapelar (empape'lar) vt 1 wrap in paper. 2 to paper (walls, etc.).

empaquetar (empake'tar) vt pack, package.

emparejar (empare'xar) vt 1 match, pair off. 2 smooth, level. vi draw abreast with, catch up.

empastar (empas'tar) vt paste. **empaste** nm (dental) filling.

empatar (empa'tar) vt tie, draw (in games, etc.). **empate** nm draw, tie.

empedernir (empeðer'nir) vt harden. **empedernirse** vr grow hard, become obdurate.

empedrar (empe'ðrar) vt pave.

empeine (em'peine) nm 1 groin. 2 instep.

empeñar (empe'nar) vt pawn, pledge. **empeñarse en** insist on. **empeñado** adj 1 pawned. 2 determined.

empeorar (empeo'rar) vt make worse, impair. vi get worse, worsen. **empeorarse** vr worsen.

empequeñecer* (empekene'θer) vt 1 belittle. 2 dwarf.

emperador (empera'ðor) nm emperor.

empezar (ie) (empe'θar) vt,vi begin.

empinar (empi'nar) vt 1 lift, raise. 2 inf drink a lot. **empinarse** vr stand on tip-toe.

empírico (em'piriko) adj empirical.

emplazar (empla'θar) vt 1 summon. 2 place, locate.

emplear (emple'ar) vt use, employ. **empleado** nm employee. **empleo** nm 1 use. 2 employment. 3 job.

empobrecer* (empoβre'θer) vt impoverish. **empobrecerse** vr become poor.

empollar (empo'Kar) vt 1 hatch. 2 inf study hard.

emponzoñar (emponθo'nar) vt poison.

emporcar (ue) (empor'kar) vt make dirty, soil.

empotrar (empo'trar) vt embed.

emprender (empren'der) vt undertake, embark on. **emprendedor** adj enterprising.

empresa (em'presa) nf 1 enterprise. 2 comm company. 3 management.

empréstito (em'prestito) nm loan.

empujar (empu'xar) vt push, shove. **empuje** nm 1 thrust, push. 2 initiative, drive. **empujón** nm violent push.

empuñar (empu'nar) vt clasp, grasp. **empuñadura** nf hilt, handle.

emular (emu'lar) vt emulate.

emulsión (emul'sjon) nf emulsion.

en (en) prep 1 on. 2 in. 3 into. 4 onto. **en casa** at home. **en avión/tren** by aeroplane/train.

enaguas (e'nagwas) nf pl petticoat.

enajenar (enaxe'nar) vt 1 transfer (property). 2 alienate. 3 madden. **enajenarse** vr 1 deprive oneself. 2 be enraptured. 3 (of friends) become estranged.

enamorar (enamo'rar) vt 1 cause to fall in love. 2 win the love of. **enamorarse** vr fall in love. **enamorado** adj in love.

enano (e'nano) nm dwarf, midget.

enarbolar (enarβo'lar) vt 1 hoist (a flag, a sail). 2 flourish.

enardecer* (enarðe'θer) vt inflame. **enardecerse** vr become impassioned.

encabestrar (enkaβes'trar) vt 1 lead by the reins. 2 dominate.

encabezar (enkaβe'θar) vt 1 head (an organization, etc.). 2 put a title to. **encabezamiento** nm heading, title.

encadenar (enkaðe'nar) vt chain, shackle. **encadenamiento** nm 1 chaining. 2 linking, connection.

encajar (enka'xar) vt, vi fit together. **encaje** nm 1 fitting. 2 socket. 3 lace, lacework.

encallar (enka'Kar) vi 1 run aground. 2 get bogged down. **encalladero** nm sandbank.

encaminar (enkami'nar) vt 1 set off (on a journey). 2 direct, give directions to. **encaminarse** vr set out for.

encandilar (enkandi'lar) vt dazzle. **encandilarse** vr (of the eyes) sparkle brightly.

encantar (enkan'tar) vt bewitch, enchant. **¡encantado!** pleased to meet you! **encantador** adj charming, delightful. **encanto** nm 1 spell, enchantment. 2 delight.

encapotar (enkapo'tar) vt muffle, cloak. **encapotarse** vr 1 cloak oneself. 2 become cloudy.

encapricharse (enkapri'tʃarse) vr follow one's whims, be obstinate. **encapricharse por** become infatuated with.

encarar (enka'rar) vt 1 aim, point. 2 face. **encararse** vr face, face up to.

encarcelar (enkarθe'lar) vt put in jail, imprison.

encarecer* (enkare'θer) vt 1 raise the price of. 2 praise. **encarecidamente** adv strongly, earnestly. **encarecimiento** nm 1 price rise. 2 exaggeration.

encargar (enkar'gar) vt 1 comm order, commission. 2 entrust. **encargarse** vr take responsibility, to undertake. **encargado** adj charged with, responsible for. nm agent, representative. **encargo** nm 1 commission, assignment. 2 order.

encarnar (enkar'nar) vt 1 personify. 2 play (a rôle in theatre etc.). **encarnado** adj 1 incarnate. 2 blood-red.

encarnizar (enkarni'θar) vt infuriate. **encarnizarse** vr 1 feed on. 2 become infuriated. **encarnizado** adj 1 inflamed, bloodshot. 2 fierce.

encasillar (enkasi'ʎar) vt file, classify.

encauzar (enkau'θar) vt channel, direct.

encender (ie) (enθen'der) vt light, set alight. **encenderse** vr catch fire. **encendedor** nm lighter. **encendido** adj burning, alight.

encerrar (ie) (enθe'rar) vt 1 shut up, enclose. 2 include, contain. **encerrarse** vr shut oneself up, go into seclusion.

encía (en'θia) nf anat gum.

encierro (en'θjerro) nm 1 penning in. 2 enclosure. 3 place of confinement.

encima (en'θima) adv above, overhead. por **encima** overhead. **encima de** on top of, upon, over.

encina (en'θina) nf ilex, evergreen oak.

encinta (en'θinta) adj pregnant.

enclavar (enkla'βar) vt nail, pierce. **enclave** nm enclave.

enclenque (en'klenke) adj weak, feeble.

encoger (enko'xer) vt shrink. **encogerse** vr shrink. **encogerse de hombros** shrug one's shoulders. **encogido** adj 1 shrunken. 2 timid. **encogimiento** nm 1 shrinking. 2 shyness.

encolar (enko'lar) vt glue.

encomendar (enkomen'der) vt entrust. **encomendarse** vr commend oneself. **encomienda** nf 1 commission. 2 tribute. 3 concession (of land).

enconar (enko'nar) vt 1 inflame. 2 provoke. **enconarse** vr become irritable. **enconado** adj 1 inflamed. 2 angry.

encontrar (ue) (enkon'trar) vt 1 find. 2 meet.

encontrarse vr 1 meet, encounter. 2 be situated.

encopetado (enkope'taðo) adj 1 of noble birth, aristocratic. 2 conceited.

encorvar (enkor'βar) vt curve. **encorvarse** vr stoop, bend over. **encorvado** adj 1 curved. 2 stooping. **encorvadura** nf curve, bend.

encrespar (enkres'par) vt 1 ruffle, ripple. 2 curl. 3 irritate. **encresparse** vr 1 ripple, curl up. 2 get angry.

encrucijada (enkruθi'xaða) nf crossroads.

encuadernar (enkwaðer'nar) vt bind (a book). **encuadernación** nf bookbinding, cover.

encuadrar (enkwa'ðrar) vt frame. **encuadre** nm frame.

encubrir* (enku'βrir) vt conceal. **encubrimiento** nm concealment.

encuentro (en'kwentro) nm 1 encounter, meeting. 2 mot collision.

encumbrar (enkum'brar) vt elevate, extol. **encumbrarse** vr 1 soar, be lofty. 2 be haughty. **encumbrado** adj lofty, elevated.

enchufar (entʃu'far) vt 1 connect, join. 2 plug in. **enchufe** nm 1 electric plug. 2 inf personal contact, connection. **enchufismo** nm use of personal contacts to get favours. **enchufado** adj well connected.

endeble (en'deβle) adj frail.

endémico (en'demiko) adj endemic.

enderezar (endere'θar) vt 1 straighten. 2 put right. **enderezarse** vr stand upright. **enderezado** adj appropriate.

endeudarse (endeu'ðarse) vr contract debts.

endiablado (endja'βlaðo) adj wicked, devilish. **endiablar** vt bedevil.

endiosar (endjo'sar) vt deify. **endiosarse** vr be conceited. **endiosado** adj conceited.

endosar (endo'sar) vt also **endorsar** endorse. **endoso** nm also **endorso** endorsement.

endulzar (endul'θar) vt sweeten.

endurecer* (endure'θer) vt harden. **endurecido** adj hardened. **endurecimiento** nm hardening.

enemigo (ene'migo) nm enemy, foe. adj hostile, inimical. **enemistar** vt set at odds, alienate.

energía (ener'xia) nf energy.

enérgico (e'nerxiko) adj 1 energetic. 2 forthright. 3 drastic (measures, etc.).

enero (e'nero) nm January.

enfadar (enfa'ðar) vt anger. **enfadarse** vr become angry. **enfado** nm anger. **enfadoso** adj annoying.

ensalada

énfasis ('enfasis) *nm,f* 1 emphasis. 2 pomposity. **enfático** *adj* 1 emphatic. 2 pompous.

enfermar (enfer'mar) *vt* make ill. *vi* fall ill. **enfermedad** *nf* illness. **enfermera** *nf* nurse. **enfermizo** *adj* sickly. **enfermo** *adj* ill, sick.

enfilar (enfi'lar) *vt* line up.

enfocar (enfo'kar) *vt* 1 focus. 2 approach (a question, etc.). **enfoque** *nm* 1 focus. 2 approach.

enfrascar (enfras'kar) *vt* put in bottles, bottle. **enfrascarse** *vr* become absorbed (in a problem, etc.).

enfrentar (enfren'tar) *vt* confront. **enfrentarse** face up to, face. **enfrente** *adv* opposite. **enfrente de** *prep* opposite, facing.

enfriar (enfri'ar) *vt* cool. **enfriarse** *vr* cool down.

enfurecer* (enfure'θer) *vt* enrage. **enfurecerse** *vr* rage, get into a rage.

enganchar (engan'tʃar) *vt* 1 hook, hitch on. 2 harness (a horse). **enganche** *nm* 1 coupling. 2 hitching-up.

engañar (enga'ɲar) *vt* deceive. **engaño** *nm* deceit, fraud. **engañoso** *adj* deceitful.

engatusar (engatu'sar) *vt* coax, persuade.

engendrar (enxen'drar) *vt* engender, breed. **engendro** *nm* 1 foetus. 2 monstrosity. 3 fantastic plan.

englobar (englo'βar) *vt* include, lump together.

engordar (engor'ðar) *vt* fatten. *vi* gain weight.

engorro (en'gorro) *nm* nuisance.

engranar (engra'nar) *vt* mesh, put in gear. *vi* interlock. **engranaje** *nm* mot gears.

engrandecer* (engrande'θer) *vt* magnify, extol. **engrandecimiento** *nm* 1 enlargement. 2 exaggeration.

engrasar (engra'sar) *vt* grease. **engrase** *nm* greasing.

engreído (engre'iðo) *adj* conceited. **engreimiento** *nm* vanity, conceit.

engrosar (engro'sar) *vt* increase, thicken. **engrosarse** *vr* expand.

engullir (engu'ʎir) *vt* bolt (food), gobble.

enhestar* (enes'tar) *vt* erect. **enhestarse** *vr* straighten. **enhiesto** *adj* 1 erect. 2 lofty.

enhorabuena (enora'βwena) *nf* congratulations. **¡enhorabuena!** well done! congratulations! **¡enhoramala!** bad luck! unluckily!

enigma (e'nigma) *nm* enigma. **enigmático** *adj* enigmatic.

enjabonar (enxaβo'nar) *vt* soap.

enjambre (en'xambre) *nm* swarm.

enjaular (enxau'lar) *vt* cage.

enjuagar (enxwa'gar) *vt* rinse. **enjuague** *nm* 1 rinse, rinsing. 2 intrigue.

enjugar (enxu'gar) *vt* wipe, dry.

enjuiciar (enxwi'(θ)ar) *vt* 1 judge. 2 law try. **enjuiciamiento** *nm* judgment, trial.

enlace (en'laθe) *nm* 1 link, connection, liaison. 2 marriage. **enlazar** *vt* 1 link, tie up. 2 marry. **enlazarse** *vr* be linked, connected.

enloquecer* (enloke'θer) *vt* madden, drive insane. **enloquecerse** *vr* go mad. **enloquecido** *adj* mad.

enlosar (enlo'sar) *vt* pave. **enlosado** *nm* flagstone.

enlucir* (enlu'θir) *vt* 1 plaster. 2 polish. **enlucido** *nm* plaster.

enlutar (enlu'tar) *vt* dress in mourning clothes.

enmascarar (enmaska'rar) *vt* mask. **enmascararse** *vr* put on a mask, disguise.

enmendar (ie) (enmen'dar) *vt* 1 correct, amend. 2 reform. **enmendarse** *vr* reform oneself. **enmienda** *nf* correction, amendment.

enmohecerse* (enmoe'θerse) *vr* become rusty or mouldy. **enmohecido** *adj* 1 rusty. 2 mouldy.

enmudecer* (enmuðe'θer) *vt* silence. **enmudecerse** *vr* fall silent.

enojar (eno'xar) *vt* anger. **enojarse** *vr* get angry. **enojado** *adj* angry. **enojo** *nm* annoyance, vexation.

enorgullecer* (enorguʎe'θer) *vt* make proud. **enorgullecerse** *vr* grow proud. **enorgullecerse de** pride oneself on.

enorme (e'norme) *adj* enormous. **enormidad** *nf* enormity, hugeness.

enrarecer* (enrare'θer) *vt* make rare or scarce. *vi* (of air) become thin.

enredar (enre'ðar) *vt* 1 catch, entangle. 2 complicate. 3 involve (someone in an affair, etc.). **enredarse** *vr* become involved, get entangled. **enredo** *nm* entanglement, awkward affair.

enrevesado (enreβe'saðo) *adj* 1 complicated, involved. 2 (of a person) noisy, ill-disciplined

enriquecer* (enrike'θer) *vt* enrich.

enrojecer* (enroxe'θer) *vt* redden, make red. **enrojecerse** *vr* blush.

enrollar (enro'ʎar) *vt* coil up.

enronquecer* (enronke'θer) *vt* make hoarse. **enronquecerse** *vr* become hoarse.

enroscar (enros'kar) *vt* curl, coil, twist. **enroscarse** coil, curl. **enroscado** *adj* coiled, curled

ensalada (ensa'laða) *nf* salad.

ensalmar (ensal'mar) vt 1 set (a bone). 2 cure (by magic).

ensalzar (ensal'θar) vt extol, praise highly. **ensalzamiento** nm praise.

ensamblar (ensam'blar) vt put together, assemble. **ensamblador** n fitter.

ensanchar (ensan'tʃar) vt grow broader, expand. **ensancharse** vr spread, extend. **ensanche** nm 1 extension, enlargement. 2 new suburb (of a town).

ensañar (ensa'ɲar) vt enrage. **ensañarse** become enraged, grow furious.

ensayar (ensa'jar) vt 1 try out, test. 2 rehearse. **ensayarse** vr rehearse, practise. **ensayo** nm 1 test, attempt. 2 essay. 3 rehearsal. **ensayo general** dress rehearsal.

enseñar (ense'ɲar) vt 1 show. 2 teach. **enseñanza** nf education.

enseres (en'seres) nm pl goods and chattels.

ensillar (ensi'ʎar) vt saddle.

ensimismarse (ensimis'marse) vr become absorbed in thought. **ensimismamiento** nm reverie, daydream.

ensordecer* (ensorðe'θer) vt deafen. **ensordecedor** adj deafening.

ensuciar (ensu'θjar) vt dirty, soil. **ensuciarse** vr become dirty.

ensueño (en'sweno) nm dream, fantasy.

entablar (enta'βlar) vt 1 cover with planks, board up. 2 set up (games, etc.). 3 table (a motion). 4 strike up a conversation. **entablado** nm planking.

entallar (enta'ʎar) vt 1 carve. 2 tailor, vi fit well.

ente ('ente) nm entity.

entender (ie) (enten'der) vt,vi understand. **entender de** know about (a subject), be versed in. **entenderse** vr 1 be understood. 2 understand one another, be on good terms. **entendido** adj 1 agreed. 2 knowledgeable. nm connoisseur.

enterar (ente'rar) vt inform, advise. **enterado** adj well-informed. **enterarse** vr find out about.

entero (en'tero) adj 1 entire, whole. 2 honest, upright.

enterrar (ie) (enter'rar) vt bury. **enterrador** nm gravedigger.

entidad (enti'ðað) nf 1 entity. 2 board, commission.

entierro (en'tjerro) nm burial, funeral.

entonar (ento'nar) vt 1 intone. 2 sing in tune. 3 tone up (muscles, etc.). vi be in tune, harmonize.

entonces (en'tonθes) adv 1 then, at that time. 2 in that case, and so, then.

entornar (entor'nar) vt half-close (the eyes, door, etc.). **entornado** adj half-closed, ajar.

entorpecer* (entorpe'θer) vt 1 stupefy. 2 hinder. **entorpecimiento** nm lethargy, torpor.

entrada (en'traða) nf 1 entrance, doorway. 2 entry, admission. 3 ticket. 4 sport gate. 5 income, takings.

entrambos (en'trambos) adj pl both.

entraña (en'traɲa) nf 1 core, essential part. 2 pl entrails, bowels. 3 pl feelings, heart. **entrañable** adj 1 intimate. 2 beloved

entrar (en'trar) vt 1 introduce, bring in. 2 mil attack, invade. 3 influence. vi enter. **el año que entra** the coming year.

entre ('entre) prep among, between. **entre que** while.

entreabierto (entrea'βjerto) adj half-open, ajar.

entrecejo (entre'θexo) nm frown.

entregar (entre'gar) vt 1 hand over, deliver. 2 surrender, give up. **entregarse** surrender, give oneself up. **entrega** nf 1 delivery, handing over. 2 instalment, part (of a novel, journal, etc.).

entrelazar (entrela'θar) vt entwine.

entremés (entre'mes) nm 1 Th short farce. 2 interlude. 3 cul side dish, hors d'oeuvre.

entremeter (entreme'ter) vt insert, introduce. **entremeterse** vr also **entrometerse** interfere. **entremetido** adj also **entrometido** interfering.

entrenar (entre'nar) vt sport train, coach. **entrenarse** vr train oneself. **entrenador** n trainer. **entrenamiento** nm training.

entresacar (entresa'kar) vt select.

entresuelo (entre'swelo) nm mezzanine, ground floor.

entretanto (entre'tanto) adv meanwhile.

entretejer (entrete'xer) vt interweave.

entretener* (entrete'ner) 1 entertain. 2 delay. **entretenerse** vr 1 amuse oneself. 2 linger. **entretenido** adj entertaining. **entretenimiento** nm entertainment.

entrever* (entre'βer) vt 1 glimpse. 2 suspect.

entrevista (entre'βista) nf interview. **entrevistar** vt interview. **entrevistarse** vr have an interview.

entristecer* (entriste'θer) vt sadden. **entristecerse** vr grow sad.

entumecer* (entume'θer) vt numb. **entumecimiento** nm numbness.

enturbiar (entur'βjar) vt 1 make cloudy. 2

muddy. **enturbiarse** *vr* grow cloudy or confused.

entusiasmar (entusjas'mar) *vt* fill with enthusiasm. **entusiasmarse** *vr* grow enthusiastic. **entusiasmo** *nm* enthusiasm. **entusiasta** *adj* enthusiastic. *nm,f* enthusiast, fan. **entusiástico** *adj* enthusiastic.

enumerar (enume'rar) *vt* enumerate. **enumeración** *nf* enumeration.

envainar (enβai'nar) *vt* sheathe.

envanecer* (enβane'θer) *vt* make conceited.

envasar (enβa'sar) *vt* 1 pack, wrap. 2 bottle. **envase** *nm* 1 act of packing. 2 bottle, container.

envejecer* (enβexe'θer) *vt* make aged, age. **envejecerse** *vr* grow old. **envejecido** *adj* aged, old-looking.

envenenar (enβene'nar) *vt* poison.

envergadura (enβerga'ðura) *nf* 1 extent, span. 2 scope.

enviar (en'βjar) *vt* send.

envidiar (enβi'ðjar) *vt* envy. **envidia** *nf* envy. **envidioso** *adj* envious.

envilecer* (enβile'θer) *vt* debase, degrade. **envilecerse** *vr* degrade, abase oneself.

envío (en'βio) *nm* dispatch, consignment, shipment.

envoltura (enβol'tura) *nf* 1 cover, wrapping. 2 envelope.

envolver (ue) (enβol'βer) *vt* 1 wrap, tie up. 2 involve, implicate.

enzarzar (enθar'θar) *vt* embroil. **enzarzarse** *vr* get involved.

épico ('epiko) *adj* epic.

epidemia (epi'ðemja) *nf* epidemic. **epidémico** *adj* epidemic

epígrafe (e'piɣrafe) *nm* epigraph, inscription.

epílogo (e'piloɣo) *nm* epilogue.

episcopado (episko'paðo) *nm* 1 bishopric, episcopate. 2 episcopacy.

episodio (epi'soðjo) *nm* episode.

epitafio (epi'tafjo) *nm* epitaph.

época ('epoka) *nf* epoch, period.

equidad (eki'ðað) *nf* equity, fairness.

equilibrar (ekili'βrar) *vt* balance. **equilibrarse** *vr* balance, poise. **equilibrio** *nm* balance, equilibrium.

equinoccio (eki'nokθjo) *nm* equinox.

equipaje (eki'paxe) *nm* 1 luggage. 2 equipment. 3 *naut* crew.

equipar (eki'par) *vt* equip, furnish.

equipo (e'kipo) *nm* 1 team. 2 equipment, gear.

equitación (ekita'θjon) *nf* 1 riding. 2 horsemanship.

equitativo (ekita'tiβo) *adj* equitable, fair.

equivalencia (ekiβa'lenθja) *nf* equivalence. **equivalente** *adj* equivalent. **equivaler** *vi* be equivalent.

equivocar (ekiβo'kar) *vt* mistake. **equivocarse** *vr* be wrong, make a mistake. **equivocación** *nf* mistake. **equivocado** *adj* mistaken.

equívoco (e'kiβoko) *nm* pun, word play. *adj* equivocal.

era ('era) *nf* era, age.

eremita (ere'mita) *nm* also **ermitaño** hermit. *nf* hermitage.

era ('era) *v* see **ser.**

eres ('eres) *v* see **ser.**

erguir* (er'gir) *vt* 1 raise. 2 straighten. **erguirse** *vr* 1 straighten. 2 (of buildings, mountains, etc.) soar. **erguido** *adj* 1 upright, straight. 2 proud.

erigir (eri'xir) *vt* erect.

erizarse (eri'θarse) *vr* bristle. **erizado** *adj* bristly.

erradicar (erraði'kar) *vt* eradicate.

errar* (er'rar) *vi* wander, roam. *vt* miss (a shot, one's way). **errarse** *vr* err. **errado** *adj* mistaken.

error (er'ror) *nm* error. **erróneo** *adj* mistaken, false, erroneous.

eructar (eruk'tar) *vi* belch.

erudición (eruði'θjon) *nf* erudition. **erudito** *nm* scholar. *adj* erudite.

es (es) *v* see **ser.**

esbelto (es'βelto) *adj* slim, slight. **esbeltez** *nf* slimness.

esbozar (esβo'θar) *vt* sketch. **esbozo** *nm* sketch.

escabechar (eskaβe'tʃar) *vt* 1 *cul* pickle. 2 dye (hair). **escabeche** *nm* vinegar sauce.

escabroso (eska'βroso) *adj* 1 rough, uneven. 2 complex. 3 risqué.

escabullirse (eskaβu'ʎirse) *vr* slip or run away.

escala (es'kala) *nf* 1 ladder. 2 scale. 3 *naut* port of call. **en gran escala** large scale. **hacer escala** call in, stop at. **escalar** *vt* 1 climb, scale. 2 escalate. **escalamiento** *nm* escalation.

escaldar (eskal'ðar) *vt* 1 scald. 2 chafe. 3 make red hot. **escaldado** *adj* 1 scalded. 2 wary.

escalera (eska'lera) *nf* stairs.

escalfar (eskal'far) *vt* *cul* poach.

escalofrío (eskalo'frio) *nm* 1 shiver. 2 *med* fever, chill.

escalón (eska'lon) *nm* 1 rung (of ladder). 2

tread, step (of stair). **3** stage (of progress, etc.). **escalonar** vt space, set at intervals, stagger.

escalpelo (eskal'pelo) nm scalpel.

escama (es'kama) nf **1** scale (of fish, lizard). **2** flake (of soap).

escamot(e)ar (eskamo'tar) vt **1** whisk away. **2** make vanish. **3** shirk. **escamoteo** nm inf swindle, trick. **escamoteador** nm **1** conjurer. **2** swindler.

escampar (eskam'par) vt clear out. vi (of weather) grow clear, improve.

escándalo (es'kandalo) nm **1** scandal. **2** row. **escandalizar** vt scandalize. vi **1** fuss. **2** cause a scandal. **escandaloso** adj **1** scandalous. **2** uproarious. **3** outrageous.

Escandinavia (eskandi'naβja) nf Scandinavia. **escandinavo** adj,n Scandinavian.

escaño (es'kaɲo) nm **1** bench. **2** seat in parliament.

escapar (eska'par) vi escape, flee. **escaparse** vr **1** escape. **2** leak. **escape** nm **1** escape. **2** leak. **3** mot exhaust. **tubo de escape** exhaust pipe.

escaparate (eskapa'rate) nm shop window.

escarabajo (eskara'βaxo) om beetle.

escaramuza (eskara'muθa) nf skirmish, quarrel.

escarbar (eskar'βar) vt **1** scratch. **2** poke. **3** investigate.

escarcha (es'kartʃa) nf frost.

escarlata (eskar'lata) adj scarlet.

escarmentar (ie) (eskarmen'tar) vt punish. vi learn by experience. **escarmiento** nm **1** punishment. **2** warning, example.

escarnecer* (eskarne'θer) vt scoff, sneer. **escarnecedor** adj scoffing. **escarnio** nm taunt.

escarola (eska'rola) nf endive.

escarpa (es'karpa) nf slope.

escasear (eskase'ar) vt skimp. vi be scarce. **escasez** nf **1** shortage, lack. **2** meanness. **escaso** adj scarce.

escena (es'θena) nf **1** scene. **2** Th stage. **escenario** nm Th stage, scenery. **escénico** adj scenic.

escéptico (es'θeptiko) adj sceptical. nm,f sceptic. **escepticismo** nm scepticism.

esclarecer* (esklare'θer) vt **1** illuminate. **2** enlighten. vi dawn. **esclarecimiento** nm **1** illumination. **2** enlightenment.

esclavitud (esklaβi'tuð) nf slavery. **esclavizar** vt enslave. **esclavo** nm slave.

esclusa (es'klusa) nf floodgate, lock.

escoba (es'koβa) nf broom, brush. **escobar** vt sweep.

escocer (ue) (esko'θer) vt annoy. vi sting, smart. **escocecerse** vr chafe.

Escocia (es'koθja) nf Scotland. **escocés** adj Scots, Scottish. n Scot.

escoger (esko'xer) vt choose. **escogido** adj selected. **escogimiento** nm choosing, choice.

escolar (esko'lar) adj scholastic. nm schoolboy.

escolta (es'kolta) nf escort. **escoltar** vt escort.

escollo (es'koʎo) nm **1** reef, rock. **2** trap, pitfall. **escollera** nf jetty, breakwater.

escombro (es'kombro) nm **1** rubbish. **2** pl dust, litter.

esconder (eskon'der) vt hide. **esconderse** vr conceal oneself.

escopeta (esko'peta) nf shotgun.

escoplo (es'koplo) nm chisel. **escoplear** vt chisel.

escoria (es'korja) nf **1** metal slag, dross. **2** scum.

escorpión (eskor'pjon) nm scorpion.

escotilla (esko'tiʎa) nf naut hatch.

escribir* (eskri'βir) vt,vi write. **escribir a máquina** type. **escribirse** vr correspond with one another.

escrito (es'krito) v see **escribir**. adj written. nm document, manuscript. **escritor** nm writer. **escritorio** nm **1** desk. **2** office.

escrúpulo (es'krupulo) nm **1** scruple, hesitation. **2** scrupulousness. **escrupuloso** adj scrupulous.

escrutinio (eskru'tinjo) nm scrutiny.

escuadra (es'kwaðra) nf **1** carpenter's square. **2** squad. **3** naut squadron. **escuadrar** vt make square.

escuálido (es'kwaliðo) adj **1** weak. **2** emaciated, skinny. **3** squalid. **escualidez** nf **1** weakness. **2** skinniness. **3** squalor.

escuchar (esku'tʃar) vt listen to. vi listen. **escucha** nf listening.

escudero (esku'ðero) nm squire or page (of a knight). **escudo** nm shield.

escudriñar (eskuðri'ɲar) vt scrutinize.

escuela (es'kwela) nf school.

escueto (es'kweto) adj unadorned, plain.

esculpir (eskul'pir) vt sculpture, engrave. **escultor** nm sculptor. **escultura** nf sculpture.

escupir (esku'pir) vt,vi spit.

escurrir (eskur'rir) vt **1** wring, squeeze dry. **2** drain. vi ooze, slide. **escurrirse** vr **1** drip, ooze. **2** slip out.

ese[1] ('ese) *adj also* **esa** that.

ese[2] ('ese) *nf* the letter S.

ése ('ese) *pron also* **ésa 1** that one. **2** the former.

esencia (e'senθja) *nf* essence. **esencial** *adj* essential.

esfera (es'fera) *nf* sphere, globe. **esférico** *adj* spherical.

esfinge (es'finxe) *nf* sphinx.

esforzar (**ue**) (esfor'θar) *vt* invigorate, strengthen. **esforzarse** *vr* make an effort.

esfuerzo (es'fwerθo) *nm* effort.

esgrimir (esgri'mir) *vt* brandish. *vi sport* fence. **esgrima** *nf* fencing.

eslabón (esla'βon) *nm* link, join. **eslabonar** *vt* link, connect.

esmaltar (esmal'tar) *vt* **1** enamel. **2** varnish (fingernails). **esmalte** *nm* enamel.

esmerado (esme'raðo) *adj* painstaking, careful. **esmerar** *vt* polish. **esmerarse** *vr* take pains.

esmeralda (esme'ralða) *nf* emerald.

eso ('eso) *pron* that thing, that. **en eso** at that moment. **eso es 1** that is to say. **2** that's right. **nada de eso** not a bit. **por eso** because of that.

esos ('esos) *adj pl also* **esas** those.

ésos ('esos) **ésas** *pron* **1** those. **2** the former. **ni por ésas** not at all.

espabilar (espaβi'lar) *vt* snuff (a candle). **espabilarse** *vr* **1** wake up. **2** look lively.

espaciar (espa'θjar) *vt* space out, spread. **espaciarse** *vr* **1** expatiate. **2** relax. **espacio** *nm* space. **espacioso** *adj* spacious. **espacial** *adj* spatial, space. **viajes espaciales** *nm pl* space travel.

espada (es'paða) *nf* sword. *nm* swordsman.

espalda (es'palda) *nf* shoulder, back. **a espaldas** behind someone's back. **volverse de espaldas** turn one's back.

espantapájaros (espanta'paxaros) *nm invar* scarecrow.

espantar (espan'tar) *vt* scare, frighten off. **espanto** *nm* fright. **espantoso** *adj* terrifying.

España (es'paɲa) *nf* Spain. **español** *adj* Spanish. *nm* **1** Spaniard. **2** Spanish (language).

esparcir (espar'θir) *vt* **1** scatter, spread. **2** sow. **3** amuse.

espárrago (es'parrago) *nm* asparagus.

espasmo (es'pasmo) *nm* spasm.

especia (es'peθja) *nf* spice.

especial (espe'θjal) *adj* special, especial. **en especial** especially. **especialidad** *nf* speciality. **especialista** *nm* specialist. **especializarse** *vr* specialize.

especie (es'peθje) *nf* **1** species. **2** kind, type.

específico (espe'θifiko) *adj* specific. **especificar** *vt* specify.

espectáculo (espek'takulo) *nm* **1** spectacle. **2** *Th* performance. **espectacular** *adj* spectacular. **espectador** *nm* spectator.

espejo (es'pexo) *nm* mirror.

esperar (espe'rar) *vt,vi* **1** hope. **2** await, wait. **3** expect. **espera** *nf* **1** wait, waiting. **2** expectation. **sala de espera** *nf* waiting room. **esperanza** *nf* hope. **esperanzador** *adj* encouraging.

esperpento (esper'pento) *nm* **1** ugly sight. **2** absurdity.

espesar (espe'sar) *vt* thicken. **espeso** *adj* thick.

espía (es'pia) *nm* spy. **espiar** *vt* spy on.

espiga (es'piga) *nf* spike, ear of corn. **espigar** *vt* glean, pick up grains.

espina (es'pina) *nf* **1** thorn. **2** spine.

espinaca (espi'naka) *nf* spinach.

espionaje (espjo'naxe) *nm* espionage.

espiral (espi'ral) *adj,nf* spiral.

espíritu (es'piritu) *nm* **1** spirit. **2** mind. **espiritual** *adj* spiritual.

espléndido (es'plendiðo) *adj* splendid, lavish. **esplendidez** *nf* splendour.

espliego (es'pljego) *nm* lavender.

espolear (espole'ar) *vt* spur, spur on.

esponja (es'ponxa) *nf* sponge. **esponjar** *vt* make fluffy, fluff up. **esponjoso** *adj* **1** spongy, porous. **2** fluffy.

esponsales (espon'sales) *nm pl* betrothal.

espontáneo (espon'taneo) *adj* spontaneous. *nm* spectator who rushes into the bullring to fight the bull. **espontaneidad** *nf* spontaneity.

esporádico (espo'raðiko) *adj* sporadic.

esposa (es'posa) *nf* **1** wife. **2** *pl* handcuffs. **esposo** *nm* husband. **esposar** *vt* handcuff.

espuela (es'pwela) *nf* spur.

espuma (es'puma) *nf* foam, froth, lather.

esquela (es'kela) *nf* **1** note, short letter. **2** obituary.

esqueleto (eske'leto) *nm* skeleton.

esquema (es'kema) *nm* scheme, sketch, diagram.

esquí (es'ki) *nm, pl* **esquís** ski. **esquiar** *vi* ski.

esquilar (eski'lar) *vt* clip, shear.

esquimal (eski'mal) *nm* Eskimo.

esquina (es'kina) *nf* (outside) corner **esquinar** *vt* form a corner with.

esquirol (eski'rol) *nm* strike-breaker, blackleg.

esquivar (eski'βar) *vt* avoid, shun. **esquivo** *adj* shy, unsociable, withdrawn.

estabilidad (estaβili'ðað) *nf* stability. **estable** *adj* stable.

establecer* (estaβle'θer) *vt* establish. **establecerse** *vr* set oneself up, establish oneself. **establecimiento** *nm* establishment.

establo (es'taβlo) *nm* cowshed.

estaca (es'taka) *nf* post, stake. **estacada** *nf* fence.

estación (esta'θjon) *nf* 1 station. 2 season.

estacionar (estaθjo'nar) *vt* park (a car). **estacionamiento** *nm* parking.

estadio (es'taðjo) *nm* 1 stadium. 2 *med* phase.

estado (es'taðo) *nm* 1 state. 2 status. **estar en estado** be pregnant. **estado mayor general** *mil* general staff.

Estados Unidos (es'taðos u'niðos) *nm pl* United States. **estadounidense** *adj* American.

estafa (es'tafa) *nf* swindle. **estafador** *nm* swindler. **estafar** *vt* swindle.

estafeta (esta'feta) *nf* 1 district post office. 2 mail.

estallar (esta'ʎar) *vi* burst, erupt. **estallido** *nm* 1 explosion. 2 outbreak.

estampar (estam'par) *vt* print, imprint. **estampa** *nf* 1 print, footprint. 2 engraving. 3 appearance.

estampida (estam'piða) *nf* stampede. **estampido** *nm* explosion.

estancar (estan'kar) *vt* block, delay. **estancarse** *vr* stagnate. **estancado** *adj* 1 stagnant. 2 at a standstill.

estanco (es'tanko) *nm* 1 state tobacco shop. 2 monopoly.

estandarte (estan'darte) *nm* banner.

estanque (es'tanke) *nm* pond.

estante (es'tante) *nm* 1 shelf. 2 bookcase.

estaño (es'taɲo) *nm* tin.

estar* (es'tar) *vi* be (in a place, temporarily, etc.). **no está** he or she is not at home. **¿estamos?** do we agree? **¡ya está!** that's it! **¿a cuántos estamos?** what's the date? **estar para** 1 be in the mood for. 2 be about to.

estático (es'tatiko) *adj* static.

estatua (es'tatwa) *nf* statue.

estatura (esta'tura) *nf* stature, height.

este[1] ('este) *adj also* **esta** this.

este[2] ('este) *adj,nm* east.

éste ('este) *pron also* **ésta** 1 this one. 2 the latter.

estela (es'tela) *nf* 1 *naut* wake. 2 trail.

estepa (es'tepa) *nf* steppe.

estera (es'tera) *nf* matting, mat.

estereofónico (estereo'foniko) *adj* stereophonic.

estereotipo (estereo'tipo) *nm* stereotype.

estéril (es'teril) *adj* 1 sterile. 2 useless. **esterilizar** *vt* sterilize.

esterlina (ester'lina) *adj* sterling.

estético (es'tetiko) *adj* aesthetic. **estética** *nf* aesthetics.

estetoscopio (estetos'kopjo) *nm* stethoscope.

estiércol (es'tjerkol) *nm* dung, manure.

estigma (es'tigma) *nm* stigma.

estilar (esti'lar) *vt* 1 wear. 2 be in the habit of using. **estilarse** *vr* be in fashion. **estilo** *nm* style.

estimar (esti'mar) *vt* 1 estimate. 2 esteem. **estima** *nf* esteem. **estimable** *adj* esteemed. **estimación** *nf* 1 estimation. 2 esteem.

estimular (estimu'lar) *vt* stimulate. **estimulante** *adj* stimulant. **estímulo** *nm* 1 stimulus. 2 stimulation.

estío (es'tio) *nm lit* summer.

estipular (estipu'lar) *vt* stipulate.

estirar (esti'rar) *vt* stretch, pull out. **estirado** *adj* taut, stretched tight. **estirón** *nm* pull, jerk.

estirpe (es'tirpe) *nf* lineage, stock.

estofa (es'tofa) *nf* 1 quilted material. 2 (of a person) quality, class.

estofar (esto'far) *vt* 1 stew. 2 quilt. **estofado** *nm* stew.

estoico (es'toiko) *adj* stoic. **estoicismo** *nm* stoicism.

estómago (es'tomago) *nm* stomach. **estomagar** *vt* 1 give indigestion to. 2 annoy.

estorbar (estor'βar) *vt* hinder. vi be in the way. **estorbo** *nm* hindrance, obstacle.

estornudar (estornu'ðar) *vi* sneeze. **estornudo** *nm* sneeze.

estos ('estos) *adj pl also* **estas** these.

éstos ('estos) *pron pl also* **éstas** 1 these. 2 the latter.

estoy (es'toi) *v see* **estar.**

estrafalario (estrafa'larjo) *adj* outlandish, eccentric.

estragar (estra'gar) *vt* 1 lay waste. 2 pervert. **estrago** *nm* ruin, havoc. **hacer estragos** wreak havoc.

estrangular (estrangu'lar) vt strangle. **estrangulador** nm 1 strangler. 2 mot choke.

estratagema (estrata'xema) nf stratagem. **estrategia** nf strategy. **estratégico** adj strategic.

estrechar (estre't∫ar) vt 1 make narrower, reduce. 2 tighten. 3 embrace, shake (hand). **estrecharse** vr get narrow. **estrechez** nf 1 narrowness. 2 stringency. 3 intimacy. **estrecho** adj 1 narrow, cramped, tight. 2 austere. 3 narrow-minded. nm straits, channel.

estrella (es'treʎa) nf star. **estrellar** vt smash, shatter. **estrellado** adj starry.

estremecer* (estreme'θer) vt shake. **estremecerse** vr tremble, shudder, shiver. **estremecimiento** nm tremor, trembling.

estrenar (estre'nar) vt 1 try on, wear for the first time. 2 Th perform for the first time. **estrenarse** vr make a début. **estreno** nm 1 début. 2 première. 3 first appearance.

estreñido (estre'niðo) adj constipated. **estreñimiento** nm constipation. **estreñirse** vr become constipated.

estrépito (es'trepito) nm noise, din, fuss. **estrepitoso** adj boisterous, noisy.

estribo (es'triβo) nm 1 stirrup. 2 running board. **perder los estribos** lose one's head, go crazy.

estribor (estri'βor) nm naut starboard.

estricto (es'trikto) adj strict, severe.

estridente (estri'ðente) adj strident.

estropajo (estro'paxo) nm 1 scourer. 2 rubbish. **estropajoso** adj 1 gristly. 2 slovenly. 3 (of speech) slurred, indistinct.

estropear (estrope'ar) vt 1 spoil. 2 maim.

estructura (estruk'tura) nf structure, framework.

estruendo (estru'endo) nm noise, din, turmoil. **estruendoso** adj noisy, uproarious.

estrujar (estru'xar) vt 1 squeeze. 2 drain. **estrujón** nm squeeze, crush.

estuario (es'twarjo) nm estuary.

estuche (es'tut∫e) nm 1 box. 2 sheath.

estudiar (estu'ðjar) vt,vi study. **estudiante** nm,f student. **estudio** nm 1 study. 2 research. 3 studio. **estudioso** adj studious.

estufa (es'tufa) nf 1 stove. 2 hot house.

estupefacto (estupe'fakto) adj astonished. **estupefaciente** nm drug, narcotic.

estupendo (estu'pendo) adj stupendous, marvellous.

estúpido (es'tupiðo) adj stupid. **estupidez** nf stupidity.

estuve (es'tuβe) v see **estar**.

etapa (e'tapa) nf 1 stage (of a journey, etc.). 2 phase. **por etapas** by stages.

éter ('eter) nm ether.

etéreo (e'tereo) adj ethereal.

eternidad (eterni'ðað) nf eternity. **eterno** adj eternal. **eternizar** vt make eternal, perpetuate.

ética ('etika) nf ethics. **ético** adj ethical.

Etiopía (Etjo'pia) nf Ethiopia. **etíope** adj,n Ethiopian.

etiqueta (eti'keta) nf 1 etiquette. 2 label. **etiquetero** adj formal, ceremonious.

eufemismo (eufe'mismo) nm euphemism. **eufemístico** adj euphemistic.

eunuco (eu'nuko) nm eunuch.

Europa (eu'ropa) nf Europe. **europeísmo** nm pro-European attitudes. **europeizar** vt Europeanize. **europeo** adj,n European.

eutanasia (euta'nasja) nf euthanasia.

evacuar (eβa'kwar) vt 1 evacuate. 2 undertake. **evacuación** nf evacuation.

evadir (eβa'ðir) vt evade. **evadirse** vr escape. **evadido** n fugitive.

evangélico (eβaŋ'xeliko) adj evangelical. **evangelio** nm gospel. **evangelista** nm evangelist.

evaporar (eβapo'rar) vt,vi evaporate. **evaporación** nf evaporation.

evasión (eβa'sjon) nf escape, flight. **evasiva** nf loophole, evasion. **evasivo** adj evasive.

evento (e'βento) nm eventuality, unforeseen event.

eventual (eβen'twal) adj 1 conditional, possible. 2 temporary. **eventualmente** adv 1 by chance. 2 circumstantially.

evidencia (eβi'ðenθja) nf 1 evidence. 2 clarity. **evidenciar** vt prove, make evident. **evidente** adj evident, obvious.

evitar (eβi'tar) vt avoid. **evitable** adj avoidable.

evocar (eβo'kar) vt evoke, invoke. **evocación** nf evocation, invocation. **evocador** adj evocative.

evolución (eβolu'θjon) nf evolution. **evolucionar** vi evolve. **evolutivo** adj evolutionary.

exacerbar (eksaθer'βar) vt exacerbate, provoke.

exactitud (eksakti'tuð) nf exactness. **exacto** adj exact, precise, correct.

exagerar (eksaxe'rar) vt exaggerate. **exagerado** adj 1 exaggerated. 2 excessive. **exageración** nf exaggeration.

exaltar (eksal'tar) vt 1 raise. 2 praise. **exaltarse** vr become excited.

examen (ek'samen) nm 1 educ examination. 2

investigation. **examen de conductor** driving test. **examinador** nm examiner.

examinar (eksami'nar) vt 1 examine, inspect closely. 2 test, question. **examinarse** vr take an examination.

exangüe (ek'sangwe) adj 1 bloodless, anaemic. 2 worn-out, weak.

exánime (ek'sanime) adj 1 lifeless. 2 unconscious. **caer exánime** fall in a faint.

exasperar (eksaspe'rar) vt 1 exasperate, annoy. 2 make worse. **exasperarse** vr become angry.

excavar (ekska'βar) vt 1 excavate. 2 hollow out.

exceder (eksθe'ðer) vt 1 exceed, surpass. **excederse** vr 1 surpass oneself. 2 go too far, overreach oneself.

excelencia (eksθe'lenθja) nf excellence, virtue. **su Excelencia** his Excellency. **excelente** adj outstanding, excellent.

excéntrico (eks'θentriko) adj,nm eccentric. **excentricidad** nf eccentricity.

excepción (eksθep'θjon) nf exception. **a excepción de** with the exception of. **hacer una excepción de** make an exception of. **excepcional** adj exceptional.

excepto (eks'θepto) prep. with the exception of.

excesivo (eksθe'siβo) adj excessive. **exceso** nm 1 excess. 2 abuse.

excitar (eksθi'tar) vt excite, stimulate. **excitarse** vr become excited.

exclamar (ekskla'mar) vi exclaim. **exclamarse contra** protest against.

excluir (eksklu'ir) vt exclude, rule out. **exclusión** nf exclusion. **exclusivo** adj exclusive, sole.

excomulgar (ekskomul'gar) vt excommunicate.

excursión (ekskur'sjon) nf excursion, outing. **excursión a pie** ramble. **ir de excursión** go on an outing.

excusar (eksku'sar) vt 1 forgive. 2 avoid. **excusarse** vr apologise. **excusa** nf excuse, pretext. **excusado** adj 1 unnecessary. 2 private.

exentar (eksen'tar) vt exempt (from). **exención** nf exemption. **exento** adj 1 exempt (from). 2 unobstructed.

exequias (ek'sekjas) nf pl funeral ceremony.

exhalar (eksa'lar) vt 1 breathe out. 2 give off (fumes, etc.). 3 utter (sigh, etc.).

exhausto (ek'sausto) adj exhausted.

exhibir (eksi'βir) vt exhibit, show, display. **exhibirse** vr show oneself. **exhibición** nf exhibition, show. **exhibicionismo** nm exhibitionism.

exhortar (eksor'tar) vt exhort.

exigir (eksi'xir) vt demand, insist on. **exigente** adj demanding.

exiguo (ek'sigwo) adj small, scanty.

eximir (eksi'mir) vt exempt from, relieve of.

existir (eksis'tir) vi exist, be. **existe la posibilidad que** it is just possible that. **existencia** nf 1 existence. 2 comm stocks, supplies. **existencialismo** nm existentialism.

éxito ('eksito) nm 1 result. 2 success. **éxito de taquilla** box-office success.

éxodo ('eksoðo) nm exodus, departure.

exonerar (eksone'rar) vt 1 exonerate. 2 free (from responsibility, weight, etc.).

exorbitante (eksorβi'tante) adj excessive.

exorcizar (eksorθi'θar) vt exorcise. **exorcismo** nm exorcism.

expansión (ekspan'sjon) nf 1 expansion. 2 relief, relaxation. 3 warmth of feeling. **expansivo** adj expansive, affectionate.

expatriar (ekspatri'ar) vt exile. **expatriarse** vr leave one's country.

expectación (ekspekta'θjon) nf expectation. **expectante** adj expectant.

expedición (ekspeði'θjon) nf 1 expedition. 2 comm shipment. 3 speed.

expedir* (ekspe'ðir) vt send, dispatch, issue. **expediente** nm 1 means device. 2 law proceedings. 3 file, record. **expediente académico** academic or school record.

expendedor (ekspende'ðor) nm,f dealer, agent. adj spending. **expendedor de billetes** booking clerk.

experiencia (ekspe'rjenθja) nf experience, skill.

experimentar (eksperimen'tar) vt 1 experience (emotion, etc.). 2 experiment (with). **experimental** adj experimental. **experimento** nm experiment.

experto (eks'perto) adj,nm expert.

expiar (eks'pjar) vt make atonement for.

expirar (ekspi'rar) vi 1 expire. 2 die.

explanar (ekspla'nar) vt 1 level, flatten. 2 explain.

explicar (ekspli'kar) vt 1 explain. 2 put forward (theory). 3 teach. **explicarse** vr 1 express oneself. 2 understand. **explicación** nf explanation. **explicativo** adj explanatory.

explícito (eks'pliθito) adj explicit, clear.

explorar (eksplo'rar) vt explore, investigate.

explosión (eksplo'sjon) nf explosion. **explosivo** adj,nm explosive

explotar (eksplo'tar) vt 1 run (a business), work (a mine), etc. 2 exploit. vt,vi explode. **explotación** nf 1 operation (of a business, factory, etc.). 2 exploitation.

exponer* (ekspo'ner) vt 1 expose, lay bare. 2 display. 3 explain. 4 phot expose. **exponerse** vr lay oneself open (to danger, etc.). **exponente** nm,f 1 one who explains, interpreter (of art, music). 2 illustration, example. adj explaining, explanatory.

exportar (ekspor'tar) vt export. **exportación** nf exportation, export. **exportador** adj exporting. nm exporter.

exposición (eksposi'θjon) nf 1 exhibition (art, etc.), showing. 2 phot exposure. 3 narrative. 4 position, location.

exprés (eks'pres) nm 1 express (train). 2 cul espresso (coffee).

expresar (ekspre'sar) vt express, state, quote, voice (opinion). **expresarse** vr 1 express oneself. 2 be stated. **expresión** nf 1 expression. 2 pl (kind) regards. **expresivo** adj affectionate.

exprimir (ekspri'mir) vt squeeze or wring (out).

expuesto (eks'pwesto) adj 1 dangerous, risky. 2 exposed.

expulsar (ekspul'sar) vt expel, banish, throw out.

exquisito (ekski'sito) adj exquisite, delicious.

éxtasis ('ekstasis) nm invar ecstasy.

extender (**ie**) (eksten'der) vt 1 extend, lengthen. 2 prolong. 3 unfold, spread out. **extenderse** vr 1 stretch oneself out. 2 talk at length. **extenderse a** or **hasta** run to, amount to.

extenso (eks'tenso) adj 1 wide, spread out, vast. 2 spacious. 3 extended. **por extenso** in great detail. **extensión** nf 1 extension, length. 2 expanse. 3 extent. **extensivo** adj extensive. **extensivo** adj applicable to.

extenuar (ekste'nwar) weaken.

exterior (ekste'rjor) adj 1 outer, external. 2 foreign. nm 1 (outward) appearance. 2 foreign countries. **al** or **por el exterior** outwardly. **del exterior** from abroad.

exterminar (ekstermi'nar) vt destroy, wipe out.

externo (eks'terno) adj external. nm day pupil.

extinguir* (ekstin'gir) vt 1 extinguish, put out. 2 wipe out. **extinción** nf extinction. **extinto** adj extinct. **extintor** nm fire extinguisher.

extirpar (ekstir'par) vt 1 stamp out, wipe out. 2 med remove.

extra ('ekstra) adj invar extra. nm bonus, extra item. nm,nf (film) extra. **extra de** in addition to.

extraer* (ekstra'er) vt 1 extract, remove. 2 release. **extracción** nf 1 extraction. 2 origin, birth. **extracto** nm 1 extract. 2 abstract (of text).

extranjero (ekstran'xero) adj foreign. nm 1 foreigner. 2 stranger. 3 foreign country. **en el extranjero** abroad. **ir al extranjero** go abroad.

extrañar (ekstra'nar) vt 1 find strange or surprising. 2 exile. 3 estrange. **es de extrañar que** it is surprising that. **extrañarse** vr be surprised.

extraordinario (ekstraorði'narjo) adj 1 uncommon. 2 strange, odd. 3 outstanding. nm special number (newspaper, etc.).

extravagancia (ekstraβa'ganθja) nf 1 extravagance. 2 strangeness. **extravagante** adj 1 extravagant. 2 odd.

extraviar (ekstra'βjar) vt 1 lose, mislay (object). 2 mislead (person). **extraviarse** vr 1 get lost. 2 stray (animal). 3 inf fall into bad habits.

extremar (ekstre'mar) vt carry to extremes, overdo. **extremarse en** make every effort to.

extremidad (ekstremi'ðað) nf 1 tip, edge, extremity. 2 pl furthest limits. **extremo** adj 1 extreme, farthest, end. 2 last. 3 desperate. **en caso extremo** as a last resort. nm 1 extreme, end. 2 great care. **al extremo de** to the point of. **de un extremo a otro** from one extreme to the other. **Extremo Oriente** Far East.

extrínseco (eks'trinseko) adj extrinsic, not inherent in.

exuberancia (eksuβe'ranθja) nf 1 exuberance, high spirits. 2 lushness. **exuberante** adj 1 abundant, lush. 2 well-rounded (figure).

exultar (eksul'tar) vi exult, triumph.

F

fábrica ('faβrika) nf 1 factory. 2 manufacture, production. **fabricar** vt 1 manufacture. 2 arch build. **fabricación** nf manufacture. **fabricante** nm manufacturer. **fabricación en serie** mass production.

fábula ('faβula) nf 1 fable, tale. 2 plot, action. 3 gossip, rumour.

fabuloso (faβu'loso) adj 1 fabulous, imaginary. 2 inf wonderful.

facción (fak'θjon) nf 1 faction, party, side. 2 anat pl features.

faceta (fa'θeta) nf facet.

fácil ('faθil) adj 1 easy, simple. 2 fluent, glib. 3 docile. **facilidad** nf facility, ease.

facilitar (faθili'tar) vt 1 facilitate. 2 supply, provide.

facsímil (fak'θimil) adj,nm facsimile.

factible (fak'tiβle) adj feasible.

factor (fak'tor) nm 1 factor, element. 2 agent.

facturar (faktu'rar) vt 1 invoice. 2 mot register (baggage). **factura** nf bill, invoice.

facultad (fakul'taδ) nf 1 power, authority. 2 ability, faculty. 3 educ faculty, school (in a university).

facultativo (faculta'tivo) adj 1 optional. 2 professional. 3 med medical. nm doctor.

facha ('fatʃa) nf inf appearance, look.

fachada (fa'tʃaδa) nf façade.

faena (fa'ena) nf 1 task, duty. 2 inf tough job. **estar de faena** be at work.

faisán (fai'san) nm pheasant.

faja ('faxa) nf 1 strip of cloth, bandage. 2 belt, zone. 3 girdle.

falaz (fa'laθ) 1 deceitful, treacherous. 2 deceptive, fallacious.

falda ('falda) nf 1 skirt. 2 lower slope of a hill. 3 lap.

falsear (false'ar) vt 1 falsify. 2 counterfeit. 3 tech bevel. vi give way, sag.

falsificar (falsifi'kar) vt 1 falsify. 2 forge. **falsificación** nf 1 falsification. 2 forgery.

falso ('falso) adj 1 false. 2 bogus, sham. **en falso** falsely. **falsedad** nf falsity.

falta ('falta) nf 1 want, need. 2 fault, failure, shortcoming. 3 sport foul, fault.

faltar (fal'tar) vi 1 be lacking. 2 be absent or missing. **faltar a la verdad** lie.

falto ('falto) adj 1 deficient, short. 2 incomplete.

fallar (fa'ʎar) vt 1 law judge, pronounce sentence on. 2 game trump. vi fail, go wrong. **falla** nf failure, defect.

fallecer* (faʎe'θer) vi 1 die. 2 run out, end. **fallecimiento** nm decease, demise.

fallir (fa'ʎir) vi 1 fail. 2 run out, expire.

fallo ('faʎo) nm 1 failure, breakdown. 2 law decision, verdict.

fama ('fama) nf reputation, fame.

familia (fa'milja) nf 1 family. 2 household.

familiar adj 1 of the family. 2 familiar. 3 ordinary, informal. nm,f 1 intimate friend. 2 relative. **familiaridad** nf familiarity.

familiarizar (familjari'θar) vt familiarize.

famoso (fa'moso) adj 1 famous. 2 inf great (friend).

fanático (fa'natiko) adj fanatical. nm 1 fanatic. 2 inf supporter, enthusiast, fan.

fanfarrón (fanfar'ron) nm 1 bully. 2 braggart. adj boastful.

fango ('fango) nm mud, mire. **fangal** nm muddy place, bog. **fangoso** adj muddy.

fantasía (fanta'sia) nf 1 fantasy. 2 whim, fancy. **joyas de fantasía** nf pl imitation jewellery.

fantasma (fan'tasma) nm ghost.

fantástico (fan'tastiko) adj 1 fantastic. 2 imaginary, unreal.

fantoche (fan'totʃe) nm 1 puppet. 2 inf non-entity, man of straw.

fardo ('farδo) nm 1 bundle, pack. 2 load, burden.

fariseo (fari'seo) nm hypocrite, Pharisee.

farmacia (far'maθja) nf chemist's shop, pharmacy. **farmacia de guardia** all-night chemist's. **farmacéutico** nm chemist, pharmacist. adj pharmaceutical.

faro ('faro) nm 1 lighthouse. 2 beacon. 3 mot headlamp.

farol (fa'rol) nm 1 lantern. 2 inf swank. **farol público** street lamp.

farsa ('farsa) nf 1 Th farce. 2 humbug. **farsante** inf fake, fraud.

fascinar (fasθi'nar) vt,vi fascinate. **fascinación** nf fascination. **fascinador** adj fascinating.

fascismo (fas'θismo) nm fascism. **fascista** adj, n fascist.

fase ('fase) nf phase, stage.

fastidiar (fasti'δjar) vt 1 annoy. 2 bore. 3 disgust. ¡**no fastidies!** 1 you're joking! 2 do not bother me! **fastidiarse** vr 1 become annoyed. 2 become bored. **fastidio** nm 1 annoyance. 2 boredom. **fastidioso** adj 1 annoying. 2 boring.

fastuoso (fas'twoso) adj 1 magnificent, splendid. 2 pompous.

fatal (fa'tal) adj 1 deadly. 2 cursed, ill fated. 3 inescapable. 4 inf horrible, awful. **fatalidad** nf 1 fate, fatality. 2 misfortune. **fatalista** adj invar fatalistic. nm,f fatalist. **fatalismo** nm fatalism.

fatigar (fati'gar) vt 1 tire. 2 annoy. **fatigarse** vr become tired or weary. **fatiga** nf 1 tiredness. 2 tech fatigue. 3 pl troubles, worries. **fatigoso** adj 1 trying, tiresome. 2 tiring. 3 difficult.

fatuidad (fatwi'δaδ) nf 1 frivolity, silliness. 2 vanity. **fatuo** adj 1 idle, foolish, inane. 2 vain.

fausto ('fausto) adj succesful, fortunate. nm glory, splendour.

favor (fa'βor) nm 1 favour, kindness. 2 help. 3 gift. **a favor de** 1 in favour of. 2 on behalf of. **de favor** complimentary (tickets, etc.). **favorable** adj favourable. **favorecer*** vt 1 favour, prefer. 2 help. **favorito** adj,nm favourite.

faz (faθ) nf 1 face. 2 front.

fe (fe) nf 1 faith, belief. 2 trust. 3 witness, testimony. 4 certificate. **a fe** in truth. **dar fe en** put trust in. **tener fe en** believe in.

fealdad (feal'ðað) nf ugliness.

febrero (fe'βrero) nm February.

febril (fe'βril) adj 1 feverish. 2 agitated.

fecundar (fekun'dar) vt fertilize. **fecundidad** nf fertility, fruitfulness. **fecundizar*** vt fertilize. **fecundo** adj 1 fertile, fruitful. 2 abundant, productive. **fecundo en** rich in, full of.

fecha ('fetʃa) nf date. **hasta la fecha** to date, up to the present.

federación (feðera'θjon) nf federation.

fehaciente (fea'θjente) adj law authentic, reliable.

felicidad (feliθi'ðað) nf 1 joy, happiness. 2 success, good fortune. **¡felicidades!** congratulations!

felicitar (feliθi'tar) vt congratulate.

feligrés (feli'gres) nm parishioner.

feliz (fe'liθ) adj 1 happy. 2 fortunate. **feliz año nuevo** happy New Year. **feliz cumpleaños** happy birthday.

felpa ('felpa) nf 1 plush, towelling. 2 inf beating, hiding. **felpudo** adj plushy. nm doormat.

femenino (feme'nino) adj feminine, female.

fenecer* (fene'θer) vt 1 cease, end. 2 die, perish.

fenómeno (fe'nomeno) nm 1 phenomenon. 2 oddity, freak. 3 person of extraordinary qualities, genius.

feo ('feo) adj 1 ugly, plain, unsightly. 2 nasty, foul. 3 unfair, cheating. **más feo que Picio** as ugly as sin. ~nm insult.

féretro ('feretro) nm coffin.

feria ('ferja) nf 1 fair. 2 festival, carnival. **feria de muestras** trade fair.

fermentar (fermen'tar) vi ferment.

ferocidad (feroθi'ðað) nf ferocity, savageness. **feroz** adj fierce, wild, savage.

férreo ('ferreo) adj 1 iron. 2 sci ferrous. 3 severe, firm.

ferretería (ferrete'ria) nf 1 hardware. 2 ironmonger's shop, hardware shop.

ferrocarril (ferrokar'ril) nm railway. **por ferrocarril** by rail.

ferroviario (ferro'βjarjo) adj railway, rail. nm railway worker.

fértil ('fertil) adj fertile, productive, abundant. **fertilidad** nf fertility, fruitfulness. **fertilizante** nm fertilizer. **fertilizar** vt fertilize.

ferviente (fer'βjente) adj intense, ardent. **fervor** nm 1 passion, ardour. 2 enthusiasm, zeal. **fervoroso** adj 1 ardent. 2 eager, enthusiastic.

festejar (feste'xar) vt 1 feast, celebrate. 2 woo. **festejo** nm 1 feast. 2 courtship. **festín** nm feast, banquet. **festividad** nf 1 festivity. 2 holiday. **festivo** adj 1 festive, merry. 2 witty. **día festivo** nm holiday.

fétido ('fetiðo) adj stinking, rotting.

feto ('feto) nm embryo, unborn child.

feudal (feu'ðal) adj feudal. **feudalismo** nm feudal system. **feudo** nm manor, feudal territory.

fiado ('fjaðo) nm trust. **combrar al fiado** buy on credit. **en fiado** on bail. **fiador** nm 1 sponsor. 2 fastener, catch. 3 trigger (of a gun).

fiambre ('fjambre) nm 1 cold cooked meat, cold dish. 2 inf dead body. 3 inf corny joke.

fiar ('fjar) vt 1 comm guarantee. 2 give credit to. 3 bail. vi confide. **fiarse de** trust in, depend on. **fianza** nf 1 comm security. 2 bail.

fibra ('fiβra) nf 1 fibre, filament. 2 energy, vigour. 3 min vein. 4 pl sinews, muscles.

ficción (fik'θjon) nf 1 fiction. 2 tall story, invention. **ficticio** adj imaginary, invented.

ficha ('fitʃa) nf 1 counter, token, disc. 2 game piece. 3 card, index card.

fidedigno (fiðe'ðigno) adj trustworthy. **fidelidad** nf loyalty, fidelity. **de alta fidelidad** hi-fi.

fideos (fi'ðeos) nm pl noodles.

fiebre ('fjeβre) nf fever. **tener fiebre** be feverish, have fever.

fiel (fjel) adj 1 loyal, trustworthy. 2 accurate, exact. 3 reliable. 4 honourable. **fiel a** true to. ~nm 1 good Christian. 2 needle (of scales, compass, etc.). 3 inspector of weights and measures. 4 pl rel the faithful.

fieltro ('fjeltro) nm 1 felt (material). 2 felt hat.

fiera ('fjera) nf 1 wild beast. 2 brute (of a person). **estar hecho una fiera** be beside oneself, be furious.

fiero ('fjero) adj wild.

fiesta ('fjesta) nf 1 rel feast day, saint's day. 2 holiday. 3 party. **estar en fiestas** be in high spirits.

figurar (figu'rar) vt 1 form, shape. 2 represent. vi figure in, appear in (book, play, etc.). **figurarse** vr imagine, believe, seem. **figura** nf 1 figure, shape. 2 face. 3 appearance. 4 gram figure, symbol. 5 inf unpleasant person. **figurado** adj 1 figurative. 2 imaginary.

fijar (fi'xar) vt 1 fix, fasten. 2 decide, settle. 3 fix one's attention on. **fijarse en** 1 resolve to. 2 pay attention to. **¡fijamos en esto!** that's settled! **fija** nf 1 hinge. 2 trowel. **fijamente** adv steadily, intently. **fijeza** nf firmness. **fijo** adj 1 decided, settled. 2 steady. 3 immovable, invariable. **fijamente** adv certainly.

fila ('fila) nf 1 row, line. 2 mil file, column. **fila india** single file.

filantropía (filantro'pia) nf philanthropy.

filete (fi'lete) nm 1 cul fillet, steak. 2 (screw) thread. 3 hem, border. 4 arch type of moulding.

filiación (filja'θjon) nf 1 affiliation, association. 2 relationship. 3 personal characteristics. **filial** adj filial. nf affiliated company, subsidiary.

filigrana (fili'grana) nf 1 filigree work. 2 watermark. 3 daintiness.

filo ('filo) nm 1 blade, cutting edge. 2 dividing line. **por filo** exactly. **tirarse un filo con** argue with, pick a quarrel with.

filón (fi'lon) nm 1 min seam, vein. 2 inf bargain, windfall.

filosofía (filoso'fia) nf philosophy. **filósofo** nm philosopher.

filtrar (fil'trar) vt filter, purify, strain. vi seep into, penetrate. **filtración** nf leakage, seepage. **filtrador** adj filtering. nm filter. **filtro** nm 1 filter, strainer. 2 lit love philtre.

fin (fin) nm 1 end, conclusion. 2 death. 3 objective, aim. **a fin de** in order to. **al fin y al cabo** when all is said and done. **en fin** at last. **por fin** at last.

final (fi'nal) adj final, last. nm end, outcome. **al final de** at the end of. **finalidad** nf aim, purpose. **finalizar** vt,vi end, finish. **finalmente** finally.

financiar (finan'θjar) vt finance. **financiero** adj financial. nm financier. **finanzas** nf pl finances.

finca ('finka) nf 1 property. 2 estate, farm land.

fineza (fi'neθa) nf 1 refinement, grace. 2 kindness. 3 gift.

fingir (fin'xir) vt 1 pretend. 2 deceive. 3 fake, appear to. **fingirse** vr pretend to be.

Finlandia (fin'landja) nf Finland. **finlandés** adj Finnish. nm 1 Finn. 2 Finnish (language).

fino ('fino) adj 1 fine, slender, delicate. 2 pure, refined. 3 precious (stone, metal, etc.). 4 sharp (point). 5 shrewd, acute, subtle.

firmar (fir'mar) vt sign. **firma** nf 1 signature. 2 business, firm.

firme ('firme) adj 1 firm, solid, hard. 2 resolute, steady. adv firmly. nm road surface. **de firme** steadily. **en lo firme** in the right. **¡firmes!** mil attention! **firmeza** nf firmness, stability.

fiscal (fis'kal) adj financial. nm 1 law treasurer. 2 law counsel for the prosecution. **fiscalizar** vt 1 supervise. 2 criticise. 3 inf interfere, pry. **fisco** nm exchequer, treasury.

física ('fisika) nf physics.

físico ('fisiko) adj physical, material. nm 1 physicist. 2 physique, body.

fisiología (fisjolo'xia) nf physiology.

fisionomía (fisjono'mia) nf 1 physiognomy. 2 outward appearance.

flaco ('flako) adj 1 skinny. 2 weak. nm weakness, defect.

flagrante (fla'grante) adj blatant, undisguised. **en flagrante** in the act.

flamante (fla'mante) adj 1 blazing. 2 brand new.

flamenco (fla'menko) adj 1 Flemish. 2 gypsy (especially Andalusian). 3 cocky, swaggering. nm 1 flamenco. 2 flamingo.

flanco ('flanko) nm side, flank. **coger por el flanco** catch unawares.

flaquear (flake'ar) vi 1 grow weak. 2 worsen (health). 3 become downhearted. **flaqueza** nf 1 thinness. 2 frailty. 3 failing, lacking.

flauta ('flauta) nf flute. **flautiste** nm,f flautist.

fleco ('fleko) nm tassel, fringe.

flecha ('fletʃa) nf arrow, dart. **flecha de dirección** traffic indicator. **flecha de mar** zool squid. **flechar** vt 1 shoot with an arrow, wound. 2 inf make a conquest. **flechazo** nm 1 arrow shot. 2 wound. 3 sudden realization. 4 love at first sight. **flechero** nm 1 archer. 2 quiver.

fletar (fle'tar) vt charter (plane, etc.). **fletamento** nm comm charter.

flexibilidad (fleksiβili'ðað) nf flexibility, adaptability. **flexible** adj flexible, supple. nm flex, wire. **flexión** nf 1 bending, flexing. 2 gram inflection.

flojo ('floxo) adj 1 loose, slack. 2 weak. 3 inf lazy.

flor (flor) nf 1 flower. 2 ornament. 3 compliment. 4 peak, best part. 5 freshness. **a flor de** on the surface. **echar flores** flatter. **en flor** 1 in flower. 2 in one's prime. **flor de lis** lily. **floral** adj floral. **florar** vi flower.

florecer* (flore'θer) vi 1 flower. 2 flourish, prosper. **florecerse** vr go mouldy. **floreciente** adj 1 flowering. 2 prospering. **florecimiento** nm flowering. **florido** adj 1 flowering. 2 ornate. 3 gram rhetorical.

flotar (flo'tar) vi 1 float. 2 flap, hang loose. **flota** nf fleet. **flotante** adj floating. **a flote** afloat.

fluctuar (fluk'twar) vi 1 fluctuate, vary. 2 hesitate.

fluidez (flui'ðeθ) nf 1 fluidity. 2 fluency. **fluido** adj fluent, flowing. **flúido** adj fluid. nm electric current.

fluir (flu'ir) vi flow, run. **fluente** adj flowing. **flujo** nm 1 stream, surge, flow. 2 rising tide. **flujo de vientre** diarrhoea. **flujo y reflujo** ebb and flow.

fluorescencia (fluores'θenθja) nf fluorescence. **fluorescente** adj fluorescent.

fluoruro (flwo'ruro) nm fluoride.

foca ('foka) nf zool seal.

foco ('foko) nm 1 focus. 2 centre, core. 3 origin, source.

fogata (fo'gata) nf bonfire, blaze.

fogón (fo'gon) nm 1 stove. 2 hearth. 3 fire (of guns). 4 naut galley.

fogoso (fo'goso) adj fiery, high-spirited, impetuous.

follaje (fo'ʎaxe) nm 1 foliage, greenery. 2 excessive decoration.

folletín (foʎe'tin) nm newspaper article or serial. **folleto** nm pamphlet, leaflet.

follón (fo'ʎon) adj 1 idle. 2 cowardly. 3 vain, proud. nm 1 good-for-nothing, lout. 2 commotion.

fomentar (fomen'tar) vt 1 encourage, provoke. 2 promote (business, etc.). **fomento** nm 1 encouragement, provocation. 2 comm productivity, development. 3 med fomentation.

fonda ('fonda) nf inn.

fondear (fonde'ar) vt 1 sound (depth of water). 2 test, examine. 3 search (a ship). vi anchor.

fondo ('fondo) nm 1 bottom (of box, etc.). 2 depth. 3 sea or river bed. 4 background. 5 pl capital, funds. **a fondo** thoroughly. **en el fondo** at heart. **estar en fondos** be well off.

fontanero (fonta'nero) nm plumber.

forajido (fora'xiðo) nm outlaw, fugitive.

forastero (foras'tero) adj strange. n stranger, alien, visitor.

forcejear (forθexe'ar) vi struggle, strive. **forcejeo** nm struggle, great effort.

forense (fo'rense) adj legal, forensic.

forjar (for'xar) vt 1 forge, beat into shape. 2 create, invent. **forja** nf 1 forge, furnace. 2 forging.

formal (for'mal) adj 1 serious. 2 courteous, correct. 3 reliable. 4 conventional. 5 well behaved. **formalidad** nf 1 formality. 2 convention. 2 seriousness.

formar (for'mar) vt 1 form, shape, make. 2 educate, train. **formarse** vr 1 develop, grow up. 2 be trained. **forma** nf 1 form, shape. 2 method, way. 3 tech mould. **de forma que** so that. **de todas formas** anyway.

formidable (formi'ðaβle) adj 1 fearful. 2 tremendous. 3 inf marvellous.

fórmula ('formula) nf 1 formula. 2 med prescription.

fornicar (forni'kar) vi fornicate.

fornido (for'niðo) adj robust.

foro ('foro) nm 1 forum. 2 law court. 3 Th back of the stage.

forraje (for'raxe) nm 1 fodder. 2 plunder, forage.

forrar (for'rar) vt 1 put a cover on. 2 line, pad (clothes). **forrarse** vr 1 inf make lots of money. 2 inf gorge oneself. **forro** nm 1 cover, sheath, coat. 2 lining, padding. **ni por el forro** not the foggiest idea.

fortalecer* (fortale'θer) vt 1 strengthen. 2 encourage. 3 mil fortify. **fortaleza** nf 1 strength. 2 courage, fortitude. 3 mil fortress.

fortuito (for'twito) adj 1 accidental. 2 random.

fortuna (for'tuna) nf 1 fate, chance. 2 good luck. 3 happiness. 4 fortune, wealth. **por fortuna** luckily. **probar fortuna** take a chance, try one's luck.

forzar (ue) (for'θar) vt 1 oblige, compel. 2 rape. 3 break into, force. 4 mil storm.

fosa ('fosa) nf 1 grave. 2 anat cavity.

fosfato (fos'fato) nm phosphate.

fósforo ('fosforo) nm 1 sci phosphorus 2 match.

fósil ('fosil) adj fossilized. nm fossil.

foso ('foso) nm 1 hole, pit, ditch 2 Th pit. 3 mil trench.

fotogénico (foto'xeniko) adj photogenic.

fotografía (fotogra'fia) nf 1 photography 2

photograph. **fotografiar** vt photograph. **fotógrafo** nm photographer.

frac (frak) nm dress coat, tails.

fracasar (fraka'sar) vi fail, come to grief. **fracaso** nm failure, disaster.

fracción (frak'θjon) nf 1 part, portion, fragment. 2 a breaking into parts, sharing out. 3 math fraction.

fractura (frak'tura) nf med fracture.

fragancia (fra'ganθja) nf fragrance, perfume.

frágil ('fraxil) adj fragile, breakable.

fragmento (frag'mento) nm part, fragment.

fragor (fra'gor) nm row, uproar.

fraguar (fra'gwar) vt 1 forge (metal). 2 plan, plot. vi harden (cement, etc.). **fragua** nf forge.

fraile ('fraile) nm friar, monk.

frambuesa (fram'bwesa) nf raspberry.

Francia ('franθja) nf France. **francés** adj French. nm 1 Frenchman. 2 French (language).

franco ('franko) adj 1 open, sincere. 2 generous, free. nm franc (coinage).

franela (fra'nela) nf flannel.

franja ('franxa) nf 1 fringe, border. 2 strip, narrow piece.

franquear (franke'ar) vt 1 release, free. 2 frank (parcel, etc.). 3 clear (path, etc.). 4 get round (obstacle). **franquearse** vr 1 reveal one's thoughts. 2 fall in with someone's wishes. **franqueo** nm 1 franking. 2 postage.

franqueza (fran'keθa) nf 1 frankness, sincerity. 2 generosity. **con franqueza** frankly.

frasco ('frasko) nm flask, small bottle.

frase ('frase) nf 1 gram sentence, phrase, expression. **frase hecha** 1 proverb. 2 cliché.

fraternal (frater'nal) adj brotherly.

fraude ('frauðe) nm 1 fraud. 2 dishonesty. **fraudulencia** nf dishonesty. **fraudulento** adj dishonest, false.

fray (frej) nm rel Friar, Brother.

frecuencia (fre'kwenθja) nf frequency. **con frequencia** often. **frecuentar** vt frequent, visit often. **frecuente** adj 1 frequent. 2 usual, common.

fregar (ie) (fre'gar) vt 1 rub, scrub. 2 wash up. **fregado** nm 1 scrubbing. 2 washing up. 3 inf mess. **fregadero** nm sink. **fregador** nm 1 mop. 2 dish-mop. **fregona** nf inf (kitchen) maid.

freír (fre'ir) vt 1 fry. 2 inf bore.

frenar (fre'nar) vt 1 mot brake. 2 restrain, check. **freno** nm 1 mot brake. 2 horse's bit, bridle. 3 restraint, check. **freno de mano**

handbrake. **poner el freno** apply the brake. **soltar el freno** release the brake.

frenesí (frene'si) nm frenzy.

frente ('frente) nm 1 front, face. 2 façade. 3 min face. nf forehead, face. **en frente** opposite.

fresa ('fresa) nf 1 strawberry. 2 strawberry plant. 3 tech drill, cutting tool.

fresco ('fresko) adj 1 cool. 2 fresh, new. 3 calm. 4 inf insolent, forward. 5 strong (wind, etc.). **ponerse fresco con** inf get fresh with. **frescura** nf 1 coolness. 2 calmness. 3 inf insolence, cheek. 4 cheeky comment.

fresno ('fresno) nm bot ash.

frialdad (frjal'ðað) nf 1 coldness. 2 indifference. 3 impotence.

fricción (frik'θjon) nf 1 friction. 2 med massage. 3 ill feeling.

frigidez (frixi'ðeθ) nf frigidity, rigidity.

fríjol (fri'xol) nm French bean.

frío ('frio) adj 1 cold, cool. 2 indifferent. nm 1 coldness. 2 indifference. **hacer frío** be cold (weather). **tener frío** feel cold.

friolera (frjo'lera) nf triviality, trifle.

frisar (fri'sar) vt frizz, curl. **frisar en** be about, border on (a certain age).

frito ('frito) v see **freír**. adj 1 fried. 2 inf worn out. nm fried food. **estar frito** inf be exhausted. **traer frito** a worry (someone).

frívolo ('friβolo) adj frivolous, superficial.

frondoso (fron'doso) adj 1 leafy. 2 lush.

frontera (fron'tera) nf frontier, border.

frotar (fro'tar) vt 1 rub. 2 strike (match) **frotación** nf 1 rubbing. **frote** nm rub.

fructífero (fruk'tifero) adj 1 bot fruit-bearing. 2 productive.

frugal (fru'gal) adj frugal, sparing.

fruncir (frun'θir) vt 1 wrinkle, ruffle. 2 pleat, gather (sewing). **fruncir las cejas** frown.

frustrar (frus'trar) vt frustrate. **frustrarse** vr 1 be frustrated. 2 fail.

fruta ('fruta) nf 1 fruit. 2 result, consequence. **frutero** adj fruit or fruit-bearing. nm 1 fruit bowl. 2 fruiterer. **fruto** nm 1 fruit. 2 product, result. **sacar fruto de** benefit from.

fue¹ ('fue) v see **ir**.

fue² ('fue) v see **ser**.

fuego ('fwego) nm 1 fire, blaze. 2 cul flame, heat. 3 med rash. 4 passion. 5 mil fire. 6 hearth. **apagar el fuego** put out the fire. **fuegos artificiales** fireworks. **pegar fuego a** set fire to.

fuelle ('fweʎe) nm 1 bellows. 2 inf gossip. 3 mot folding hood.

fuente ('fwente) nf 1 fountain, spring. 2 source, origin. 3 cul large dish.

fuera ('fwera) adv outside, out. **desde fuera** from outside. **estar fuera** be away (from home). **ir fuera** go outside. **por fuera** on the outside. **fuera de** prep 1 except. 2 in addition to. **fuera de alcance** out of reach.

fuero ('fwero) nm 1 law. 2 charter. 3 privilege. 4 pl inf airs and graces.

fuerte ('fwerte) adj 1 strong. 2 energetic. 3 tough, hard. 4 loud. 5 concentrated. 6 heavy. nm 1 strong point. 2 mil fortress. **fuerza** nf 1 strength. 2 loudness. 3 energy. 4 effort. 5 intensity. 6 electric current. 7 violence. 8 pl armed forces.

fugarse (fu'garse) vr 1 run away, escape. 2 leak. **fuga** nf 1 escape. 2 elopement. 3 leak (gas, etc.). 4 mus fugue. **fugaz** adj brief, fleeting. **fugitivo** adj fugitive.

fulano (fu'lano) nm 1 what's-his-name. 2 nobody. **fulano de tal** Mr so-and-so.

fulcro ('fulkro) nm fulcrum.

fulgor (ful'gor) nm 1 glow, brilliant light. 2 brilliance (quality).

fulminante (fulmi'nante) adj 1 med grave, mortal (illness). 2 thundering, explosive.

fumar (fu'mar) vt,vi smoke. **prohibido fumar** no smoking. **fumarse** vr inf squander, fritter away.

fumigar (fumi'gar) vt fumigate. **fumigarse** vr inf get lost.

función (funk'θjon) nf 1 function, operation. 2 performance, show. 3 pl duties, responsibilities.

funcionar (funkθjo'nar) vt function, operate, work, go (machine, etc.).

funda ('funda) nf cover, case.

fundar (fun'dar) vt 1 found, establish. 2 base (theory). **fundarse (en)** vr be founded (on). **fundado** adj justified. **fundamental** adj essential. **fundamento** nm 1 arch foundation. 2 good reason, grounds. 3 reliability.

fundir (fun'dir) vt 1 fuse, join together. 2 melt. 3 tech smelt. **fundición** nf 1 foundry. 2 fusing. 3 melting. 4 tech smelting.

fúnebre ('funeβre) adj 1 funerary. 2 gloomy.

funesto (fu'nesto) adj ill fated, gloomy, disastrous.

furgón (fur'gon) nm 1 wagon. 2 truck. **furgoneta** nf van.

furia ('furja) nf 1 fury, rage. 2 frenzy. 3 speed.

furioso adj 1 furious. 2 mad. 3 violent. **ponerse furioso** become furious.

furor (fu'ror) nm 1 fury, rage. 2 madness. 3 passion. 4 violence. **con furor** furiously. **hacer furor** be fashionable.

furtivo (fur'tiβo) adj secretive, sly.

fusible (fu'siβle) nm fuse.

fusil (fu'sil) nm rifle.

fusión (fu'sjon) nf fusion, union.

fuste ('fuste) nm 1 wood. 2 wooden shaft (of spear, column, etc.). 3 wooden saddle. **de poco fuste** of little importance.

fútbol ('futβol) nm football.

fútil ('futil) adj frivolous, trivial.

futuro (fu'turo) adj,nm future.

G

gabán (ga'βan) nm overcoat.

gabardina (gaβar'ðina) nf 1 raincoat. 2 gabardine.

gabinete (gaβinete) nm 1 study, studio, laboratory. 2 pol cabinet.

gacela (ga'θela) nf gazelle.

gaceta (ga'θeta) nf gazette.

gachas (ga'tʃas) nf pl porridge.

gacho ('gatʃo) adj drooping.

gafas ('gafas) nf pl spectacles. **gafas de sol** sunglasses.

gajo ('gaxo) nm 1 twig. 2 clump (of herbs). 3 slice (of orange).

gala ('gala) nf 1 formal dress. 2 pomp, elegance. **estar de gala** be in formal dress. **hacer gala de** show off, display. **tener a gala** be proud of.

galán (ga'lan) nm Th leading man.

galante (ga'lante) adj polite, charming. **galantear** vi flirt.

galardón (galar'ðon) nm reward, prize. **galardonar** vt award prize to.

galeón (gale'on) nm galleon.

galera (ga'lera) nf galley, prison.

galería (gale'ria) nf 1 gallery. 2 tunnel, corridor. 3 veranda.

Gales ('gales) nm Wales. **galés** adj,n Welsh. nm Welsh (language).

galgo ('galgo) nm greyhound.

galón[1] (ga'lon) nm 1 silk band. 2 mil stripe. **quitar los galones a** demote.

galón[2] (ga'lon) nm gallon.

galopar (galo'par) vi gallop. **galope** nm gallop. **a medio galope** at a canter.

galvanizar

galvanizar (galβani'θar) vt galvanize.
gallardo (ga'ʎarðo) adj 1 graceful. 2 dashing.
galleta (ga'ʎeta) nf biscuit.
gallina (ga'ʎina) nf hen. **gallo** nm cock.
gamuza (ga'muθa) nf chamois (leather).
gana ('gana) nf 1 wish. 2 appetite. **de buena/mala gana** willingly/unwillingly. **tener ganas de** want to.
ganadería (ganaðe'ria) nf 1 cattle-farming. 2 ranch, cattle farm. 3 livestock. **ganadero** nm cattle-farmer. adj of cattle. **ganado** nm cattle, livestock.
ganar (ga'nar) vt 1 win, get, gain. 2 earn. vi 1 win. 2 do well. **ganancia** nf earnings, profit. **ganancioso** adj profitable.
gancho ('gantʃo) nm hook.
gansada (gan'saða) nf stupid behaviour. **ganso** nm goose.
garaje (ga'raxe) nm garage.
garantizar (garanti'θar) vt guarantee. **garantía** nf guarantee, warranty. **bajo garantía** under guarantee.
garbanzo (gar'βanθo) nm chickpea.
garbo ('garβo) nm 1 jauntiness. 2 refinement, gracefulness.
garganta (gar'ganta) nf throat.
gárgara ('gargara) nf gargle.
gárgola ('gargola) nf gargoyle.
garita (ga'rita) nf 1 cab (of a lorry). 2 hut.
garra ('garra) nf claw.
garrafa (gar'rafa) nf decanter.
garrote (gar'rote) nm 1 bar, stick. 2 garrotte. **dar garrote a** execute.
garza ('garθa) nf heron.
gas (gas) nm gas.
gasa ('gasa) nf gauze.
gaseosa (gase'osa) nf carbonated water.
gasolina (gaso'lina) nf petrol.
gastar (gas'tar) vt 1 spend, consume. 2 waste, wear out. **gasto** nm expenditure.
gatillo (ga'tiʎo) nm 1 trigger. 2 dentist's forceps.
gato ('gato) nm 1 cat. 2 mot jack. **gatear** vi crawl on all fours. **a gatas** on all fours. **buscarle tres patas al gato** look for trouble.
gavilán (gaβi'lan) nm hawk.
gavilla (ga'βiʎa) nf sheaf.
gaviota (ga'βjota) nf seagull.
gazapo (ga'θapo) nm 1 small rabbit. 2 slip of the tongue.
gelatina (xela'tina) nf gelatine.
gelignita (xelig'nita) nf gelignite.
gemelo (xe'melo) adj twin. nm 1 twin. 2 pl

72

cufflinks. 3 pl opera glasses. **los Gemelos** Gemini.
gemir (xe'mir) vi groan. **gemido** nm groan.
genealogía (xenealo'xia) nf genealogy.
generación (xenera'θjon) nf generation.
generalizar (xenerali'θar) vt,vi generalize, make general. **general** adj general. nm m. general. **generalidad** nf majority. **generalización** nf generalization. **por lo general** in general.
genérico (xe'neriko) adj generic. **género** nm 1 kind. 2 gram gender. 3 genre. 4 material (cloth). 5 pl general groceries, goods.
generosidad (xenerosi'ðað) nf generosity. **generoso** adj generous.
genética (xe'netika) nf genetics.
genial (xe'njal) adj 1 brilliant. 2 inf nice.
genio ('xenjo) nm 1 temper. 2 genius. **estar de mal genio** be in a bad temper.
gente ('xente) nf people. **gente baja** lower classes.
gentil (xen'til) adj 1 charming, courteous. 2 re pagan, gentile. **gentileza** nf politeness, kindness.
gentío (xen'tio) nm crowd.
genuino (xe'nwino) adj genuine.
geografía (xeogra'fia) nf geography. **geográfico** adj geographical. **geógrafo** nm geographer.
geología (xeolo'xia) nf geology. **geológico** ac geological. **geólogo** nm geologist.
geometría (xeome'tria) nf geometry. **geométrico** adj geometrical.
geranio (xe'ranjo) nm geranium.
gerencia (xe'renθja) nf management. **gerente** nm manager.
germinar (xermi'nar) vi germinate. **germen** nm 1 germ. 2 seed.
gesticular (xestiku'lar) vi gesticulate. **gesticulación** nf gesture.
gestión (xes'tjon) nf negotiation, business.
gesto ('xesto) nm 1 face. 2 gesture. **hacer un gesto** make a face or gesture.
gigante (xi'gante) nm giant.
gimnasia nf gymnastics. **gimnasta** nm,f gymnast. **gimnasio** nm gymnasium.
ginebra (xi'neβra) nf gin.
gira ('xira) nf tour.
giralda (xi'ralda) nf weathercock.
girar (xi'rar) vt 1 turn. 2 comm draw, issue. vi 1 turn, rotate. 2 swing. 3 comm do business. **girar un cheque** send a cheque. **giro** nm 1 turn, rotation. 2 comm draft. 3 tendency.

gitano (xi'tano) adj,n gypsy.

glacial (gla'θjal) adj freezing.

glándula ('glandula) nf gland.

glicerina (gliθe'rina) nf glycerine.

global (glo'βal) adj complete. **globo** nm globe.

gloriarse (glo'rjarse) vr boast. **gloria** nf 1 glory. 2 puff-pastry cake.

glosar (glo'sar) vt annotate. **glosa** nf annotation. **glosario** nm glossary.

glotón (glo'ton) adj greedy.

gobernar (ie) (goβer'nar) vt govern, control. **gobernación** nf government. **gobierno** nm 1 government. 2 control.

goce ('goθe) nm enjoyment.

gol ('gol) nm goal.

golfo ('golfo) nm 1 gulf, bay. 2 lout.

golondrina (golon'drina) nf zool swallow.

golosina (golo'sina) nf sweet. **goloso** adj fond of sweets.

golpear (golpe'ar) vt strike. **golpe** nm blow. **golpe de estado** coup d'état. **golpe de gracia** coup de grâce.

goma ('goma) nf 1 rubber. 2 (rubber) tyre. **goma pegante** glue.

gordo ('gorðo) adj fat. nm fat (of meat). **gordura** nf fatness.

gorila (go'rila) nf gorilla.

gorjear (gorxe'ar) vi chirp, trill. **gorjeo** nm chirping.

gorra ('gorra) nf 1 peaked cap. 2 inf sponger.

gorrión (gor'rjon) nm sparrow.

gorro ('gorro) nm cap.

gotear (gote'ar) vi drip. **gota** nf drop. **gotera** nf 1 leak. 2 gutter. 3 dripping.

gótico ('gotiko) adj Gothic.

gozar (go'θar) vt enjoy, have. vi enjoy oneself. **gozo** nm joy.

gozne ('goθne) nm hinge.

grabar (gra'βar) vt 1- engrave. 2 record. 3 imprint. **grabado** nm engraving, print. **grabadora** nf tape-recorder.

gracia (gra'θja) nf 1 grace. 2 humour. **gracias** thank you. **me hace gracia** it amuses me. **tener gracia** be amusing. **gracioso** adj humorous.

grada ('graða) nf 1 step. 2 tier of seats.

grado ('graðo) nm 1 grade. 2 degree.

gradual (gra'ðwal) adj gradual.

grajo ('graxo) nm rook.

gramática (gra'matika) nf grammar.

gramo ('gramo) nm gramme.

gramófono (gra'mofono) nm gramophone.

gran (gran) adj see **grande**.

Gran Bretaña (gran bre'taɲa) nf Great Britain.

grana[1] ('grana) nf 1 small seed. 2 seeding time.

grana[2] ('grana) n scarlet.

granada (gra'naða) nf 1 pomegranate. 2 grenade, shell. **granado** nm pomegranate tree.

grande ('grande) adj big, great. **grandeza** nf size, greatness.

grandioso (gran'djoso) adj grandiose, grand.

granel (gra'nel) nm heap.

granero (gra'nero) nm granary.

granito (gra'nito) nm granite.

granizar (grani'θar) vi hail. **granizo** nm hail.

granja ('granxa) nf farm. **granjero** nm farmer.

grano ('grano) nm 1 grain, corn. 2 pimple.

grapa ('grapa) nf staple, clamp.

grasa ('grasa) nf grease, fat. **grasiento** adj greasy, dirty.

gratificar (gratifi'kar) vt gratify, reward. **gratificación** nf bonus, prize.

gratis ('gratis) adv free of charge.

gratitud (grati'tuð) nf gratitude. **grato** adj pleasing.

gratuito (gra'twito) adj 1 free of charge. 2 gratuitous.

gravamen (gra'βamen) nm 1 tax. 2 obligation. **gravar** vt impose a burden on. **gravar impuestos a** or **sobre** impose taxes on.

grave ('graβe) adj grave, serious. **gravedad** nf gravity.

gravitar (graβi'tar) vi gravitate.

graznar (graθ'nar) vi croak. **graznido** nm croak, squawk.

Grecia ('greθja) nf Greece. **griego** adj,n Greek. nm 1 Greek (language). 2 inf gibberish, incomprehensible speech.

greda ('greða) nf clay. **gredoso** adj clayey.

gremio ('gremjo) nm 1 guild. 2 pol union. **gremio obrero** trade union.

greña ('greɲa) nf tangle (esp. of hair). **greñudo** adj dishevelled.

grey (grej) nf congregation.

grieta ('grjeta) nf crack.

grifo ('grifo) nm tap. **al grifo** on draught.

grillo ('griʎo) nm 1 cricket. 2 pl fetters.

gris (gris) adj grey.

gritar (gri'tar) vi shout. **grito** nm shout, cry.

Groenlandia (groen'landja) nf Greenland. **groenlandés** adj Greenland. nm Greenlander.

grosella (gro'seʎa) nf currant. **grosella espinosa** gooseberry.

grosería (grose'ria) nf vulgarity. **grosero** adj vulgar.

grotesco (gro'tesko) adj grotesque.

grúa ('grua) *nf tech* crane.
grueso (gru'eso) *adj* thick, heavy. *nm* thickness.
grulla ('gruʎa) *nf zool* crane.
grumete (gru'mete) *nm* cabin boy.
gruñir (gru'ɲir) *vi* growl. **gruñido** *nm* growl.
grupo ('grupo) *nm* group, unit.
gruta ('gruta) *nf* grotto.
guadaña (gwa'ðaɲa) *nf* scythe.
guante ('gwante) *nm* glove.
guapo ('gwapo) *adj* handsome.
guardar (gwar'ðar) *vt* guard, keep. **guarda** *nm* guard, keeper. *nf* guard, custody. **guardarropa** *nm* cloakroom. *nm,f* cloakroom attendant.
guardia ('gwarðja) *nf* guard, police force. *nm* policeman. **Guardia Civil** *nf* Civil Guard.
guardián (gwar'ðjan) *nm* guardian.
guardilla (gwar'ðiʎa) *nf* attic.
guarida (gwa'riða) *nf* den, lair.
guarnecer* (gwarne'θer) *vt* **1** equip, adorn. **2** *cul* garnish. **guarnición** *nf* **1** *mil* garrison. **2** garnish. **3** *pl* fittings.
guasa ('gwasa) *nf* joke.
gubernamental (guβernamen'tal) *adj* governmental.
guerra ('gerra) *nf* war. **guerrear** *vi* fight. **guerrero** *nm* warrior. *adj* warlike. **guerrilla** *nf* guerrilla war. **guerrillero** *nm* guerrilla.
guía ('gia) *nf* guide (book). *nm* guide (person). **guía sonora** soundtrack.
guiar (gi'ar) *vt* guide.
guija ('gixa) *nf* pebble.
guiñar (gi'ɲar) *vi* wink.
guión (gi'on) *nm* **1** hyphen. **2** film or radio script. **3** subtitles. **4** summary.
guisa ('gisa) *nf* way, manner. **a guisa de** like.
guisado (gi'saðo) *nm* stew. **guisar** *vt* cook, prepare. **guiso** *nm* stewed dish.
guisante (gi'sante) *nm* pea.
guitarra (gi'tarra) *nf* guitar.
gula ('gula) *nf* greed.
gusano (gu'sano) *nm* worm.
gustar (gus'tar) *vi* please. **gusto** *nm* **1** pleasure. **2** taste. **de buen/mal gusto** in good/bad taste. **¡mucho gusto!** how do you do?
gutural (gutu'ral) *adj* guttural.

H

ha (a) *v* see **haber.**
haba ('aβa) *nf* broad bean.
habeis (a'βeis) *v* see **haber.**
haber* (a'βer) have. **haber de** have to.
habichuela (aβi'tʃwela) *nf* kidney bean.
hábil ('aβil) *adj* capable, skilful, able. **habilidad** *nf* ability.
habilitar (aβili'tar) *vt* enable. **habilitación** *nf* **1** qualification. **2** financing.
habitar (aβi'tar) *vi* live, dwell. **habitación** *nf* room. **habitante** *nm* inhabitant.
hábito ('aβito) *nm* habit.
habitual (aβi'twal) *adj* habitual.
hablar (a'βlar) *vt,vi* speak. **habla** *nf* speech. **hablador** *nm* speaker. *adj* talkative.
hablilla (a'βliʎa) *nf* **1** rumour, gossip. **2** gossip. **habladuría** *nf* gossip, idle talk.
hacedero (aθe'ðero) *adj* practicable.
hacendado (aθen'daðo) *nm* landowner.
hacer* (a'θer) *vt* do, make. **hacer calor/frío** (of weather) be hot/cold. **hace mucho tiempo que** it is a long time since. **hacerse** *vr* become.
hacia ('aθja) *prep* (of time) towards, about.
hacienda (a'θjenda) *nf* estate.
hacina (a'θina) *nf* **1** pile. **2** haystack.
hacha ('atʃa) *nf* axe.
hada ('aða) *nm* fairy.
hado ('aðo) *nm* fate.
hago ('ago) *v* see **hacer.**
halagar (ala'gar) *vt* flatter. **halago** *nm* flattery. **halagüeño** *adj* flattering.
halcón (al'kon) *nm* falcon.
hálito ('alito) *nm* breath.
hallar (a'ʎar) *vt* find. **hallarse** *vr* be situated. **hallazgo** *nm* find, discovery.
hamaca (a'maka) *nf* hammock.
hambre ('ambre) *nf* hunger. **tener hambre** be hungry. **hambriento** *adj* hungry.
han (an) *v* see **haber.**
haragán (ara'gan) *adj* lazy. **haraganear** *vi* laze.
harapiento (ara'pjento) *adj* ragged. **harapo** *nm* rag.
harina (a'rina) *nf* flour.
hartar (ar'tar) *vt* bore, exasperate. **hartarse** *vr* **1** be exasperated. **2** *sl* stuff oneself (with food). **harto** *adj* **1** bored, exasperated. **2** satiated.
has (as) *v* see **haber.**
hasta ('asta) *prep* up to, until. *adv* even.

hastío (as'tio) *nm* disgust, weariness.

hato ('ato) *nm* **1** sheep-pen. **2** flock. **3** pack.

hay ('aj) *v imp* there is. **hay que** one must.

haya ('aja) *nf* beech.

haz[1] (aθ) *nm* bundle, sheaf.

haz[2] (aθ) *nf* face.

hazmerreír (aθmerre'ir) *nm* laughing-stock.

he (e) *v* see **haber.**

hebilla (e'βiʎa) *nf* buckle.

hebra ('eβra) *nf* **1** thread. **2** grain (wood).

hebreo (e'βreo) *adj,n* Hebrew. *nm* Hebrew (language).

hechicero (etʃi'θero) *nm* wizard. **hechicería** *nf* sorcery. **hechizar** *vt* bewitch. **hechizo** *nm* magic spell.

hecho ('etʃo) *v* see **hacer.** *adj* **1** ready-made. **2** well-cooked. *nm* fact. **hechura** *nf* making, handiwork. **de hecho** *law* de facto.

hediondo (e'ðjondo) *adj* **1** stinking. **2** repugnant. **hedor** *nm* stink, stench.

helar (ie) (e'lar) *vt* freeze. **helado** *nm* ice-cream.

helecho (e'letʃo) *nm* fern.

hélice ('eliθe) *nf* **1** helix. **2** propeller.

helicóptero (eli'koptero) *nm* helicopter.

hembra ('embra) *nf* **1** female. **2** nut (of a screw).

hemorragia (emor'raxja) *nf* haemorrhage.

hemorroides (emor'rojðes) *nf pl* piles.

hemos ('emos) *v* see **haber.**

henchirse* (en'tʃirse) *vr* swell up.

hender (ie) (en'der) *vt* split. **hendedura** *nf* split.

heno ('eno) *nm* hay.

herbaje (er'βaxe) *nm* pasture. **herbicida** *nm* herbicide. **herbívoro** *adj* herbivorous.

heredar (ere'ðar) *vt* inherit. **heredero** *nm* heir. **hereditario** *adj* hereditary.

hereje (e'rexe) *nm* heretic. **herejía** *nf* heresy.

herencia (e'renθja) *nf* inheritance.

herir (ie) (e'rir) *vt* wound. **herida** *nf* wound. **herido** *nm* casualty.

hermano (er'mano) *nm* brother. **hermana** *nf* sister. **hermandad** *nf* brotherhood.

hermético (er'metiko) *adj* hermetic.

hermoso (er'moso) *adj* **1** beautiful, handsome. **hermosura** *nf* beauty, splendour.

héroe ('eroe) *nm* hero. **heroico** *adj* heroic. **heroísmo** *nm* heroism.

heroína[1] (e'roina) *nf* heroine.

heroína[2] (ero'ina) *nf* heroin.

herramienta (erra'mjenta) *nf* tool.

herrar (ie) (er'rar) *vt* shoe (a horse). **herradura** *nf* horseshoe.

herrería (erre'ria) *nf* forge. **herrero** *nm* blacksmith.

herrumbre (er'rumbre) *nf* rust.

hervir (ie) (er'βir) *vt,vi* boil. **hervor** *nm* **1** boiling. **2** fervour. **hervidero** *nm inf* crowd.

hez (eθ) *nf,pl* **heces** dregs.

híbrido. ('iβriðo) *adj* hybrid.

hice ('iθe) *v* see **hacer.**

hidalgo (i'ðalgo) *nm* nobleman. **hidalguía** *nf* nobility.

hidráulico (i'ðrauliko) *adj* hydraulic.

hidroala (iðro'ala) *nf* hovercraft.

hidroavión (iðroa'βjon) *nm* seaplane.

hidroeléctrico (iðroe'lektriko) *adj* hydroelectric.

hidrógeno (i'ðroxeno) *nm* hydrogen.

hiedra ('jeðra) *nf* ivy.

hielo ('jelo) *nm* ice.

hiena ('jena) *nf* hyena.

hierba ('jerβa) *nf* **1** grass. **2** herb.

hierro ('jerro) *nm* iron. **hierro colado** cast iron.

hígado ('igaðo) *nm* liver.

higiene (i'xjene) *nf* hygiene. **higiénico** *adj* hygienic.

higo ('igo) *nm* fig. **higuera** *nf* fig-tree.

hijo ('ixo) *nm* **1** son. **2** *pl* children. **hija** *nf* daughter. **hijastro** *nm* stepson.

hilar (i'lar) *vt* spin. **hilandera** *nf* spinner. **hilandería** *nf* **1** spinning. **2** spinning mill.

hilera (i'lera) *nf* rank, row.

himno ('imno) *nm* hymn. **himno nacional** national anthem.

hincapié (inka'pje) *nm* foothold. **hacer hincapié** stand firm.

hincar (in'kar) *vt* drive in.

hinchar (in'tʃar) *vt* inflate. **hincharse** *vr* **1** swell up. **2** put on airs. **3** *inf* stuff oneself (with food). **hinchazón** *nm* **1** *med* swelling. **2** *inf* conceit, arrogance.

hinojo (i'noxo) *nm* fennel.

hipnosis (ip'nosis) *nf* hypnosis. **hipnótico** *adj* hypnotic.

hipo ('ipo) *nm* hiccups.

hipocondria (ipokon'dria) *nf* hypochondria.

hipocresía (ipokre'sia) *nf* hypocrisy.

hipócrita (i'pokrita) *adj invar* hypocritical. *nm,f invar* hypocrite.

hipopótamo (ipo'potamo) *nm* hippopotamus.

hipotecar (ipote'kar) *vt* mortgage. **hipoteca** *nf* mortgage.

hipótesis (i'potesis) *nf* hypothesis. **hipotético** *adj* hypothetical.

hirsuto (ir'suto) *adj* hairy.
hispánico (is'paniko) *adj* Hispanic.
hispanoamericano (ispanoameri'kano) *adj,n* Spanish American.
histerectomía (isterekto'mia) *nf* hysterectomy.
histeria (i'sterja) *nf* hysteria. **histérico** *adj* hysterical.
historia (is'torja) *nf* 1 history. 2 story. **historiador** *nm* historian. **histórico** *adj* historical.
hizo ('iθo) *v* see **hacer.**
hogar (o'gar) *nm* hearth, home.
hogaza (o'gaθa) *nf* loaf (of bread).
hoja ('oxa) *nf* 1 leaf. 2 sheet (of metal, etc.). 3 form, questionnaire. **hoja de afeitar** razor blade.
hojear (oxe'ar) *vt* leaf through.
Holanda (o'landa) *nf* Holland. **holandés** *adj* Dutch. ~*nm* 1 Dutchman. 2 Dutch (language).
holgar (ue) (ol'gar) *vi* 1 be idle. 2 be unnecessary. 3 strike, quit work. **holgazán** *adj* idle. **holgura** *nf* comfort, ease.
hollar (ue) (o'ʎar) *vt* leave footprints on.
hollín (o'ʎin) *nm* soot.
hombre ('ombre) *nm* man. **¡sí, hombre!** of course!
hombro ('ombro) *nm* shoulder.
homenaje (ome'naxe) *nm* homage.
homicida (omi'θiðja) *nm* murderer. **homicidio** *nm* murder.
homogéneo (omo'xeneo) *adj* homogeneous.
homólogo (o'mologo) *adj* corresponding, alike.
honda ('onda) *nf* sling, catapult.
hondo ('ondo) *adj* deep. **hondonada** *nf* ravine. **hondura** *nf* depth.
honestidad (onesti'ðað) *nf* honour. **honesto** *adj* honourable.
hongo ('ongo) *nm* 1 mushroom. 2 bowler hat.
honor (o'nor) *nm* honour. **honorífico** *adj* honorific. **honorario** *nm* fee, honorarium.
honrar (on'rar) *vt* honour. **honra** *nf* honour.
hora ('ora) *nf* hour. **¿qué hora es?** what is the time?
horario (o'rarjo) *nm* 1 timetable. 2 hours of work.
horca ('orka) *nf* 1 gallows. 2 pitchfork.
horda ('orða) *nf* horde.
horizonte (ori'θonte) *nm* horizon.
hormiga (or'miga) *nf* 1 ant. 2 *pl* pins and needles.
hormigón (ormi'gon) *nm* concrete.
hormiguear (ormige'ar) *vi* itch. **hormigueo** *nm* itching.

hormona (or'mona) *nf* hormone.
horno ('orno) *nm* oven. **hornillo** *nm* ring (on a cooker).
horóscopo (o'roskopo) *nm* horoscope.
horquilla (or'kiʎa) *nf* hairpin.
horrendo (or'rendo) *adj* fearful.
horrible (or'riβle) *adj* horrible.
horror (or'ror) *nm* horror. **horrozizar** *vt* horrify.
hortaliza (orta'liθa) *nf* green vegetable.
horticultura (ortikul'tura) *nf* horticulture.
hosco ('osko) *adj* grim.
hospedar (ospe'ðar) *vt* give a room to, put up. **hospedarse** *vr* lodge. **hospedaje** *nm* lodging. **hospedería** *nf* inn.
hospicio (os'piθjo) *nm* orphanage, workhouse.
hospital (ospi'tal) *nm* hospital.
hospitalidad (ospitali'ðað) *nf* hospitality.
hostelero (oste'lero) *nm* hosteller. **hostelería** *nf* hotel business. **hostería** *nf* inn.
hostia ('ostja) *nf* rel host.
hostigar (osti'gar) *vt* punish, beat.
hostil (os'til) *adj* hostile. **hostilidad** *nf* hostility.
hoy ('oi) *adv* today. **hoy (en) día** the present day. **de hoy en mañana** any day now. **de hoy en ocho días** a week today.
hoyo ('ojo) *nm* pit.
hoyuelo (o'jwelo) *nm* dimple.
hoz (oθ) *nf* sickle.
hubo ('uβo) *v* see **haber.**
hueco ('weko) *adj* empty. ~*nm* hole, space.
huelga ('welga) *nf* strike (industrial). **huelguista** *nm* striker.
huelgo ('welgo) *nm* 1 breath. 2 space, room. 3 tech play, tolerance.
huelo ('welo) *v* see **oler.**
huella ('weʎa) *nf* footprint. **huella digital** fingerprint.
huérfano ('werfano) *nm* orphan.
huerta ('werta) *nf* 1 vegetable garden. 2 irrigated land. **huerto** *nm* 1 small vegetable garden. 2 orchard.
hueso ('weso) *nm* bone. **huesudo** *adj* bony.
huésped ('wespeð) *nm* 1 guest. 2 host.
hueva ('weβa) *nf* 1 roe (of fish). 2 *pl* spawn.
huevo ('weβo) *nm* egg.
huida ('wiða) *nf* flight, escape.
huir* (wir) *vi* flee.
hule¹ ('ule) *nm* 1 oilskin. 2 rubber.
hule² ('ule) *nm* goring (bullfight).
hulla ('uʎa) *nf* coal.
humanidad (umani'ðað) *nf* 1 humanity. 2 *pl cap educ* Arts. **humano** *adj* human. **humanismo** *nm* humanism.

umear (ume'ar) vi smoke. **humareda** nf pall of smoke.

umedad (ume'ðað) nf humidity, moisture. **humedecer** vt moisten, wet. **húmedo** adj humid.

umildad (umil'ðað) nf humility. **humilde** adj humble.

umillar (umi'ʎar) vt humiliate.

umo ('umo) nm smoke.

umor (u'mor) nm humour. **humorada** nf witticism.

undir (un'dir) vt sink.

lungría (un'gria) nf Hungary. **húngaro** adj,n Hungarian. **húngaro** Hungarian (language).

uracán (ura'kan) nm hurricane.

urgar (ur'gar) vt poke.

urón (u'ron) nm ferret.

urtadillas (urta'ðiʎas) **a hurtadillas** adv secretively, stealthily.

urtar (ur'tar) vt steal. **hurto** nm 1 theft. 2 stolen object.

usmear (usme'ar) vt scent, track.

uso ('uso) nm spindle.

uyente (u'jente) adj fugitive.

uyó (u'jo) v see **huir**.

I

bérico (i'βeriko) adj Iberian. **ibero** adj,n Iberian.

ctericia (ikte'riθja) nf jaundice.

da (i'ða) nf 1 journey. 2 departure.

dea (i'ðea) nf idea.

deal (iðe'al) adj,nm 1 ideal. 2 abstract, imaginary. **idealismo** nm idealism. **idealista** nm,f idealist. adj invar idealistic.

dealizar (ideali'θar) vt idealize.

déntico (i'ðentiko) adj identical. **identidad** nf identity.

dentificar (iðentifi'kar) vt identify. **identificación** nf identification.

deología (iðeolo'xia) nf ideology. **ideológico** adj ideological.

dilio (i'ðiljo) nm idyll. **idílico** adj idyllic.

dioma (i'ðjoma) nm language. **idiomático** adj idiomatic.

diosincrasia (iðjosin'krasja) nf idiosyncrasy.

diota (i'ðjota) nm,f idiot. **idiotez** nf idiocy.

dólatra (i'ðolatra) nm idolater. adj idolatrous, heathen. **idolatrar** vt worship. **idolatría** nf idolatry.

dolo ('iðolo) nm idol.

idóneo (i'ðoneo) adj apt, appropriate.

iglesia (i'glesja) nf church.

ignominia (igno'minja) nf ignominy. **ignominioso** adj ignominious.

ignorancia (igno'ranθja) nf ignorance. **ignorante** adj ignorant.

ignorar (igno'rar) vt be unaware of.

igual (i'gwal) adj same, equal. **igualar** vt equalize. **igualación** nf equalization. **igualdad** nf equality.

ijada (i'xaða) nf flank, side.

ilegal (ile'gal) adj illegal.

ileso (i'leso) adj unharmed.

ilógico (i'loxiko) adj illogical.

iluminar (ilumi'nar) vt illuminate. **illuminación** nf illumination.

ilusión (ilu'sjon) nf illusion, dream.

ilusionarse (ilusjo'narse) vr delude oneself. **ilusionismo** nm conjuring trick. **ilusionista** nm,f conjurer.

ilustrar (ilus'trar) vt illustrate. **ilustración** nf 1 illustration. 2 enlightenment, learning.

ilustre (i'lustre) adj illustrious.

imagen (i'maxen) nf image.

imaginar (imaxi'nar) vt,vi imagine. **imaginación** nf imagination. **imaginativo** adj imaginary.

imán (i'man) nm magnet.

imbécil (im'beθil) adj imbecile. **imbecilidad** nf imbecility.

imborrable (imbor'raβle) adj unforgettable.

imbuir (imbu'ir) vt imbue.

imitar (imi'tar) vt copy. **imitación** nf copy.

impaciencia (impa'θjenθja) nf impatience. **impaciente** adj impatient.

impacto (im'pakto) nm impact.

impalpable (impal'paβle) adj impalpable, intangible.

impar (im'par) adj math odd.

imparcial (impar'θjal) adj impartial.

impartir (impar'tir) vt 1 impart (a teaching). 2 give (orders).

impasibilidad (impasiβili'ðað) nf impassivity. **impasible** adj impassive.

impávido (im'paβiðo) adj fearless. **impavidez** nf fearlessness.

impecable (impe'kaβle) adj perfect.

impedir (i) (impe'ðir) vt impede. **impedimento** nm impediment.

impeler (impe'ler) vt drive.

impenitente (impeni'tente) adj impenitent.

imperar (impe'rar) vt rule.

imperativo (impera'tiβo) *adj* imperative. *nm gram* imperative.

imperceptible (imperθep'tiβle) *adj* imperceptible.

imperdible (imper'ðiβle) *nm* safety pin.

imperdonable (imperðo'naβle) *adj* unforgivable.

imperfección (imperfek'θjon) *nf* imperfection. **imperfecto** *adj* imperfect. *nm gram* imperfect.

imperial (impe'rjal) *adj* imperial. **imperialismo** *nm* imperialism. **imperialista** *adj, nm,f* imperialist.

imperio (im'perjo) *nm* empire.

impermeable (imperme'aβle) *adj* waterproof, impermeable. *nm* mackintosh.

impersonal (imperso'nal) *adj* impersonal

impertinencia (imperti'nenθja) *nf* 1 impudence. 2 inappropriateness. **impertinente** *adj* 1 impudent. 2 inappropriate.

imperturbable (impertur'βaβle) *adj* imperturbable.

ímpetu ('impetu) *nm* impetus. **impetuoso** *adj* impetuous.

impío (im'pio) *adj* irreligious, godless.

implacable (impla'kaβle) *adj* implacable.

implantar (implan'tar) *vt* implant.

implicar (impli'kar) *vt* imply.

implícito (im'pliθito) *adj* implicit.

implorar (implo'rar) *vt* beg.

imponer (impo'ner) *vt* impose. **imponente** *adj* 1 imposing. 2 *inf* smashing.

impopular (impopu'lar) *adj* unpopular.

importancia (impor'tanθja) *nf* importance. **importante** *adj* important.

importar (impor'tar) *vt* 1 import. 2 *comm* amount to. *vi* be important. **importación** *nf* import. **importe** *nm* amount.

importunar (importu'nar) *vt* annoy. **importuno** *adj* impertinent.

imposible (impo'siβle) *adj* impossible. **imposibilidad** *nf* impossibility. **imposibilitar** *vt* 1 make impossible. 2 make incapable.

imposición (imposi'θjon) *nf* 1 tax. 2 *comm* deposit.

impostor (impos'tor) *nm* impostor. **impostura** *nf* fraud.

impotencia (impo'tenθja) *nf* impotence. **impotente** *adj* impotent.

impracticable (imprakti'kaβle) *adj* impracticable.

imprecar (impre'kar) *vt* curse.

impregnar (impreg'nar) *vt* impregnate.

imprenta (im'prenta) *nf* 1 press. 2 printing.

imprescindible (impresθin'diβle) *adj* indispensable.

impresión (impre'sjon) *nf* impression. **impresionar** *vt* impress. **impresionismo** *nf* Ar impressionism.

impreso (im'preso) *v see* **imprimir.** *adj* printed.

imprevisto (impre'βisto) *adj* unexpected.

imprimir (impri'mir) *vt* print.

improbabilidad (improβaβili'ðað) *nf* improbability. **improbable** *adj* improbable.

ímprobo ('improβo) *adj* wicked.

improcedente (improθe'ðente) *adj law* inadmissible.

improductivo (improðuk'tiβo) *adj* unproductive.

impropicio (impro'piθjo) *adj* unpropitious.

impropiedad (impropje'ðað) *nf* impropriety. **impropio** *adj* improper, inappropriate.

improvisar (improβi'sar) *vt* improvise.

improvisto (impro'βisto) *adj* unforeseen.

imprudencia (impru'ðenθja) *nf* imprudence. **imprudente** *adj* imprudent.

impúdico (im'puðiko) *adj* shameless, immodest. **impudor** *nm* 1 shamelessness. 2 cynicism.

impuesto (im'pwesto) *nm* 1 tax. 2 duty.

impugnar (impug'nar) *vt* 1 oppose. 2 confute. 3 impugn.

impulsar (impul'sar) *vt* drive, impel. **impulsión** *nf* 1 impulse. 2 impetus. **impulso** *nm* 1 impulse, urge. 2 pressure, force.

impune (im'pune) *adj* unpunished.

impureza (impu'reθa) *nf* 1 impurity, foulness. 2 dishonesty. 3 obscenity.

imputar (impu'tar) *vt* impute, ascribe. **imputación** *nf* imputation, accusation.

inacabable (inaka'βaβle) *adj* endless, interminable.

inaccesible (inakθe'siβle) *adj* inaccessible.

inacción (inak'θjon) *nf* inaction, rest.

inaceptable (inakθep'taβle) *adj* unacceptable.

inactividad (inaktiβi'ðað) *nf* inactivity. **inactivo** *adj* inactive.

inadaptable (inaðap'taβle) *adj* unadaptable.

inadecuado (inaðe'kwaðo) *adj* inadequate.

inadmisible (inaðmi'siβle) *adj* inadmissible.

inadvertencia (inaðβer'tenθja) *nf* inadvertence, carelessness.

inagotable (inago'taβle) *adj* inexhaustible.

inaguantable (inagwan'taβle) *adj* unbearable, intolerable.

inajenable (inaxe'naβle) *adj* inalienable.

inalterable (inalte'raβle) *adj* unchangeable.

inanición (inani'θjon) nf 1 med exhaustion, weakness. 2 starvation.

inanimado (inani'maðo) adj inanimate.

inaplicable (inapli'kaβle) adj inapplicable.

inapreciable (inapre'θjaβle) adj priceless, invaluable.

inapto (in'apto) adj unsuited.

inasequible (inase'kiβle) adj unattainable.

inaudible (inau'ðiβle) adj inaudible.

inaudito (inau'ðito) adj unheard-of, extraordinary, outrageous.

inaugurar (inaugu'rar) vt inaugurate. **inauguración** nf inauguration.

incalculable (inkalku'laβle) adj incalculable.

incandescencia (incandes'θenθja) nf incandescence. **incandescente** adj incandescent.

incansable (inkan'saβle) adj indefatigable.

incapacidad (inkapaθi'ðað) nf incapacity.

incapacitar (inkapaθi'tar) vt incapacitate, disable, disqualify.

incapaz (inka'paθ) adj incapable, unfit.

incautarse (inkau'tarse) vr law confiscate (property).

incauto (in'kauto) adj incautious, careless.

incendiar (inθen'djar) vt set on fire. **incendiario** adj incendiary. **incendio** nm fire.

incentivo (inθen'tiβo) nm incentive.

incertidumbre (inθerti'ðumbre) nf uncertainty.

incesante (inθe'sante) adj incessant, uninterrupted.

incesto (in'θesto) nm incest. **incestuoso** adj incestuous.

incidencia (inθi'ðenθja) nf incidence.

incidental (inθiðen'tal) adj incidental, accidental.

incidente (inθi'ðente) adj incidental, chance. nm incident, happening.

incienso (in'θjenso) nm incense.

incierto (in'θjerto) adj uncertain.

incinerar (inθine'rar) vt 1 cremate. 2 incinerate.

incipiente (inθi'pjente) adj incipient.

incisión (inθi'sjon) nf incision, cut.

incisivo (inθi'siβo) adj incisive, sharp.

incitar (inθi'tar) vt instigate. **incitación** nf instigation.

incivil (inθi'βil) adj impolite. **incivilidad** nf impoliteness.

inclemencia (inkle'menθja) nf inclemency. **inclemente** adj inclement.

inclinar (inkli'nar) vt incline. **inclinarse** vr be inclined to. **inclinación** nf inclination.

incluir* (inklu'ir) vt include. **inclusión** nf inclu-

sion. **inclusive** prep including. adv even. **incluso** adv even.

incógnito (in'kognito) adj unknown.

incoherencia (inkoe'renθja) nf incoherence. **incoherente** adj incoherent.

incoloro (inko'loro) adj colourless.

incomodar (inkomo'ðar) vt annoy, molest. **incómodo** adj 1 annoying. 2 uncomfortable.

incompatibilidad (inkompatiβili'ðað) nf incompatibility. adj incompatible.

incompetente (inkompe'tente) adj incompetent. **incompetencia** nf incompetence.

incompleto (inkom'pleto) adj incomplete.

incomprensible (inkompren'siβle) adj incomprehensible.

incomunicado (inkomuni'kaðo) adj isolated.

inconcebible (inkonθe'βiβle) adj inconceivable.

inconcluso (inkon'kluso) adj unfinished, inconclusive.

incondicional (inkondiθjo'nal) adj unconditional.

inconfundible (inkonfun'diβle) adj unmistakeable.

incongruente (inkongru'ente) adj incongruous. **incongruencia** nf incongruity.

inconmensurable (inkonmensu'raβle) adj immeasurable.

inconmovible (inkonmo'βiβle) adj immovable.

inconsciencia (inkons'θjenθja) nf med unconsciousness. **inconsciente** adj 1 unconscious. 2 irresponsible.

inconsecuencia (inkonse'kwenθja) nf inconsequence. **inconsecuente** adj inconsequential.

inconsiderado (inkonsiðe'raðo) adj ill-considered.

inconstancia (inkon'stanθja) nf inconstancy. **inconstante** adj inconstant.

incontestable (inkontes'taβle) adj indisputable.

incontinencia (inkonti'nenθja) nf incontinence. **incontinente** adj incontinent.

inconveniencia (inkonβe'njenθja) nf inconvenience. **inconveniente** adj inconvenient. nm objection, impediment.

incorporar (inkorpo'rar) vt incorporate. **incorporarse** vr sit up. **incorporarse a** become a member of.

incorrección (inkorrek'θjon) nf inexactitude. **incorrecto** adj incorrect.

incorregible (inkorre'xiβle) adj incorrigible.

incorruptible (inkorrup'tiβle) adj incorruptible. **incorrupto** adj incorrupt.

incredulidad (inkreðuli'ðaθ) *nf* incredulity. **incrédulo** *adj* sceptical.

increíble (inkre'iβle) *adj* incredible.

incremento (inkre'mento) *nm* increase.

increpar (inkre'par) *vt* reproach.

incriminar (inkrimi'nar) *vt* inculpate.

incrustar (inkrus'tar) *vt* encrust.

incubar (inku'βar) *vt* incubate.

inculcar (inkul'kar) *vt* inculcate.

inculto (in'kulto) *adj* uneducated, uncouth.

incumbencia (inkum'benθja) *nf* duty, obligation.

incurable (inku'raβle) *adj* incurable.

incurrir (inkur'rir) *vi* 1 commit. 2 become liable to. 3 incur.

indagar (inda'gar) *vt* investigate. **indagación** *nf* investigation.

indebido (inde'βiðo) *adj* 1 unjust. 2 improper.

indecente (inde'θente) *adj* indecent.

indecible (inde'θiβle) *adj* indescribable.

indecisión (indeθi'sjon) *nf* indecision. **indeciso** *adj* indecisive.

indecoroso (indeko'roso) *adj* indecorous.

indefectible (indefek'tiβle) *adj* inevitable, infallible.

indefenso (inde'fenso) *adj* defenceless.

indefinible (indefi'niβle) *adj* indefinable. **indefinido** (inde'finido) *adj* indefinite.

indeleble (inde'leβle) *adj* indelible.

indemne (in'demne) *adj* unharmed. **indemnidad** *nf* indemnity. **indemnizar** *vt* indemnify, compensate.

independencia (indepen'denθja) *nf* independence. **independiente** *adj* independent.

indescriptible (indeskrip'tiβle) *adj* indescribable.

indeseable (indese'aβle) *adj* undesirable.

indeterminado (indetermi'naðo) *adj* 1 indeterminate. 2 undetermined.

India ('indja) *nf* India. **indio** *adj,n* Indian.

indiano (indi'ano) *adj,n* South American. *nm* Spaniard who has become rich in South America.

indicar (indi'kar) *vt* indicate. **indicación** *nf* indication. **indicado** *adj* suitable. **indicador** *nm* indicator. **indicativo** *adj,n* indicative. **indicativo de nacionalidad** *mot* nationality plate.

índice ('indiθe) *nm* 1 index. 2 hand (of a clock, etc.). 3 index finger.

indicio (in'diθjo) *nm* 1 sign. 2 *pl law* evidence.

indiferencia (indife'renθja) *nf* indifference. **indiferente** *adj* indifferent.

indígena (in'dixena) *adj,n* native.

indigestión (indixes'tjon) *nf* indigestion. **indigestible** *adj* indigestible.

indignar (indig'nar) *vt* annoy, anger.

indirecta (indi'rekta) *nf* indirect suggestion. **indirecto** *adj* indirect.

indiscreción (indiskre'θjon) *nf* indiscretion. **indiscreto** *adj* indiscreet.

indiscutible (indisku'tiβle) *adj* unquestionable.

indisoluble (indiso'luβle) *adj* indissoluble.

indispensable (indispen'saβle) *adj* indispensable.

indisponer* (indispo'ner) *vt* upset. **indisponerse** *vr med* 1 feel unwell. 2 fall ill.

indistinto (indis'tinto) *adj* indistinct.

individual (indiβi'ðwal) *adj* individual, private. **individualidad** *nf* individuality. **individuo** *nm* individual.

indivisible (indiβi'siβle) *adj* indivisible. **indiviso** *adj* undivided.

índole ('indole) *nm* nature, inclination.

indolencia (indo'lenθja) *nf* sloth, apathy. **indolente** *adj* apathetic, slothful.

indómito (in'domito) *adj* untamed.

indubitable (induβi'taβle) *adj* indubitable.

inducir* (indu'θir) *vt* 1 persuade. 2 *phil* infer. 3 *tech,sci* induce. **inducción** *nf* 1 induction. 2 inducement.

indudable (indu'ðaβle) *adj* unquestionable.

indulgencia (indul'xenθja) *nf* indulgence. **indulgente** *adj* indulgent.

indultar (indul'tar) *vt* pardon. **indulto** *nm law* pardon.

indumentaria (indumen'tarja) *nf* dress, costume.

industria (in'dustrja) *nf* industry.

inédito (i'neðito) *adj* unpublished.

inefable (ine'faβle) *adj* ineffable.

ineficacia (inefi'kaθja) *nf* ineffectiveness. **ineficaz** *adj* inefficient.

ineludible (inelu'ðiβle) *adj* inevitable.

ineptitud (inepti'tuð) *nf* ineptitude. **inepto** *adj* inept.

inequívoco (ine'kiβoko) *adj* unmistakeable.

inercia (i'nerθja) *nf* 1 laziness. 2 *sci* inertia.

inerme (i'nerme) *adj* unarmed.

inerte (in'erte) *adj* 1 *sci* inert. 2 *inf* sluggish, slow.

inesperado (inespe'raðo) *adj* unexpected.

inestable (ines'taβle) *adj* unsteady.

inevitable (ineβi'taβle) *adj* inevitable.

inexactitud (ineksakti'tuð) *nf* inaccuracy. **inexacto** *adj* inaccurate.

inexperto (ineks'perto) adj inexperienced.

inexplicable (inekspli'kaβle) adj inexplicable.

infalibilidad (infaliβili'ðað) nf infallibility. **infalible** adj infallible.

infamar (infa'mar) vt dishonour. **infame** adj 1 infamous. 2 dishonourable. **infamia** nf 1 infamy. 2 dishonour.

infancia (in'fanθja) nf infancy. **infante** adj infant. nm prince.

infatigable (infati'gaβle) adj indefatigable.

infausto (in'fausto) adj ill-omened.

infectar (infek'tar) vt infect. **infección** nf infection. **infeccioso** adj infectious.

infeliz (infe'liθ) adj unhappy.

inferior (infe'rjor) adj 1 lower. 2 inferior.

inferir (ie) (infe'rir) vt 1 infer. 2 inflict (a wound, etc.).

infernal (infer'nal) adj infernal.

infestar (infes'tar) vt infest.

infiel (infi'el) adj 1 unfaithful. 2 inaccurate.

infierno (in'fjerno) nm hell.

ínfimo ('infimo) adj lowest.

infinidad (infini'ðað) nf infinity. **infinito** adj infinite.

inflación (infla'θjon) nf inflation.

inflamar (infla'mar) vt 1 inflame. 2 set alight. **inflamarse** vr become inflamed. **inflamación** nf 1 inflammation. 2 combustion.

inflar (in'flar) vt inflate.

inflexible (inflek'siβle) adj inflexible.

infligir (infli'xir) vt inflict.

influencia (influ'enθja) nf influence.

influir* (influ'ir) vt influence, affect. **influencia** nf influence. **influyente** adj influential.

influjo (in'fluxo) nm 1 influence. 2 flood (tide).

información (informa'θjon) nf 1 information. 2 character reference.

informal (infor'mal) adj 1 informal. 2 unreliable. **informalidad** nf 1 informality. 2 unreliability.

informar (infor'mar) vt inform. vi law plead. **informe** nm 1 announcement. 2 item of information.

infortunio (infor'tunjo) nm misfortune.

infracción (infrak'θjon) nf offence, breach.

infranqueable (infranke'aβle) adj 1 inaccessible. 2 unsurmountable.

infringir (infrin'xir) vt infringe, break (one's word, oath, etc.).

infructuoso (infruk'twoso) adj fruitless.

infundado (infun'daðo) adj unfounded.

infundir (infun'dir) vt instil.

ingeniería (inxenje'ria) nf engineering. **ingeniero** nm engineer.

ingenio (in'xenjo) nm 1 talent, wit, intuition. 2 device.

ingenuo (in'xenwo) adj 1 frank. 2 simple, credulous.

ingerir (ie) (inxe'rir) vt consume (food).

Inglaterra (ingla'terra) nf England. **inglés** adj English. nm 1 Englishman. 2 English (language).

ingratitud (ingrati'tuð) nf ingratitude. **ingrato** adj 1 ungrateful. 2 unpleasant. 3 unrewarding.

ingrediente (ingre'ðjente) nm ingredient.

ingresar (ingre'sar) vi 1 enter, join. 2 be admitted (to hospital). vt deposit (money). **ingreso** nm 1 entry. 2 comm deposit. 3 pl revenue, income.

inhábil (i'naβil) adj unfit, incapable. **día inhábil** non-working day.

inhabilitar (inaβili'tar) vt 1 disqualify, declare unfit. 2 disable. **inhabilitación** nf 1 declaration of unfitness. 2 endorsement (licence).

inhabitable (inaβi'taβle) adj uninhabitable. **inhabitado** adj uninhabited.

inhalar (ina'lar) vt inhale. **inhalación** nf inhalation.

inherente (ine'rente) adj inherent, innate.

inhibir (ini'βir) vt 1 inhibit. 2 law impede, stay. **inhibirse** vr abstain.

inhospitalario (inospita'larjo) adj inhospitable.

inhumano (inu'mano) adj inhuman.

inhumar (inu'mar) vt bury.

inicial (ini'θjal) adj,nf initial.

iniciar (ini'θjar) vt initiate (into a society, etc.).

inicuo (i'nikwo) adj evil, wicked. **iniquidad** nf iniquity, evil.

injerir (ie) (inxe'rir) vt insert.

injertar (inxer'tar) vt med,bot graft. **injerto** nm graft, grafting.

injuriar (inxuri'ar) vt 1 insult. 2 injure. **injuria** nf 1 insult, outrage. 2 injury. **injurioso** adj 1 insulting. 2 harmful.

injusticia (inxus'tiθja) nf injustice. **injusto** adj unjust.

inmediato (inme'ðjato) adj immediate.

inmejorable (inmexo'raβle) adj unsurpassable.

inmemorial (inmemo'rjal) adj immemorial.

inmenso (in'menso) adj immense.

inmerecido (inmere'θiðo) adj undeserved.

inmigrar (inmi'grar) vi immigrate. **inmigración** nf immigration. **inmigrante** nm immigrant.

inminente (inmi'nente) adj imminent. **inminencia** nf imminence.

inmiscuir* (inmisku'ir) vt mix. **inmiscuirse** vr interfere.

81

inmoderado (inmoðe'raðo) adj excessive.

inmodestia (inmo'ðestja) nf immodesty. **inmodesto** adj immodest.

inmoral (inmo'ral) adj immoral. **inmoralidad** nf immorality.

inmortal (inmor'tal) adj,n immortal. **inmortalidad** nf immortality. **inmortalizar** vt immortalize.

inmóvil (in'moβil) adj 1 immobile. 2 immovable. **inmovilizar** vt immobilizᵉ

inmueble (in'mweβle) nm 1 property. 2 pl real estate.

inmundo (in'munðo) adj dirty, foul.

inmunidad (inmuni'ðað) nf immunity. **inmunizar** vt immunize.

inmutar (inmu'tar) vt alter. **inmutarse** vr change countenance.

innato (in'nato) adj innate.

innecesario (inneθe'sarjo) adj unnecessary.

innegable (inne'gaβle) adj undeniable.

innoble (in'noβle) adj ignoble.

innocuo (in'nokwo) adj also **inocuo** innocuous.

innovar (inno'βar) vt renovate.

innumerable (innume'raβle) adj innumerable.

inobediente (inoβe'ðjente) adj disobedient.

inocencia (ino'θenθja) nf innocence. **inocente** adj innocent.

inocular (inoku'lar) vt 1 inoculate. 2 pervert, infect.

inofensivo (inofen'siβo) adj harmless.

inolvidable (inolβi'ðaβle) adj unforgettable.

inopinado (inopi'naðo) adj unexpected, surprising.

inoportuno (inopor'tuno) adj inopportune.

inoxidable (inoksi'ðaβle) adj stainless (steel).

inquebrantable (inkeβran'taβle) adj unbreakable.

inquietar (inkje'tar) vt disquiet, disturb. **inquieto** adj restless. **inquietud** nf restlessness, disquiet.

inquilino (inki'lino) nm 1 lodger, tenant. 2 parasite. **inquilinato** nm 1 rent. 2 lease.

inquirir (inki'rir) vt examine, scrutinize.

inquisición (inkisi'θjon) nf 1 inquisition, tribunal. 2 enquiry, investigation. **inquisidor** nm inquisitor.

insaciable (insa'θjaβle) adj insatiable.

insalubre (insa'luβre) adj unhealthy.

insano (in'sano) adj 1 mad. 2 unhealthy.

inscribir (inskri'βir) vt 1 inscribe. 2 enroll. **inscripción** nf 1 inscription. 2 enrolment. **inscrito** adj 1 inscribed. 2 enrolled.

insecto (in'sekto) nm insect.

inseguridad (inseguri'ðað) nf insecurity. **inseguro** adj insecure, unsafe.

insensatez (insensa'teθ) nf stupidity, foolishness. **insensato** adj stupid, foolish.

insensible (insen'siβle) adj 1 insensitive. 2 impassive. 3 imperceptible.

insepulto (inse'pulto) adj unburied.

insertar (inser'tar) vt 1 insert. 2 graft.

inservible (inser'βiβle) adj useless.

insidioso (insi'ðjoso) adj insidious.

insigne (in'signe) adj distinguished.

insignia (in'signja) nf also **insignias** insignia.

insignificancia (insignifi'kanθja) nf insignificance. **insignificante** adj insignificant.

insincero (insin'θero) adj insincere.

insinuar (insi'nwar) vt insinuate. **insinuarse** vr ingratiate oneself.

insípido (in'sipiðo) adj tasteless, insipid.

insistir (insis'tir) vt insist. **insistencia** nf insistence.

insociable (inso'θjaβle) adj unsociable.

insolación (insola'θjon) nf sunstroke.

insolencia (inso'lenθja) nf insolence. **insolente** adj insolent, arrogant.

insólito (in'solito) adj unusual.

insoluble (inso'luβle) adj 1 insoluble. 2 indissoluble.

insolvencia (insol'βenθja) nf insolvency. **insolvente** adj insolvent, penniless.

insomne (in'somne) adj,n insomniac. **insomnio** nm insomnia.

insondable (inson'ðaβle) adj unfathomable.

insoportable (insopor'taβle) adj insufferable.

inspección (inspek'θjon) nf inspection. **inspeccionar** vt inspect. **inspector** nm inspector.

inspirar (inspi'rar) vt 1 breathe in. 2 inspire. **inspiración** nf inspiration.

instalar (insta'lar) vt instal, establish. **instalación** nf installation.

instancia (ins'tanθja) nf petition, application.

instante (ins'tante) nm instant. **instantáneo** adj instantaneous. **por instantes** continually.

instaurar (instau'rar) vt restore, re-establish.

instigar (insti'gar) vt incite.

instintivo (instin'tiβo) adj instinctive. **instinto** nm instinct.

instituir (institu'ir) vt institute. **institución** nf institution. **instituto** nm 1 institute. 2 grammar school.

instruir (instru'ir) vt instruct. **instrucción** nf 1 instruction. 2 education. **instructivo** adj instructive. **instructor** nm instructor.

instrumento (instru'mento) *nm* instrument.

insubordinar (insuβorði'nar) *vt* make rebellious. **insubordinable** *adj also* **insubordinado** rebellious. **insubordinación** *nf* insubordination.

insuficiencia (insufi'θjenθja) *nf* 1 insufficiency. 2 incapability. **insuficiente** *adj* 1 insufficient. 2 incapable.

insufrible (insu'friβle) *adj* unbearable.

insulso (in'sulso) *adj* dull.

insular (insu'lar) *adj* insular.

insultar (insul'tar) *vt* insult, provoke. **insulto** *nm* insult.

insuperable (insupe'raβle) *adj* insuperable.

insurgente (insur'xente) *adj* rebellious. *nm,f* rebel.

insurrección (insurrek'θjon) *nf* rebellion. **insurreccionar** *vt* incite to rebel. **insurreccionarse** *vr* rebel.

intacto (in'takto) *adj* intact.

intachable (inta'tʃaβle) *adj* irreproachable.

integrar (inte'grar) *vt* 1 integrate, complete. 2 construct, form. **integración** *nf* integration. **integral** *adj also* **integrante** integral.

íntegro ('integro) *adj* entire. **integridad** *nf* 1 integrity, chastity. 2 entirety.

intelecto (inte'lekto) *nm* intellect. **intelectual** *adj,n* intellectual. **intelectualidad** *nf* intelligentsia.

inteligencia (inteli'xenθja) *nf* 1 intelligence. 2 meaning (of word). 3 relationship, agreement. **inteligente** *adj* intelligent. **inteligible** *adj* intelligible.

intemperie (intem'perje) *nf* bad weather.

intempestivo (intempes'tiβo) *adj* inopportune.

intención (inten'θjon) *nf* intention, meaning.

intenso (in'tenso) *adj* intense.

intentar (inten'tar) *vt* 1 attempt, try. 2 intend. **intento** *nm* 1 intent, design. 2 attempt.

intercalar (interka'lar) *vt* insert.

intercambio (inter'kambjo) *nm* interchange.

interceder (interθe'ðer) *vi* intercede. **intercesión** *nf* intercession.

interceptor (interθep'tor) *nm* interceptor.

interdicción (interðik'θjon) *nf*, *also* **interdicto** *nm* prohibition.

interés (inte'res) *nm* 1 interest, concern. 2 import, advantage. 3 *comm* interest.

interesar (intere'sar) *vt* interest. **interesado** *adj* self-seeking. *n* person concerned. **interesante** *adj* interesting. **interesarse por** *or* **en** be interested in.

interferencia (interfe'renθja) *nf* interference.

ínterin ('interin) *nm* interim. **interino** *adj* provisional, interim.

interior (inte'rjor) *adj* interior, inner, internal.

interjección (interxek'θjon) *nf* interjection.

intermediario (interme'ðjarjo) *adj,nm* intermediary. **intermedio** *adj* intermediate. *n Th* interval.

interminable (intermi'naβle) *adj* interminable.

intermisión (intermi'sjon) *nf* intermission.

intermitente (intermi'tente) *adj* intermittent.

internacional (internaθjo'nal) *adj* international.

internar (inter'nar) *vt* intern, confine. **internarse** *vr* penetrate. **interno** *adj* boarding. *nm* 1 boarder. 2 *med* houseman. **escuela interna** boarding school.

interpelar (interpe'lar) *vt* 1 appeal for help to. 2 buttonhole, demand an answer. **interpelación** *nf* plea, appeal.

interponer (interpo'ner) *vt* 1 interpose. 2 lodge (a complaint, etc.).

interpretar (interpre'tar) *vt* interpret. **interpretación** *nf* interpretation. **intérprete** *nm,f* interpreter.

interrogar (interro'gar) *vt* question. **interrogación** *nf* 1 question. 2 question mark. **interrogativo** *adj* interrogative. **interrogatorio** *nm* questionnaire.

interrumpir (interrum'pir) *vt* interrupt. **interrupción** *nf* interruption. **interruptor** *nm tech* switch.

intervalo (inter'βalo) *nm* interval, distance.

intervenir (interβe'nir) *vt,vi* 1 take part in. 2 intervene. 3 *med* operate on. 4 *comm* audit. **intervención** *nf* 1 *pol* intervention. 2 audit. 3 *med* operation. **interventor** *nm* 1 auditor. 2 supervisor (of a train).

intestado (intes'taðo) *adj* intestate.

intestino (intes'tino) *adj* internal. *nm* intestine. **intestinal** *adj* intestinal.

intimar (inti'mar) *vt* intimate, declare, notify. **intimarse** *vr* become intimate. **intimación** *nf* declaration. **intimidad** *nf* intimacy. **íntimo** *adj* intimate.

intimidar (intimi'ðar) *vt* intimidate.

intolerable (intole'raβle) *adj* intolerable. **intolerancia** *nf* intolerance. **intolerante** *adj* intolerant.

intoxicar (intoksi'kar) *vt* poison. **intoxicación** *nf* intoxication, poisoning.

intraducible (intraðu'θiβle) *adj* untranslatable.

intranquilidad (intrankili'ðað) *nf* restlessness, disquiet. **intranquilo** *adj* restless, worried.

intransigencia (intransi'xenθja) *nf* intransigence. **intransigente** *adj* intransigent.

intransitable (intransi'taβle) *adj* impassable.

intransitivo (intransi'tiβo) *adj gram* intransitive.

intratable (intra'taβle) *adj* 1 unmanageable. 2 unsociable.

intrepidez (intrepi'ðeθ) *nf* valour. **intrépido** *adj* intrepid, brave, fearless.

intrigar (intri'gar) *vi,vt* intrigue.

intrincado (intrin'kaðo) *adj* 1 intricate. 2 confused.

intrínseco (in'trinseko) *adj* intrinsic.

introducir (introðu'θir) *vt* introduce. **introducción** *nf* introduction.

intrusión (intru'sjon) *nf* intrusion. **intruso** *adj* intrusive. *nm* intruder.

intuición (intwi'θjon) *nf* intuition.

inundar (inun'dar) *vt* flood. **inundación** *nf* flood.

inusitado (inusi'taðo) *adj* obsolete, rare.

inútil (i'nutil) *adj* useless. **inutilidad** *nf* uselessness. **inutilizar** *vt* render useless.

invadir (inβa'ðir) *vt* invade.

invalidar (inβali'ðar) *vt* invalidate, abolish. **inválido** (in'βaliðo) *adj,n* invalid.

invariable (inβa'rjaβle) *adj* invariable.

invasión (inβa'sjon) *nf* invasion. **invasor** *adj* invading. *nm* invader.

invencible (inβen'θiβle) *adj* invincible, unconquerable.

inventar (inβen'tar) *vt* invent. **invención** *nf* invention. **inventivo** *adj* inventive. **invento** *nm* invention. **inventor** *nm* inventor.

inventario (inβen'tarjo) *nm* inventory.

invernáculo (inβer'nakulo) *nm* also **invernadero** hot-house.

invernar (ie) (inβer'nar) *vt* pass the winter, hibernate. **invernada** *nf* 1 winter. 2 hibernation. **invernal** *adj* wintry.

inverosímil (inβero'simil) *adj* improbable.

invertir (ie) (inβer'tir) *vt* 1 invert. 2 *comm* invest. **inversión** *nf* 1 inversion. 2 *comm* investment.

investigar (inβesti'gar) *vt* investigate. **investigación** *nf* investigation. **investigador** *nm* researcher.

investir* (inβes'tir) *vt* 1 invest. 2 confer upon. **investidura** *nf* investiture.

inveterado (inβete'raðo) *adj* confirmed, rooted.

invicto (in'βikto) *adj* undefeated.

invierno (in'βjerno) *nm* winter.

inviolable (inβjo'laβle) *adj* inviolable.

invitar (inβi'tar) *vt* 1 invite. 2 treat (to drinks). **invitación** *nf* invitation.

invocar (inβo'kar) *vt* invoke. **invocación** *nf* invocation.

involuntario (inβolun'tarjo) *adj* 1 automatic. 2 unintended.

inyección (injek'θjon) *nf* injection.

inyectar (injek'tar) *vt* inject. **inyectable** *nm* injectable. **inyector** *nm* nozzle.

iodo ('joðo) *nm* iodine.

ir (ir) *vi* 1 go. 2 walk. **irse** *vr* go away.

ira ('ira) *nf* anger. **iracundo** *adj* 1 furious. 2 irascible.

Irak (i'rak) *nm* Iraq. **iraquí** *adj,n* Iraqui.

Irán (i'ran) *nm* Iran. **iraní** *adj,n* Iranian.

irguió (irgi'o) *v* see **erguir**.

iris ('iris) *nm* iris (of the eye). **arco iris** *nm* rainbow.

Irlanda (ir'landa) *nf* Ireland. **irlandés** *adj,n* Irishman. *nm* Irish (language).

ironía (iro'nia) *nf* irony. **irónico** *adj* ironic.

irracional (irraθjo'nal) *adj* irrational.

irradiar (irra'ðjar) *vt* radiate. **irradiación** *nf* irradiation.

irrazonable (irraθo'naβle) *adj* unreasonable.

irreal (irre'al) *adj* unreal.

irreconciliable (irrekonθi'ljaβle) *adj* irreconcilable.

irreflexión (irreflek'sjon) *nf* hastiness. **irreflexivo** *adj* hasty.

irrefrenable (irrefre'naβle) *adj* uncontrollable.

irregular (irregu'lar) *adj* irregular, anomalous. **irregularidad** *nf* irregularity.

irreligioso (irreli'xjoso) *adj* impious.

irremediable (irreme'ðjaβle) *adj* 1 irreparable. 2 incurable.

irresoluto (irreso'luto) *adj* 1 indecisive. 2 perplexed.

irrespetuoso (irrespe'twoso) *adj* irreverent.

irresponsable (irrespon'saβle) *adj* irresponsible.

irrigar (irri'gar) *vt* irrigate. **irrigación** *nf* irrigation. **irrigador** *nm* sprinkler.

irritabilidad (irritaβili'ðað) *nf* irascibility. **irritable** *adj* irascible.

isla ('isla) *nf* island.

Islandia (is'landja) *nf* Iceland. **islandés** *adj* Icelandic. *nm* 1 Icelander. 2 Icelandic (language).

isleño (is'leno) *adj* island. *nm* islander.

Israel (is'rael) *nm* Israel. **israelí** *adj,n* Israeli. **israelita** *adj,n* Israelite.

istmo ('istmo) *nm* isthmus.

Italia (i'talja) nf Italy. **italiano** adj,n Italian. nm Italian (language).

itinerario (itine'rarjo) nm itinerary.

izar (i'θar) vt hoist.

izquierdo (iθ'kjerðo) adj left. **a la izquierda** on or to the left. **la izquierda** also **los izquierdistas** pol the left wing.

J

jabalí (xaβa'li) nm boar.

jabalina (xaβa'lina) nf javelin.

jabón (xa'βon) nm soap. **jabonar** vt soap, wash. **jabonoso** adj soapy.

jaca ('xaka) nf pony.

jacinto (xa'θinto) nm hyacinth.

jactarse (xak'tarse) vr boast, brag. **jactancia** nf boasting. **jactancioso** adj boastful.

jadear (xaðe'ar) vt pant, gasp. **jadeante** adj panting.

jalear (xale'ar) vt 1 urge on (dogs in hunting). 2 clap, stamp in time to a song, dance, etc. **jaleo** nm 1 audience participation (in flamenco, etc.). 2 row. **armar un jaleo** or **estar de jaleo** kick up a row.

jamás (xa'mas) adv never. **nunca jamás** never ever.

jamón (xa'mon) nm ham.

Japón (xa'pon) nm Japan. **japonés** adj,n Japanese. nm Japanese (language).

jaque ('xake) nm check (in chess).

jaqueca (xa'keka) nf migraine.

jarabe (xa'raβe) nm syrup.

jarana (xa'rana) nf drinking bout, spree.

jardín (xar'ðin) nm garden. **jardinería** nf gardening. **jardinero** nm gardener.

jarra ('xarra) nf deep earthenware jar. **jarro** nm earthenware jug. **jarrón** nm vase.

jaula ('xaula) nf cage.

jazmín (xaθ'min) nm jasmine.

jefatura (xefa'tura) nf headquarters. **jefe** nm 1 chief, head. 2 manager, boss.

jengibre (xen'xiβre) nm ginger.

jerarquía (xerar'kia) nf hierarchy. **jerárquico** adj hierarchical.

jerez (xe'reθ) nm sherry.

jerga ('xerga) nf also **jerigonza** jargon.

jeringa (xe'ringa) nf syringe.

jeroglífico (xero'glifiko) adj,nm hieroglyph.

jersey (xer'sei) nm jersey.

Jerusalén (xerusa'len) nm Jerusalem.

jesuita (xesu'ita) adj,n Jesuit.

jeta ('xeta) nf 1 protruding mouth, snout. 2 fam face. **poner jeta** pout.

jilguero (xil'gero) nm goldfinch.

jinete (xi'nete) nm rider.

jirafa (xi'rafa) nf giraffe.

jocosidad (xokosi'ðað) nf joviality, cheer. **jocoso** adj cheerful, humorous.

jofaina (xo'faina) nf washbowl.

jornada (xor'naða) nf 1 journey, day's journey. 2 day's work. 3 Th act. **jornal** nm wage, day's wage. **jornalero** nm day-labourer.

joroba (xo'roβa) nf 1 hump. 2 bother. **jorobado** adj,n hunchback (person).

jota ('xota) nf 1 the letter j. 2 folk dance.

joven ('xoβen) adj young. nm,f, pl **jóvenes** youth, young person.

joya ('xoja) nf jewel. **joyería** nf jewellery. **joyero** nm jeweller.

jubilar (xuβi'lar) vt pension off, superannuate, retire. **jubilación** nf 1 pension. 2 retirement. **jubilado** nm pensioner.

jubileo (xuβi'leo) nm jubilee.

júbilo ('xuβilo) nm rejoicing.

judaísmo (xuða'ismo) nm Judaism.

judía (xu'ðia) nf 1 string bean. 2 (kidney) bean. **judiada** (xu'ðjaða) nf 1 cruelty, cruel action. 2 comm extortion.

judicial (xuði'θjal) adj judicial.

judío (xu'ðio) adj Jewish. nm Jew.

juego ('xwego) nm 1 game, play. 2 gaming, gambling. 3 set, assembly.

juerga ('xwerga) nf sl party, spree.

jueves ('xweβes) nm Thursday.

juez (xweθ) nm judge.

jugar (ue) (xu'gar) vi,vt play. **jugarse** vr gamble. **jugada** nf game go, move. **jugador** nm player.

juglar (xu'glar) nm minstrel.

jugo ('xugo) nm juice. **jugoso** adj juicy.

juguetear (xugete'ar) vi frolic. **juguete** nm toy, plaything.

juicio ('xwiθjo) nm judgment. **juicioso** adj 1 good. 2 sensible.

julio ('xuljo) nm July.

jumento (xu'mento) nm donkey, ass.

junco ('xunko) nm reed.

jungla ('xungla) nf jungle.

junio ('xunjo) nm June.

junquillo (xun'kiʎo) nm garden reed, bullrush.

juntar (xun'tar) vt join, assemble. **junta** nf 1 assembly. 2 tech joint, washer. 3 junta. **la junta directiva** the board of directors. **junto** adj,adv together, joint. **junto a** prep near.

juramentar (xuramen'tar) vt swear in. **juramento** nm 1 oath. 2 swearword.

jurar (xu'rar) vi,vt swear. **jurado** nm jury, juror.

jurídico (xu'riðiko) adj juridical.

jurisconsulto (xuriskon'sulto) nm legal expert. **jurisdicción** nf jurisdiction. **jurisprudencia** nf jurisprudence. **jurista** nm jurist.

justa ('xusta) nf joust, competition.

justicia (xus'tiθja) nf 1 justice. 2 tribunal.

justificar (xustifi'kar) vt justify. **justificación** nf justification.

justo ('xusto) adj just, correct.

juvenil (xuβe'nil) adj youthful.

juventud (xuβen'tuð) nf youth.

juzgar (xuθ'gar) vt judge. **juzgado** nm court.

K

kilo ('kilo) nm kilo.

kilogramo (kilo'gramo) nm kilogramme.

kilolitro (kilo'litro) nm kilolitre.

kilómetro (ki'lometro) nm kilometre. **kilométrico** adj kilometric.

kilovatio (kilo'βatjo) nm kilowatt.

kiosco ('kjosko) nm kiosk.

L

la (la) def art f the. pron 3rd pers s 1 her, it. 2 fml you. 3 that, that one.

laberinto (laβe'rinto) nm labyrinth, maze.

labio ('laβjo) nm lip. **labial** adj,n labial.

labor (la'βor) nf 1 work, handiwork. 2 knitting.

laborar (laβo'rar) vt work, till. **laborioso** adj 1 industrious. 2 laborious. **laborista** adj Labour (Party).

labrar (la'βrar) vt 1 till, cultivate. 2 work, fashion. **labrador** nm ploughman, farmer. **labranza** nf 1 farming. 2 farmland. **labriego** adj, nm peasant.

laca ('laka) nf lacquer, varnish.

lacayo (la'kajo) nm lackey.

lacerar (laθe'rar) vt 1 wound. 2 damage (fruit). **laceración** nf laceration, damage.

lacio ('laθjo) adj limp, creased, lank.

lacrar[1] (la'krar) vt infect. **lacra** nf blemish, scar.

lacrar[2] (la'krar) vt seal. **lacre** nm sealing wax.

lacrimoso (lakri'moso) adj tearful.

lácteo ('lakteo) adj milky. **vía láctea** nf Milky Way.

ladear (laðe'ar) vt overturn, tip, tilt.

ladera (la'ðera) nf slope.

lado ('laðo) nm side. **al lado de** beside.

ladrar (la'ðrar) vi bark. **ladrido** nm barking.

ladrillo (la'ðriλo) nm brick, tile.

ladrón (laðˈron) nm thief.

lagarto (la'garto) nm lizard.

lago ('lago) nm lake.

lágrima ('lagrima) nf tear, drop.

laguna (la'guna) nf 1 pond, lagoon. 2 gap.

laico ('laiko) adj secular.

lamentar (lamen'tar) vt 1 lament. 2 regret. **lamentación** nf lamentation. **lamento** nm lament.

lamer (la'mer) vt lick.

lámina ('lamina) nf 1 sheet (of metal). 2 plate (of a book). **laminar** vt laminate.

lámpara ('lampara) nf lamp.

lana ('lana) nf wool.

lance ('lanθe) nm 1 throw. 2 occasion, opportunity.

lanceta (lan'θeta) nf lancet.

lancha ('lantʃa) nf launch.

langosta (lan'gosta) nf 1 lobster. 2 locust.

languidecer* (langiðe'θer) vi languish. **languidez** nf languor. **lánguido** adj languid.

lanudo (la'nuðo) adj woolly.

lanza ('lanθa) nf spear.

lanzar (lan'θar) vt 1 throw, fling. 2 evict. **lanzarse** vr rush, jump. **lanzamiento** nm ejection.

lapicero (lapi'θero) nm pencil-holder.

lápida ('lapiða) nf slab (of stone).

lápiz ('lapiθ) nm pencil.

lapso ('lapso) nm lapse.

largar (lar'gar) vt free, loosen. **largarse** vr run away.

largo ('largo) adj long. nm length. **a lo largo de** along, the length of. **dar largas** a delay.

laringe (la'ringe) nf larynx.

larva ('larβa) nf larva.

lascivo (las'θiβo) adj lascivious. **lascivia** nf lasciviousness.

lástima ('lastima) nf pity. **¡qué lástima!** what a pity! **lastimar** vt hurt.

lastre ('lastre) nm ballast.

lata ('lata) nf 1 tin, can. 2 inf nuisance.

latente (la'tente) adj latent.

lateral (late'ral) adj lateral.

látigo ('latigo) nm whip. **latigazo** nm whiplash.

latín (la'tin) nm Latin.

latir (la'tir) vi (of the heart) beat. **latido** nm heartbeat.

latitud (lati'tuð) nf 1 breadth. 2 geog latitude.
latón (la'ton) nm brass.
latoso (la'toso) adj inf annoying.
latrocinio (latro'θinjo) nm theft.
laúd (la'uð) nm lute.
laudable (lau'ðaβle) adj praiseworthy.
laurel (lau'rel) nm 1 bay tree. 2 bayleaf. 3 laurel, chaplet.
lava ('laβa) nf lava.
lavabo (la'βaβo) nm 1 washbasin. 2 toilet.
lavar (la'βar) vt wash, clean. **lavadero** nm laundry (place). **lavadora** nf washing machine.
laxante (lak'sante) nm laxative.
lazo ('laθo) nm 1 loop, lasso. 2 bootlace.
leal (le'al) adj loyal. **lealdad** nf loyalty.
lebrel (le'βrel) nm greyhound.
lección (lek'θjon) nf lesson.
lector (lek'tor) nm 1 reader. 2 lecturer. **lectura** nf reading matter.
leche ('letʃe) nf milk. **lechería** nf dairy. **lechero** nm milkman.
lecho ('letʃo) nm bed.
lechón (le'tʃon) nm suckling pig.
lechuga (le'tʃuga) nf lettuce.
lechuza (le'tʃuθa) nf owl.
leer* (le'er) vt read.
legación (lega'θjon) nf legation. **legado** nm delegate.
legal (le'gal) adj lawful. **legalizar** vt legalize, authenticate. **legalización** nf legalization, authentication.
legar (le'gar) vt bequeath. **legado** nm bequest, legacy.
legendario (lexen'darjo) adj legendary.
legión (le'xjon) nf legion.
legislar (lexis'lar) vi legislate. **legislación** nf legislation.
legitimar (lexiti'mar) vt 1 prove, justify. 2 legitimize. **legítimo** adj legitimate, real.
lego ('lego) adj lay. nm layman.
legua ('legwa) nf league.
legumbre (le'gumbre) nf vegetable.
lejanía (lexa'nia) nf distance, far-away place. **lejano** adj far-away.
lejía (le'xia) nf bleach.
lejos ('lexos) adv far away.
lema ('lema) nm motto.
lengua ('lengwa) nf 1 tongue. 2 language. **soltar la lengua** inf be indiscreet.
lenguado (len'gwaðo) nm sole (fish).
lenguaje (len'gwaxe) nm language.
lengüeta (len'gweta) nf tongue of a shoe, tab.

lenidad (leni'ðað) nf lenience, mildness.
lente ('lente) nm lens. **lentes de contacto** contact lenses.
lenteja (len'texa) nf lentil.
lentitud (lenti'tuð) nf slowness. **lento** adj sluggish.
leña ('leɲa) nf firewood. **leñador** nm woodcutter.
león (le'on) nm lion.
lepra ('lepra) nf leprosy. **leproso** adj leprous. nm leper.
lesión (le'sjon) nf injury. **lesionar** vt injure.
letanía (leta'nia) nf 1 litany. 2 sl interminable list.
letargo (le'targo) nm lethargy.
letra ('letra) nf 1 letter of the alphabet. 2 handwriting, script. 3 lyrics. 4 comm draft. 5 pl cap literature, Arts. **letras de molde** block letters.
leva ('leβa) nf tech spoke.
levadizo (leβa'ðiθo) adj able to be raised. **puente levadizo** nm drawbridge.
levadura (leβa'ðura) nf yeast.
levantar (leβan'tar) vt raise, set up. **levantarse** vr 1 stand up, get up. 2 rebel. **levantamiento** nm revolt.
leve ('leβe) adj slight.
léxico ('leksiko) adj lexical. nm 1 vocabulary. 2 lexicon, dictionary.
ley (lej) nf law.
leyó (le'jo) v see **leer.**
leyenda (le'jenda) nf legend.
liar (ljar) vt bind, tie up.
libélula (li'βelula) nf dragonfly.
liberal (liβe'ral) adj generous. adj, n liberal. **liberalidad** nf generosity. **liberalismo** nm liberalism. **liberalizar** vt liberalize.
libertar (liβer'tar) vt liberate, free. **libertad** nf liberty, freedom. **libertador** nm liberator.
libertinaje (liβerti'naxe) nm licentiousness. **libertino** nm libertine.
libra ('libra) nf pound. **libra esterlina** pound sterling.
librar (li'βrar) vt 1 free, exempt. 2 expedite, draw (letters of exchange, etc.). **libranza** nf draft, bill of exchange.
libre ('liβre) adj free.
librería (liβre'ria) nf 1 bookshop. 2 bookshelf. **librero** nm bookseller.
libreta (li'βreta) nf 1 notebook. 2 cashbook.
libro ('liβro) nm book.
licenciar (liθen'θjar) vt license. **licenciarse** vr

graduate. **licencia** nf 1 licence. 2 mil leave. **licenciado** adj, nm graduate.

licencioso (liθen'θjoso) adj dissolute.

lícito ('liθito) adj authorized.

licor (li'kor) nm 1 liquor. 2 liqueur.

líder ('liðer) nm leader.

lidiar (li'ðjar) vi fight (bulls). **lidia** nf bullfight. **lidiador** nm bullfighter.

liebre ('ljeβre) nf hare.

lienzo ('ljenθo) nm linen, canvas.

liga ('liga) nf 1 garter. 2 alloy. 3 league.

ligamento (liga'mento) nm ligament.

ligar (li'gar) vt,vi unite, bind together. **ligadura** nf bond. **ligazón** nm bond, tie-beam.

ligereza (lixe'reθa) nf 1 lightness, agility. 2 flippant remark. **ligero** adj 1 light, agile. 2 slight, unimportant.

lija ('lixa) nf sandpaper.

lila ('lila) nf lilac.

limar (li'mar) vt file, sand. **lima** nf 1 file. 2 polishing, filing.

limitar (limi'tar) vt limit. **limitación** nf limitation. **límite** nm limit, boundary.

limón (li'mon) nm lemon. **limonada** nf lemonade. **limonero** nm lemon tree.

limosna (li'mosna) nf alms.

limpiabotas (limpja'βotas) nm invar bootblack.

limpiar (lim'pjar) vt clean. **limpieza** nf 1 cleaning. 2 cleanness. **limpio** adj clean.

linaje (li'naxe) nm lineage.

linaza (li'naθa) nf linseed.

lince ('linθe) nm lynx.

lindar (lin'dar) vi adjoin. **lindero** adj adjoining. nm boundary.

lindo ('lindo) adj pretty. **lindeza** nf prettiness.

línea ('linea) nf line. **lineal** adj linear.

lingüista (lin'gwista) nm linguist. **lingüística** nf linguistics.

lino ('lino) nm linen.

linóleo (li'noleo) nm linoleum.

linterna (lin'terna) nf torch.

lío ('lio) nm 1 parcel. 2 fuss, trouble.

liquidar (liki'ðar) vt 1 comm liquidate, settle up. 2 sci liquify. **liquidación** nf 1 liquidation. 2 clearance sale.

líquido ('likiðo) nm liquid. **líquido imponible** net taxable amount. ~adj 1 liquid. 2 comn net. **liquidez** nf fluidity.

lira ('lira) nf 1 lyre. 2 lit type of verse, stanza.

lírica ('lirika) nf lyric poetry. **lírico** adj lyric. nm lyric poet.

lirio ('lirjo) nm iris.

liso ('liso) adj smooth.

lisonjear (lisonxe'ar) vt flatter. **lisonja** nf flattery. **lisonjero** adj flattering.

lista ('lista) nf list.

listo ('listo) adj 1 ready. 2 inf clever.

litera (li'tera) nf 1 berth. 2 bunk, litter.

literato (lite'rato) adj well-read. nm man of letters. **literatura** nf literature.

litigar (liti'gar) vt,vi dispute (in law), litigate. **litigio** nm lawsuit.

litografía (litogra'fia) nf lithograph.

litoral (lito'ral) adj coastal. nm coast.

litro ('litro) nm litre.

liturgia (litur'xia) nf liturgy.

liviano (li'βjano) adj 1 slight, trivial. 2 lewd. **liviandad** nf triviality, frivolity.

lo (lo) def art m the. pron 3rd pers s 1 him, it. 2 that, what.

loable (lo'aβle) adj praiseworthy.

lobo ('loβo) nm wolf.

lóbrego ('loβrego) adj gloomy.

lóbulo ('loβulo) nm lobe.

local (lo'kal) adj local. nm place, locale.

localizar (lokali'θar) vt locate.

loción (lo'θjon) nf lotion.

loco ('loko) adj mad. nm madman.

locomoción (lokomo'θjon) nf locomotion. **locomotora** nf locomotive.

locuaz (lo'kwaθ) adj talkative.

locura (lo'kura) nf madness.

locutor (lo'kutor) nm 1 radio announcer, commentator. 2 news reader.

lodo ('loðo) nm mud.

lógica ('loxika) nf logic. **lógico** adj logical.

lograr (lo'grar) vt 1 obtain. 2 perfect, achieve. **logro** nm 1 success, achievement. 2 gain, usury.

loma ('loma) nf hill.

lombriz (lom'briθ) nf earthworm.

lomo ('lomo) nm 1 back (of an animal). 2 loin (of meat).

lona ('lona) nf canvas, sailcloth.

Londres ('londres) nm London.

longaniza (longa'niθa) nf pork sausage.

longitud (lonxi'tuð) nf longitude. **longitud de onda** wavelength.

lonja ('lonxa) nf 1 slice (of food). 2 comm market.

loro ('loro) nm parrot.

lote ('lote) nm comm lot. **lotería** nf lottery. **lotero** nm lottery-ticket seller.

loza ('loθa) nf crockery.

lozano (lo'θano) adj 1 radiant, healthy. 2 (of greenery) lush. 3 proud.

lubrificar (luβrifi'kar) vt lubricate. **lubrificante** adj, nm lubricant.

lucidez (luθi'δeθ) nf lucidity, brightness. **lúcido** adj lucid, clear, shining.

luciérnaga (lu'θjernaga) nf glow-worm.

lucir (lu'θir) vi shine, be distinguished. vt show off.

lucro ('lukro) nm profit.

luchar (lu'tʃar) vi struggle. **lucha** nf struggle.

luego ('lwego) adv then, later. **luego que** conj as soon as. **desde luego** of course. **hasta luego** goodbye.

lugar (lu'gar) nm 1 place. 2 occasion, opportunity.

lúgubre ('luguβre) adj lugubrious.

lujo ('luxo) nm luxury. **lujoso** adj luxurious.

lujuria (lu'xurja) nf lust. **lujurioso** adj lecherous.

lumbre ('lumbre) nf light, flame. **lumbrera** nf 1 luminary. 2 tech vent. 3 skylight. 4 bright and learned person.

luminoso (lumi'noso) adj bright.

luna ('luna) nf moon. **luna de miel** honeymoon.

lunes ('lunes) nm Monday.

lupa ('lupa) nf magnifying glass.

lustrar (lus'trar) vt polish. **lustre** nm 1 polish. 2 lustre.

luto ('luto) nm mourning.

Luxemburgo (luxem'burgo) nm Luxemburg.

luz (luθ) nf light. **a todas luces** at any rate.

LL

llaga ('ʎaga) nf ulcer.

llama ('ʎama) nf flame.

llamar (ʎa'mar) vt 1 call. 2 name. **llamar la atención** attract the attention. **llamarse** vr be called, be named. **llamada** nf call, telephone call.

llamear (ʎame'ar) vi flame, blaze.

llana ('ʎana) nf trowel.

llano ('ʎano) adj 1 flat. 2 plain. nm plain.

llanta ('ʎanta) nf tyre.

llanto ('ʎanto) nm lament, weeping.

llanura (ʎa'nura) nf plain.

llave ('ʎaβe) nf 1 key. 2 spanner.

llegar (ʎe'gar) vi arrive, reach. **llegar a** end up at.

llenar (ʎe'nar) vt fill up. **lleno** adj full.

llevar (ʎe'βar) vt 1 take. 2 wear, bear. 3 spend, pass (time, life, etc.). **llevarse** vr take away. **llevarse bien** get on well together.

llorar (ʎo'rar) vi weep, cry. vt mourn. **llorón** adj weeping. nm cry-baby.

llover (ʎo'βer) vi rain.

lloviznar (ʎoβiθ'nar) vi drizzle. **llovizna** nf drizzle.

lluvia ('ʎuβja) nf 1 rain. 2 shower. **lluvioso** adj rainy, wet.

M

macabro (ma'kaβro) adj macabre.

macarrón (makar'ron) nm 1 macaroon. 2 pl macaroni.

maceta (ma'θeta) nf flowerpot.

macilento (maθi'lento) adj 1 faded. 2 lean, gaunt.

macis (ma'θis) nf invar cul mace.

macizo (ma'θiθo) adj massive, solid, stout. nm 1 mass, clump. 2 flowerbed.

machacar (matʃa'kar) vt crush, pound, grind. vi harp on a matter, go on about something.

machete (ma'tʃete) nm 1 cutlass. 2 large knife.

macho ('matʃo) adj 1 male, masculine. 2 strong. nm 1 male. 2 inf he-man. 3 mule. 4 sledgehammer.

madeja (ma'δexa) nf 1 skein, hank. 2 mop of hair.

madera¹ (ma'δera) nm Madeira wine.

madera² (ma'δera) nf 1 wood, timber. 2 disposition, aptitude. **maderaje** nm wood(work). **maderero** nm 1 timber merchant. 2 carpenter. **madero** nm beam, log.

madrastra (ma'δrastra) nf stepmother.

madre (maδre) nf mother. **madre adoptiva** foster mother. **madre política** mother-in-law.

madreselva (maδres'elβa) nf honeysuckle.

Madrid (ma'δriδ) nm Madrid. **madrileño** adj of Madrid. nm native or inhabitant of Madrid.

madriguera (maδri'gera) nf den, burrow.

madrina (ma'δrina) nf 1 godmother. 2 protectress. **madrina de boda** bridesmaid.

madrugar (maδru'gar) vi get up early. **madrugada** nf early morning, dawn.

madurar (maδu'rar) vt,vi ripen, mature. **madurez** nf ripeness, maturity. **maduro** adj ripe, mature, mellow.

maestría (maes'tria) nf mastery, skill. **maestro** adj 1 masterly, skilled. 2 main, master. nm master, teacher. **magistral** adj masterly.

magia ('maxia) nf magic. **mágico** adj magic(al). nm magician.

magistrado (maxi'straδo) nm magistrate.

89

magnánimo (mag'nanimo) adj magnanimous.

magnético (mag'netiko) adj magnetic.

magnetofón (magneto'fon) nm also **magnetófono** tape recorder.

magnífico (mag'nifiko) adj magnificent.

magnitud (magni'tuð) nf size, magnitude.

mago ('mago) nm magician, wizard.

magro ('magro) adj 1 thin, lean. 2 (of land) poor.

magullar (magu'ʎar) vt bruise, damage, mangle. **magulladura** nf bruise.

maíz (ma'iθ) nm maize.

majadero (maxa'ðero) adj silly, boring. nm 1 bore. 2 pestle.

majar (ma'xar) vt 1 pound, crush. 2 bother.

majestad (maxes'tað) nf majesty. **majestuoso** adj majestic, stately.

majo ('maxo) adj smart, dashing. nm 1 dandy, fop. **maja** nf belle.

mal (mal) adj see **malo**. adv badly, wrongly, poorly. nm 1 evil, wrong. 2 illness, harm, misfortune. **de mal en peor** from bad to worse. **echar a mal** 1 despise. 2 waste. **llevar a mal** take offence at. **mal que bien** rightly or wrongly, anyhow. **menos mal que** luckily, a good job that.

malaconsejado (malakonse'xaðo) adj unwise, ill-advised.

malbaratar (malbara'tar) vt 1 sell off cheaply. 2 squander.

malcontento (malkon'tento) adj discontented, hard to please. nm malcontent.

malcriado (malkri'aðo) adj bad-mannered, ill-bred.

maldad (mal'dað) nf evil, act of wickedness.

maldecir* (malde'θir) vt curse. vi slander. **maldición** nf curse. **maldito** adj damned, accursed.

maleficio (male'fiθjo) nm curse, spell.

maleta (ma'leta) nf 1 (suit)case. 2 boot of a car. **hacer la maleta** pack.

malévolo (ma'leβolo) adj 1 malicious, spiteful. 2 malignant. **malevolencia** nf malevolence, ill-will, spite.

maleza (ma'leθa) nf scrub, thicket.

malgastar (malgas'tar) vt waste, squander. **malgastador** nm, adj spendthrift.

malhechor (male'tʃor) nm wrongdoer, criminal. **malhecho** nm misdeed.

malhumorado (malumo'raðo) adj ill-tempered, cross, surly.

malicia (ma'liθja) nf malice, naughtiness, wickedness. **malicioso** adj spiteful, mischievous, wicked.

malignidad (maligni'ðað) nf evil, malice, malignancy. **maligno** adj evil, harmful.

malintencionado (malintenθjo'naðo) adj hostile, ill-disposed.

malo ('malo) adj also **mal** 1 bad, evil, 2 obnoxious. 3 cunning. **estar malo** be ill.

malograr (malo'grar) vt spoil, waste. **malograrse** vr fail, come to naught. **malogrado** adj unlucky. **malogro** nm failure, untimely end.

malsano (mal'sano) adj 1 unhealthy. 2 sick. 3 insanitary.

malta ('malta) nf malt.

Malta ('malta) nf Malta. **maltés**, adj,n Maltese. nm Maltese (language).

maltratar (maltra'tar) vt ill-treat, abuse, damage. **maltrato** nm ill-treatment, abuse.

malva ('malβa) nf 1 mallow. 2 marshmallow.

malvado (mal'βaðo) adj wicked, evil. nm villain.

malla ('maʎa) nf 1 mesh, net(work). 2 coat of mail. **hacer malla** knit.

Mallorca (ma'ʎorka) nf Majorca. **mallorquín** adj,n Majorcan.

mamá (ma'ma) nf also **mama** mummy, mother.

mamar (ma'mar) vt 1 suck. 2 absorb, acquire. 3 achieve. **mamarse** vr inf get drunk.

mamífero (ma'mifero) adj,nm mammal.

mampostería (mamposte'ria) nf masonry.

manada (ma'naða) nf 1 herd, flock, pack. 2 crowd. 3 handful.

manantial (manantí'al) nm spring, fountain, source, origin.

manar (ma'nar) vi run, flow, abound in.

mancebo (man'θeβo) nm 1 youth. 2 bachelor. 3 shop assistant.

manco ('manko) adj 1 one-armed, one-handed. 2 armless. 3 maimed. nm cripple, one-armed person.

mancomunar (mankomu'nar) vt unite, combine. **mancomunidad** nf union, association, commonwealth.

manchar (man'tʃar) vt stain, make dirty, mark. **mancha** nf spot, mark, blemish, stain.

mandar (man'dar) vt 1 order, command. 2 send. vi give orders. **mandamiento** nm 1 order, warrant. 2 rel commandment.

mandatario (manda'tarjo) nm 1 agent. 2 attorney. 3 leader. **mandato** nm order, mandate, writ. **mandato internacional** international money order.

mandíbula (man'diβula) nf jaw.

mando ('mando) nm 1 command. 2 authority.

manejar (mane'xar) vt handle, operate, manage. **manejarse** vr manage. **manejable** adj manageable. **manejo** nm 1 handling, operation. 2 shrewdness. 3 intrigue.

manera (ma'nera) nf 1 way, manner, mode. 2 kind, type. 3 fashion, style. **de ninguna manera** by no means, certainly not. **de todas maneras** at any rate.

manga ('manga) nf 1 sleeve. 2 hose, spout. **tener manga ancha** be easygoing.

mango [1] ('mango) nm mango (tree).

mango [2] ('mango) nm handle, shaft, stick.

manguera (man'gera) nf hose, tube.

manía (ma'nia) nf 1 mania, rage. 2 whim, fad, oddity.

maníaco (ma'niako) adj maniac(al). nm maniac.

maniatar (manja'tar) vt handcuff, manacle.

manicomio (mani'komjo) nm lunatic asylum.

manifestar (le) (manifes'tar) vt 1 show, demonstrate. 2 declare. 3 expose.

manifiesto (mani'fjesto) adj manifest, obvious. nm pol manifesto.

maniobrar (manio'βrar) vt handle, operate. vt,vi manoeuvre. **maniobra** nf handling, manoeuvre, move.

manipular (manipu'lar) vt manipulate.

maniquí (mani'ki) nm 1 mannequin, model. 2 puppet.

manivela (mani'βela) nf mot crank.

mano ('mano) nf 1 hand. 2 paw. 3 game hand, round, turn. **a mano** by hand. **a (la) mano** at hand, handy. **de segunda mano** second hand. **coger con las manos en la masa** catch red-handed. **darse las manos** to shake hands.

manojo (ma'noxo) nm handful, bunch.

manosear (manose'ar) vt 1 handle. 2 paw. 3 fondle.

mansión (mansi'on) nf mansion.

manso ('manso) adj 1 gentle, meek, mild. 2 tame. **mansedumbre** nf 1 gentleness. 2 tameness.

manta ('manta) nf 1 blanket. 2 shawl. 3 rug.

manteca (man'teka) nf 1 lard. 2 fat. 3 butter.

mantecado (mante'kaðo) nm 1 ice-cream. 2 shortbread, type of biscuit.

mantel (man'tel) nm tablecloth.

mantener (mante'ner) vt 1 hold. 2 maintain. 3 defend. **mantenimiento** nm maintenance, upkeep.

mantequera (mante'kera) nf 1 churn. 2 butter dish. **mantequilla** nf butter.

mantilla (man'tiʎa) nf mantilla, shawl.

manto ('manto) nm cloak. **mantón** nm shawl.

manual (manu'al) adj manual. nm manual, handbook.

manubrio (ma'nubrio) nm 1 handle, crank, winch. 2 barrel organ.

manufactura (manufak'tura) nf 1 manufacture. 2 factory. **manufacturar** vt manufacture.

manuscrito (manus'krito) nm manuscript.

manzana (man'θana) nf 1 apple. 2 block of flats. **manzano** nm apple tree. **manzanilla** nf 1 camomile (tea). 2 type of dry sherry.

maña ('maɲa) nf 1 skill. 2 ingenuity. 3 trick, ruse, vice.

mañana (ma'ɲana) nf morning. adv tomorrow. **mañana por la mañana** tomorrow morning. **pasado mañana** the day after tomorrow.

mañoso (ma'ɲoso) adj clever, skilful, crafty.

mapa ('mapa) nm 1 map. 2 chart.

máquina ('makina) nf 1 machine. 2 locomotive. 3 edifice. 4 scheme. **máquina de escribir** typewriter. **máquina de fotografiar** camera.

maquinación (makina'θjon) nf machination, scheme, plotting. **maquinal** adj automatic. **maquinar** vt,vi plot.

mar (mar) nm,f sea, ocean.

maraña (ma'raɲa) nf 1 thicket, tangle. 2 mess.

maravillar (maraβi'ʎar) vt wonder, marvel. **maravilla** nf 1 wonder, marvel. 2 marigold. **maravilloso** adj wonderful, marvellous.

marcar (mar'kar) vt 1 mark, show. 2 dial. vt,vi sport score. **marca** nf mark, make, brand.

marcial (marθi'al) adj 1 martial. 2 military.

marco ('marko) nm 1 frame, framework. 2 setting. 3 mark (German coin).

marchar (mar'tʃar) vi 1 go, move. 2 work, function. 3 march. **marcharse** vr go away, leave. **marcha** nf 1 march, progress, course. 2 mot gear. **marcha atrás** reverse gear. **poner en marcha** mot start.

marchitar (martʃi'tar) vt,vi wither, fade, shrivel. **marchito** adj faded, shrunken.

marea (ma'rea) nf tide.

marearse (mare'arse) vr 1 feel (sea) sick. 2 be sick. **mareado** adj (sea) sick, dizzy. **mareo** nm 1 sickness, nausea. 2 bore, nuisance.

marfil (mar'fil) nm ivory.

margarina (marga'rina) nf margarine.

margarita (marga'rita) nf 1 daisy. 2 pearl.

margen ('marxen) nm 1 border, edge, margin. 2 space. 3 occasion, motive. 4 comm profit. nf bank (of a river).

marica (ma'rika) *nf* magpie. *nm inf* sissy. **maricón** *nm sl* homosexual.

marido (ma'riðo) *nm* husband.

marina (ma'rina) *nf* 1 navy. 2 seamanship. 3 coast. **marinero** *adj* seafaring, seaworthy, seamanlike. *nm* sailor, mariner. **marino** *adj* marine. *nm* sailor, seaman.

mariposa (mari'posa) *nf* butterfly. **mariposa nocturna** moth.

mariscal (maris'kal) *nm* 1 marshal. 2 major general.

mariscos (ma'riskos) *nm pl* shellfish, seafood.

marítimo (ma'ritimo) *adj* maritime.

marmita (mar'mita) *nf* stew-pot, casserole.

mármol ('marmol) *nm* marble.

marmóreo (mar'moreo) *adj* 1 marble. 2 stony.

marqués (mar'kes) *nm* marquis. **marquesa** *nf* marchioness.

marrano (mar'rano) *adj* filthy, dirty. *nm* pig, boar.

marrón (mar'ron) *adj* chestnut brown, maroon. *nm* 1 chestnut (colour). 2 marron glacé.

Marruecos (marru'ekos) *nm* Morocco. **marroquí** *adj,n* Moroccan.

martes ('martes) *nm invar* Tuesday. **martes de carnaval** Shrove Tuesday.

martillar (marti'ʎar) *vt* hammer. **martillo** *nm* hammer.

martín (mar'tin) *nm* **martín pescador** kingfisher.

martinete (marti'nete) *nm* 1 drop-hammer. 2 pile-driver.

mártir ('martir) *nm,f* martyr. **martirio** *nm* martyrdom.

marzo ('marθo) *nm* March.

mas (mas) *conj* but.

más (mas) *adj invar* more. *adv* 1 more. 2 most. 3 besides. *conj* and, plus.

masa ('masa) *nf* 1 dough. 2 mortar. 3 mass, volume.

masaje (ma'saxe) *nm* massage. **masajista** *nm,f* masseur, masseuse.

mascar (mas'kar) *vt,vi* 1 chew. 2 *inf* mumble.

máscara ('maskara) *nf* mask, disguise.

mascarada (maska'raða) *nf* 1 masquerade. 2 charade.

masculino (masku'lino) *adj* masculine, manly, male. *nm gram* masculine.

masón (ma'son) *nm* freemason. **masonería** *nf* freemasonry.

masticar (masti'kar) *vt* masticate, chew.

mástil ('mastil) *nm* 1 mast. 2 pole.

mastín (mas'tin) *nm* 1 mastiff. 2 bulldog.

mata ('mata) *nf* 1 bush, shrub. 2 *pl* thicket, grove. **mata de pelo** head or mop of hair.

matar (ma'tar) *vt,vi* 1 kill, slay, slaughter. 2 put out (light). 3 *game* mate. **matadero** *nm* slaughterhouse. **matador** *nm* bullfighter. **matanza** *nf* slaughter, killing.

mate[1] ('mate) *nm* (check)mate.

mate[2] ('mate) *adj* dull, unpolished.

matemáticas (mate'matikas) *nf pl* mathematics. **matemático** *adj* mathematical. *nm* mathematician.

materia (ma'terja) *nf* 1 matter. 2 subject. **materia prima** raw material. **material** *adj* material. **materialismo** *nm* materialism.

maternal (mater'nal) *adj* maternal. **maternidad** *nf* motherhood, maternity. **materno** *adj* maternal.

matinal (mati'nal) *adj* morning.

matiz (ma'tiθ) *nm* shade, hue, tint, hint. **matizar** *vt* blend.

matorral (mator'ral) *nm* 1 thicket. 2 shrub.

matricular (matriku'lar) *vt,vi* register, enrol, license. **matrícula** *nf* 1 register. 2 registration, matriculation. 3 licence plate.

matrimonio (matri'monjo) *nm* 1 matrimony, marriage. 2 married couple. **cama matrimonial** or **de matrimonio** *nf* double bed.

matriz (ma'triθ) *nf* 1 womb. 2 mould, die. 3 matrix.

matrona (ma'trona) *nf* 1 matron. 2 midwife.

matutino (matu'tino) *adj* (early) morning.

matute (ma'tute) *nm* smuggling, contraband.

maullar (mau'ʎar) *vi* mew. **maullido** *nm* mewing.

máxima ('maksima) *nf* maxim.

máxime ('maksime) *adv* especially, all the more so.

máximo ('maksimo) *adj,nm* maximum.

maya[1] ('maja) *adj,n* Mayan. *nm* Mayan (language).

maya[2] ('maja) *nf* daisy.

mayo ('majo) *nm* May.

mayonesa (majo'nesa) *nf* mayonnaise.

mayor (ma'jor) *adj* 1 older, elder. 2 major, main. 3 larger. 4 adult. *nm* 1 chief, boss, elder. 2 *pl* elders (and betters). 3 *pl* ancestors. **al por mayor** wholesale. **mayoral** *nm* foreman, manager of a farm.

mayorazgo (majo'raθgo) *nm* 1 primogeniture. 2 entailed estate. 3 first born.

mayordomo (major'ðomo) *nm* butler, steward.

mayoría (majo'ria) *nf* 1 majority, greater part. 2 adult status.

mayorista (majo'rista) *nm,f* wholesaler.

mayúscula (ma'juskula) *nf* capital letter.

maza ('maθa) *nf* 1 mace, club. 2 hammer. 3 bat, stick.

mazapán (maθa'pan) *nm* marzipan.

mazmorra (maθ'morra) *nf* dungeon.

me (me) *pron 1st pers s* me, myself.

mear (me'ar) *vt,vi* urinate. **mearse** *vr* wet oneself.

mecánica (me'kanika) *nf* mechanics. **mecánico** *adj* mechanical. *nm* mechanic, fitter.

mecanógrafa (meka'nografa) *nf* typist. **mecanografía** *nf* typing.

mecer (me'θer) *vt* swing, rock, sway. **mecedora** *nf* rocking chair.

mecha ('metʃa) *nf* wick, fuse. **mechero** *nm* 1 cigarette-lighter. 2 burner, jet.

medalla (me'ðaʎa) *nf* medal.

media ('meðja) *nf* 1 stocking. 2 *math* mean.

mediados (me'ðjaðos) *prep* **a mediados de** in the middle of.

mediano (me'ðjano) *adj* middling, average, mediocre.

medianoche (meðja'notʃe) *nf* midnight.

mediante (me'ðjante) *prep* by means of, through.

mediar (me'ðjar) *vi* 1 mediate, intervene. 2 be in the middle, lie between.

medicina (meði'θina) *nf* medicine.

médico ('meðiko) *adj* medical. *nm* doctor, physician.

medida (me'ðiða) *nf* 1 measure(ment). 2 step, move. 3 moderation. **a medida que** according as, in step with.

medio ('meðjo) *adj* 1 half. 2 middle. 3 medium, average. *adv* half, partly. *nm* 1 middle. 2 medium, mean. 3 way, method. 4 *pl* resources. 5 *pl* circumstances. **a medias** by halves, partly. **de por medio** in between, in the way. **por medio de** by means or way of.

mediocre (me'ðjokre) *adj* mediocre. **mediocridad** *nf* mediocrity.

mediodía (meðjo'ðia) *nm* 1 midday, noon. 2 south.

medir (i) (me'ðir) *vt,vi* 1 measure. 2 *lit* scan.

meditar (meði'tar) *vt* ponder, meditate on. *vi* think, meditate, muse. **meditabundo** *adj* pensive.

mediterráneo (meðiter'raneo) *adj* Mediterranean. **mar mediterráneo** *nm* Mediterranean Sea.

medrar (me'ðrar) *vi* thrive, prosper, grow. **medra** *nf* growth, prosperity.

medroso (me'ðroso) *adj* timid, fearful.

médula ('meðula) *nf* 1 *anat* marrow. 2 essence, substance.

medusa (me'ðusa) *nf* jellyfish.

Méjico ('mexiko) *nm* Mexico. **mejicano** *adj,n* Mexican.

mejilla (me'xiʎa) *nf* cheek.

mejor (me'xor) *adj* better, best. *adv* 1 better, best. 2 rather. **a lo mejor** probably, most likely. rather.

mejorar (mexo'rar) *vt* improve, better. **mejora** *nf* improvement.

melancolía (melanko'lia) *nf* melancholy. **melancólico** *adj* melancholy, sad, gloomy.

melena (me'lena) *nf* mane, long hair.

melindroso (melin'droso) *adj* squeamish, finicky.

melocotón (meloko'ton) *nm* peach.

melodía (melo'ðia) *nf* melody, tune. **melódico** *adj* melodic.

melón (me'lon) *nm* melon.

meloso (me'loso) *adj* 1 honeyed, sweet. 2 sickly.

mella ('meʎa) *nf* notch, dent.

mellizo (me'ʎiθo) *adj,n* twin.

membrana (mem'brana) *nf* membrane.

membrillo (mem'briʎo) *nm* quince.

memorable (memo'rable) *adj* memorable.

memoria (me'morja) *nf* 1 memory, remembrance. 2 report, record.

mencionar (menθjo'nar) *vt* mention, name.

mendigar (mendi'gar) *vt,vi* beg. **mendigo** *nm* beggar.

menear (mene'ar) *vt* 1 move, shake, wag, wave. 2 conduct (business).

menester (menes'ter) *nm* 1 duty. 2 occupation. 3 need, want. **ser menester** be necessary.

menguar (men'gwar) *vt,vi* lessen, decrease. **mengua** *nf* 1 decrease, decline. 2 loss. 3 discredit.

menguado (men'gwaðo) *adj* 1 decreased. 2 cowardly, wretched, miserable. *nm* coward, wretch.

menopausia (meno'pausja) *nf* menopause.

menor (me'nor) *adj* 1 minor. 2 younger. 3 lesser, least. *nm* minor. **al por menor** retail.

Menorca (me'norka) *nf* Minorca.

menos ('menos) *adj* less, fewer. *adv* except, minus, less. **al, a lo, or por lo menos** at least. **echar de menos** miss.

menoscabar (menoska'βar) *vt* 1 reduce. 2 impair. 3 discredit. **menoscabo** *nm* 1 reduction. 2 detriment.

menospreciar (menospre'θjar) vt 1 scorn, despise. 2 underrate. **menospreciable** adj contemptible. **menosprecio** nm 1 scorn. 2 undervaluation. 3 disrespect.

mensaje (men'saxe) nm message. **mensajero** nm messenger.

mensual (mensu'al) adj monthly.

menta ('menta) nf peppermint.

mental (men'tal) adj mental, intellectual. **mentalidad** nf mentality, mind.

mente ('mente) nf mind, intelligence.

mentecato (mente'kato) adj silly, stupid. nm fool.

mentir (ie) (men'tir) vi tell lies. **mentira** nf 1 lie. 2 deceitfulness.

menudear (menuðe'ar) vt repeat frequently. vi happen often.

menudencia (menu'ðenθia) nf 1 trifle, small thing. 2 pl odds and ends, minute detail. 3 pl offal.

menudo (me'nuðo) adj small, tiny, minute, petty. nm 1 small change. 2 pl offal, giblets. **a menudo** often.

meñique (me'ɲike) adj tiny. nm little finger.

meollo (me'oʎo) nm 1 anat marrow. 2 brains. 3 essence, core, gist.

mercado (mer'kaðo) nm market. **Mercado Común** Common Market. **mercader** nm merchant. **mercadería** nf merchandise, goods.

merced (mer'θeð) nf 1 favour. 2 mercy.

mercurio (mer'kurjo) nm mercury.

merecer* (mere'θer) vt,vi deserve, be worthy of. **merecimiento** nm deserts, merit.

merendar (ie) (meren'dar) vt have for lunch. vi have lunch, a snack, a picnic.

merengue (me'renge) nm meringue.

meridiano (meri'ðjano) nm meridian. **meridional** adj southern.

merienda (me'rjenda) nf 1 afternoon tea. 2 snack. 3 picnic.

mérito ('merito) nm merit, worth, value.

merluza (mer'luθa) nf 1 hake. 2 sl drunkenness.

mermar (mer'mar) vt reduce, decrease. vi decrease. **merma** nf reduction, wastage, loss.

mermelada (merme'laða) nf jam, marmalade.

mero ('mero) adj mere, pure, simple.

merodear (meroðe'ar) vi maraud, pillage.

mes (mes) nm month.

mesa ('mesa) nf table, desk.

meseta (me'seta) nf 1 plateau. 2 arch landing.

mesón (me'son) nm inn, hostelry. **mesonero** nm innkeeper, landlord.

mestizo (mes'tiθo) adj,nm half-caste.

mesura (me'sura) nf 1 moderation. 2 gravity, dignity. 3 courtesy.

meta ('meta) nf 1 goal, aim. 2 sport goal. **guardameta** nm goalkeeper.

metafísica (meta'fisika) nf metaphysics.

metáfora (me'tafora) nf metaphor.

metal (me'tal) nm 1 metal. 2 mus brass. 3 timbre. **metálico** adj metallic, metal. nm coin, cash.

metalurgia (meta'lurxia) nf metallurgy.

meteoro (mete'oro) nm meteor. **meteórico** adj meteoric.

meter (me'ter) vt 1 put in, insert, introduce. 2 wager. **meterse** vr interfere in, meddle in. **meterse con 1** quarrel with. 2 accost.

meticuloso (metiku'loso) adj meticulous.

método (me'toðo) nm method, manner. **metódico** adj methodical.

métrico ('metriko) adj metric(al).

metro ('metro) nm 1 metre. 2 ruler, tape. 3 underground railway.

metrópoli (me'tropoli) nf metropolis.

mezclar (meθ'klar) vt 1 mix, blend. 2 shuffle. **mezcla** nf mixture, blend.

mezcolanza (meθko'lanθa) nf jumble, hotchpotch.

mezquindad (meθkin'dað) nf meanness, pettiness. **mezquino** adj mean.

mezquita (meθ'kita) nf mosque.

mi (mi) poss pron 1st pers s my.

mí (mi) pron 1st pers s me, myself.

miaja ('mjaxa) nf crumb, bit.

mico ('miko) nm monkey.

micrófono (mi'krofono) nm 1 microphone. 2 mouthpiece.

microscopio (mikro'skopjo) nm microscope.

miedo (mi'eðo) nm fear. **tener miedo** be afraid. **miedoso** adj fearful, timid.

miel (mi'el) nf honey.

miembro (mi'embro) nm 1 limb. 2 member.

mientes (mientes) nf pl ¡ni por mientes! not on your life! **parar mientes en** consider carefully.

mientras (mi'entras) conj while, as long as, whereas. adv meanwhile, meantime. **mientras tanto** meanwhile.

miércoles (mi'erkoles) nm Wednesday. **miércoles de ceniza** Ash Wednesday.

mies (mjes) nf 1 ripe corn. 2 pl cornfields.

miga ('miga) nf 1 crumb. 2 substance. **hacer buenas migas con** get on well with.

mil (mil) adj,nm thousand. **milésimo** adj thousandth. **miles de** masses of. **mil gracias** many thanks.

milagro (mi'lagro) nm miracle, wonder, marvel. **milagroso** adj miraculous.

milicia (mi'liθja) nf 1 militia. 2 military service.

militar (mili'tar) adj 1 military. 2 warlike. nm soldier. vi 1 serve as a soldier. 2 militate.

milla ('miλa) nf mile.

millar (mi'λar) nm thousand. **a millares** in thousands.

millón (mi'λon) nm million. **millonésimo** adj millionth. **millonario** nm millionaire.

mimar (mi'mar) vt spoil, pamper. **mimo** nm 1 petting. 2 mime.

mimbre ('mimbre) nm,f wicker.

minar (mi'nar) vt mine. **mina** nf mine, deposit, store.

mineral (mine'ral) adj,nm mineral. **minero** nm miner.

mínimo ('minimo) adj, nm minimum.

ministerio (minis'terjo) nm ministry, office.

ministro (mi'nistro) nm minister. **primer ministro** prime minister.

minoría (mino'ria) nf minority.

minucioso (minu'θjoso) adj 1 meticulous. 2 minute.

minúscula (mi'nuskula) nf small letter.

minuta (mi'nuta) nf 1 agenda, list. 2 menu.

mío ('mio) poss pron 1st pers s my, mine.

miope (mi'ope) adj shortsighted. **miopía** nf myopia.

mirar (mi'rar) vt 1 look. 2 consider. **mira** nf 1 sight. 2 intention. **con miras a** with a view to. **mirada** nf look, glance. **mirador** nm 1 viewpoint. 2 balcony. **miramiento** nm 1 courtesy. 2 caution.

mirlo ('mirlo) nm blackbird.

mirra ('mirra) nf myrrh.

misa ('misa) nf rel mass. **misa mayor** high mass.

miserable (mise'raβle) adj wretched, miserable. **miseria** nf poverty, wretchedness.

misericordia (miseri'korðja) nf pity, compassion, mercy.

misión (mi'sjon) nf mission.

mismo ('mismo) adj 1 same. 2 very. 3 self. **por lo mismo** for this reason. **aquí mismo** right here.

misterio (mis'terjo) nm 1 mystery, secret. 2 mystery play. **misterioso** adj mysterious.

místico ('mistiko) adj mystic(al). **misticismo** nm mysticism.

mitad (mi'tað) nf 1 half. 2 middle.

mítico ('mitiko) adj mythical.

mitigar (miti'gar) vt mitigate, reduce.

mitin ('mitin) nm pol meeting.

mito ('mito) nm myth. **mitología** nf mythology.

mixto ('miksto) adj mixed.

mobiliario (moβi'ljarjo) nm furniture.

mocedad (moθe'ðað) nf 1 youth. 2 youthful prank.

moción (mo'θjon) nf 1 motion. 2 proposal.

moco ('moko) nm 1 mucus. 2 inf brat. **mocoso** adj snivelling.

mochila (mo'tʃila) nf rucksack, pack.

moda ('moða) nf fashion, style. **de moda** fashionable. **pasado de moda** out-dated.

modales (mo'ðales) nm pl manners.

modelo (mo'ðelo) nm model, pattern. nf fashion model.

moderar (moðe'rar) vt moderate, control. **moderado** adj moderate.

moderno (mo'ðerno) adj modern.

modestia (mo'ðestja) nf modesty. **modesto** adj modest.

módico ('moðiko) adj moderate, reasonable (price).

modificar (moðifi'kar) vt modify.

modismo (mo'ðismo) nm idiom, phrase.

modista (mo'ðista) nf dressmaker.

modo ('moðo) nm 1 way, manner, method. 2 mood. 3 mus mode. **de modo que** so that. **de todos modos** in any case.

modorra (mo'ðorra) nf drowsiness.

modular (moðu'lar) vt modulate.

mofar (mo'far) vi mock, jeer. **mofarse** vr mock, sneer at. **mofa** nf mockery.

mohín (mo'in) nm grimace, pout. **mohíno** adj gloomy, sulky, peevish.

moho ('moo) nm 1 rust. 2 mould, mildew. **mohoso** adj rusty, mouldy.

mojar (mo'xar) vt wet, moisten, drench.

mojigato (moxi'gato) adj hypocritical, prudish.

mojón (mo'xon) nm landmark.

moldar (mol'dar) vt mould. **molde** nm mould.

molécula (mo'lekula) nf molecule.

moler (ue) (mo'ler) vt 1 grind, crush, pound. 2 weary, bore.

molestar (moles'tar) vt annoy, upset. **molestarse** vr put oneself out. **molestia** nf trouble, bother. **molesto** adj 1 annoying. 2 upset.

molinero (moli'nero) nm miller. **molino** nm mill, grinder.

molusco (mo'lusko) *nm* mollusc.

mollera (mo'ʎera) *nf* 1 crown of the head. 2 *inf* brains. **cerrado de mollera** dim-witted, dense.

momentáneo (momen'taneo) *adj* momentary.

momento (mo'mento) *nm* 1 moment, instant. 2 momentum. 3 importance.

momia ('momja) *nf* mummy (corpse).

monarca (mo'narka) *nm* monarch. **monarquía** *nf* monarchy. **monárquico** *adj* monarchic(al), royalist.

monasterio (monas'terjo) *nm* monastery.

mondar (mon'dar) *vt* prune, trim, peel, clean.

moneda (mo'neða) *nf* 1 coin. 2 currency, money. **monedero** *nm* purse, wallet.

monitor (moni'tor) *nm* 1 monitor. 2 assistant (teacher). **monitorio** *adj* admonitory.

monja ('monxa) *nf* nun, sister. **monje** *nm* monk, friar.

mono[1] ('mono) *nm* monkey, ape.

mono[2] ('mono) *adj* pretty, lovely.

monólogo (mo'nologo) *nm* monologue.

monopolizar (monopoli'θar) *vt* monopolize. **monopolio** *nm* monopoly.

monosílabo (mono'silaβo) *adj* monosyllabic. *nm* monosyllable.

monstruo ('monstruo) *nm* monster. **monstruoso** *adj* monstrous.

monta ('monta) *nf* 1 mounting. 2 amount, value. **montacargas** *nm invar* service lift.

montaña (mon'taɲa) *nf* mountain. **montañés** *adj* mountain, highland. *nm* highlander. **montañismo** *nm* mountaineering. **montañoso** *adj* mountainous.

montar (mon'tar) *vt* 1 mount, ride. 2 set up, assemble. *vi* mount, ride.

monte ('monte) *nm* 1 mountain, hill. 2 woodland, scrub.

montera (mon'tera) *nf* 1 bullfighter's hat. 2 cloth cap. **montero** *nm* huntsman.

montón (mon'ton) *nm* heap, pile, mass.

monumento (monu'mento) *nm* monument, memorial.

moño ('moɲo) *nm* bun, topknot.

mora[1] ('mora) *nf* 1 blackberry. 2 mulberry.

mora[2] ('mora) *nf* 1 delay. 2 default.

morada (mo'raða) *nf* 1 dwelling, abode. 2 period of residence.

morado (mo'raðo) *adj* purple, violet. *nm* bruise.

moral (mo'ral) *adj* moral. *nf* morality. **moraleja** *nf* moral. **moralidad** *nf* morality.

morar (mo'rar) *vi* reside, dwell, stay.

mórbido ('morβiðo) *adj* 1 morbid. 2 diseased.

morboso (mor'βoso) *adj* morbid, unhealthy.

morcilla (mor'θiʎa) *nf* blood sausage, black pudding.

mordaz (mor'ðaθ) *adj* sarcastic, scathing.

mordaza (mor'ðaθa) *nf* gag, muzzle.

morder (ue) (mor'ðer) *vt,vi* bite, gnaw, eat away. **mordisco** *nm* bite.

moreno (mo'reno) *adj* 1 brown, swarthy. 2 dark-haired.

morera (mo'rera) *nf* mulberry tree.

morfina (mor'fina) *nf* morphine.

moribundo (mori'βundo) *adj* moribund.

morir (mo'rir) *vi* 1 die. 2 fade. **morir de hambre** starve to death. **morirse por** be dying to, be keen on.

moro ('moro) *adj* Moorish. *nm* Moor.

moroso (mo'roso) *adj* slow, sluggish, tardy.

morral (mor'ral) *nm* 1 haversack. 2 game-bag.

morriña (mor'riɲa) *nf* homesickness.

mortaja (mor'taxa) *nf* shroud.

mortal (mor'tal) *adj* mortal. **mortalidad** *nf* mortality.

mortandad (mortan'dað) *nf* massacre, carnage.

mortero (mor'tero) *nm* mortar.

mortífero (mor'tifero) *adj* deadly, lethal.

mortificar (mortifi'kar) *vt* mortify.

mosca ('moska) *nf* fly.

moscardón (moskar'ðon) *nm* 1 blowfly. 2 hornet.

mosquete (mos'kete) *nm* musket. **mosquetero** *nm* musketeer.

mosquito (mos'kito) *nm* mosquito, gnat.

mostaza (mos'taθa) *nf* mustard.

mostrar (ue) (mos'trar) *vt* 1 show, point out, explain. 2 prove. **mostrador** *nm* counter, bar.

mote ('mote) *nm* nickname.

motín (mo'tin) *nm* revolt, uprising.

motivar (moti'βar) *vt* cause, give rise to. **motivo** *nm* motive, reason, cause. **con motivo de** owing to.

motor (mo'tor) *nm* motor, engine. **motorista** *nm* motorcyclist. **motorizado** *adj* motorized.

mover (ue) (mo'βer) *vt,vi* move. **moverse** *vr* stir, get a move on.

móvil ('moβil) *adj* mobile. *nm* motive.

movilizar (moβili'θar) *vt* mobilize. **movilización** *nf* mobilization.

movimiento (moβi'mjento) *nm* movement, motion, activity.

moza ('moθa) *nf* 1 girl. 2 servant, maid. **mozo** *nm* 1 youth. 2 waiter. 3 porter.

mucosidad (mukosi'ðað) *nf* mucus. **mucoso** *adj* mucous.

muchacha (mu'tʃatʃa) nf 1 girl. 2 maid, servant. muchacho nm boy, lad.

muchedumbre (mutʃe'ðumbre) nf crowd, mass.

mucho ('mutʃo) adj much, a lot, great. adv much, a lot, a great deal. con mucho by far, easily.

mudar (mu'ðar) vt,vi change, alter. mudarse vr 1 move house. 2 change one's clothes. mudanza nf 1 change. 2 removal.

mudo ('muðo) adj dumb, mute. mudez nf dumbness.

mueble ('mweβle) nm piece of furniture.

mueca ('mweka) nf grimace.

muela ('mwela) nf molar, tooth.

muelle ('mweʎe) nm 1 tech spring, watch spring. 2 wharf, dock, pier, quay.

muérdago ('mwerðago) nm mistletoe.

muerte ('mwerte) nf 1 death. 2 murder. estar a la muerte be at death's door.

muerto ('mwerto) v see morir. adj dead, lifeless. nm corpse.

muestra ('mwestra) nf 1 sign, proof. 2 example, sample, pattern.

muevo ('mwevo) v see mover.

mugir (mu'xir) vi moo, bellow, roar. mugido nm roar, howl.

mujer (mu'xer) nf woman, wife.

mulo ('mulo) nm mule.

muleta (mu'leta) nf 1 crutch. 2 bullfighter's cape or its supporting stick.

multar (mul'tar) vt fine, penalize. multa nf fine, penalty.

múltiple ('multiple) adj 1 math complex, multiple. 2 pl numerous.

multiplicar (multipli'kar) vt multiply, increase.

multitud (multi'tuð) nf crowd, multitude.

mullir (mu'ʎir) vt fluff up, soften, loosen.

mundo ('mundo) nm world, earth. todo el mundo everybody. mundial adj world-wide, universal.

munición (muni'θjon) nf 1 ammunition. 2 stores, provisions.

municipal (muniθi'pal) adj municipal. municipio nm town, town council.

muñeca (mu'ɲeθa) nf 1 doll, puppet. 2 wrist.

muralla (mu'raʎa) nf wall, rampart.

murciélago (mur'θjelago) nm zool bat.

murmullo (mur'muʎo) nm murmur, whispering, rustling.

murmurar (murmu'rar) vi 1 murmur, whisper. 2 gossip. 3 grumble. murmuración nf backbiting, gossip.

muro ('muro) nm external wall.

músculo ('muskulo) nm muscle. muscular adj muscular.

museo (mu'seo) nm museum, gallery.

musgo ('musgo) nm moss.

música ('musika) nf music. musical adj musical. músico nm musician, player.

muslo ('muslo) nm thigh.

mustio ('mustjo) adj 1 faded. 2 tired.

mutación (muta'θjon) nf change, mutation.

mutilar (muti'lar) vt 1 mutilate. 2 cripple. 3 spoil. mutilado nm disabled person.

mutual (mu'twal) adj mutual. mutuo adj mutual, joint.

muy ('muj) adv very, greatly, highly, most.

N

nabo ('nabo) nm turnip.

nácar ('nakar) nm mother-of-pearl, nacre.

nacer* (na'θer) vi 1 be born. 2 begin, originate. nacido adj born. naciente adj rising, growing. nacimiento nm birth, nativity.

nación (na'θjon) nf nation. nacional adj 1 national. 2 native, domestic. nm native. nacionalidad nf nationality.

nada ('naða) nf nothing. adv not at all. por nada by no means.

nadar (na'ðar) vi swim. nadador nm swimmer.

nadie ('naðje) pron nobody, no one, none.

naipe ('naipe) nm playing card.

nalga ('nalga) nf buttock.

naranja (na'ranxa) nf orange.

narciso (nar'θiso) nm narcissus.

narcótico (nar'kotiko) adj narcotic. nm 1 narcotic, sleeping pill. 2 pl narcotic drugs. narcotizar vt drug.

nariz (na'riθ) nf, pl narices nose. narizudo adj big-nosed.

narrar (nar'rar) vt narrate, tell. narración nf narration.

nata ('nata) nf cream, curd.

natación (nata'θjon) nf swimming.

natal (na'tal) adj 1 natal. 2 native. natalicio adj,nm birthday. natalidad nf birth rate.

nativo (na'tiβo) adj,nm native. natividad nf nativity. nato adj 1 born. 2 natural.

natural (natu'ral) adj natural. nm,f 1 native. 2 inhabitant. naturaleza nf 1 nature. 2 naturalization.

naufragar (naufra'gar) vi be shipwrecked. nau-

97

fragio nm shipwreck. **náufrago** adj shipwrecked. nm a shipwrecked person.

náusea ('nausea) nf nausea.

náutico ('nautiko) adj nautical.

naval (na'βal) adj naval.

nave ('naβe) nf 1 ship. 2 arch nave.

navegar (naβe'gar) vt sail, navigate. **navegación** nf navigation, sailing. **navegador** nm also **navegante** navigator, voyager.

navío (na'βio) nm ship.

neblina (ne'βlina) nf mist, fog.

necesario (neθe'sarjo) adj necessary. **necesidad** nf 1 necessity. 2 need, poverty. 3 pl hardships.

necesitar (neθesi'tar) vt need, require.

necio ('neθjo) adj 1 foolish. 2 stupid. 3 imprudent. **necedad** nf 1 foolishness. 2 stupidity. 3 nonsense.

nefasto (ne'fasto) adj unlucky, ill-fated.

negar (ie) (ne'gar) vt deny, refuse. **negación** nf 1 negation. 2 denial. **negativa** nf 1 negation. 2 denial, refusal. **negativo** adj 1 negative. 2 math minus. adj,nm phot negative.

negligencia (negli'xenθja) nf negligence. **negligente** adj negligent.

negociar (nego'θjar) vt negotiate, trade. **negociante** nm businessman. **negocio** nm business, transaction.

negro ('negro) adj 1 black. 2 Negro. nm Negro. **negroide** adj negroid. **negrura** nf blackness.

nene ('nene) nm baby.

nenúfar (ne'nufar) nm waterlily.

nervio ('nerβjo) nm 1 nerve. 2 anat tendon. **tener los nervios en punta** be on edge. **tener nervio** be brave. **nerviosidad** nf nervousness. **nervioso** adj nervous, edgy. **crisis nerviosa** nf nervous breakdown.

neto ('neto) adj 1 clear, neat. 2 comm net.

neumático (neu'matiko) adj pneumatic. nm tyre.

neurótico (neu'rotiko) adj,nm neurotic.

neutro ('neutro) adj 1 neutral. 2 neuter.

nevar (ie) (ne'βar) vi snow. **nevada** nf snowfall. **nevado** adj snow-covered.

nevera (ne'βera) nf refrigerator.

ni (ni) conj neither, nor.

nicho ('nitʃo) nm niche.

nido ('niðo) nm nest.

niebla ('njeβla) nf fog.

nieto ('njeto) nm 1 grandson. 2 pl grandchildren.

nieve (njeβe) nf snow.

nilón (ni'lon) nm nylon.

ninguno (nin'guno) adj, pron also **ningún** no, no-one, not any.

niña ('niɲa) nf 1 girl. 2 anat pupil. **niñez** nf childhood. **niño** adj 1 young. 2 childish. nm boy, child.

níquel ('nikel) nm nickel.

nítido ('nitiðo) adj bright, clear.

nitrógeno (ni'troxeno) nm nitrogen.

nivelar (niβe'lar) vt make level. **nivel** nm level.

no (no) adv no, not.

noble ('noβle) adj noble. nm nobleman. **nobleza** nf nobility.

noción (no'θjon) nf 1 notion, idea. 2 pl rudiments.

nocivo (no'θiβo) adj harmful.

nocturno (nok'turno) adj night, nocturnal. nm mus nocturne.

noche ('notʃe) nf night. **Nochebuena** nf Christmas Eve. **Nochevieja** nf New Year's Eve.

nogal (no'gal) nm walnut tree.

nómada ('nomaða) adj nomadic. nm,f nomad.

nombrar (nom'brar) vt 1 name. 2 nominate. 3 mention. **nombramiento** nm nomination, appointment. **nombre** nm 1 name. 2 noun. **nombre artístico** pseudonym. **nombre de pila** Christian name.

nómina ('nomina) nf 1 list. 2 comm payroll.

non (non) adj math odd. nm odd number.

nonagésimo (nona'xesimo) adj ninetieth.

nordeste (nor'ðeste) nm 1 northeast. 2 northeaster (wind).

noria ('norja) nf waterwheel.

norma ('norma) nf norm, rule. **normal** adj normal, regular. **normalidad** nf normality.

noroeste (noro'este) adj nm northwest. nm 1 northwest. 2 northwester (wind).

norte ('norte) adj,nm north.

Noruega (no'rwega) nf Norway. **noruego** adj 1 Norwegian. 2 Norse. nm 1 Norwegian (man). 2 Norseman. 3 Norwegian (language).

nos (nos) pron 1st pers pl us, ourselves.

nosotros (no'sotros) pron 1st pers pl 1 we. 2 us, ourselves.

nostalgia (nos'talxja) nf nostalgia. **nostálgico** adj 1 homesick. 2 nostalgic.

notar (no'tar) vt 1 note, notice, perceive. 2 note down. **nota** nf 1 note, memo. 2 comm account. 3 educ grade, marks. 4 mus note. **notable** adj notable.

notario (no'tarjo) nm notary. **notaría** nf notary's office.

noticiar (noti'θjar) vt notify. **noticiero** adj

containing news. **nm** newspaper. **noticia(s)** nf (pl) news, information.

notificar (notifi'kar) vt notify, inform.

notorio (no'torjo) adj notorious, well-known.

novato (no'βato) adj inexperienced. **nm** novice.

novedad (noβe'ðað) nf 1 newness. 2 novelty. 3 latest news or fashion.

novela (no'βela) nf novel. **novelesco** adj 1 fictional. 2 fantastic, unbelievable. **novelista** nm,f novelist.

noveno (no'βeno) adj ninth.

noventa (no'βenta) adj ninety.

novia ('noβja) nf 1 girlfriend, fiancée. 2 bride. **noviazgo** nm engagement, betrothal.

novicio (no'βiθjo) nm 1 beginner, novice. 2 rel novice.

noviembre (no'βjembre) nm November.

novilla (no'βiʎa) nf heifer. **novillada** nf bullfight for novice bullfighters and young bulls. **novillero** nm novice bullfighter. **novillo** nm bullock. **hacer novillos** play truant.

nube ('nuβe) nf cloud. **por las nubes 1** astronomical (prices, figures, etc.). 2 (praise, etc.) to the skies. **estar en las nubes** be daydreaming.

nublado (nu'βlaðo) adj cloudy, overcast.

núcleo ('nukleo) nm 1 nucleus. 2 core. 3 bot kernel, stone.

nudillo (nu'ðiʎo) nm knuckle.

nudo ('nuðo) nm knot.

nuera ('nwera) nf daughter-in-law.

nuestro ('nwestro) poss adj our.

nueva ('nweβa) nf piece of news.

Nueva Zelanda ('nweβa θe'landa) nf New Zealand.

nueve ('nweβe) adj,nm nine.

nuez (nweθ) nf bot nut, walnut. **nuez de la garganta** Adam's Apple.

nulidad (nuli'ðað) nf nullity. **nulo** adj null, nil.

numerar (nume'rar) vt number. **numeral** adj,nm numeral.

número ('numero) nm 1 number. 2 quantity. 3 size. **numérico** adj numerical. **numeroso** adj numerous.

nunca ('nunka) adv 1 never. 2 ever. ¡**nunca jamás!** not on your life! never! **más que nunca** more than ever.

nuncio ('nunθjo) nm nuncio.

nupcial (nup'θjal) adj nuptial. **nupcias** nf pl wedding.

nutria ('nutrja) nf otter.

nutrir (nu'trir) vt feed, nourish. **nutritivo** adj nutritious.

Ñ

ñaque ('ɲake) nm junk.

ñoño ('ɲoɲo) adj 1 doddery. 2 characterless. 3 timid. **ñoñería** nf also **ñoñez** 1 senility. 2 lack of character. 3 shyness.

O

o (o) conj or. **o...o** either...or.

oasis (o'asis) nm oasis.

obcecar (oβθe'kar) vt blind, deceive. **obcecación** nf blindness, stubbornness.

obedecer* (oβeðe'θer) vt,vi obey.

obediencia (oβe'ðjenθja) nf obedience. **obediente** adj obedient.

obertura (oβer'tura) nf overture.

obesidad (oβesi'ðað) nf obesity. **obeso** adj obese.

obispo (o'βispo) nm bishop. **obispado** nm bishopric.

objetar (oβxe'tar) vt,vi object (to). **objeción** nf objection. **objetividad** nf objectivity. **objetivo** adj,nm objective. **objeto** nm object. **objetor** nm objector.

oblicuo (o'βlikwo) adj oblique.

obligar (oβli'gar) vt oblige, compel, force. **obligarse** vr agree, promise to do something. **obligación** nf obligation.

obrar (o'βrar) vt 1 work, operate. 2 make, construct, build. 3 put into practice. vi 1 work. 2 behave, act. **obra** nf work. **obra maestra** masterpiece. **obrero** adj working. nm workman.

obsceno (oβs'θeno) adj obscene. **obscenidad** nf obscenity.

obscurecer* (oβskure'θer) vt also **oscurecer** obscure, darken. vi grow dark. **obscuridad** nf obscurity, darkness. **obscuro** adj obscure, dark.

obsequiar (oβseki'ar) vt 1 shower with gifts. 2 give a present to. **obsequio** nm 1 gift. 2 courtesy. **obsequioso** adj attentive.

observar (oβser'βar) vt observe. **observación** nf observation. **observador** nm observer. **observancia** nf observance. **observante** adj observant, observing. **observatorio** nm observatory.

obsesión (oβse'sjon) nf obsession. **obsesionante** adj obsessive. **obseso** adj obsessed.

obstáculo (oβs'takulo) nm obstacle.

obstante (oβs'tante) prep in spite of. **no obstante** nevertheless, however.

obstar (oβs'tar) vi oppose, obstruct.

obstetricia (obste'triθja) nf obstetrics.

obstinarse (oβsti'narse) vr be obstinate, stand firm. **obstinación** nf obstinacy. **obstinado** adj obstinate.

obstruir* (oβstru'ir) vt 1 obstruct. 2 seal up, stop up. **obstrucción** nf obstruction. **obstructivo** adj obstructive. **obstructor** adj obstructing.

obtener* (oβte'ner) vt obtain.

obturar (oβtu'rar) vt plug, stop up. **obturador** nm 1 stopper. 2 mot choke.

obtuso (oβ'tuso) adj obtuse.

obvio (' oββjo) adj obvious.

oca ('oka) nf goose.

ocasión (oka'sjon) nf 1 occasion. 2 opportunity, chance. **ocasional** adj accidental.

ocasionar (okasjo'nar) vt 1 cause. 1 stir up, excite. 2 endanger.

ocaso (o'kaso) nm 1 sunset. 2 west. 3 decline.

occidental (okθiðen'tal) adj western, occidental. **occidente** nm west, occident.

océano (o'θeano) nm ocean.

ocio ('oθjo) nm 1 idleness. 2 leisure. **ociosidad** nf idleness. **ocioso** adj idle. nm idler.

ocre ('okre) nm ochre.

octágono (ok'tagono) adj octagonal. nm octagon.

octava (ok'taβa) nf octave.

octavo (ok'taβo) adj eighth.

octogésimo (okto'xesimo) adj eightieth.

octubre (ok'tuβre) nm October.

ocular (oku'lar) adj ocular. nm 1 lens. 2 eye-piece. **oculista** nm,f oculist.

ocultar (okul'tar) vt conceal. **ocultación** nf concealment. **ocultista** adj,nm,f occultist. **oculto** adj hidden, unknown.

ocupar (oku'par) vt occupy. **ocuparse con** be engaged in. **ocupación** nf occupation. **ocupado** adj occupied, busy. **ocupante** adj occupying. nm occupant.

ocurrir (okur'rir) vi occur. **ocurrencia** nf 1 occurrence. 2 witticism. 3 bright idea. **ocurrente** adj witty, clever.

ochenta (o'tʃenta) adj,nm eighty.

ocho ('otʃo) adj,nm eight.

odiar (o'ðjar) vt hate. **odio** nm hate. **odiosidad** nf odiousness. **odioso** adj odious, hateful. nm detestable person.

odorífero (oðo'rifero) adj odoriferous, fragrant.

oeste (o'este) nm 1 west. 2 westerly wind.

ofender (ofen'der) vt offend.

ofensa (o'fensa) nf offence, insult. **ofensiva** nf mil offensive. **ofensivo** adj offensive. **ofensor** adj offending. nm offender.

oferta (o'ferta) nf 1 offer. 2 comm supply.

oficial (ofi'θjal) adj official. nm officer, official.

oficina (ofi'θina) nf office.

oficio (o'fiθjo) nm job, work, duty.

oficioso (ofi'θjoso) adj 1 unofficial, informal. 2 helpful, attentive. 3 officious, intrusive.

ofrecer* (ofre'θer) vt offer. **ofrecerse** vr volunteer, offer one's services. **¿qué se le ofrece?** what would you like? **ofrecimiento** nm offer.

ofrendar (ofren'dar) vt give, contribute. **ofrenda** nf offering, gift

ofuscar (ofus'kar) vt blind, dazzle.

oída (o'iða) nf hearing. **oíble** adj audible. **oído** nm 1 ear. 2 hearing.

oigo (o'igo) v see **oír.**

oír* (o'ir) vt hear.

ojal (o'xal) nm buttonhole.

ojalá (oxa'la) interj let's hope so! if only it would! conj if only, I hope.

ojear[1] (oxe'ar) vt eye, examine. **ojeada** nf glance.

ojear[2] (oxe'ar) vt 1 drive, chase away. 2 beat (in hunting).

ojo ('oxo) nm 1 eye. 2 span (of a bridge). **¡ojo!** interj look out! **ojo de la llave** keyhole.

ola ('ola) nf wave.

olé (o'le) interj bravo!

óleo ('oleo) nm Art, rel oil. **oleoducto** nm pipeline. **oleosidad** nf oiliness.

oler (ue) (o'ler) vt,vi smell.

olfatear (olfate'ar) vt sniff, smell at.

oliva (o'liba) nf olive.

olmo ('olmo) nf elm tree.

olor (o'lor) nm smell. **oloroso** adj fragrant.

olvidar (olβi'ðar) vt forget. **olvidadizo** adj forgetful. **olvido** nm 1 forgetfulness. 2 oblivion.

olla ('oʎa) nf 1 cul pan, pot. 2 cul meat and vegetable stew. 3 eddy, whirlpool. **olla exprés** pressure cooker.

ombligo (om'bligo) nm 1 navel. 2 umbilical cord.

ominoso (omi'noso) adj ominous.

omisión (omi'sjon) nf 1 omission. 2 neglect. **omiso** adj careless.

omitir (omi'tir) vt omit.

ómnibus ('omniβus) nm omnibus.

omnipotencia (omnipo'tenθja) nf omnipotence. **ommipotente** adj omnipotent.

once ('onθe) adj, nm eleven.

onda ('onda) nf wave. **ondear** vt wave. vi wave, undulate. **ondearse** vr swing.

ondular (ondu'lar) vt wave. vi undulate. **ondulado** adj undulating. nm wave (of hair).

oneroso (one'roso) adj onerous.

onza ('onθa) nf ounce.

opaco (o'pako) adj 1 opaque. 2 dull.

opción (op'θjon) nf option.

ópera ('opera) nf opera.

operar (ope'rar) vt,vi operate. **operable** adj operable. **operación** nf operation. **operario** nm operator, worker. **operativo** adj operative.

opinar (opi'nar) vi judge, give an opinion. **opinión** nf opinion.

opio ('opjo) nm opium.

oponer* (opo'ner) vt 1 oppose, resist. 2 hinder. 3 contradict, dispute. **oponerse a** compete for.

oportunidad (oportuni'ðað) nf opportunity. **oportunista** nm,f opportunist. **oportuno** adj opportune.

oposición (oposi'θjon) nf 1 opposition. 2 pl competition for a post.

opresión (opre'sjon) nf oppression. **opresivo** adj oppressive. **opresor** nm oppressor.

oprimir (opri'mir) vt 1 oppress. 2 depress, press down.

optar (op'tar) vt,vi opt, choose. **optante** nm chooser. **optativo** adj optional. nm gram optative.

óptico ('optiko) adj optic, optical. nm optician.

optimismo (opti'mismo) nm optimism. **optimista** adj optimistic. nm optimist.

óptimo ('optimo) adj optimum, best.

opuesto (o'pwesto) adj opposed, opposite.

opulencia (opu'lenθja) nf opulence. **opulento** adj opulent.

oquedad (oke'ðað) nf 1 hollow, cavity. 2 hollowness (of words, etc).

oráculo (o'rakulo) nm oracle.

orador (ora'ðor) nm orator, public speaker.

orar (o'rar) vi 1 pray, harangue. vt beg, plead. **oración** nf 1 prayer. 2 oration, speech. 3 gram sentence. **oracional** nm prayer book.

orbe ('orβe) nm orb, sphere.

órbita ('orβita) nf orbit. **orbitar** vt orbit.

orden ('orðen) nm order, sequence. nf order, command.

ordenar (orðe'nar) vt 1 order, command. 2 put

in order, tidy. 3 ordain. **ordenación** nf 1 arrangement, order, array. 2 ordinance. **ordenanza** nf 1 order, method. 2 statute, law. 3 command. nm mil orderly.

ordeñar (orðe'nar) vt milk.

ordinal (orði'nal) adj,nm ordinal.

ordinario (orði'narjo) adj ordinary. **ordinariez** nf vulgarity.

oreja (o'rexa) nf 1 ear. 2 flap of shoe.

orfebre (or'feβre) nm goldsmith, silversmith. **orfebrería** nf gold or silver work.

orfeón (orfe'on) nm choral society.

orgánico (or'ganiko) adj organic.

organismo (orga'nismo) nm organism.

organizar (organi'θar) vt organize. **organización** nf organization. **organizado** adj 1 well-organized. 2 sci organic. **organizador** adj organizing.

órgano ('organo) nm organ. **organista** nf organist.

orgía (or'xia) nf also **orgia** orgy.

orgullo (or'ɣuʎo) nm pride. **orgulloso** adj proud.

orientarse (orjen'tarse) vr find one's bearings. **orientación** nf orientation.

oriente (o'rjente) nm orient. **oriental** adj oriental, eastern.

orificio (ori'fiθjo) nm orifice, hole.

origen (o'rixen) nm origin.

original (orixi'nal) adj,nm original. **originador** nm originator. **originalidad** nf originality. **originar** vt,vi originate.

orilla (o'riʎa) nf edge, border.

oriundo (o'rjundo) adj native of, originating from.

orlar (or'lar) vt border, edge. **orla** nf border, trimming.

ornamentar (ornamen'tar) vt adorn, decorate. **ornamentación** nf ornamentation. **ornamento** nm ornament.

ornato (or'nato) nm ornament, adornment.

ornitología (ornitolo'xia) nf ornithology.

oro ('oro) nm gold. **oro batido** gold leaf. **oropel** nm tinsel.

orquesta (or'kesta) nf also **orquestra** orchestra. **orquestación** nf orchestration. **orquestar** vt orchestrate.

orquídea (or'kiðea) nf orchid.

ortiga (or'tiga) nf nettle.

ortodoxo (orto'ðokso) adj orthodox. **ortodoxia** nf orthodoxy.

ortografía (ortogra'fia) nf orthography, spelling.

oruga (o'ruga) nf caterpillar.

os (os) pron 2nd pers pl you.

osa ('osa) nf she-bear. **Osa Mayor** Ursa Major.

osadía (osa'ðia) nf daring, boldness. **osado** adj daring, bold. **osar** vi dare.

oscilar (osθi'lar) vi oscillate, swing. **oscilación** nf oscillation.

oscuro (os'kuro) adj dark, obscure, dull.

ostensible (osten'siβle) adj ostensible, apparent. **ostentación** nf ostentation, show. **ostentativo** adj also **ostentoso** ostentatious.

ostentar (osten'tar) vt show, display.

ostra ('ostra) nf oyster.

otear (ote'ar) vt make out, perceive.

otoño (o'toɲo) nm autumn.

otorgar (otor'gar) vt grant, confer.

otro ('otro) adj,pron 1 s another. 2 pl other.

ovación (oβa'θjon) nf ovation. **ovacionar** vt applaud.

óvalo ('oβalo) nm oval.

ovario (o'βarjo) nm ovary.

oveja (o'βexa) nf sheep, ewe. nm ram. **ovejuno** adj sheep.

ovillo (o'βiʎo) nm 1 ball (of wool, etc.). 2 tangle.

oxidar (oksi'ðar) vt rust.

óxido ('oksiðo) nm oxide.

oxígeno (ok'sixeno) nm oxygen.

oye ('oje) v see **oír**.

oyente (o'jente) nm,f 1 listener. 2 educ unregistered student. adj hearing.

P

pabellón (paβe'ʎon) nm 1 pavilion. 2 bell tent. 3 flag. 4 ward, hospital wing.

pacer (pa'θer) vt,vi graze, pasture.

paciencia (pa'θjenθja) nf patience. **paciente** adj,n patient. **pacienzudo** adj patient, long-suffering.

pacificar (paθifi'kar) vt pacify, calm. **pacificación** nf pacification. **pacificador** adj pacifying, peace-making.

pacífico (pa'θifiko) adj pacific, peaceful. **el Océano Pacífico** the Pacific Ocean. **pacifismo** nm pacifism.

pacotilla (pako'tiʎa) nf inferior merchandise, junk. **de pacotilla** of poor quality, shoddy.

pactar (pak'tar) vt,vi agree, make a pact. **pacto** nm pact, agreement, covenant.

padecer* (paðe'θer) vt,vi suffer. **padecimiento** nm suffering.

padrastro (pa'ðrastro) nm stepfather.

padre ('paðre) nm 1 father. 2 pl parents. **padrenuestro** nm Lord's prayer. **padrino** nm 1 godfather. 2 best man. 3 patron. 4 pl godparents. **padrinazgo** nm 1 act of being a godfather, best man, sponsor, etc. 2 patronage, sponsorship.

padrón (pa'ðron) nm 1 poll, census. 2 tech pattern. 3 blot, disgrace. 4 inf indulgent father.

paga ('paga) nf payment, pay. **pagadero** adj payable, due. **pagado** adj 1 paid. 2 self satisfied. **pago** adj paid, paid up. nm payment.

pagano (pa'gano) adj,nm pagan.

pagar (pa'gar) vt,vi 1 pay. 2 atone for. **pagarse** vr 1 be content with. 2 be conceited about.

página ('paxina) nf page.

país (pa'is) nm 1 country. 2 region.

paisaje (pai'saxe) nm countryside, scenery.

paisano (pai'sano) adj of the same country. nm fellow countryman. **vestido de paisano** in civilian clothes, in mufti.

paja ('paxa) nf straw.

pájaro ('paxaro) nm bird.

paje ('paxe) nm pageboy.

Pakistán (pakis'tan) nm Pakistan. **Pakistaní** adj,n Pakistani.

pala ('pala) nf shovel, scoop.

palabra (pa'labra) nf word.

palacio (pa'laθjo) nm 1 palace. 2 mansion.

paladar (pala'ðar) nm palate.

paladear (palaðe'ar) vt taste, savour.

palanca (pa'lanka) nf 1 lever, crowbar. 2 inf influence.

palangana (palan'gana) nf washbasin.

palco ('palko) nm Th box.

Palestina (pales'tina) nf Palestine.

paleta (pa'leta) nf 1 shovel, trowel. 2 Art palette. 3 tech blade, vane. 4 anat shoulder blade.

paliar (pali'ar) vt alleviate.

palidecer* (paliðe'θer) vi become pale. **palidez** nf paleness.

pálido ('paliðo) adj pale, pallid.

palillo (pa'liʎo) nm 1 toothpick. 2 small stick.

paliza (pa'liθa) nf beating.

palma ('palma) nf 1 anat palm. 2 palm tree. **palmada** nf light blow, slap. **dar palmas** clap, applaud.

palmatoria (palma'torja) nf 1 candlestick. 2 cane.

palmo ('palmo) nm measure of approx. 21

cms. **palmo a palmo** inch by inch, little by little.

paloma (pa'loma) *nf* 1 dove. 2 pigeon. **palomar** *nm* dovecote.

palpable (pal'paβle) *adj* palpable, tangible.

palpar (pal'par) *vt* touch, feel.

palpitar (palpi'tar) *vi* palpitate, throb. **palpitación** *nf* throb, palpitation.

paludismo (palu'δismo) *nm* malaria.

palurdo (pa'lurδo) *adj, nm* rustic.

palustre[1] (pa'lustre) *adj* marshy.

palustre[2] (pa'lustre) *nm* trowel.

pan (pan) *nm* 1 bread. 2 loaf.

pana ('pana) *nf* 1 velveteen. 2 corduroy.

panal (pa'nal) *nm* honeycomb.

Panamá (pana'ma) *nm* Panama.

pancarta (pan'karta) *nf* placard.

pandereta (pande'reta) *nf* tambourine.

pandilla (pan'diλa) *nf* group, gang.

pánico ('paniko) *adj, nm* panic.

pantalón (panta'lon) *nm also* **pantalones** trousers.

pantalla (pan'taλa) *nf* 1 screen. 2 lampshade.

pantano (pan'tano) *nm* 1 marsh, bog. 2 reservoir, lake. **pantanal** *nm* marshland. **pantanoso** *adj* marshy.

pantera (pan'tera) *nf* panther.

pantorrilla (pantor'riλa) *nf anat* calf.

panza ('panθa) *nf* belly.

pañal (pa'ɲal) *nm* nappy.

pañería (paɲe'ria) *nf* drapery. **pañero** *nm* draper. **pañete** *nm* light cloth. **paño** *nm* cloth.

pañuelo (pa'ɲwelo) *nm* 1 headscarf. 2 handkerchief.

papa[1] ('papa) *nm* pope.

papa[2] ('papa) *nf* potato.

papá (pa'pa) *nm inf* dad, daddy.

papada (pa'paδa) *nf* double chin.

papagayo (papa'gajo) *nm* parrot.

papamoscas (papa'moskas) *nm invar* 1 *zool* fly catcher. 2 simpleton.

papel (pa'pel) *nm* paper. **papeleo** *nm* 1 paper work. 2 *inf* red tape. **papelera** *nf* 1 wastepaper basket. 2 desk. **papelería** *nf* 1 stationery. 2 stationer's shop.

papera (pa'pera) *nf* 1 goitre. 2 *pl* mumps.

paquete (pa'kete) *nm* packet.

par (par) *adj* equal, even. *nm* pair. **pares y nones** odds or evens.

para ('para) *prep* for, to. **¿para qué?** why? what for?

parabrisas (para'βrisas) *nm invar* windscreen.

paracaídas (paraka'iδas) *nm invar* parachute. **paracaidista** *nm* parachutist.

parachoques (para'tʃokes) *nm invar* 1 *mot* bumper. 2 shock absorber.

parada (pa'raδa) *nf* 1 stop, stopping place. 2 stoppage, shutdown. 3 *mil* parade. **paradero** *nm* 1 stopping place. 2 lodgings. 3 whereabouts. **parado** *adj* 1 motionless, stopped. 2 unemployed.

paradoja (para'δoxa) *nf* paradox. **paradójico** *adj* paradoxical.

parador (para'δor) *nm* tourist hotel.

parafina (para'fina) *nf* paraffin wax.

paráfrasis (pa'rafrasis) *nf invar* paraphrase.

paraguas (pa'ragwas) *nm invar* umbrella.

paraíso (para'iso) *nm* 1 paradise. 2 *Th* gallery, the gods.

paralela (para'lela) *nf* parallel. **paralelo** *adj, nm* parallel.

parálisis (pa'ralisis) *nf* paralysis. **paralítico** *adj, nm* paralytic. **paralizar** *vt* paralyse.

páramo ('paramo) *nm* wilderness, waste land, moor.

parangón (paran'gon) *nm* 1 comparison. 2 paragon, model.

parapeto (para'peto) *nm* 1 parapet. 2 barricade.

parar (pa'rar) *vt, vi* stop, halt. **parar en mal** come to a bad end.

pararrayos (parar'rajos) *nm invar* lightning conductor.

parásito (pa'rasito) *adj* parasitic. *nm* parasite.

parasol (para'sol) *nm* parasol.

parcela (par'θela) *nf* plot of land.

parcial (par'θjal) *adj* partial. **parcialidad** *nf* 1 partiality, bias. 2 group, faction.

parco ('parko) *adj* frugal, sparing.

pardo ('parδo) *adj* brown, dark.

parecer[*] (pare'θer) *vi* appear, seem. **parecerse** *vr* resemble. ~*nm* opinion. **parecido** *adj* similar, like. *nm* resemblance.

pared (pa'red) *nf* (interior) wall.

pareja (pa'rexa) *nf* 1 pair, couple. 2 partner.

parentela (paren'tela) *nf* 1 relations. 2 parentage. **parentesco** *nm* kinship, relationship.

paréntesis (pa'rentesis) *nm invar* parenthesis, bracket.

paridad (pari'δaδ) *nf* 1 parity, equality. 2 comparison.

pariente (pa'rjente) *nm* relative.

parir (pa'rir) *vt, vi* bear, give birth.

París (pa'ris) *nm* Paris.

parla ('parla) *nf* chatter, gossip.

parlamentar (parlamen'tar) *vi* 1 converse. 2

parley. **parlamentario** adj parliamentary. nm member of parliament. **parlamento** nm parliament.

parlanchín (parlan'tʃin) adj gossipy, indiscreet. nm talkative person, gossip.

parlar (par'lar) vi chatter.

paro ('paro) nm 1 stoppage, standstill. 2 unemployment.

parpadear (parpaðe'ar) vi 1 blink, wink (the eye). 2 flicker, twinkle. **parpadeo** nm wink, blink.

párpado ('parpaðo) nm eyelid.

parque ('parke) nm park.

párrafo ('parrafo) nm paragraph.

parricida (parri'θiða) nm,f parricide (person). **parricidio** nm parricide (act).

parrilla (par'riʎa) nf gridiron, cooking grill.

párroco ('parroko) nm parish priest.

parroquia (par'rokja) nf 1 parish. 2 clientele. **parroquial** adj parochial, parish. **parroquiano** nm 1 parishioner. 2 client.

parsimonia (parsi'monja) nf 1 parsimony, frugality. 2 deliberateness.

parte ('parte) nf 1 part. 2 place. 3 law party. 4 Th role. 5 report.

partición (parti'θjon) nf division, partition.

participar (partiθi'par) vt notify, inform. vi participate. **participación** nf 1 participation. 2 notice, notification. 3 comm share. **participante** nm,f participant.

partícipe (par'tiθipe) nm,f participant.

participio (parti'θipjo) nm participle.

partícula (par'tikula) nf particle.

particular (partiku'lar) adj 1 particular. 2 private. nm 1 particular, detail. 2 private individual.

particularizar (partikulari'θar) vt 1 specify, itemize. 2 single out (a person). **particularizarse** vr be characterized, distinguished. **particularidad** nf 1 particularity, characteristic. 2 intimacy.

partida (par'tiða) nf 1 departure. 2 certificate. 3 comm entry, item. 4 game (of cards, chess, etc.).

partidario (parti'ðarjo) adj partisan. nm supporter.

partido (par'tiðo) adj divided. nm 1 pol party. 2 sport game, match. **tomar partido** take sides. **sacar partido** benefit from.

partir (par'tir) vt divide, cut up. vi leave, depart. **a partir de ahora** from now on.

partitura (parti'tura) nf mus score.

parto ('parto) nm childbirth, delivery.

parvo ('parβo) adj small, little.

párvulo ('parβulo) adj 1 small. 2 humble. nm child, infant.

pasa ('pasa) nf raisin.

pasada (pa'saða) nf passage. **mala pasada** dirty trick, bad turn. **pasadero** adj tolerable, passable.

pasado (pa'saðo) adj, nm past. **la semana pasada** last week. **pasado mañana** day after tomorrow.

pasador (pasa'ðor) nm 1 fastener, pin, bolt. 2 filter. 3 pl shoelaces, cufflinks.

pasaje (pa'saxe) nm 1 passage, voyage. 2 fare. 3 passageway. **pasajero** adj transient, passing. nm passenger.

pasamano (pasa'mano) nm handrail, bannister.

pasaporte (pasa'porte) nm passport.

pasar (pa'sar) vt 1 pass, give. 2 cross. 3 pierce, penetrate. 4 spend (time). **pasarlo bien/mal** have a good/bad time. vi 1 pass, go. 2 happen, occur. **pasar por alto** overlook. **pasar de la raya** be too much, be the last straw.

pasatiempo (pasa'tjempo) nm hobby, pastime.

pascua ('paskwa) nf rel feast. **Pascua de Navidad** Christmas. **Pascua de Resurrección** Easter. **¡felices pascuas!** Merry Christmas.

pase ('pase) nm pass.

pasear (pase'ar) vt 1 take for a walk. 2 parade, exhibit. vi go for a walk or ride. **paseo** nm 1 stroll. 2 outing. 3 walk, promenade.

pasillo (pa'siʎo) nm passage, corridor.

pasión (pa'sjon) nf passion.

pasividad (pasiβi'ðað) nf passivity. **pasivo** adj passive, inactive. nm comm liabilities, debit.

pasmar (pas'mar) vt 1 astound, amaze. 2 chill (to the marrow). **pasmado** adj 1 amazed. 2 chilled. 3 idiotic. **pasmo** nm 1 astonishment. 2 chill.

paso ('paso) nm 1 step, pace. 2 geog pass. **paso a nivel** level crossing. **paso a paso** step by step.

pasta ('pasta) nf 1 paste. 2 dough, pastry. 3 pasta.

pastar (pas'tar) vt.vi graze.

pastel (pas'tel) nm 1 cake. 2 art pastel. **pastelería** nf 1 pastry shop. 2 pastry-making. 3 pastry. **pastelero** nm pastry cook.

pastilla (pas'tiʎa) nf tablet, pill.

pasto ('pasto) nm grass, fodder.

pastor (pas'tor) nm 1 shepherd. 2 clergyman.

pastorear (pastore'ar) vt 1 pasture. 2 tend (a flock).

pata ('pata) nf zool paw, leg. **meter la pata** inf put one's foot in it.

patada (pa'taða) nf 1 kick. 2 stamp.

patalear (patale'ar) vi 1 stamp. 2 kick about.

patán (pa'tan) nm yokel, oaf.

patata (pa'tata) nf potato.

patear (pate'ar) vt,vi 1 kick. 2 stamp.

patente (pa'tente) adj obvious. nm comm patent.

paternal (pater'nal) adj paternal. **paternidad** nf paternity. **paterno** adj paternal.

patético (pa'tetiko) adj 1 pathetic. 2 poignant.

patíbulo (pa'tiβulo) nm gallows.

patillas (pa'tiʎas) nf pl whiskers, sideboards.

patín (pa'tin) nm skate. **patinar** vi 1 skate. 2 skid. **patinadero** nm skating rink. **patinazo** nm 1 skid. 2 mistake.

patio ('patjo) nm courtyard, patio.

pato ('pato) nm duck.

patología (patolo'xia) nf pathology. **patológico** adj pathological. **patólogo** nm pathologist.

patraña (pa'traɲa) nf 1 tall story. 2 fib.

patria ('patrja) nf native land.

patriarca (pa'trjarka) nm patriarch.

patricio (pa'triθjo) adj,nm patrician.

patrimonio (patri'monjo) nm 1 inheritance. 2 heritage.

patriota (pa'trjota) nm,f patriot. **patriótico** adj patriotic. **patriotismo** nm patriotism.

patrocinar (patroθi'nar) vt sponsor. **patrocinador** nm sponsor. **patrocinio** nm sponsorship.

patrón (pa'tron) nm 1 patron. 2 owner. 3 pattern, model. **patronato** nm 1 patronage. 2 comm employer's association. 3 board of trustees.

patrulla (pa'truʎa) nf patrol.

paulatinamente (paulatina'mente) adv gradually.

pausa ('pausa) nf 1 pause. 2 mus rest. **pausado** adj slow, deliberate.

pauta ('pauta) nf 1 lines, guide lines. 2 ruler.

pávido ('paβiðo) adj timid, fearful.

pavimentar (paβimen'tar) vt pave, surface. **pavimento** nm pavement.

pavo ('paβo) nm turkey. **pavo real** peacock.

pavor (pa'βor) nm terror. **pavoroso** adj awesome, dreadful, terrifying.

payaso (pa'jaso) nm clown, buffoon.

paz (paθ) nf peace. **hacer las paces** make peace.

peaje (pe'axe) nm toll.

peca ('peka) nf spot, freckle.

pecar (pe'kar) vi sin. **pecado** nm sin.

pécora ('pekora) nf 1 sheep, head of sheep. 2 inf cunning or crafty woman.

peculiar (peku'ljar) adj 1 peculiar. 2 characteristic. **peculiaridad** nf 1 peculiarity. 2 characteristic.

pechera (pe'tʃera) nf front of a dress or shirt.

pecho ('petʃo) nm 1 chest, bosom. 2 courage, heart. **tomar a pecho** take to heart.

pechuga (pe'tʃuga) nf cul breast (of chickens, etc.).

pedagogía (peðago'xia) nf pedagogy. **pedagogo** nm 1 schoolmaster. 2 mentor.

pedal (pe'ðal) nm pedal.

pedante (pe'ðante) adj pedantic. nm pedant. **pedantería** nf pedantry.

pedazo (pe'ðaθo) nm piece, fragment.

pedernal (peðer'nal) nm flint.

pedestal (peðes'tal) nm pedestal.

pedestre (pe'ðestre) adj pedestrian.

pediatría (peðja'tria) nf paediatrics.

pedicuro (peði'kuro) nm chiropodist.

pedir (i) (pe'ðir) vt ask for, request. **pedido** nm comm order. **pedigüeño** adj importunate, insistent. **pedimento** nm 1 petition. 2 law claim.

pedregal (peðre'gal) nm stony ground. **pedregoso** adj stony, rocky.

pedrería (peðre'ria) nf jewels.

pedrisco (pe'ðrisko) nm hailstorm.

pegar (pe'gar) vt 1 hit, strike. 2 fasten, stick, glue. 3 med infect. vi 1 stick. 2 take effect. **pegar fuego** set fire to. **pegar un tiro** shoot. **pega** nf 1 heating. 2 trick, joke. 3 problem, difficulty. **pegajoso** adj 1 sticky. 2 med infectious.

peinar (pei'nar) vt comb. **peinado** nm coiffure. **peinador** nm 1 hairdresser. 2 dressing-gown. **peine** nm comb.

pelado (pe'laðo) adj bare, barren.

pelar (pe'lar) vt 1 peel, skin. 2 shear.

peldaño (pel'daɲo) nm step, stair.

pelear (pele'ar) vi fight, brawl, row. **pelea** nf fight, brawl. **peleador** adj quarrelsome, belligerent.

peliagudo (pelja'guðo) adj tricky, difficult.

pelícano (pe'likano) nm pelican.

película (pe'likula) nf film.

peligrar (peli'grar) vi be in danger. **peligro** nm danger. **peligroso** adj dangerous.

pelmazo (pel'maθo) nm also **pelma** 1 dull person. 2 crushed mass.

pelo ('pelo) nm hair.

pelota (pe'lota) nf ball. **en pelota** naked.

pelotón (pelo'ton) nm mil platoon, squad.

peltre ('peltre) nm pewter.

peluca (pe'luka) nf wig.

pelusa (pe'lusa) nf 1 down, fine hair. 2 inf jealousy.

pelleja (pe'ʎexa) nf also **pellejo** nm skin, hide.

pellizcar (peʎiθ'kar) vt pinch, nip. **pellizco** nm pinch, nip.

pena ('pena) nf 1 grief, sorrow. 2 penalty, punishment. 3 pain.

penal (pe'nal) adj penal. nm prison. **penalidad** nf 1 hardship. 2 law penalty.

penar (pe'nar) vt punish, penalize. vi suffer, grieve.

pender (pen'der) vi 1 hang. 2 law be pending. **pendiente** adj 1 hanging. 2 pending. nm earring. nf hill, slope.

pene ('pene) nm penis.

penetrar (pene'trar) vt penetrate, pierce. **penetrable** adj penetrable. **penetración** nf penetration. **penetrante** adj penetrating.

penicilina (peniθi'lina) nf penicillin.

península (pe'ninsula) nf peninsula.

penitencia (peni'tenθja) nf penitence, penance. **penitencial** adj penitential. **penitente** adj,n penitent.

penoso (pe'noso) adj 1 painful, distressing. 2 difficult.

pensar (ie) (pen'sar) vi think. **pensar en** think about. **pensamiento** nm thought.

pensión (pen'sjon) nf 1 pension, allowance. 2 pension, boarding house.

penúltimo (pe'nultimo) adj penultimate.

penumbra (pe'numbra) nf half-light, dimness.

penuria (pe'nurja) nf penury, scarcity.

peña ('pena) nf 1 cliff. 2 mountain top. 3 group (of friends).

peón (pe'on) nm 1 labourer. 2 foot-soldier. 3 pedestrian. 4 game pawn.

peor (pe'or) adj,adv 1 worse. 2 worst.

pepino (pe'pino) nm cucumber.

pepita (pe'pita) nf pip.

pequeño (pe'keno) adj small.

pera ('pera) nf 1 pear. 2 light switch. **peral** nm pear tree.

percance (per'kanθe) nm mishap.

percatarse (perka'tarse) vr notice.

percibir (perθi'ßir) vt 1 perceive. 2 comm earn, receive (salary). **percepción** nf 1 perception. 2 idea. 3 comm collection. **perceptible** adj 1 perceptible. 2 comm receivable. **perceptivo** adj perceptive.

percusión (perku'sjon) nf percussion.

percha ('pertʃa) nf 1 pole, support. 2 coat rack or hanger.

perder (ie) (per'ðer) vt lose. **pérdida** nf loss, waste. **perdido** adj lost.

perdiz (per'ðiθ) nf partridge.

perdonar (perðo'nar) vt pardon, excuse. **perdón** nm pardon.

perdurar (perðu'rar) vi last, endure.

perecer (pere'θer) vi perish. **perecedero** adj perishable.

peregrinar (peregri'nar) vi 1 travel, voyage. 2 rel go on a pilgrimage. **peregrino** adj 1 wandering, travelling. 2 migratory. nm pilgrim.

perejil (pere'xil) nm bot parsley.

perenne (pe'renne) adj perennial, everlasting.

perentorio (peren'torjo) adj 1 peremptory. 2 urgent. 3 decisive.

pereza (pe'reθa) nf laziness, idleness. **perezoso** adj lazy, idle.

perfección (perfek'θjon) nf perfection. **perfeccionamiento** nm perfection, improvement. **perfecto** adj perfect.

perfidia (per'fiðja) nf perfidy, treachery. **pérfido** ('perfiðo) adj perfidious, treacherous.

perfilar (perfi'lar) vt outline. **perfil** nm 1 profile. 2 outline.

perforar (perfo'rar) vt 1 perforate. 2 drill. **perforación** nf 1 perforation. 2 drilling. **perforadora** nf 1 punch. 2 drill.

perfumar (perfu'mar) vt perfume, scent. **perfume** nm perfume, scent. **perfumería** nf perfume shop.

pericia (pe'riθja) nf skill, expertise.

periferia (peri'ferja) nf periphery.

perímetro (pe'rimetro) nm perimeter.

periódico (pe'rjoðiko) adj periodic. nm 1 newspaper. 2 periodical.

periodismo (perjo'ðismo) nm journalism. **periodista** nm,f journalist. **periodístico** adj journalistic.

período (pe'rioðo) nm 1 period. 2 gram sentence.

peripecia (peri'peθja) nf 1 incident. 2 pl adventures.

perjudicar (perxuði'kar) vt 1 harm. 2 prejudice.

perjuicio (per'xwiθjo) nm harm, damage, detriment.

perjurar (perxu'rar) vi 1 perjure oneself. 2 swear, curse.

perla ('perla) nf pearl.

permanecer (permane'θer) vi remain, stay.

permanencia (perma'nenθja) nf 1 permanence.

2 stay. **permanente** adj permanent. nf perm (hairdressing).

permiso (per'miso) nm 1 permission. 2 permit, licence. 3 leave. **con permiso** excuse me, if I may. **permisible** adj permissible. **permisivo** adj permissive.

permitir (permi'tir) vt permit, allow. **no permite?** may I?

permutar (permu'tar) vt 1 math permute. 2 exchange. **permuta** nf barter, exchange. **permutación** nf permutation.

pernicioso (perni'θjoso) adj pernicious, injurious.

pernoctar (pernok'tar) vi stay overnight.

pero ('pero) conj but, yet.

perogrullada (perogru'ʎaða) nf platitude.

perorar (pero'rar) vi make a speech.

perpendicular (perpendiku'lar) adj,nf perpendicular.

perpetrar (perpe'trar) vt perpetrate. **perpetración** nf perpetration.

perpetuar (perpe'twar) vt perpetuate. **perpetuidad** nf perpetuity. **perpetuo** adj perpetual.

perplejidad (perplexi'ðað) nf 1 perplexity. 2 hesitation. **perplejo** adj bewildered, perplexed.

perro ('perro) nm dog.

persecución (perseku'θjon) nf 1 pursuit, chase, hunt. 2 persecution.

perseguir (perse'gir) vt 1 pursue, chase, hunt down. 2 persecute.

perseverar (perseβe'rar) vi persevere. **perseverancia** nf perseverance, persistence. **perseverante** adj persevering, persistent.

persiana (per'sjana) nf 1 Venetian blind. 2 shutter.

persistir (persis'tir) vi persist. **persistencia** nf persistence. **persistente** adj persistent.

persona (per'sona) nf person. **personaje** nm 1 personage, celebrity. 2 Th character. **personal** adj personal. nm personnel. **personalidad** nf personality.

personarse (perso'narse) vr appear in person.

personificar (personifi'kar) vt personify, embody.

perspectiva (perspek'tiβa) nf 1 perspective. 2 view, scene. 3 outlook, prospect.

perspicacia (perspi'kaθja) nf perspicacity, shrewdness. **perspicaz** adj perspicacious, shrewd.

persuadir (perswa'ðir) vt persuade. **persuasión** nf 1 persuasion. 2 conviction. **persuasivo** adj persuasive.

pertenecer (pertene'θer) vi 1 belong to. 2 pertain to. **perteneciente** adj 1 belonging, member. 2 relevant. **pertenencia** nf 1 ownership. 2 pl possessions, property.

pértiga ('pertiga) nf pole.

pertinacia (perti'naθja) nf persistence, pertinacity. **pertinaz** adj persistent, pertinacious. **pertinencia** nf relevance, pertinence. **pertinente** adj pertinent.

pertrechar (pertre'tʃar) vt supply, equip.

perturbar (pertur'βar) vt disturb, perturb. **perturbación** nf disturbance.

Perú (pe'ru) nm Peru. **peruano** adj,n Peruvian.

pervertir (ile) (perβer'tir) vt pervert, corrupt. **perversión** (perβer'sjon) nf 1 perversion. 2 wickedness. **perverso** adj perverse. **pervertido** adj perverted. nm pervert.

pesa ('pesa) nf weight. **pesadez** nf 1 weight, heaviness. 2 slowness. 3 drowsiness.

pesadilla (pesa'ðiʎa) nf nightmare.

pesado (pe'saðo) adj 1 heavy. 2 slow. 3 boring. nm boring person. **pesadumbre** nf grief, sorrow.

pésame ('pesame) nm condolence, sympathy. **mi sentido pésame** my deepest regrets or sympathy.

pesar (pe'sar) vt weigh.

pescar (pes'kar) vt 1 fish. 2 catch. **pesca** nf 1 fishing. 2 catch of fish. **pescadería** nf fish shop. **pescadero** nm fishmonger. **pescado** nm fish. **pescador** nm fisherman. **pesquería** nf fishery.

pescuezo (pes'kweθo) nm neck.

pesebre (pe'seβre) nm manger, crib.

pesimismo (pesi'mismo) nm pessimism. **pesimista** adj pessimistic. nm,f pessimist.

pésimo ('pesimo) adj terrible, extremely bad.

peso ('peso) nm 1 weight. 2 scales. 3 comm peso (currency).

pesquisa (pes'kisa) nf investigation, search.

pestañear (pestaɲe'ar) vi blink. **pestaña** nf 1 eyelash. 2 anat,bot fringe. **pestañeo** nm blink.

peste ('peste) nf plague, epidemic. **echar pestes** curse, fume. **pesticida** nm pesticide. **pestífero** adj pestiferous. 2 foul.

pestilencia (pesti'lenθja) nf 1 pestilence, plague. 2 stink, stench. **pestilente** adj 1 pestilent. 2 foul-smelling.

pestillo (pes'tiʎo) nm latch, bolt.

petaca (pe'taka) nf cigarette case.

pétalo ('petalo) nm petal.

petardo (pe'tarðo) nm firework.

107

petición (peti'θjon) nf 1 plea, request. 2 petition.

petirrojo (petir'roxo) nm robin.

peto ('peto) nm 1 bodice. 2 breastplate.

pétreo ('petreo) adj stony.

petrificar (petrifi'kar) vt petrify.

petróleo (pe'troleo) nm min oil. **petrolero** nm 1 naut tanker. 2 oilman. adj oil.

petulancia (petu'lanθja) nf 1 petulance. 2 vanity. **petulante** adj 1 petulant. 2 vain.

peyorativo (pejora'tiβo) adj pejorative.

pez (peθ) nm fish. nf pitch, tar.

pezón (pe'θon) nm 1 anat teat, nipple. 2 bot stalk.

pezuña (pe'θuɲa) nf hoof.

piadoso (pja'ðoso) adj pious, devout.

piano ('pjano) nm piano. **pianista** nm,f pianist.

piar (pjar) vi cheep, chirp.

piara ('pjara) nf herd, drove (esp. of pigs).

picadillo (pika'ðiʎo) nm minced meat.

picante (pi'kante) adj 1 cul hot, highly-seasoned. 2 sharp, piquant.

picaporte (pika'porte) nm 1 doorlatch. 2 door knocker.

picar (pi'kar) vt 1 prick, sting. 2 chop (meat). **picarse** vr 1 go rotten. 2 be piqued or annoyed. **picado** adj 1 minced, chopped. 2 perforated. 3 bitten, stung. 4 offended. **picador** nm picador (bullfight). **picadura** nf 1 prick. 2 bite, sting.

picardía (pikar'ðia) nf mischief, roguery.

pícaro ('pikaro) nm scoundrel. adj inf naughty. **picaresco** adj lit picaresque.

pico ('piko) nm 1 beak, spout. 2 peak. 3 pickaxe.

picotear (pikote'ar) vt peck. vi inf chatter. **picotero** adj, n chatterbox.

pichón (pi'tʃon) nm pigeon.

pie (pje) nm 1 foot. 2 bottom. **al pie de la letra** literally, word for word. **dar pie a/para** give cause to/for. **en pie de** on the basis of.

piedad (pje'ðað) nf 1 piety. 2 pity.

piedra ('pjeðra) nf stone.

piel (pjel) nf skin.

pienso ('pjenso) nm fodder.

pierna ('pjerna) nf leg.

pieza ('pjeθa) nf 1 piece, part. 2 roll (of material). **quedarse de una sola pieza** be flabbergasted.

pigmento (pig'mento) nm pigment.

pijama (pi'xama) nm pyjamas.

pila¹ ('pila) nf 1 heap, pile. 2 battery.

pila² ('pila) nf 1 sink. 2 fountain. 3 font. **nombre de pila** Christian name.

pilar (pi'lar) nm pillar.

píldora ('pildora) nf pill.

pilón (pi'lon) nm pillar.

piloto (pi'loto) nm pilot.

piltrafa (pil'trafa) nf piece of offal, scrap.

pillar (pi'ʎar) vt inf catch. **pillaje** nm pillage, sack.

pillo ('piʎo) adj 1 villainous. 2 naughty. nm 1 villain. 2 scamp. **pillastre** nm also **pilluelo** rascal (child).

pimienta (pi'mjenta) nf pepper. **pimiento** nm pepper (vegetable). **pimentón** nm 1 red pepper. 2 paprika.

pimpollo (pim'poʎo) nm 1 sapling. 2 beauty (young person or child).

pináculo (pi'nakulo) nm pinnacle.

pinar (pi'nar) nm pine forest.

pincel (pin'θel) nm paintbrush. **pincelada** nf brush-stroke.

pinchar (pin'tʃar) vt puncture. **pincharse** vr mot have a puncture. **pinchazo** nm 1 mot puncture. 2 med injection. **pincho** nm 1 spike, skewer. 2 pl cul snacks.

pingo ('pingo) nm 1 shred, rag. 2 inf prostitute. 3 pl inf odds and ends.

pino ('pino) nm pine tree. **pinocha** nf pine needle.

pintar (pin'tar) vt paint. **pintarse** vr make oneself up. **pinta** nf 1 spot. 2 inf appearance. **pintura** nf 1 painting. 2 paint.

pinzas ('pinθas) nf pl tweezers, pincers.

pinzón (pin'θon) nm finch.

piña ('piɲa) nf 1 pineapple. 2 pine cone.

piñón (pi'ɲon) nm pinion.

pío¹ ('pio) nm chirp, chirping.

pío² ('pio) adj 1 pious. 2 merciful.

piojo ('pjoxo) nm louse.

pipa ('pipa) nf pipe.

pique ('pike) nm pique, resentment.

piqueta (pi'keta) nf pickaxe.

piquete (pi'kete) nm 1 prick, cut. 2 hole. 3 picket (of strikers).

piragua (pi'ragwa) nf canoe.

pirámide (pi'ramiðe) nf pyramid.

pirata (pi'rata) nm pirate. **piratería** nf piracy.

Pirineos (piri'neos) nm pl Pyrenees.

piropear (pirope'ar) vt pay compliments to, flatter. **piropo** nm compliment, flattery.

pirotecnia (piro'teknja) nf fireworks.

pirueta (pi'rweta) nf pirouette.

pisar (pi'sar) *vt* tread, trample. *vi* tread. **pisada** *nf* step, footprint.

piscina (pis'θina) *nf* swimming pool.

piscolabis (pisko'laβis) *nm invar inf* snack.

piso ('piso) *nm* **1** floor, storey. **2** flat, apartment.

pisotear (pisote'ar) *vt* **1** trample. **2** *inf* abuse.

pista ('pista) *nf* track. **pista de baile** dance floor.

pistola (pis'tola) *nf* **1** pistol. **2** *tech* spray. **pistolero** *nm* gunman.

pistón (pis'ton) *nm* piston.

pitar (pi'tar) *vi* whistle. **pito** *nm* whistle.

pitón (pi'ton) *nm* python.

pizarra (pi'θarra) *nf* slate, blackboard.

pizca ('piθka) *nf* **1** crumb. **2** pinch.

placa ('plaka) *nf* plate, sheet (metal, photographic, etc.).

placer* (pla'θer) *vt* please. *nm* pleasure. **placentero** *adj* pleasant.

plácido ('plaθiðo) *adj* placid.

plagar (pla'gar) *vt* plague. **plaga** *nf* plague, pest.

plagiar (pla'xjar) *vt* plagiarize. **plagio** *nm* plagiarism, copy.

plan (plan) *nm* **1** plan. **2** basis.

plana ('plana) *nf* **1** page. **2** trowel. **en primera plana 1** on the front page. **2** important.

plancton ('plankton) *nm* plankton.

planchar (plan'tʃar) *vt* iron (clothes). **plancha** *nf* **1** iron. **2** plate (printing). **3** slab (concrete).

planear (plane'ar) *vt* plan. *vi* glide. **planeador** *nm* glider.

planeta (pla'neta) *nm* planet.

planicie (pla'niθje) *nf* level, flat surface.

planificar (planifi'kar) *vt* plan. **planificación** *nf* planning. **planificación familiar** family planning.

plano ('plano) *adj* flat, level. *nm* **1** plane, dimension. **2** plan, diagram. **3** *phot* shot, angle. **primer plano** foreground (picture).

plantar (plan'tar) *vt* plant, set up. **plantarse** *vr* establish oneself. **planta** *nf* **1** plant. **2** ground plan. **3** *anat* sole. **4** *tech* plant. **plantación** *nf* plantation. **plante** *nm* programme. **plantío** *nm* **1** planting. **2** land planted or ready to be planted. **plantón** *nm* **1** *bot* seedling. **2** *mil* sentry.

plantear (plante'ar) *vt* put, pose (question, etc.).

plantel (plan'tel) *nm bot* nursery.

plantilla (plan'tiʎa) *nf* **1** sole (of shoe). **2** template.

plasma ('plasma) *nm* plasma.

plástico ('plastiko) *adj,nm* plastic.

plata ('plata) *nf* silver.

plataforma (plata'forma) *nf* **1** platform. **2** oil rig. **3** *Th* stage.

plátano ('platano) *nm* **1** banana. **2** plane tree.

platea (pla'tea) *nf Th* orchestra pit.

platear (plate'ar) *vt* silverplate. **platero** *nm* silversmith.

plática ('platika) *nf* talk, chat.

platillo (pla'tiʎo) *nm* saucer.

platino (pla'tino) *nm* platinum.

plato ('plato) *nm* **1** plate. **2** *cul* course. **un plato típico** a local delicacy.

platónico (pla'toniko) *adj* platonic.

playa ('plaja) *nf* **1** beach. **2** seaside.

plaza ('plaθa) *nf* **1** town square. **2** place, seat.

plazo ('plaθo) *nm* **1** time limit. **2** *comm* instalment. **comprar a plazos** buy on hire-purchase.

pleamar (plea'mar) *nf* high tide.

plebe ('pleβe) *nf* proletariat. **plebeyo** *adj* proletarian.

plegar (ie) (ple'gar) *vt* fold. **plegable** *adj* pliable, folding.

pleitear (pleite'ar) *vi* start legal proceedings. **pleito** *nm* lawsuit.

plenitud (pleni'tuð) *nf* fullness. **pleno** *adj* complete.

pliego ('pljego) *nm* **1** sheaf of papers. **2** folder.

pliegue ('pljege) *nm* **1** crease. **2** pleat, tuck.

plomo ('plomo) *nm* **1** lead, plumb. **2** *tech* fuse-wire.

pluma ('pluma) *nf* **1** feather. **2** pen. **plumaje** *nm* plumage.

plural (plu'ral) *adj,nm* plural.

pluscuamperfecto (pluskwamper'fekto) *nm* pluperfect.

poblar (ue) (po'βlar) *vt* populate, inhabit. **población** *nf* **1** population. **2** village. **poblado** *nm* built-up area.

pobre ('poβre) *adj* poor. *nm* pauper. **pobreza** *nf* poverty.

pocilga (po'θilga) *nf* pigsty.

poción (po'θjon) *nf* potion.

poco ('poko) *adj* **1** little (quantity). **2** *pl* few. **poco** or **un poco** *adv* a little, not much. **poco a poco** gradually. **poco interesante** not very interesting. **por poco** nearly.

podar (po'ðar) *vt* prune. **podadera** *nf* pruning shears.

poder (ue) (po'ðer) *vi* **1** can, be able. **2** be possible. **poder** *nm* power. **poderío** *nm* authority. **poderoso** *adj* powerful. **no puedo**

más I can do no more. **no puedo menos** I can't help it. **puede ser** maybe.

poema (po'ema) *nm* poem. **poesía** *nf* 1 poetry. 2 poem. **poeta** *nm* poet. **poética** *nf* art of poetry, poetics. **poético** *adj* poetic.

polaco (po'lako) *adj* Polish. *nm* 1 Pole. 2 Polish (language).

polaridad (polari'ðað) *nf* polarity.

polea (po'lea) *nf* pulley.

polémica (po'lemika) *nf* polemic, argument.

polen ('polen) *nm* pollen.

policía (poli'θia) *nm* policeman. *nf* police force. **policíaco** *adj also* **policial** police. **novela policíaca** *nf* detective novel.

polígono (po'ligono) *nm* 1 building site. 2 housing estate. 3 *math* polygon.

polilla (po'liʎa) *nf* moth.

pólipo ('polipo) *nm* polyp.

política (po'litika) *nf* 1 politics. 2 political manifesto. 3 political policy. **político** *adj* political. *nm* politician.

póliza (po'liθa) *nf* 1 fiscal stamp, certificate. 2 policy. **póliza de seguro** insurance policy.

polizón (poli'θon) *nm* 1 stowaway. 2 vagrant.

polo ('polo) *nm* 1 pole. 2 *tech* terminal. 3 *sport* polo. 4 polo-neck sweater.

Polonia (po'lonja) *nf* Poland.

poltrona (pol'trona) *nf* easy chair.

polvareda *nf* 1 cloud of dust. 2 altercation. **pólvora** *nf* gunpowder. **polvoriento** *adj* dusty.

polvo ('polbo) *nm* 1 dust. 2 *pl* powder.

polla ('poʎa) *nf* pullet. **pollo** *nm* chicken.

pómez ('pomeθ) *nf* pumice.

pomo ('pomo) *nm* 1 doorknob. 2 pommel. 3 fruit.

pompa ('pompa) *nf* 1 pomp. 2 *pl* bubbles.

pómulo ('pomulo) *nm* cheekbone.

ponche ('pontʃe) *nm* punch.

poncho ('pontʃo) *nm* poncho.

ponderar (ponde'rar) *vt* 1 ponder. 2 estimate. 3 esteem. **ponderación** *nf* consideration, esteem.

ponente (po'nente) *nm* 1 proposer (of motion, etc.). 2 spokesman.

poner* (po'ner) *vt* put (down, up, on, etc.). **ponerse** *vr* 1 put on (clothes). 2 set (sun). **poner con** connect (telephone). **poner la radio** turn on the radio. **ponerse bravo** get angry. **ponerse rojo** turn red.

pongo ('pongo) *v* see **poner.**

pontificado (pontifi'kaðo) *nm* papacy. **pontifical** *adj* papal. **pontífice** *nm* pope.

pontón (pon'ton) *nm* pontoon.

ponzoña (pon'θoɲa) *nf* poison. **ponzoñoso** *adj* poisonous.

popa ('popa) *nf* poop, stern.

populacho (popu'latʃo) *nm* mob.

popular (popu'lar) *adj* popular. **popularidad** *nf* popularity. **popularizar** *vt* popularize.

poquedad (poke'ðað) *nf* 1 paucity. 2 timidity.

poquito (po'kito) *adj* very little. *nm* a little bit.

por (por) *prep* 1 for. 2 to. 3 from. 4 by. 5 through, about (place). 6 in exchange for. **por ciento** percent. **por la noche** at or in the night. **¿por qué?** why?

porcelana (porθe'lana) *nf* porcelain.

porcentaje (porθen'taxe) *nm* percentage.

porción (por'θjon) *nf* portion.

porche ('portʃe) *nm* 1 porch. 2 arcade.

porfiar (por'fjar) *vi* insist. **porfía** *nf* insistence, persistence.

pormenor (porme'nor) *nm* detail.

pornografía (pornogra'fia) *nf* pornography. **porno** *nm* pore. **poroso** *adj* porous.

porque ('porke) *conj* because.

porquería (porke'ria) *nf sl* rubbish, trash.

porra ('porra) *nf* truncheon. **porrazo** *nm* blow, beating.

porrón (por'ron) *adj* dull, stupid.

portador (porta'ðor) *nm comm* bearer.

portal (por'tal) *nm* portal, entrance.

portamonedas (portamo'neðas) *nm invar* wallet.

portarse (por'tarse) *vr* behave.

portátil (por'tatil) *adj* portable.

portazgo (por'taθgo) *nm* toll, road-tax.

portazo (por'taθo) *nm* bang. **dar un portazo** slam the door.

porte ('porte) *nm* 1 postage, transport costs. 2 behaviour. 3 bearing (of a person). **franco de porte** postage paid.

portento (por'tento) *nm* prodigy. **portentoso** *adj* prodigious.

portería (porte'ria) *nf* porter's lodge. **portero** *nm* doorman, porter.

portezuela (porte'θwela) *nf* door (of car).

pórtico ('portiko) *nm* portico.

portilla (por'tiʎa) *nf* porthole.

Portugal (portu'gal) *nm* Portugal. **portugués** *adj,nm* Portuguese. *nm* Portuguese (language).

porvenir (porβe'nir) *nm* future.

pos (pos) *prep* **en pos de** behind, after.

posada (po'saða) *nf* 1 lodging. 2 inn. 3 dwelling, home.

posar (po'sar) vt place, put down. **posarse** vr settle. **pose** nm pose, posture. **poso** nm sediment.

poseer* (pose'er) vt possess. **posesión** nf possession.

posibilitar (posiβili'tar) vt facilitate.

posible (po'siβle) adj possible. **posibilidad** possibility, opportunity.

posición (posi'θjon) nf position.

positivo (posi'tiβo) adj positive. nm tech,phot

posponer* (pospo'ner) vt 1 postpone. 2 put below. 3 think less of.

postal (pos'tal) adj postal. nf postcard.

poste ('poste) nm pole, post.

postergar (poster'gar) vt pass over, put aside.

posteridad (posteri'ðað) nf posterity. **posterior** adj 1 later. 2 latter. 3 rear.

postizo (pos'tiθo) adj artificial.

postrar (pos'trar) vt prostrate.

postre ('postre) nm dessert.

postular (postu'lar) vt postulate, demand.

póstumo ('postumo) adj posthumous.

postura (pos'tura) nf 1 posture. 2 stand.

potable (po'taβle) adj drinkable.

potaje (po'taxe) nm stew.

potasio (po'tasjo) nm potassium.

pote ('pote) nm pot, jar.

potencia (po'tenθja) nf capability, potential. **potencia en caballos** horsepower. **potencial** adj potential. **potentado** nm potentate. **potente** adj powerful.

potestad (potes'tað) nf authority.

potro ('potro) nm 1 colt. 2 rack (tortura). **potrero** nm paddock.

pozo ('poθo) nm well.

práctica ('praktika) nf practice, exercise. **practicable** adj usable. **practicar** vt practise. **práctico** adj 1 practical. 2 practised, expert.

pradera (pra'ðera) nf 1 meadow. 2 prairie. **prado** nm meadow, field.

preámbulo (pre'ambulo) nm preamble.

precario (pre'karjo) adj precarious.

precaución (prekau'θjon) nf 1 precaution. 2 caution.

preceder (preθe'ðer) vt,vi precede.

precepto (pre'θepto) nm precept.

preciarse (pre'θjarse) vr boast. **precio** nm price, value.

precioso (pre'θjoso) adj 1 valuable. 2 beautiful.

precipicio (preθi'piθjo) nm precipice.

precipitar (preθipi'tar) vt hasten, precipitate.

precipitarse vr throw oneself headlong. **precipitoso** adj rash.

precisar (preθi'sar) vt,vi 1 need, be necessary. 2 clarify. **preciso** adj 1 necessary. 2 precise. **precisión** nf precision.

preconizar (prekoni'θar) vt praise.

precoz (pre'koθ) adj precocious. **precosidad** nf precocity.

precursor (prekur'sor) nm forerunner.

predecesor (preðeθe'sor) nm predecessor.

predecir* (preðe'θir) vt foretell. **predicción** nf prediction.

predestinar (preðesti'nar) vt predestine.

prédica ('preðika) nf sermon. **predicar** vt,vi preach.

predilección (preðilek'θjon) nf predilection.

predisponer* (preðispo'ner) vt predispose. **predisposición** nf predisposition.

predominar (preðomi'nar) vi predominate. vt dominate. **predominante** adj predominant. **predominio** nm predominance.

preeminencia (preemi'nenθja) nf pre-eminence. **preeminente** adj pre-eminent.

prefacio (pre'faθjo) nm preface.

prefecto (pre'fekto) nm prefect. **prefectura** nf prefecture.

preferir (ie) (prefe'rir) vt prefer. **preferencia** nf preference.

prefijo (pre'fixo) nm prefix.

pregonar (prego'nar) vt announce. **pregón** nm announcement. **pregonero** nm street-crier.

preguntar (pregun'tar) vt 1 ask. 2 question. vi inquire. **pregunta** nf question.

prejuicio (pre'xwiθjo) nm prejudice.

prejuzgar (prexuθ'gar) vt prejudge.

prelado (pre'laðo) nm prelate.

preliminar (prelimi'nar) adj,nm preliminary.

preludio (pre'luðjo) nm prelude.

prematuro (prema'turo) adj premature.

premeditar (premeði'tar) vt premeditate. **premeditación** nf premeditation.

premiar (pre'mjar) vt reward. **premio** nm 1 prize. 2 comm premium.

premisa (pre'misa) nf proposition, premise.

premura (pre'mura) nf urgency.

prenda ('prenda) nf 1 pledge. 2 garment. **prendero** nm second-hand dealer, pawnbroker. **dejar en prenda** pawn.

prender (pren'der) vt take, catch. vi catch, get caught. **prendimiento** nm capture, arrest.

prensa ('prensa) nf press. **prensar** vt press.

preñado (pre'ɲaðo) adj 1 bulging. 2 pregnant. **preñar** vt make pregnant.

preocupar (preoku'par) vt worry. **preocupación** nf worry.

preparar (prepa'rar) vt prepare. **preparación** nf preparation.

preponderar (preponde'rar) vi be in the majority. **preponderancia** nf preponderance.

prerrogativa (prerroga'tiβa) nf prerogative.

presa[1] ('presa) nf 1 prey, victim. 2 claw. 3 hold, clutch.

presa[2] ('presa) nf 1 dam. 2 ditch.

presagiar (presa'xjar) vt presage. **presagio** nm omen.

présbita ('presβita) adj invar long-sighted.

presbítero (pres'βitero) nm priest.

prescindir (presθin'dir) vi dispense with. **prescindible** adj dispensable.

prescribir (preskri'βir) vt prescribe. **prescripción** nf prescription.

presenciar (presen'θjar) vt attend, witness. **presencia** nf presence.

presentar (presen'tar) vt 1 present. 2 introduce (a person).

presente (pre'sente) adj,nm present.

presentir (ie) (presen'tir) vt have forebodings of. **presentimiento** nm foreboding.

preservar (preser'βar) vt protect. **preservación** nf protection.

presidencia (presi'ðenθja) nf presidency. **presidente** nm president.

presidiario (presi'ðjarjo) nm convict. **presidio** nm 1 prison. 2 penal sentence. 3 pol praesidium.

presidir (presi'ðir) vt preside over. vi preside.

presilla (pre'siʎa) nf loop, fastener.

presión (pre'sjon) nf pressure.

preso ('preso) adj under arrest. nm prisoner.

préstamo ('prestamo) nm loan.

prestar (pres'tar) vt lend. **prestador** nm lender. **prestamista** nm money-lender. **prestatario** nm borrower.

presteza (pres'teθa) nf promptness.

prestidigitador (prestiðixita'ðor) nm conjurer.

prestigio (pres'tixjo) nm prestige. **prestigioso** adj prestigious.

presto ('presto) adj prompt. adv at once.

presumir (presu'mir) vi 1 presume. 2 be presumptuous. **presumido** adj presumptuous.

presunción (presun'θjon) nf presumption. **presunto** adj presumed. **presuntuoso** adj conceited.

presuponer* (presupo'ner) vt presuppose.

presupuesto (presu'pwesto) nm budget.

presura (pre'sura) nf haste. **presuroso** adj hasty.

pretender (preten'der) vt 1 claim. 2 aspire to. 3 allege. **pretendiente** nm 1 claimant. 2 suitor.

pretensión (preten'sjon) nf 1 claim. 2 pretension.

pretexto (pre'teksto) nm pretext.

prevalecer* (preβale'θer) vi prevail.

prevaricar (preβari'kar) vi prevaricate.

prevención (preβen'θjon) nf 1 preparation, precaution. 2 police station. **preventivo** adj preventive.

prevenir (preβe'nir) vt 1 prepare. 2 prevent, foresee. 3 warn.

prever (pre'βer) vt foresee.

previo ('preβjo) adj previous. nm playback (film).

previsión (preβi'sjon) nf foresight. **previsión social** social security.

prieto ('prjeto) adj 1 dark (colour). 2 tight, packed.

prima ('prima) nf premium, bonus.

primario (pri'marjo) adj primary. **primacía** nf primacy.

primavera (prima'βera) nf 1 spring, springtime. 2 primrose. **primaveral** adj 1 spring. 2 fresh, virginal.

primero (pri'mero) adj 1 first. 2 foremost. adv first.

primitivo (primi'tiβo) adj original, primitive.

primo ('primo) nm cousin.

primogénito (primo'xenito) adj first-born.

primor (pri'mor) nm beauty. **primoroso** adj beautiful.

princesa (prin'θesa) nf princess.

principal (prinθi'pal) adj,nm 1 principal. 2 comm capital.

príncipe ('prinθipe) nm prince.

principiar (prinθi'pjar) vt begin. **principio** nm 1 beginning. 2 principle.

pringar (prin'gar) vt 1 baste. 2 soil (with grease). **pringoso** adj greasy.

prior (pri'or) nm prior. **prioridad** nf priority.

prisa ('prisa) nf hurry.

prisión (pri'sjon) nm imprisonment. **prisionero** nm prisoner.

prisma ('prisma) nm prism. **prismático** adj prismatic.

privar[1] (pri'βar) vt deprive. **privarse** vr forgo **privado** adj private.

privar[2] (pri'βar) vi be favourite. **privado** nm favourite. **privanza** nf favour, period of favour.

privilegiar (priβile'xjar) vt favour, grant privilege to. **privilegio** nm **1** privilege. **2** concession.

pro (pro) prep **en pro de** on behalf of.

proa ('proa) nf **1** naut bows, prow. **2** aviat nose.

probable (pro'βaβle) adj probable. **probabilidad** nf probability.

probar (ue) (pro'βar) vt,vi **1** test, try. **2** taste. **3** prove. **probador** nm fitting-room. **probatorio** adj serving as evidence. **probeta** nf **1** test tube. **2** cylinder.

problema (pro'βlema) nm problem.

proceder (proθe'ðer) vi **1** procede. **2** originate. **3** be appropriate. **proceder** nm also **procedimiento 1** procedure. **2** law proceedings. **procedencia** nf origin. **procedente** adj **1** originating from. **2** appropriate.

procesar (proθe'sar) vt law try, prosecute. **procesado** nm accused, defendant. **procesal** adj law legal. **proceso** nm **1** process. **2** trial, prosecution.

proclamar (prokla'mar) vt proclaim. **proclama** nf also **proclamación** proclamation.

procrear (prokre'ar) vt,vi procreate.

procurar (proku'rar) vt **1** attempt, try. **2** obtain, succeed. **procuración** nf law proxy. **procurador** nm law attorney.

prodigar (proði'gar) vt lavish, squander. **prodigarse** be prodigal.

prodigio (pro'ðixjo) nm prodigy. **prodigioso** adj prodigious.

pródigo ('proðigo) adj prodigal, lavish.

producir* (proðu'θir) vt produce. **producirse** vr come about, take place. **producción** nf production. **productividad** nf productivity. **productivo** adj productive. **producto** nm **1** product. **2** produce. **3** profit. **productor** adj producing. nm producer.

proeza (pro'eθa) nf deed.

profanar (profa'nar) vt profane. **profano** adj profane.

profecía (profe'θia) nf prophecy.

proferir (ie) (profe'rir) vt utter.

profesar (profe'sar) vt profess. **profesión** nf profession. **profesional** adj professional. **profesor** nm teacher, professor.

profeta (pro'feta) nm prophet.

prófugo ('profugo) nm fugitive.

profundidad (profundi'ðað) nf depth. **profundo** adj deep, profound.

profundizar (profundi'θar) vt deepen.

profusión (profu'sjon) nf profusion. **profuso** adj profuse.

programa (pro'grama) nm programme.

progresar (progre'sar) vi progress. **progresivo** adj progressive. **progreso** nm progress.

prohibir (proi'βir) vt prohibit. **prohibición** nf prohibition.

prohijar (proi'xar) vt adopt.

prójimo ('proximo) nm **1** fellow man. **2** neighbour.

prole ('prole) nf offspring.

proletario (prole'tarjo) adj,nm proletarian.

prolífico (pro'lifiko) adj prolific.

prolijo (pro'lixo) adj longwinded.

prólogo ('prologo) nm prologue.

prolongar (prolon'gar) vt prolong.

promediar (prome'ðjar) vt **1** bisect. **2** math average. vi be midway. **promedio** nm average.

promesa (pro'mesa) nf promise.

prometer (prome'ter) vt,vi promise. **prometerse** vr expect.

prominencia (promi'nenθja) nf bump, hillock. **prominente** adj prominent.

promiscuo (pro'miskwo) adj **1** motley. **2** ambiguous.

promontorio (promon'torjo) nm promontory.

promover (ue) (promo'βer) vt promote. **promoción** nf promotion. **promotor** nm promoter.

promulgar (promul'gar) vt promulgate.

pronombre (pro'nombre) nm pronoun.

pronosticar (pronosti'kar) vt predict, forecast. **pronóstico** (pro'nostiko) nm prediction, forecast.

prontitud (pronti'tuð) nf promptness, quickness. **pronto** adj quick, prompt. adv quickly, at once.

pronunciar (pronun'θjar) vt pronounce. **pronunciación** nf pronunciation.

propagar (propa'gar) vt propagate. **propaganda** nf **1** advertisement. **2** propaganda.

propalar (propa'lar) vt make public.

propenso (pro'penso) adj inclined, prone.

propicio (pro'piθjo) adj propitious.

propiedad (propje'ðað) nf **1** property. **2** comm copyright. **propietario** nm owner.

propina (pro'pina) nf tip (money) .

propio ('propjo) adj **1** own, particular. **2** proper.

proponer* (propo'ner) vt propose.

proporción (propor'θjon) nf proportion. **proporcionar** vt provide.

proposición (proposi'θjon) nf proposition.

propósito (pro'posito) nm purpose. **a propó-**

propuesta

sito on purpose. **a propósito de** with regard to.

propuesta (pro'pwesta) nf proposal.

propulsar (propul'sar) vt tech drive. **propulsión** nf propulsion.

prorrata (pror'rata) nf quota. **a prorrata** adv pro rata.

prórroga ('prorroga) nf 1 respite. 2 extension.

prorrogar (prorro'gar) vt 1 adjourn. 2 defer.

prorrumpir (prorrum'pir) vi break out.

prosa ('prosa) nf prose. **prosaico** adj prosaic.

proscribir (proskri'βir) vt outlaw, ban.

prosecución (proseku'θjon) nf continuation.

proseguir (i) (prose'gir) vt,vi continue.

prospecto (pros'pekto) nm prospectus.

prosperar (prospe'rar) vi prosper. **prosperidad** nf prosperity. **próspero** adj prosperous.

prostituir (prostitu'ir) vt prostitute. **prostitución** nf prostitution. **prostituta** nf prostitute.

protagonista (protago'nista) nm,f Th protagonist, hero

protección (protek'θjon) nf protection. **protector** adj protective. nm protector.

proteger (prote'xer) vt protect. **protegido** nm protégé.

proteína (prote'ina) nf protein.

protestar (protes'tar) vi protest. vt bounce (a cheque) **protesta** nf protest. **protestación** nf protestation. **protestante** nm,f Protestant.

protocolo (proto'kolo) nm protocol, formalities.

prototipo (proto'tipo) nm prototype.

protuberancia (protuβe'ranθja) nf protuberance

provecho (pro'βetʃo) nm advantage, profit. **provechoso** adj advantageous, profitable.

proveer (proβe'er) vt 1 provide. 2 deal with **proveedor** nm 1 supplier. 2 dealer.

provenir proβe'nir) vi originate.

proverbio (pro'βerβjo) nm proverb.

providencia (proβi'ðenθja) nf 1 providence, forethought. 2 law ruling.

provincia (pro'βinθja) nf province. **provincial** adj provincial. **provinciano** nm 1 provincial 2 inf boor

provisión (proβi'sjon) nf provision. **provisional** adj provisional.

provocar (proβo'kar) vt provoke. **provocación** nf provocation. **provocador** adj also **provocativo** provocative.

próximo ('proksimo) adj next, nearest.

proyectar projek'tar) vt 1 project, throw (out). 2 plan design. **proyectil** nm projectile.

proyecto nm plan, project. **proyector** nm 1 phot projector. 2 spotlight.

prudencia (pru'ðenθja) nf prudence. **prudencial** adj (of an action) wise. **prudente** adj (of a person) wise.

prueba ('prweβa) nf 1 proof. 2 test. **a prueba de** proof against.

prurito (pru'rito) nm 1 med itch. 2 urge.

psicoanálisis (psikoa'nalisis) nm psychoanalysis.

psicología (psikolo'xia) nf psychology. **psicológico** adj psychological. **psicólogo** nm psychologist.

psiquiatría (psikia'tria) nf psychiatry. **psiquiatra** nm psychiatrist. **psiquiatrico** adj psychiatric.

púa ('pua) nf 1 spine. 2 tooth. 3 needle.

pubertad (puβer'tað) nf puberty.

publicar (puβli'kar) vt publish. **publicación** nf publication. **publicidad** nf publicity, advertising.

público ('puβliko) adj,nm public.

pude ('puðe) v see **poder.**

púdico ('puðiko) adj chaste, modest.

pudiente (pu'ðjente) adj rich.

pudor (pu'ðor) nm modesty. **pudoroso** adj chaste, modest.

pudrir* (pu'ðrir) vt rot.

pueblo (pu'weβlo) nm 1 pol people. 2 provincia town.

puente ('pwente) nm bridge.

puerco ('pwerko) nm pig.

pueril (pwe'ril) adj childish.

puerro (pu'werro) nm leek.

puerta ('pwerta) nf 1 door. 2 gate. **puerto** nm 1 port. 2 mountain pass.

pues (pwes) adv 1 then, so. 2 inf well. conj for since.

puesta ('pwesta) nf 1 setting (of sun). 2 game stake. **puesta en escena** stage management.

puesto ('pwesto) v see **poner.** nm place, post **puesto que** conj since, given that.

pugnar (pug'nar) vi fight. **pugnaz** ad pugnacious.

pujar (pu'xar) vi strain. **pujante** adj 1 straining 2 powerful

pulcritud (pulkri'tuð) nf neatness. **pulcro** adj neat.

pulga ('pulga) nf flea.

pulgada (pul'gaða) nf inch. **pulgar** nm thumb.

pulir (pu'lir) vt polish. **pulimiento** nm polish.

pulmón (pul'mon) nm lung.

pulmonía (pulmo'nia) nf pneumonia.

pulpa ('pulpa) nf pulp.
púlpito ('pulpito) nm pulpit.
pulsar (pul'sar) vi pulsate. **pulso** nm 1 pulse. 2 wrist. 3 steadiness (of the hand).
pulsera (pul'sera) nf bracelet.
pulverizar (pulβeri'θar) vt pulverize.
pulla ('puʎa) nf 1 obscenity. 2 taunt.
punción (pun'θjon) nf med puncture.
punición (puni'θjon) nf punishment. **punible** adj punishable. **punitivo** adj punitive.
punta ('punta) nf point, tip.
puntapié (puntapi'e) nm kick.
puntear (punte'ar) vt 1 tick (off). 2 perforate, stitch.
puntería (punte'ria) nf aim.
puntilla (pun'tiʎa) nf 1 tack, nib. 2 lace.
punto ('punto) nm 1 point, spot. 2 full stop. 3 stitch.
puntual (pun'twal) adj 1 reliable. 2 punctual. **puntualidad** nf 1 reliability. 2 punctuality.
puntualizar (puntwali'θar) vt 1 clarify. 2 work out in detail.
punzar (pun'θar) vt pierce. **punzada** nf puncture, prick.
puñado (pu'ɲaðo) nm handful. **puñada** nf also **puñetazo** nm punch, blow. **puño** nm 1 fist. 2 handle, knob.
puñal (pu'ɲal) nm dagger. **puñalada** nf stab.
pupila (pu'pila) nf pupil (eye).
pupilaje (pupi'laxe) nm boarding (house). **pupilo** nm law ward.
pupitre (pu'pitre) nm desk.
puré (pu're) nm purée.
pureza (pu'reθa) nf purity.
purgar (pur'gar) vt purge, purify. **purgarse** vr med take a purge. **purgante** adj also **purgativo** purgative.
purgatorio (purga'torjo) nm purgatory.
purificar (purifi'kar) vt purify. **purificación** nf purification.
puritano (puri'tano) adj,n puritan.
puro ('puro) adj pure, simple. nm cigar.
púrpura ('purpura) nf purple.
puse ('puse) v see **poner**.
pusilánime (pusi'lanime) adj cowardly.
pústula ('pustula) nf med pustule, pimple.
puta ('puta) nf inf prostitute.
putrefacción (putrefak'θjon) nf rot, decay.
pútrido ('putriðo) adj putrid.
puya ('puja) nf goad.

Q

que (ke) pron who, that, which. conj that, than.
qué (ke) pron, adj what? ¡**qué raro!** how extraordinary!
quebrantar (keβran'tar) vt shatter. **quebranto** nm exhaustion.
quebrar (ie) (ke'βrar) vt break. vi go bankrupt. **quebrado** adj 1 broken, rough. 2 weakened. 3 bankrupt. **quebradura** nf crack, break.
quedar (ke'ðar) vi 1 stay, remain. 2 be, lie (in a place). **quedarse** vr 1 stay behind. 2 grow calm (sea). **quedar bien** give a good impression. **quedar en nada** come to nothing.
quedo ('keðo) adj quiet. adv quietly. **queda** nf curfew.
quehacer (kea'θer) nm chore.
quejarse (ke'xarse) vr complain. **queja** nf complaint. **quejido** nm moan.
quemar (ke'mar) vt burn. vi be scalding. **quemadura** nf burn. **quemazón** nf burning, smarting.
quepo ('kepo) v see **caber**.
querella (ke'reʎa) nf 1 quarrel. 2 law complaint. nm plaintiff. **querellar** vt reprimand. **querellarse** vr law make a complaint.
querer (ie) (ke'rer) vt,vi 1 want. 2 love, like. nm affection. **querido** adj dear.
queso ('keso) nm cheese.
quiá (ki'a) interj never!
quicio ('kiθjo) nm hinge.
quiebra ('kjeβra) nf 1 fissure, break. 2 bankruptcy. **quiebro** nm mus trill.
quien (kjen) pron 1 who. 2 whom. 3 whoever.
quieto ('kjeto) adj still. **quietud** nf stillness.
quijote (ki'xote) nm quixotic person.
quilate (ki'late) nm carat.
quilla ('kiʎa) nf keel.
quimera (ki'mera) nf 1 false notion, hallucination. 2 unjustified suspicion. 3 quarrel.
química (ki'mika) nf chemistry. **químico** adj chemical. nm chemist.
quincalla (kin'θaʎa) nf 1 hardware. 2 small wares. 3 ironmongery. **quincallero** nm 1 dealer in hardware or small wares. 2 ironmonger.
quince ('kinθe) adj, nm fifteen.
quincena (kin'θena) nf fortnight.
quincuagésimo (kinkwa'xesimo) adj fiftieth.
quinta ('kinta) nf 1 country estate. 2 mil call-up.
quintal (kin'tal) nm hundredweight.

quinteto (kin'teto) *nm* quintet.

quinto ('kinto) *adj* fifth.

quiosco ('kjosko) *nm* kiosk.

quirúrgico (ki'rurxiko) *adj* surgical.

quise ('kise) *v* see **querer**.

quisquilla (kis'kiʎa) *nf* 1 quibble. 2 *zool* shrimp. **quisquilloso** *adj* quibbling.

quiste ('kiste) *nm* cyst.

quitar (ki'tar) *vt* remove, take away. **quitarse** *vr* 1 withdraw. 2 get rid of, take off, undress. **quitamanchas** *nm invar* stain-remover.

quitasol (kita'sol) *nm* parasol.

quizá(s) (ki'θa) *adv* perhaps.

R

rábano ('raβano) *nm* radish.

rabiar (raβi'ar) *vi* rage, rave. **rabia** *nf* 1 rage, fury. 2 *med* rabies. **rabioso** *adj* 1 *med* rabid. 2 raging, furious.

rabo ('raβo) *nm* tail.

racial (ra'θjal) *adj* racial.

racimo (ra'θimo) *nm* bunch of grapes, bunch.

raciocinar (raθjoθi'nar) *vi* reason, consider rationally. **raciocinio** *nm* reason.

ración (ra'θjon) *nf* 1 ration, portion. 2 *math* ratio.

racional (raθjo'nal) *adj* reasonable.

racionar (raθjo'nar) *vt* share, ration. **racionamiento** *nm* rationing.

racha ('ratʃa) *nf* 1 gust (of wind). 2 stroke of luck.

radiactivo (raðjak'tivo) *adj also* **radioactivo** radioactive. **radiactividad** *nf* radioactivity.

radiar (ra'ðjar) *vt* radiate. **radiación** *nf* radiation. **radiador** *nm* radiator. **radiante** *adj* radiant.

radicar (raði'kar) *vi* take or have roots. **radical** *adj* radical.

radio[1] ('raðjo) *nf* radio. **radiodifusión** *nf* broadcasting. **radiografía** *nf* 1 X-ray. 2 radiography. **radiología** *nf* radiology. **radiólogo** *nm* radiologist. **radioyente** *nm,f* listener (to the radio).

radio[2] ('raðjo) *nm* 1 radius. 2 spoke (wheel). **radiogente** (raðjo'jente) *nm,f* listener (to the radio).

raer (ra'er) *vt* scrape.

raíz (ra'iθ) *nf* root.

rajar (ra'xar) *vt* crack, split. **raja** *nf also* **rajadura** 1 split, crack. 2 slice, sliver.

ralea (ra'lea) *nf* sort, kind.

rallar (ra'ʎar) *vt* grate (cheese, etc.). **rallador** *nm* grater.

rama ('rama) *nf* branch. **ramada** *nf also* **ramaje** *nm* foliage. **ramal** *nm* 1 *mot* branch, sideroad. 2 halter.

rambla ('rambla) *nf* 1 riverbed. 2 avenue.

ramificarse (ramifi'karse) *vr* ramify, branch off. **ramificación** *nf* ramification.

ramillete (rami'ʎete) *nm* bouquet of flowers.

ramo ('ramo) *nm* 1 *comm* branch, department. 2 branch (of a tree).

rampa ('rampa) *nf* ramp.

ramplón (ram'plon) *adj* vulgar.

rana ('rana) *nf* frog.

rancio ('ranθjo) *adj* 1 rancid. 2 ancient. 3 old-fashioned. **rancidez** *nf* 1 age, antiquity. 2 mustiness, rancidness.

rancho ('rantʃo) *nm* 1 farmhouse. 2 hut. 3 *mil* communal meal.

rango ('rango) *nm* rank.

ranura (ra'nura) *nf* slot.

rapaz (ra'paθ) *adj* rapacious. **rapacidad** *nf* rapacity.

rápido (ra'piðo) *adj* swift. *adv* quickly. **rapidez** *nf* rapidity.

rapiña (ra'piɲa) *nf* robbery.

raptar (rap'tar) *vt* abduct. **rapto** *nm* abduction.

raqueta (ra'keta) *nf* racquet.

rareza (ra'reθa) *nf* 1 rarity. 2 oddity. **raro** *adj* 1 odd. 2 rare, remarkable.

ras (ras) *nm* 1 ground level. 2 level. **a ras de** level with.

rascacielos (raska'θjelos) *nm invar* skyscraper.

rascar (ras'kar) *vt* scrape, scratch.

rasgar (ras'gar) *vt* tear, rip. **rasgón** *nm* tear. **rasguño** *nm* 1 scratch. 2 *Art* sketch.

rasgo ('rasgo) *nm* 1 stroke, flourish. 2 feature, characteristic.

raso ('raso) *adj* 1 smooth. 2 level. 3 (of the sky) clear.

raspar (ras'par) *vt* scrape, file down. **raspa** *nf* 1 ear of corn. 2 fishbone.

rastra ('rastra) *nf* 1 string of garlic, dry fruit, etc. 2 harrow. 3 sledge. 4 trawling dredge.

rastrear (rastre'ar) *vt* 1 drag, dredge, harrow. 2 track, hunt.

rastrillar (rastri'ʎar) *vt* rake up. **rastrillo** *nm* rake.

rastro ('rastro) *nm* 1 track, trace. 2 rake.

rastrojo (ras'troxo) *nm* stubble.

rasurar (rasu'rar) *vt* shave.

rata ('rata) *nf* rat.

ratería (rate'ria) nf petty thieving. **ratero** nm petty thief.

ratificar (ratifi'kar) vt ratify.

rato ('rato) nm while, period of time.

ratón (ra'ton) nm mouse. **ratonera** nf mousetrap.

rayar (ra'jar) vt 1 stripe. 2 cross out. 3 scratch (furniture, etc.). **rayar en** border on. **raya** nf 1 stripe, line. 2 trouser crease. 3 boundary. 4 parting (of hair).

rayo ('rajo) nm 1 ray, beam. 2 lightning.

raza ('raθa) nf race, breed.

razón (ra'θon) nf 1 reason. 2 rationale. **tener razón** be right.

razonar (raθo'nar) vt argue out, justify. **razonable** adj reasonable.

reacción (reak'θjon) nf reaction. **reaccionar** vi react. **reaccionario** adj,n reactionary. **reactivo** nm reagent. **reactor** nm 1 reactor. 2 aviat jet.

reacio (re'aθjo) adj stubborn.

real[1] (re'al) adj real.

real[2] (re'al) adj royal.

realce (re'alθe) nm 1 highlight. 2 importance.

realizar (reali'θar) vt 1 fulfil. 2 comm realize.

realzar (real'θar) vt 1 highlight. 2 art emboss.

reanimar (reani'mar) vt revive.

reanudar (reanu'ðar) vt renew.

rebajar (reβa'xar) vt 1 lower. 2 comm reduce, discount. 3 weaken (a drink). **rebaja** nf 1 discount, reduction. 2 pl comm sale.

rebanada (reβa'naða) nf slice.

rebaño (re'βaɲo) nm flock.

rebasar (reβa'sar) vt exceed.

rebatir (reβa'tir) vt repel, refute. **rebato** nm 1 call to arms. 2 surprise attack.

rebeca (re'βeka) nf cardigan.

rebelarse (reβe'larse) vr rebel. **rebelde** adj rebellious. nm,f rebel. **rebelión** nf rebellion.

rebosar (reβo'sar) vi overflow.

rebotar (reβo'tar) vt,vi bounce, turn back. **rebote** nm 1 bounce, rebound. 2 ricochet.

rebozar (reβo'θar) vt wrap up. **rebozo** nm muffler.

rebuscar (reβus'kar) vt search out. **rebuscado** adj elaborate.

rebuznar (reβuθ'nar) vi bray. **rebuzno** nm bray.

recado (re'kaðo) nm 1 message. 2 gift.

recaer[*] (reka'er) vi relapse. **recaída** nf relapse.

recalcar (rekal'kar) vt 1 emphasize. 2 press, squeeze.

recalcitrante (rekalθi'trante) adj recalcitrant.

recalentar (ie) (rekalen'tar) vt reheat. **recalentarse** vr overheat.

recambio (re'kambjo) nm 1 spare part. 2 replacement, refill.

recargar (rekar'gar) vt 1 overload. 2 tech recharge. **recargo** nm comm surcharge.

recatarse (reka'tarse) vr 1 act modestly. 2 be cautious. **recato** nm 1 modesty. 2 caution.

recaudar (rekau'ðar) vt comm, pol collect (debts, taxes). **recaudo** nm 1 comm collection (tax). 2 safekeeeping.

recelar (reθe'lar) vt,vi suspect. **recelo** nm suspicion. **receloso** adj suspicious.

recepción (reθep'θjon) nf reception. **recepcionista** nf receptionist.

receptáculo (reθep'takulo) nm receptacle.

receptor (reθep'tor) nm receiver.

recesión (reθe'sjon) nf comm,pol recession.

receta (re'θeta) nf 1 recipe. 2 prescription.

recibir (reθi'βir) vt 1 receive. 2 welcome. **recibo** nm receipt.

recién (re'θjen) adv recently, just. **reciente** adj recent, new.

recinto (re'θinto) nm precinct.

recio ('reθjo) adj tough.

recipiente (reθi'pjente) nm 1 receptacle. 2 recipient.

reciprocar (reθipro'kar) vt reciprocate. **recíproco** adj reciprocal.

recitar (reθi'tar) vt recite. **recital** nm recital.

reclamar (rekla'mar) vt claim. vi law appeal. **reclamación** nf 1 claim. 2 complaint. **reclamo** nm 1 advertisement. 2 lure (for birds).

reclinar (rekli'nar) vt lean.

reclusión (reklu'sjon) nf 1 seclusion. 2 imprisonment. **recluso** adj,n 1 recluse. 2 convict.

recluta (re'kluta) nf recruitment. nm recruit.

recobrar (reko'βrar) vt 1 recover. 2 reclaim.

recoger (reko'xer) vt collect, gather. **recogerse** vr withdraw, retire.

recolección (rekolek'θjon) nf 1 harvest. 2 recollection. 3 compilation.

recomendar (ie) (rekomen'dar) vt 1 recommend. 2 praise. **recomendación** nf recommendation.

recompensar (rekompen'sar) vt 1 compensate. 2 reward. **recompensa** nf 1 compensation. 2 reward.

reconciliarse (rekonθi'ljarse) vr reconcile oneself. **reconciliación** nf reconciliation.

recóndito (re'kondito) adj obscure.

reconocer[*] (rekono'θer) vt 1 recognize. 2

117

acknowledge. **3** inspect. **reconocible** adj recognizable. **reconocimiento** nm **1** recognition. **2** acknowledgement. **3** inspection.

reconquista (rekon'kista) nf reconquest.

reconstituir (rekonstitu'ir) vt reconstitute.

reconstruir (rekonstru'ir) vt reconstruct.

reconvenir (rekonβe'nir) vt reprimand.

recopilar (rekopi'lar) vt **1** compile. **2** law codify. **recopilación** nf **1** summary. **2** law code.

recordar (ue) (rekor'ðar) vt, vi **1** remember. **2** remind. **3** recall.

recorrer (rekor'rer) vt **1** travel about. **2** look over, survey. **3** overhaul. **recorrido** nm route, stretch of journey.

recortar (rekor'tar) vt trim, cut back. **recortarse** vr stand out, show up. **recorte** nm **1** cutout. **2** cutting.

recoveco (reko'βeko) nm **1** street-corner. **2** nook.

recrearse (rekre'arse) vr entertain oneself. **recreo** nm recreation.

recriminar (rekrimi'nar) vt reproach.

recrudecer (rekruðe'θer) vt make worse.

rectángulo (rek'tangulo) nm rectangle. adj rectangular, right-angled. **rectangular** adj rectangular.

rectificar (rektifi'kar) vt rectify, correct.

rectitud (rekti'tuð) nf rectitude. **recto** adj **1** straight. **2** upright, honest.

rector (rek'tor) nm head (of a school or university).

recua ('rekwa) nf mule train.

recuento (re'kwento) nm count, reckoning.

recuerdo (re'kwerðo) nm **1** memory. **2** souvenir. **3** pl regards, best wishes.

recular (reku'lar) vi recoil.

recuperar (rekupe'rar) vt recuperate, retrieve.

recurrir (reku'rir) vi **1** resort. **2** revert. **recurrir a** have recourse to.

recurso (re'kurso) nm **1** recourse. **2** pl comm funds, resources.

recusar (reku'sar) vt refuse.

rechazar (retʃa'θar) vt **1** repel. **2** reject. **rechazo** nm rebuff.

rechinar (retʃi'nar) vi creak.

rechoncho (re'tʃontʃo) adj thickset.

red (reð) nf **1** net. **2** network.

redactar (reðak'tar) vt **1** edit. **2** draft. **redacción** nf **1** editing. **2** editorial office or staff. **redactor** nm editor.

redención (reden'θjon) nf redemption. **redentor** nm redeemer.

redimir (reði'mir) vt redeem.

rédito ('reðito) nm comm interest, return.

redoblar (reðo'βlar) vt **1** fold, bend. **2** redouble. **3** beat (a drum). **redoble** nm drum roll.

redondear (reðonde'ar) vt round off. **redondo** adj round.

reducir* (reðu'θir) vt reduce. **reducción** nf reduction.

redundar (reðun'dar) vi redound. **redundancia** nf redundancy.

reduzco (re'ðuθko) v see **reducir**.

reembolsar (reembol'sar) vt reimburse. **reembolsable** adj refundable. **reembolso** nm refund.

reemplazar (reempla'θar) vt replace. **reemplazable** adj replaceable. **reemplazo** nm replacement.

referencia (refe'renθja) nf reference.

referéndum (refe'rendum) nm referendum.

referir (ie) (refe'rir) vt **1** relate, retell. **2** refer. **referirse a** refer to.

refinar (refi'nar) vt refine. **refinadura** nf process of refining. **refinamiento** nm refinement. **refinería** nf refinery.

reflector (reflek'tor) nm reflector.

reflejar (refle'xar) vt, vi reflect. **reflejo** nm **1** reflection. **2** reflex. adj reflex, reflected.

reflexionar (refleksjo'nar) vt, vi reflect on, consider.

reflexivo (reflek'siβo) adj, nm reflexive.

reflujo (re'fluxo) nm ebb.

reformar (refor'mar) vt **1** reform. **2** alter. **reforma** nf reform, reformation. **reformación** nf reform, reformation. **reformador** nm reformer. **reformatorio** nm reformatory.

reforzar (ue) (refor'θar) vt reinforce.

refractario (refrak'tarjo) adj **1** ovenproof. **2** obstinate.

refrán (re'fran) nm proverb.

refregar (ie) (refre'gar) vt scrub.

refrenar (refre'nar) vt hold back, curb.

refrescar (refres'kar) vt refresh. vi cool. **refrescante** adj cooling. **refresco** nm refreshment, long drink.

refrigerar (refrixe'rar) vt **1** cool. **2** refrigerate. **refrigeración** nf cooling system. **refrigerador** nm refrigerator.

refuerzo (re'fwerθo) nm reinforcement.

refugiarse (refu'xjarse) vr take refuge, flee. **refugiado** nm refugee. **refugio** nm refuge, shelter.

refulgir (reful'xir) vi shine brightly. **refulgencia** nf brilliance.

refundir (refun'dir) vt **1** recast. **2** reconstruct.

refunfuñar (refunfu'ɲar) vi 1 growl. 2 grumble.

refutar (refu'tar) vt refute.

regadera (rega'ðera) nf watering-can. **regadío** adj also **regadizo** irrigable.

regalar (rega'lar) vt 1 give (a present). 2 pamper, indulge. **regalo** nm present.

regaliz (rega'liθ) nm liquorice.

regañar (rega'ɲar) vt 1 reprimand. 2 inf nag. vi 1 grumble. 2 quarrel.

regar (ie) (re'gar) vt irrigate, water.

regatear (regate'ar) vt haggle over. vi haggle, bargain. **regateo** nm haggling.

regazo (re'gaθo) nm anat lap.

regencia (re'xenθja) nf regency.

regenerar (rexene'rar) vt regenerate. **regeneración** nf regeneration.

regentar (rexen'tar) vt occupy temporarily. **regente** nm 1 regent. 2 head man.

régimen ('reximen) nm 1 regime. 2 diet.

regimiento (rexi'mjento) nm 1 regiment. 2 government.

región (re'xjon) nf region. **regional** adj regional. **regionalismo** nm regionalism.

regir (i) (re'xir) vt govern.

registrar (rexis'trar) vt 1 register, record. 2 search, inspect. **registro** nm 1 registration. 2 register. 3 register office. 4 search, inspection.

reglar (re'glar) vt 1 rule (with lines). 2 regulate, adjust. **regla** nf rule, ruler.

regocijar (regoθi'xar) vt cheer, delight. **regocijo** nm rejoicing.

regresar (regre'sar) vi return. **regreso** nm return.

regular (regu'lar) vt regulate. adj regular, ordinary. **regulación** nf regulation, control. **regulador** nm control, regulator. **regularidad** nf regularity.

regularizar (regulari'θar) vt standardize.

rehabilitar (reaβili'tar) vt rehabilitate.

rehacer (rea'θer) vt 1 remake. 2 do again. **rehacerse** vr 1 rally, gain strength again. 2 get well.

rehén (re'en) nm hostage.

rehuir (reu'ir) vt avoid, shrink from.

rehusar (reu'sar) vt refuse.

reimprimir (reimpri'mir) vt reprint. **reimpresión** nf reprint.

reina ('reina) nf queen.

reinar (rei'nar) vi reign, rule. **reino** nm kingdom.

reincidir (reinθi'ðir) vi fall back, relapse.

reintegrar (reinte'grar) vt 1 reintegrate. 2 comm

reimburse. **reintegro** nm 1 reimbursement, refund. 2 withdrawal (from a bank account).

reír (re'ir) vi laugh. vt mock. **reírse de** have a laugh at.

reiterar (reite'rar) vt repeat.

reivindicar (reiβindi'kar) vt 1 vindicate. 2 claim. **reivindicación** nf 1 vindication. 2 claim.

reja ('rexa) nf 1 grating, grille. 2 ploughshare. **rejilla** nf 1 small grating. 2 luggage rack.

rejuvenecer (rexuβene'θer) vt rejuvenate.

relación (rela'θjon) nf 1 relation. 2 ratio. 3 account, telling (of a story). 4 pl relations, connections. 5 pl intercourse.

relacionar (relaθjo'nar) vt relate.

relajar (rela'xar) vt 1 relax. 2 slacken.

relámpago (re'lampago) nm lightning. **relampaguear** vi flash with lightning.

relatar (rela'tar) vt relate, narrate. **relato** nm account, story.

relatividad (relatiβi'ðað) nf relativity. **relativo** adj,nm relative.

relevar (rele'βar) vt 1 relieve. 2 Art carve in relief. **relevo** nm relief, change (of guard, etc.).

relicario (reli'karjo) nm 1 locket. 2 reliquary.

relieve (re'ljeβe) nm 1 art relief, embossing. 2 prominence, eminence.

religión (reli'xjon) nf religion. **religiosidad** nf religiosity. **religioso** adj religious. nm member of a religious order.

reliquia (re'likja) nf relic.

reloj (re'lox) nm clock.

relucir (relu'θir) vi gleam. **reluciente** adj shining, gleaming.

relumbrar (relum'brar) vi 1 be dazzling. 2 shine.

rellenar (reʎe'nar) vt refill, stuff. **relleno** adj stuffed. nm stuffing, filling.

remachar (rema'tʃar) vt hammer in, rivet. **remache** nm rivet.

remanente (rema'nente) adj surplus.

remanso (re'manso) nm backwater.

remar (re'mar) vi row.

rematar (rema'tar) vt 1 put an end to, finish or kill off. 2 comm sell off. vi finish off. **remate** nm finishing touch.

remediar (reme'ðjar) vt remedy. **remedio** nm remedy.

remendar (ie) (remen'dar) vt mend, repair. **remendón** nm cobbler.

remesa (re'mesa) nf 1 remittance. 2 shipment.

remiendo (re'mjendo) nm repair, patch.

remilgado (remil'gaðo) *adj* prudish. **remilgo** *nm* prudery.

remirado (remi'raðo) *adj* overcautious.

remisión (remi'sjon) *nf* 1 remission. 2 *comm* consignment. **remiso** *adj* remiss.

remitir (remi'tir) *vt* 1 remit. 2 refer, entrust.

remo ('remo) *nm* oar.

remojar (remo'xar) *vt* soak.

remolacha (remo'latʃa) *nf* beetroot.

remolcar (remol'kar) *vt* tow. **remolque** *nm* 1 towing. 2 twrope. 3 trailer.

remolino (remo'lino) *nm* 1 eddy, whirl. 2 throng.

remontar (remon'tar) *vt* 1 climb, surmount. 2 remount. **remontarse** *vr* rise. **remontarse a** amount to, reach.

remordimiento (remorði'mjento) *nm* remorse.

remoto (re'moto) *adj* remote.

remover (ue) (remo'ßer) *vt* 1 remove. 2 stir.

remunerar (remune'rar) *vt* remunerate. **remuneración** *nf* remuneration.

renacer (rena'θer) *vi* 1 be reborn. 2 revive. **renacentista** *adj* Renaissance. **renacimiento** *nm* Renaissance.

renacuajo (rena'kwaxo) *nm* tadpole.

rencilla (ren'θiʎa) *nf* 1 feud. 2 grudge.

rencor (ren'kor) *nm* bitterness. **rencoroso** *adj* bitter.

rendir (i) (ren'dir) *vt* 1 yield, give. 2 reduce, defeat. **rendirse** *vr* 1 surrender. 2 exhaust oneself.

renegar (ie) (rene'gar) *vt* 1 deny. 2 detest. *vi* 1 renounce, turn renegade. 2 grumble. **renegado** *adj,n* renegade. **reniego** *nm* 1 oath, curse. 2 complaint. 3 blasphemy.

renglón (ren'glon) *nm* 1 line (of printing). 2 *comm* entry (in accounts).

reno ('reno) *nm* reindeer.

renombrado (renom'braðo) *adj* renowned. **renombre** *nm* renown.

renovar (ue) (reno'ßar) *vt* renew, renovate. **renovación** *nf* renewal, renovation.

rentar (ren'tar) *vt comm* yield. **renta** *nf* 1 *comm* yield. 2 income.

renunciar (renun'θjar) *vt* renounce. *vi* resign. **renuncia** *nf* resignation.

reñir (i) (re'ɲir) *vt* scold. *vi* quarrel.

reo ('reo) *nm* 1 accused. 2 culprit.

reojo (re'oxo) *adv* **de reojo** sideways, out of the corner of the eyes.

reorganizar (reorgani'θar) *vt* reorganize.

reparar[1] (repa'rar) *vt* 1 repair. 2 make amends.

reparación *nf* 1 repair. 2 amends. **reparo** *nm* repair.

reparar[2] (repa'rar) *vi* stay, stop. **reparar en** notice, take notice of. **reparo** *nm* 1 hesitation, doubt. 2 criticism.

repartir (repar'tir) *vt* 1 share out. 2 *comm* deliver. **reparto** *nm* 1 sharing out, distribution. 2 *comm* delivery.

repasar (repa'sar) *vt* go over, check. **repaso** *nm* revision, check.

repatriar (repatri'ar) *vt* repatriate.

repeler (repe'ler) *vt* 1 repel. 2 reject. **repelente** *adj* 1 repellent. 2 resistant.

repente (re'pente) **de repente** *adv* suddenly. **repentino** *adj* sudden.

repercutir (reperku'tir) *vi* rebound. **repercusión** *nf* repercussion.

repertorio (reper'torjo) *nm* 1 handbook, list. 2 repertory.

repetir (i) (repe'tir) *vt* repeat. **repetirse** *vr* recur. **repetición** *nf* repetition.

repisa (re'pisa) *nf* 1 shelf. 2 mantelpiece.

replegar (ie) (reple'gar) *vt* fold back.

repleto (re'pleto) *adj* full.

réplica ('replika) *nf* 1 retort. 2 *law* answer (to charge). 3 copy.

replicar (repli'kar) *vt* argue.

repliegue (repli'ege) *nm* crease.

repoblación (repoßla'θjon) *nf* repopulation.

repollo (re'poʎo) *nm* cabbage.

reponer[*] (repo'ner) *vt* replace, restore. **reponerse** *vr med* recover.

reportar (repor'tar) *vt* bring, carry. **reportarse** *vr* regain one's composure. **reportaje** *nm* newspaper report. **repórter** *nm also* **reportero** reporter.

reposar (repo'sar) *vi* rest. **reposo** *nm* repose.

repostería (reposte'ria) *nf* confectionery, confectioner's. **repostero** *nm* confectioner.

reprender (repren'der) *vt* scold, reprehend. **reprensible** *adj* reprehensible. **reprensión** *nf* reprimand.

represalia (repre'salja) *nf* reprisal.

representar (represen'tar) *vt* 1 represent. 2 *Th* play, act. **representación** *nf* 1 representation. 2 *Th* production. **representante** *nm,f* 1 *pol* representative. 2 *Th* actor. **representativo** *adj* representative.

represión (repre'sjon) *nf* suppression.

reprimenda (repri'menda) *nf* reprimand.

reprimir (repri'mir) *vt* suppress.

reprobar (ue) (repro'ßar) *vt* condemn.

réprobo ('reproβo) *adj* reprobate.

reprochar (repro'tʃar) vt reproach. **reproche** nm reproach.

reproducir* (reproðu'θir) vt reproduce. **reproducción** nf reproduction.

reptil (rep'til) adj,nm reptile.

república (re'puβlika) nf republic. **republicano** adj,nm republican.

repudiar (repu'ðjar) vt repudiate. **repudio** nm repudiation.

repuesto (re'pwesto) 1 replacement, spare part. 2 store, larder. 3 sideboard.

repugnar (repug'nar) vt 1 nauseate. 2 hate. **repugnancia** nf repugnance. **repugnante** adj repugnant.

repulsivo (repul'siβo) adj repulsive. **repulsión** nf repulsion.

reputar (repu'tar) vt 1 esteem. 2 prize. **reputación** nf reputation.

requebrar (ie) (reke'βrar) vt flatter.

requemar (reke'mar) vt scorch.

requerir (ie) (reke'rir) vt require.

requesón (reke'son) nm 1 cottage cheese. 2 curd.

requisar (reki'sar) vt requisition.

res (res) nf head of cattle.

resabio (re'saβjo) nm aftertaste.

resaca (re'saka) nf 1 undercurrent, undertow. 2 inf hangover.

resaltar (resal'tar) vi stick out.

resarcir (resar'θir) vt repay, compensate.

resbalar (resβa'lar) vi slip. **resbaladizo** adj slippery. **resbalón** nm slip, skid.

rescatar (reska'tar) vt rescue, recover, redeem. **rescate** nm 1 rescue, recovery. 2 ransom.

rescindir (resθin'dir) vt 1 repeal. 2 cancel. **rescisión** nf 1 repeal. 2 cancellation.

rescoldo (res'koldo) nm cinders, embers.

resecar (rese'kar) vt parch. **reseco** adj lean, parched.

resentirse (ie) (resen'tirse) vr resent, take offence. **resentirse de** suffer from, feel the effects of. **resentido** adj resentful. **resentimiento** nm resentment.

reseñar (rese'ɲar) vt review, report on. **reseña** nf review, report.

reservar (reser'βar) vt reserve. **reservarse** vr save one's strength. **reserva** nf 1 reservation, doubt. 2 reserve, stock. 3 geog reserve. 4 discretion. 5 reservation, booking.

resfriar (resfri'ar) vi turn cold. **resfriarse** vr catch cold.

resguardar (resgwar'ðar) vt safeguard. **resguardo** nm 1 safeguard. 2 comm guarantee, security.

residencia (resi'ðenθja) nf 1 residence. 2 educ hostel. **residente** adj,n resident.

residir (resi'ðir) vi reside.

residuo (re'siðwo) nm residue.

resignar (resig'nar) vt resign. **resignación** nf resignation.

resina (re'sina) nf resin.

resistir (resis'tir) vt,vi 1 resist. 2 put up with, endure. **resistirse** vr 1 resist. 2 refuse. **resistencia** nf 1 resistance. 2 endurance. **resistente** adj 1 durable. 2 resistant.

resolución (resolu'θjon) nf 1 resolution. 2 decision.

resolver (ue) (resol'βer) vt resolve, settle, decide.

resollar (ue) (reso'ʎar) vi pant, puff.

resonar (ue) (reso'nar) vi resound. **resonancia** nf resonance. **resonante** adj resonant.

resoplar (reso'plar) vi breathe heavily. **resoplido** nm snort, puff.

resorte (re'sorte) nm 1 means, resort. 2 sl strings, influence. 3 spring, elasticity.

respaldar (respal'ðar) vt back, support. **respaldarse** lean back. **respaldo** nm 1 back (of a chair, etc.), support. 2 wall.

respecto (res'pekto) prep **respecto a** or **de** with respect to.

respetar (respe'tar) vt respect. **respeto** nm respect. **respetuoso** adj respectful.

respirar (respi'rar) vt,vi breathe. **respiración** nf respiration, breath. **respiro** nm 1 breathing. 2 reprieve.

resplandecer* (resplande'θer) vi glitter. **resplandeciente** adj glittering. **resplandor** nm glitter, glint.

responder (respon'der) vi reply, respond. **responder de** or **por** be answerable for.

responsable (respon'saβle) adj responsible. **responsabilidad** nf responsibility.

respuesta (res'pwesta) nf response.

resquebrajar (ie) (reskeβra'xar) vt split, crack.

resquemar (reske'mar) vt scald. **resquemor** nm 1 burn. 2 heartburn. 3 resentment.

resquicio (res'kiθjo) nm chink.

restablecer* (restaβle'θer) vt re-establish. **restablecimiento** nm 1 re-establishment. 2 med recovery.

restallar (resta'ʎar) vi crackle.

restante (res'tante) adj remaining.

restar (res'tar) vt subtract. vi remain.

restaurante (restau'rante) nm restaurant.

restaurar (restau'rar) vt restore. **restauración** nf restoration.

restituir (restitu'ir) vt restore, give back. **restitución** nf restitution.

resto ('resto) nm remainder, rest.

restregar (ie) (restre'gar) vt rub, scrub.

restricción (restrik'θjon) nf restriction. **restrictivo** adj restrictive.

restringir (restrin'xir) vt restrict.

resucitar (resuθi'tar) vt,vi resuscitate.

resuello (re'sweλo) nm breath, breathing.

resuelto (re'swelto) adj resolved, determined.

resultar (resul'tar) vi result, turn out. **resultado** nm result.

resumir (resu'mir) vt summarize. **resumen** nm summary.

retablo (re'taβlo) nm altarpiece.

retaguardia (reta'gwarδja) nf rearguard.

retal (re'tal) nm remnant.

retama (re'tama) nf bot broom.

retardar (retar'δar) vt retard, delay. **retardo** nm delay.

retén (re'ten) nm 1 catch, reserve. 2 mil reserve.

retener (rete'ner) vt retain. **retención** nf retention.

retina (re'tina) nf retina.

retintín (retin'tin) nm jingle.

retirar (reti'rar) vt withdraw. **retiro** nm 1 seclusion, retreat. 2 withdrawal.

reto ('reto) nm challenge.

retocar (reto'kar) vt retouch. **retoque** nm retouching.

retorcer (ue) (retor'θer) vt twist. **retorcido** adj 1 involved. 2 devious.

retórica (re'torika) nf rhetoric.

retornar (retor'nar) vt,vi return. **retorno** nm return.

retractar (retrak'tar) vt retract. **retracción** nf retraction. **retractable** adj also **retráctil** retractable.

retraer (retra'er) vt withdraw. **retraído** adj shy.

retrasar (retra'sar) vt delay. **retrasarse** vr be late. **retraso** nm delay.

retratar (retra'tar) vt portray. **retrato** nm portrait.

retrete (re'trete) nm lavatory.

retribuir (retriβu'ir) vt repay. **retribución** nf repayment.

retroceder (retroθe'δer) vi retreat. **retroceso** nm 1 retreat. 2 comm slump.

retruécano (retru'ekano) nm pun.

retumbar (retum'bar) vi resound.

reuma ('reuma) nm rheumatism. **reumático** adj rheumatic.

reunir (reu'nir) vt 1 unite. 2 collect. **reunirse** vr meet, assemble. **reunión** nf 1 meeting. 2 party.

revalidar (reβali'δar) vt confirm, ratify.

revancha (re'βantʃa) nf revenge.

revelar (reβe'lar) vt 1 reveal. 2 phot develop. **revelación** nf revelation. **revelado** nm phot developing.

revendedor (reβende'δor) nm retailer.

reventar (ie) (reβen'tar) vt,vi burst. **reventarse** vr blow up. **reventón** nm 1 bursting. 2 mot puncture.

reverberar (reβerβe'rar) vi 1 shimmer. 2 reverberate. **reverbero** or **reverberación** nm 1 reverberation. 2 reflector.

reverdecer (reβerδe'θer) vi 1 grow green. 2 grow young.

reverenciar (reβeren'θjar) vt revere. **reverencia** nf 1 reverence. 2 bow. **reverendo** adj 1 revered. 2 Reverend.

reversión (reβer'sjon) nf reversion. **reversible** adj reversible.

revés (re'βes) nm 1 reverse, back. 2 setback. **al revés** the wrong way round.

revisar (reβi'sar) vt revise, review. **revisión** nf 1 revision, review. 2 comm audit. **revista** nf 1 review. 2 journal, magazine.

revivir (reβi'βir) vt revive.

revocar (reβo'kar) vt revoke. **revocación** nf revocation.

revolcar (ue) (reβol'kar) vt knock over. **revolcarse** vr wallow.

revoltillo (reβolti'λo) nm confusion, mess.

revoltoso (reβol'toso) adj unruly.

revolución (reβolu'θjon) nf revolution. **revolucionario** adj revolutionary.

revolver (ue) (reβol'βer) vt 1 turn over. 2 disturb. **revolverse** vr turn around.

revólver (re'βolβer) nm revolver.

revoque (re'βoke) nm stucco, plaster.

revuelta (re'βwelta) nf 1 turn, bend. 2 disturbance.

revuelto (re'βwelto) adj disturbed, disorderly.

rey (rej) nm king.

reyerta (re'jerta) nf brawl, fight.

rezagar (reθa'gar) vt 1 overtake. 2 leave behind. **rezagarse** vr leave behind, straggle. **rezago** nm remainders, stragglers.

rezar (re'θar) vt pray for. vi pray. **rezo** nm prayers, praying.

rezumarse (reθu'marse) vr ooze, leak out.

riachuelo (rja'tʃwelo) nm stream.

ribera (ri'βera) nf river-bank.

ribete (ri'βete) nm border, trimmings (clothes, etc.).

ricino (ri'θino) nm castor-oil plant. **aceite de ricino** nm castor oil.

rico ('riko) adj 1 rich. 2 delicious.

ridiculizar (riðikuli'θar) vt ridicule. **ridículo** adj ridiculous. nm ridicule. **ridiculez** nf ridiculousness, absurdity.

riego ('rjeɣo) nm irrigation.

riel (rjel) nm rail, track.

rienda ('rjenda) nf rein.

riesgo ('rjesɣo) nm risk.

rifar (ri'far) vt raffle. **rifa** nf 1 raffle. 2 argument, quarrel.

rifle ('rifle) nm rifle.

rígido ('rixiðo) adj 1 rigid. 2 stern. **rigidez** nf rigidity.

rigor (ri'ɣor) nm 1 strictness, severity. 2 rigour. **riguroso** adj rigorous, severe.

rimar (ri'mar) vt,vi rhyme. **rima** nf rhyme.

rimbombante (rimbom'bante) adj bombastic.

rincón (rin'kon) nm corner, nook.

rinoceronte (rinoθe'ronte) nm rhinoceros.

riña ('riɲa) nf 1 quarrel. 2 fight.

riñón (ri'ɲon) nm kidney.

río[1] ('rio) nm river.

río[2] ('rio) v see **reír**.

ripio ('ripjo) nm 1 rubble. 2 waste.

riqueza (ri'keθa) nf wealth.

risa ('risa) nf 1 laugh. 2 laughter. **risueño** adj 1 smiling. 2 cheerful.

ristre ('ristre) nm **en ristre** all set, ready.

ritmo ('ritmo) nm rhythm. **rítmico** adj rhythmic.

rito ('rito) nm rite. **ritual** adj,nm ritual.

rival (ri'βal) adj,n rival.

rivalizar (riβali'θar) vi rival, compete. **rivalidad** nf rivalry.

rizar (ri'θar) vt 1 curl. 2 ripple. **rizado** adj curly. **rizo** nm 1 curl. 2 ripple.

robar (ro'βar) vt 1 steal. 2 rob. **robo** nm robbery.

roble ('roβle) nm oak.

robustecer* (roβuste'θer) vt strengthen. **robusto** adj robust.

roca ('roka) nf min rock.

roce ('roθe) nm graze, rub.

rociar (ro'θjar) vt sprinkle. **rocío** nm dew.

rocín (ro'θin) nm nag, old horse.

rodapié (roða'pje) nm skirting board.

rodar (ue) (ro'ðar) vi,vt roll. **rodaja** nf 1 roller. 2 slice. **rodaje** nm 1 wheels. 2 shooting (of a film). 3 mot running-in.

rodear (roðe'ar) vt encircle, surround. vi go round. **rodeo** nm 1 evasive remark. 2 rodeo.

rodezno (ro'ðeθno) nm 1 waterwheel. 2 cogwheel.

rodilla (ro'ðiʎa) nf knee.

rodillo (ro'ðiʎo) nm 1 roller. 2 rolling pin.

roer (ro'er) vt 1 gnaw. 2 corrode.

rogar (ue) (ro'ɣar) vi,vt beg. **rogación** nf petition.

rojo ('roxo) adj red. nm 1 red. 2 rouge.

rollizo (ro'ʎiθo) adj plump, round.

rollo ('roʎo) nm 1 roll. 2 phot film.

romance (ro'manθe) nm ballad. adj,nm lit Romance. **romancero** nm ballad collection.

romántico (ro'mantiko) adj romantic. **romanticismo** nm lit Romanticism.

romería (rome'ria) nf pilgrimage. **romero** nm 1 pilgrim. 2 bot rosemary.

romo ('romo) adj 1 snub-nosed. 2 obtuse (person).

rompecabezas (rompeka'βeθas) nm invar 1 puzzle, brain-teaser. 2 jigsaw puzzle.

rompeolas (rompe'olas) nm invar breakwater.

romper (rom'per) vt,vi break. **rompimiento** nm 1 breaking. 2 break.

ron (ron) nm rum.

roncar (ron'kar) vi 1 snore. 2 roar.

ronco ('ronko) adj hoarse.

rondar (ron'dar) vt,vi 1 haunt, frequent. 2 patrol. 3 prowl. **ronda** nf 1 night watch, patrol. 2 round (drinks, cards, etc.).

ronquedad (ronke'ðað) nf also **ronquera** huskiness, hoarseness.

ronquido (ron'kiðo) nm snore.

ronronear (ronrone'ar) vi purr.

ronzal (ron'θal) nm halter.

roña ('roɲa) nf 1 scab. 2 mange. 3 grime. 4 mean person. **roñoso** adj 1 mangy. 2 grimy. 3 mean. **roñería** nf meanness.

ropa ('ropa) nf clothing. **ropero** nm wardrobe. **ropa interior** underclothes.

roque ('roke) nm rook (chess).

rosa ('rosa) nf rose. **rosado** adj pink. **rosal** nm 1 rosebush. 2 rose garden.

rosario (ro'sarjo) nm rosary.

rosca ('roska) nf 1 ring. 2 coil. 3 thread (of a screw). **hacer la rosca** flatter.

rostro ('rostro) nm 1 face. 2 rostrum.

rotación (rota'θjon) nf rotation.

roto ('roto) adj broken. nm break, hole. **rotura** nf rupture, break.

rotular (rotu'lar) vt label. **rótulo** nm 1 label. 2 poster.

rotundo (ro'tundo) adj 1 round. 2 peremptory.

roturar (rotu'rar) vt plough up (ground).

rozar (ro'θar) vt,vi rub, graze. **rozarse** vr 1 get worn, chafed. 2 be in close contact. **rozadura** nf graze, chafe.

rubí (ru'βi) nm, pl **rubíes** ruby.

rubio ('ruβjo) adj blond.

rubor (ru'βor) nm blush.

rúbrica ('ruβrika) nf 1 rubric, heading. 2 flourish (of a signature).

rudeza (ru'ðeθa) nf roughness. **rudo** adj rough, plain.

rudimento (ruði'mento) nm rudiment.

rueca ('rweka) nf distaff, spinning wheel.

rueda ('rweða) nf 1 wheel. 2 circle.

ruedo ('rweðo) nm 1 turn, revolution. 2 hem. 3 bullring.

ruego ('rwego) nm request.

rugir (ru'xir) vi roar. **rugido** nm roar, bellow.

rugoso (ru'goso) adj wrinkled.

ruibarbo (rui'βarβo) nm rhubarb.

ruido ('ruiðo) nm noise. **ruidoso** adj noisy.

ruin (ru'in) adj mean, contemptible. **ruindad** nf meanness.

ruina ('ruina) nf 1 ruin. 2 ruins, remains. **ruinoso** adj ruinous.

ruiseñor (ruise'ɲor) nm nightingale.

rumbo ('rumbo) nm 1 direction, course. 2 inf pomp, ostentation. **rumboso** adj 1 splendid, lavish. 2 generous.

rumiar (ru'mjar) vt digest, ruminate. **rumiante** adj,n ruminant.

rumor (ru'mor) nm 1 rumour. 2 murmur. **rumoroso** adj murmuring (of a stream, etc.).

ruptura (rup'tura) nf rupture.

rural (ru'ral) adj rural.

Rusia ('rusja) nf Russia. **ruso** adj,n Russian. nm Russian (language).

rústico ('rustiko) adj rustic.

ruta ('ruta) nf route, way.

rutina (ru'tina) nf routine. **rutinario** adj routine, everyday.

S

sábado ('saβaðo) nm Saturday.

sabana (sa'βana) nf savannah.

sábana ('saβana) nf sheet.

sabañón (saβa'ɲon) nm chilblain.

saber* (sa'βer) vt 1 know. 2 know how. vi

taste. **saber a** taste of. **saber de** know about. **sabio** adj wise. nm learned man. **sabiduría** nf wisdom.

sabor (sa'βor) nm 1 taste. 2 flavour.

saborear (saβore'ar) vt savour, relish. **saborearse** vr 1 anticipate. 2 relish the thought of.

sabotear (saβote'ar) vt sabotage. **sabotaje** nm sabotage.

sabroso (sa'βroso) adj 1 tasty, delicious. 2 racy, daring.

sacabocados (sakaβo'kaðos) nm invar tech punch.

sacacorchos (saka'kortʃos) nm,pl **sacacorchos** corkscrew.

sacar (sa'kar) vt 1 take out. 2 buy (tickets). 3 sport serve. 4 bring out, publish.

sacerdote (saθer'ðote) nm priest.

saciar (sa'θjar) vt satisfy, appease. **saciedad** nf satiety.

saco ('sako) nm 1 bag, sack. 2 plunder. **entrar a saco** sack, plunder.

sacramento (sakra'mento) nm sacrament.

sacrificar (sakrifi'kar) vt sacrifice. **sacrificio** nm 1 sacrifice. 2 slaughter.

sacrilegio (sakri'lexjo) nm sacrilege.

sacro ('sakro) adj sacred.

sacudir (saku'ðir) vt shake, jolt. **sacudida** nf shake, jolt.

sádico ('saðiko) adj sadistic. **sadismo** nm sadism. **sadista** nm,f sadist.

saeta (sa'eta) nf 1 arrow. 2 dart. 3 hand (of a watch). 4 brief religious song.

sagacidad (sagaθi'ðað) nf shrewdness. **sagaz** adj shrewd, wise.

sagrado (sa'graðo) adj sacred, holy. nm sanctuary.

sajón (sa'xon) adj Saxon.

sal (sal) nf 1 salt. 2 wit, charm.

sala ('sala) nf 1 drawing room. 2 hall (of theatre, etc.). **sala de espera** waiting room.

salar (sa'lar) vt salt. **salado** adj 1 salty. 2 witty.

salario (sa'larjo) nm salary, pay.

salchicha (sal'tʃitʃa) nf sausage.

saldar (sal'dar) vt settle, pay off. **saldo** nm 1 payment. 2 clearance sale. 3 comm balance.

salero (sa'lero) nm 1 salt cellar. 2 wit. 3 charm.

salgo ('salgo) v see **salir**.

salida (sa'liða) nf 1 departure. 2 exit. 3 rising (of sun, moon). 4 Th appearance, entry. 5. outcome.

saliente (sa'ljente) nm 1 projection. 2 salient. adj overhanging, jutting out.

salir* (sa'lir) vi 1 emerge, come out. 2 depart,

leave. 3 rise (sun, moon, etc.). 4 *Th* make an entry. 5 happen, turn out. **salirse** *vr* 1 get away from the point. 2 leak.

salmón (sal'mon) *nm* salmon.

salmuera (sal'mwera) *nf* brine, pickling fluid.

salón (sa'lon) *nm* 1 large hall. 2 drawing room.

salpicar (salpi'kar) *vt* 1 splash, spatter. 2 sprinkle. **salpicadura** *nf* splash, sprinkle.

salsa ('salsa) *nf cul* sauce, gravy.

saltamontes (salta'montes) *nm invar* grasshopper.

saltar (sal'tar) *vt* 1 jump. 2 miss out, skip. 3 blow up (with explosives). *vi* 1 jump, leap. 2 blow up, explode.

saltear (salte'ar) *vt* 1 rob, hold up. 2 attack by surprise, assail. **salteador** *nm* robber.

salto ('salto) *nm* 1 leap, jump. 2 hop. **salto de altura** high diving. **salto mortal** somersault. **salto de agua** waterfall.

salubre (sa'luβre) *adj* healthy. **salubridad** *nf* healthiness.

salud (sa'luð) *nf* 1 health. **¡salud!** *interj* 1 cheers, good health. 2 cheerio, goodbye.

saludar (salu'ðar) *vt* 1 greet. 2 salute. **le saluda atentamente** yours faithfully. **saludo** *nm* 1 greeting. 2 *pl* regards, best wishes.

salvaje (sal'βaxe) *adj* 1 *bot, zool* wild. 2 savage. *nm* savage.

salvar (sal'βar) *vt* 1 rescue, save. 2 except. 3 cross, clear (an obstacle). **salvador** *nm* saviour. **salvamento** *nm* rescue, salvage. **bote de salvamento** *nm* lifeboat.

salvedad (salβe'ðað) *nf* proviso, qualification. **con la salvedad de que** with the proviso that.

salvia ('salβja) *nf bot* sage.

salvo ('salβo) *adv* except, saving. **a salvo** safe, out of danger. **poner a salvo** rescue. **salvo que** unless. ~*adj* safe. **sano y salvo** safe and sound.

salvoconducto (salβokon'dukto) *nf* safe conduct.

san (san) *adj* see **santo**.

sanar (sa'nar) *vt* heal, cure. *vi* get better, regain one's health. **sanatorio** *nm* sanatorium.

sandalia (san'dalja) *nf* sandal.

sandía (san'dia) *nf* watermelon.

sanear (sane'ar) *vt* 1 drain. 2 repair (damage). 3 insure. **saneamiento** *nm* 1 drainage. 2 cleaning-up. 3 law security, insurance.

sangrar (san'grar) *vt* 1 *med* bleed. 2 drain off. *vi* bleed. **sangre** *nf* blood.

sangría (san'gria) *nf* 1 *cul* a drink of red wine and fruit. 2 *med* bleeding, blood-letting. **sangriento** *adj* bloody, bloodstained.

sanguijuela (sangi'xwela) *nf* leech.

sanguíneo (san'gineo) *adj* 1 of or like blood. 2 sanguine.

sanidad (sani'ðað) *nf* health, healthiness. **sanitario** *adj* sanitary. **sano** *adj* 1 healthy, wholesome. 2 intact, unbroken.

santa ('santa) *nf* saint. See also **santo**.

santiamén (santja'men) *nm* **en un santiamén** in a flash.

santificar (santifi'kar) *vt* sanctify, consecrate, hallow. **santificación** *nf* sanctification.

santiguar (santi'gwar) *vt* bless. **santiguarse** *vr* cross oneself.

santo ('santo) *adj* 1 sacred, holy. 2 saintly. **santo y bueno** all well and good. ~*nm* 1 saint. 2 *mil* password. 3 saint's day.

santuario (san'twarjo) *nm* sanctuary, shrine.

saña ('sana) *nf* fury, rage. **sañudo** *adj* 1 furious, enraged. 2 vicious.

sapo ('sapo) *nm* toad.

saquear (sake'ar) *vt* loot, plunder. **saqueo** *nm* plunder. **saqueador** *nm* looter.

sarampión (saram'pjon) *nm* measles.

sarcasmo (sar'kasmo) *nm* sarcasm. **sarcástico** *adj* sarcastic.

sardina (sar'ðina) *nf* sardine.

sargento (sar'xento) *nm* sergeant.

sarna ('sarna) *nf* scabies. **sarnoso** *adj* 1 mangy. 2 itchy.

sartén (sar'ten) *nf* frying pan.

sastre ('sastre) *nm* tailor. **sastrería** *nf* 1 tailoring. 2 tailor's shop.

satélite (sa'telite) *nm* satellite.

sátira ('satira) *nf* satire. **satírico** *adj* satirical. **satirizar** *vt* satirize.

satisfacer* (satisfa'θer) *vt* satisfy. **satisfacerse** *vr* content oneself. **satisfacción** *nf* satisfaction. **satisfactorio** *adj* satisfactory. **satisfecho** *adj* satisfied.

saturar (satu'rar) *vt* saturate. **saturación** *nf* saturation.

sauce ('sauθe) *nm bot* willow.

savia ('saβja) *nf* sap.

saya ('saja) *nf* skirt, petticoat. **sayo** *nm* smock.

sazonar (saθo'nar) *vt* 1 ripen, mature. 2 *cul* season. **sazón** *nf* 1 time. 2 *cul* flavour. **a la sazón** then, at that moment. **en sazón** ripe. **sazonado** *adj* 1 ripe. 2 *cul* seasoned.

se[1] (se) *pron* 1 himself, herself, itself, themselves. 2 each other. 3 oneself.

se[2] (se) *v see* **saber**.

sebo ('seβo) nm grease, fat. **seboso** adj greasy, fatty.

secar (se'kar) vt dry. **secador** nm drying place, drier. **secadora** nf drier. **secano** nm dry barren land. **secante** adj drying. nm blotting paper.

sección (sek'θjon) nf section.

seco ('seko) adj 1 dry, withered. 2 brusque, cold. 3 (of sound) dull. **a secas** curtly, abruptly.

secretario (sekre'tarjo) nm secretary. **secretaría** nf 1 secretariat. 2 secretary's office.

secreto (se'kreto) nm 1 secret. 2 secrecy. adj secret, confidential. **secretear** vi whisper, exchange confidences.

secta ('sekta) nf sect.

secuaz (se'kwaθ) nm follower, supporter.

secuestrar (sekwes'trar) vt 1 kidnap. 2 hijack. **secuestrador** nm 1 kidnapper. 2 hijacker. **secuestro** nm 1 kidnap. 2 hijack.

secundar (sekun'dar) vt second, support.

sed (seð) nf thirst. **tener sed** be thirsty.

seda ('seða) nf silk.

sedante (se'ðante) nm sedative. adj calming, sedative.

sede ('seðe) nf seat (of government, etc.). **Santa Sede** Holy See.

sedería (seðe'ria) nf silk goods.

sedición (seði'θjon) nf sedition. **sedicioso** nm rebel. adj seditious.

sediento (se'ðjento) adj thirsty.

sedimento (seði'mento) nm sediment. **sedimentar** vt deposit.

seducir* (seðu'θir) vt 1 seduce. 2 charm, captivate. **seducción** nf seduction. **seductor** nm seducer. adj seductive.

segar (ie) (se'gar) vt mow, reap. **segadora** nf 1 mower, mowing machine. 2 reaper.

seglar (se'glar) nm layman. adj secular.

segregar (segre'gar) vt 1 segregate. 2 anat secrete. **segregación** nf 1 segregation. 2 secretion.

seguida (se'giða) nf continuation. **coger la seguida** get into the swing. **en seguida** straight away. **seguidamente** adv immediately after.

seguido (se'giðo) adj continuous, unbroken. **todo seguido** straight ahead.

seguir (i) (se'gir) vt 1 follow. 2 pursue. 3 continue. **seguidor** nm follower.

según (se'gun) prep according to. adv it all depends.

segundo (se'gundo) adj,nm second.

segundón (segun'don) nm second son.

seguridad (seguri'ðað) nf 1 security, safety. 2 certainty. **seguro** adj 1 safe. 2 sure. nm 1 safety catch. 2 insurance.

seis ('seis) adj,nm six.

selección (selek'θjon) nf selection. **selecto** adj select, choice.

selva ('selβa) nf 1 forest. 2 jungle. **selvoso** adj wooded, forested.

sello ('seʎo) nm 1 postage stamp. 2 seal. 3 hallmark. **sellado** adj sealed. nm sealing, stamping.

semáforo (se'maforo) nm 1 semaphore. 2 traffic lights.

semana (se'mana) nf week.

semblante (sem'blante) nm 1 face. 2 appearance.

sembrar (ie) (sem'brar) vt 1 sow. 2 scatter.

semejar (seme'xar) vi be like, resemble. **semejante** adj similar. nm equal, like. **semejanza** nf similarity.

semestre (se'mestre) nm semester. **semestral** adj half-yearly.

semilla (se'miʎa) nf seed. **semillero** nm 1 seedbed, nursery. 2 hotbed.

seminario (semi'narjo) nm 1 seminar. 2 eccl seminary. 3 seedbed, nursery.

senado (se'naðo) nm senate. **senador** nm senator.

sencillez (senθi'ʎeθ) nf 1 simplicity. 2 simple-mindedness. **sencillo** adj 1 easy. 2 simple, unsophisticated.

senda ('senda) nf path. **sendero** nm path.

sendos ('sendos) adj pl 1 each. 2 both.

senectud (senek'tuð) nf old age.

senil (se'nil) adj senile.

seno ('seno) nm 1 bosom, breast. 2 haven, refuge.

sensación (sensa'θjon) nf sensation. **sensacional** adj sensational.

sensatez (sensa'teθ) nf good sense. **sensato** adj sensible.

sensibilidad (sensiβili'ðað) nf 1 sensibility. 2 sensitivity. **sensible** adj 1 sensitive, responsive. 2 perceptible. 3 regrettable.

sensiblería (sensiβle'ria) nf sentimentality. **sensiblero** adj sentimental.

sensitivo (sensi'tiβo) adj 1 relating to the sense. 2 sensitive.

sensual (sen'swal) adj sensual. **sensualidad** nf sensuality.

sentar (ie) (sen'tar) vt 1 place, locate. 2

establish. 3 suit, agree with. **sentarse** *vr* 1 sit down. 2 settle. **sentada** *nf* sit-in.

sentencia (sen'tenθja) *nf* 1 *law* sentence. 2 ruling. **sentenciar** *law* *vt* sentence. *vi* lay down ruling. **sentencioso** *adj* 1 pithy. 2 sententious

sentido (sen'tiðo) *nm* 1 sense. 2 meaning. 3 direction. *adj* 1 susceptible, touchy. 2 offended.

sentimiento (senti'mjento) *nm* 1 feeling, emotion. 2 sentiment. 3 grief, regret. **sentimental** *adj* 1 sentimental. 2 emotional.

sentir (ie) (sen'tir) *vt* 1 feel. 2 hear. 3 regret. **lo siento mucho** I am very sorry. **sentirse** *vr* feel. **sentirse enfermo** feel ill.

seña ('seɲa) *nf* 1 mark. 2 sign. 3 *pl* name and address.

señal (se'ɲal) *nf* 1 signal. 2 sign. 3 mark.

señalar (seɲa'lar) *vt* 1 point out, point to. 2 denote. 3 mark. **señalarse** *vr* make one's mark. **señalado** *adj* 1 marked out, singled out. 2 distinguished.

señor (se'ɲor) *nm* 1 gentleman. 2 mister. **señora** *nf* 1 lady. 2 wife. 3 madam. **señorita** *nf* Miss.

separar (sepa'rar) *vt* separate. **separarse** *vr* 1 separate, come free. 2 cut oneself off. **separación** *nf* separation. **separado** *adj* separate. **separatismo** *nm* separatism.

septentrional (septentrijo'nal) *adj* northern.

séptico ('septiko) *adj* septic.

septiembre (sep'tjembre) *nm* September.

séptimo ('septimo) *adj* seventh.

septuagésimo (septwa'xesimo) *adj* seventieth.

sepulcro (se'pulkro) *nm* tomb, grave.

sepultar (sepul'tar) *vt* bury. **sepultura** *nf* 1 burial. 2 grave. **sepulturero** *nm* gravedigger.

sequedad (seke'ðað) *nf* 1 dryness. 2 brusqueness.

sequía (se'kia) *nf* drought.

séquito ('sekito) *nm* entourage, followers.

ser* (ser) *vi* be. **siendo así que** since. **a no ser por** but for. **sea lo que sea** come what may. **~nm** being.

serenar (sere'nar) *vt* calm, quieten. **sereno** *adj* 1 serene, calm. 2 (of weather) settled, calm. *nm* 1 night watchman. 2 night dew. **serenidad** *nf* calmness.

serie ('serje) *nf* series.

seriedad (serje'ðað) *nf* seriousness. **serio** *adj* 1 grave, solemn. 2 serious, responsible. **tomar en serio** take seriously.

sermón (ser'mon) *nm* sermon.

serpentear (serpente'ar) *vi* 1 wriggle. 2 meander. **serpenteo** *nm* wriggling, twisting.

serpiente (ser'pjente) *nf* snake.

serrano (ser'rano) *adj* of the mountains. *nm* highlander.

serrar (ie) (ser'rar) *vt* saw. **serrín** *nm* sawdust.

servicio (ser'viθjo) *nm* 1 service. 2 *pl* toilet, lavatory. **estar de servicio** be on duty. **servicial** *adj* helpful.

servidor (serβi'ðor) *nm* servant. **servidumbre** *nf* servitude. **servil** *adj* servile.

servilleta (serβi'ʎeta) *nf* napkin.

servir (i)* (ser'βir) *vt* serve.

sesenta (se'senta) *adj* sixty.

sesgar (ses'gar) *vt* slant, twist to one side. **sesgo** *nm* slant, twist. *adj* sloped, biased.

sesión (sesi'on) *nf* 1 session. 2 *Th* performance.

seso ('seso) *nm* brain.

seta ('seta) *nf* mushroom.

setenta (se'tenta) *adj* seventy.

seto ('seto) *nm* fence.

seudónimo (seu'ðonimo) *nm* pseudonym.

severidad (seβeri'ðað) *nf* severity. **severo** *adj* 1 severe. 2 strict, harsh.

sexagésimo (seksa'xesimo) *adj* sixtieth.

sexo ('sekso) *nm* sex. **sexual** *adj* sexual.

sexto ('seksto) *adj* sixth.

si (si) *conj* 1 if. 2 whether.

sí¹ (si) *adv* 1 yes. 2 certainly. **sí que es** of course it is.

sí² (si) *pron* 3rd pers s himself, herself, itself. **sí mismo** himself. **entre sí** among themselves. **de por sí** in itself.

siderurgia (siðe'rurxja) *nf* iron and steel industry.

sidra ('siðra) *nf* cider.

siega ('sjega) *nf* reaping, harvesting.

siembra ('sjembra) *nf* sowing.

siempre ('sjempre) *adv* always. **siempre que** 1 whenever. 2 provided that.

sien (sjen) *nf* anat temple.

siento ('sjento) *v* see **sentir**.

sierra ('sjerra) *nf* 1 saw. 2 sierra, mountain range.

siervo ('sjerβo) *nm* 1 slave. 2 servant.

siesta ('sjesta) *nf* siesta.

siete ('sjete) *adj,nm* seven.

sífilis ('sifilis) *nm* syphilis.

sifón (si'fon) *nm* 1 soda water. 2 syphon.

sigilo (si'xilo) *nm* secrecy. **sigiloso** *adj* 1 secret. 2 discreet.

siglo ('siglo) *nm* century.

signar (sig'nar) *vt* sign, seal.

significar (signifiˈkar) vt 1 mean, signify. 2 express. **significarse** vr become famous or notorious. **significado** adj well-known. nm meaning, significance.

signo (ˈsigno) nm sign.

siguiente (siˈgjente) adv following.

sílaba (ˈsilaβa) nf syllable.

silbar (silˈβar) vt 1 whistle. 2 hiss. **silbido** nm 1 whistle. 2 hiss.

silencio (siˈlenθjo) nm silence. **silenciar** vt silence. **silencioso** adj silent.

silueta (siˈlweta) nf silhouette, outline.

silvestre (silˈβestre) adj bot wild.

silla (ˈsiʎa) nf 1 chair, seat. 2 saddle. **sillon** nm armchair.

sima (ˈsima) nf abyss.

símbolo (ˈsimbolo) nm symbol. **simbólico** adj symbolic. **simbolizar** vt symbolize.

simetría (simeˈtria) nf symmetry. **simétrico** adj symmetrical.

simiente (siˈmjente) nf seed.

símil (ˈsimil) adj similar. nm 1 comparison. 2 simile.

similar (simiˈlar) adj similar.

simpatía (simpaˈtia) nf 1 affection. 2 friendliness, likeableness. 3 mutual support, sympathy.

simpático (simˈpatiko) adj nice, pleasant.

simpatizar (simpatiˈθar) vi get on well, become friends.

simple (ˈsimple) adj 1 simple. 2 simple-minded. **simplemente** adv merely.

simplificar (simplifiˈkar) vt simplify. **simplificación** nf simplification.

simulacro (simuˈlakro) nm 1 image. 2 semblance.

simular (simuˈlar) vt simulate. **simulado** adj simulated, sham.

simultáneo (simulˈtaneo) adj simultaneous.

sin (sin) prep without. **sin que** conj without.

sinagoga (sinaˈgoga) nf synagogue.

sincero (sinˈθero) adj sincere. **sinceridad** nf sincerity.

sindicato (sindiˈkato) nm 1 syndicate. 2 trade union. **sindical** adj trade-union.

sinfín (sinˈfin) nm un sinfín de a large number of, a great many.

sinfonía (sinfoˈnia) nf symphony. **sinfónico** adj symphonic.

singular (singuˈlar) adj 1 singular. 2 exceptional. **singularizar** vt single out. **singularizarse** vr excel.

siniestro (siˈnjestro) adj 1 left (opposite of right). 2 sinister. nm catastrophe. **siniestrado** nm victim (of an accident).

sino (ˈsino) nm fate, destiny. conj but, except.

sinrazón (sinraˈθon) nf injustice.

sinsabor (sinsaˈβor) nm trouble, worry.

sintaxis (sinˈtaksis) nf syntax. **sintáctico** adj syntactic.

síntesis (ˈsintesis) nf invar synthesis. **sintético** adj synthetic.

sintió (sinˈtjo) v see **sentir.**

síntoma (ˈsintoma) nm symptom. **sintomático** adj symptomatic.

sintonizar (sintoniˈθar) vt tech tune.

siquiera (siˈkjera) adv 1 even if, even though. 2 at least. **ni siquiera** not even.

sirena (siˈrena) nf 1 siren, mermaid. 2 siren, foghorn.

sirviente (sirˈβjente) nm servant.

sisar (siˈsar) vt 1 pilfer. 2 cheat. **sisa** nf theft, pilfering.

sistema (sisˈtema) nm system, method.

sitiar (siˈtjar) vt 1 besiege. 2 surround.

sitio (ˈsitjo) nm 1 place. 2 room, space. 3 siege.

situar (siˈtwar) vt situate. **situación** nf situation. **situado** adj situated.

so (so) prep under.

sobaco (soˈβako) nm armpit.

sobado (soˈβaðo) adj shabby, well-worn.

sobar (soˈβar) vt 1 crumple. 2 knead. 3 fondle.

soberanía (soβeraˈnia) nf sovereignty. **soberano** adj,nm sovereign.

soberbia (soˈβerβja) nf 1 pride. 2 magnificence, pomp. **soberbio** adj 1 proud. 2 superb.

sobornar (soβorˈnar) vt bribe. **soborno** nm 1 bribe. 2 bribery.

sobrar (soˈβrar) vt exceed. vi remain, be left over. **de sobra** more than enough. **sobradamente** adv amply, only too well. **sobrado** adj superfluous. **sobrante** adj spare, surplus. nm surplus.

sobre (ˈsoβre) prep on, upon, over.

sobrecama (soβreˈkama) nm bedspread.

sobrecargar (soβrekarˈgar) vt overload.

sobrecejo (soβreˈθexo) nm frown.

sobrecoger (soβrekoˈxer) vt 1 scare, startle. **sobrecogerse** vr 1 be scared. 2 be overcome.

sobremanera (soβremaˈnera) adv exceedingly.

sobremesa (soβreˈmesa) nf 1 dessert. 2 table cover. 3 period after dinner (for conversation, etc.).

sobrenatural (soβrenatuˈral) adj supernatural.

sobrepasar (soβrepaˈsar) vt surpass.

sobreponer (soβrepoˈner) vt 1 superimpose. 2

put before. **sobreponerse** vr **1** win through, overcome. **2** master oneself.

sobresalir (soβresa'lir) vi **1** jut out, project. **2** be outstanding, excel.

sobresaltar (soβresal'tar) vt startle. **sobresalto** nm scare, shock. **de sobresalto** suddenly.

sobretodo (soβre'todo) nm overcoat.

sobrevenir* (soβreβe'nir) vi happen suddenly.

sobrevivir (soβreβi'βir) vi survive. **sobreviviente** nm survivor.

sobriedad (soβrje'ðað) nf sobriety. **sobrio** adj sober, moderate.

sobrino (so'βrino) nm nephew. **sobrina** nf niece.

socarrón (sokar'ron) adj sarcastic.

socavar (soka'βar) vt undermine. **socavón** nm **1** cavity. **2** subsidence.

sociable (so'θjaβle) adj sociable.

socialismo (soθja'lismo) nm socialism. **socialista** nm socialist.

sociedad (soθje'ðað) nf **1** society. **2** comm company. **socio** nm member (of club, etc.).

sociología (soθjolo'xia) nf sociology. **sociólogo** nm sociologist.

socorrer (sokor'rer) vt help. **socorrido** adj **1** useful, helpful. **2** trite, hackneyed. **3** well-provided. **socorro** nm help, assistance.

soez (so'eθ) adj obscene, vulgar.

sofocar (sofo'kar) vt **1** suffocate, stifle, smother. **2** embarrass, make blush. **sofoco** nm **1** suffocation. **2** embarrassment.

soga ('soga) nf rope, cord.

sois (sojs) v see **ser.**

soja ('soxa) nf soya.

sojuzgar (soxuθ'gar) vt subdue.

sol (sol) nm sun.

solapa (so'lapa) nf **1** flap. **2** lapel. **3** slyness. **solapado** adj sly. **solapar** vt overlap.

solar (so'lar) nm **1** piece of ground, site. **2** ancestral home. adj solar.

solaz (so'laθ) nm relaxation, solace. **solazar** vt distract, amuse.

soldado (sol'daðo) nm soldier.

soldar (ue) (sol'dar) vt solder, weld. **soldador** nm soldering iron. **soldadura** nf welding.

soledad (sole'ðað) nf loneliness, solitude.

solemne (so'lemne) adj solemn. **solemnidad** nf solemnity.

soler (ue) (so'ler) vi be in the habit of, be accustomed to.

solera (so'lera) nf **1** prop, support. **2** typical character. **3** vintage.

solicitar (soliθi'tar) vt **1** request. **2** apply for. **3** canvass. **solicitante** nm, f applicant.

solícito (so'liθito) adj solicitous, careful, concerned about.

solicitud (soliθi'tuð) nf **1** solicitude. **2** application. **3** petition.

solidaridad (soliðari'ðað) nf solidarity. **solidarizarse** vr side with, declare support for.

sólido ('soliðo) adj solid, firm, sound. **solidez** nf **1** hardness. **2** solidity.

solitario (soli'tarjo) adj lonely, solitary. nm recluse, hermit.

solo ('solo) adj **1** alone. **2** single, unique. **3** mus solo. **a solas** by oneself.

sólo ('solo) adv only, merely.

soltar (ue) (sol'tar) vt **1** let go, release, untie. **soltarse** vr begin, start to be fluent.

soltero (sol'tero) nm bachelor. adj single, unmarried. **soltera** nf spinster. **solterona** nf old maid.

soltura (sol'tura) nf looseness, ease of movement. **hablar con soltura** speak fluently.

soluble (so'luβle) adj soluble. **solubilidad** nf solubility. **solución** nf solution. **solucionar** vt solve.

solvencia (sol'βenθja) nf comm solvency. **solvente** adj solvent.

sollozar (soλo'θar) vi sob. **sollozo** nm sob.

sombra ('sombra) nf shadow, shade.

sombrero (som'brero) nm hat.

sombrilla (som'briλa) nf parasol.

sombrío (som'brio) adj **1** shady, dark. **2** sombre, gloomy.

somero (so'mero) adj superficial.

someter (some'ter) vt **1** conquer, overwhelm. **2** subordinate. **3** submit (to trial, etc.).

somnífero (som'nifero) nm sleeping pill.

somnolencia (somno'lenθja) nf sleepiness.

somos ('somos) v see **ser.**

son[1] (son) nm **1** sound. **2** rumour.

son[2] (son) v see **ser.**

sonar (ue) (so'nar) vt,vi **1** ring. **2** sound. **sonarse** vr blow one's nose. **sonado** adj sensational, talked-about.

sondear (sonde'ar) vt **1** naut sound, take soundings of. **2** bore, drill. **3** sound out (opinion, etc.). **sondeo** nm **1** tech boring, drilling. **2** inquiry, investigation.

soneto (so'neto) nm sonnet.

sonido (so'niðo) nm sound.

sonoro (so'noro) adj **1** sonorous. **2** sound.

sonreír* (sonre'ir) vi smile. **sonriente** adj smiling. **sonrisa** nf smile.

sonrojar (sonro'xar) *vt* make blush, embarrass. **sonrojarse** *vr* blush, flush. **sonrojo** *nm* 1 blush. 2 insult.

soñar (ue) (so'ɲar) *vt,vi* dream. **soñar con** dream of. **soñar despierto** to daydream. **soñador** *adj* dreamy. *nm* dreamer.

soñoliento (soɲo'ljento) *adj* drowsy, sleepy.

sopa ('sopa) *nf* 1 soup. 2 *sl* hangover. **sopa juliana** vegetable soup. **hecho una sopa** soaked to the skin.

sopapo (so'papo) *nm* blow, punch.

soplar (so'plar) *vt* 1 blow away. 2 blow out, inflate. 3 whisper. 4 *Th* prompt. **soplarse** *vr* gobble (food). **soplado** *adj* smartly dressed. **soplo** *nm* 1 gust. 2 puff of breath.

sopor (so'por) *nm* drowsiness.

soportar (sopor'tar) *vt* 1 carry. 2 withstand, endure. **soportable** *adj* bearable. **soporte** *nm* support.

sorber (sor'βer) *vt* 1 sip, suck. 2 soak up, absorb. **sorbo** *nm* 1 sip. 2 gulp.

sordera (sor'ðera) *nf* deafness.

sórdido ('sorðiðo) *adj* squalid. **sordidez** *nf* squalor.

sordo ('sorðo) *adj* 1 deaf. 2 muffled.

sordomudo (sorðo'muðo) *adj* deaf and dumb.

sorprender (sorpren'der) *vt* surprise. **sorprendente** *adj* surprising. **sorpresa** *nf* surprise.

sortear (sorte'ar) *vt* 1 draw lots for, raffle. 2 avoid, swerve round. **sorteo** *nm* 1 raffle, draw. 2 *sport* toss.

sortija (sor'tixa) *nf* 1 ring. 2 curl (of hair).

sortilegio (sorti'lexjo) *nm* 1 sorcery. 2 charm.

sosegar (ie) (sose'gar) *vt* calm, quieten. **sosiego** *nm* calm, quiet.

soslayar (sosla'jar) *vt* 1 lay obliquely. 2 avoid, get round. **al soslayo** aslant, obliquely. **de soslayo** sidelong, from the side.

soso ('soso) *adj* 1 tasteless. 2 dull, insipid.

sospechar (sospe'tʃar) *vt* suspect. **sospecha** *nf* suspicion. **sospechoso** *adj* suspicious, suspect.

sostener* (soste'ner) *vt* 1 prop up, support. 2 sustain, nourish. 3 maintain. 4 defend. **sostenerse** *vr* 1 support oneself upright. 2 continue unchanged. 3 support oneself, keep going. **sostén** *nm* 1 support, prop. 2 brassière. 3 sustenance. **sostenido** *adj* sustained, continuous. **sostenimiento** *nm* support, maintenance.

sota ('sota) *nf* game jack.

sotana (so'tana) *nf* rel cassock.

sótano ('sotano) *nm* basement, cellar.

soto ('soto) *nm* thicket, copse.

soviet (so'βjet) *nm, pl* **soviets** Soviet. **soviético** *adj* Soviet.

soy (soj) *v* see **ser.**

su (su) *poss adj* 1 his, her, its. 2 your. 3 their.

suave ('swaβe) *adj* 1 smooth. 2 gentle, mild. **suavidad** *nf* 1 smoothness. 2 mildness.

suavizar (swaβi'θar) *vt* 1 smooth. 2 calm down, soothe.

subarrendar (ie) (suβarren'dar) *vt* sublet. **subarriendo** *nm* sublet.

subasta (su'βasta) *nf* auction. **subastar** *v* auction.

subconsciencia (subkons'θjenθja) *nf* subconscious. **subconsciente** *adj* subconscious.

subdesarrollado (suβðesarro'ʎaðo) *adj* underdeveloped. **subdesarrollo** *nm* underdevelopment.

súbdito ('suβðito) *nm pol* subject, citizen.

subdividir (suβðiβi'ðir) *vt* subdivide. **subdivisión** *nf* subdivision.

subir (su'βir) *vt* 1 raise, lift. 2 ascend, go up. 3 promote. *vi* rise, go up. **subir al coche** get into the car. **subirse** *vr* 1 rise, climb. 2 become proud or conceited. **subida** *nf* 1 climb, ascent. 2 rise. **subido** *adj* (of colour) bright, strong.

súbito ('suβito) *adj* sudden. *adv* suddenly.

sublevar (suβle'βar) *vt* rouse, stir up. **sublevarse** *vr* revolt, rebel. **sublevación** *nf* rebellion.

sublime (su'βlime) *adj* sublime, lofty.

submarino (subma'rino) *adj* underwater. *nm* submarine.

subordinado (suβorði'naðo) *adj* subordinate.

subrayar (suβra'jar) *vt* 1 underline, underscore. 2 emphasize. **subrayado** *nm* 1 underlining. 2 emphasis.

subsanar (suβsa'nar) *vt* 1 repair. 2 excuse (fault, etc.). 3 overcome (problem). **subsanable** *adj* 1 excusable. 2 easily remedied.

subscribir (suβskri'βir) *vt* 1 subscribe to. 2 ratify, endorse.

subsidio (suβ'siðjo) *nm* subsidy, grant, allowance.

subsistir (suβsis'tir) *vi* subsist, survive. **subsistencia** *nf* subsistence. **subsistente** *adj* 1 enduring. 2 surviving.

substancia (su'stanθja) *nf* substance. **substancial** *adj* substantial. **substancioso** *adj* substantial, solid.

substituir* (sustitu'ir) *vt,vi* substitute. **substi-**

tución nf substitution. **substitutivo** adj substitute. **substituto** nm substitute.

substraer* (sustra'er) vt 1 remove, steal. 2 subtract. **substraerse** vr withdraw, retire. **substracción** 1 removal, theft. 2 subtraction.

subterfugio (sußter'fuxjo) nm subterfuge.

subterráneo (sußter'raneo) adj subterranean.

subtítulo (suß'titulo) nm subtitle.

suburbio (su'ßurßjo) nm 1 slum. 2 shanty town. 3 outskirts.

subvención (sußßen'θjon) nf subsidy. **subvencionar** vt subsidize.

subyugar (subju'gar) vt subjugate.

suceder (suθe'ðer) vi happen. vt 1 succeed. 2 inherit. **sucederse** follow one another, be consecutive. **suceso** nm 1 event. 2 news item. 3 outcome, result.

sucesión (suθe'sjon) nf 1 succession. 2 inheritance. **sucesivo** adj consecutive, following.

suciedad (suθje'ðað) nf dirt, dirtiness. **sucio** adj 1 dirty. 2 vile, mean..

sucumbir (sukum'bir) vi succumb.

sucursal (sukur'sal) nm branch (of office, bank, etc.).

sud (suð) adj,nm south.

sudamericano (suðameri'kano) adj,n South American.

sudar (su'ðar) vt,vi sweat.

sudeste (suð'este) adj,nm south-east.

sudoeste (suðo'este) adj,nm south-west.

sudor (su'ðor) nm sweat. **sudoroso** adj also **sudoriento** sweaty.

Suecia ('sweθja) nf Sweden. **sueco** adj Swedish. nm 1 Swede. 2 Swedish (language).

suegro ('swegro) nm father-in-law.

suela ('swela) nf sole (of shoe).

sueldo ('·weldo) nm salary, pay.

suelo ('swelo) nm 1 soil. 2 ground. 3 floor.

suelto ('swelto) adj 1 free, untied, loose. 2 separate. 3 flowing, fluent. nm loose change.

sueño ('sweɲo) nm 1 dream. 2 sleep. **tener sueño** be sleepy.

suero ('swero) nm 1 buttermilk, whey. 2 serum.

suerte ('swerte) nf 1 luck, chance. 2 fate, lot. 3 sort, kind. **echar suertes** draw lots.

suéter ('sweter) nm sweater.

suficiencia (sufi'θjenθja) nf 1 sufficiency, adequacy. 2 conceit, smugness. **suficiente** adj 1 sufficient. 2 smug, conceited.

sufragar (sufra'gar) vt 1 comm defray. 2 support, aid. **sufragio** nm 1 vote. 2 suffrage. 3 aid.

sufrir (su'frir) vt,vi 1 suffer. 2 tolerate, with-

stand. **sufrido** adj 1 long-suffering. 2 durable, long-lasting. **sufrimiento** nm 1 suffering. 2 long-suffering, patience.

sugerir (ie) (suxe'rir) vt 1 suggest. 2 hint. **sugerencia** nf suggestion.

sugestión (suxes'tjon) nf 1 suggestion. 2 hint. **sugestionar** vt hypnotize. **sugestionable** adj gullible, suggestible.

suicidarse (swiθi'ðarse) vr commit suicide. **suicida** adj suicidal. nm suicidal case. **suicidio** nm suicide. ·

Suiza ('swiθa) nf Switzerland. **suizo** adj,n Swiss.

sujetar (suxe'tar) vt 1 grasp, clamp, fasten. 2 conquer, subdue. **sujetarse** vr 1 abide by. 2 subject oneself to.

sujeto (su'xeto) nm 1 individual, person. 2 gram subject. adj 1 secured, locked. 2 tight.

sumar (su'mar) vt 1 add. 2 summarize. 3 amount to. **sumarse** vr join, enlist. **suma** nf 1 addition. 2 sum. **sumamente** adv highly, extremely.

sumergir (sumer'xir) vt 1 submerge. 2 plunge. **sumersión** nf submersion.

suministrar (suminis'trar) vt provide, supply. **suministros** nm pl supplies, provisions.

sumir (su'mir) vt submerge, sink.

sumisión (sumi'sjon) nf 1 submission. 2 submissiveness. **sumiso** adj submissive, docile.

sumo ('sumo) adj extreme, great.

suntuoso (sun'twoso) adj sumptuous. **suntuosidad** nf sumptuousness.

supe ('supe) v see **saber.**

supeditar (supeði'tar) vt 1 subdue. 2 subordinate.

superar (supe'rar) vt 1 surpass, excel. 2 overcome (difficulty, etc.). **superarse** vr excel, stand out.

superávit (supe'raßit) nm surplus.

superchería (supertʃe'ria) nf swindle, fraud.

superficial (superfi'θjal) adj superficial. **superficie** nf 1 surface. 2 area.

superfluo (su'perfluo) adj superfluous. **superfluidad** nf superfluity.

superior (supe'rjor) adj 1 superior. 2 upper(most). nm superior, better.

supermercado (supermer'kaðo) nm supermarket.

superstición (supersti'θjon) nf superstition. **supersticioso** adj superstitious.

supervivencia (superßi'ßenθja) nf survival. **superviviente** adj surviving. nm,f survivor.

suplantar (suplan'tar) vt supplant.

suplemento (suple'mento) *nm* supplement. **suplementario** *adj* supplementary, extra. **horas suplementarias** *nf pl* overtime.

suplente (su'plente) *adj,n* substitute.

súplica ('suplika) *nf* 1 petition. 2 request. **suplicar** *vt* 1 beg for, petition for. 2 implore. 3 *law* appeal.

suplicio (su'pliθjo) *nm* torture.

suplir (su'plir) *vt* make up for, substitute.

suponer* (supo'ner) *vt* 1 suppose. 2 involve, require, entail.

suposición (suposi'θjon) *nf* supposition.

supremo (su'premo) *adj* supreme.

suprimir (supri'mir) *vt* suppress. **supresión** *nf* suppression, elimination.

supuesto (su'pwesto) *adj* supposed, self-styled. **nombre supuesto** *nm* assumed name. ~*nm* assumption, hypothesis. **¡por supuesto!** of course.

sur (sur) *adj* southern. *nm* south.

surcar (sur'kar) *vt* score, furrow. **surco** *nm* furrow, rut.

surgir (sur'xir) *vi* 1 arise, emerge. 2 spout or soar up.

surtido (sur'tiðo) *adj* mixed, assorted. **bien surtido** well-stocked, well-supplied. ~*nm* assortment, choice.

surtidor (surti'ðor) *nm* fountain, spout. **surtidor de gasolina** petrol pump.

surtir (sur'tir) *vt* supply, provide. *vi* spout, gush.

susceptibilidad (susθeptiβili'ðað) *nf* susceptibility. **susceptible** *adj* susceptible.

suscitar (susθi'tar) *vt* agitate, stir up. **suscitar interés** arouse interest.

suscribir (suskri'βir) *vt* 1 sign (a contract, etc.). 2 agree to, endorse.

susodicho (suso'ðitʃo) *adj* aforementioned.

suspender (suspen'der) *vt* 1 suspend, hang up. 2 adjourn. 3 suspend from duty. 4 fail. 5 astound. **suspense** *nm* suspense. **suspensión** *nf* 1 suspension. 2 adjournment. 3 astonishment. **suspenso** *adj* 1 failed. 2 suspended.

suspicacia (suspi'kaθja) *nf* 1 suspicion. 2 misgiving. **suspicaz** *adj* suspicious.

suspirar (suspi'rar) *vi* sigh. **suspirado** *adj* desired, longed-for. **suspiro** *nm* sigh.

sustancia (sus'tanθja) *nf see* **substancia**.

sustentar (susten'tar) *vt* 1 support. 2 maintain. 3 nourish. **sustento** *nm* 1 support. 2 sustenance.

sustituir* (sustitu'ir) *vt,vi see* **substituir**.

susto ('susto) *nm* fright. **dar susto** frighten, scare.

susurrar (susur'rar) *vi* 1 whisper. 2 rustle. 3 hum. **susurro** *nm* 1 whispering. 2 humming.

sutil (su'til) *adj* 1 subtle. 2 fine, light. **sutileza** *nf* fineness, subtlety.

sutura (su'tura) *nf med* suture.

suyo ('sujo) *poss pron 3rd pers s* 1 his, hers, its. 2 theirs. 3 yours. **de suyo** in itself. **ir a lo suyo** go one's own way.

T

tabaco (ta'βako) *nm* tobacco.

taberna (ta'βerna) *nf* tavern, public house.

tabique (ta'βike) *nm* partition, dividing wall.

tabla ('taβla) *nf* 1 plank, board. 2 *pl Th* the stage. 3 *pl* game stalemate. **hacer** or **quedar (en) tablas** reach a stalemate. **tabla de planchar** ironing board.

tabular (taβu'lar) *vt* tabulate. *adj* tabular.

taburete (taβu'rete) *nm* stool.

tacaño (ta'kaɲo) *adj* mean, stingy. **tacañería** *nf* meanness.

tácito ('taθito) *adj* tacit.

taco ('tako) *nm* 1 stopper. 2 oath, swearword. 3 billiard cue. 4 *inf* mess.

tacón (ta'kon) *nm* heel. **taconazo** *nm* blow or tap with the heel.

taconear (takone'ar) *vi* tap the ground with the heels. **taconeo** *nm* flamenco tap-dancing.

tacto ('takto) *nm* 1 touch. 2 sense of touch. 3 tact.

tachar (ta'tʃar) *vt* 1 cross out, erase. 2 criticize. 3 denounce. **tachadura** *nf* erasure.

tahona (ta'ona) *nf* bakery.

taimado (tai'maðo) *adj* crafty, sly.

tajar (ta'xar) *vt* slice, cut. **tajada** *nf* 1 *cul* chunk. 2 cut, share (of money, etc.). **tajadera** *nf* chopper. **tajante** *adj* cutting, biting. **tajo** *nm* 1 cut, slash. 2 cliff, cleft.

tal (tal) *adj* such, such a. *pron* such a one, such a person. **con tal de que** provided that. **¿qué tal?** 1 how are you? 2 how is it? **tal como** such as. **tal cual** such-and-such. *adv* so, in such a way.

taladrar (tala'ðrar) *vt* bore, drill. **taladro** *nm* bore, drill.

talante (ta'lante) *nm* 1 mood. 2 appearance, look. **estar de buen talante** be well disposed.

talar (ta'lar) *vt* cut down, fell.

talco ('talko) *nm* talcum powder.

talega (ta'lega) *nf* 1 (money) bag. 2 nappy.

talento (ta'lento) *nm* talent. **talentoso** *adj also* **talentudo** talented.

talón (ta'lon) *nm* heel.

talonario (talo'narjo) *nm* 1 wad (of tickets, etc.) 2 book of cheques, tickets).

talud (ta'luð) *nm* slope.

tallar (ta'ʎar) *vt* 1 carve, shape. 2 *game* deal. **talla** *nf* 1 carving, sculpture. 2 height, stature. 3 size (of clothes, etc.) 4 reward.

talle (ta'ʎe) *anat* 1 waist. 2 figure, frame.

taller (ta'ʎer) *nm* 1 workshop. 2 factory.

tallo (ta'ʎo) *nm bot* shoot, stem.

tamaño (ta'maɲo) *nm* size. *adj* so big, such a big.

tambalearse (tambale'arse) *vr* stagger. **tambaleante** *adj* 1 staggering. 2 swaying.

también (tam'bjen) *adv* also, too.

tambor (tam'bor) *nm* drum.

Támesis ('tamesis) *nm* Thames.

tamiz (ta'miθ) *nm* sieve.

tampoco (tam'poko) *adv* neither.

tan (tan) *adv* so.

tanda ('tanda) *nf* 1 batch. 2 shift (at work, etc.).

tangible (tan'xiβle) *adj* tangible.

tanque ('taŋke) *nm* tank.

tantear (tante'ar) *vt* 1 guess, estimate roughly. 2 weigh up, consider. 3 test. 4 *sport* keep the score of. **tanteo** *nm* 1 reckoning, rough guess. 2 trial, test. 3 *sport* score, scoring.

tanto ('tanto) *adj,adv* 1 so or as much. 2 so long. **hasta tanto que** until. **no es para tanto** it's not that bad. ~*nm* 1 *comm* amount. 2 *sport* point. **estar al tanto** be up to date, be informed. **un tanto** rather, somewhat. **veinte y tantos** twenty and a bit more.

tañer (ta'ɲer) *vt mus* play.

tapar (ta'par) *vt* 1 cover. 2 stop, plug. **tapa** *nf* 1 cover. 2 plug. 3 *cul* snack, tit-bits. **tapete** *nm* table cover. **estar sobre el tapete** be under discussion.

tapia ('tapja) *nf* (garden) wall.

tapicería (tapiθe'ria) *nf* 1 tapestry. 2 upholstery.

tapizar (tapi'θar) *vt* 1 upholster. 2 carpet. **tapiz** *nm* 1 tapestry. 2 carpet.

tapón (ta'pon) *nm* 1 plug, bung. 2 stopper. **taponar** *vt* 1 plug. 2 stopper.

taquigrafía (takigra'fia) *nf* shorthand. **taquígrafo** *nm* shorthand writer.

taquilla (ta'kiʎa) *nf* 1 booking office, box office. 2 *Th* takings.

tararear (tarare'ar) *vt,vi* hum.

tardar (tar'ðar) *vi* 1 take a long time. 2 be late. **tardanza** *nf* slowness.

tarde ('tarðe) *nf* 1 afternoon. 2 evening. *adv* late.

tarea (ta'rea) *nf* task.

tarifa (ta'rifa) *nf* 1 tariff. 2 rate.

tarima (ta'rima) *nf* stand, low platform.

tarjeta (tar'xeta) *nf* card.

tarro ('tarro) *nm* jar.

tarta ('tarta) *nf cul* tart, cake.

tartamudear (tartamuðe'ar) *vt,vi* stutter, stammer. **tartamudeo** *nm* stammer, stutter.

tasar (ta'sar) *vt* 1 fix (price). 2 value, estimate. **tasa** *nf* 1 estimate, valuation. 2 fixed price, official rate. **tasa de cambio** rate of exchange.

tatarabuelo (tatara'βwelo) *nm* great-great-grandfather.

tatuaje (ta'twaxe) *nm* tattoo. **tatuar** *vt* tattoo.

tauromaquia (tauro'makja) *nf* art of bullfighting.

taxi ('taksi) *nm* taxi. **taxímetro** *nm* taximeter. **taxista** *nm* taxi-driver.

taza ('taθa) *nf* cup.

te (te) *pron 2nd pers s fam* you, to you.

té (te) *nm* tea.

teatro (te'atro) *nm* theatre. **teatral** *adj* theatrical.

tecla ('tekla) *nf* key. **teclado** *nm* keyboard. **teclear** *vt mus* strum.

técnica ('teknika) *nf* technique. **técnico** *adj* technical. *nm* technician. **tecnológico** *adj* technological.

techado (te'tʃaðo) *nm also* **techo**, **techumbre** roof.

tedio ('teðjo) *nm* tedium.

teja ('texa) *nf* tile. **tejado** *nm* tiled roof.

tejer (te'xer) *vt* 1 weave. 2 fashion. 3 spin. **tejido** *nm* 1 weave, woven material. 2 *anat* tissue.

tejón (te'xon) *nm* badger.

tela ('tela) *nf* 1 fabric, cloth. 2 film, skin. 3 matter, material, subject.

telar (te'lar) *nm* loom.

telaraña (tela'raɲa) *nf* cobweb.

telefonear (telefone'ar) *vt* telephone. **teléfono** *nm* telephone.

telegrafiar (telegra'fjar) *vt* telegraph. **telegrafía** *nf* telegraphy. **telégrafo** *nm* telegraph.

telegrama (tele'grama) *nm* telegram.

telepatía (telepa'tia) *nf* telepathy. **telepático** *adj* telepathic.

telescopio (teles'kopjo) *nm* telescope. **telescópico** *adj* telescopic.

televisión (teleβi'sjon) *nf* television. **televi-**

133

sado adj televised. **televisor** nm television set.

telón (te'lon) nm Th curtain. **telón de acero** Iron Curtain.

tema ('tema) nm theme.

temblar (tem'blar) vi tremble, shake. **temblor** nm shiver, shudder. **temblor de tierra** earthquake. **tembloroso** adj trembling, shaking.

temer (te'mer) vt,vi fear, be afraid. **temerario** adj rash. **temeridad** nf temerity, rashness. **temor** nm fear, dread.

temperamento (tempera'mento) nm temperament, nature.

temperatura (tempera'tura) nf temperature.

tempestad (tempes'taθ) nf storm. **tempestuoso** adj stormy.

templar (tem'plar) vt 1 temper, moderate. 2 warm up (temperature, liquid). 3 mus tune up.

temple ('temple) nm 1 temper (of steel, etc.). 2 mood. 3 state of the weather.

templo ('templo) nm 1 temple. 2 church.

temporada (tempo'raða) nf 1 season. 2 period.

temporal (tempo'ral) adj 1 temporary. 2 secular, worldly. nm rough weather.

temprano (tem'prano) adv,adj early.

tenacidad (tenaθi'ðaθ) nf tenacity.

tenaz (te'naθ) adj 1 tenacious. 2 tough. **tenazas** nf pl 1 pincers. 2 pliers.

tendedero (tende'ðero) nm 1 clothes-line. 2 place for hanging clothes.

tendencia (ten'denθja) nf tendency, trend.

tender (ie) (ten'der) vt 1 stretch, spread out. 2 hang out (washing). vi incline, tend, have a tendency. **tenderse** vr stretch out, lie down.

tendero (ten'ðero) nm shopkeeper.

tendón (ten'don) nm tendon, sinew.

tenebroso (tene'βroso) adj dark, gloomy.

tenedor (tene'ðor) nm 1 fork. 2 holder, keeper. **tenedor de libros** bookkeeper.

teneduría (teneðu'ria) nf bookkeeping.

tenencia (te'nenθja) nf tenancy, tenure.

tener* (te'ner) vt 1 have, possess. 2 keep. 3 hold. **tener veinte años** be twenty years old. **tener hambre/sed/calor/frío** be hungry/thirsty/hot/cold. **tener que** have to. **tenerse** vr stand, stand up. **tenerse en mucho** have a high opinion of oneself.

tengo ('tengo) v see **tener**.

teniente (te'njente) nm lieutenant. **teniente coronel** lieutenant-colonel.

tenis ('tenis) nm tennis.

tenor[1] (te'nor) nm mus tenor.

tenor[2] (te'nor) nm meaning, sense.

tensión (ten'sjon) nf tension. **tensión arterial** blood pressure. **tenso** adj tense, taut.

tentación (tenta'θjon) nf temptation.

tentáculo (ten'takulo) nm tentacle.

tentar (ie) (ten'tar) vt 1 touch, feel. 2 grope, feel one's way. 3 try, attempt. 4 tempt. **tentativa** nf attempt. **tentativo** adj tentative.

tentempié (tentem'pje) nm inf snack.

tenue ('tenwe) adj 1 tenuous. 2 thin, slight. **tenuidad** nf tenuousness.

teñir* (te'ɲir) vt dye, colour.

teología (teolo'xia) nf theology. **teológico** adj theological. **teólogo** nm theologian.

teoría (teo'ria) nf theory. **teórico** adj theoretical.

tercero (ter'θero) adj,n third.

terciar (ter'θjar) vt 1 divide into three. 2 place diagonally. vi mediate.

tercio ('terθjo) nm 1 third. 2 mil regiment.

terciopelo (terθjo'pelo) nm velvet.

terco ('terko) adj 1 stubborn, obstinate. 2 hard material.

tergiversar (terxiβer'sar) vt distort, twist, misrepresent.

terminar (termi'nar) vt end, finish, complete.

término ('termino) nm end. **dar término a** bring to an end.

termo ('termo) nm Thermos bottle.

termodinámica (termoði'namika) nf thermodynamics.

termómetro (ter'mometro) nm thermometer.

termonuclear (termonukle'ar) adj thermonuclear.

termostato (termos'tato) nm thermostat.

ternera (ter'nera) nf 1 female calf. 2 veal. **ternero** nm male calf.

terneza (ter'neθa) nf also **ternura** nf 1 tenderness. 2 fondness. 3 pl endearing words.

terquedad (terke'ðaθ) nf 1 stubbornness. 2 toughness.

terraplén (terra'plen) nm 1 embankment. 2 terrace. 3 slope.

terraza (ter'raθa) nf 1 terrace. 2 flat roof. 3 balcony. 4 outdoor cafe.

terremoto (terre'moto) nm earthquake.

terreno (ter'reno) adj earthly, terrestrial. nm 1 land, soil. 2 plot. 3 area. **ceder/perder/ganar terreno** give/lose/gain ground.

terrestre (ter'restre) adj terrestrial.

terrible (ter'riβle) adj terrible, awful.

territorial (territo'rjal) adj territorial. **territorio** nm territory.

terrón (ter'ron) nm 1 lump (of sugar, salt, etc.). 2 clod.

terror (ter'ror) nm terror. **terrorismo** nm terrorism. **terrorista** nm,f terrorist.

terso ('terso) adj 1 smooth, polished. 2 terse.

tertulia (ter'tulja) nf 1 social gathering. 2 group.

tesis ('tesis) nf invar thesis.

tesón (te'son) nm tenacity, firmness, persistence.

tesoro (te'soro) nm treasure. **tesorería** nf 1 treasury. 2 treasurership. **tesorero** nm treasurer.

testa ('testa) nf head.

testar (tes'tar) vi make a will. **testamento** nm will, testament.

testarudo (testa'ruðo) adj stubborn, obstinate.

testificar (testifi'kar) vt attest, testify. **testigo** nm witness, one who testifies.

teta ('teta) nf 1 teat, nipple. 2 breast, udder.

tetera (te'tera) nf teapot.

tétrico ('tetriko) adj 1 gloomy. 2 sullen.

textil (teks'til) adj, nm textile.

texto ('teksto) nm 1 text. 2 textbook.

textura (teks'tura) nf texture.

tez (teθ) nf complexion, skin.

ti (ti) pron 2nd pers s fam you, yourself.

tía ('tia) nf aunt.

tibio ('tiβjo) adj lukewarm.

tiburón (tiβu'ron) nm shark.

tiempo ('tjempo) nm 1 time. 2 weather.

tienda ('tjenda) nf 1 shop, store. 2 tent.

tienta ('tjenta) nf 1 med probe. 2 shrewdness, cleverness. 3 (in bullfighting) test of bullocks for fierceness. **a tientas** gropingly, haphazardly.

tiento ('tjento) nm 1 touch, feel. 2 tact. **a tiento** by touch, gropingly.

tierno ('tjerno) adj 1 tender. 2 fresh.

tierra ('tjerra) nf 1 earth, world. 2 land, soil, ground. 3 country, homeland. **tierra natal** native land.

tieso ('tjeso) adj 1 stiff, rigid. 2 strong, firm. adv 1 stiffly. 2 firmly.

tiesto ('tjesto) nm 1 piece of pottery. 2 flowerpot.

tifo ('tifo) nm also **tifus** typhus. **tifo asiático** cholera.

tifón (ti'fon) nm 1 typhoon. 2 waterspout.

tigre ('tigre) nm tiger.

tijeras (ti'xeras) nf pl 1 scissors. 2 shears.

tilín (ti'lin) nm sound of bell.

tilo ('tilo) nm linden tree.

timar (ti'mar) vt cheat. **timador** nm swindler, cheat.

timbrar (tim'brar) vt stamp. **timbre** nm 1 seal. 2 stamp-duty. 3 bell. 4 mus timbre.

tímido ('timiðo) adj timid. **timidez** nf timidity.

timo ('timo) nm 1 hoax. 2 swindle.

tímpano ('timpano) nm 1 eardrum. 2 kettledrum.

tina ('tina) nf tub.

tinglado (tin'glaðo) nm 1 shed. 2 roof. 3 machination, intrigue.

tiniebla(s) (ti'njeβla) nf (pl) darkness, obscurity.

tino ('tino) nm 1 good judgment, tact. 2 skill, knack. 3 aim.

tinta ('tinta) nf 1 ink. 2 hue, tint.

tinte ('tinte) nm 1 dyeing. 2 paint, dye. **tintero** nm inkwell.

tintín (tin'tin) nm tinkle, clinking.

tinto ('tinto) adj dyed. **vino tinto** nm red wine.

tintorería (tintore'ria) nf dry-cleaner's, dyer's. **tintorero** nm dry-cleaner, dyer. **tintura** nf dye.

tío ('tio) nm uncle.

tiovivo (tjo'βiβo) nm merry-go-round.

típico ('tipiko) adj 1 typical. 2 native.

tiple ('tiple) nm treble. nf 1 soprano. 2 chorus girl.

tipo ('tipo) nm 1 type, model. 2 sl fellow, guy.

tira ('tira) nf long strip.

tirada (ti'raða) nf 1 throw. 2 stretch (of time). 3 edition.

tirado (ti'raðo) adj comm very cheap.

tirador (tira'ðor) nm 1 marksman. 2 handle, knob.

tiranía (tira'nia) nf tyranny. **tirano** nm tyrant. adj tyrannical.

tirante (ti'rante) nm 1 arch brace. 2 strap. 3 pl braces. adj taut.

tirar (ti'rar) vt,vi 1 throw, cast. 2 pull, draw.

tiritar (tiri'tar) vi shiver.

tiro ('tiro) nm 1 throw. 2 shot.

tirón (ti'ron) nm tug, jerk, pull.

tiroteo (tiro'teo) nm firing, gunshots.

tisis ('tisis) nf tuberculosis.

titubear (tituβe'ar) vi 1 hesitate. 2 totter. 3 stammer.

titular (titu'lar) adj titular. nm,f holder of an office. nm newspaper headline. vt 1 name. 2 entitle.

título ('titulo) nm 1 title. 2 diploma, degree.

tiza ('tiθa) nf chalk.

tiznar (tiθ'nar) *vt* stain, smear. **tiznado** *adj* grimy.

toalla (to'aʎa) *nf* towel.

tobillo (to'βiʎo) *nm* ankle.

tocadiscos (toka'ðiskos) *nm invar* record-player.

tocado (to'kaðo) *adj* touched, crazy. **tocado de la cabeza** touched in the head.

tocador (toka'ðor) *nm* **1** dressing table. **2** powder room. **3** *mus* player.

tocante (to'kante) *adj* touching. **tocante a** concerning.

tocar (to'kar) *vt* **1** touch, feel. **2** touch upon (a subject). **3** *mus* play. *vi* be one's turn. **en lo que toca a** with regard to.

tocino (to'θino) *nm* bacon, salt pork.

todavía (toða'βia) *adv* yet, still.

todo ('toðo) *adj* all, every, whole. *nm* entirety. **todos** *pron* everybody. **con todo** nevertheless, all the same.

toldo ('toldo) *nm* **1** awning. **2** sunshade.

tolerar (tole'rar) *vt* tolerate. **tolerancia** *nf* tolerance. **tolerante** *adj* tolerant.

tomar (to'mar) *vt* **1** take, seize. **2** receive. **3** eat, drink. **toma** *nf* **1** taking, seizure. **2** portion. **3** *med* dose. **4** take (in films).

tomate (to'mate) *nm* tomato.

tomillo (to'miʎo) *nm* thyme.

tomo ('tomo) *nm* **1** bulk. **2** volume, tome. **3** importance.

ton (ton) *nm* motive, reason.

tonel (to'nel) *nm* barrel.

tonelada (tone'laða) *nf* ton. **tonelaje** *nm* tonnage.

tónico ('toniko) *nm,adj* tonic.

tono ('tono) *nm* **1** pitch, tone. **2** manner.

tontería (tonte'ria) *nf* foolishness. **tonto** *adj* foolish, stupid, ignorant.

topacio (to'paθjo) *nm* topaz.

topar (to'par) *vi* **1** collide. **2** encounter, meet.

tope ('tope) *nm* **1** top, end. **2** summit.

tópico ('topiko) *nm* topic. *adj* topical.

topo ('topo) *nm* mole.

topografía (topogra'fia) *nf* topography.

toque ('toke) *nm* **1** touch, tap. **2** peal of bells.

torbellino (torβe'ʎino) *nm* whirlwind.

torcer (ue) (tor'θer) *vt* twist, bend, turn. **torcerse** *vr* **1** turn sour. **2** be dislocated. **torcido** *adj* twisted, bent.

tordo ('torðo) *nm zool* thrush.

torear (tore'ar) *vi* fight a bull. **toreo** *nm* bullfighting. **torero** *nm* bull-fighter.

tormenta (tor'menta) *nf* storm. **tormentoso** *adj* stormy.

tormentar (tormen'tar) *vt* torment. **tormento** *nm* torment, anguish, pain.

tornar (tor'nar) *vt,vi* **1** return. **2** change. **tornarse** *vr* **1** become. **2** change.

tornasol (torna'sol) *nm* **1** sunflower. **2** litmus.

torneo (tor'neo) *nm* tournament.

tornillo (tor'niʎo) *nm* **1** screw. **2** *mech* vice. **torniquete** *nm* tourniquet. **torno** *nm* lathe. **en torno a** round, about.

toro ('toro) *nm* **1** bull. **2** *pl* bullfight.

toronja (to'ronxa) *nf* grapefruit.

torpe ('torpe) *adj* **1** stupid. **2** slow, torpid. **torpeza** *nf* **1** torpor. **2** clumsiness. **3** impurity, obscenity.

torre ('torre) *nf* tower.

torrente (tor'rente) *nm* torrent. **torrencial** *adj* torrential.

tórrido (tor'riðo) *adj* torrid.

torta ('torta) *nf* **1** round cake or bread. **2** *inf* slap.

tortilla (tor'tiʎa) *nf* omelette.

tortuga (tor'tuga) *nf* **1** turtle. **2** tortoise.

tortura (tor'tura) *nf* torture. **tortuoso** *adj* tortuous.

tos (tos) *nf* cough.

tosco ('tosko) *adj* **1** coarse. **2** rude, uncouth.

toser (to'ser) *vi* cough.

tostar (ue) (tos'tar) *vt* toast. **tostada** *nf* toasted bread. **tostado** *adj* **1** tanned. **2** toasted.

total (to'tal) *nm* total.

tóxico ('toksiko) *nm* poison. *adj* poisonous.

tozudo (to'θuðo) *adj* stubborn.

traba ('traβa) *nf* **1** obstacle. **2** brace, clasp.

trabajar (traβa'xar) *vt* **1** work. **2** till. **3** form, shape. **trabajador** *nm* worker, labourer. *adj* hard-working. **trabajo** *nm* work.

trabalenguas (traβa'lengwas) *nm invar* tongue-twister.

trabar (tra'βar) *vt* **1** fasten, clasp, grasp, join. **2** engage in. **trabazón** *nf* union, juncture. **trabe** *nf* arch beam.

tracción (trak'θjon) *nf* traction.

tractor (trak'tor) *nm* tractor.

tradición (traði'θjon) *nf* tradition.

traducir (traðu'θir) *vt* **1** translate. **2** interpret. **traducción** *nf* translation. **traducible** *adj* translatable. **traductor** *nm* translator.

traer (tra'er) *vt* **1** bring, carry, fetch. **2** lead. **3** occasion, bring about.

traficar (trafi'kar) *vi* **1** deal, trade. **2** journey, go, keep on the move. **traficante** nm dealer, trader. **tráfico** nm traffic.

tragaluz (traga'luθ) nf skylight.

tragar (tra'gar) vt swallow. **tragarse** vr accept, believe. **trago** nm 1 drink. 2 swig.

tragedia (tra'xeðja) nf tragedy. **trágico** adj tragic.

traicionar (traiθjo'nar) vt betray. **traición** nf treason, disloyalty. **traicionero** adj treacherous. **traidor** nm traitor.

traje[1] ('traxe) nm 1 suit. 2 dress. 3 costume. **traje de baño** swimming costume.

traje[2] ('traxe) v see **traer**.

trajín (tra'xin) nm 1 carriage. 2 coming and going. **trajinar** vt cart (goods). vi travel back and forth.

tramar (tra'mar) vt 1 weave. 2 plan, plot.

tramitar (trami'tar) vt transact, proceed with. **trámite** nm 1 transaction. 2 procedure. 3 law proceedings.

tramo ('tramo) nm piece, section, area (of ground).

trampear (trampe'ar) vt cheat, swindle, trick. **trampa** nf 1 trap. 2 fraud. **tramposo** nm 1 swindler. 2 a person who does not pay his debts.

trampolín (trampo'lin) nm trampoline, springboard.

trancar (tran'kar) vt bar (window, door). **tranca** nf bar (across window, door).

tranco ('tranko) nm stride.

trance ('tranθe) nm emergency, difficult situation.

tranquilizar (trankili'θar) vt calm. **tranquilidad** nf tranquillity. **tranquilo** adj tranquil.

transacción (transak'θjon) nf transaction.

transatlántico (transat'lantiko) adj transatlantic. nm naut liner.

transbordar (transβor'ðar) vt transfer, change (trains, etc.). **transbordador** nm ferry. **transbordo** nm transfer.

transcribir* (transkri'βir) vt transcribe.

transcurrir (transku'rir) vi pass, elapse. **transcurso** nm lapse of time.

transeúnte (transe'unte) adj transitory, transient. nm passer-by.

transferir (ie) (transfe'rir) vt transfer. **transferible** adj transferable.

transformar (transfor'mar) vt transform. **transformación** nf transformation.

tránsfuga ('transfuga) nm deserter.

transgredir (transgre'ðir) vt transgress, violate.

transgresión nf transgression. **transgresor** nm transgressor.

transido (tran'siðo) adj overwhelmed.

transigir (transi'xir) vi 1 compromise. 2 yield. 3 tolerate.

transitar (transi'tar) vi 1 pass by, pass along. 2 travel along the road.

tránsito ('transito) nm 1 transit. 2 traffic.

transitorio (transi'torjo) adj transitory.

transmitir (transmi'tir) vt transmit. **transmisión** nf transmission. **transmisora** nf 1 transmitter. 2 radio station.

transparencia (transpa'renθja) nf transparency. **transparente** adj transparent.

transpirar (transpi'rar) vi 1 perspire. 2 transpire.

transponer* (transpo'ner) vt 1 transpose, exchange. 2 transplant. **transponerse** vr (of the sun) set.

transportar (transpor'tar) vt transport. **transportación** nf transportation. **transporte** nm transport, conveyance.

tranvía (tran'βia) nm 1 tram. 2 tramway.

trapaza (tra'paθa) nf swindle, trick.

trapecio (tra'peθjo) nm trapeze.

trapo ('trapo) nm 1 rag. 2 pl old clothes.

traquetear (trakete'ar) vt,vi agitate, shake. vi make a loud noise, crack. **traqueteo** nm 1 shaking. 2 cracking. 3 clatter.

tras (tras) prep after, behind.

trascender (ie) (trasθen'ðer) 1 go beyond. 2 smell. **trascender a** 1 be suggestive of, reek of. 2 have effect upon. **trascendencia** nf 1 significance, importance. 2 transcendence. **trascendental** adj 1 important. 2 transcendental.

trasegar (ie) (trase'gar) vt 1 move about. 2 turn upside down, upset (things). **trasiego** nm 1 upset. 2 change, switch.

trasero (tra'sero) adj back, hind, rear. nm 1 rump. 2 behind, buttocks. 3 pl predecessors.

trasladar (trasla'ðar) vt move, transfer to another place. **traslado** nm 1 transfer. 2 copy.

traslucirse* (traslu'θirse) vr 1 be translucent. 2 be revealed, become clear.

trasnochar (trasno'tʃar) vi be up all or most of the night.

traspasar (traspa'sar) vt 1 pierce, go through. 2 pass, cross over. 3 trespass. 4 sell (business premises, etc.). **traspaso** nm transfer, sale.

trasplantar (trasplan'tar) vt transplant. **trasplantarse** vr migrate. **trasplante** nm transplant.

trasquilar (traski'lar) *vt* shear, clip.

traste ('traste) *nm mus* fret.

trasto ('trasto) *nm* 1 piece of furniture. 2 rubbish. 3 *pl* utensils, tools.

trastornar (trastor'nar) *vt* 1 upset, disarrange. 2 trouble, disturb. 3 drive insane. **trastorno** *nm* 1 upheaval, disturbance. 2 mental disorder.

trasunto (tra'sunto) *nm* 1 copy. 2 likeness.

tratar (tra'tar) 1 treat, handle (a subject, etc.). 2 deal with, trade. 3 call, accuse. *vi* try. **tratarse** *vr* 1 have dealings with. 2 be on speaking terms.

través (tra'βes) *nm* 1 *arch* crossbeam. 2 reversal, calamity. **al través** across.

travesero (traβe'sero) *adj* transverse.

travesura (traβe'sura) *nf* prank.

traviesa (tra'βjesa) *nf* 1 (railway) sleeper. 2 *arch* rafter.

travieso (tra'βjeso) *adj* 1 lively, mischievous. 2 transverse.

trayecto (tra'jekto) *nm* 1 journey. 2 distance. **trayectoria** *nf* trajectory.

trazar (tra'θar) *vt* trace, plot, delineate. **trazo** *nm* sketch, plan.

trébol ('treβol) *nm* clover.

trece ('treθe) *adj,nm* thirteen.

trecho ('tretʃo) *nm* space, distance, stretch.

tregua ('tregwa) *nf* 1 truce. 2 rest, respite.

treinta ('treinta) *adj* thirty.

tremendo (tre'mendo) *adj* tremendous.

trémulo ('tremulo) *adj* tremulous.

tren (tren) *nm* train.

trenzar (tren'θar) *vt* braid. **trenza** *nf* plait, braid.

trepar (tre'par) *vi* climb. **trepa** *nf* climbing. **trepador** *nm* climber.

trepidar (trepi'ðar) *vi* quiver, tremble.

tres (tres) *adj, nm* three.

triángulo ('triangulo) *nm* triangle.

tribu ('triβu) *nm,f* tribe.

tribuna (tri'βuna) *nf* 1 tribune. 2 stage, platform.

tributar (triβu'tar) *vt* pay. **tributo** *nm* tribute, tax. **tributario** *nm, adj* tributary.

trigo ('trigo) *nm* wheat. **trigal** *nm* wheat-field.

trigésimo (tri'xesimo) *adj* thirtieth.

trillar (tri'ʎar) *vt* 1 thresh, beat. 2 mash. **trillado** *adj* threshed. **trillador** *nm* thresher.

trimestre (tri'mestre) *nm educ* three-month term.

trinar (tri'nar) *vi* trill, warble.

trincar (trin'kar) *vt* 1 tie up. 2 lash. 3 break, chop. *vt,vi* drink.

trinchar (trin'tʃar) *vt* slice. **trinchador** *nm* carving knife. **trinchera** *nf* 1 trench. 2 trench coat.

trineo (tri'neo) *nm* sledge, sleigh.

trinidad (trini'ðað) *nf* trinity.

tripa ('tripa) *nf* 1 *anat* intestine. 2 *inf* tummy.

triple ('triple) *adj* triple.

trípode ('tripoðe) *nm* tripod.

tripulación (tripula'θjon) *nf* crew of a ship or aircraft.

triscar (tris'kar) *vt* mingle. *vi* (of lambs) frisk.

triste ('triste) *adj* sad, gloomy. **tristeza** *nf* sadness.

triturar (tritu'rar) *vt* grind, crush.

triunfar (trjun'far) *vi* triumph. **triunfal** *adj* triumphal. **triunfante** *adj* triumphant. **triunfo** *nm* 1 triumph, victory. 2 *game* trumps.

trivial (tri'βjal) *adj* trivial. **trivialidad** *nf* triviality.

triza ('triθa) *nf* shred, fragment.

trocar (ue) (tro'kar) *vt* exchange. **trocarse** *vr* change into.

trochemoche (trotʃe'motʃe) *adv* **a trochemoche** helter-skelter.

trofeo (tro'feo) *nm* trophy.

trole ('trole) *nm* trolley.

tromba ('tromba) *nf* whirlwind. **tromba de agua** heavy rainfall, downpour.

trombón (trom'bon) *nm* trombone.

trompa ('trompa) *nf* 1 horn. 2 humming top. 3 (of an elephant) trunk.

trompeta (trom'peta) *nf* trumpet.

tronar (ue) (tro'nar) *vi* thunder, roar. **tronada** *nf* thunderstorm.

tronco ('tronko) *nm* 1 tree trunk. 2 stem.

trono ('trono) *nm* throne.

tropa ('tropa) *nf* troop.

tropel (tro'pel) *nm* crowd. **en tropel** in a mad rush.

tropezar (ie) (trope'θar) *vi* stumble, trip. **tropezar con** run across, run into.

trópico ('tropiko) *nm* tropic. **tropical** *adj* tropical.

trotar (tro'tar) *vi* trot. **trote** *nm* trot.

trozo ('troθo) *nm* piece, bit.

truco ('truko) *nm* trick.

trucha ('trutʃa) *nf* trout.

trueno ('trweno) *nm* thunder.

trueque ('trweke) *nm* exchange, barter.

trufa ('trufa) *nf* truffle.

truncar (trun'kar) *vt* shorten, truncate.

tu (tu) *poss adj* 2nd pers s fam your.

tú (tu) *pron* 2nd pers s fam you.

tubo ('tuβo) *nm* tube, pipe.

tuerca ('twerka) *nf* nut.

tuerto ('twerto) *adj* one-eyed. *nm* wrong.

tuétano ('twetano) *nm anat* marrow.

tufo ('tufo) *nm* 1 vapour, fume. 2 stink.

tul (tul) *nm* tulle.

tulipán (tuli'pan) *nm* tulip.

tumba[1] ('tumba) *nf* tomb.

tumba[2] ('tumba) *nf* tumble.

tumbar (tum'bar) *vt* knock over. *vi* fall over. **tumbarse** *vr* lie down, sprawl. **tumbo** *nm* 1 tumble. 2 jolt.

túmido (tu'miðo) *adj* swollen.

tumor (tu'mor) *nm* tumour.

tumulto (tu'multo) *nm* turmoil, tumult. **tumultuoso** *adj* tumultuous.

tunante (tu'nante) *nm* rogue, crook.

túnel ('tunel) *nm* tunnel.

túnica ('tunika) *nf* tunic.

tuno ('tuno) *nm* rascal.

tupé (tu'pe) *nm* toupee.

tupido (tu'piðo) *adj* matted, entangled.

turba ('turba) *nf* crowd.

turbar (tur'βar) *vt* disturb, alarm. **turbarse** *vr* 1 become disturbed. 2 be embarrassed. **turbado** *adj* 1 upset. 2 embarrassed.

turbina (tur'βina) *nf* turbine.

turbulento (turβu'lento) *adj* turbulent, unruly. **turbulencia** *nf* turbulence.

turco *adj* Turkish. *nm* Turk.

turismo (tu'rismo) *nm* 1 tourism. 2 passenger car.

turnar (tur'nar) *vi* take turns. **turno** *nm* shift, turn.

turquesa (tur'kesa) *nf* turquoise.

Turquía (tur'kia) *nf* Turkey. **turquesco** *adj* Turkish. *nm* Turkish (language).

turrón (tur'ron) *nm cul* almond sweet, nougat.

tutear (tute'ar) *vt* address familiarly by using *tú*. **tutearse** *vr* be on familiar terms, call one another *tú*.

tutela (tu'tela) *nf* guardianship, tutelage.

tutor (tu'tor) *nm* 1 tutor. 2 guardian.

tuve ('tuβe) *v* see **tener**.

tuyo ('tujo) *poss pron* 2nd pers *s fam* yours.

U

u (u) *conj* (before **o** or **ho**) or.

ubicar (ubi'kar) *vi* lie, be situated.

ubicuidad (uβikui'ðað) *nf* ubiquity.

ubre ('uβre) *nf* udder.

ufanarse (ufa'narse) *vr* boast. **ufano** *adj* proud, vain. **ufanía** *nf* pride, conceit.

ujier (u'xjer) *nm* usher.

úlcera ('ulθera) *nf* ulcer. **ulceroso** *adj* ulcerous.

ulterior (ulte'rjor) *adj* further, farther. **ulteriormente** *adv* later.

ultimar (ulti'mar) *vt* conclude, bring to an end. **ultimación** *nf* conclusion.

último ('ultimo) *adj* last, most recent. **por último** finally.

ultrajar (ultra'xar) *vt* outrage, abuse. **ultraje** *nm* outrage. **ultrajoso** *adj* offensive, abusive.

ultramarino (ultrama'rino) *adj* overseas.

ultranza (ul'tranθa) **a ultranza** *adv* at all costs, to the last, out-and-out.

umbral (um'bral) *nm* threshold.

umbrío (um'brio) *adj also* **umbroso** shaded, shady.

un (un) *indef art m also* **una** *f* a, an. *adj,n* one.

unánime (u'nanime) *adj* unanimous. **unanimidad** *nf* unanimity.

unción (un'θjon) *nf* anointing, unction. **extremaunción** *nf rel* extreme unction.

uncir (un'θir) *vt* yoke.

undécimo (un'deθimo) *adj* eleventh.

undoso (un'doso) *adj also* **ondoso** wavy, rippling.

undular (undu'lar) *vi also* **ondular** undulate, be wavy.

ungir (un'xir) *vt* anoint, rub with oil.

ungüento (un'gwento) *nm* ointment.

único ('uniko) *adj* 1 only, single. 2 unique. **hijo único** *nm* only child.

unidad (uni'ðað) *nf* 1 unity. 2 unit.

unificar (unifi'kar) *vt* unify.

uniformar (unifor'mar) *vt* make uniform or standard. **uniforme** *adj,nm* uniform. **uniformidad** *nf* uniformity, evenness.

unión (u'njon) *nf* union.

Unión Soviética (u'njon so'βjetika) *nf* Soviet Union.

unir (u'nir) *vt* 1 unite, join. 2 *cul* mix.

unísono (u'nisono) *adj* on the same tone. **al unísono** in unison, unanimous.

universidad (uniβersi'ðað) *nf* university. **universitario** *adj* of or belonging to a university.

universo (uni'βerso) *nm* universe. **universal** *adj* universal. **universalidad** *nf* universality.

uno ('uno) *adj* 1 one. 2 sole, only. *pron* 1 one. 2 someone.

unos ('unos) *pron pl* some, a few.

untar (un'tar) *vt* 1 smear. 2 oil. **untadura** *nf* 1 ointment. 2 anointing.

uña ('uɲa) *nf anat* 1 nail. 2 claw. 3 hoof.

uranio (u'ranjo) *nm* uranium.

urbanidad (urβani'ðað) *nf* courtesy. **urbano** *adj* 1 urban. 2 polite. 3 urbane.

urbanizar (urβani'θar) *vt* build on, develop. **urbanización** *nf* urban development scheme. **urbanizado** *adj* built-up.

urdir (ur'ðir) *vt* 1 warp. 2 contrive, scheme.

urgencia (ur'xenθja) *nf* 1 urgency. 2 emergency. **urgente** *adj* urgent.

urgir (ur'xir) *vt* 1 be urgent. 2 be urgently needed.

urna ('urna) *nf* 1 urn. 2 ballot box.

urraca (ur'raka) *nf* magpie.

usanza (usan'θa) *nf* usage, custom.

usar (u'sar) *vt* 1 use. 2 wear (clothes). *vi* be accustomed. **uso** *nm* 1 use. 2 practice. 3 usage, custom. **al uso** according to custom.

usted (us'ted) *pron 2nd pers s fml,pl* **ustedes** you.

usual (u'swal) *adj* usual.

usufructo (usu'frukto) *nm* use, enjoyment.

usura (u'sura) *nf* usury. **usurero** *nm* usurer.

usurpar (usur'par) *vt* usurp. **usurpación** *nf* usurpation.

utensilio (uten'siljo) *nm* 1 utensil. 2 *pl* tools.

útero ('utero) *nm* uterus.

útil ('util) *adj* useful. **utilidad** *nf* utility, usefulness.

utilizar (utili'θar) *vt* utilize, use.

uva ('uβa) *nf* grape.

V

va (ba) *v see* **ir.**

vaca ('baka) *nf* 1 cow. 2 *cul* beef.

vacación (baka'θjon) *nf* 1 vacation. 2 *pl* holidays.

vacante (ba'kante) *adj* vacant. *nf* vacancy.

vaciar (ba'θjar) *vt* 1 empty, drain. 2 pour out.

vacilar (baθi'lar) *vi* hesitate. **vacilante** *adj* unsteady, wobbly. **vacilación** *nf* vacillation, hesitancy.

vacío (ba'θio) *adj* empty. *nm* 1 emptiness, void. 2 vacuum.

vacunar (baku'nar) *vt* vaccinate.

vacuo ('bakwo) *adj* 1 empty. 2 vacuous, emptyheaded.

vadear (baðe'ar) *vt* 1 ford. 2 wade across. 3 overcome (problems, etc.). **vado** *nm* ford.

vagar (ba'gar) *vi* wander, roam. *nm* 1 free time, leisure. 2 ease.

vago ('bago) *adj* 1 vague. 2 lazy. *nm* tramp, idler. **vaguedad** *nf* vagueness.

vagón (ba'gon) *nm* 1 railway carriage. 2 wagon.

vagoneta (bago'neta) *nm* mot pick-up, light truck.

vahear (bae'ar) *vi* steam. **vaho** *nm* vapour.

vahido (ba'iðo) *nm* dizzy spell, dizziness.

vaina ('baina) *nf* 1 sheath, scabbard. 2 *pl* green beans.

vainilla (bai'niʎa) *nf* vanilla.

vaivén (bai'βen) *nm* 1 fluctuation, oscillation. 2 swinging movement.

vajilla (ba'xiʎa) *nf* crockery, dishes.

vale ('bale) *nm comm* promissory note, voucher.

valedero (bale'ðero) *adj* valid.

valentía (balen'tia) *nf* 1 bravery, courage. 2 bold or courageous act.

valer * (ba'ler) *vt* 1 be worth, cost. 2 be worthy. 3 be all right. 4 equal.

valeroso (bale'roso) *adj* brave.

valgo ('balgo) *v see* **valer.**

valía (ba'lia) *nf* worth, value.

validar (bali'ðar) *vt* validate, ratify. **validación** *nf* 1 validation. 2 ratification.

válido ('baliðo) *adj* valid. **validez** *nf* validity.

valiente (ba'ljente) *adj* 1 brave, courageous. 2 strong, powerful.

valija (ba'lixa) *nf* 1 case, valise. 2 mail bag.

valimiento (bali'mjento) *nm* 1 value. 2 goodwill, favour.

valioso (ba'ljoso) *adj* valuable, useful.

valor (ba'lor) *nm* 1 value, price. 2 valour. 3 *pl comm* bonds, assets.

valorar (balo'rar) *vt* value, assess. **valoración** *nf* assessment, valuation.

valsar (bal'sar) *vi* waltz. **vals** *nm* waltz.

valuar (ba'lwar) *vt* value, assess.

válvula ('balβula) *nf* valve.

vallar (ba'ʎar) *vt* enclose, fence in. **valla** *nf* fence.

valle ('baʎe) *nm* valley.

vampiro (bam'piro) *nm* vampire.

vanagloriarse (banaglo'rjarse) *vr* boast. **vanagloria** *nf* boasting, vainglory.

vándalo ('bandalo) *nm* vandal.

vanguardia (ban'gwarðja) *nf* 1 vanguard. 2 avant-garde.

vano ('bano) *adj* 1 useless. 2 imaginary, groundless. 3 conceited, vain. **en vano** in vain. **vanidad** *nf* 1 vanity. 2 futility, uselessness. **vanidoso** *adj* vain, conceited.

vapor (ba'por) *nm* 1 steam. 2 vapour, mist. 3 steamship. 4 *med* faintness. **vaporizar** *vt* vaporize. **vaporización** nf vaporization. **vaporoso** adj 1 steamy. 2 filmy, tenuous.

vaquero (baˈkero) nm cowboy.

vaqueta (baˈketa) nf cowhide.

vara (ˈbara) nf 1 stick, pole. 2 wand. 3 baton (of office). 4 lance.

varar (baˈrar) vt launch. **vararse** vr naut run aground. **varado** adj stranded, aground. **varadura** nf 1 launching. 2 running aground.

variar (baˈrjar) vt,vi vary, change. **variación** nf variation, change. **variado** adj mixed, assorted.

varilla (baˈriʎa) nf 1 bot twig, wand. 2 rib (of an umbrella, fan).

vario (ˈbarjo) adj 1 varied, assorted. 2 pl several.

varón (baˈron) adj,nm male. **varonil** adj 1 manly, virile. 2 male.

vasco (ˈbasko) adj also **vascongado** Basque. nm 1 Basque. 2 Basque (language).

vasija (baˈsixa) nf container, vessel.

vaso (ˈbaso) nm 1 cul glass. 2 glassful. 3 anat,naut vessel.

vástago (ˈbastaɣo) nm 1 bot shoot, sprout. 2 offspring.

vasto (ˈbasto) adj vast. **vastedad** nf vastness.

vaticinar (batiθiˈnar) vt predict, prophesy. **vaticinador** nm prophet. **vaticinio** nm prophecy.

vatio (ˈbatjo) nm watt.

vecinal (beθiˈnal) adj local. **vecindad** nf neighbourhood. **vecino** nm 1 neighbour. 2 resident. adj neighbouring.

vedar (beˈðar) vt prohibit. **veda** nf 1 prohibition. 2 sport close season. **vedado** nm reserve, restricted area.

vega (ˈbeɣa) nf plain, fertile lowland.

vegetación (beɣetaˈθjon) nf vegetation. **vegetal** adj vegetable. **vegetar** vi 1 vegetate. 2 grow.

vehemencia (beeˈmenθja) nf vehemence. **vehemente** adj vehement.

vehículo (beˈikulo) nm vehicle.

veinte (ˈbeinte) adj twenty.

vejar (beˈxar) vt annoy, vex. **vejación** nf vexation.

vejez (beˈxeθ) nf old age.

vejiga (beˈxiɣa) nf 1 anat bladder. 2 med blister.

vela (ˈbela) nf naut sail.

velar (beˈlar) vt keep watch over. vi stay awake. **vela** nf 1 vigil. 2 candle.

veleidad (beleiˈðað) nf 1 whim, fancy. 2 capriciousness.

velero (beˈlero) nm 1 sailing ship. 2 glider.

velo (ˈbelo) nm veil.

velocidad (beloθiˈðað) nf speed, velocity. **velocímetro** nm speedometer. **veloz** adj fast.

vello (ˈbeʎo) nm fluff, down. **velloso** adj downy.

vena (ˈbena) nf 1 anat vein. 2 streak, trait. 3 min vein, seam.

venado (beˈnaðo) nm 1 deer. 2 cul venison.

venal (beˈnal) adj 1 corrupt, venal. 2 comm marketable.

vencer (benˈθer) vt conquer, defeat. vi 1 triumph, succeed. 2 comm expire. **vencedor** adj victorious. nm conqueror. **vencimiento** nm 1 giving way, collapse. 2 comm expiry.

vendar (benˈdar) vt bandage. **venda** nf also **vendaje** nm bandage.

vendaval (bendaˈβal) nm gale.

vender (benˈder) vt sell. **vendedor** nm seller, salesman.

vendimia (benˈdimja) nf grape harvest. **vendimiar** vt harvest (grapes).

veneno (beˈneno) nm poison. **venenoso** adj poisonous.

venerar (beneˈrar) vt venerate. **veneración** nf veneration.

venero (beˈnero) nm 1 water spring. 2 source, origin.

vengar (benˈgar) vt avenge. **vengarse** vr take revenge. **vengador** adj avenging. nm avenger. **venganza** nf revenge. **vengativo** adj vindictive.

vengo (ˈbengo) v see **venir.**

venia (ˈbenja) nf 1 pardon. 2 permission, leave.

venida (beˈniða) nf 1 coming, arrival. 2 return. **venidero** adj future.

venir (beˈnir) vi come. **venir bien** suit, be convenient.

venta (ˈbenta) nf 1 comm sale. 2 rural inn. **venta a plazos** hire purchase.

ventaja (benˈtaxa) nf advantage. **ventajoso** adj advantageous.

ventana (benˈtana) nf window.

ventilar (bentiˈlar) vt ventilate. **ventilación** nf ventilation. **ventilador** nm ventilator, fan.

ventosa (benˈtosa) nf vent.

ventoso (benˈtoso) adj windy.

ventrílocuo (benˈtrilokwo) nm ventriloquist.

ventura (benˈtura) nf joy, happiness.

ver (ber) vt see. nm 1 view, opinion. 2 looks, appearance.

vera (ˈbera) nf verge, edge.

veracidad (beraθiˈðað) nf truth.

verano (beˈrano) nm summer.

veras ('beras) nf pl truth. **de veras** in truth, really, for real.

veraz (be'raθ) adj truthful.

verbo ('berβo) nm verb.

verdad (ber'ðað) nf truth. **verdadero** adj 1 true. 2 real, genuine. 3 trustworthy, truthful.

verde ('berðe) adj 1 green. 2 immature, young. 3 obscene.

verdugo (ber'ðugo) nm hangman, executioner.

verdulero (berðu'lero) nm greengrocer.

veredicto (bere'ðikto) nm verdict.

vergonzoso (bergon'θoso) adj 1 timid, shy. 2 shameful.

vergüenza (ber'gwenθa) nf 1 timidity. 2 shame, disgrace.

verídico (be'riðiko) adj truthful.

verificar (berifi'kar) vt 1 check, inspect. 2 verify. **verificarse** vr prove true, be realized.

verosímil (bero'simil) adj likely, probable. **verosimilitud** nf likeliness, probability.

verruga (ber'ruga) nf wart.

versado (ber'saðo) adj versed, skilful.

versar (ber'sar) vi spin, revolve. **versar sobre** deal with.

versátil (ber'satil) adj 1 adaptable, versatile. 2 fickle.

versículo (ber'sikulo) nm verse (of Bible).

versificar (bersifi'kar) vt,vi versify.

versión (ber'sjon) nf version.

verso ('berso) nm 1 verse. 2 line of poetry.

vértebra ('berteβra) nf vertebra.

verter (ie) (ber'ter) vt 1 pour, spill. 2 translate.

vertical (berti'kal) adj vertical.

vértice ('bertiθe) nm apex.

vértigo ('bertigo) nm vertigo, dizziness. **vertiginoso** adj giddy, dizzy.

vesícula (be'sikula) nf blister, vesicle.

vestíbulo (bes'tiβulo) nm 1 entrance hall. 2 Th lobby, foyer.

vestido (bes'tiðo) nm dress.

vestigio (bes'tixjo) nm vestige, trace.

vestir (i) (bes'tir) vt clothe, dress, put on.

veta ('beta) nf 1 vein, streak. 2 grain of wood.

veterano (bete'rano) adj,nm veteran.

veterinaria (beteri'narja) nf veterinary science. **veterinario** nm vet.

veto ('beto) nm veto.

vez (beθ) nf 1 time. 2 one's turn in a queue. **a veces** sometimes. **de una vez** once and for all. **de vez en cuando** from time to time. **en vez de** instead of. **muchas veces** often. **tal vez** perhaps. **una vez** once.

142

vía ('bia) nf 1 road, route. 2 track (railway). **vía aérea** air mail. **en vías de** in the process of.

viable ('bjaβle) adj viable, feasible.

viajar (bja'xar) vi travel. **viaje** nm journey. **viajero** nm 1 traveller. 2 passenger.

víbora ('biβora) nf viper.

vibrar (bi'βrar) vi,vt vibrate, shake. **vibración** nf vibration.

viciar (bi'θjar) vt 1 corrupt. 2 adulterate. **viciado** adj corrupt, foul. **vicio** nm 1 vice. 2 blemish. **vicioso** adj 1 vicious, depraved. 2 blemished, faulty.

vicisitud (biθisi'tuð) nf mishap.

víctima ('biktima) nf victim.

victoria (bik'torja) nf victory.

vid (bið) nf vine.

vida ('biða) nf life.

vidriar (bi'ðrjar) vt glaze. **vidriera** nf stained glass. **vidrio** nm glass. **vidrioso** adj glassy.

viejo ('bjexo) adj old. nm old man.

viento ('bjento) nm wind.

vientre ('bjentre) nm 1 belly. 2 bowels.

viernes ('bjernes) nm Friday.

viga ('biga) nf timber, beam.

vigencia (bi'xenθja) nf 1 validity, effectiveness. 2 social norm, convention. **en vigencia** in effect, effective. **vigente** adj valid, in force.

vigésimo (bi'xesimo) adj twentieth.

vigilar (bixi'lar) vt watch over. **vigilia** nf 1 watchfulness. 2 vigil.

vigor (bi'gor) nm vigour. **vigoroso** adj vigorous.

vil (bil) adj despicable, vile. **vileza** nf vileness.

vilo ('bilo) adv **en vilo** 1 in the air, aloft, suspended. 2 in suspense, up in the air.

villa ('biʎa) nf 1 villa. 2 town.

villancico (biʎan'θiko) nm Christmas carol.

villanía (biʎa'nia) nf 1 low birth. 2 villainy. ⸱ obscene remark. **villano** adj 1 low, coarse. ⸱ villainous. nm base person, cad.

vinagre (bi'nagre) nm vinegar.

vínculo ('binkulo) nm link, tie.

vindicar (bindi'kar) vt vindicate.

vino¹ ('bino) nm wine. **vinícola** adj relating t⸱ wine or wine-growing. **vino tinto** red wine⸱ **vino de solera** vintage wine.

vino² ('bino) v see **venir**.

viña ('bina) nf vineyard.

viñeta (bi'neta) nf vignette.

violar (bjo'lar) vt 1 violate. 2 rape. **violación** n⸱ 1 violation. 2 rape.

violencia (bjo'lenθja) nf 1 violence. 2 emba⸱

rassment. **violento** adj **1** violent. **2** embarrassing, awkward.

violentar (bjolen'tar) vt **1** force. **2** twist (words). **3** break in. **4** do violence to.

violeta (bjo'leta) adj,nf violet.

violín (bjo'lin) nm violin.

violón (bjo'lon) nm double bass.

virar (bi'rar) vi **1** change direction. **2** swerve. **3** naut tack.

virgen ('birxen) adj,nf virgin.

viril (bi'ril) adj virile. **virilidad** nf virility.

virtual (bir'twal) adj **1** virtual. **2** potential.

virtud (bir'tuð) nf virtue. **virtuoso** adj virtuous.

viruela (bi'rwela) nf smallpox.

virulencia (biru'lenθja) nf virulence. **virulento** adj virulent.

visado (bi'saðo) nm visa.

visaje (bi'saxe) nm grimace, wry face.

viscoso (bis'koso) adj viscous. **viscosidad** nf viscosity.

visera (bi'sera) nf **1** peak of cap. **2** eyeshade.

visible (bi'sible) adj visible. **visibilidad** nf visibility.

visión (bi'sjon) nf **1** eyesight. **2** vision, fantasy. **3** view.

visitar (bisi'tar) vt **1** visit. **2** inspect. **visita** nf **1** visit. **2** visitor.

vislumbrar (bislum'brar) vt glimpse. **vislumbre** nf glimpse, glimmer.

viso ('biso) nm **1** appearance. **2** glint.

visón (bi'son) nm mink.

víspera ('bispera) nf eve.

vista ('bista) nf **1** eyesight. **2** look, gaze. **a primera vista** at first sight. **con vistas de** with a view to. **tener vista** be far-sighted.

visto ('bisto) v see **ver**. adj **1** seen. **2** evident. **por lo visto** apparently. **muy visto** out of date. **visto que** seeing that.

vistoso (bis'toso) adj gaudy, showy.

visual (bi'swal) adj visual.

vital (bi'tal) adj vital. **vitalidad** nf vitality.

vitamina (bita'mina) nf vitamin.

vitorear (bitore'ar) vt acclaim, cheer. **vítor** nm cheer.

vítreo ('bitreo) adj vitreous.

vituperar (bitupe'rar) vt condemn. **vituperio** nm **1** condemnation. **2** pl abuse. **vituperioso** adj abusive, insulting.

viuda ('bjuða) nf widow. **viudo** adj widowed. nm widower. **viudez** nf widowhood.

vivacidad (biβaθi'ðað) nf sprightliness, liveliness. **vivaz** adj **1** long-lived. **2** sprightly, sharp-witted.

víveres ('biβeres) nm pl provisions.

vivero (bi'βero) nm bot nursery.

viveza (bi'βeθa) nf liveliness.

vivienda (bi'βjenda) nf **1** housing. **2** residence, dwelling.

vivificar (biβifi'kar) vt bring to life.

vivir (bi'βir) vt,vi live. **¿quién vive?** who goes there? **~**nm way of life.

vivo ('biβo) adj **1** living, alive. **2** vivid, sharp.

vizconde (biθ'konde) nm viscount.

vocablo (bo'kaβlo) nm word. **vocabulario** nm vocabulary.

vocación (boka'θjon) nf vocation.

vocal (bo'kal) adj vocal. nm member of a committee, board, etc. nf vowel.

vocear (boθe'ar) vt **1** shout to. **2** acclaim. **3** advertise by shouting. vi boast. **voceador** adj loud-mouthed. nm town crier.

vociferar (boθife'rar) vt,vi shout, scream.

vocinglero (boθin'glero) adj loud-mouthed, talkative. **vocinglería** nf uproar.

volante (bo'lante) adj flying. nm **1** steering wheel. **2** shuttlecock. **3** sport winger.

volar (ue) (bo'lar) vt blow up, demolish. vi fly. **volarse** vr fly away.

volátil (bo'latil) adj volatile. **volatilidad** nf volatility.

volcán (bol'kan) nm volcano. **volcánico** adj volcanic.

volcar (ue) (bol'kar) vt upset, knock over. vi turn over. **volcarse** vr tip over, overturn.

volición (boli'θjon) nf volition.

voltaje (bol'taxe) nm voltage.

voltear (bolte'ar) vt **1** turn over, roll over. **2** throw up in the air, toss. **3** peal (bells). vi roll over. **voltereta** nf somersault.

voltio ('boltjo) nm volt.

volubilidad (boluβili'ðað) nf fickleness. **voluble** adj **1** fickle. **2** bot climbing, twining.

volumen (bo'lumen) nm volume. **voluminoso** adj voluminous.

voluntad (bolun'tað) nf **1** will. **2** intention. **3** desire.

voluntario (bolun'tarjo) adj voluntary. nm volunteer.

voluptuoso (bolup'twoso) adj voluptuous.

volver (ue) (bol'βer) vt **1** turn round, turn, return. **2** turn inside out. vi return. **volver en sí** regain consciousness. **volverse** vr **1** turn round. **2** become, turn into.

vomitar (bomi'tar) vt,vi vomit, cough up. **vómito** nm vomit.

voracidad (boraθi'ðað) *nf* voraciousness. **voraz** *adj* voracious.

vórtice ('bortiθe) *nm* whirlpool.

vosotros (bo'sotros) *pron* 2nd pers pl fam you.

votar (bo'tar) *vt,vi* vote. **voto** *nm* 1 vote. 2 vow. 3 *pl* wishes. **mejores votos** best wishes.

voy (boj) *v* see **ir**.

voz (boθ) *nf* 1 voice. 2 rumour. 3 vote, say. 4 word. **hacer** or **dar voces** shout.

vuelco ('bwelko) *nm* tumble, spill.

vuelo ('bwelo) *nm* 1 flight. 2 fullness (clothes). **vuelo fletado** charter flight.

vuelta ('bwelta) *nf* 1 turn. 2 revolution (of a wheel). 3 rotation. 4 change, reversal. 5 return. 6 walk, stroll. 7 *also pl* change (of money).

vuelto ('bwelto) *v* see **volver**.

vuestro ('bwestro) *poss adj* 2nd pers s your. *poss pron* 2nd pers s yours.

vulcanizar (bulkani'θar) *vt* vulcanize.

vulgar (bul'gar) *adj* 1 vulgar. 2 commonplace, trivial. **vulgaridad** *nf* 1 vulgarity. 2 triviality. **vulgarizar** *vt* popularize. **vulgarmente** *adv* commonly, ordinarily. **vulgo** *nm* common people.

vulnerar (bulne'rar) *vt* damage, harm. **vulnerable** *adj* vulnerable. **vulnerabilidad** *nf* vulnerability.

X

xilófono (ksi'lofono) *nm* xylophone.

Y

y (i) *conj* and.

ya (ja) *adv* 1 already. 2 now, finally. *interj* of course! **ya que** since, seeing that. **ya no** no longer.

yacimiento (jaθi'mjento) *nm geol* bed, deposit.

yanqui ('janki) *adj* Yankee, North American.

yarda (jarða) *nf* yard.

yate (jate) *nm* yacht.

yedra ('jeðra) *nf* ivy.

yegua ('jegwa) *nf* mare.

yelmo ('jelmo) *nm* helmet.

yema ('jema) *nf* 1 egg yolk. 2 fingertip. 3 *bot* bud, shoot.

yerba ('jerβa) *nf* 1 grass. 2 herb.

yergo ('jergo) *v* see **erguir**.

yermo ('jermo) *adj* barren, waste.

yerno ('jerno) *nm* son-in-law.

yerro ('jerro) *v* see **errar**. *nm* error, lapse.

yeso ('jeso) *nm* 1 plaster. 2 gypsum.

ye-yé (je'je) *inf adj* trendy. *nm,f* trendy member of the modern generation.

yo (jo) *pron* 1st pers s I.

yodo ('joðo) *nm* iodine.

yogur (jo'gur) *nm* yoghurt.

yugo ('jugo) *nm* yoke.

Yugo(e)slavia (jugoes'laβja) *nf* Yugoslavia. **yugo(e)slavo** *adj,nm* Yugoslav.

yunque ('junke) *nm* anvil.

yunta ('junta) *nf* team of oxen.

yute ('jute) *nm* jute.

yuxtaponer (jukstapo'ner) *vt* juxtapose. **yuxtaposición** *nf* juxtaposition.

Z

zafar (θa'far) *vt* make lighter. **zafarse** *vr* run or slip away.

zafio ('θafjo) *adj* uncouth.

zafiro (θa'firo) *nm* sapphire.

zaga ('θaga) *nf* rear. **ir a la zaga** lag behind.

zaguán (θa'gwan) *nm* hallway, entry.

zaherir (ie) (θae'rir) *vt* 1 reproach. 2 wound, mortify. **zaherimiento** *nm* 1 blame, criticism. 2 mortification.

zalamería (θalame'ria) *nf* flattery. **zalamero** *adj* flattering.

zamarra (θa'marra) *nf* sheepskin jacket.

zambo ('θambo) *adj* knock-kneed.

zambullir (θambu'ʎir) *vt* plunge, dip. **zambullirse** *vr* dive. **zambullida** *nf* dive.

zampar ('θampar) *vt* 1 hide (an object) away hurriedly. 2 eat greedily. **zampabollos** *nm invar* glutton.

zanahoria (θana'orja) *nf* carrot.

zancada (θan'kaða) *nf* stride.

zanco ('θanko) *nm* stilt.

zancudo (θan'kuðo) *adj* long-legged.

zángano ('θangano) *nm* 1 drone (bee). 2 idler, sponger.

zangolotear (θangolote'ar) *vt* fiddle with. **zangolotearse** *vr* rattle, clatter.

zanja ('θanxa) *nf* trench, ditch.

zapa ('θapa) *nf* spade.

zapatear (θapate'ar) *vt* kick with the shoe. *vi* 1 tap. 2 tap-dance.

zapatería (θapate'ria) *nf* 1 shoemaking. 2 shoemaker's shop. **zapatero** *nm* shoemaker.

zapatilla (θapa'tiʎa) nf slipper.

zapato (θa'pato) nm shoe.

zar (θar) nm tsar.

zarandear (θarande'ar) vt shake about.

zaraza (θa'raθa) nf chintz.

zarcillo (θar'θiʎo) nm earring.

zarco ('θarko) adj pale blue.

zarpa ('θarpa) nf paw, claw.

zarpar (θar'par) vi naut set sail.

zarza ('θarθa) nf bramble. **zarzamora** nf blackberry.

zarzuela (θar'θwela) nf light opera, musical comedy.

zigzaguear (θigθage'ar) vi zig-zag.

zinc (θink) nm zinc.

zócalo ('θokalo) nm 1 arch plinth. 2 skirting board.

zona ('θona) nf zone.

zoología (θoolo'xia) nf zoology. **zoológico** adj zoological. **zoólogo** nm zoologist.

zoquete (θo'kete) nm 1 block of wood. 2 chunk of bread. 3 blockhead.

zorro ('θorro) nm fox. adj cunning. **zorra** nf 1 vixen. 2 cheap woman, tart.

zozobrar (θoθo'βrar) vi 1 naut capsize. 2 collapse, be ruined. 3 worry.

zueco ('θweko) nm clog.

zumbar ('θumbar) vi buzz. vt tease, annoy. **zumbido** nm buzzing noise.

zumbón (θum'bon) adj bantering, joking. nm joker, teaser.

zumo ('θumo) nm juice.

zurcir (θur'θir) vt darn, patch. **zurcido** nm darning, mending.

zurdo ('θurðo) adj left-handed.

zurrar (θur'rar) vt 1 tech tan (leather). 2 inf give a beating to. 3 inf criticize harshly, defeat in an argument. **zurriago** nm whip.

zurrón (θur'ron) nm pouch, small bag.

zutano (θu'tano) nm so-and-so.

A

a, an (ə, ən; *stressed* ei, æn) *indef art* un *ms.* una *fs.*

aback (ə'bæk) *adv* atrás. **taken aback** desconcertado, perplejo.

abandon (ə'bændən) *vt* abandonar, dejar. **abandonment** *n* abandono *m.*

abate (ə'beit) *vt,vi* bajar, disminuir, aminorar. **abatement** *n* disminución *f.* abatimiento *m.*

abbess ('æbis) *n* abadesa *f.*

abbey ('æbi) *n* abadía *f.*

abbot ('æbət) *n* abad *m.*

abbreviate (ə'bri:vieit) *vt* abreviar. **abbreviation** *n* abreviación *f.*

abdicate ('æbdikeit) *vt,vi* abdicar, renunciar. **abdication** *n* abdicación *f.* renuncia *f.*

abdomen ('æbdəmən) *n* abdomen *m.* vientre *m.* **abdominal** *adj* abdominal.

abduct (æb'dʌkt) *vt* secuestrar, raptar. **abduction** *n* secuestro, rapto *m.* **abductor** *n* secuestrador, raptor *m.*

abet (ə'bet) *vt* instigar, inducir, patrocinar.

abhor (əb'hɔ:) *vt* aborrecer, detestar, odiar, despreciar. **abhorrence** *n* odio, horror *m.* aversión *f.* **abhorrent** *adj* aborrecible, detestable.

abide* (ə'baid) *vi* permanecer, continuar. *vt* aguantar, aceptar. **abide by** atenerse a, cumplir con.

ability (ə'biliti) *n* 1 habilidad, capacidad *f.* 2 talento *m.* 3 alcance *m.*

abject ('æbdʒekt) *adj* abyecto, vil, despreciable, bajo. **abjection** *n* 1 abyección *f.* 2 servilismo *m.*

ablative ('æblətiv) *n* ablativo *m.*

ablaze (ə'bleiz) *adj* en llamas, ardiente.

able ('eibəl) *adj* hábil, inteligente, fuerte, capaz. **be able** poder, ser capaz. **able-bodied** *adj* robusto, sano.

abnormal (æb'nɔ:məl) *adj* 1 anormal. 2 excepcional. **abnormality** *n* anormalidad *f.* **abnormally** *adv* excepcionalmente.

aboard (ə'bɔ:d) *adv* a bordo.

abode¹ (ə'boud) *n* domicilio *m.*

abode² (ə'boud) *v see* **abide.**

abolish (ə'bɔliʃ) *vt* 1 abolir. 2 revocar, anular. **abolition** *n* abolición *f.*

abominable (ə'bɔminəbəl) *adj* abominable.

Aborigine (æbə'ridʒini) *n* aborigen *m.*

abort (ə'bɔ:t) *vt,vi* 1 abortar. 2 frustrar. **abortion** *n* aborto *m.* **abortive** *adj* abortivo, frustrado, malogrado.

abound (ə'baund) *vi* abundar.

about (ə'baut) *prep* alrededor de, cerca de, hacia, acerca de, sobre. *adv* alrededor, más o menos.

above (ə'bʌv) *prep* por encima de, sobre, superior a. *adv* arriba, encima. **aboveboard** *adv* abiertamente.

abrasion (ə'breiʒən) *n* 1 raspadura *f.* 2 rasguño *m.* 3 *tech* abrasión *f.* **abrasive** *adj* 1 raspante. 2 *tech* abrasivo.

abreast (ə'brest) *adv* de frente. **abreast of** *or* **with** al corriente de.

abridge (ə'bridʒ) *vt* abreviar.

abroad (ə'brɔ:d) *adv* 1 en el extranjero. 2 fuera.

abrupt (ə'brʌpt) *adj* abrupto, brusco. **abruptly** *adv* precipitadamente, bruscamente. **abruptness** *n* precipitación, aspereza, brusquedad *f.*

abscess ('æbses) *n* absceso *m.*

abscond (əb'skɔnd) *vi* fugarse.

absent (*adj* 'æbsənt; *v* əb'sent) *adj* ausente. *vr* ausentarse. **absent-minded** *adj* absorto, distraído, despistado. **absent-mindedness** *n* distracción *f.* despiste *m.* **absence** *n* ausencia *f.* **absentee** *n* ausente *m,f.* absentista *m,f.* **absenteeism** *n* absentismo *m.*

absolute ('æbsəlu:t) *adj* absoluto, total.

absolve (əb'zɔlv) *vt* absolver. **absolution** *n* absolución *f.*

absorb (əb'zɔ:b) *vt* 1 absorber, empapar, chupar. 2 preocupar. **absorbent** *adj* absorbente. **absorption** *n* absorción *f.*

abstain (əb'stein) *vi* abstenerse. **abstention** *n*

abstención f. **abstinence** n abstinencia, sobriedad f.

abstract (adj,n 'æbstrækt; v əb'strækt) adj abstracto. n resumen, sumario m. vt abstraer, resumir. **abstract art** n arte abstracto m.

absurd (əb'sə:d) adj absurdo, disparatado. **absurdity** n absurdo, disparate m.

abundance (ə'bʌndəns) n abundancia f. **abundant** adj abundante, suficiente.

abuse (v ə'bju:z; n ə'bju:s) vt 1 abusar. 2 injuriar. n 1 abuso m. 2 injurias f pl. **abusive** adj 1 abusivo. 2 injurioso.

abyss (ə'bis) n abismo m. sima f. **abysmal** adj abismal, profundo.

academy (ə'kædəmi) n academia f. **academic** adj,n académico.

accelerate (ək'seləreit) vt acelerar, apresurar. vi acelerarse, apresurarse. **acceleration** n aceleración f. apresuramiento m. **accelerator** n acelerador m.

accent (n 'æksənt; v æk'sent) n acento m. vt acentuar. **accentuate** vt acentuar.

accept (ək'sept) vt aceptar, acoger. **acceptance** n 1 aceptación f. 2 acogida favorable f.

access ('ækses) n acceso m.

accessory (ək'sesəri) adj accesorio, adicional. n 1 accesorio m. 2 law cómplice m,f.

accident ('æksidənt) n 1 accidente m. 2 casualidad f. **by accident** por casualidad, sin querer. **accidental** adj accidental, casual, fortuito.

acclaim (ə'kleim) vt aclamar, vitorear, celebrar. n aclamación, ovación f. aplauso m.

acclimatize (ə'klaimətaiz) vt aclimatar.

accommodate (ə'kɔmədeit) vt 1 acomodar, complacer. 2 alojar. **accommodating** adj complaciente. **accommodation** n 1 acomodación, adaptación f. facilidades f pl. 2 alojamiento m.

accompany (ə'kʌmpəni) vt acompañar. **accompaniment** n acompañamiento m.

accomplice (ə'kʌmplis) n cómplice m,f.

accomplish (ə'kʌmpliʃ) vt cumplir, realizar, completar, lograr. **accomplishment** n cumplimiento, logro, éxito m. realización f.

accord (ə'kɔ:d) vt,vi 1 conceder, otorgar. 2 concordar. **accord with** concordar con. ~n acuerdo, convenio m. **of one's own accord** espontáneamente. **accordance** n acuerdo m. **in accordance with** de acuerdo con, conforme a. **according to** según, conforme a. **accordingly** adv en consecuencia, en conformidad.

accordion (ə'kɔ:diən) n acordeón m.

accost (ə'kɔst) vt abordar.

account (ə'kaunt) n 1 cuenta f. relato m. 2 importancia f. **of no account** de poca importancia. **on account of** a causa de. **on no account** de ninguna manera. **take into account** tener en cuenta. ~vi dar cuenta de, justificar. **account for** responder de, dar una explicación de. **accountant** n contable m,f. contador m.

accumulate (ə'kju:mjuleit) vt acumular. **accumulation** n acumulación f. montón m.

accurate ('ækjurət) adj exacto, preciso. **accuracy** n exactitud, precisión f. **accurately** adv con exactitud, con precisión.

accuse (ə'kju:z) vt acusar, delatar. **accusation** n acusación f.

accustom (ə'kʌstəm) vt acostumbrar, habituar. vi soler.

ace (eis) n as m. **within an ace of** a dos dedos de.

ache (eik) n dolor m. **headache** dolor de cabeza. **toothache** dolor de muelas. ~vi doler.

achieve (ə'tʃi:v) vt acabar, realizar, lograr, alcanzar. **achievement** n realización, hazaña f. logro m.

acid ('æsid) adj ácido, agrio. n ácido m. **acidity** n acidez f.

acknowledge (ək'nɔlidʒ) vt 1 reconocer, aceptar. 2 comm acusar recibo. **acknowledgment** n 1 reconocimiento m. gratitud f. 2 comm acuso de recibo m.

acne ('ækni) n acné m.

acorn ('eikɔːn) n bellota f.

acoustic (ə'ku:stik) adj acústico. **acoustics** n acústica f.

acquaint (ə'kweint) vt enterar, dar a conocer, familiarizar. **acquaintance** n 1 conocimiento m. 2 conocido m.

acquiesce (ækwi'es) vi consentir, someterse. **acquiescence** n aquiescencia f. consentimiento m. **acquiescent** adj conforme, aquiescente.

acquire (ə'kwaiə) vt adquirir. **acquisition** n adquisición f. **acquisitive** adj adquisitivo.

acquit (ə'kwit) vt 1 absolver, exculpar. 2 cumplir, desempeñar. **acquittal** n absolución f. descargo m.

acre ('eikə) n acre m. terrenos m pl.

acrimony ('ækriməni) n acrimonia f. **acrimonious** adj áspero, mordaz.

147

acrobat ('ækrəbæt) n acróbata m,f. **acrobatic** adj acrobático.

across (ə'krɔs) prep a través, al través de, contra. adv al través, de través.

acrylic (ə'krilik) adj acrílico.

act (ækt) vt,vi actuar, obrar, representar, fingir. n 1 acto, m. 2 law acta f. decreto m. 3 Th acto m. jornada f. **catch in the act** coger con las manos en la masa.

action ('ækʃən) n 1 acto m. acción f. 2 law demanda f. proces m. 3 mil batalla f. **put out of action** inutilizar.

active ('æktiv) adj 1 activo. 2 vigoroso. **activate** vt activar. **activist** n activista m,f. **activity** n actividad f.

actor ('æktə) n actor m. protagonista m,f.

actress ('æktris) n actriz f.

actual ('æktʃuəl) adj 1 actual. 2 real, efectivo.

acupuncture ('ækjupʌŋktʃə) n acupuntura f.

acute (ə'kju:t) adj agudo, penetrante.

adamant ('ædəmənt) adj firme, seguro, inflexible.

Adam's apple ('ædəmz) n nuez de la garganta f.

adapt (ə'dæpt) vt 1 adaptar, ajustar. 2 arreglar. **adaptability** n adaptabilidad f. **adaptable** adj adaptable.

add (æd) vt,vi añadir, aumentar. **add up** sumar. **adding machine** n máquina sumadora f. **addition** n adición, suma f. aumento m. **in addition to** además de. **additional** adj adicional, suplementario. **additive** n aditivo m.

addendum (ə'dendəm) n, pl **addenda** apéndice, suplemento m. adición f.

adder ('ædə) n víbora f.

addict (n 'ædikt; v ə'dikt) n adicto, partidario m. **be addicted to** 1 ser adicto a, ser aficionado a. 2 estar enviciado con. **drug-addict** toxicómano m. **addiction** n 1 afición f. 2 toxicomanía f.

addled ('ædld) adj huero.

address (ə'dres) vt 1 (a letter) dirigir. 2 (a meeting) pronunciar un discurso ante. 3 (oneself) dirigirse. n 1 dirección f. señas f pl. 2 discurso m. 3 destreza f. **address book** n cuaderno de direcciones m.

adenoids ('ædinɔidz) n vegetaciones adenoideas, glándulas adenoides f pl.

adept ('ædept) n experto m. adj versado, hábil, consumado.

adequate ('ædikwət) adj suficiente, adecuado. **adequacy** n suficiencia f.

adhere (əd'hiə) vi 1 adherirse. 2 observar,

cumplir. **adherent** adj adherente, adhesivo. n adherente m,f. partidario m. **adhesion** n adhesión f.

adhesive (əd'hi:siv) adj adhesivo, engomado. n adhesivo m.

adjacent (ə'dʒeisənt) adj adyacente, contiguo.

adjective ('ædʒiktiv) n adjetivo m.

adjourn (ə'dʒə:n) vt aplazar, levantar la sesión. **adjournment** n suspensión f.

adjudicate (ə'dʒu:dikeit) vt adjudicar. **adjudication** n juicio m.

adjust (ə'dʒʌst) vt ajustar. **adjustable** adj ajustable.

ad-lib (æd'lib) adv a voluntad. vt,vi improvisar.

administer (əd'ministə) vt administrar. **administration** n administración f. **administrative** adj administrativo. **administrator** n administrador m.

admiral ('ædmərəl) n almirante m. **admiralty** n almirantazgo m.

admire (əd'maiə) vt admirar, contemplar. **admirable** adj admirable. **admiration** n admiración f. **admirer** n admirador m.

admit (əd'mit) vt admitir, dar entrada. **admission** n admisión f. entrada f. **admittance** n admisión f.

ado (ə'du:) n trabajo m. dificultad f.

adolescence (ædə'lesəns) n adolescencia f. **adolescent** adj,n adolescente.

adopt (ə'dɔpt) vt adoptar, escoger, aceptar. **adoption** n adopción f. **adoptive** adj adoptivo.

adore (ə'dɔ:) vt adorar. **adorable** adj adorable. **adoration** n adoración f. **adorer** n adorador m. **adoringly** adv apasionadamente.

adorn (ə'dɔ:n) vt adornar.

adrenaline (ə'drenəlin) n adrenalina f.

Adriatic (eidri'ætik) n Adriático m. **Adriatic (Sea)** n (Mar) Adriático m.

adrift (ə'drift) adv a la deriva.

adroit (ə'drɔit) adj hábil, diestro.

adulation (ædju'leiʃən) n adulación f. **adulator** n adulador m. **adulatory** adj adulador.

adult ('ædʌlt) adj,n adulto.

adulterate (ə'dʌltəreit) vt adulterar. **adulteration** n adulteración f.

adultery (ə'dʌltəri) n adulterio m. corrupción f. **adulterer** n adúltero m. **adulterous** adj adúltero.

advance (əd'vɑ:ns) vt,vi avanzar, adelantar. n avance, adelanto, progreso m. **in advance** de antemano. **advancement** n promoción f.

advantage (əd'vɑ:ntidʒ) n ventaja, superiorida

f. **take advantage of** aprovechar(se) de. **have the advantage of** llevar ventaja a. **advantageous** *adj* ventajoso.

advent ('ædvent) *n* advenimiento *m.*

adventure (əd'ventʃə) *n* aventura *f.* **adventurer** *n* aventurero *m.* **adventurous** *adj* audaz.

adverb ('ædvə:b) *n* adverbio *m.*

adverse ('ædvə:s) *adj* adverso, hostil. **adversity** *n* adversidad, desgracia *f.*

advertise ('ædvətaiz) *vt* anunciar, advertir. **advertisement** *n* anuncio, aviso *m.* **advertising** *n* publicidad *f. adj* publicitario.

advise (əd'vaiz) *vt* aconsejar, avisar. **advice** *n* consejo, aviso *m.* **advisable** *adj* aconsejable, conveniente. **adviser** *n* consejero, asesor *m.* **advisory** *adj* consultivo.

advocate (*n* 'ædvəkət; *v* 'ædvəkeit) *n* abogado, defensor *m. vt* abogar por, propugnar, defender.

Aegean (i'dʒi:ən) *adj* Egeo. **Aegean (Sea)** *n* (Mar) Egeo *m.*

aerate ('ɛəreit) *vt* ventilar, airear.

aerial ('ɛəriəl) *adj* aéreo. *n* antena *f.*

aerodynamics (ɛəroudai'næmiks) *n* aerodinámica *f.*

aeronautics (ɛərə'nɔ:tiks) *n* aeronáutica *f.* **aeronautical** *adj* aeronáutico.

aeroplane ('ɛərəplein) *n* avión, aeroplano *m.*

aesthetic (is'θetik) *adj* estético.

afar (ə'fɑ:) *adv* lejos.

affable ('æfəbəl) *adj* afable. **affability** *n* afabilidad *f.*

affair (ə'fɛə) *n* 1 asunto, negocio *m.* 2 amorio *m.*

affect[1] (ə'fekt) *vt* afectar, conmover, impresionar, influir, atacar. **affected** *adj* conmovido, afectado.

affect[2] (ə'fekt) *vt* 1 aparentar, fingir. 2 *inf* dárselas de. **affected** *adj* amanerado, cursi. **affectation** *n* afectación *f.* cursilería *f.*

affection (ə'fekʃən) *n* 1 afecto, cariño *m.* 2 *med* afección *f.* **affectionate** *adj* afectuoso, cariñoso.

affiliate (ə'filieit) *vi* **affiliate to** *or* **with** afiliarse a. **affiliation** *n* afiliación *f.*

affinity (ə'finiti) *n* afinidad *f.*

affirm (ə'fə:m) *vt* afirmar, declarar, asegurar. *vr* afirmarse. **affirmation** *n* afirmación, aseveración *f.* **affirmative** *adj* afirmativo.

affix (*v* ə'fiks; *n* 'æfiks) *vt* fijar, pegar, añadir. *n gram* afijo *m.*

afflict (ə'flikt) *vt* afligir, aquejar. **affliction** *n* aflicción *f.* dolor *m.*

affluent ('æfluənt) *adj* opulento, acaudalado, rico. **affluence** *n* afluencia, opulencia *f.* **the affluent society** *n* la sociedad opulenta *f.*

afford (ə'fɔ:d) *vt* 1 dar, proporcionar. 2 costear, darse el lujo.

affront (ə'frʌnt) *vt* afrentar. *n* afrenta, injuria *f.* insulto *m.*

Afghanistan (æf'gænistɑ:n, -stæn) *n* Afganistán *m.* **Afghan** *adj,n* afgano.

afloat (ə'flout) *adv* a flote, a nado, en el mar.

afoot (ə'fut) *adv* 1 a pie. 2 en proyecto.

aforesaid (ə'fɔ:sed) *adj* susodicho.

afraid (ə'freid) *adj* temeroso. **be afraid** temer, tener miedo.

Africa ('æfrikə) *n* África *f.* **African** *adj,n* africano.

aft (ɑ:ft) *adv* a popa, en popa.

after ('ɑ:ftə) *prep* 1 después de. 2 detrás. 3 según. **time after time** repetidas veces. ~*adv* 1 después. 2 detrás. *adj* posterior, ulterior. **after-effect** *n* efecto secundario *m.* consecuencias *f pl.* **aftermath** *n* consecuencias *f pl.* **afternoon** *n* tarde *f.* **good afternoon** buenas tardes. **afterthought** *n* ocurrencia tardía *f.* reparo *m.* **afterwards** *adv* después, más tarde.

again (ə'gen) *adv* otra vez, de nuevo, nuevamente.

against (ə'genst) *prep* 1 contra, junto a. 2 en contra de. **be against** oponerse. **over against** enfrente de.

age (eidʒ) *n* 1 edad *f.* 2 época *f.* siglo *m.* 3 vejez *f.* **of age** mayor de edad. **under age** menor de edad. ~*vt,vi* envejecer. **aged** *adj* viejo, anciano, envejecido.

agency ('eidʒənsi) *n* agencia, mediación *f.*

agenda (ə'dʒendə) *n* agenda *f.*

agent ('eidʒənt) *n* agente, representante *m,f.*

aggravate ('ægrəveit) *vt* 1 agravar, empeorar. 2 *inf* exasperar, molestar.

aggregate (*adj,n* 'ægrigit; *v* 'ægrigeit) *adj,nm* agregado. *vt* agregar, juntar.

aggression (ə'greʃən) *n* agresión *f.* **aggressive** *adj* 1 agresivo. 2 emprendedor.

aggrieved (ə'gri:vd) *adj* agraviado, ofendido.

aghast (ə'gɑ:st) *adj* 1 horrorizado. 2 pasmado.

agile ('ædʒail) *adj* ágil. **agility** *n* agilidad *f.*

agitate ('ædʒiteit) *vt* agitar, alborotar. **agitation** *n* agitación *f.* alboroto *m.* **agitator** *n* agitador, instigador *m.*

aglow (ə'glou) *adj* encendido.

agnostic (æg'nɔstik) adj,n agnóstico.

ago (ə'gou) adv hace. **long ago** hace mucho tiempo.

agog (ə'gɔg) adj ansioso, ávido.

agony ('ægəni) n agonía f. **agonize** vi agonizar.

agree (ə'gri:) vi concordar, estar de acuerdo. **agreeable** adj 1 agradable. 2 dispuesto. **agreement** n acuerdo m.

agriculture ('ægrikʌltʃə) n agricultura f. **agricultural** adj agrícola.

aground (ə'graund) adv varado, encallado.

ahead (ə'hed) adv delante, adelante. **be ahead** ir delante. **get ahead** adelantarse. **go ahead!** ¡adelante! **straight ahead** todo seguido.

aid (eid) vt ayudar. n ayuda f. ayudante m,f. **first aid** primeros auxilios m pl. **in aid of** a beneficio de.

ailment ('eilmənt) n dolencia f. achaque m. **ailing** adj enfermizo, achacoso.

aim (eim) vt,vi 1 apuntar. 2 aspirar, pretender. n. 1 puntería f. 2 meta f.

air (εə) n 1 aire m. 2 aspecto, porte m. **by air** por avión. **on the air** en la radio. ~vt airear, ventilar.

airbed n colchón neumático m.

airborne ('εəbɔ:n) adj 1 en el aire. 2 aerotransportado.

air-conditioning n aire acondicionado m.

aircraft ('εəkra:ft) n avión m.

aircraft carrier n port(a)aviones m invar.

airfield ('εəfi:ld) n campo de aviación m.

airforce ('εəfɔ:s) n aviación f.

air-hostess n azafata f.

air lift n puente aéreo m.

airline ('εəlain) n línea aérea f.

airmail ('εəmeil) n correo aéreo m.

airman ('εəmən) n aviador m.

airport ('εəpɔ:t) n aeropuerto m.

air-raid n bombardeo aéreo m.

airtight ('εətait) adj hermético.

airy ('εəri) adj 1 airoso. 2 bien ventilado.

aisle (ail) n nave lateral f. pasillo m.

ajar (ə'dʒɑ:) adj entreabierto, entornado.

alabaster ('æləbɑ:stə) n alabastro m.

alarm (ə'lɑ:m) n alarma f. vt alarmar. **alarm clock** n despertador m.

alas (ə'læs) interj ¡ay!

Albania (æl'beiniə) n Albania f. **Albanian** adj,n albanés.

albatross ('ælbətrɔs) n albatros m.

albeit (ɔ:l'bi:it) conj aunque, bien que.

album ('ælbəm) n álbum m.

alchemy ('ælkəmi) n alquimia f. **alchemist** n alquimista m.

alcohol ('ælkəhɔl) n alcohol m. **alcoholic** adj,n alcohólico.

alcove ('ælkouv) n alcoba f.

alderman ('ɔ:ldəmən) n 1 teniente de alcalde m. 2 regidor m.

ale (eil) n cerveza f.

alert (ə'lə:t) adj,nm alerta.

algebra ('ældʒibrə) n álgebra f.

Algeria (æl'dʒiəriə) n Argelia f. **Algerian** adj,n argelino.

alias ('eiliəs) adv,nm alias.

alibi ('ælibai) n coartada f.

alien ('eiliən) adj ajeno, extranjero. n extranjero m. **alienate** vt enajenar, alienar. **alienation** n enajenación, alienación f.

alight[1] (ə'lait) adj encendido, iluminado.

alight[2] (ə'lait) vi 1 bajar, apearse. 2 posarse. 3 descargar.

align (ə'lain) vt alinear.

alike (ə'laik) adj semejante, parecido.

alimentary (æli'mentəri) adj alimenticio.

alimony ('æliməni) n mantenimiento de divorcio m.

alive (ə'laiv) adj 1 vivo, viviente. 2 activo, vivaz. 3 sensible. **alive with** rebosante de.

alkali ('ælkəlai) n álcali m.

all (ɔ:l) adj todo. **all day** todo el día. ~pron todo ms. todos mpl. toda fs. todas fpl. n todo m. totalidad f. adv todo, enteramente. **all but** casi, menos. **all right** ¡está bien! **at all** en lo más mínimo. **not at all** en absoluto, de ninguna manera.

allay (ə'lei) vt apaciguar, calmar.

allege (ə'ledʒ) vt alegar.

allegiance (ə'li:dʒəns) n lealtad f.

allegory ('æligəri) n alegoría f. **allegorical** adj alegórico.

allergy ('ælədʒi) n alergia f. **allergic** adj alérgico.

alleviate (ə'li:vieit) vt aliviar. **alleviation** n alivio m.

alley ('æli) n 1 paseo m. 2 callejón m. **alleyway** n callejón, pasadizo m. **blind alley** callejón sin salida m.

alliance (ə'laiəns) n alianza f.

allied (ə'laid, 'ælaid) adj aliado.

alligator ('æligeitə) n caimán m.

alliteration (əlitə'reiʃən) n aliteración f.

allocate ('æləkeit) vt asignar, repartir. **allocation** n asignación f. reparto m.

allot (ə'lɔt) vt asignar. **allotment** n lote m. asignación, parcela f.

allow (ə'lau) vt permitir, admitir, conceder. **allow for** tener en cuenta. **allowance** n 1 concesión f. 2 dieta f. 3 subsidio m. pensión f.

alloy ('ælɔi) n aleación f. vt alear, mezclar.

allude (ə'lu:d) vi aludir. **allusion** n alusión f. **allusive** adj alusivo.

allure (ə'luə) n atractivo m. fascinación f. vt atraer, seducir, tentar. **alluring** adj atractivo, tentador.

ally (v ə'lai; n 'ælai) vr aliarse, unirse, emparentar. n aliado m.

almanac ('ɔ:lmənæk) n almanaque m.

almond ('ɑ:mənd) n almendra f. **almond tree** n almendro m.

almost ('ɔ:lmoust) adv casi.

alms (ɑ:mz) n limosna f.

aloft (ə'lɔft) adv 1 arriba, en lo alto. 2 naut en la arboladura.

alone (ə'loun) adj solo. adv solamente, sólo.

along (ə'lɔŋ) adv a lo largo, adelante. prep a lo largo de, a lo largo por. **alongside** adv al lado. prep junto a, al lado de.

aloof (ə'lu:f) adv distante.

aloud (ə'laud) adv en voz alta.

alphabet ('ælfəbet) n alfabeto m. **alphabetical** adj alfabético.

alpine ('ælpain) adj alpino, alpestre.

Alps (ælps) n Alpes mpl.

already (ɔ:l'redi) adv ya, previamente.

also ('ɔ:lsou) adv también, además.

altar ('ɔ:ltə) n altar m.

alter ('ɔ:ltə) vt alterar, cambiar. **alteration** n alteración, reforma f. cambio m.

alternate (v 'ɔ:ltəneit; adj ɔ:l'tə:nit) vt,vi alternar, variar. adj alterno, alternativo. **alternative** n alternativa f. adj alternativo.

although (ɔ:l'ðou) conj aunque.

altitude ('æltitju:d) n altitud, altura f.

alto ('æltou) adj,n alto, contralto f.

altogether (ɔ:ltə'geðə) adv 1 en total, en conjunto. 2 enteramente, del todo.

aluminium (ælju'miniəm) n aluminio m.

always ('ɔ:lweiz) adv siempre.

am (əm; stressed æm) v see **be**.

amalgamate (ə'mælgəmeit) vt amalgamar, unir. vi amalgamarse.

amass (ə'mæs) vt acumular, amontonar.

amateur ('æmətə) n aficionado m.

amaze (ə'meiz) vt asombrar, dejar atónito. **amazement** n asombro m.

ambassador (æm'bæsədə) n embajador m.

amber ('æmbə) n ámbar m.

ambidextrous (æmbi'dekstrəs) adj ambidextro.

ambiguous (æm'bigjuəs) adj ambiguo. **ambiguity** n ambigüedad f.

ambition (æm'biʃən) n ambición f. anhelo m. **ambitious** adj ambicioso.

ambivalent (æm'bivələnt) adj ambivalente.

amble ('æmbəl) vi 1 andar despacio. 2 amblar. n paso de andadura f.

ambulance ('æmbjuləns) n ambulancia f.

ambush ('æmbuʃ) n emboscada f. vt emboscar.

amenable (ə'mi:nəbəl) adj 1 dócil, tratable. 2 law responsable.

amend (ə'mend) vt enmendar, rectificar. **amendment** n enmienda f. **amends** n reparación, compensación f. **make amends** indemnizar, dar satisfacción.

amenity (ə'mi:niti) n amenidad f.

America (ə'merikə) n America f. **American** adj,n Americano.

amethyst ('æmiθist) n amatista f.

amiable ('eimiəbəl) adj afable, amistoso.

amicable ('æmikəbəl) adj amigable, amistoso.

amid (ə'mid) also **amidst** prep entre, en medio de.

amiss (ə'mis) adv mal, fuera de lugar, impropiamente. **take amiss** llevar a mal.

ammonia (ə'mouniə) n amoníaco m.

ammunition (æmju'niʃən) n municiones f pl.

amnesty ('æmnəsti) n amnistía f.

amoeba (ə'mi:bə) n ameba f.

among (ə'mʌŋ) prep entre, en medio de.

amorous ('æmərəs) adj amoroso, enamoradizo.

amorphous (ə'mɔ:fəs) adj amorfo.

amount (ə'maunt) n 1 cantidad f. 2 importe m. vi 1 sumar, ascender a. 2 equivaler.

ampere ('æmpɛə) n amperio m.

amphetamine (æm'fetəmi:n) n anfetamina f.

amphibian (æm'fibiən) adj,n anfibio m. **amphibious** adj anfibio.

amphitheatre ('æmfiθiətə) n anfiteatro m.

ample ('æmpəl) adj 1 amplio. 2 abundante. 3 bastante.

amplify ('æmplifai) vt amplificar, ampliar. **amplifier** n amplificador m.

amputate ('æmpjuteit) vt amputar. **amputation** n amputación f.

amuse (ə'mju:z) vt divertir, entretener, distraer. **amusement** 1 diversión f. 2 pasatiempo, recreo m. **amusing** adj gracioso, divertido.

an (ən; stressed æn) indef art see **a**.

anachronism (ə'nækrənizəm) n anacronismo m. **anachronistic** adj anacrónico.

151

anaemia (ə'ni:miə) n anemia f.

anaesthetic (ænis'θetik) n,adj anestésico. **anaesthetist** n anestesista m,f. **anaesthetize** vt anestesiar.

anagram ('ænəgræm) n anagrama m.

anal ('einl) adj anal.

analogy (ə'næləʤi) n analogía f. **analogous** adj análogo.

analysis (ə'nælisis) n, pl **analyses** análisis m. **analyse** vt analizar. **analytic** or **analytical** adj analítico.

anarchy ('ænəki) n anarquía f. **anarchist** n anarquista m,f.

anatomy (ə'nætəmi) n anatomía f.

ancestor ('ænsəstə) n antepasado m. **ancestral** adj ancestral. **ancestry** n linaje m.

anchor ('æŋkə) n ancla, áncora f. vt,vi anclar, fijar.

anchovy ('ænt∫əvi) n anchoa f.

ancient ('ein∫ənt) adj antiguo.

ancillary (æn'siləri) adj auxiliar.

and (ən, ænd; stressed ænd) conj y, e.

Andalusia n Andalucía f. **Andalusian** n,adj andaluz.

Andorra (æn'dɔ:rə) n Andorra f.

anecdote ('ænikdout) n anécdota f.

anemone (ə'neməni) n anémona f.

anew (ə'nju:) adv de nuevo, otra vez.

angel ('einʤəl) n ángel m. **angelic** adj angélico.

anger ('æŋgə) n cólera, ira f. vt enojar, enfadar, encolerizar.

angle[1] ('æŋgəl) n 1 ángulo m. 2 punto de vista m.

angle[2] ('æŋgəl) vi pescar con caña. **angle for** _ inf ir a la caza de. **angler** n pescador de caña m.

Anglican ('æŋglikən) adj,n anglicano.

angry ('æŋgri) adj enojado, enfadado, encolerizado. **get angry** enojarse, montar en cólera.

anguish ('æŋgwi∫) n angustia f.

angular ('æŋgjulə) adj angular, anguloso.

animal ('æniməl) n animal m. bestia f. adj animal.

animate (adj 'ænimət; v 'ænimeit) vt animar. adj animado.

aniseed ('ænisi:d) n anís m.

ankle ('æŋkəl) n tobillo m.

annals ('ænlz) n anales m pl.

annex (ə'neks) vt 1 anexar, agregar. 2 adjuntar. **annexe** n anexo m.

annihilate (ə'naiəleit) vt aniquilar. **annihilation** n aniquilación f.

anniversary (æni'və:səri) n aniversario m.

annotate ('ænəteit) vt,vi anotar, glosar.

announce (ə'nauns) vt anunciar, proclamar. **announcement** n anuncio, aviso m.

annoy (ə'nɔi) vt molestar, fastidiar. **annoyed** adj enojado. **annoying** adj molesto.

annual ('ænjuəl) adj anual.

annul (ə'nʌl) vt 1 anular. 2 law abrogar. **annulment** n anulación f.

anode ('ænoud) n ánodo m.

anoint (ə'nɔint) vt ungir, consagrar.

anomaly (ə'nɔməli) n anomalía f. **anomalous** n anómalo m.

anonymous (ə'nɔniməs) adj anónimo. **anonymity** n anonimato m.

another (ə'nʌðə) adj otro. pron otro m. otra f.

answer ('ɑ:nsə) vt,vi contestar, responder, replicar. **answer for** responder de. n respuesta f.

ant (ænt) n hormiga f.

antagonize (æn'tægənaiz) vt antagonizar. **antagonism** n antagonismo m. **antagonist** n antagonista m,f. **antagonistic** adj antagónico.

Antarctic (æn'tɑ:ktik) adj antártico.

antelope ('æntiloup) n antílope m.

antenna (æn'tenə) n, pl **-ae** or **-as** antena f.

anthem ('ænθəm) n motete m. **national anthem** himno nacional m.

anthology (æn'θɔləʤi) n antología f.

anthropology (ænθrə'pɔləʤi) n antropología f.

anti-aircraft adj antiaéreo.

antibiotic (æntibai'ɔtik) n antibiótico m.

antibody ('æntibɔdi) n anticuerpo m.

anticipate (æn'tisipeit) vt 1 anticiparse a. 2 prever. 3 esperar. **anticipation** n 1 anticipación f. 2 expectación f.

anticlimax (ænti'klaimæks) n anticlímax m. decepción f.

anticlockwise (ænti'klɔkwaiz) adj en dirección contraria a las agujas del reloj.

antics ('æntiks) n payasadas f pl.

anticyclone (ænti'saikloun) n anticiclón m.

antidote ('æntidout) n antídoto m.

antifreeze ('æntifri:z) n anticongelante m. adj anticuado.

antique (æn'ti:k) adj antiguo. n antigüedad f. **antique dealer** n anticuario m. **antiquated** adj anticuado. **antiquity** n antigüedad f.

anti-Semitic adj antisemítico. **anti-Semitism** n antisemitismo m.

antiseptic (ænti'septik) adj,n antiséptico m.

antithesis (æn'tiθəsis) n antítesis f.

antler ('æntlə) n asta f. cuerno m.

anus ('einəs) n ano m.

anvil ('ænvil) n yunque m.

anxious ('æŋkʃəs) adj ansioso, inquieto, deseoso. **be anxious** inquietarse. **anxiety** n ansiedad f.

any ('eni) adj algún, cualquier invar. ningún. pron alguno ms. alguna fs. algunos m pl. algunas f pl. cualquiera invar. ninguno ms. ninguna fs. adv algo. **anybody** pron alguien, cualquiera, nadie. **anyhow** adv 1 de todos modos. 2 de cualquier modo. **anyone** pron see anybody. **anything** pron algo, cualquier cosa, nada. **anyway** see anyhow. **anywhere** adv en cualquier parte, en todas partes, en ninguna parte.

apart (ə'pɑːt) adv aparte.

apartment (ə'pɑːtmənt) n 1 apartamento m. habitación f. 2 piso m.

apathy ('æpəθi) n apatía f. **apathetic** adj apático.

ape (eip) n 1 mono m. 2 imitador m. vt imitar.

aperitive (ə'peritiv) n aperitivo m.

aperture ('æpətʃə) n abertura f.

apex ('eipeks) n ápice m. cúspide f.

apiece (ə'piːs) adv por persona, cada uno.

apology (ə'pɒlədʒi) n 1 disculpa f. 2 apología f. **apologetic** adj lleno de disculpas. **apologize** vi disculparse, pedir perdón.

apostle (ə'pɒsəl) n apóstol m.

apostrophe (ə'pɒstrəfi) n apóstrofo m. apóstrofe m,f.

appal (ə'pɔːl) vt horrorizar, pasmar, consternar. **appalling** adj espantoso.

apparatus (æpə'reitəs) n aparato m.

apparent (ə'pærənt) adj 1 aparente. 2 evidente, manifiesto, claro.

appeal (ə'piːl) vi 1 law apelar. 2 interesar, atraer. n. 1 law apelación f. 2 llamamiento m. 3 atractivo m.

appear (ə'piə) vi 1 aparecer. 2 parecer. 3 law comparecer. **appearance** n 1 aparición f. 2 apariencia f. 3 law comparecencia f. **put in an appearance** hacer acto de presencia.

appease (ə'piːz) vt apaciguar, satisfacer. **appeasement** n apaciguamiento m.

appendix (ə'pendiks) n apéndice m. **appendicitis** n apendicitis f.

appetite ('æpətait) n apetito m.

applaud (ə'plɔːd) vt,vi aplaudir. **applause** n aplauso m.

apple ('æpəl) n manzana f. **apple tree** n manzano m.

apply (ə'plai) vt 1 aplicar. 2 referir. 3 solicitar. vi aplicarse, referirse. **appliance** n aparato, dis-

positivo m. **applicable** adj aplicable. **applicant** n aspirante m,f. candidato m. suplicante m,f. **application** n 1 aplicación f. 2 solicitud f.

appoint (ə'pɔint) vt 1 señalar. 2 nombrar.

appointment (ə'pɔintmənt) n 1 designación f. 2 nombramiento m. 3 cita f. **make an appointment** citarse, pedir hora.

appraise (ə'preiz) vt evaluar, tasar. **appraisal** n valoración f.

appreciate (ə'priːʃieit) vt 1 apreciar. 2 percibir. 3 aumentar de valor. **appreciable** adj apreciable. **appreciation** n 1 apreciación f. aprecio m. 2 percepción f. 3 aumento de valor m.

apprehend (æpri'hend) vt 1 prender, capturar. 2 aprehender, percibir, comprender. 3 temer. **apprehension** n 1 captura f. 2 percepción f. 3 aprensión f. **apprehensive** adj aprensivo, receloso.

apprentice (ə'prentis) n aprendiz m. **apprenticeship** n aprendizaje m.

approach (ə'prouts) vi 1 acercarse, aproximarse. 2 abordar, dirigirse. n 1 acercamiento m. 2 aproximación f. 3 acceso m. 4 método m.

appropriate (adj ə'proupriət; v ə'prouprieit) adj apropiado. vt 1 apropiarse. 2 destinar, asignar.

approve (ə'pruːv) vt,vi aprobar. **approval** n aprobación f. **on approval** a prueba.

approximate (ə'prɒksimət; v ə'prɒksimeit) adj aproximado. vt,vi aproximar(se). **approximation** n aproximación f.

apricot ('eiprikɒt) n albaricoque m.

April ('eiprəl) n abril m.

apron ('eiprən) n delantal, mandil m.

apse (æps) n ábside m,f.

apt (æpt) adj 1 apto. 2 propenso.

aptitude ('æptitjuːd) n aptitud f.

aquarium (ə'kweəriəm) n acuario m.

Aquarius (ə'kweəriəs) n Acuario m.

aquatic (ə'kwætik) adj acuático.

aqueduct ('ækwədʌkt) n acueducto m.

Arabia (ə'reibiə) n Arabia. **Arab** n,adj árabe. **Arabic** adj árabe, arábigo.

arable ('ærəbəl) adj arable.

arbitrary ('ɑːbitrəri) adj arbitrario.

arbitrate ('ɑːbitreit) vt arbitrar. **arbitration** n arbitraje m. **arbitrator** n 1 arbitrador, árbitro m. 2 tercero m.

arc (ɑːk) n arco m.

arcade (ɑː'keid) n 1 arcada f. 2 pasaje, pasadizo m. 3 soportales m pl.

arch (ɑːtʃ) n 1 arch arco m. 2 bóveda f. vt,vi arquear, abovedar. **archway** n arcada f.

archaeology (ɑ:ki'ɔlədʒi) n arqueología f. **archaeologist** n arqueólogo m.

archaic (ɑ:'keiik) adj arcaico.

archbishop (ɑ:tʃ'biʃəp) n arzobispo m.

archduke (ɑ:tʃ'dju:k) n archiduque m.

archery ('ɑ:tʃəri) n tiro con arco m. **archer** n arquero m.

archetype ('ɑ:kitaip) n arquetipo m.

archipelago (ɑ:ki'peləgou) n pl **-os** or **-oes** archipiélago m.

architect ('ɑ:kitekt) n arquitecto m. **architecture** n arquitectura f.

archives ('ɑ:kaivz) n archivo m.

Arctic ('ɑ:ktik) adj ártico. **the Arctic** n el Ártico m.

ardent ('ɑ:dnt) adj ardiente, apasionado, fervoroso.

ardour ('ɑ:də) n ardor m. **arduous** adj arduo.

are (ə; stressed ɑ:) v1 see **be**.

area ('ɛəriə) n 1 área, superficie f. 2 zona f.

arena (ə'ri:nə) n arena f. campo de combate m.

Argentina (ɑ:dʒən'ti:nə) n Argentina f. **Argentinian** adj,n argentino m.

argue ('ɑ:gju:) vt argüir, sostener. vi disputar, discutir. **argument** n 1 argumento m. 2 disputa, discusión f. **argumentative** adj 1 argumentativo. 2 argumentador.

arid ('ærid) adj árido. **aridity** n aridez f.

Aries ('ɛəri:z) n Aries m.

arise* (ə'raiz) vi surgir, aparecer, alzarse.

aristocracy (æri'stɔkrəsi) n aristocracia f. **aristocrat** n aristócrata m,f. **aristocratic** adj aristocrático.

arithmetic (ə'riθmətik) n aritmética f.

arm[1] (ɑ:m) n 1 brazo m. 2 rama f. **arm in arm** de bracete. **at arm's length** a distancia. **within arm's reach** al alcance de la mano. **armchair** n sillón m. **armful** n brazada f. **armpit** n axila f.

arm[2] (ɑ:m) n arma f. vt armar. vr armarse. **arms** n pl 1 armas f. armamentos m. 2 escudo, blasón m.

armour ('ɑ:mə) n armadura f.

army ('ɑ:mi) n ejército m.

arose (ə'rouz) v see **arise**.

around (ə'raund) adv alrededor, por todos lados. prep alrededor de, en torno de.

arouse (ə'rauz) vt despertar, excitar.

arrange (ə'reindʒ) vt arreglar, ajustar, disponer, concertar. **arrangement** n arreglo, convenio m.

array (ə'rei) n 1 formación f. 2 hilera f. 3 despliegue m. vt desplegar.

arrears (ə'riəz) n pl atrasos, pagos atrasados m pl.

arrest (ə'rest) vt 1 arrestar. 2 parar. 3 prorrogar. 4 llamar. n arresto m. detención f. **under arrest** preso, detenido. **arresting** adj impresionante.

arrive (ə'raiv) vi llegar. **arrival** n 1 llegada f. 2 advenimiento m.

arrogant ('ærəgənt) adj arrogante. **arrogance** n arrogancia f.

arrow ('ærou) n flecha, saeta f. **arrowroot** n arrurruz m.

arsenic ('ɑ:snik) n arsénico m.

arson ('ɑ:sən) n incendio premeditado m.

art (ɑ:t) n arte m. **fine arts** bellas artes f pl. **art gallery** museo de arte m. **artful** adj 1 artero, astuto. 2 ingenioso.

artery ('ɑ:təri) n arteria f. **arterial** adj 1 arterial. 2 principal.

arthritis (ɑ:'θraitis) n artritis f.

artichoke ('ɑ:titʃouk) n alcachofa f.

article (ɑ:'tikəl) n artículo, objeto m. cosa f. vt contratar(se), poner(se) de aprendiz.

articulate (v ɑ:'tikjuleit: adj ɑ:'tikjulət) adj 1 articulado. 2 claro, distinto. 3 capaz de hablar bien. vt articular.

artificial (ɑ:ti'fiʃəl) adj artificial. **artificial respiration** respiración artificial f.

artillery (ɑ:'tiləri) n artillería f.

artist ('ɑ:tist) n artista m,f. **artistic** adj artístico.

as (əz; stressed æz) conj 1 como, ya que. 2 cuando, mientras, a medida que. **as for, as to** en cuanto a. **as from** a partir de. **as good as** tan bueno como. **as it were** por decirlo así. **as well** también. **as well as** así como.

asbestos (æs'bestəs) n asbesto m.

ascend (ə'send) vt,vi ascender. **ascension** n ascensión f.

ascertain (æsə'tein) vt averiguar, determinar.

ash[1] (æʃ) n ceniza f. **ashtray** n cenicero m.

ash[2] (æʃ) n fresno m.

ashamed (ə'ʃeimd) adj avergonzado. **be ashamed** avergonzarse.

ashore (ə'ʃɔ:) adv a tierra, en tierra. **go ashore** desembarcar. **run ashore** encallar.

Ash Wednesday n Miércoles de Ceniza m.

Asia ('eiʃə) n Asia f. **Asian** adj,n asiático.

aside (ə'said) adv aparte, a un lado. n aparte m.

ask (ɑ:sk) vt,vi 1 preguntar. 2 pedir. 3 invitar. **ask a question** hacer una pregunta. **ask for trouble, ask for it** inf buscársela. **for the asking** sin más que pedirlo.

askew (ə'skju:) adv ladeado.

asleep (ə'sli:p) *adj* dormido. **fall asleep** dormirse.

asparagus (ə'spærəgəs) *n* espárrago *m*.

aspect ('æspekt) *n* aspecto *m*.

asphalt ('æsfælt) *n* asfalto *m*.

aspire (ə'spaiə) *vi* aspirar.

aspirin ('æsprin) *n* aspirina *f*.

ass (æs) *n* asno, burro *m*.

assassinate (ə'sæsineit) *vt* asesinar. **assassin** *n* asesino *m*.

assault (ə'sɔ:lt) *n* 1 *mil* asalto *m*. 2 agresión *f*. *vt* asaltar, agredir.

assemble (ə'sembəl) *vt* 1 reunir, juntar. 2 *tech* montar 3 *mil* formar. *vi* reunirse. **assembly** *n* 1 asamblea *f*. 2 *tech* montaje *m*. **assembly hall** sala de actos *f*. **assembly line** cadena de montaje *f*.

assent (ə'sent) *n* asentimiento *m*. *vi* asentir.

assert (ə'sə:t) *vt* 1 afirmar, aseverar, declarar. 2 hacer valer. **assertion** *n* afirmación, aserción *f*.

assess (ə'ses) *vt* evaluar, tasar, asesorar. **assessment** *n* valoración *f*.

asset (æset) *n* 1 posesión *f*. 2 *inf* ventaja *f*. **assets** *n pl comm* activo *m*.

assign (ə'sain) *vt* 1 asignar, consignar. 2 *law* traspasar. **assignment** *n* asignación *f*.

assimilate (ə'simileit) *vt* asimilar.

assist (ə'sist) *vt,vi* ayudar, auxiliar, asistir. **assistance** *n* ayuda, asistencia *f*. **assistant** *n* ayudante auxiliar *m,f*.

assizes (ə'saiziz) *n pl* sesión de un tribunal jurídico *f*.

associate (ə'souʃieit) *vt* asociar, juntar. *vi* asociarse, juntarse. *n* 1 socio *m*. 2 compañero *m*. 3 cómplice *m,f*. **association** *n* asociación *f*.

assort (ə'sɔ:t) *vi* convenir, concordar. **assortment** *n* 1 surtido *m*. 2 colección, variedad *f*.

assume (ə'sju:m) *vt* 1 asumir. 2 suponer. **assumption** *n* 1 asunción *f*. 2 suposición *f*.

assure (ə'ʃuə) *vt* asegurar, garantizar. **assurance** *n* 1 seguridad *f*. 2 garantía *f*. 3 desenvoltura *f*. 4 *comm* seguro *m*.

asterisk ('æstərisk) *n* asterisco *m*.

asthma ('æsmə) *n* asma *f*.

astonish (ə'stɔniʃ) *vt* asombrar. **astonishment** *n* asombro *m*.

astound (ə'staund) *vt* pasmar, aturdir.

astray (ə'strei) *adv* extraviado, descarriado. **go astray** extraviarse.

astride (ə'straid) *adv* a horcajadas.

astrology (ə'strɔlədʒi) *n* astrología *f*.

astronaut ('æstrənɔ:t) *n* astronauta *m,f*.

astronomy (ə'strɔnəmi) *n* astronomía *f*. **astronomer** *n* astrónomo *m*. **astronomical** *adj* astronómico.

astute (ə'stju:t) *adj* astuto.

asunder (ə'sʌndə) *adv* separadamente, en dos, a pedazos.

asylum (ə'sailəm) *n* 1 asilo *m*. 2 manicomio *m*.

at (ət; *stressed* æt) *prep* en, a. **at last** por último. **at least** por lo menos. **at work** trabajando.

ate (eit, et) *v see* **eat**.

atheism ('eiθiizəm) *n* ateísmo *m*. **atheist** *n* ateo *m*.

Athens ('æθinz) *n* Atenas. **Athenian** *adj,n* ateniense.

athlete ('æθli:t) *n* atleta *m,f*. **athletic** *adj* atlético. **athletics** *n* atletismo *m*.

Atlantic (ət'læntik) *n* Atlántico *m*. *adj* atlántico.

atlas ('ætləs) *n* atlas *m*.

atmosphere ('ætməsfiə) *n* atmósfera *f*.

atom ('ætəm) *n* átomo *m*. **atomic** *adj* atómico.

atone (ə'toun) *vi* expiar, reparar.

atrocious (ə'trouʃəs) *adj* atroz. **atrocity** *n* atrocidad *f*.

attach (ə'tætʃ) *vt* 1 atar, pegar, adherir. 2 atribuir, conceder. 3 *comm* adjuntar.

attaché (ə'tæʃei) *n* agregado *m*.

attack (ə'tæk) *vt* atacar. *n* ataque *m*.

attain (ə'tein) *vt* alcanzar, lograr. **attainable** *adj* asequible. **attainment** *n* logro *m*, consecución *f*.

attempt (ə'tempt) *vt* intentar. *n* intento *m*, tentativa *f*.

attend (ə'tend) *vt,vi* atender, asistir. **attendance** *n* asistencia *f*. **attendant** *adj* 1 concomitante. 2 acompañante. *n* 1 criado, ordenanza *m*. 2 acomodador *m*. **attention** *n* atención *f*. **attentive** *adj* atento.

attic ('ætik) *n* desván *m*.

attire (ə'taiə) *n* atavío, adorno *m*. *vt* ataviar, vestir.

attitude ('ætitju:d) *n* actitud *f*.

attorney (ə'tə:ni) *n* 1 apoderado *m*. 2 abogado *m*. **power of attorney** poder *m*.

attract (ə'trækt) *vt* atraer, llamar. **attraction** *n* atracción *f*. atractivo *m*. **attractive** *adj* atrayente, atractivo.

attribute (*v* ə'tribju:t; *n* 'ætribju:t) *vt* atribuir, imputar, achacar. *n* atributo *m*.

atypical (ei'tipikəl) *adj* atípico.

aubergine ('oubəʒi:n) *n* berenjena *f*.

auburn ('ɔ:bən) *adj* castaño rojizo.

auction ('ɔ:kʃən) vt subastar. n subasta f.
audacious (ɔ:'deiʃəs) adj audaz, atrevido.
audible ('ɔ:dibəl) adj audible.
audience ('ɔ:diəns) n 1 auditorio, público m. 2 audiencia f.
audiovisual (ɔ:diou'viʒuəl) adj audiovisual.
audit ('ɔ:dit) vt intervenir, examinar. n intervención f. exámen oficial de cuentas m. **auditor** n revisor de cuentas m.
audition (ɔ:'diʃən) n audición f.
auditorium (ɔ:di'tɔ:riəm) n auditorio m.
August ('ɔ:gəst) n agosto m.
aunt (ɑ:nt) n tía f.
au pair (ou 'pɛə) n ayudante doméstica a cambio de alojamiento y manutención f.
aura ('ɔ:rə) n aura f. aureola f.
austere (ɔ:'stiə) adj austero.
Australia (ɔ'streiliə) n Australia f. **Australian** adj,n australiano.
Austria ('ɔstriə) n Austria f. **Austrian** adj,n austríaco.
authentic (ɔ:'θentik) adj auténtico.
author ('ɔ:θə) n autor m.
authority (ɔ:'θɔriti) n autoridad f. **on the best authority** de beuna tinta. **authoritarian** adj autoritario. **authoritative** adj 1 autorizado. 2 autoritario. **authorize** vt autorizar.
autistic (ɔ:'tistik) adj autístico.
autobiography (ɔ:təbai'ɔgrəfi) n autobiografía f. **autobiographical** adj autobiográfico.
autograph ('ɔ:təgrɑ:f) n autógrafo m. vt firmar, dedicar.
automatic (ɔ:tə'mætik) adj automático.
automation (ɔ:tə'meiʃən) n automatización f.
autonomous (ɔ:'tɔnəməs) adj autónomo. **autonomy** n autonomía f.
autumn ('ɔ:təm) n otoño m.
auxiliary (ɔ:g'ziliəri) adj auxiliar.
available (ə'veiləbəl) adj disponible.
avalanche ('ævəla:nʃ) n avalancha f. alud m.
avenge (ə'vendʒ) vt vengar, vindicar.
avenue ('ævənju:) n avenida f.
average ('ævəridʒ) n promedio m. **on average** por regla general. ~adj medio. vt calcular el término medio. resultar por término medio.
aversion (ə'və:ʃən) n aversión f.
aviary ('eiviəri) n pajarera f.
aviation (eivi'eiʃən) n aviación f.
avid ('ævid) adj ávido. **avidity** n avidez f.
avocado (ævə'ka:dou) n aguacate m.
avoid (ə'vɔid) vt evitar, eludir. **avoidable** adj evitable, eludible.
await (ə'weit) vt esperar, aguardar.

awake* (ə'weik) vt despertar. vi despertarse. adj despierto, alerta. **awaken** vt,vi 1 despertar. 2 poner al corriente. 3 darse cuenta.
award (ə'wɔ:d) vt 1 conceder, otorgar. 2 law adjudicar, sentenciar. n 1 premio m. 2 adjudicación f. 3 law sentencia f. 4 mil condecoración f.
aware (ə'wɛə) adj consciente, enterado. **become aware of** enterarse de, darse cuenta de. **awareness** n conciencia f. conocimiento m.
away (ə'wei) adv ausente, en otro lugar, fuera.
awe (ɔ:) n 1 temor, espanto m. 2 veneración, reverencia f. **awe-inspiring** adj imponente, temible. **awe-struck** adj atemorizado, asustado, aterrado.
awful ('ɔ:fəl) adj tremendo, espantoso. **awfully** adv inf muy, excesivamente.
awkward ('ɔ:kwəd) adj 1 torpe, desmañado. 2 embarazoso, difícil, peliagudo.
awoke (ə'wouk) v see **awake**.
axe (æks) n hacha f. vt inf reducir, cortar.
axis ('æksis) n, pl **axes** eje m.
axle ('æksəl) n tech eje m.
azalea (ə'zeiliə) n azalea f.

B

babble ('bæbəl) vi 1 balbucear. 2 murmurar. n 1 balbuceo m. 2 murmullo m.
baboon (bə'bu:n) n mandril m.
baby ('beibi) n niño, nene, bebé m. adj infantil. **babyhood** n niñez, infancia f. **baby-sitter** n cuidaniños m,f invar.
bachelor ('bætʃələ) n 1 soltero m. 2 educ licenciado m.
back (bæk) n 1 anat espalda f. 2 dorso m. 3 final m. 4 sport defensa m. adj trasero, posterior, de atrás. adv 1 atrás. 2 de vuelta. vt apoyar, respaldar. vi retroceder. **back out** echarse atrás, desdecirse.
backache ('bækeik) n dolor de espaldas.
backbone ('bækboun) n 1 espinazo m. 2 firmeza f.
backdate ('bækdeit) vt poner fecha atrasada.
backfire ('bækfaiə) n mot petardeo m. vi 1 petardear. 2 inf salir el tiro por la culata.
backgammon ('bækgæmən) n chaquete m.
background ('bækgraund) n 1 fondo m. 2 antecedentes m pl. 3 educación f.
backhand ('bækhænd) n revés m. **backhanded** adj 1 de revés. 2 irónico.

backing ('bækiŋ) n 1 apoyo m. garantía f. 2 refuerzo, forro m. 3 contrafuerte m.

backlash ('bæklæʃ) n reacción f.

backlog ('bæklɔg) n 1 atrasos m pl. 2 comm pedidos pendientes m pl.

backstage (bæk'steidʒ) adv entre bastidores.

backward ('bækwəd) adj 1 vuelto hacia atrás. 2 atrasado. **backwards** adv hacia atrás.

backwater ('bækwɔ:tə) n 1 remanso m. 2 lugar atrasado m.

bacon ('beikən) n tocino, bacón m.

bacteria (bæk'tiəriə) n pl bacteria f.

bad (bæd) adj 1 malo. 2 dañoso, nocivo. **bad-tempered** adj 1 de mal genio. 2 malhumorado.

bade (beid) v see **bid.**

badge (bædʒ) n 1 insignia, divisa f. 2 distintivo m.

badger ('bædʒə) n tejón m. vt molestar.

badminton ('bædmintən) n volante m.

baffle ('bæfəl) vt 1 frustrar. 2 confundir, desconcertar.

bag (bæg) n 1 bolsa f. 2 saco m. 3 valija f. vt ensacar. **baggy** adj holgado. **baggage** n equipaje m. **bagpipes** n pl gaita f.

bail (beil) n fianza, caución f. vt poner bajo fianza, caucionar.

bailiff ('beilif) n alguacil m.

bait (beit) n 1 cebo, señuelo m. vt 1 poner cebo en. 2 azuzar.

bake (beik) vt 1 cocer al horno. 2 endurecer, calcinar. **baker** n panadero m. **bakery** n panadería f. **baking powder** n levadura en polvo f.

balance ('bæləns) n 1 equilibrio m. 2 comm balance m. 3 balanza f. vt,vi 1 equilibrar. 2 comm saldar.

balcony ('bælkəni) n 1 balcón m. 2 anfiteatro m.

bald (bɔ:ld) adj calvo. **baldness** n calvicie f.

bale[1] (beil) n 1 fardo m. 2 bala f. vt embalar.

bale[2] (beil) vt naut ahicar, baldear. **bale out** aviat lanzarse en paracaídas.

ball[1] (bɔ:l) n 1 bola f, esfera f. 2 sport pelota f. balón m. **ball-bearing** n cojinete de bolas m. **ball-point pen** n bolígrafo m. **play ball** inf cooperar.

ball[2] (bɔ:l) n baile m. **fancy-dress ball** baile de disfraces. **ballroom** n salón de baile m.

ballad ('bæləd) n romance m. balada f.

ballast ('bæləst) n lastre m. vt lastrar.

ballet ('bælei) n 1 ballet m. 2 danza f.

ballistic (bə'listik) adj balístico. **ballistics** n balística f.

balloon (bə'lu:n) n globo m. vi subir en globo. **balloonist** n ascensionista m.

ballot ('bælət) n 1 votación f. 2 sufragio m. 3 papeleta de votación f. vi votar. **ballot-box** n urna electoral f.

Baltic ('bɔ:ltik) adj báltico. **Baltic Sea** n Mar Báltico m.

bamboo (bæm'bu:) n bambú m.

ban (bæn) n 1 prohibición f. 2 bando, edicto m. 3 excomunión f. destierro m. vt prohibir, proscribir, excomulgar.

banal (bə'nɑ:l) adj trivial, vulgar. **banality** n trivialidad f.

banana (bə'nɑ:nə) n plátano m.

band[1] (bænd) n grupo m. banda f. 2 mus orquesta, banda f. vi agruparse, asociarse.

band[2] (bænd) n faja, tira, banda f. **bandage** n venda f. vendaje m. vt vendar.

bandit ('bændit) n bandido m.

bandy ('bændi) vt intercambiar. **bandy about** divulgar, esparcir.

bang (bæŋ) n 1 detonación f. estallido m. 2 golpe m. vt,vi golpear, cerrar con estrépito. **be bang on** sl dar en el clavo. ~interj ¡pum!

bangle ('bæŋgəl) n ajorca f. brazalete m.

banish ('bæniʃ) vt desterrar. **banishment** n destierro m.

banister ('bænistə) n barandilla f. pasamano m.

bank[1] (bæŋk) n 1 ribera, orilla f. 2 loma f. terraplén m. vt estancar, amontonar.

bank[2] (bæŋk) n banco m. **savings bank** caja de ahorros f. **bank account** n cuenta bancaria f. **bank holiday** n día festivo m. **banknote** n billete de banco m. ~vt depositar dinero. **bank on** inf contar con. **banker** n banquero m.

bankrupt ('bæŋkrʌpt) adj insolvente, quebrado. **become bankrupt** quebrar. **bankruptcy** n quiebra, bancarrota f.

banner ('bænə) n bandera f. estandarte m.

banquet ('bæŋkwit) n banquete m. vt,vi banquetear.

baptize (bæp'taiz) vt bautizar. **baptism** n 1 bautismo m. 2 bautizo m.

bar (bɑ:) n 1 barra f. 2 bar m. 3 mus compás m. 4 impedimento m. vt 1 atrancar. 2 impedir, obstruir. 3 excluir. **barmaid** n camarera f. **barman** n mozo de bar m.

barbarian (bɑ:'beəriən) adj,n bárbaro m. **barbaric** adj barbárico. **barbarity** n barbaridad f. **barbarous** adj bárbaro.

barbecue

barbecue ('bɑ:bikju:) n parrillada, barbacoa f. asado a la parrilla m.

barber ('bɑ:bə) n barbero, peluquero m. **barber's shop** barbería f.

barbiturate (bɑ:'bitjurət) n barbitúrico m.

Barcelona (bɑ:si'lounə) n Barcelona f.

bare (bɛə) adj desnudo, desprovisto, descubierto, escaso. vt desnudar, descubrir. **barefaced** adj descarado. **barefoot** adj descalzo. **barely** adv apenas.

bargain ('bɑ:gin) n 1 pacto, convenio m. 2 ganga f. vi regatear, negociar.

barge (bɑ:dʒ) n gabarra, barcaza f. v **barge in** inf irrumpir. **barge into** inf entrometerse.

baritone ('bæritoun) n barítono m.

bark[1] (bɑ:k) n ladrido m. vi ladrar.

bark[2] (bɑ:k) n bot corteza f.

barley ('bɑ:li) n cebada f.

barn (bɑ:n) n granero m.

barometer (bə'rɔmitə) n barómetro m.

baron ('bærən) n 1 barón m. 2 potentado m. **baroness** n baronesa f. **baronet** n baronet m.

barracks ('bærəks) n cuartel m.

barrage ('bærɑ:ʒ) n 1 presa f. 2 mil cortina de fuego f.

barrel ('bærəl) n 1 tonel, barril m. cuba f. 2 tech cilindro, tambor m. 3 cañón m.

barren ('bærən) adj estéril, árido.

barricade ('bærikeid) n barricada f. vt barrear, parapetarse.

barrier ('bæriə) n barrera f.

barrister ('bæristə) n abogado m.

barrow ('bærou) n carretilla f.

barter ('bɑ:tə) vt,vi trocar, permutar. n trueque, intercambio m.

base[1] (beis) n base f. vt basar.

base[2] (beis) adj bajo, vil. **baseness** n bajeza, vileza f.

baseball ('beisbɔ:l) n béisbol m.

basement ('beismənt) n sótano m.

bash (bæʃ) vt 1 golpear, apalear. 2 hacer añicos.

bashful ('bæʃfəl) adj tímido, vergonzoso.

basic ('beisik) adj básico, fundamental.

basil ('bæzəl) n albahaca f.

basin ('beisən) n 1 jofaina. f. 2 lavabo m. 3 escudilla f. tazón m. 4 geog cuenca f.

basis ('beisis) n, pl **bases** base f. fundamento m.

bask (bɑ:sk) vi tomar el sol, tostarse.

basket ('bɑ:skit) n cesta, canasta f. cesto m. **basketball** n baloncesto m.

bass[1] (beis) n 1 mus bajo m. 2 contrabajo m.

bass[2] (bæs) n zool róbalo m.

bassoon (bə'su:n) n bajón m.

bastard ('bɑ:stəd) n bastardo m.

baste ('beist) vt untar, rociar con grasa.

bat[1] (bæt) n maza f. palo m. **off one's own bat** sin ayuda. vt,vi 1 golpear, pegar. 2 pestañear.

bat[2] (bæt) n zool murciélago m.

batch (bætʃ) n 1 hornada f. 2 remesa, tanda f.

bath (bɑ:θ) n 1 baño m. 2 bañera f. **have a bath** tomar un baño. vt bañar. **bathrobe** n albornoz m. **bathroom** n cuarto de baño m.

bathe (beið) vt,vi bañar. **bathing costume** n traje de baño, bañador m. **bathing trunks** n pl pantalones de baño m pl.

baton ('bætən) n 1 mus batuta f. 2 mil bastón de mando m.

battalion (bə'tæliən) n batallón m.

batter[1] ('bætə) vt 1 apalear, magullar. 2 mil cañonear. **battering** n paliza f. castigo m.

batter[2] ('bætə) n cul pasta f. batido m.

battery ('bætəri) n batería, pila f. **storage battery** acumulador m.

battle ('bætl) n batalla f. combate m. **pitched battle** batalla campal. ~vi batallar, combatir, luchar. **battlefield** n campo de batalla m. **battleship** n acorazado m.

bawl (bɔ:l) vt,vi vocear, desgañitarse.

bay[1] (bei) n geog bahía f. golfo m.

bay[2] (bei) n arch galería, nave, crujía f. **bay window** mirador m.

bay[3] (bei) n bot laurel m.

bay[4] (bei) vi aullar, ladrar. n aullido, ladrido m. **at bay** acorralado. **keep at bay** mantener a raya.

bayonet ('beiənit) n bayoneta f. vt pasar a la bayoneta.

be* (bi:) vi 1 ser, existir. 2 estar, encontrarse, haber. **be off** marcharse.

beach (bi:tʃ) n playa f. vt varar. **beachcomber** n raquero m.

beacon ('bi:kən) n 1 faro, fanal m. atalaya f. 2 guía f. 3 semáforo intermitente m.

bead (bi:d) n cuenta, perla f. abalorio m. vt 1 ensartar. 2 perlar.

beak (bi:k) n 1 pico m. 2 nariz f. **beaked** adj picudo.

beaker ('bi:kə) n vaso alto m.

beam (bi:m) n 1 arch viga f. 2 rayo luminoso m. vt,vi 1 emitir rayos luminosos, irradiar. 2 vi sonreír radiantemente.

158

bean (biːn) n judía, alubia f. **broad bean** haba f.

bear[1] (bɛə) vt 1 soportar, aguantar, sufrir. 2 llevar. 3 producir, rendir. 4 parir, dar a luz. **bear in mind** tener presente. **bearing** n 1 porte, aspecto m. 2 relación f. 3 pl situación, orientación f. **lose one's bearings** desorientarse. **take one's bearings** orientarse.

bear[2] (bɛə) n oso m. **teddy-bear** n osito de felpa m.

beard (biəd) n barba f. vt desafiar. **bearded** adj barbudo. **beardless** adj imberbe, lampiño.

beast (biːst) n bestia f. **beastly** adj 1 bestial. 2 inf molesto, desagradable.

beat[1] (biːt) vt 1 batir. 2 apalear, dar una paliza a. 3 vencer, superar. vi pulsar, latir. n 1 med latido m. 2 mus compás, ritmo m.

beauty ('bjuːti) n belleza, hermosura, f. **beautiful** adj hermoso, bello. **beautify** vt embellecer.

beaver ('biːvə) n castor m.

became (bi'keim) v see **become**.

because (bi'kɔːz) conj porque. **because of** a causa de.

beckon ('bekən) vt,vi llamar con señas, hacer señas, atraer.

become[1] (bi'kʌm) vi 1 hacerse, volverse, ponerse, convertirse en. 2 vt sentar bien, favorecer. **becoming** adj 1 decoroso, correcto. 2 que sienta bien, favorecedor.

bed (bed) n 1 cama f. lecho m. 2 tech base f. apoyo m. capa f. **bedding** n 1 ropa de cama f. 2 colchón m. **bedridden** adj encamado. **bedroom** n dormitorio m. **bed-sitter** n salón con cama m. **bedspread** n colcha f. cubrecama m. **flower bed** macizo de flores m. **river bed** cauce m. **go to bed** acostarse. **take to one's bed** encamarse.

bedbug ('bedbʌg) n chinche m.

bedraggled (bi'drægəld) adj enlodado, salpicado de barro.

bee (biː) n abeja f. **bee line** n línea recta f. **beehive** n colmena f.

beech (biːtʃ) n haya f.

beef (biːf) n carne de vaca f. **beefy** adj 1 que sabe a carne. 2 inf fornido.

been (biːn) v see **be**.

beer (biə) n cerveza f.

beet (biːt) n remolacha f.

beetle ('biːtl) n 1 zool escarabajo m. 2 tech pisón m.

befall (bi'fɔːl) vt,vi acontecer, acaecer, suceder.

before (bi'fɔː) adv 1 delante. 2 antes. conj antes

(de) que. prep delante de, ante, antes de. **beforehand** adv de antemano.

befriend (bi'frend) vt,vi amistarse, favorecer, patrocinar.

beg (beg) vt,vi 1 suplicar, rogar. 2 mendigar, pordiosear. **I beg your pardon?** ¿cómo dice? **beg the question** ser una petición de principio. **beggar** n mendigo, pordiosero m. **beggarly** adj indigente.

begin[1] (bi'gin) vt,vi empezar, comenzar, iniciar. **to begin with** en primer lugar. **beginner** n principiante m,f. **beginning** n principio, comienzo m.

begrudge (bi'grʌdʒ) vt 1 conceder de mala gana, escatimar. 2 envidiar.

behalf (bi'hɑːf) n **on behalf of** en nombre de.

behave (bi'heiv) vi 1 comportarse, portarse. 2 funcionar. vr portarse bien. **behaviour** n 1 comportamiento m. conducta f. 2 funcionamiento m.

behind (bi'haind) adv detrás, atrás. **be behind** ir con retraso. **fall behind** retrasarse. ~prep detrás de, tras. **behindhand** adv retrasado, con retraso.

behold (bi'hould) vt 1 contemplar. 2 advertir. interj ¡mira(d)! ¡aquí está!

beige (beiʒ) adj beige.

being (biːiŋ) n 1 ser m. 2 existencia f. **well-being** n bienestar m.

belch (beltʃ) vt arrojar, echar. vi eructar. n eructo m.

belfry ('belfri) n campanario m.

Belgium ('beldʒəm) n Bélgica f. **Belgian** adj,n belga m,f.

believe (bi'liːv) vt,vi 1 creer, pensar. 2 opinar. 3 dar crédito a. **make-believe** n ficción, simulación f. simulacro m. **belief** n 1 creencia f. 2 fe f. 3 opinión f.

bell (bel) n campana, campanilla f. **electric bell** timbre m. **bellringer** n campanero m.

belligerent (bə'lidʒərənt) adj beligerante.

bellow ('belou) vi bramar, rugir. n bramido m.

bellows ('belouz) n pl fuelle m.

belly ('beli) n vientre m. barriga, panza f. **bellyful** n hartazgo, hartón m.

belong (bi'lɔŋ) vi 1 pertenecer. 2 corresponder. **belongings** n pl 1 posesiones, cosas f pl. 2 inf bártulos m.

below (bi'lou) adv debajo, abajo. prep (por) debajo de.

belt (belt) n 1 cinturón m. 2 tech correa f. 3 zona f. vt 1 ceñir. 2 azotar con una correa.

bench (bentʃ) n 1 banco m. 2 tribunal m.

bend

---

bend* (bend) n **1** curva f. recodo m. **2** naut gaza f. **go round the bend** volverse loco. ~vt,vi **1** doblar, torcer. **2** inclinar, encorvarse.

beneath (bi'ni:θ) adv debajo, abajo. prep (por) debajo de.

benefit ('benifit) vt,vi beneficiar, sacar provecho. n **1** beneficio m. **2** subsidio m. **beneficial** adj beneficioso, provechoso. **beneficiary** n beneficiario m.

benevolent (bi'nevələnt) adj benévolo, caritativo.

bent (bent) v see **bend.**

bereave* (bi'ri:v) vt **1** despojar, arrebatar. **2** afligir. **bereavement** n **1** aflicción f. duelo m. **2** fallecimiento m.

beret ('berei) n boina f.

berry ('beri) n baya f.

berth (bə:θ) n **1** naut fondeadero m. amarradero m. **2** naut camarote m. **3** litera f.

beside (bi'said) prep **1** junto a, cerca de. **2** comparado con. **beside oneself** fuera de sí. **besides** adv además, también. prep **1** además de. **2** excepto.

besiege (bi'si:dʒ) vt asediar, sitiar.

best (best) adj mejor, óptimo. adv mejor. **at best** a lo más. ~n lo mejor neu. **for the best** con la mejor intención. **make the best of it** sacar el mejor partido posible. **best man** n padrino de boda m. **best-seller** n éxito de librería m.

bestow (bi'stou) vt conferir, otorgar.

bet* (bet) n apuesta f. vt apostar. **better** n apostador m. **betting shop** n establecimiento de apuestas m.

betray (bi'trei) vt traicionar, delatar. **betrayal** n **1** traición f. **2** revelación f.

better ('betə) adj mejor, superior. **get better** mejorar(se). ~adv mejor. **better off** en mejor posición. **so much the better** tanto mejor ~vt,vi mejorar(se), progresar.

between (bi'twi:n) prep entre. **in between** en medio.

beverage ('bevridʒ) n bebida f.

beware (bi'weə) vi precaverse, guardarse. interj ¡cuidado!

bewilder (bi'wildə) vt aturdir, aturrullar, desconcertar. **bewilderment** n aturdimiento m. perplejidad f.

beyond (bi'jɔnd) adv más allá, más lejos. prep **1** más allá de, fuera de, superior a. **2** además de. ~n más allá m.

biannual (bai'ænjuəl) adj bianual.

bias ('baiəs) n **1** sesgo m. diagonal f. **2** propen-

sión, predisposición f. prejuicio m. vt **1** sesgar. **2** torcer(se), influir en. **biased** adj parcial, predispuesto.

bib (bib) n babero m.

Bible ('baibəl) n Biblia f. **biblical** adj bíblico.

bibliography (bibli'ɔgrəfi) n bibliografía f.

biceps ('baiseps) n biceps m.

bicker ('bikə) vi altercar, reñir.

bicycle ('baisikəl) n bicicleta f.

bid* (bid) vt,vi **1** ordenar, mandar. **2** pujar. n **1** oferta, postura f. **2** tentativa f. **no bid** game paso. **bidder** n postor m. **bidding** n **1** orden f. **2** postura f.

biennial (bai'eniəl) adj bienal.

big (big) adj **1** grande. **2** grueso. **3** abultado. **4** importante.

bigamy ('bigəmi) n bigamia f. **bigamist** n bígamo m. **bigamous** adj bígamo.

bigot ('bigət) n fanático m. **bigotry** n fanatismo m. intolerancia f.

bikini (bi'ki:ni) n bikini m.

bile (bail) n med bilis f. **bilious** adj bilioso.

bilingual (bai'liŋgwəl) adj bilingüe.

bill¹ (bil) n **1** comm cuenta, factura f. letra de cambio f. **2** law proyecto de ley m. **3** anuncio, programa m. **bill of sale** escritura de venta f. ~vt **1** enviar una cuenta a. **2** Th anunciar.

bill² (bil) n zool pico m.

billiards ('biliədz) n pl billar m.

billion ('biliən) n **1** billón m. **2** US mil millones m pl.

bin (bin) n cubo m. papelera f.

binary ('bainəri) adj binario.

bind* (baind) vt,vi **1** atar, ligar. **2** vendar. **3** encuadernar. **4** aglutinar. **5** obligar. n mus ligadura f. **binding** adj obligatorio. n **1** ligadura f. **2** encuadernación f. **3** aglutinante m.

binoculars (bi'nɔkjuləz) n pl gemelos m pl.

biography (bai'ɔgrəfi) n biografía f. **biographer** n biógrafo m. **biographical** adj biográfico.

biology (bai'ɔlədʒi) n biología f. **biological** adj biológico. **biologist** n biólogo m.

birch (bə:tʃ) n **1** bot abedul m. **2** vara f. vt varear.

bird (bə:d) n **1** ave f. pájaro m. **2** sl chica f. **bird of prey** ave de rapiña. **bird's eye view** n vista de pájaro. **birdcage** n jaula f.

birth (bə:θ) n **1** nacimiento m. **2** med parto m. **3** linaje m. **4** origen, comienzo m. **give birth to 1** dar a luz. **2** med parir. **birth certificate** n partida de nacimiento f. **birth control** n control de la natalidad *m*. **birthday** *n* cumpleaños *m pl*.

biscuit ('biskit) *n* galleta *f*. bizcocho *m*.

bishop ('biʃəp) *n* obispo *m*. **bishopric** *n* obispado *m*.

bit¹ (bit) *n* 1 trozo *m*. trocito *m*. pedacito *m*. 2 bocado *m*. 3 *inf* moneda *f*. **not a bit** ni pizca. *adv* (un) poco. **bit by bit** poco a poco.

bit² (bit) *n* freno *m*.

bitch (bitʃ) *n* 1 perra *f*. 2 *inf* zorra *f*.

bite* (bait) *n* 1 mordedura *f*. mordisco *m*. picadura *f*. 3 bocado *m*. 4 mordacidad *f*. *vt,vi* 1 morder. 2 picar. **biting** *adj* mordaz, penetrante.

bitter ('bitə) *adj* amargo, áspero. *n* cerveza clara *f*. **bitterness** *n* amargura, aspereza *f*.

bizarre (bi'zɑː) *adj* raro, grotesco.

black (blæk) *adj* 1 negro. 2 aciago, funesto. *n* negro *m*. **blacken** *vt,vi* 1 ennegrecer. 2 denigrar.

blackberry ('blækbəri) *n* zarzamora *f*.

blackbird ('blækbəːd) *n* mirlo *m*.

blackboard ('blækbɔːd) *n* pizarra *f*. encerado *m*.

blackcurrant (blæk'kʌrənt) *n* grosella negra *f*. casis *m*.

blackleg ('blæklɛg) *n* esquirol *m*.

blackmail ('blækmeil) *n* chantaje *m*. *vt* hacer chantaje. **blackmailer** *n* chantajista *m,f*.

black market *n* mercado negro *m*.

blackout ('blækaut) *n* 1 apagón *m*. 2 desmayo *m*. amnesia temporal *f*. *vi* desmayarse.

black pudding *n* morcilla *f*.

blacksmith ('blæksmiθ) *n* herrero *m*.

bladder ('blædə) *n* vejiga *f*.

blade (bleid) *n* 1 hoja *f*. filo *m*. 2 pala, paleta *f*.

blame (bleim) *vt* culpar. *n* culpa *f*. **blameless** *adj* 1 intachable. 2 inocente.

blancmange (blə'mɔnʒ) *n* natillas de leche *f pl*.

blank (blæŋk) *adj* 1 en blanco, vacío. 2 desconcertado. **blank verse** verso libre. ~*n* 1 blanco, hueco *m*. 2 vacío *m*.

blanket ('blæŋkit) *n* manta *f*. **wet blanket** aguafiestas *m,f*. ~*vt* 1 mantear. 2 encubrir. *adj* general, comprensivo.

blare (blɛə) *vi* sonar muy fuerte. *vt* vociferar. *n* 1 trompetazo *m*. 2 estrépito *m*.

blaspheme (blæs'fiːm) *vi* blasfemar. **blasphemous** *adj* blasfemo. **blasphemy** *n* blasfemia *f*.

blast (blɑːst) *n* 1 ráfaga *f*. soplo *m*. 2 explosión, sacudida *f*. 3 carga de explosivos *f*. 4 trompetazo *m*. **blast furnace** alto horno. ~*vt* 1 volar, destruir. 2 marchitar.

blatant ('bleitnt) *adj* 1 descarado. 2 vocinglero.

blaze (bleiz) *n* 1 hoguera *f*. 2 llamarada *f*. *vi* 1 arder, encenderse, inflamarse. 2 enardecerse. **blazer** *n* chaqueta deportiva *f*.

bleach (bliːtʃ) *vt,vi* blanquear, descolorar. *n* lejía *f*.

bleak (bliːk) *adj* 1 desierto, pelado. 2 crudo.

bleat (bliːt) *n* balido *m*. *vi* balar.

bleed* (bliːd) *vi* sangrar, desangrar.

blemish ('blemiʃ) *n* defecto *m*. mancha *f*. *vt* manchar, empañar.

blend (blend) *vt,vi* mezclar, combinar. *n* mezcla, combinación *f*.

bless (bles) *vt* 1 bendecir. 2 favorecer. **blessing** *n* bendición *f*.

blew (bluː) *v* see **blow**¹.

blind (blaind) *adj* ciego. *n* 1 persiana *f*. 2 pretexto *m*. *vt* cegar. **blindfold** *n* venda *f*. *vt* vendar los ojos de. **blindness** *n* ceguera *f*.

blink (bliŋk) *n* 1 parpadeo, guiño *m*. 2 destello *m*. *vi* parpadear, guiñar. **blinkers** *n pl* anteojeras *f pl*.

bliss (blis) *n* bienaventuranza *f*. embeleso *m*. **blissful** *adj* bienaventurado, dichoso.

blister ('blistə) *n* ampolla *f*. *vt* hacer ampollas en.

blizzard ('blizəd) *n* ventisca *f*.

bloat (blout) *vt,vi* hinchar.

blob (blɔb) *n* 1 gota. 2 borrón *m*.

bloc (blɔk) *n* bloque *m*.

block (blɔk) *n* 1 bloque *m*. 2 tajo *m*. 3 *arch* manzana *f*. 4 obstáculo *m*. *vt* bloquear, tapar.

blond (blɔnd) *adj* rubio. **blonde** *n* rubia *f*.

blood (blʌd) *n* 1 sangre *f*. 2 parentesco *m*. **bloodless** *adj* 1 exangüe. 2 incruento. **blood pressure** *n* presión arterial *f*. **bloodshed** *n* matanza *f*. **bloodstream** *n* corriente sanguínea *f*. **bloodthirsty** *adj* sanguinario. **bloody** *adj* 1 sangriento. 2 *sl* maldito. *adv sl* muy.

bloom (bluːm) *n* 1 flor *f*. 2 florecimiento *m*. 3 lozanía *f*. *vi* florecer, lozanear. **blooming** *adj* floreciente.

blossom ('blɔsəm) *n* flor *f*. *vi* florecer.

blot (blɔt) *n* borrón *m*. tachadura *f*. *vt* 1 manchar, tachar. 2 empañar. 3 secar. **blotting paper** *n* papel secante *m*. **blotch** *n* 1 mancha *f*. 2 *med* erupción *f*.

blouse (blauz) *n* blusa *f*.

blow*¹ (blou) *vi* 1 soplar. 2 sonar. 3 inflar.

blow over pasar. **blow up** estallar, reventar. ∼n soplo m.

blow[2] (blou) n golpe m. bofetada f.

blubber ('blʌbə) n llanto m. vi gimotear.

blue (blu:) adj,n azul m. **bluish** adj azulado. **the blues** melancolía, murria f.

bluebell ('blu:bel) n jacinto silvestre m.

blueprint ('blu:print) n bosquejo, proyecto m.

bluff (blʌf) vt,vi fanfarronear, embaucar. n fanfarronada f.

blunder ('blʌndə) vi desatinar. n desatino m.

blunt (blʌnt) adj 1 desafilado, embotado. 2 despuntado. 3 franco, brusco. vt embotar, despuntar, desafilar. **bluntness** n 1 embotamiento m. 2 franqueza, brusquedad f.

blur (blə:) vt,vi 1 emborronar, manchar. 2 empañar, hacer borroso. n 1 borrón m. 2 contorno borroso m. **blurred** adj borroso.

blush (blʌʃ) vi ruborizarse, sonrojarse. n rubor, sonrojo m.

boar (bɔ:) n verraco m. **wild boar** jabalí m.

board (bɔ:d) n 1 tabla f. 2 tablero m. 3 comm junta f. **go by the board** tirar por la borda. **on board** naut a bordo. ∼vt 1 entablar. 2 naut abordar. 3 hospedar. **boarding house** n pensión f. casa de huéspedes f.

boast (boust) vi jactarse, presumir. n baladronada, ostentación f. alarde m. **boaster** n fanfarrón, pavero m. **boastful** adj jactancioso.

boat (bout) n 1 barca, lancha f. bote m. 2 barco, buque m. vi navegar, ir en bote. **boatsman** n barquero m.

bob (bɔb) vi bambolear. vt menear. n 1 balanceo m. 2 sacudida f.

bodice ('bɔdis) n corpiño m.

body ('bɔdi) n 1 cuerpo m. 2 cadáver m. 3 mot carrocería f. 4 tech armazón f. **able-bodied** robusto, sano. **busybody** n entrometido m. **bodily** adj corporal, corpóreo. **bodyguard** n guardaespaldas m invar.

bog (bɔg) n pantano m. ciénaga f.

bohemian (bə'hi:miən) adj bohemio.

boil[1] (bɔil) vt,vi hervir. **boil over** irse, sobrarse un líquido. ∼n hervor m. **boiler** n caldera f. **boiling point** n punto de ebullición m.

boil[2] (bɔil) n furúnculo, divieso m.

boisterous ('bɔistərəs) adj bullicioso, borrascoso, tormentoso. **boisterousness** n tumulto, bullicio m.

bold (bould) adj 1 atrevido, audaz. 2 claro, vigoroso. **boldness** n atrevimiento m. audacia f.

Bolivia (bə'liviə) n Bolivia f. **Bolivian** adj,n boliviano m.

bolster ('boulstə) n 1 travesaño m. 2 almohada f. vt 1 apoyar, sostener. 2 alentar.

bolt (boult) n 1 cerrojo, pestillo m. 2 tech perno m. 3 rayo m. 4 saeta f. 5 salida repentina f. vt 1 pasar el cerrojo. 2 tech empernar. 3 engullir. vi desbocarse.

bomb (bɔm) n bomba f. vt,vi bombardear. **bombard** vt bombardear. **bombardment** n bombardeo m. **bomber** n bombardero m.

bond (bɔnd) n 1 lazo, vínculo m. 2 comm obligación f. bono m. 3 comm fianza f. vt comm 1 obligar por fianza. 2 poner en depósito. **bondage** n esclavitud f.

bone (boun) n hueso m. **make no bones about** inf no andarse con rodeos. **bony** adj huesudo.

bonfire ('bɔnfaiə) n hoguera, fogata, falla f.

bonnet ('bɔnit) n 1 gorra f. 2 mot capó m.

bonus ('bounəs) n extra m. prima f.

booby trap ('bu:bi) n trampa explosiva f.

book (buk) n 1 libro m. **bookcase** n librería f. estante para libros m. **booking office** n taquilla f. despacho de billetes m. **bookkeeping** n teneduría de libros f. **booklet** n folleto, opúsculo m. **bookmaker** n corredor profesional de apuestas m. **bookseller** n librero m. **bookshop** n librería f. **bookstall** n puesto de libros m. **bookworm** n 1 polilla f. 2 ratón de biblioteca m. ∼vt 1 asentar, anotar, apuntar. 2 reservar.

boom (bu:m) n 1 comm augue repentino m. 2 estampido m. vi 1 prosperar, estar en bonanza. 2 retumbar.

boost (bu:st) vt 1 inf empujar. 2 fomentar, animar. 3 tech recargar. n inf empujón m.

boot (bu:t) n 1 bota f. 2 mot maleta f. **get the boot** ser despedido. **to boot** también. ∼vt patear.

booth (bu:θ) n cabina f.

booze (bu:z) vi inf emborracharse. n 1 bebida alcohólica f. 2 sl morapio m. 3 borrachera f.

border ('bɔ:də) n 1 borde m. 2 frontera f. 3 orla, cenefa f. vt,vi 1 lindar. 2 ribetear. adj fronterizo. **borderline** adj dudoso, incierto.

bore[1] (bɔ:) vt 1 taladrar. n 1 tech taladro m. sonda f. 2 mil calibre m. alma f.

bore[2] (bɔ:) vt aburrir, dar la lata. n 1 pesado, pelmazo m. 2 inf rollo m. **boredom** n aburrimiento m. **boring** adj aburrido, pesado.

bore[3] (bɔ:) v see **bear**[1].

born (bɔ:n) adj nato, innato. **be born** nacer.

borne (bɔ:n) v see **bear**[1].

borough ('bʌrə) n 1 villa f. 2 municipio m.

borrow ('bɔrou) vt pedir prestado. **borrower** n prestatario m.

bosom ('buzəm) n 1 seno m. 2 pecho m.

boss (bɔs) n 1 jefe, patrón m. 2 cacique m. vt dirigir, mandar, dominar.

botany ('bɔtəni) n botánica f. **botanical** adj botánico.

both (bouθ) adj,pron ambos, los dos.

bother ('bɔðə) vt molestar. n molestia, lata f.

bottle ('bɔtl) n botella f. frasco m. vt embotellar.

bottom ('bɔtəm) n 1 fondo m. 2 casco m. 3 anat trasero m. adj más bajo. **bottomless** adj 1 sin fondo. 2 insondable.

bough (bau) n rama f.

bought (bɔ:t) v see **buy**.

boulder ('bouldə) n canto rodado m.

bounce (bauns) vi rebotar, botar. n rebote m. **bouncing** adj fuerte, vigoroso.

bound[1] (baund) v see **bind**.

bound[2] (baund) n salto, brinco m. vi saltar, brincar, botar.

bound[3] (baund) n límite, lindero m. vt limitar, deslindar. **boundless** adj ilimitado. **boundary** n límite, lindero m.

bound[4] (baund) adj destinado, con rumbo a.

bountiful ('bauntiful) adj liberal, generoso.

bouquet (bu'kei) n 1 ramillete, ramo m. 2 aroma m.

bourgeois ('buəʒwa:) adj burgués.

bout (baut) n 1 turno m. 2 med ataque m.

bow[1] (bau) vi 1 inclinarse, hacer una reverencia. 2 someterse. n 1 inclinación, reverencia f. saludo m. 2 lazo m.

bow[2] (bau) n proa f.

bow[3] (bou) n arco m.

bowels ('bauəlz) n pl intestinos m pl. entrañas f pl.

bowl[1] (boul) n tazón, bol m. escudilla f.

bowl[2] (boul) n sport bola, bocha f. vi jugar a las bochas. **bowl over** hacer rodar. **bowler** n jugador de bochas m. **bowler hat** hongo m.

box[1] (bɔks) n 1 caja f. cajón m. 2 palco m. 3 bot boj m. vt encajonar. **box number** n apartado m. **box office** n taquilla f. **be good box office** ser taquillero.

box[2] (bɔks) vt,vi boxear. n cachete m. **boxer** n boxeador m. **boxing** n boxeo m.

boy (bɔi) n niño, muchacho, chico, joven m. **boyhood** n niñez, juventud f. **boyfriend** n novio m.

boycott ('bɔikɔt) vt boicotear. n boicot m.

brace (breis) n 1 tirante, refuerzo m. 2 tech abrazadera f. 3 corchete m. 4 par, berbiquí m. vt reforzar, trabar. **braces** n pl tirantes m pl. **bracing** adj vigorizador, tónico.

bracelet ('breislət) n pulsera f.

bracket ('brækit) n 1 arch repisa f. 2 tech puntal m. 3 brazo m. 4 corchete, paréntesis m. vt 1 poner entre corchetes. 2 agrupar.

brag (bræg) vi jactarse de, fanfarronear.

braid (breid) n 1 trenza f. 2 trencilla f. galón m. vt 1 trenzar. 2 galonear.

Braille (breil) n alfabeto para ciegos, Braille m.

brain (brein) n 1 med cerebro m. 2 sesos m pl. vt romper la crisma. **brains** n pl talento m. **brainwash** vt lavar el cerebro. **brainy** adj sesudo, talentudo.

braise (breiz) vt estofar, guisar.

brake (breik) n freno m. vt,vi frenar.

branch (brɑ:ntʃ) n 1 rama f. 2 sección f. 3 ramal m. 4 comm sucursal f. vi 1 ramificarse, bifurcarse. 2 bot echar ramas.

brand (brænd) n 1 comm marca f. 2 tizón m. 3 hierro de marcar m. vt marcar. **brand-new** adj enteramente nuevo.

brandish ('brændiʃ) vt blandir.

brandy ('brændi) n coñac m.

brash (bræʃ) adj inf insolente, descarado.

brass (brɑ:s) n 1 latón m. 2 mus cobre m. 3 inf pasta f. **brassy** adj 1 de latón. 2 presuntuoso.

brassiere ('bræziə) n also **bra** sostén m.

brave (breiv) adj valiente, bravo. vt desafiar, arrostrar. **bravery** n valentía f. valor m.

brawl (brɔ:l) n riña f. alboroto m. vi alborotar, armar camorra.

bray (brei) vi rebuznar. n rebuzno m.

brazen ('breizən) adj 1 de latón. 2 desvergonzado.

Brazil (brə'zil) n Brasil m. **Brazilian** adj,n brasileño m.

breach (bri:tʃ) n 1 brecha f. 2 ruptura f. 3 infracción, violación f. vt,vi 1 abrir brecha. 2 romper.

bread (bred) n pan m. **breadcrumb** n migaja f. **breadcrumbs** pan rallado m. **breadwinner** n cabeza de familia m.

breadth (bredθ) n 1 anchura f. ancho m. 2 amplitud, tolerancia f.

break[1] (breik) n 1 ruptura f. 2 abertura, grieta f. 3 pausa, interrupción f. 4 descanso, recreo m. vt romper, quebrantar, quebrar. **break away** desprenderse. **break down** 1 derribar. 2 enfermar. 3 echarse a llorar. 4 tener una avería. **break in** forzar la entrada. **break out**

163

breakfast

estallar. **break up 1** desmenuzar. **2** disolver. **breakdown** n **1** colapso m. crisis f. **2** mot avería f. **breakthrough** n avance m.

breakfast ('brekfəst) n desayuno m. vi desayunarse.

breast (brest) n pecho m. **make a clean breast of it** confesarlo todo con franqueza. **breaststroke** n brazada de pecho, braza f.

breath (breθ) n **1** aliento m. respiración. f. **2** soplo m. **under one's breath** en voz baja. **waste one's breath** gastar saliva. **breathless** adj sin aliento. **breathtaking** adj **1** vertiginoso. **2** pasmoso.

breathe (bri:ð) vt,vi **1** respirar. **2** exhalar. **3** inspirar.

breed* (bri:d) n raza, casta f. vt,vi **1** criar, reproducirse, engendrar. **2** educar. **breeding** n **1** cría f. **2** crianza, educación f.

breeze (bri:z) n brisa f. **breezy** adj ventilado, oreado.

brew (bru:) vt **1** fabricar (cerveza). **2** infusionar. n poción f. **brewery** n fábrica de cerveza f.

bribe (braib) n soborno m. vt sobornar. **briber** n sobornador m. **bribery** n soborno m.

brick (brik) n ladrillo m. vt cerrar con ladrillos, cegar. **bricklayer** n albañil m.

bride (braid) n novia, desposada f. **bridal** adj nupcial. **bridegroom** n novio, desposado m. **bridesmaid** n dama de honor f.

bridge¹ (bridʒ) n puente m. **drawbridge** puente levadizo. **suspension bridge** puente colgante. ~vt tender un puente.

bridge² (bridʒ) n game bridge m.

bridle ('braidl) n brida f. freno m. vt enfrenar, refrenar. vi picarse.

brief (bri:f) adj breve. n **1** resumen, memorial m. **2** law autos jurídicos m pl. **3** breve m. vt dar instrucciones. **briefcase** n cartera f.

brigade (bri'geid) n brigada f. **brigadier** n brigadier m.

bright (brait) adj **1** brillante, claro. **2** alegre, vivo. **3** listo, agudo. **brighten** vt,vi **1** abrillantar. **2** aclarar. **3** mejorar, avivar. **brightness** n **1** brillantez f. **2** viveza f. **3** talento m.

brilliant ('briliant) adj brillante.

brim (brim) n **1** borde m. **2** ala de sombrero f.

bring* (briŋ) vt traer, conducir, llevar. **bring about** ocasionar. **bring down 1** rebajar. **2** mil derribar. **bring forth** producir. **bring forward 1** presentar. **2** adelantar. **bring in 1** introducir. **2** rendir. **bring off** conseguir. **bring on** causar, inducir. **bring out 1** sacar,

revelar. **2** publicar. **3** alentar. **bring together** reunir. **bring up** criar, educar.

brink (briŋk) n borde m. orilla f.

brisk (brisk) adj enérgico, vigoroso, animado.

bristle ('brisl) n cerda f. vi erizarse.

Britain ('britn) n Gran Bretaña f. **British** adj británico. **Briton** n británico m.

brittle ('britl) adj quebradizo, frágil.

broad (brɔ:d) adj **1** ancho. **2** amplio, extenso. **3** general, aproximado. **broadly** adj **1** en general. **2** plenamente. **broadness** n **1** anchura f. **2** amplitud f. liberalismo m. **broad-minded** adj de miras amplias, liberal, tolerante.

broad bean n haba verde f.

broadcast ('brɔ:dka:st) vt,vi **1** emitir, radiar. **2** diseminar, divulgar. n emisión f. programa radiofónico m. **broadcasting** n radiodifusión f. **broadcasting station** n emisora f.

broaden ('brɔ:dn) vt,vi **1** ensanchar. **2** ampliar.

broccoli ('brɔkəli) n brécoles m pl.

brochure ('brəuʃə) n folleto m.

broke (brouk) v see **break**. adj inf sin blanca.

broken ('broukən) v see **break.**

broker ('broukə) n corredor de bolsa·m.

bronchitis (brɔŋ'kaitis) n bronquitis f.

bronze (brɔnz) n bronce m.

brooch (broutʃ) n broche m.

brood (bru:d) n **1** camada, nidada f. **2** progenie, prole f. vi empollar. **brood on** or **over** rumiar, meditar.

brook (bruk) n arroyo m.

broom (bru:m) n **1** escoba f. **2** retama f.

brothel ('brɔθəl) n burdel, prostíbulo m.

brother ('brʌðə) n hermano m. **brotherhood** n fraternidad f. **brotherly** adj fraternal. **brother-in-law** n cuñado, hermano político m.

brought (brɔ:t) v see **bring.**

brow (brau) n **1** ceja f. **2** frente f. **3** cumbre f. **browbeat** vt intimidar verbalmente.

brown (braun) adj pardo, castaño, moreno. vt **1** poner moreno, tostar. **2** dorar. n color pardo, etc. m. **brownish** adj parduzco.

browse (brauz) vi hojear. vt pacer, ramonear.

bruise (bru:z) n contusión f. magulladura f. cardenal m. vt magullar, machacar.

brunette (bru:'net) n morena f.

brush (brʌʃ) n **1** cepillo m. **2** brocha f. pincel m. vt **1** cepillar. **2** rozar.

brusque (bru:sk) adj brusco, rudo.

Brussels ('brʌsəlz) n Bruselas. **Brussels sprout** n col de Bruselas f.

brute (bru:t) n bruto m. bestia m,f. adj bruto.

brutal *adj* brutal, salvaje. **brutality** *n* brutalidad *f.* **brutalize** *vt* brutalizar.

bubble ('bʌbəl) *n* burbuja *f.* *vi* burbujear, borbotear.

buck[1] (bʌk) *n* 1 gamo *m.* 2 macho *m.*

buck[2] (bʌk) *vi* corcovear.

bucket ('bʌkit) *n* cubo, balde *m.*

buckle ('bʌkəl) *n* hebilla *f.* *vt* abrochar. *vi* doblegarse.

bud (bʌd) *n* 1 brote *m.* pimpollo *m.* 2 capullo *m.* *vi* 1 brotar. 2 florecer.

Buddhism ('budizəm) *n* budismo *m.* **Buddhist** *adj,n* budista *m,f.*

budget ('bʌdʒit) *n* presupuesto *m.* *vi* presupuestar.

buffalo ('bʌfəlou) *n, pl* **-oes** *or* **-os** búfalo *m.*

buffer ('bʌfə) *n* tope, amortiguador *m.*

buffet[1] ('bufei) *n* buffet *m.*

buffet[2] ('bʌfit) *n* bofetón *m.* bofetada *f.* *vt* abofetear, golpear.

bug (bʌg) *n* 1 chinche *f.* 2 bicho *m.* 3 *inf* microbio, virus *m.*

bugle ('bjuːgəl) *n* corneta *f.* **bugler** *n* corneta *m.*

build* (bild) *vt,vi* 1 construir. 2 edificar. 3 establecer, fundar. **builder** *n* constructor, maestro de obras *m.* **building** *n* 1 edificio *m.* 2 construcción *f.* **building site** *n* solar *m.* **building society** *n* cooperativa de la vivienda *f.*

bulb (bʌlb) *n* 1 *bot* bulbo *m.* 2 bombilla *f.* 3 ampolla *f.*

bulge (bʌldʒ) *n* comba, hinchazón *f.* bulto *m.* *vi* combarse, bombearse, abultar.

bulk (bʌlk) *n* 1 bulto, volumen, tamaño *m.* 2 grueso *m.* **in bulk** a granel. **bulkiness** *n* volumen, bulto *m.* **bulky** *adj* voluminoso.

bull (bul) *n* toro *m.* **bullfight** *n* corrida de toros *f.* *vt,vi* torear. **bullfighter** *n* torero *m.* **bullring** *n* plaza de toros *f.* **bull's-eye** *n* centro del blanco *m.*

bulldog ('buldɔg) *n* dogo, perro de presa *m.*

bulldozer ('buldouzə) *n* excavadora *f.* buldózer *m.* **bulldoze** *vt inf* intimidar.

bullet ('bulit) *n* bala *f.* **bullet-proof** *adj* a prueba de bala.

bulletin ('bulətin) *n* boletín *m.* **news bulletin** boletín informativo.

bullion ('buliən) *n* oro en barras *m.* plata en barras *f.*

bully ('buli) *n* matón *m.* *vt* intimidar, amedrantar.

bum (bʌm) *n* 1 *inf* posaderas *f pl.* pompis *m.* 2 *inf* holgazán *m.*

bump (bʌmp) *n* 1 trompazo, topetón *m.* 2 sacudida *f.* 3 comba, giba *f.* 4 protuberancia *f.* 5 chichón *m.* *vt* 1 dar un trompazo a. 2 chocar, topar. **bumper** *n* parachoques *m invar. adj* abundante.

bun (bʌn) *n* 1 bollo *m.* 2 moño *m.*

bunch (bʌntʃ) *n* 1 manojo *m.* 2 ranco *m.* 3 racimo *m.* 4 *inf* pandilla *f.* montón *m.*

bundle ('bʌndl) *n* 1 lío, paquete *m.* 2 haz *m.* manojo *m.* *vt* envolver, liar.

bungalow ('bʌŋgəlou) *n* chalet *m.*

bungle ('bʌŋgəl) *n* chapucería, torpeza *f.* *vt* chapucear, echar a perder. **bungler** *n* chapucero *m.* **bungling** *adj* chapucero, torpe.

bunk (bʌŋk) *n* 1 litera *f.* 2 *inf* palabrería *f.*

bunker ('bʌŋkə) *n* 1 refugio, bunker *m.* 2 carbonera *f.* 3 *sport* hoya de arena *f.*

buoy (bɔi) *n* boya *f.* flotador *m.* **buoyant** *adj* boyante. **buoyancy** *n* fluctuación *f.* capacidad de recuperación *f.*

burden ('bəːdn) *n* carga *f.* *vt* cargar, gravar.

bureau ('bjuərou) *n* 1 oficina, agencia *f.* departamento *m.* 2 escritorio *m.*

bureaucracy (bjuˈrɔkrəsi) *n* burocracia *f.* **bureaucrat** *n* burócrata *m,f.* **bureaucratic** *adj* burocrático.

burglar ('bəːglə) *n* ladrón, escalador *m.* **burglar alarm** *n* alarma contra ladrones *f.* **burglary** *n* robo *m.* **burgle** *vt* robar, escalar.

burn* (bəːn) *vt* 1 quemar, abrasar. 2 requemar, curtir. *vi* arder. *n* quemadura *f.* **burner** *n* quemador *m.* **burning** *adj* ardiente, abrasador.

burrow ('bʌrou) *n* madriguera *f.* *vi* socavar, minar.

burst* (bəːst) *vt* 1 reventar, estallar, romper. 2 irrumpir. 3 rebosar. 4 brotar. *n* 1 reventón *m.* 2 estallido *m.*

bury ('beri) *vt* 1 enterrar, sepultar. 2 ocultar. **burial** *n* entierro *m.* **burial ground** *n* cementerio, camposanto *m.*

bus (bʌs) *n, pl* **-es** *or* **-ses** autobús *m.* **bus-stop** parada de autobús *f.*

bush (buʃ) *n* 1 arbusto *m.* 2 matorral *m.*

bushy ('buʃi) *adj* 1 espeso. 2 matoso. 3 peludo.

business ('biznis) *n* 1 negocio, comercio *m.* empresa *f.* 2 ocupación *f.* 3 asunto *m.* 4 tarea *f.* **mind one's own business** no meterse donde no le llaman. **businessman** *n* hombre de negocios *m.* **business-like** *adj* metódico, práctico.

165

bust¹ (bʌst) n busto m.

bust² (bʌst) n inf 1 reventón m. 2 fracaso m. **go bust** quebrar. vt romper, reventar, estropear.

bustle ('bʌsəl) n bullicio m. animación, bulla f. vi 1 bullir. 2 afanarse. **bustling** adj bullicioso.

busy ('bizi) adj 1 ocupado, atareado. 2 activo. **busybody** entrometido.

but (bət; stressed bʌt) conj pero, sino. prep excepto. adv solamente.

butcher ('butʃə) n carnicero m. vt 1 matar. 2 destrozar, hacer una carnicería con. **butcher's shop** n carnicería f.

butler ('bʌtlə) n mayordomo m.

butt¹ (bʌt) n 1 cabo, mango m. 2 culata f.

butt² (bʌt) n 1 blanco m. 2 meta f. objeto m.

butt³ (bʌt) vt dar cabezadas contra, embestir. **butt in** inf entrometerse, interrumpir.

butter ('bʌtə) n mantequilla f. vt untar con mantequilla. **buttercup** n ranúnculo m. **butterfly** n mariposa f.

buttocks ('bʌtəks) n pl nalgas f pl.

button ('bʌtn) n botón m. vt abotonar.

buttress ('bʌtrəs) n arch contrafuerte m. vt apoyar, reforzar.

buy* (bai) vt comprar. n compra f. **buyer** n comprador m.

buzz (bʌz) n zumbido m. vi zumbar. **buzzer** n timbre, silbato m.

by (bai) prep 1 por, a, de. 2 cerca de. adv 1 cerca, al lado. 2 a un lado, aparte. **by the way** a propósito. **by and large** en generales. **by-election** n elecciones complementarias f pl. **bylaw** n estatuto m. ley local f. **bypass** n desviación f. vt 1 desviar. 2 evitar. **by-product** n subproducto m. **bystander** n espectador m. circunstante m,f.

C

cab (kæb) n taxi, coche de alquiler m. **cabman** n cochero m.

cabaret ('kæbərei) n cabaret m.

cabbage ('kæbidʒ) n col f. repollo m.

cabin ('kæbin) n 1 cabaña f. 2 naut camarote m. **cabin cruiser** n motonave f.

cabinet ('kæbinət) n 1 armario m. vitrina f. 2 gabinete m. 3 pol consejo de ministros m. **medicine cabinet** botiquín m.

cable ('keibəl) n cable m. vt,vi cablegrafiar.

cackle ('kækəl) vi cacarear. n cacareo m.

cactus ('kæktəs) n, pl -ti or -tuses cacto m.

cadence ('keidns) n 1 cadencia f. 2 compás m.

cadet (kə'det) n mil cadete m.

cafe ('kæfei) n 1 café m. 2 restaurante m.

cafeteria (kæfi'tiəriə) n cafetería f.

caffeine ('kæfi:n) n cafeína f.

cage (keidʒ) n jaula f. vt enjaular.

cake (keik) n 1 pastel m. 2 (of soap) pastilla f. vi endurecerse.

calamity (kə'læməti) n calamidad f.

calcium ('kælsiəm) n calcio m.

calculate ('kælkjuleit) vt,vi calcular. **calculable** adj calculable. **calculation** n cálculo m. calculación f. **calculator** n calculador m.

calendar ('kælində) n calendario m.

calf¹ (ka:f) n, pl **calves** zool ternero, becerro m.

calf² (ka:f) n, pl **calves** anat pantorrilla f.

calibre ('kælibə) n 1 calibre m. 2 talento m.

call (kɔ:l) vt llamar. **call for** pedir, exigir. **call off** cancelar, abandonar. **call on** 1 visitar. 2 invitar. **call up** 1 evocar. 2 convocar. 3 llamar por teléfono. **call upon** visitar. ~n 1 llamada f. llamamiento m. 2 grito m. 3 visita f.

callbox ('kɔ:lbɔks) n cabina telefónica f.

calling ('kɔ:liŋ) n vocación, profesión f.

callous ('kæləs) adj insensible, duro.

calm (ka:m) n calma, tranquilidad f. sosiego m. adj 1 calmoso. 2 tranquilo, sosegado. vt,vi 1 calmar. 2 tranquilizar.

calorie ('kæləri) n caloría f.

Cambodia (kæm'boudiə) n Camboya f.

came (keim) v see **come**.

camel ('kæməl) n camello m.

camera ('kæmrə) n 1 máquina fotográfica f. 2 cámara f. **cameraman** n cameraman m.

camouflage ('kæməfla:ʒ) n camuflaje m. vt camuflar.

camp¹ (kæmp) n campamento m. vi acampar. **camp-bed** n cama plegable f. **camping site** n camping m.

camp² (kæmp) adj inf 1 afeminado. 2 homosexual.

campaign (kæm'pein) n campaña f. **election campaign** campaña electoral. vi hacer campaña.

campus ('kæmpəs) n recinto universitario, campus m.

can*¹ (kæn) vi 1 poder. 2 saber.

can² (kæn) n lata f. bote m. vt enlatar. **canned** adj enlatado, en conserva. **canning** n enlatado m.

Canada ('kænədə) n Canadá m. **Canadian** n,adj canadiense m,f.

canal (kə'næl) n canal m.

canary ('kɛəri) n canario m.

Canary Islands n pl (Islas) Canarias f pl.

cancel ('kænsəl) vt, vi **1** cancelar. **2** tachar. **cancel out** destruirse, anularse. **cancellation** n cancelación, anulación f.

cancer ('kænsə) n cáncer m. **cancerous** adj canceroso.

candid ('kændid) adj franco, sincero.

candidate ('kændidət) n candidato m.

candle ('kændl) n vela, candela f. **candlestick** n **1** candelero m. **2** candelabro m.

candour ('kændə) n franqueza f.

cane (kein) n **1** caña f. **2** bastón m. **3** palmeta f. vt azotar, castigar con la palmeta.

canine ('keinain) n, adj canino m.

cannabis ('kænəbis) n marijuana f.

cannibal ('kænəbəl) n caníbal m, f. adj antropófago. **cannibalism** n canibalismo m.

cannon ('kænən) n **1** cañón m. **2** carambola f. **cannonade** n cañoneo m. **cannonball** n bala de cañón f.

cannot ('kænɔt) v see **can**[1].

canoe (kə'nu:) n canoa f. vi ir en canoa.

canon[1] ('kænən) n canon m. **canon law** derecho canónico m. **canonize** vt canonizar. **canonization** n canonizacion f.

canon[2] ('kænən) n canónigo m.

canopy ('kænəpi) n dosel, baldaquín m.

canteen (kæn'ti:n) n **1** cantina f. **2** cantimplora f.

canter ('kæntə) n medio galope m. vi ir a medio galope.

canton ('kæntɔn) n cantón m.

canvas ('kænvəs) n **1** lona f. **2** cañamazo m. **3** art tela f. lienzo m.

canvass ('kænvəs) vt escrutinar, sondear. vi solicitar apoyo. **canvassing** n **1** sondeo m. **2** solicitación de apoyo f.

canyon ('kænjən) n desfiladero m. cañada f.

cap (kæp) n **1** gorra f. **2** casquete m. vt coronar, rematar.

capable ('keipəbəl) adj capaz, hábil. **capability** n capacidad, habilidad f.

capacity (kə'pæsiti) n **1** capacidad f. **2** mot cilindrada f.

cape[1] (keip) n capa f.

cape[2] (keip) n cabo m.

caper ('keipə) n cul alcaparra f.

capital ('kæpitl) n **1** capital f. **2** mayúscula f. **3** capital m. **capitalism** n capitalismo m. **capitalist** n capitalista m, f. **capitalistic** adj capitalista. **capitalize** vt capitalizar. **capitalization** n capitalización f.

capricious (kə'prɪʃəs) adj caprichoso. **caprice** or **capriciousness** n capricho m.

Capricorn ('kæprikɔ:n) n Capricornio m.

capsicum ('kæpsikam) n pimiento m.

capsize ('kæpsaiz) vt **1** volcar. **2** hacer zozobrar.

capsule ('kæpsju:l) n cápsula f.

captain ('kæptin) n capitán m. vt capitanear.

caption ('kæpʃən) n **1** encabezamiento m. **2** pie, subtítulo m. vt poner subtítulos.

captivate ('kæptiveit) vt cautivar.

captive ('kæptiv) n, adj cautivo m. **captivity** n cautividad f.

capture ('kæptʃə) vt **1** capturar. **2** tomar. **3** captar. n **1** captura, toma f. **2** presa f.

car (ka:) n **1** coche m. **2** vagón m. **car park** n aparcamiento m.

caramel ('kærəməl) n azúcar quemado, caramelo m.

carat ('kærət) n quilate m.

caravan ('kærəvæn) n **1** caravana f. **2** mot remolque m.

caraway ('kærəwei) n alcaravea f.

carbohydrate (ka:bou'haidreit) n carbohidrato m. fécula f.

carbon ('ka:bən) n **1** carbono m. **2** carbón m. **carbonic** adj carbónico. **carbonize** vt carbonizar(se). **carbon dioxide** n bióxido de carbono m. **carbon paper** n papel carbón m.

carburettor (ka:bju'retə) n carburador m.

carcass ('ka:kəs) n **1** res muerta f. **2** cadáver de animal m. **3** armazón f.

card (ka:d) n **1** tarjeta f. **2** ficha f. **3** naipe m. carta f. **4** carnet m. **cardboard** n cartón m. **card index** n fichero m.

cardigan ('ka:digən) n rebeca f.

cardinal ('ka:dinl) n cardenal m. adj cardinal.

care (kɛə) n **1** cuidado m. **2** esmero m. **3** cuita f. **4** cargo m. **care of 1** en casa de. **2** a manos de. **take care of** cuidar de. ~vi importar, preocuparse. **care for 1** cuidar. **2** querer, desear. **3** gustar. **care to** tener ganas de. **carefree** adj despreocupado. **careful** adj **1** cuidadoso. **2** esmerado. **3** cauteloso. **be careful** tener cuidado. **carefulness** n cuidado, esmero m. cautela f. **careless** adj **1** descuidado, dejado. **2** desatento, desaplicado.

caretaker ('kɛəteikə) n **1** conserje, portero m. **2** custodio m.

career (kə'riə) n carrera, profesión f. vi correr a) carrera tendida.

caress (kə'res) vt acariciar. n caricia f.

cargo ('ka:gou) n, pl **cargoes** cargamento m. carga f.

Caribbean (kæri'biən) n Caribe m. adj caribe. **Caribbean Sea** n Mar Caribe m.

caricature ('kærikətjuə) n caricatura f. vt caricaturizar. **caricaturist** n caricaturista m,f.

carnal ('ka:nl) adj carnal. **carnality** n carnalidad f.

carnation (ka:'neiʃən) n clavel m.

carnival ('ka:nivəl) n carnaval m.

carnivorous (ka:'nivərəs) adj carnívoro.

carol ('kærəl) n villancico m.

carpenter ('ka:pintə) n carpintero m. **carpentry** n carpintería f.

carpet ('ka:pit) n alfombra f. vt alfombrar.

carriage ('kæridʒ) n 1 carruaje, carro m. 2 vagón m. 3 comm porte m. **carriageway** n carretera, calzada f.

carrier ('kæriə) n 1 portador m. 2 empresa de transportes f. **aircraft carrier** n portaviones m invar. **carrier bag** n bolsa f. **carrier pigeon** n paloma mensajera f.

carrot ('kærət) n zanahoria f.

carry ('kæri) vt 1 llevar, acarrear. 2 sostener. **carry forward** comm pasar. **carry out** realizar, llevar a cabo.

carrycot ('kærikət) n cuna portátil f.

cart (ka:t) n carro m. carreta f. vt carretear.

cartilage ('ka:tlidʒ) n cartílago m.

carton ('ka:tn) n cartón, envase m.

cartoon (ka:'tu:n) n 1 caricatura f. chiste m. 2 dibujos animados m pl. película de dibujos f. 3 Art cartón m.

cartridge ('ka:tridʒ) n cartucho m.

carve (ka:v) vt 1 trinchar. 2 tallar, esculpir. **carving** n talla, escultura f.

cascade (kæ'skeid) n cascada f. vi caer en cascada.

case[1] (keis) n 1 caso m. 2 argumento convincente m. **in case** 1 en caso de que. 2 por si acaso. **in any case** en todo caso.

case[2] (keis) n 1 caja f. 2 estuche m. funda f. 3 vitrina f. 4 bastidor, marco m. vt 1 encajonar. 2 enfundar. **casing** n 1 envoltura, cubierta f. 2 cerco m.

cash (kæʃ) n 1 dinero contante m. 2 pago al contado m. **cash desk** n caja f. **cash in on** inf sacar provecho de, aprovecharse. **cash on delivery** pago contra recibo. **cash register** n caja registradora f. **in cash** en metálico. vt cobrar, hacer efectivo.

cashier[1] (kæ'ʃiə) n cajero m.

cashier[2] (kæ'ʃiə) vt despedir, destituir.

cashmere ('kæʃ'miə) n cachemira f. casimir m.

casket ('ka:skit) n cofrecito, joyero m.

casserole ('kæsəroul) n cacerola f.

cassette (kə'set) n cassette m.

cassock ('kæsək) n sotana f.

cast[*] (ka:st) vt, vi 1 echar, arrojar. 2 desechar. 3 tech fundir, moldear. **cast off** 1 abandonar. 2 naut desamarrar. ~n 1 vaciado m. 2 molde m. 3 reparto m. 4 estampa f. matriz m. **cast iron** n hierro colado m. adj duro, fuerte. **castaway** n náufrago m.

castanets (kæstə'nets) n pl castañuelas f pl.

caste (ka:st) n casta f.

castle ('ka:səl) n 1 castillo m. 2 torre f.

castrate (kæ'streit) vt castrar. **castration** n castración f.

casual ('kæʒuəl) adj 1 casual. 2 indiferente, descuidado. **casualty** n 1 accidente m. 2 víctima f. 3 mil baja f.

cat (kæt) n 1 gato m. **cat's eye** n cimofana f.

catalogue ('kætələg) n catálogo m. vt catalogar.

catamaran (kætəmə'ræn) n catamarán m.

catapult ('kætəpʌlt) n catapulta, honda f.

cataract ('kætərækt) n catarata f.

catarrh (kə'ta:) n catarro m.

catastrophe (kə'tæstrəfi) n catástrofe f. **catastrophic** adj catastrófico.

catch (kætʃ) vt 1 coger, agarrar, atrapar. 2 prender. **catch on** 1 prender. 2 inf caer en la cuenta. **catch out** inf pillar. ~n 1 cogida f. 2 presa, pesca f. 3 pestillo m. 4 trampa f.

catechism ('kætikizəm) n catecismo m. **catechize** vt catequizar.

category ('kætigəri) n categoría f. **categorical** adj categórico. **categorize** vt categorizar.

cater ('keitə) vi 1 proveer. 2 abastecer. **caterer** n 1 proveedor m. 2 hostelero m. **catering** n abastecimiento m.

caterpillar ('kætəpilə) n oruga f.

cathedral (kə'θi:drəl) n catedral f.

cathode ('kæθoud) n cátodo m. **cathode ray** n rayo catódico m.

catholic ('kæθlik) n católico m. adj 1 católico. 2 universal. 3 ortodoxo. **catholicism** n catolicismo m. **catholicity** n catolicidad f.

cattle ('kætl) n ganado m.

caught (kɔ:t) v see **catch.**

cauliflower ('kɔliflauə) n coliflor f.

cause (kɔ:z) n causa f. vt causar. **causal** adj causal. **causality** n causalidad f. **causeless** adj infundado, sin causa.

causeway ('kɔ:zwei) n 1 arrecife m. 2 terraplén m. 3 acera f.

caustic ('kɔ:stik) adj cáustico.

caution n 1 cautela f. 2 advertencia, amonestación f. vt advertir, amonestar. **cautionary** adj amonestador. **cautious** adj cauteloso, precavido.

cavalry ('kævəlri) n caballería f.

cave (keiv) n cueva, caverna f.

caviar ('kævia:) n caviar m.

cavity ('kæviti) n cavidad f.

cayenne (kei'en) n pimentón m.

cease (si:s) vt,vi cesar. **cease-fire** n cese de hostilidades m. tregua f.

cedar ('si:də) n cedro m.

cedilla (si'dilə) n cedilla f.

ceiling ('si:liŋ) n 1 techo m. 2 límite m. tope f.

celebrate ('selabreit) vt,vi celebrar, festejar. **celebrated** adj célebre, celebrado. **celebration** n celebración f.

celebrity (si'lebriti) n celebridad f.

celery ('seləri) n apio m.

celestial (si'lestiəl) adj celestial.

celibate ('selibət) n,adj célibe. **celibacy** n celibato m.

cell (sel) n 1 celda f. 2 med célula f. 3 celdilla f.

cellar ('selə) n 1 sótano m. 2 bodega f.

cello ('tʃelou) n violoncelo m. **cellist** n violoncelista m,f.

Cellophane ('seləfein) n Tdmk celofán m.

Celt (kelt) n celta m,f. **Celtic** adj céltico, celta. **Celtic** (language) n céltico m.

cement (si'ment) n cemento m. vt cimentar.

cemetery ('semətri) n cementerio m.

censor ('sensə) n censor m. vt censurar. **censorious** adj hipercrítico, criticón. **censorship** n censura f.

censure ('senʃə) n censura f. vt censurar. **censurable** adj censurable.

census ('sensəs) n censo m.

cent (sent) n centavo m.

centenary (sen'ti:nəri) n centenario m. **centenarian** n,adj centenario m. **centennial** adj centenario.

centigrade ('sentigreid) adj centígrado.

centimetre ('sentimi:tə) n centímetro m.

centipede ('sentipi:d) n ciempiés m invar.

centre ('sentə) n centro m. **centre-forward** n delantero centro m. **centre-half** n medio centro m. ~vi centrar. **central** adj central. **central heating** n calefacción central f. **centralize** vi,vt centralizar. **centralization** n centralización f.

century ('sentʃəri) n siglo m.

ceramic (si'ræmik) adj cerámico. **ceramics** n pl cerámica f.

cereal ('siəriəl) n,adj cereal m.

ceremony ('serəməni) n ceremonia f. **ceremonial** n,adj ceremonial m. **ceremonious** adj ceremonioso.

certain ('sə:tn) adj cierto. **make certain** asegurarse, cerciorarse. **certainty** n certeza f.

certify ('sə:tifai) vt 1 certificar. 2 garantizar. **certificate** n 1 certificado, título m. 2 partida f.

chaffinch ('tʃæfintʃ) n pinzón m.

chain (tʃein) n cadena f. vt encadenar.

chair (tʃɛə) n 1 silla f. 2 cátedra f. 3 presidencia f. vt presidir. **chairman** n presidente m.

chalet ('ʃælei) n chalet m.

chalk (tʃɔ:k) n 1 yeso m. 2 tiza f. 3 creta f. vt 1 marcar con tiza. 2 apuntar. **chalky** adj 1 yesoso. 2 cretáceo.

challenge ('tʃæləndʒ) n 1 desafío, reto m. 2 law recusación f. vt desafiar, retar. **challenger** n desafiador, retador m.

chamber ('tʃeimbə) n 1 cámara f. 2 recámara f. **chambermaid** n doncella, camarera f. **chamber music** n música de cámara f.

chamberlain ('tʃeimbəlin) n chambelán m.

chameleon (kə'mi:liən) n camaleón m.

chamois ('ʃæmwa:) n invar gamuza f.

champagne (ʃæm'pein) n champaña m.

champion ('tʃæmpiən) n 1 campeón m. 2 paladín m. vt 1 defender. 2 abogar. **championship** n campeonato m.

chance (tʃɑ:ns) n 1 casualidad, suerte f. azar m. 2 ocasión, oportunidad f. 3 posibilidad f. 4 riesgo m. adj casual, fortuito. vi acaecer. **chance upon** tropezarse con.

chancellor ('tʃɑ:nsələ) n canciller m. **chancellery** n cancillería f.

chandelier (ʃændə'liə) n araña f.

change (tʃeindʒ) n 1 cambio m. 2 muda f. 3 vuelta f. **for a change** por cambiar. ~vt,vi 1 cambiar, mudar. 2 hacer transbordo. **changeable** adj cambiable, cambiante, inestable.

channel ('tʃænl) n 1 canal m. 2 vía f. cauce m. vt 1 acanalar. 2 encauzar.

Channel Islands n pl Islas Normandas f pl.

chant (tʃɑ:nt) n cantilena f. canto m. vt,vi entonar.

chaos ('keiɔs) n caos m. **chaotic** adj caótico.

chap[1] (tʃæp) vt,vi agrietar. n grieta f.

chap[2] (tʃæp) n inf tipo, sujeto m.

chapel ('tʃæpəl) n 1 capilla f. 2 templo m.

chaperon ('ʃæpəroun) n 1 acompañanta f. 2 inf carabina f. vt acompañar.

chaplain ('tʃæplin) n capellán m.

169

chapter

chapter ('tʃæptə) n 1 capítulo m. 2 rel cabildo m.

char[1] (tʃɑ:) vt, vi carbonizar.

char[2] (tʃɑ:) n inf asistenta, mujer de la limpieza f.

character ('kærɪktə) n 1 carácter m. 2 personaje m. **in character** conforme al tipo. **characterize** vt caracterizar. **characterization** n caracterización f. **characteristic** adj característico.

charcoal ('tʃɑ:koul) n 1 carbón de leña m. 2 carboncillo m.

charge (tʃɑ:dʒ) n 1 carga f. 2 cargo m. 3 precio, coste m. **in charge of** encargado de. **take charge of** hacerse cargo de. ~vt 1 cargar. 2 mandar, encomendar. 3 law acusar.

chariot ('tʃærɪət) n carro de combate m.

charisma (kə'rɪzmə) n carisma m.

charity ('tʃærɪti) n 1 caridad f. 2 obra benéfica f. **charitable** adj 1 caritativo. 2 benéfico.

charm (tʃɑ:m) n 1 encanto hechizo m. 2 amuleto m. vt encantar, hechizar. **charming** adj encantador.

chart (tʃɑ:t) n 1 tabla f. 2 gráfico m. 3 naut carta de navegar f. vt 1 tabular. 2 trazar.

charter ('tʃɑ:tə) n 1 law carta f. 2 comm flete m. vt 1 estatuir. 2 fletar. 3 alquilar.

chase (tʃeis) vt perseguir, dar caza. n persecución, caza f.

chasm ('kæzəm) n abismo m. sima f.

chassis ('tʃæsi) n invar chasis m. armazón f.

chaste (tʃeist) adj casto, honesto. **chastity** n castidad f.

chasten ('tʃeisən) vt 1 corregir. 2 castigar. 3 depurar.

chastise (tʃæ'staiz) vt castigar.

chat (tʃæt) vi charlar. n charla f. **chatty** adj hablador.

chatter ('tʃætə) vi 1 chacharear. 2 castañetear. n 1 cháchara f. parloteo m. 2 castañeteo m. **chatterbox** n inf charlatán m.

chauffeur ('ʃoufə) n chófer m.

chauvinism ('ʃouvɪnɪzəm) n chauvinismo m. **chauvinist** (n,adj chauvinista m,f.

cheap (tʃi:p) adj 1 barato. 2 de mal gusto. 3 de pacotilla. **cheapen** vt abaratar.

cheat (tʃi:t) vi hacer trampa. vt engañar, estafar. n 1 trampa f. 2 tramposo m.

check (tʃek) vt 1 parar, impedir. 2 refrenar. 3 comprobar. 4 controlar. n 1 parada, súbita. 2 impedimento m. restricción f. 3 comprobación f. 4 control m. inspección f. **checkpoint** n control m. **check-up** n 1 revisión f. 2 med reconocimiento general m.

checkmate ('tʃekmeit) n jaque mate. vt dar el mate.

cheek (tʃi:k) 1 mejilla f. carrillo m. 2 inf desfachatez f. **cheekbone** n pómulo m. **cheeky** adj descarado, fresco.

cheer (tʃiə) n 1 regocijo, buen humor m. vt 1 alegrar. 2 vitorear. **cheerful** adj alegre, animado, jovial. **cheerfulness** n alegría, jovialidad f. **cheerio** interj inf ¡hasta luego!

cheese (tʃi:z) n queso m. **cheesecake** n pastel de queso m.

cheetah ('tʃi:tə) n leopardo indio m.

chef (ʃef) n jefe de cocina m.

chemical ('kemikəl) adj químico. n sustancia química f.

chemist ('kemist) n 1 químico m. 2 farmacéutico m. **chemist's shop** n farmacia f.

chemistry ('kemistri) n química f.

cheque (tʃek) n cheque m. **chequebook** n talonario de cheques m. **cheque card** n tarjeta de crédito f.

cherish ('tʃeriʃ) vt 1 querer, apreciar. 2 cuidar. 3 mimar.

cherry ('tʃeri) n cereza f.

cherub ('tʃerəb) n querubín m.

chess (tʃes) n ajedrez m. **chess-board** n tablero de ajedrez m. **chessman** n pieza de ajedrez f. **chess set** n juego de ajedrez m.

chest (tʃest) n 1 anat pecho m. 2 arca f. cofre m. **chest of drawers** n cómoda f.

chestnut ('tʃesnʌt) n castaña f. **chestnut tree** n castaño m.

chew (tʃu:) vt, vi mascar, masticar. **chewing gum** n chicle m.

chick (tʃik) n pollito, polluelo m.

chickpea ('tʃikpi:) n garbanzo m.

chicken ('tʃikən) n pollo m. polla, gallina f. **chicken pox** n varicela f.

chicory ('tʃikəri) n achicoria f.

chief (tʃi:f) adj principal, primero. n jefe m. **chieftain** n jefe, cacique m.

chilblain ('tʃilblein) n sabañón m.

child (tʃaild) n, pl **children** 1 niño m. 2 hijo m. **with child** encinta. **childbirth** n parto m. **childhood** n niñez, infancia f. **childish** adj infantil, pueril. **childlike** adj aniñado.

Chile ('tʃili) n Chile m. **Chilean** n,adj chileno m.

chill (tʃil) vt, vi 1 enfriar. 2 helar. 3 congelar. n 1 escalofrío m. 2 resfriado m. **chilly** adj 1 frío. 2 desapacible. 3 friolero.

chilli ('tʃili) n chile m.

170

chime (tʃaim) vi repicar, sonar. n 1 carillón m. 2 repique m.

chimney ('tʃimni) n chimenea f. **chimney-sweep** n limpiachimeneas m invar.

chimpanzee (tʃimpænˈziː) n chimpancé m.

chin (tʃin) n barbilla f. mentón m. **double chin** papada f.

china ('tʃainə) n 1 porcelana f. 2 loza f.

China ('tʃainə) n China f. **Chinese** n,adj chino m. **Chinese** (language) n chino m.

chink¹ (tʃiŋk) n grieta f. resquicio m.

chink² (tʃiŋk) n tintineo m. vi,vt tintinear.

chip (tʃip) n 1 astilla f. 2 lasca f. 3 ficha f. **chips** n pl patatas fritas f pl. ~vt 1 astillar. 2 cincelar. **chip in** inf interrumpir, cortar.

chiropody (kiˈrɔpədi) n pedicura f. **chiropodist** n pedicuro m.

chirp (tʃəːp) vi,vt gorjear, piar. n gorjeo, pio m. **chirpy** adj inf alegre.

chisel ('tʃizəl) n cincel m. vt cincelar.

chivalry ('ʃivəlri) n 1 caballería f. 2 caballerosidad f. **chivalrous** adj caballeroso.

chives (tʃaivz) n pl cebollino m.

chlorine ('klɔːriːn) n cloro m.

chlorophyll ('klɔrəfil) n clorofila f.

chocolate ('tʃɔklit) n chocolate m.

choice (tʃɔis) n 1 elección f. 2 preferencia f. 3 surtido m. adj selecto, escogido.

choir (kwaiə) n coro m.

choke (tʃouk) vt,vi 1 estrangular, ahogar. 2 atascar. n 1 obturador m. 2 mot aire m.

cholera ('kɔlərə) n cólera m.

choose* (tʃuːz) vt,vi elegir, escoger, optar. **choosy** adj inf delicado, exigente.

chop (tʃɔp) 1 tajo m. 2 cul chuleta f. vt cortar, tajar. **chop off** tronchar. **chop up** trinchar.

chop² (tʃɔp) vi (of wind) vivrar. **choppy** adj (of the sea) agitado.

chopstick ('tʃɔpstik) n palillo chino m.

chord (kɔːd) n 1 cuerda f. 2 mus acorde m.

chore (tʃɔː) n tarea rutinaria f. **chores** n pl quehaceres domésticos m pl.

choreography (kɔriˈɔgrafi) n coreografía f. **choreographer** n coreógrafo m.

chorus ('kɔːrəs) n coro m. **choral** adj coral.

chose (tʃouz) v see **choose.**

chosen ('tʃouzən) v see **choose.**

Christ (kraist) n Cristo m.

christen ('krisən) vt bautizar. **christening** n 1 bautizo m. 2 bautismo m.

Christian ('kristʃən) adj,n cristiano m. **Christian name** n nombre de pila m. **Christianity** n cristiandad f. **christianize** vt cristianizar.

Christmas ('krisməs) n Navidad f. Navidades f pl. **Father Christmas** n Papá Noel m. ~adj navideño. **Christmas Eve** n Nochebuena f. **Christmas tree** n árbol de Navidad m.

chromatic (krəˈmætik) adj cromático.

chrome (kroum) n cromo m.

chromium ('kroumiəm) n cromo m.

chromosome ('krouməsoum) n cromosoma m.

chronic ('krɔnik) adj crónico.

chronicle ('krɔnikəl) n crónica f. vt historiar.

chronology (krəˈnɔlədʒi) n cronología f. **chronological** adj cronológico.

chrysalis ('krisəlis) n crisálida f.

chrysanthemum (kriˈzænθiməm) n crisantemo m.

chubby ('tʃʌbi) adj 1 rollizo. 2 mofletudo.

chuck (tʃʌk) vt tirar, arrojar.

chuckle ('tʃʌkəl) vi reirse entre dientes, soltar una risita. n risita f.

chunk (tʃʌŋk) n pedazo, trozo m. **chunky** adj grueso, rechoncho.

church (tʃəːtʃ) n iglesia f. **Church of England** Iglesia anglicana. **churchgoer** n fiel, devoto m. **churchyard** n cementerio, camposanto m.

churn (tʃəːn) n 1 mantequera f. 2 lechera f. vt batir.

chute (ʃuːt) n 1 salto de agua m. 2 rampa de caída f. vertedero m. 3 paracaídas m invar.

chutney ('tʃʌtni) n salsa picante f.

cicada (siˈkɑːdə) n cigarra f.

cider ('saidə) n sidra f.

cigar (siˈgɑː) n puro m. **cigarette** n cigarrillo, pitillo m. **cigarette lighter** n mechero m.

cinder ('sində) n ceniza f.

cinecamera ('sinikæmrə) n cámara cinematográfica f.

cinema ('sinəmə) n cine m. **cinematographic** adj cinematográfico.

cinnamon ('sinəmən) n canela f.

circle ('səːkəl) n círculo m. vt circundar, cercar. **circular** adj,n circular f. **circulate** vi circular. vt hacer circular, poner en circulación. **circulation** n circulación f.

circuit ('səːkit) n circuito m. **circuitous** adj tortuoso, indirecto.

circumcise ('səːkəmsaiz) vt circuncidar. **circumcision** n circuncisión f.

circumference (səˈkʌmfərəns) n circunferencia f.

circumflex ('səːkəmfleks) n circunflejo m.

circumscribe ('səːkəmskraib) vt circunscribir. **circumscription** n circunscripción f.

circumstance ('səːkəmstæns) n circunstancia

f. **under no circumstances** de ninguna manera. **circumstantial** *adj* 1 circunstancial. 2 circunstanciado, detallado.

circus ('sə:kəs) *n* 1 circo *m.* 2 plaza redonda, glorieta *f.*

cistern ('sistən) *n* 1 tanque, depósito *m.* 2 cisterna *f.*

cite (sait) *vt* 1 citar. 2 *mil* mencionar. **citation** *n* 1 citación. 2 *mil* mención *f.*

citizen ('sitizən) *n* ciudadano *m.* **citizenship** *n* ciudadanía *f.*

citrus ('sitrəs) *n* cidro *m.* **citrus fruits** *n pl* agrios *m pl.*

city ('siti) *n* ciudad *f. adj* ciudadano, municipal.

civic ('sivik) *adj* cívico.

civil ('sivəl) *adj* 1 civil. 2 cortés. **civil service** *n* cuerpo de funcionarios *m.* **civil servant** *n* funcionario *m.* **civil engineering** *n* ingeniería de caminos *f.* **civil war** *n* guerra civil *f.*

civilian (si'viliən) *adj* civil. *n* paisano *m.*

civilize ('sivilaiz) *vt* civilizar. **civilization** *n* civilización *f.*

claim (kleim) *n* 1 demanda *f.* 2 petición *f.* 3 pretensión *f.* 4 concesión *f. vt* 1 demandar. 2 reclamar. 3 pretender. **claimant** *n* 1 *law* demandante *m,f.* 2 pretendiente *m,f.*

clam (klæm) *n* almeja *f.*

clamber ('klæmbə) *vi* trepar.

clammy ('klæmi) *adj* húmedo, pegajoso.

clamour ('klæmə) *n* 1 clamor *m.* 2 clamoreo *m. vi* 1 clamar. 2 clamorear, vociferar.

clamp (klæmp) *n* 1 abrazadera *f.* 2 tornillo de banco *m.* 3 montón, amontonamiento *m. vt* afianzar, sujetar, apretar los tornillos.

clan (klæn) *n* clan *m.*

clandestine (klæn'destin) *adj* clandestino.

clang (klæŋ) *n* estrépito, estruendo *m. vi* sonar estrepitosamente: **clanger** *n inf* plancha *f.*

clank (klæŋk) *n* golpeteo metálico *m. vi* golpetear, resonar.

clap (klæp) *n* 1 palmada *f.* 2 palmoteo, aplauso *m. vi* 1 aplaudir. 2 dar palamadas, batir palmas. **clapper** *n* badajo *m.*

claret ('klærət) *n* clarete *m.*

clarify ('klærifai) *vt* aclarar. **clarification** *n* aclaración *f.* **clarity** *n* claridad *f.*

clarinet (klæri'net) *n* clarinete *m.*

clash (klæʃ) *n* 1 choque, encuentro *m.* 2 estruendo, fragor *m.* 3 conflicto *m.* incompatibilidad *f. vi* 1 chocar. 2 pelear.

clasp (klɑ:sp) *n* 1 cierre *m.* 2 corchete *m.* 3 apretón *m. vt* abrochar.

class (klɑ:s) *n* clase *f. vt* clasificar. **classify** *vt*

clasificar. **classification** *n* clasificación *f.* **classy** *adj inf* elegante.

classroom ('klɑ:srum) *n* aula, clase *f.*

classic ('klæsik) *adj,n* clásico *m.* **classical** *adj* clásico. **classics** *n pl* clásicas *f pl.*

clatter ('klætə) *n* 1 estruendo *m.* 2 repiqueto *m. vi* repiquetear, martillear.

clause (klɔ:z) *n* cláusula *f.*

claustrophobia (klɔstrə'foubiə) *n* claustrofobia *f.*

claw (klɔ:) *n* 1 garra *f.* 2 pinza *f.* 3 *tech* garfio, gancho *m. vt,vi* arañar, desgarrar.

clay (klei) *n* arcilla *f.* barro *m.*

clean (kli:n) *adj* 1 limpio. 2 nítido, definido. *vt* limpiar, asear. **cleanliness** *n* 1 limpieza *f.* aseo *m.* 2 esmero *m.*

cleanse (klenz) *vt* limpiar, purificar.

clear (kliə) *adj* 1 claro. 2 despejado. 3 evidente. *adv* claramente, perfectamente. *vt,vi* 1 aclarar. 2 despejar. 3 *law* absolver. **clearance** *n* 1 claro *m.* 2 acreditación *f.* 3 *tech* espacio muerto *m.* **clearance sale** *n* liquidación *f.*

clef (klef) *n* clave *f.*

clench (klentʃ) *vt* apretar, cerrar.

clergy (klæg) *n* clero *m.* **clergyman** *n* clérigo *m.*

clerical ('klerikəl) *adj* 1 de oficina. 2 clerical. **clerical error** *n* error de copia *m.*

clerk (klɑ:k) *n* 1 empleado, secretario *m.* oficinista *m,f.* 2 *law* escribano *m.*

clever ('klevə) *adj* 1 listo, inteligente. 2 hábil, diestro. 3 ingenioso. **cleverness** *n* 1 habilidad *f.* 2 ingenio *m.*

cliché ('kli:ʃei) *n* cliché *m.* frase hecha *f.*

click (klik) *n* 1 taconeo *m.* 2 chasquido *m. vi,vt* 1 taconear. 2 chasquear.

client ('klaiənt) *n* cliente *m,f.*

cliff (klif) *n* 1 acantilado *m.* 2 risco *m.*

climate ('klaimit) *n* 1 clima *m.* 2 ambiente *m.* **climatic** *adj* climático.

climax ('klaimæks) *n* 1 punto culminante, colmo *m.* 2 apogeo *m.* 3 climax *m.*

climb (klaim) *vt,vi* 1 subir. 2 trepar. 3 escalar. *n* subida, escalada *f.* ascenso *m.* **climber** *n* escalador *m.* alpinista *m,f.*

cling¹ (kliŋ) *vi* 1 adherirse, pegarse, agarrarse. 2 abrazarse. **clinging** *adj* 1 ceñido. 2 pegajoso.

clinic ('klinik) *n* clínica *f.* **clinical** *adj* clínico.

clip¹ (klip) *vt* 1 cortar. 2 trasquilar. 3 abreviar. *n* 1 tijeretada *f.* 2 esquileo *m.*

clip² (klip) *n* 1 grapa *f.* 2 sujetapapeles *m invar. vt* sujetar, prender.

clitoris ('klitəris) *n* clítoris *m.*

cloak (klouk) n capa f. manto m. vt **1** encapotar. **2** encubrir. **cloakroom** n **1** guardarropa m. **2** lavabos m pl.

clock (klɔk) n reloj m. **alarm clock** n despertador m. ~vt registrar. **clocktower** n campanario m. **clockwise** en la dirección de las agujas del reloj. **clockwork** n aparato de relojería m.

clog (klɔg) n **1** zueco m. **2** traba f. vt **1** atascar. **2** estorbar.

cloister (ˈklɔistə) n claustro m. vt enclaustrar.

close vt,vi (klouz) **1** cerrar. **2** terminar. n **1** (klouz) final m. conclusión f. **2** (klous) cercado m. adj (klous) **1** cercano, próximo. **2** tupido. **3** detallado, exacto. **4** sofocante. adv (klous) cerca. **close-up** n primer plano m.

closet (ˈklɔzit) n **1** wáter, lavabo m. **2** armario m.

clot (klɔt) n **1** grumo m. **2** coágulo, cuajarón m. **3** med embolia m. vi cuajarse, coagularse.

cloth (klɔθ) n **1** tela f. paño m. **2** trapo m. **table-cloth** n mantel m.

clothe (klouð) vt **1** vestir. **2** cubrir, revestir. **clothes** n pl ropa f. vestidos m pl. **clothes brush** n cepillo para la ropa m. **clothes line** n cuerda para tender la ropa f. **clothes peg** n pinza f.

cloud (klaud) n nube f. nubarrón m. vt,vi nublar. **cloudburst** n chaparrón m. **cloudless** adj sin nubes. **cloudy** adj **1** nebuloso. **2** turbio.

clove (klouv) n clavo de especia m.

clover (ˈklouvə) n trébol m.

clown (klaun) n payaso m. vi hacer el payaso.

club (klʌb) n **1** porra f. **2** sport palo m. **3** club m. vt aporrear. **club together** asociarse.

clue (kluː) n pista f. indicio m.

clump (klʌmp) n **1** arboleda f. matorral m. **2** grupo m. vi andar pesadamente.

clumsy (ˈklʌmzi) adj **1** torpe, desmañado. **2** chapucero. **clumsiness** n torpeza, desmaña f.

clung (klʌŋ) v see **cling.**

cluster (ˈklʌstə) n **1** grupo m. **2** racimo m. vi agruparse, arracimarse.

clutch (klʌtʃ) n **1** apretón m. **2** mot embrague m. **3** nidada f. vt agarrar(se), apretar.

clutter (ˈklʌtə) n desorden m. confusión f. vt llenar desordenadamente, atestar.

coach (koutʃ) n **1** coche m. diligencia, carroza f. **2** sport entrenador m. **3** educ instructor, profesor particular m. vt entrenar, enseñar.

coagulate (kouˈægjuleit) vt coagular.

coal (koul) n carbón m. hulla f. **live coal** n brasa f. **coalfield** n yacimiento de carbón m. **coalmine** n mina de carbón f.

coalition (kouəˈliʃən) n coalición f.

coarse (kɔːs) adj basto, tosco, grosero. **coarseness** n tosquedad, grosería f.

coast (koust) n costa f. litoral m. vi costear. **coastguard** n guardacostas m invar. **coastline** n litoral m.

coat (kout) n **1** chaqueta f. abrigo m. **2** pelo m. lana f. vt cubrir. **coat-hanger** n percha f.

coax (kouks) vt engatusar.

cobble (ˈkɔbəl) n guijarro m. vt **1** empedrar. **2** remendar.

cobbler (ˈkɔblə) n zapatero m.

cobra (ˈkoubrə) n cobra f.

cobweb (ˈkɔbweb) n telaraña f.

cock¹ (kɔk) n gallo, macho de ave m. **cocky** adj engreído.

cock² (kɔk) vt **1** amartillar. **2** aguzar.

cockle (ˈkɔkəl) n zool berberecho m.

cockpit (ˈkɔkpit) n **1** aviat cabina f. **2** reñidero de gallos m.

cockroach (ˈkɔkroutʃ) n cucaracha f.

cocktail (ˈkɔkteil) n cóctel m.

cocoa (ˈkoukou) n **1** cacao m. **2** chocolate m.

coconut (ˈkoukənʌt) n coco m.

cocoon (kəˈkuːn) n capullo m.

cod (kɔd) n bacalao m.

code (koud) n **1** law código m. **2** cifra f. vt cifrar. **highway code** código de la circulación m.

codeine (ˈkoudiːn) n codeína f.

coeducation (kouedjuˈkeiʃən) n coeducación f.

coerce vt forzar, obligar. **coercion** n coerción f.

coexist (kouigˈzist) vi coexistir. **coexistence** n coexistencia f.

coffee (ˈkɔfi) n café m. **black coffee** café solo. **white coffee** café con leche. **coffee bar** n cafetería f. **coffee bean** n grano de café m. **coffee pot** n cafetera f. **coffee table** n mesita de café f.

coffin (ˈkɔfin) n ataúd m.

cog (kɔg) n diente m. rueda dentada f.

cognac (ˈkɔnjæk) n coñac m.

cohabit (kouˈhæbit) vi cohabitar. **cohabitation** n cohabitación f.

cohere (kouˈhiə) vi adherirse, pegarse, enlazarse. **coherent** adj coherente, lógico. **coherence** n coherencia f.

coil (kɔil) n **1** rollo m. **2** tech carrete m. vt arrollar, enrollar.

coin (kɔin) n moneda f. vt acuñar. **coinage** n acuñación f.

173

coincide (kouin'said) *vi* coincidir, estar de acuerdo. **coincidence** *n* coincidencia, casualidad *f*.

colander ('kʌləndə) *n* escurridor *m*.

cold (kould) *adj,n* frío *m*. **cold-blooded** *adj* 1 *zool* de sangre fría. 2 insensible.

collaborate (kə'læbəreit) *vi* colaborar. **collaboration** *n* colaboración *f*. **collaborator** *n* colaborador *m*.

collapse (kə'læps) *n* 1 colapso *m*. 2 hundimiento *m*. *vi* sufrir colapso.

collar ('kɔlə) *n* 1 cuello *m*. 2 *zool* collar *m*. *vt* prender por el cuello. **collarbone** *n* clavícula *f*.

colleague ('kɔli:g) *n* colega *m*.

collect (kə'lekt) *vt* reunir, acumular, cobrar, coleccionar. *vi* reunirse, congregarse. **collection** *n* 1 colección *f*. 2 montón *m*. 3 recaudación *f*. **collective** *adj* colectivo. **collector** *n* coleccionador *m*.

college ('kɔlidʒ) *n* 1 colegio *m*. 2 escuela *f*. **collegiate** *adj* colegial, colegiado.

collide (kə'laid) *vi* chocar. **collision** *n* choque *m*. colisión *f*.

colloquial (kə'loukwiəl) *adj* familiar, popular. **colloquialism** *n* expresión familiar *m*.

Cologne (kə'loun) *n* Colonia *f*.

Colombia (kə'lʌmbiə) *n* Colombia *f*. **Colombian** *adj,n* colombiano.

colon ('koulən) *n* 1 dos puntos *m pl*. 2 *anat* colon *m*.

colonel ('kə:nl̩) *n* coronel *m*.

colony ('kɔləni) *n* colonia *f*. **colonial** *adj* colonial. *n* colono *m*. **colonist** *n* colonizador, colono *m*. **colonize** *vt* colonizar. **colonization** *n* colonización *f*.

colossal (kə'lɔsəl) *adj* colosal.

colour ('kʌlə) *n* color *m*. **be off colour** estar indispuesto. **colour-bar** *n* barrera racial *f*. **colour-blind** *adj* daltoniano. **colour-blindness** *n* daltonismo *m*. **colour film** *n* película en colores *f*. **colourful** *adj* lleno de color. ~*vt* colorear, colorar. *vi* sonrojarse.

colt (koult) *n* potro *m*.

column ('kɔləm) *n* columna *f*. **columnist** *n* periodista, columnista *m,f*.

coma ('koumə) *n* coma *m*.

comb (koum) *n* peine *m*. *vt* peinar.

combat ('kɔmbæt) *n* combate *m*. *vt* combatir, luchar contra. **combatant** *n* combatiente *m*.

combine (*n* 'kɔmbain; *v* kəm'bain) *n* monopolio *m*. *vt* combinar, reunir.

combustion (kəm'bʌstʃən) *n* combustión *f*.

come* (kʌm) *vi* venir. **come across** encontrar, dar con. **come along!** ¡vamos! **come back** volver. **come in** entrar. **comeback** *n* restablecimiento *m*. **come off** 1 desprenderse. 2 tener lugar. 3 tener éxito.

comedy ('kɔmədi) *n* comedia *f*. **musical comedy** 1 opereta *f*. 2 zarzuela *f*. **comedian** *n* cómico *m*. **comedienne** *n* cómica *f*. **comic** *adj* cómico, divertido, entretenido. *n* tebeo *m*. **comical** *adj* cómico.

comet ('kɔmit) *n* cometa *m*.

comfort ('kʌmfət) *n* consuelo, alivio, confort *m*. comodidad *f*. bienestar *m*. *vt* consolar, aliviar. **comfortable** *adj* cómodo, confortable. **comforting** *adj* consolador.

comma ('kɔmə) *n* coma *f*. **inverted commas** comillas *f pl*.

command (kə'mɑ:nd) *n* orden *f*. mandato, mando *m*. **be in command** estar al mando. *vt* mandar, ordenar. **commandant** *n* comandante *m*. **commanding** *adj* imponente, dominante. **commandment** *n* mandamiento *m*.

commemorate (kə'meməreit) *vt* conmemorar. **commemoration** *n* conmemoración *f*. **commemorative** *adj* conmemorativo.

commence (kə'mens) *vt* comenzar, empezar. **commencement** *n* comienzo *m*.

commend (kə'mend) *vt* encomendar, recomendar, alabar, elogiar. **commendable** *adj* recomendable. **commendation** *n* alabanza *f*. encomio *m*.

comment ('kɔment) *n* comentario *m*. *vi* comentar, observar. **commentary** *n* comentario *m*. **commentator** *n* comentador *m*.

commerce ('kɔmə:s) *n* comercio *m*. **commercial** *adj* 1 comercial. 2 mercantil. *n* emisión publicitaria *f*. **commercial traveller** *n* agente comercial, viajante *m*. **commercialism** *n* mercantilismo *m*. **commercialize** *vt* comercializar.

commission (kə'miʃən) *n* 1 comisión. 2 mil graduación *f*. *vt* nombrar, comisionar. **commissioner** *n* comisario *m*.

commit (kə'mit) *vt* cometer, hacer, entregar. **commitment** *n* obligación *f*.

committee (kə'miti) *n* comité *m*. comisión *f*.

commodity (kə'mɔditi) *n* mercancía *f*. artículo *m*.

common ('kɔmən) *adj* 1 común. 2 público. 3 frecuente. 4 ordinario. *n* campo común, ejido *m*. **commoner** *n* plebeyo *m*. **commonly** *adv* generalmente. **Common Market** *n* Mercado

Común m. **commonplace** adj común, trivial. n cosa común f. **commonsense** adj racional, lógico. n sentido común m. **commonwealth** n república f.

commotion (kə'mouʃən) n tumulto m.

commune[1] (kə'mju:n) vi 1 conversar. 2 meditar. 3 comulgar. **communion** n comunión f.

commune[2] ('kɔmju:n) n comuna f. **communal** adj comunal.

communicant (kə'mju:nikənt) n comulgante m,f.

communicate (kə'mju:nikeit) vt comunicar. **communication** n comunicación f. **communicative** adj comunicativo.

communism ('kɔmjunizəm) n comunismo m. **communist** n comunista m,f.

community (kə'mju:niti) n comunidad, sociedad f. **community centre** n centro social m.

commute (kə'mju:t) vt conmutar. vi viajar a diario.

compact[1] (kəm'pækt) adj compacto, conciso. vt comprimir.

compact[2] ('kɔmpækt) n 1 pacto, convenio m. 2 polvera f.

companion (kəm'pæniən) n compañero m. **companionable** adj sociable. **companionship** n compañerismo m.

company ('kʌmpəni) n 1 compañía f. 2 sociedad, empresa f.

compare (kəm'pɛə) vt comparar. **comparable** adj comparable. **comparative** adj 1 relativo. 2 gram comparativo. **comparison** n comparación f.

compartment (kəm'pɑ:tmənt) n compartimiento, departamento m.

compass ('kʌmpəs) n 1 brújula f. 2 alcance m. vt rodear.

compassion (kəm'pæʃən) n compasión f. **compassionate** adj compasivo.

compatible (kəm'pætibəl) adj compatible. **compatibility** n compatibilidad f.

compel (kəm'pel) vt 1 obligar. 2 imponer.

compensate ('kɔmpənseit) vt 1 compensar. 2 indemnizar. **compensation** n 1 compensación f. 2 indemnización f. 3 recompensa f.

compete (kəm'pi:t) vi competir. **competition** n 1 competencia f. 2 concurso m. **competitive** adj competidor, competitivo. **competitor** n 1 competidor m. 2 opositor m.

competent ('kɔmpitənt) adj competente, capaz, hábil. **competence** n competencia, capacidad f.

compile (kəm'pail) vt compilar, recopilar. **compilation** n compilación f.

complacent (kəm'pleisənt) adj complaciente. **complacence** also **complacency** n satisfacción de si mismo f.

complain (kəm'plein) vi quejarse. **complaint** n 1 queja f. 2 law querella, demanda f.

complement ('kɔmplimənt) n complemento m. vt complementar. **complementary** adj complementario.

complete (kəm'pli:t) adj completo, entero. vt completar, terminar. **completion** n cumplimiento m. terminación f.

complex ('kɔmpleks) adj complejo, complicado. n complejo m. **complexity** n complejidad f.

complexion (kəm'plekʃən) n 1 tez f. cutis m. 2 aspecto m.

complicate ('kɔmplikeit) vt complicar. **complicated** adj complicado. **complication** n complicación f.

compliment ('kɔmplimənt) n cumplido, piropo m. **compliments** n pl saludos m pl. ~vt felicitar. **complimentary** adj 1 lisonjero. 2 de regalo.

comply (kəm'plai) vi 1 obedecer. 2 conformarse.

component (kəm'pounənt) adj,n componente.

compose (kəm'pouz) vt componer. **be composed of** constar de, componerse de. **composer** n compositor m. **composition** n composición f. **composure** n serenidad, calma f.

composite ('kɔmpəzit) adj compuesto.

compound[1] (adj,n 'kɔmpaund; v kəm'paund) adj,n compuesto m. vt componer.

compound[2] ('kɔmpaund) n recinto m.

comprehend (kɔmpri'hend) vt comprender. **comprehensible** adj comprensible. **comprehension** n comprensión f. **comprehensive** adj extenso, comprensivo. **comprehensive school** n colegio integrado m.

compress (n 'kɔmpres; v kəm'pres) n compresa f. vt comprimir. **compression** n compresión f.

comprise (kəm'praiz) vt comprender, abarcar.

compromise ('kɔmprəmaiz) n compromiso, arreglo m. vt comprometer, arreglar. **compromising** adj comprometedor.

compulsion (kəm'pʌlʃən) n obligación, compulsión f. **compulsive** adj compulsivo. **compulsory** adj obligatorio.

compute (kəm'pju:t) vt computar, calcular. **computer** n computador m. calculadora f.

comrade ('kɔmrəd, -reid) n camarada, compañero m.

concave ('kɔŋkeiv) *adj* cóncavo. **concavity** *n* concavidad *f.*

conceal (kən'si:l) *vt* ocultar, disimular. **concealed** *adj* 1 oculto. 2 disimulado. **concealment** *n* encubrimiento *m.* disimulación *f.*

concede (kən'si:d) *vt* conceder.

conceit (kən'si:t) *n* presunción *f.* engreimiento *m.* **conceited** *adj* presumido, engreído.

conceive (kən'si:v) *vi* concebir. *vt* 1 imaginar. 2 concebir. **conceivable** *adj* concebible.

concentrate ('kɔnsəntreit) *n* concentrado *m.* *vt* concentrar. **concentration** *n* concentración *f.* **concentration camp** *n* campo de concentración *m.*

concentric (kən'sentrik) *adj* concéntrico.

concept ('kɔnsept) *n* concepto *m.* **conception** *n* 1 concepción *f.* 2 concepto *m.* idea *f.*

concern (kən'sə:n) *n* 1 asunto, negocio *m.* interés *m.* 3 preocupación *f.* 4 empresa *f.* *vt* interesar, concernir. **concerned** *adj* inquieto, preocupado. **concerning** *prep* sobre, a cerca de.

concert ('kɔnsət) *n* concierto *m.* **concert hall** *n* sala de conciertos *f.*

concertina (kɔnsə'ti:nə) *n* concertina *f.*

concerto (kən'tʃɛətou) *n* concierto *m.*

concession (kən'seʃən) *n* concesión *f.*

concise (kən'sais) *adj* conciso. **concision** *n* concisión *f.*

conclude (kən'klu:d) *vt* terminar, concluir. **concluding** *adj* final. **conclusion** *n* conclusión, terminación *f.* **conclusive** *adj* conclusivo.

concoct (kən'kɔkt) *vt* 1 confeccionar. 2 inventar. 3 tramar. **concoction** *n* 1 confección *f.* 2 trama *f.*

concrete ('kɔŋkri:t) *adj* 1 concreto. 2 *tech* de hormigón. *n tech* hormigón *m.*

concussion (kən'kʌʃən) *n* conmoción cerebral *f.*

condemn (kən'dem) *vt* 1 condenar. 2 censurar. **condemned** *adj* condenado. **condemnation** *n* condenación *f.* **condemnatory** *adj* condenador.

condense (kən'dens) *vt* 1 condensar. 2 abreviar. **condensation** *n* 1 condensación *f.* 2 compendio *m.* **condenser** *n* condensador *m.*

condescend (kɔndi'send) *vi* condescender, dignarse. **condescending** *adj* superior. **condescension** *n* aire de superioridad *m.*

condition (kən'diʃən) *n* 1 condición *f.* 2 estado *m.* *vt* condicionar, determinar. **conditional** *adj* condicional. **conditionally** *adv* con reservas.

condolence (kən'douləns) *n* pésame *m.*

condone (kən'doun) *vt* condonar.

conduct (*n* 'kɔndʌkt; *v* kən'dʌkt) *n* conducta *f.* comportamiento *m.* *vt* conducir, dirigir. *vi mus* llevar la batuta. **conduct oneself** comportarse. **conduction** *n* conducción *f.*

conductor (kən'dʌktə) *n* 1 *mus* director. 2 *mot* cobrador *m.* 3 (of lightning) pararrayos *m invar.*

cone (koun) *n* cono *m.*

confectioner (kən'fekʃənə) *n* confitero *m.*

confederate (*adj,n* kən'fedərət; *v* kən'fedəreit) *adj, n* confederado *m.* *vt* confederar. **confederacy** *n* confederación *f.*

confer (kən'fə:) *vt* conferir, conceder, otorgar. *vi* conferir, consultar. **conference** *n* conferencia *f.*

confess (kən'fes) *vt* confesar. **confession** *n* confesión *f.* **confessional** *n* confesionario *m.*

confetti (kən'feti) *n* confeti *m.*

confide (kən'faid) *vt* confiar. **confidence** *n* 1 confianza *f.* 2 confidencia *f.* **confidence man** *n* timador *m.* **confident** *adj* seguro de sí mismo, lleno de confianza. **confidential** *adj* confidencial. **confidentially** *adv* en confianza.

confine (kən'fain) *n* confín, límite *m.* *vt* 1 encerrar. 2 limitar. **confined** *adj* reducido. **confinement** *n* 1 encierro *m.* 2 *med* parto *m.*

confirm (kən'fə:m) *vt* confirmar. **confirmation** *n* confirmación *f.* **confirmed** *adj* inveterado.

confiscate ('kɔnfiskeit) *vt* confiscar. **confiscation** *n* confiscación *f.*

conflict (*v* kən'flikt; *n* 'kɔnflikt) *vi* luchar. *n* conflicto *m.* **conflicting** *adj* contradictorio.

conform (kən'fɔ:m) *vi* conformarse. **conformist** *adj,n* conformista *m,f.* **conformity** *n* conformidad *f.*

confound (kən'faund) *vt* confundir.

confront (kən'frʌnt) *vt* hacer frente a, confrontar. **confrontation** *n* confrontación *f.*

confuse (kən'fju:z) *vt* 1 confundir. 2 desconcertar. **confused** *adj* confuso, perplejo. **confusing** *adj* confuso, desconcertante. **confusion** *n* confusión *f.*

congeal (kən'dʒi:l) *vt* congelar, coagular.

congenial (kən'dʒi:niəl) *adj* congenial, agradable.

congested (kən'dʒestid) *adj* 1 superpoblado. 2 *med* congestionado. **congestion** *n* congestión *f.*

Congo ('kɔŋgou) *n* el Congo *m.*

congratulate (kən'grætjuleit) *vt* felicitar. **congratulations** *n pl* felicitaciones *f pl. interj* ¡enhorabuena!

congregate ('kɔŋgrigeit) vi congregarse. **congregation** n 1 congregación f. 2 asamblea f. 3 (in church) los fieles m pl. **congregational** adj congregacionalista.

congress ('kɔŋgres) n congreso m.

conical ('kɔnikəl) adj cónico.

conifer ('kɔnifə) n conífera f. **coniferous** adj conífero.

conjugal ('kɔndʒugəl) adj conyugal.

conjugate ('kɔndʒugeit) vt conjugar. **conjugation** n conjugación f.

conjunction (kən'dʒʌŋkʃən) n conjunción f. **conjunctive** adj conjuntivo.

conjure ('kʌndʒə) vt conjurar. vi hacer juegos de manos. **conjurer** n ilusionista m. **conjuring trick** n juego de manos m.

connect (kə'nekt) vt 1 juntar, unir. 2 conectar, poner en comunicación. **connection** n 1 unión, comunicación f. 2 relación f.

connoisseur (kɔnə'sə:) n entendido, experto m.

connotation (kɔnə'teiʃən) n connotación f.

conquer ('kɔŋkə) vt vencer. **conqueror** n conquistador, vencedor rn. **conquest** n conquista f.

conscience ('kɔnʃəns) n conciencia f. **conscientious** adj concienzudo.

conscious ('kɔnʃəs) adj 1 consciente. 2 intencional. **be conscious** med tener conocimiento. **consciousness** n consciencia f.

conscript (kən'skript) n recluta m. vt reclutar. **conscription** n servicio militar obligatorio m.

consecrate ('kɔnsikreit) vt consagrar. **consecration** n consagración f.

consecutive (kən'sekjutiv) adj consecutivo.

consent (kən'sent) n consentimiento m. vi consentir.

consequence ('kɔnsikwəns) n consecuencia f. resultado m. **consequent** adj consiguiente.

conserve (kən'sə:v) n conserva f. vt conservar. **conservation** n conservación f. **conservative** adj,n pol conservador. adj conservativo, moderado. **conservatory** n invernadero m.

consider (kən'sidə) vt considerar, tomar en cuenta. **considerable** adj considerable. **consideration** n 1 consideración f. 2 retribución f. **considerate** adj considerado.

consign (kən'sain) vt 1 consignar. 2 enviar. **consignment** n consignación f.

consist (kən'sist) vi consistir, constar. **consistency** n consistencia f. **consistent** adj consecuente, lógico. **consistently** adv 1 sin excepción, constantemente. 2 consecuentemente.

console (kən'soul) vt consolar.

consolidate (kən'sɔlideit) vt consolidar.

consonant ('kɔnsənənt) adj,n consonante f.

conspicuous (kən'spikjuəs) adj visible, evidente.

conspire (kən'spaiə) vi conspirar. **conspiracy** n conspiración, conjuración f. **conspirator** n conspirador m.

constable ('kɔnstəbəl) n policía, guardia m. **constabulary** n policía f.

constant ('kɔnstənt) adj,n constante f.

constellation (kɔnstə'leiʃən) n constelación f.

constipation (kɔnsti'peiʃən) n estreñimiento m. **constipate** vt estreñir.

constitute ('kɔnstitju:t) vt constituir. **constituency** n distrito electoral m. **constituent** adj constitutivo, integrante. n 1 constitutivo, componente m. 2 elector m. **constitution** n constitución f. **constitutional** adj constitucional. n paseo m.

constrain (kən'strein) vt constreñir, obligar. **constraint** n 1 encierro m. 2 fuerza f.

constrict (kən'strikt) vt estrechar, apretar.

construct (kən'strʌkt) vt construir. **construction** n 1 construcción f. 2 interpretación f. **constructive** adj constructivo. **constructor** n constructor m.

consul ('kɔnsəl) n cónsul m. **consular** adj consular. **consulate** n consulado m.

consult (kən'sʌlt) vt consultar. **consultation** n consulta, consultación f. **consultant** n 1 asesor m. 2 med especialista m,f.

consume (kən'sju:m) vt consumir, utilizar. **consumer** n consumidor m. **consumption** n consumición f. 2 med tisis f.

contact ('kɔntækt) n contacto m. vt ponerse en contacto con. **contact lenses** n pl lentes de contacto, microlentillas f pl.

contagious (kən'teidʒəs) adj contagioso. **contagion** n contagio m.

contain (kən'tein) vt contener. **container** n 1 envase m. 2 caja f. 3 recipiente m.

contaminate (kən'tæmineit) vt contaminar. **contamination** n contaminación f.

contemplate ('kɔntəmpleit) vt 1 contemplar. 2 pensar. **contemplation** n contemplación f. **contemplative** adj contemplativo.

contemporary (kən'tempərəri) adj,n contemporáneo m.

contempt (kən'tempt) n desprecio, desdén m. **contemptible** adj despreciable, vil. **contemptuous** adj desdeñoso.

content

content[1] ('kɔntent) n contenido m. **contents** n pl cóntenido m.

content[2] (kən'tent) adj contento, satisfecho. n contento m. satisfacción f. vt contentar, satisfacer. **contentment** n contento m.

contest (n 'kɔntest; v kən'test) n 1 contienda, lucha f. 2 concurso m. vt 1 impugnar, atacar. 2 defender. **contestant** n contendiente m,f.

context ('kɔntekst) n contexto m.

continent ('kɔntinənt) adj,n continente m. **the Continent** el continente europeo. **continental** adj continental.

contingency (kən'tindʒənsi) n contingencia f.

continue (kən'tinjuː) vt,vi continuar, seguir. **continual** adj continuo, incesante. **continually** adv constantemente. **continuation** n continuación f. **continuity** n continuidad f. **continuous** adj continuo.

contour ('kɔntuə) n contorno m.

contraband ('kɔntrəbænd) n contrabando m.

contraception (kɔntrə'sepʃən) n anticoncepción m. **contraceptive** adj,n anticonceptivo m. **contraceptive pill** n píldora anticonceptiva f.

contract (n 'kɔntrækt; v kən'trækt) n contrato m. vt contraer. **contraction** n contracción f. **contractor** n contratista m.

contradict (kɔntrə'dikt) vt 1 contradecir. 2 desmentir. **contradiction** n contradicción f. **contradictory** adj contradictorio.

contralto (kən'træltou) n contralto m,f.

contraption (kən'træpʃən) n ingenio m.

contrary ('kɔntrəri) adj,n contrario m.

contrast (v kən'trɑːst; n 'kɔntrɑːst) n contraste m. **in contrast** por contraste. **in contrast to** a diferencia de. ~vt poner en contraste, comparar. **contrasting** adj que hace contraste.

contravene (kɔntrə'viːn) vt contravenir. **contravention** n contravención f.

contribute (kən'tribjuːt) vt,vi contribuir. **contribution** n contribución f. **contributor** n contribuyente m.

contrive (kən'traiv) vt inventar, idear. **contrived** adj artificial. **contrivance** n invención f.

control (kən'troul) n 1 mando m. 2 inspección f. vt 1 controlar, mandar. 2 dirigir. **controller** n inspector m. **controlling** adj predominante.

controversy ('kɔntrəvəːsi, kən'trɔvəsi) n controversia f. **controversial** adj discutible.

convalesce (kɔnvə'les) vi convalecer. **convalescence** n convalecencia f.

convenience (kən'viːniəns) n 1 conveniencia, comodidad f. 2 ventaja f. **convenient** adj 1 cómodo, práctico. 2 oportuno.

convent ('kɔnvənt) n convento m.

convention (kən'venʃən) n 1 convención f. 2 asamblea f. congreso m. **conventional** adj convencional.

converge (kən'vəːdʒ) vi convergir. **convergence** n convergencia f. **converging** adj convergente.

converse (adj,n 'kɔnvəːs; v kən'vəːs) adj contrario, inverso. n 1 math inversa f. vi conversar, hablar. **conversation** n conversación f. **conversational** adj 1 familiar. 2 locuaz. **conversationalist** n conversador m.

convert (v kən'vəːt; n 'kɔnvəːt) vt convertir, transformar. n converso m,f. **conversely** adv a la inversa. **conversion** n conversión f. **conversion table** n tabla da conversión f.

convex ('kɔnveks) adj convexo.

convey (kən'vei) vt 1 transportar, llevar. 2 comunicar. **conveyance** n 1 transporte m. 2 law escritura de traspaso f.

convict (v kən'vikt; n 'kɔnvikt) vt condenar. n presidiario m. **conviction** n 1 convicción, creencia f. 2 law condena f.

convince (kən'vins) vt convencer. **convincing** adj convincente.

convoy ('kɔnvɔi) n convoy m. vt convoyar.

cook (kuk) n cocinero m. vt,vi cocinar. **cooking** n cocina f. **cooker** n cocina f. **cookery** n arte de cocina m. **cookery book** n libro de cocina m.

cool (kuːl) adj 1 fresco. 2 tranquilo, imperturbable. 4 frío, indiferente. n fresco m. vt enfriar, refrescar.

coop (kuːp) n gallinero m. **coop up** encerrar.

cooperate (kou'ɔpəreit) vi cooperar, colaborar. **cooperation** n cooperación f. **cooperative** adj cooperativo. **cooperative society** n cooperativa f.

coordinate (n kou'ɔːdnət; v kou'ɔːdineit) n math coordenada. vt coordinar. **coordination** n coordinación f.

cope[1] (koup) vi arreglarse bien. **cope with** poder con.

cope[2] (koup) n rel capa pluvial f.

Copenhagen (koupən'heigən) n Copenhague m.

copper[1] ('kɔpə) n min cobre m. **copper plate** plancha de cobre f. **coppery** adj cobrizo.

copper[2] ('kɔpə) n inf polizonte m.

copulate ('kɔpjuleit) vi copularse. **copulation** n cópula f.

copy ('kɔpi) n 1 copia f. 2 ejemplar m. **fair copy** n copia en limpio f. **rough copy** n borrador m. ~vt copiar, imitar. **copyright** n derecho de propiedad literaria m.

coral ('kɔrəl) n coral m. adj coralino, decoral.

cord (kɔ:d) n 1 cuerda f. 2 med cordón m. 3 pana. vt encordelar.

cordial ('kɔ:diəl) adj cordial. n cordial m. **cordiality** n cordialidad f.

cordon ('kɔ:dn) n cordón m. **cordon off** acordonar.

corduroy ('kɔ:dərɔi) n pana f.

core (kɔ:) n 1 centro, corazón m. 2 esencia f.

cork (kɔ:k) n 1 corcho m. 2 tapón m. vt tapar con corcho. **corkscrew** n sacacorchos m invar.

corn[1] (kɔ:n) 1 trigo m. 2 maíz m. **corny** adj inf gastado, trillado. **cornflour** n harina de maíz f. **cornflower** n aciano m.

corn[2] (kɔ:n) n med callo m.

corner ('kɔ:nə) n 1 esquina f. 2 ángulo m. 3 rincón m. 4 curva f. 5 aprieto m. vt 1 arrinconar. 2 detener, cazar. 3 acaparar.

cornet ('kɔ:nit) n mus corneta f.

coronary ('kɔrənəri) adj coronario. **coronary thrombosis** n trombosis coronaria f.

coronation (kɔrə'neiʃən) n coronación f.

corporal[1] ('kɔ:pərəl) adj corporal.

corporal[2] ('kɔ:prəl) n cabo m.

corporation (kɔ:pə'reiʃən) n 1 corporación f. 2 sociedad anónima f. **corporate** adj colectivo, corporativo.

corps (kɔ:) n invar cuerpo m. **army corps** cuerpo de ejército. **diplomatic corps** cuerpo diplomático.

corpse (kɔ:ps) n cadáver m.

correct (kə'rekt) adj correcto, exacto, justo. vt corregir, rectificar. **correction** n corrección, rectificación f. **corrective** adj correctivo.

correlate ('kɔrəleit) vt correlacionar. vi tener correlación. **correlation** n correlación f.

correspond (kɔri'spɔnd) vi 1 corresponder. 2 escribirse. **correspondence** n correspondencia f. **correspondent** n 1 correspondiente m,f. 2 (of a newspaper) corresponsal m,f.

corridor ('kɔridɔ:) n pasillo, corredor m.

corrode (kə'roud) vt corroer. **corrosion** n corrosión f.

corrupt (kə'rʌpt) adj corrompido. vt corromper. **corruption** n corrupción f.

corset ('kɔ:sit) n faja f.

Corsica ('kɔ:sikə) n Córcega f.

cosmetic (kɔz'metik) adj,n cosmético m.

cosmopolitan (kɔzmə'pɔlitən) adj, n cosmopolita m,f.

cosmos ('kɔzmɔs) n cosmos m. **cosmic** adj cósmico.

cost[*] (kɔst) n 1 precio m. 2 costo, coste m. costa f. **cost of living** coste de la vida m. **at all costs** a todo trance. ~vt calcular el coste de. vi costar, valer. **costly** adj costoso.

costume ('kɔstju:m) n traje m.

cosy ('kouzi) adj 1 cómodo, agradable. 2 acogedor, amistoso.

cot (kɔt) n cuna, camita de niño f.

cottage ('kɔtidʒ) n casita de campo f. chalet m. **cottage cheese** n requesón m.

cotton ('kɔtn) n algodón m. **cottonwool** n algodón hidrófilo m.

couch (kautʃ) n sofá m. vt acostar.

cough (kɔf) n tos f. vi toser.

could (kud; unstressed kəd) v see **can**[1].

council ('kaunsəl) n 1 consejo m. junta f. 2 concilio m. 3 ayuntamiento m. **councillor** n concejal m.

counsel ('kaunsəl) n 1 consejo m. 2 law abogado m. vt aconsejar. **counsellor** n consejero m.

count[1] (kaunt) n cuenta f. cálculo m. vt contar, calcular. vi contar. **countdown** n cuenta hacia atrás f.

count[2] (kaunt) n conde m.

counter[1] ('kauntə) n 1 mostrador, contador m. 2 ficha f. **under the counter** sl por la trastienda.

counter[2] ('kauntə) adj contrario. vt contradecir, contrarrestar.

counterattack ('kauntərətæk) n contraataque m. vt contraatacar.

counterfeit ('kauntəfit) adj falso, falsificado. n falsificación f. vt falsificar.

counterfoil ('kauntəfɔil) n talón m.

counterpart ('kauntəpɑ:t) n contraparte f.

countess ('kauntis) n condesa f.

country ('kʌntri) n 1 país m. 2 campo m. **countryman** n 1 campesino. 2 compatriota m. **countryside** n campo m.

county ('kaunti) n condado m. **county council** n diputación provincial f.

coup (ku:) n golpe m. **coup d'état** n golpe de estado m.

couple ('kʌpəl) n 1 par m. 2 pareja f. **married couple** n matrimonio m. ~vt juntar, unir.

coupon ('ku:pɔn) n cupón m.

courage ('kʌridʒ) n valor m. valentía f. **courageous** adj valiente.

courgette (kuə'ʒet) n calabacín m.

courier ('kuriə) n 1 estafeta f. 2 agente de turismo m,f.

course (kɔ:s) n 1 curso m. dirección f. 2 naut rumbo m. 3 plato m. 4 pista f. campo m. **in due course** a su tiempo. **of course** por supuesto. ~vt cazar.

court (kɔ:t) n 1 corte f. 2 tribunal m. 3 sport pista, cancha f. 4 patio m. vt cortejar. vi estar en relaciones, ser novios. **courtier** n cortesano m. **courtly** adj cortés, elegante. **court-martial** n consejo de guerra m. vt someter a un consejo de guerra. **courtship** n noviazgo m. **courtyard** n patio m.

courteous ('kɔ:tiəs) adj cortés. **courtesy** n cortesía f.

cousin ('kʌzən) n primo m. **first cousin** n primo carnal m.

cove (kouv) n cala f.

covenant ('kʌvənənt) n pacto, convenio m.

cover ('kʌvə) n 1 cubierta, tapa f. 2 cubierto m. vt cubrir, tapar. **cover charge** n precio del cubierto m. **coverage** n alcance m.

cow (kau) n 1 vaca f. 2 hembra f. vt intimidar, acobardar. **cowboy** n vaquero m.

coward ('kauəd) n cobarde m.

cower ('kauə) vi agacharse, accurrucarse.

coy (kɔi) adj tímido, reservado.

crab (kræb) n cangrejo m. **crab apple** n manzana silvestre f. **crabbed** adj 1 amargado. 2 desapacible. 3 (of writing) indecifrable.

crack (kræk) n 1 grieta, hendedura f. 2 crujido m. 3 chasquido m. 4 chiste m. vt,vi chasquear, crujir.

cracker ('krækə) n petardo m.

crackle ('krækəl) n crujido m. crepitación f. vi crepitar, crujir. **crackling** n 1 crujido. 2 cul chicharrón m.

cradle ('kreidl) n cuna f. vt mecer, acunar.

craft (krɑ:ft) n 1 oficio, empleo m. 2 destreza f. 3 astucia f. **craftsman** n artesano m. **craftsmanship** n artesanía f. **crafty** adj astuto, socarrón.

cram (kræm) vt 1 embutir, rellenar. 2 cebar. 3 educ inf empollar.

cramp[1] (kræmp) n med calambre m.

cramp[2] (kræmp) tech grapa f. vt engrapar, estorbar.

crane (krein) n 1 zool grulla f. 2 tech grúa f.

crash (kræʃ) n 1 estruendo, estrépito, estallido m. 2 accidente, choque m. 3 comm quiebra f.

vt estrellar. vi 1 caer con estrépito. 2 tener un accidente. 3 fracasar, quebrar. **crash-helmet** n casco protector m.

crate (kreit) n cajón de embalaje m.

crater ('kreitə) n cráter m.

crave (kreiv) vt 1 suplicar, implorar. 2 anhelar, ansiar. **craving** n ansia f.

crawl (krɔ:l) n arrastramiento m. vi 1 arrastrarse. 2 andar a gatas.

crayfish ('kreifiʃ) n ástaco, cangrejo de río m.

crayon ('kreiən) n lápiz de tiza m.

craze (kreiz) n 1 manía, locura f. 2 moda f. **crazed** adj enloquecido. **crazy** adj loco, chiflado.

creak (kri:k) n crujido, chirrido m. vi crujir, chirriar.

cream (kri:m) n 1 nata f. 2 crema f. vt 1 desnatar. **creamy** adj cremoso.

crease (kri:s) n 1 pliegue m. 2 arruga f. 3 raya f. vt 1 arrugar. 2 plegar. **crease-resistant** adj inarrugable.

create (kri'eit) vt crear. **creation** n creación f. **creative** adj creador.

creature ('kri:tʃə) n criatura f.

creche (kreʃ) n 1 guardería infantil f. 2 rel belén m.

credentials (kri'denʃəlz) n pl credenciales f pl.

credible ('kredibəl) adj creíble. **credibility** n credibilidad f.

credit ('kredit) n crédito m. **on credit** a crédito. ~vt 1 creer. 2 acreditar. **creditable** adj estimable, honorable. **creditor** n acreedor m. **credit card** n tarjeta de crédito m.

creep (kri:p) vi 1 arrastrarse. 2 ir cautelosamente. n inf pelotillero m. **creepy** adj horripilante.

cremate (kri'meit) vt incinerar. **cremation** n incineración f. **crematorium** n horno crematorio m.

creosote n creosota f.

crept (krept) v see **creep**.

crescent ('kresənt) adj creciente. n 1 media luna f. 2 calle en forma de semicírculo f.

cress (kres) n berro, mastuerzo m.

crest (krest) n 1 cresta f. 2 cima, cumbre f. **crested** adj crestado. **crestfallen** adj alicaído.

crevice ('krevis) n grieta, hendedura f.

crew (kru:) n 1 tripulación f. 2 banda, pandilla f.

crib (krib) n 1 pesebre m. 2 educ inf chuleta f. vt plagiar.

cricket[1] ('krikit) n zool grillo m.

cricket[2] ('krikit) n criquet m.

crime ('kraim) n crimen, delito m. **criminal** adj,n criminal m.

crimson ('krimzən) adj,n carmesí m.

cringe (krindʒ) vi agacharse, encogerse. **cringing** adj servil.

crinkle ('kriŋkəl) n arruga f. vi arrugarse.

cripple ('kripəl) n lisiado, mutilado m. vt lisiar, mutilar.

crisis ('kraisis) n, pl **crises** crisis f.

crisp (krisp) adj 1 crespo, rizado. 2 crujiente, tostado. **crisps** n pl patatas fritas a la inglesa f pl.

criterion (krai'tiəriən) n, pl **criteria** criterio m.

criticize ('kritisaiz) vt criticar. **critic** n crítico m. **critical** adj crítico. **criticism** n crítica f.

croak (krouk) n graznido m. vi 1 graznar. 2 croar. 3 gruñir.

crochet ('krouʃei) n croché, labor de ganchillo m.

crockery ('krɔkəri) n loza, vajilla f.

crocodile ('krɔkədail) n cocodrilo m.

crocus ('kroukəs) n bot azafrán m.

crook (kruk) n 1 cayado m. 2 criminal, ladrón m. vt encorvar.

crooked ('krukid) adj 1 torcido, encorvado. 2 inf torcido, avieso.

crop (krɔp) n 1 cosecha f. cultivo m. 2 látigo m. vt cortar, recortar. **crop up** surgir.

croquet ('kroukei) n croquet m.

cross (krɔs) n cruz f. vt atravesar, cruzar. adj 1 cruzado. 2 malhumorado. 3 transversal, oblicuo. **cross-examination** n law repregunta, interrogación f. **cross-eyed** adj bizco. **cross-fire** n fuego cruzado m. **crossing** n cruce m. travesía f. **level crossing** paso a nivel m. **crossroads** n cruce m. encrucijada f. **cross-word puzzle** crucigrama m.

crotchet ('krɔtʃit) n 1 mus negra f. 2 capricho m. excentricidad f.

crouch (krautʃ) vi agacharse, encogerse.

crow[1] (krou) n cuervo m. corneja f. **as the crow flies** en línea recta.

crow[2] (krou) n canto, cacareo m. vi cantar, cacarear.

crowd (kraud) n multitud, muchedumbre f. gentío m. vt amontonar. vi congregarse. **crowded** adj lleno, atestado.

crown (kraun) n 1 corona f. 2 copa f. 3 cumbre f. vt coronar. **crowning** adj supremo.

crucial ('kru:ʃəl) adj decisivo, crítico.

crucify ('kru:sifai) vt crucificar. **crucifix** n crucifijo m.

crude (kru:d) adj 1 crudo. 2 tosco. 3 ordinario. **crude oil** n aceite crudo m.

cruel ('kruəl) adj cruel. **cruelty** n crueldad f.

cruise (kru:z) n crucero, viaje por mar m. vi cruzar, navegar. **cruiser** n crucero m.

crumb (krʌm) n migaja, miga f.

crumble ('krʌmbəl) vt desmenuzar, desmigajar. vi desmoronarse. **crumbly** adj desmenuzable.

crumple ('krʌmpəl) vt 1 ajar. 2 plegar.

crunch (krʌntʃ) n 1 crujido m. 2 inf punto decisivo m. vt ronzar, mascar. vi crujir. **crunchy** adj crujiente.

crusade (kru:'seid) n cruzada f. vi participar en una cruzada.

crush (krʌʃ) n 1 agolpamiento m. 2 aplastamiento m. vt 1 aplastar. 2 aniquilar, destruir. **crushing** adj aplastante.

crust (krʌst) n 1 corteza f. 2 mendrugo m.

crustacean (krʌs'teiʃən) n crustáceo m.

crutch (krʌtʃ) n muleta f.

cry (krai) n grito m. vi 1 gritar. 2 llorar. **crybaby** n llorón m.

crypt (kript) n cripta f.

crystal ('kristl) adj cristalino. n cristal m. **crystallize** vt cristalizar.

cub (kʌb) n cachorro m.

cube (kju:b) n 1 cubo m. 2 terrón m. vt cubicar. **cubic** adj cúbico. **cubicle** n 1 cubículo m. 2 caseta f.

cuckoo ('kuku:) n cuco, cuclillo m.

cucumber ('kju:kʌmbə) n pepino m.

cuddle ('kʌdl) n abrazo m. caricia f. vt abrazar amorosamente. vi abrazarse.

cue[1] (kju:) n pie, apunte m. entrada f.

cue[2] (kju:) n game taco m.

cuff[1] (kʌf) n puño m. **cufflinks** n pl gemelos m pl. **off the cuff** de improviso.

cuff[2] (kʌf) n bofetada f. vt abofetear.

culinary ('kʌlinri) adj culinario.

culprit ('kʌlprit) n culpado, culpable m.

cult (kʌlt) n culto m.

cultivate ('kʌltiveit) vt cultivar. **cultivated** adj culto, refinado. **cultivation** n cultivo m.

culture ('kʌltʃə) n 1 cultura f. 2 cultivo m. **cultural** adj cultural. **cultured** adj culto.

cumbersome ('kʌmbəsəm) adj molesto, incómodo.

cunning ('kʌniŋ) adj astuto, taimado. n astucia f.

cup (kʌp) n 1 taza f. 2 rel cáliz m. 3 sport copa f. **cupful** n taza f.

cupboard ('kʌbəd) n armario m.

curate ('kjuəreit) n cura m.

curator (kju'reitə) n director, conservador m.
curb (kə:b) n freno, estorbo m. vt refrenar.
curdle ('kə:dl) vt cuajar. vi cuajarse. **curd** n cuajada f.
cure (kjuə) n cura f. vt curar.
curfew ('kə:fju:) n toque de queda m.
curious ('kjuəriəs) adj curioso. **curiosity** n curiosidad f.
curl (kə:l) n 1 rizo, bucle m. 2 espiral f. vt 1 rizar. 2 ondular. 3 fruncir. vi 1 rizarse. 2 arrollarse. **curler** n bigudí m. **curly** adj rizado.
currant ('kʌrənt) n 1 pasa. 2 grosella f.
current ('kʌrənt) adj corriente, actual. n corriente f. **current affairs** actualidades f pl. **current account** n cuenta corriente f. **currency** n moneda f.
curry ('kʌri) n cari, curry m. vt preparar con cari. **curry powder** n especias en polvo f pl.
curse (kə:s) n 1 maldición f. 2 palabrota f. 3 calamidad f. vt maldecir. vi blasfemar, echar pestes. **cursed** adj maldito.
curt (kə:t) adj brusco, seco. **curtness** n brusquedad f.
curtail (kə:'teil) vt acortar, reducir. **curtailment** n acortamiento m. restricción f.
curtain ('kə:tn) n 1 cortina f. 2 telón m. **iron curtain** n telón de acero m.
curtsy ('kə:tsi) n reverencia f. vi hacer una reverencia.
curve (kə:v) n curva f. vi encorvarse, torcerse. **curved** adj curvo, encorvado.
cushion ('kuʃən) n 1 cojín, almohadón m. 2 banda f. vt amortiguar. **cushy** adj inf fácil, agradable.
custard ('kʌstəd) n natillas f pl.
custody ('kʌstədi) n custodia f. **be in custody** estar detenido. **custodian** n custodio m.
custom ('kʌstəm) n 1 costumbre f. 2 clientela, parroquia f. **customs** n pl aduana f. **customary** adj acostumbrado, de costumbre. **customer** n 1 cliente m,f. 2 inf tío, sujeto m.
cut (kʌt) n 1 corte m. 2 cortadura f. 3 tajada, parte f. 4 reducción f. **short cut** n atajo m. ~vt 1 cortar. 2 reducir. vi 1 cortar. 2 cruzarse. **cut across** atajar. adj 1 cortado. 2 tallado. **cut-price** adj a precio reducido. **cutting** n 1 recorte m. 2 desmonte m. 3 bot esqueje m. adj 1 cortante. 2 mordaz.
cute (kju:t) adj inf 1 mono. 2 astuto, listo.
cuticle ('kju:tikəl) n cutícula f.
cutlery ('kʌtləri) n cubiertos m pl. cuchillería f.
cutlet ('kʌtlit) n chuleta f.

cycle ('saikəl) n 1 ciclo m. 2 bicicleta f. vi ir en bicicleta. **cyclical** adj cíclico. **cycling** n ciclismo m. **cyclist** n ciclista m,f.
cyclone ('saikloun) n ciclón m,f.
cygnet ('signit) n pollo de cisne m.
cylinder ('silində) n cilindro m. **cylindrical** adj cilíndrico.
cymbal ('simbəl) n platillo m.
cynic ('sinik) n cínico m. **cynical** adj cínico, escéptico.
cypress ('saiprəs) n ciprés m.
Cyprus ('saiprəs) n Chipre f. **Cypriot** adj,n chipriota m,f.
czar (za:) n zar m.
Czechoslovakia (tʃekəslə'vækiə) n Checoslovaquia f. **Czech** adj,n checo. **Czech** (language) n checo m.

D

dab (dæb) n 1 pequeña cantidad f. 2 gota f. vt tocar ligeramente.
dabble ('dæbəl) vt 1 salpicar, mojar. 2 chapotear. **dabble in** interesarse en por pasatiempo.
dad (dæd) n inf papá m.
daffodil ('dæfədil) n narciso trompón m.
daft (da:ft) adj estúpido.
dagger ('dægə) n daga f. puñal m.
dahlia ('deiliə) n dalia f.
daily ('deili) adj diario, cotidiano. adv a diario, cada día. n 1 diario m. 2 dom asistenta f.
dainty ('deinti) adj delicado, fino.
dairy ('dɛəri) n lechería f.
daisy ('deizi) n margarita f.
dam[1] (dæm) n presa f. dique m. vt represar. **dam up** cerrar, tapar.
dam[2] (dæm) n zool madre f.
damage ('dæmidʒ) n 1 daño, perjuicio m. 2 avería f. **damages** law daños y perjuicios m pl. ~vt 1 dañar, perjudicar. 2 averiar. **damaging** adj perjudicial.
damn (dæm) vt 1 condenar. 2 maldecir. **damn it!** ¡maldito sea! **damned** adj maldito, condenado. ~adv inf muy, terriblemente. **damning** adj damnificador. **damnable** adj detestable. **damnation** n condenación f.
damp (dæmp) adj 1 húmedo. 2 mojado. n humedad f. **dampen** vt 1 humedecer, mojar. 2 amortiguar. 3 desalentar.
damson ('dæmzən) n ciruela damascena f.

dance (da:ns) n baile m. danza f. vi bailar, danzar. **dancer** n bailador, bailarín m.

dandelion ('dændilaiən) n diente de león m.

dandruff ('dændrʌf) n caspa f.

Dane (dein) n danés m. **Danish** adj danés, dinamarqués. **Danish** (language) n danés m.

danger ('deindʒə) n peligro m. **dangerous** adj peligroso, arriesgado.

dangle ('dæŋgəl) vt colgar, dejar colgado.

Danube ('dænju:b) n Danubio m.

dare (dɛə) vt 1 arriesgar. 2 desafiar. vi atreverse. **daredevil** adj,n temerario m. **daring** adj atrevido, osado.

dark (da:k) adj 1 oscuro. 2 moreno. n oscuridad f. tinieblas f pl. **be in the dark** inf no saber nada en absoluto. **darken** vt 1 oscurecer. 2 hacer más oscuro. **darkness** n oscuridad f.

darling ('da:liŋ) adj,n querido m.

darn (da:n) vt zurcir.

dart (da:t) n 1 dardo m. 2 game rehilete m. 3 movimiento rápido m. vi lanzarse, precipitarse. **dartboard** n blanco m.

dash (dæʃ) n 1 pequeña cantidad f. 2 rasgo m. 3 guión m. 4 carrera f. **make a dash for** precipitarse hacia. vt romper, estrellar. vi precipitarse. **dashing** adj brioso, gallardo. **dashboard** n tablero de instrumentos m.

data ('deitə) n pl datos m pl. **data processing** n proceso de datos m.

date¹ (deit) n 1 fecha f. 2 inf cita f. **be up to date** tener ideas modernas. **out of date** anticuado. **to date** hasta la fecha. **date line** n línea de cambio de fecha f. ~vt fechar.

date² (deit) n dátil m. **date palm** n palmera datilera f.

daughter ('dɔ:tə) n hija f. **daughter-in-law** n nuera, hija política f.

dawdle ('dɔ:dl) vi holgazanear, perder el tiempo. **dawdler** n holgazán m.

dawn (dɔ:n) n alba f. amanecer m. vi amanecer. **dawn on** caer en la cuenta.

day (dei) n 1 día m. 2 jornada f. **the day after tomorrow** pasado mañana. **from day to day** de día en día. **daybreak** n amanecer m. **daydream** n ensueño m. vi soñar despierto. **daylight** n luz del día f. **in broad daylight** en pleno día.

daze (deiz) n aturdimiento m. vt aturdir. **be in a daze** estar aturdido. **dazed** adj aturdido.

dazzle ('dæzəl) n brillo m. vt deslumbrar. **dazzling** adj deslumbrante, deslumbrador.

dead (ded) adj 1 muerto. 2 desierto. 3 apagado. **deadly** adj 1 mortal. 2 fatal. **deadline** n

fecha tope f. límite, plazo m. **deadlock** n 1 parálisis f. 2 punto muerto m. **deaden** vt 1 amortiguar. 2 aliviar.

deaf (def) adj sordo. **deaf-aid** n aparato del oído m. **deaf-mute** n sordomudo m. **deafen** vt ensordecer. **deafening** adj ensordecedor. **deafness** n sordera f.

deal¹ (di:l) n 1 negocio m. transacción f. 2 pacto, convenio m. 3 reparto m. **a great deal** muchísimo. ~vt 1 dar. 2 descargar. 3 repartir. vi negociar, comerciar. **deal with** tratar de.

dean (di:n) n 1 rel deán m. 2 educ decano m.

dear (diə) adj 1 querido. 2 estimado. 3 caro, costoso. n persona simpática f. **oh dear!** interj ¡caramba!

death (deθ) n 1 muerte f. 2 fallecimiento m. **deathly** adj 1 mortal. 2 profundo.

debase (di'beis) vt 1 degradar. 2 (coins) alterar.

debate (di'beit) n 1 discusión f. 2 debate m. vt,vi discutir. vt debatir.

debit ('debit) n 1 debe m. 2 cargo m. vt cargar.

debris ('deibri) n escombros m pl.

debt (det) n deuda f. **debtor** n deudor m.

decade ('dekeid) n decenio m.

decadent ('dekədənt) adj decadente. **decadence** n decadencia f.

decant (di'kænt) vt decantar. **decanter** n jarra, garrafa f.

decay (di'kei) n 1 decadencia f. decaimiento m. 2 pudrición, putrefacción. f. 3 caries f. vt deteriorar, pudrir. vi 1 decaer. 2 pudrirse.

decease (di'si:s) n 1 fallecimiento m. vi fallecer. **deceased** adj,n difunto.

deceit (di'si:t) n 1 engaño, fraude m. 2 mentira f. **deceitful** or **deceptive** adj engañoso.

deceive (di'si:v) vt 1 engañar. 2 defraudar.

December (di'sembə) n diciembre m.

decent ('di:sənt) adj 1 decente. 2 simpático, amable. **decency** n 1 decencia f. 2 bondad f.

decibel ('desibel) n decibelio m.

decide (di'said) vt decidir, determinar. vi resolver. **decided** adj decidido, resuelto.

deciduous (di'sidjuəs) adj de hoja caduca.

decimal ('desiməl) adj,n decimal f. **decimal point** n coma de decimales f.

decipher (di'saifə) vt descifrar.

decision (di'siʒən) n decisión f. **decisive** adj decisivo, concluyente. **decisively** adv con decisión.

deck (dek) n 1 cubierta f. 2 piso m. 3 game baraja f. **deckchair** n hamaca, tumbona f.

declaration (deklə'reiʃən) n declaración f.

declare (di'klɛə) vt declarar, afirmar. vi pronunciarse. **nothing to declare** nada de declarar. **declared** adj abierto, manifiesto.

decline (di'klain) n 1 declinación f. descenso m. 2 baja f. 3 decaimiento m. vt,vi 1 rehusar. 2 gram declinar. **declension** n declinación f.

decorate ('dekəreit) vt decorar, adornar. **interior decorating** decoración del hogar f. **decoration** n 1 adorno m. 2 decoración f. **decorative** adj hermoso, elegante. **decorator** n decorador m.

decoy (n 'di:kɔi: v di'kɔi) n 1 señuelo m. 2 reclamo m. vt atraer con señuelo.

decrease (di'kri:s) n disminución f. vt disminuir, reducir.

decree (di'kri:) n decreto m. vt decretar.

decrepit (di'krepit) adj decrépito.

dedicate ('dedikeit) vt dedicar. **dedication** n 1 dedicación f. 2 dedicatoria f. 3 devoción f.

deduce (di'dju:s) vt deducir.

deduct (di'dʌkt) vt restar, rebajar, descontar. **deduction** n 1 deducción, conclusión f. 2 descuento m. rebaja f.

deed (di:d) n 1 hecho m. acción f. 2 hazaña f. 3 law escritura f.

deep (di:p) adj 1 profundo, hondo. 2 bajo. 3 insondable. **deep-freeze** n congeladora f.

deer (diə) n ciervo m.

deface (di'feis) vt desfigurar, mutilar.

default (di'fɔ:lt) n 1 omisión f. descuido m. 2 falta f. incumplimiento m. vi 1 faltar, delinquir. 2 sport dejar de presentarse.

defeat (di'fi:t) n derrota f. vt vencer, derrotar.

defect (n 'di:fekt; v di'fekt) n defecto m. vi desertar. **defection** n deserción, defección f. **defective** adj 1 defectuoso. 2 defectivo.

defence (di'fens) n defensa f. **defenceless** adj indefenso. **defend** vt defender. **defender** n defensor m. **defensive** adj defensivo.

defer (di'fə:) vt aplazar, diferir. **deference** n deferencia f. respeto m. **in deference to** por respeto a. **deferential** adj deferente, cortés, respetuoso.

defiant (di'faiənt) adj desafiador. **defiance** n desafío, reto m.

deficient (di'fiʃənt) adj deficiente. **deficiency** n deficiencia f.

deficit ('defisit) n déficit m. adj deficitario.

define (di'fain) vt 1 definir. 2 caracterizar. **definition** n definición f.

definite ('defənit) adj 1 determinado, definido. 2 preciso.

deflate (di'fleit) vt,vi 1 desinflar. 2 comm

reducir la inflación. **deflation** n comm deflación f.

deform (di'fɔ:m) vt deformar, desfigurar. **deformation** n deformación f.

defraud (di'frɔ:d) vt defraudar, engañar, estafar. **defrauder** n defraudador m.

defrost (di'frɔst) vt deshelar.

deft (deft) adj hábil, mañoso. **deftness** n habilidad, destreza, maña f.

defunct (di'fʌŋkt) adj difunto, muerto.

defy (di'fai) vt 1 desafiar, retar, provocar. 2 contravenir.

degenerate (di'dʒenərit) adj,n degenerado m.

degrade (di'greid) vt degradar, envilecer.

degree (di'gri:) n 1 grado m. 2 educ titulo m.

dehydrate (di'haidreit) vt deshidratar.

deity ('deiiti) n 1 deidad f. 2 dios m.

dejected (di'dʒektid) adj desanimado, abatido, desalentado. **dejection** n abatimiento, desaliento m.

delay (di'lei) n retraso m. tardanza, dilación f. vt retardar, diferir. vi tardar.

delegate (n 'deligət; v 'deligeit) n 1 delegado m. 2 substituto. vt delegar, disputar.

delete (di'li:t) vt borrar, tachar. **deletion** n supresión f.

deliberate (adj di'libərət; v di'libəreit) adj deliberado, premeditado. vt deliberar, reflexionar, pensar. **deliberation** n 1 discusión f. 2 reflexión f.

delicate ('delikət) adj 1 delicado. 2 exquisita. 3 fino. **delicacy** n delicadeza, finura f. 2 exquisitez f.

delicatessen (delikə'tesən) n tienda de fiambres y manjares delicados f.

delicious (di'liʃəs) adj delicioso.

delight (di'lait) n 1 deleite m. 2 delicia f. placer m. vt deleitar, agradar, recrear. **delightful** adj delicioso, precioso.

delinquency (di'liŋkwənsi) n delincuencia f. **delinquent** adj,n delincuente.

deliver (di'livə) vt 1 liberar, librar, salvar. 2 entregar, transmitir. 3 despachar, servir. 4 dar, descargar. **delivery** n 1 entrega f. reparto de correo m. 2 med parto m.

delta ('deltə) n geog delta m.

delude (di'lu:d) vt engañar. **delusion** n engaño, error m. ilusión f.

delve (delv) vt cavar, ahondar.

demand (di'mɑ:nd) n 1 demanda, solicitación f. 2 pregunta, reclamación f. vt pedir, exigir, preguntar. **demanding** adj exigente.

democracy (di'mɔkrəsi) n democracia f. **demo-**

cratic adj democrático. **democrat** n demócrata m,f.

demolish (di'mɔliʃ) vt 1 demoler. 2 arrasar. 3 derruir. **demolition** n demolición f.

demon ('di:mən) n demonio, diablo m.

demonstrate ('demənstreit) vt demostrar, probar, exponer. **demonstration** n demostración f.

demoralize (di'mɔrəlaiz) vt desmoralizar.

demure (di'mjuə) adj 1 grave, serio. 2 modesto.

den (den) n 1 guarida f. cubil m. 2 lugar de retiro, cueva f.

denial (di'naiəl) n negación, contradicción f.

denim ('denim) n dril de algodón m.

Denmark ('denma:k) n Dinamarca.

denomination (dinɔmi'neiʃən) n 1 denominación f. 2 secta f. grupo religioso m. 3 categoría f. **denominator** n denominador m.

denote (di'nout) vt denotar.

denounce (di'nauns) vt denunciar.

dense (dens) adj denso. **density** n densidad f.

dent (dent) n mella, abolladura f.

dental ('dentl) adj dental, dentista. **dentist** n dentista m. **dentistry** n odontología, cirugía dental f. **denture** n dentadura f.

deny (di'nai) vt negar, desmentir.

deodorant (di'oudərənt) n desodorante m.

depart (di'pa:t) vi 1 partir, irse. 2 apartarse, salirse. 3 dejar. **departure** n partida, salida f.

department (di'pa:tmənt) n departamento m. sección f. **department store** almacenes m pl.

depend (di'pend) vi depender. **dependence** n dependencia f. **dependent** adj dependiente, subordinado.

depict (di'pikt) vt 1 describir. 2 pintar.

deplete (di'pli:t) vt vaciar, agotar. **depletion** n agotamiento m.

deplore (di'plɔ:) vt deplorar, lamentar.

deport (di'pɔ:t) vt deportar. **deportation** n deportación f.

depose (di'pouz) vt deponer.

deposit (di'pɔzit) n 1 depósito m. 2 min yacimiento m.

depot ('depou) n depósito, almacén m.

deprave (di'preiv) vt depravar.

depreciate (di'pri:ʃieit) vt depreciar. vi depreciarse, perder valor.

depress (di'pres) vt deprimir. **depression** n depresión f.

deprive (di'praiv) vt privar, desposeer.

depth (depθ) n 1 profundidad, hondura f. 2 fondo m.

deputize ('depjutaiz) vt diputar. **deputation** n diputación, delegación f. **deputy** n 1 diputado m. 2 sustituto m. adj 1 vice, segundo. 2 suplente.

derail (di'reil) vt hacer descarrilar.

derelict ('derəlikt) adj derelicto, abandonado.

deride (di'raid) vt ridiculizar. **derision** n irrisión f.

derive (di'raiv) vt derivar. vi provenir. **derivation** n derivación f.

derogatory (di'rɔgətri) adj despectivo, rebajante.

descend (di'send) vt,vi descender, bajar. **descendant** adj descendiente.

descent (di'sent) n 1 descenso m. bajada f. 2 descendencia hereditaria f.

describe (di'skraib) vt describir. **description** n 1 descripción f. 2 especie f. tipo m.

desert[1] ('dezət) n desierto m.

desert[2] (di'zə:t) vt abandonar, desertar. **deserter** n desertor m.

deserve (di'zə:v) vt merecer.

design (di'zain) vt 1 diseñar. 2 proyectar. 3 dibujar. n 1 proyecto, plan m. 2 objeto, propósito m. 3 dibujo, modelo m.

designate ('dezigneit) vt 1 nombrar. 2 denominar. 3 señalar. 4 designar.

desire (di'zaiə) n deseo m. vt desear.

desk (desk) n pupitre, escritorio m.

desolate ('desələt) adj desolado, desierto, triste.

despair (di'spɛə) n desesperación, desesperanza f. vi desesperar.

desperate ('despərət) adj desesperado.

despise (di'spaiz) vt despreciar.

despite (di'spait) prep a pesar de.

despondent (di'spɔndənt) adj desanimado, abatido. **despondency** n desaliento, abatimiento m.

dessert (di'zə:t) n postre m. **dessertspoon** n cuchara de postres f.

destine ('destin) vt destinar. **destination** n destinación f. **destiny** n destino, hado m. suerte f.

destitute ('destitju:t) adj indigente, menesteroso.

destroy (di'strɔi) vt destruir, destrozar.

detach (di'tætʃ) vt despegar.

detail ('di:teil) n 1 detalle, pormenor m. 2 mil destacamento m. vt detallar, enumerar.

detain (di'tein) vt 1 detener. 2 retener **detention** n detención f.

detect (di'tekt) vt 1 detectar. 2 descubrir. **detective** n detective m.

deter (di'tə:) vt disuadir. **deterrent** n 1 freno m. 2 mil fuerza disuasiva f. adj disuasivo.

detergent (di'tə:dʒənt) n detergente m.

deteriorate (di'tiəriəreit) vi deteriorarse.

determine (di'tə:min) vt determinar. **determination** n determinación f.

detest (di'test) vt detestar, aborrecer, odiar.

detonate ('detəneit) vi detonar. vt hacer estallar.

detour ('di:tuə) n rodeo m. vuelta f. vi hacer un rodeo, desviarse.

detract (di'trækt) vi **detract from** desvirtuar.

devalue (di'vælju:) vt devaluar.

devastate ('devəsteit) vt devastar.

develop (di'veləp) vt 1 desarrollar. 2 explotar. vi desarrollarse, evolucionar. **development** n desarrollo m. evolución f.

deviate ('di:vieit) vi desviarse. **devious** adj 1 taimado. 2 tortuoso.

device (di'vais) n mecanismo, aparato m.

devil ('devəl) n diablo m. **devil's advocate** n abogado del diablo m. **devilish** adj diabólico.

devise (di'vaiz) vt idear, planear.

devoid (di'vɔid) adj desprovisto, falto.

devote (di'vout) vt dedicar. **devotedly** adv con fervor, devotamente. **devotee** n devoto m. **devotion** n 1 devoción f. 2 dedicación f.

devour (di'vauə) vt devorar.

devout (di'vaut) adj devoto, piadoso.

dew (dju:) n rocío m.

dexterous ('dekstrəs) adj 1 diestro, hábil. 2 ágil.

diabetes (daiə'bi:ti:z) n diabetes f. **diabetic** adj,n diabético.

diagnosis (daiəg'nousis) n, pl **diagnoses** diagnóstico m.

diagonal (dai'agənl) adj,n diagonal f.

diagram ('daiəgræm) n diagrama, esquema m.

dial ('daiəl) n 1 esfera del reloj f. 2 cuadrante m. **sun dial** reloj de sol m. vt marcar.

dialect ('daiəlekt) n dialecto m.

dialogue ('daiəlɔg) n diálogo m.

diameter (dai'æmitə) n diámetro m.

diamond ('daiəmənd) n diamante m.

diaphragm ('daiəfræm) n diafragma m.

diarrhoea (daiə'riə) n diarrea f.

diary ('daiəri) n diario m.

dice (dais) n pl dados m pl.

dictate (v dik'teit; n 'dikteit) vt dictar, mandar, imponer. n orden f. mandato m. **dictation** n dictado m. **dictator** n dictador m. **dictatorship** n dictadura f.

dictionary ('dikʃənri) n diccionario m.

186

did (did) v see **do.**

die[1] (dai) vi morir, fallecer.

die[2] (dai) n 1 tech cuño, troquel m. matriz f. 2 game dado m.

diesel ('di:zəl) n diesel m.

diet ('daiət) n dieta f. régimen m. vi estar a dieta.

differ ('difə) vi 1 diferir. 2 discrepar. **difference** n diferencia f. **it makes no difference** da lo mismo. **different** adj diferente, distinto. **differential** adj diferencial. **differentiate** vt distinguir.

difficult ('difikəlt) adj difícil, arduo. **difficulty** n dificultad f.

dig[*] (dig) vt cavar, excavar. n 1 excavación f. 2 codazo m. 3 alojamiento m.

digest (n 'daidʒest; v dai'dʒest) n 1 resumen m. 2 law digesto m. vt 1 digerir. 2 resumir. **digestion** n digestión f.

digit ('didʒit) n digito m. **digital** adj digital.

dignity ('digniti) n dignidad f. **dignified** adj 1 dignificado. 2 digno, solemne.

dilapidated (di'læpideitid) adj ruinoso.

dilemma (di'lemə) n dilema m.

diligent ('dilidʒənt) adj diligente.

dilute (dai'lu:t) vt diluir, aguar.

dim (dim) adj 1 obscuro. 2 débil. 3 apagado. v obscurecer.

dimension (di'menʃən) n dimensión f.

diminish (di'miniʃ) vt disminuir.

diminutive (di'minjutiv) adj diminutivo, diminuto.

dimple ('dimpəl) n hoyuelo m.

din (din) n estruendo, estrépito m.

dine (dain) vi comer. **dining car** n vagón restaurante m. **dining room** n comedor m.

dinghy ('diŋgi) n naut bote m.

dingy ('dindʒi) adj sucio, negruzco.

dinner ('dinə) n cena, comida f.

dinosaur ('dainɔsɔ:) n dinosauro m.

diocese ('daiəsis) n diócesis f.

dip (dip) vt 1 sumergir, zambullir. 2 mojar. n zambullida f. 2 pendiente f. declive m.

diphthong ('difθɔŋ) n diptongo m.

diploma (di'ploumə) n diploma m.

diplomacy (di'plouməsi) n diploɾɑacia f. **diplomat** n diplomático m. **diplomatic** adj diplomático.

direct (di'rekt) adj directo. vt 1 dirigir, mandar. **direct object** n gram complemento directo m. **direction** n 1 dirección f. 2 instrucciones f pl. **director** n director m. **board o**

disparage

directors n consejo de administración m. **directory** n 1 directorio m. 2 guía f.

dirt (dɜːt) n 1 polvo m. 2 suciedad f. **dirty** adj 1 sucio. 2 malo, bajo.

disability (disəˈbiliti) n incapacidad f. **disabled** adj incapacitado, mutilado.

disadvantage (disədˈvɑːntidʒ) n desventaja f.

disagree (disəˈgriː) vi discrepar, no estar de acuerdo.

disappear (disəˈpiə) vi desaparecer.

disappoint (disəˈpɔint) vt defraudar, decepcionar.

disapprove (disəˈpruːv) vi desaprobar, censurar.

disarm (disˈɑːm) vt desarmar. **disarmament** n desarme m.

disaster (diˈzɑːstə) n desastre m.

disc (disk) n disco m. **disc jockey** n presentador de discos m.

discard (diˈskɑːd) vt descartar, desechar.

discern (diˈsəːn) vt discernir. **discernible** adj perceptible. **discerning** adj perspicaz.

discharge (n ˈdistʃɑːdʒ; v disˈtʃɑːdʒ) n 1 descarga f. 2 liberación f. 3 descargue m. 4 pago m. 5 supuración f. vt 1 descargar. 2 exonerar. 3 cumplir.

disciple (diˈsaipəl) n discípulo m.

discipline (ˈdisəplin) n disciplina f. vt disciplinar.

disclose (disˈklouz) vt revelar.

discomfort (disˈkʌmfət) n molestia f. malestar m. vt incomodar, molestar.

disconnect (diskəˈnekt) vt 1 desenchufar, desconectar. 2 disociar, separar.

disconsolate (disˈkɔnsələt) adj desconsolado.

discontinue (diskənˈtinjuː) vt descontinuar.

discord (ˈdiskɔːd) n 1 discordia f. 2 mus disonancia f.

discotheque (ˈdiskətek) n discoteca f.

discount (ˈdiskaunt) n descuento m. rebaja f. vt descontar, rebajar.

discourage (disˈkʌridʒ) vt 1 desanimar. 2 disuadir.

discover (disˈkʌvə) vt descubrir. **discovery** n descubrimiento m.

discredit (disˈkredit) n descrédito m. vt desacreditar.

discreet (disˈkriːt) adj 1 discreto. 2 prudente.

discrepancy (disˈkrepənsi) n discrepancia f.

discrete (disˈkriːt) adj discreto.

discretion (disˈkreʃən) n 1 discreción f. 2 prudencia f.

discriminate (disˈkrimineit) vt distinguir. **discriminate against** vt discriminar contra.

discuss (disˈkʌs) vt discutir, tratar. **discussion** n discusión f. debate m.

disease (diˈziːz) n enfermedad f.

disembark (disimˈbɑːk) vt,vi desembarcar. **disembarkation** n desembarque m.

disfigure (disˈfigə) vt desfigurar.

disgrace (disˈgreis) n 1 desgracia f. vergüenza f. vt deshonrar.

disgruntled (disˈgrʌntəld) adj malhumorado.

disguise (disˈgaiz) n disfraz m. vt disfrazar.

disgust (disˈgʌst) n 1 repugnancia f. 2 disgusto m. vt repugnar. **disgusting** adj repugnante.

dish (diʃ) n plato m. fuente f. **dishcloth** n paño de cocina m.

dishearten (disˈhɑːtn) vt desanimar.

dishevelled (diˈʃevəld) adj despeinado.

dishonest (disˈɔnist) adj tramposo, falso.

dishonour (disˈɔnə) n deshonra f. deshonor m. vt deshonrar.

disillusion (disiˈluːʒən) n desilusión f. vt desilusionar.

disinfect (disinˈfekt) vt desinfectar. **disinfectant** n,adj desinfectante m.

disinherit (disinˈherit) vt desheredar.

disintegrate (disˈintigreit) vi desintegrarse, desmoronarse. **disintegration** n disgregación, desintegración f.

disinterested (disˈintrəstid) adj desinteresado.

disjointed (disˈdʒɔintid) adj dislocado, desarticulado.

dislike (disˈlaik) n aversión, antipatía f. vt aborrecer, tener aversión a or antipatía a.

dislocate (ˈdisləkeit) vt dislocar. **dislocation** n 1 dislocación f. 2 anat descoyuntamiento m.

dismal (ˈdizməl) adj 1 triste. 2 sombrío.

dismantle (disˈmæntl) vt desmantelar.

dismay (disˈmei) n 1 consternación f. 2 desaliento m. vt consternar.

dismiss (disˈmis) vt 1 descartar. 2 licenciar, despedir. 3 dar por terminado. **dismissal** n despedida m.

dismount (disˈmaunt) vt desmontar.

disobey (disəˈbei) vt,vi desobedecer. **disobedient** adj desobediente. **disobedience** n desobediencia f.

disorder (disˈɔːdə) n 1 desorden, disturbio m. 2 med trastorno m. vt desordenar.

disorganized (disˈɔːgənaizd) adj desorganizado.

disown (disˈoun) vt repudiar, rechazar.

disparage (disˈpæridʒ) vt desacreditar, despre-

187

ciar. **disparagement** n menosprecio, descrédito m.

dispassionate (dis'pæʃənət) adj desapasionado, imparcial.

dispatch (dis'pætʃ) n 1 despacho m. 2 expedición f. 3 comunicación f. vt despachar, expedir.

dispel (dis'pel) vt dispersar.

dispense (dis'pens) vt 1 dispensar. 2 administrar. **dispense with** prescindir de. **dispensary** n dispensario m.

disperse (dis'pə:s) vt dispersar.

displace (dis'pleis) vt 1 desplazar. 2 desalojar. **displacement** n cambio de sitio m.

display (dis'plei) n 1 despliegue m. 2 exhibición f. vt 1 desplegar. 2 exhibir.

displease (dis'pli:z) vt 1 desagradar. 2 ofender, disgustar.

dispose (dis'pouz) vt disponer, arreglar. **disposable** adj disponible. **disposal** n 1 disposición, colocación f. 2 enajenación f. **disposition** n 1 disposición f. 2 tendencia f. 3 humor m.

disprove (dis'pru:v) vt refutar.

dispute (dis'pju:t) n 1 disputa f. 2 litigio m. vt,vi 1 disputar. 2 poner en duda, cuestionar.

disqualify (dis'kwolifai) vt descalificar, incapacitar. **disqualification** n 1 descalificación f. 2 inhabilitación f.

disregard (disri'ga:d) n 1 descuido m. 2 desprecio m. 3 desconsideración f. vt 1 despreciar. 2 pasar por alto.

disreputable (dis'repjutəbəl) adj 1 de mala fama, despreciable. 2 bajo. **disrepute** n 1 deshonra f. descrédito m.

disrespect (disri'spekt) n 1 falta de respeto f. desacato m. **disrespectful** adj irrespetuoso.

disrupt (dis'rʌpt) vt 1 desorganizar. 2 trastornar. 3 romper. **disruption** n 1 desorganización f. 2 ruptura f.

dissatisfy (di'sætisfai) vt 1 desagradar. 2 no dar satisfacción. **dissatisfaction** n descontento m.

dissect (di'sekt) vt 1 disecar. 2 seccionar. **dissection** n disección f.

dissent (di'sent) n 1 disentimiento m. disidencia f. vt 1 disentir. 2 disidir.

dissimilar (di'simila) adj desigual, disímil. **dissimilarity** n 1 disimilitud f. 2 disparidad f.

dissociate (di'souʃieit) vt disociar.

dissolve (di'zɔlv) vt disolver. vi 1 disolverse. 2 desaparecer.

dissuade (di'sweid) vt disuadir.

distance ('distəns) n distancia f. vt distanciar. **distant** adj distante, lejano.

distaste (dis'teist) n disgusto m. aversión f. **distasteful** adj desagradable, repugnante.

distil (dis'til) vt destilar. **distillation** n destilación f. **distillery** n destilería f.

distinct (dis'tiŋkt) adj distinto, preciso, claro. **distinction** n distinción f. **distinctive** adj distintivo, característico.

distinguish (dis'tiŋgwiʃ) vt distinguir. **distinguished** adj eminente.

distort (dis'tɔ:t) vt torcer, falsear. **distortion** n distorsión f. torcimiento m.

distract (dis'trækt) vt 1 distraer. 2 perturbar, enloquecer. **distraction** n distracción f.

distraught (dis'trɔ:t) adj 1 distraído. 2 enloquecido.

distress (dis'tres) n 1 dolor m. aflicción f. 2 miseria f. infortunio m. vt afligir, apenar.

distribute (dis'tribju:t) vt distribuir, repartir. **distribution** n distribución f. repartimiento m.

district ('distrikt) n 1 distrito m. 2 región f. 3 sector m.

distrust (dis'trʌst) vt desconfiar. **distrustful** adj desconfiado.

disturb (dis'tə:b) vt 1 molestar, perturbar. 2 desordenar, alterar. 3 inquietar. **disturbance** n 1 perturbación f. 2 desorden, tumulto, disturbio m. 3 trastorno m.

ditch (ditʃ) n 1 zanja f. 2 trinchera f.

ditto ('ditou) n ídem, lo mismo.

divan (di'væn) n diván m.

dive (daiv) vi 1 zambullirse. 2 aviat picar. n 1 zambullida f. 2 salto m. **diving board** n trampolín m.

diverge (dai'və:dʒ) vi divergir.

diverse (dai'və:s) adj 1 diverso, diferente. 2 variado. **diversity** n diversidad f.

divert (dai'və:t) vt 1 divertir, entretener. 2 desviar, apartar. **diversion** n 1 diversión, distracción f. 2 desviación f.

divide (di'vaid) vt dividir, partir. vi dividirse, separarse. **divisible** adj divisible. **division** n 1 división f. 2 desunión f.

dividend ('dividend) n dividendo m.

divine (di'vain) adj divino. vt adivinar. **divinity** n 1 divinidad f. 2 teología f.

divorce (di'vɔ:s) n divorcio m. vi divorciarse.

divulge (di'vʌldʒ) vt divulgar.

dizzy ('dizi) adj 1 vertiginoso. 2 aturdido. **dizziness** n 1 vértigo m. 2 desvanecimiento m.

do* (du:) vt hacer. vi hacer, obrar, portarse. do

away with eliminar. **do up** atar, arreglar. **how do you do?** ¿cómo está Usted?

docile ('dousail) adj dócil.

dock[1] (dɔk) n 1 dique m. 2 muelle m. **dockyard** n 1 astillero m. 2 arsenal m.

dock[2] (dɔk) vt 1 descolar, recortar. 2 rebajar.

dock[3] (dɔk) bot n malva silvestre, romaza f.

doctor ('dɔktə) n 1 doctor m. 2 médico m. vt 1 medicinar. 2 inf adulterar.

doctrine ('dɔktrin) n doctrina f.

document ('dɔkjumənt) n documento m. vt documentar. **documentary** adj,n documental m.

dodge (dɔdʒ) vt esquivar, evitar, eludir. n regate m. maña f.

does (dʌz) v see **do**.

dog (dɔg) n perro m. **dog days** n pl caniculares m pl. **dogged** adj tenaz. ~vt seguir los pasos de.

dogma ('dɔgmə) n dogma m. **dogmatic** adj dogmático.

dole (doul) n 1 limosna f. 2 subsidio de paro m. **be on the dole** estar parado.

doll (dɔl) n muñeca f.

dollar ('dɔlə) n dólar m.

dolphin ('dɔlfin) n delfín m.

domain (də'mein) n dominio m. propiedad f.

dome (doum) n arch cúpula f. domo m.

domestic (də'mestik) adj 1 doméstico. 2 interno. **domesticate** vt domesticar.

dominate ('dɔmineit) vt dominar. **dominant** adj dominante. **domineer** vt,vi dominar, tiranizar. **domineering** adj dominante.

dominion (də'miniən) n dominio m.

donate (dou'neit) vt donar. **donation** n donativo, regalo m.

done (dʌn) v see **do**.

donkey ('dɔŋki) n burro m.

donor ('dounə) n donador, donante m.

doom (du:m) n 1 condena f. 2 perdición f. 3 juicio final m. **doomsday** n día del juicio final m. ~vt condenar.

door (dɔ:) n puerta f. **doorbell** n timbre m. campanilla f. **doorhandle** n mano de la puerta, empuñadura f. **doorknob** n tirador de puerta, botón m. **doorknocker** n llamador m. aldaba f. **doormat** n felpudo m.

dope (doup) n 1 inf narcótico m. droga f. 2 grasa lubrificante m. vi drogarse, narcotizarse.

dormant ('dɔ:mənt) adj durmiente, inactivo, latente.

dormitory ('dɔ:mitri) n dormitorio m.

dormouse ('dɔ:maus) n zool lirón m.

dose (dous) n dosis f. vt dar una dosis. **dosage** n dosificación, dosis f.

dot (dɔt) n punto m. vt puntear.

dote (dout) vi 1 chochear. 2 idolatrar. **dote on** estar chocho por.

double ('dʌbəl) adj,n doble m. vt 1 doblar. 2 redoblar. **double bass** n mus contrabajo m. **double-cross** n traición f. vt traicionar. **double-decker bus** n autobús de dos pisos m.

doubt (daut) n duda f. vt,vi dudar. **doubtful** adj dudoso, incierto.

dough (dou) n masa, pasta f. **doughnut** n buñuelo m.

dove (dʌv) n paloma f. **dovecote** n palomar f.

dowdy ('daudi) adj poco atractivo.

down[1] (daun) adv abajo. **down with...!** ¡...abajo! **upside down** al revés.

down[2] (daun) n plumón m. pelusa f.

downcast ('daunka:st) adj deprimido, abatido, bajo.

downfall ('daunfɔ:l) n 1 caída f. 2 ruina f. hundimiento m.

downhearted (daun'ha:tid) adj descorazonado, desalentado.

downhill ('daunhil) adv cuesta abajo.

downpour ('daunpɔ:) n chaparrón, chubasco m.

downright ('daunrait) adv 1 en absoluto, categóricamente. 2 francamente. adj directo, franco, claro.

downstairs (daun'stɛəz) adv escalera abajo. **go downstairs** bajar la escalera. ~n la planta baja f.

downstream (daun'stri:m) adv río abajo, corriente abajo.

downtrodden ('dauntrɔdn) adj oprimido, tiranizado.

downward ('daunwəd) adj descendente.

downwards ('daunwədz) adv hacia abajo, de arriba abajo.

dowry ('dauəri) n dote f.

doze (douz) vi dormitar. n sueño ligero m.

dozen ('dʌzən) n docena f.

drab (dræb) adj 1 pardo. 2 monótono.

draft (dra:ft) n 1 plan, esquema m. 2 comm giro m. letra de cambio f. vt 1 redactar. 2 llamar al servicio militar.

drag (dræg) vt arrastrar. **drag on** prolongar. n 1 estorbo m. 2 inf lata f.

dragon ('drægən) n dragón m. **dragonfly** n libélula f.

drain (drein) n 1 zanja f. 2 desagüe m. vt vaciar

drake

desaguar. **drainage** n desagüe. **drainpipe** n tubo de desagüe.

drake (dreik) n pato m.

dram (dræm) n 1 dracma f. 2 trago de bebida m.

drama ('drɑːmə) n drama m. **dramatic** adj dramático. **dramatist** n dramaturgo m. **dramatize** vt dramatizar.

drank (dræŋk) v see **drink**.

drape (dreip) n colgadura f. vt 1 cubrir con ropa. 2 recoger en pliegues.

draper ('dreipə) n pañero m. **drapery** n 1 pañería f. 2 colgaduras f pl.

drastic ('dræstik) adj 1 drástico. 2 enérgico.

draught (drɑːft) n 1 corriente de aire f. 2 trago m. **draughty** adj lleno de corrientes de aire. **draughts** n pl game juego de damas m. **draughtsman** n delineante m.

draw* (drɔː) n 1 sport empate m. 2 rifa f. sorteo m. vt 1 sacar, extraer. 2 arrastrar. 3 sortear. vi 1 tirar arrostrando. 2 atraer. 3 dibujar. 4 desenvainar la espada. 5 game empatar. **drawbridge** n puente levadizo m. **drawer** n 1 cajón m. 2 comm girador m. **drawers** n pl calzoncillos m pl. **drawing** n dibujo m. **drawing board** tablero de dibujo m. **drawing pin** n chincheta f. **drawing room** n salón m.

drawl (drɔːl) n voz lenta f. vt pronunciar lentamente. vi arrastrar las palabras.

dread (dred) n 1 miedo m. 2 terror, pavor m. vt temer. **dreadful** adj 1 terrible. 2 espantoso.

dream* (driːm) n sueño m. vi,vt soñar.

dreary ('driəri) adj 1 triste. 2 lúgubre. 3 monótono.

dredge (dredʒ) n draga m. vt dragar.

dregs (dregz) n pl 1 heces f pl. 2 sedimento m.

drench (drentʃ) vt 1 mojar. 2 empapar. 3 saturar.

dress (dres) n 1 vestido m. 2 ropa f. **evening dress** 1 traje de noche m. 2 traje de etiqueta m. **dressmaker** n costurera, modista f. ~vt 1 vestir. 2 cul aliñar. vi vestirse. **dress up** vestirse de etiqueta. **dress circle** n anfiteatro m. **dress rehearsal** n ensayo general m.

dresser[1] ('dresə) n 1 persona que ayuda a vestir f. 2 él que se viste de manera especial m.

dresser[2] ('dresə) n tocador m.

dressing ('dresiŋ) n 1 acción de vestir f. 2 cul aderezo, condimento m. 3 med vendaje m. **dressing-gown** n bata f. peinador m. **dressing-room** n cuarto de vestir m. **dressing-table** n mueble tocador m.

drew (druː) v see **draw**.

dribble ('dribəl) n 1 goteo m. 2 sport regate m. vi gotear. vt sport regatear.

drift (drift) n 1 naut deriva f. 2 montón m. 3 tendencia f. 4 intención f. vi 1 ir sin rumbo. 2 desviar. 3 amontonar.

drill (dril) n 1 tech taladro, perforador m. 2 mil instrucción f. vt 1 taladrar, perforar. 2 entrenar. 3 enseñar instrucción a.

drink* (driŋk) n 1 bebida f. 2 trago m. vt,vi beber. **drinkable** adj potable. **drinking water** n agua potable m.

drip (drip) n 1 goteo m. 2 gota f. vi gotear, chorrear. **drip-dry** adj de lava y pon.

drive* (draiv) n 1 paseo m. 2 impulso, empuje m. 3 calzada f. vt 1 empujar, mover. 2 conducir, guiar. vi mot conducir. **driver** n mot conductor, chófer m. **driving licence** n permiso de conducir. **driving test** n examen de conducir m.

drivel ('drivəl) n tonterías f pl. vi decir tonterías.

drizzle ('drizəl) vi lloviznar. n llovizna f.

drone[1] (droun) n zángano, abejón m.

drone[2] (droun) vi zumbar.

droop (druːp) vi 1 marchitarse. 2 desanimarse. **drooping** adj bajo, caído.

drop (drɔp) n 1 gota f. 2 descenso m. caída f. 3 pastilla f. vt 1 dejar caer. 2 abandonar. 3 omitir. 4 bajar. vi 1 caer. 2 descender. **drop out** vi 1 desaparecer. 2 quedarse atrás, rezagarse.

drought (draut) n sequía f.

drove (drouv) v see **drive**.

drown (draun) vt 1 ahogar. 2 inundar. vi ahogarse.

drowse (drauzi) vi dormitar. **drowsy** adj soñoliento. **be drowsy** tener sueño.

drudge (drʌdʒ) n esclavo m. vi trabajar penosamente. **drudgery** n trabajo penoso m.

drug (drʌg) n 1 droga f. narcótico m. vt drogar, narcotizar.

drum (drʌm) n 1 tambor m. 2 bombo m. 3 barril m. vi mus tocar el tambor. **drummer** n tambor m.

drunk (drʌŋk) v see **drink**. **drunken** adj borracho, bebido m. **drunkenness** n borrachera f.

dry (drai) adj 1 seco. 2 árido. vt secar. **dry-clean** vt lavar en seco.

dual ('djuəl) adj doble. **duality** n dualidad f. **dual carriageway** n pista doble f.

dubious ('djuːbiəs) adj 1 dudoso. 2 ambiguo.

duchess ('dʌtʃis) n duquesa f.

duck[1] (dʌk) n pato m. **duckling** n patito m.

duck[2] (dʌk) *vt* chapuzar. *vi* agacharse.

duct (dʌkt) *n* conducto, canal, tubo *m*.

dud (dʌd) *n* **1** fracaso, fracasado *m*. **2** *mil* granada fallida *f*. *adj* defectuoso, inútil.

due (dju:) *adj* **1** debido. **2** merecido. **3** conveniente. **4** esperado. *n* deuda *f*. merecido *m*.

duel ('djuəl) *n* duelo *m*. *vi* batirse en duelo. **duellist** *n* duelista *m*.

duet (dju'et) *n mus* dúo *m*.

dug (dʌg) *v* see **dig**.

duke (dju:k) *n* duque *m*.

dull (dʌl) *adj* **1** sombrío. **2** deslustrado. **3** sordo. **4** torpe. **5** tonto, estúpido. *vt* **1** embotar. **2** entristecer.

dumb (dʌm) *adj* mudo *m*. **dumbfound** *vt* **1** confundir. **2** dejar atónito. **dumbfounded** *adj* confuso, pasmado, atónito.

dummy ('dʌmi) *n* **1** maniquí, muñeco *m*. **2** tonto, zoquete *m*. **3** *game* muerto *m*. *adj* falso.

dump (dʌmp) *n* **1** depósito de basuras *m*. montón *m*. *vt* **1** vaciar, descargar. **2** dejar.

dunce (dʌns) *n* tonto, ignorante *m*.

dune (dju:n) *n* duna *f*.

dung (dʌŋ) *n* estiércol *m*.

dungeon ('dʌndʒən) *n* calabozo *m*. mazmorra *f*.

duplicate (*adj,n* 'dju:plikət; *v* 'dju:plikeit) *adj* duplicado. *n* duplicado, doble *m*. copia *f*. *vt* duplicar.

durable ('djuərəbəl) *adj* durable.

duration (djuə'reiʃən) *n* duración *f*.

during ('djuəriŋ) *prep* durante.

dusk (dʌsk) *n* crepúsculo, anochecer *m*. **dusky** *adj* **1** obscuro. **2** sombrío. **3** pardo.

dust (dʌst) *n* polvo *m*. **dusty** *adj* polvoriento. ~*vt* quitar el polvo a. **dustbin** *n* cajón de basura *m*. **duster** *n* **1** trapo, paño *m*. **2** plumero *m*. **3** guardapolvo *m*. **dustman** *n* basurero *m*. **dustpan** *n* recogedor de basura *m*.

Dutch (dʌtʃ) *adj,n* holandés. **Dutchman** *n* holandés *m*.

duty ('dju:ti) *n* **1** deber *m*. obligación *f*. **2** derechos de aduana *m pl*. impuesto *m*. **on duty 1** de servicio. **2** de guardia. **duty-free** *adj* libre de derechos de aduana. **dutiful** *adj* obediente.

duvet ('du:vei) *n* colcha de plumón *f*.

dwarf (dwɔ:f) *n,adj* enano *m*. *vt* empequeñecer.

dwell* (dwel) *vt* habitar, morar, vivir. **dwelling** *n* **1** morada *f*. **2** residencia *f*. **3** casa *f*.

dwindle ('dwindl) *vi* disminuir, mermar, reducirse.

dye (dai) *n* tintura *f*. tinte *m*. *vt* teñir, colorar.

dyke (daik) *n* **1** dique *m*. presa *f*. **2** zanja *f*.

dynamic (dai'næmik) *adj* dinámico.

dynamite ('dainəmait) *n* dinamita *f*. *vt* volar con dinamita.

dynasty ('dinəsti) *n* dinastía *f*. **dynastic** *adj* dinástico.

dysentery ('disəntri) *n med* disentería *f*.

E

each (i:tʃ) *adj* cada *invar*. *pron* cada uno *m*. cada una *f*. **each other** (el) uno a(l) otro. ~*adv* por persona.

eager ('i:gə) *adj* ansioso, anhelante. **be eager for** ansiar. **be eager to** tener vivos deseos de. **eagerness** *n* ansia *f*. anhelo *m*.

eagle ('i:gəl) *n* águila *f*.

ear[1] (iə) *n* **1** oreja *f*. **2** oído *m*. **eardrum** *n* tímpano *m*. **earmark** *vt* **1** reservar. **2** destinar. **earphones** *n pl* auriculares *m pl*. **earring** *n* pendiente *m*.

ear[2] (iə) *n bot* espiga *f*.

earl (ə:l) *n* conde *m*.

early ('ə:li) *adj* **1** temprano, precoz. **2** primero, primitivo. *adv* **1** temprano, pronto. **2** a principios.

earn (ə:n) *vt* **1** ganar. **2** devengar. **earnings** *n pl* **1** ingresos *m pl*. **2** ganancias *f pl*.

earnest ('ə:nist) *adj* **1** serio, formal. **2** fervoroso, ardiente. **in earnest** en serio.

earth (ə:θ) *n* tierra *f*. *vt tech* conectar a tierra. **earthenware** *n* loza de barro *f*. **earthly** *adj* terrenal. **earthquake** *n* terremoto *m*. **earthworm** *n* lombriz de tierra *f*. **earthy** *adj* **1** terroso. **2** mundano. **3** grosero, basto.

earwig ('iəwig) *n* tijereta *f*.

ease (i:z) *n* **1** facilidad *f*. soltura *f*. **2** desenvoltura *f*. **3** comodidad *f*. **4** alivio *m*. *vt* aliviar, mitigar.

easel ('i:zəl) *n* caballete *m*.

east (i:st) *n* este, oriente *m*. *adj* del este, oriental. *adv* al este. **easterly** *adj* este, del este. **eastern** *adj* del este, oriental. **eastward** *adv* al este. **eastwards** *adv* hacia el este.

Easter ('i:stə) *n* Pascua de Resurrección *f*.

easy ('i:zi) *adj* **1** fácil. **2** cómodo, holgado. **3** pausado. **easygoing** *adj* **1** acomodadizo. **2** indolente, holgazán. **3** sereno.

eat* (i:t) *vt,vi* comer. **eat away** corroer. **eat into** desgastar, reducir. **eat up** comerse, devorar.

eavesdrop (ˈiːvzdrɔp) *vi* fisgonear, escuchar a escondidas. **eavesdropper** *n* fisgón *m*.

ebb (eb) *n* reflujo, menguante *m*. *vi* **1** bajar, menguar. **2** decaer.

ebony (ˈebəni) *n* ébano *m*.

eccentric (ikˈsentrik) *adj,n* excéntrico *m*. **eccentricity** *n* excentricidad *f*.

ecclesiastical (ikliːziˈæstikəl) *also* **ecclesiastic** *adj* eclesiástico.

echo (ˈekou) *n, pl* **echoes** eco *m*. *vi* resonar, hacer eco.

eclair (eiˈklɛə) *n* bizcocho relleno *m*.

eclipse (iˈklips) *n* eclipse *m*. *vt* eclipsar.

ecology (iːˈkɔlədʒi) *n* ecología *f*. **ecological** *adj* ecológico. **ecologist** *n* ecólogo *m*.

economy (iˈkɔnəmi) *n* economía *f*. **economic** *adj* económico. **economics** *n pl* economía política *f*. económicas *f pl*. **economist** *n* economista *m,f*. **economize** *vi* economizar.

ecstasy (ˈekstəsi) *n* éxtasis *m*. **ecstatic** *adj* extático.

Ecuador (ˈekwədɔː) *n* El Ecuador *m*. **Ecuadorian** *adj,n* ecuatoriano.

eczema (ˈeksimə) *n* eczema *m*.

edge (edʒ) *n* **1** filo *m*. **2** borde, margen *m*. **3** canto *m*. **4** extremo *m*. *vt* **1** afilar. **2** orlar, ribetear. **edgeways** *adj* de canto. **edgy** *adj inf* nervioso.

edible (ˈedibəl) *adj* comestible.

edict (ˈiːdikt) *n* edicto *m*.

edit (ˈedit) *vt* editar. **editor** *n* **1** editor *m*. **2** redactor en jefe *m*.

edition (iˈdiʃən) *n* edición *f*.

editorial (ediˈtɔːriəl) *adj,n* editorial *m*. **editorial staff** redacción *f*.

educate (ˈedjukeit) *vt* **1** educar. **2** instruir. **educated** *adj* culto. **education** *n* educación *f*. **educational** *adj* educacional.

eel (iːl) *n* anguila *f*.

eerie (ˈiəri) *adj* misterioso.

effect (iˈfekt) *n* **1** efecto *m*. **2** impresión *f*. **side effect** efecto secundario. ~*vt* efectuar. **effective** *adj* **1** eficaz. **2** efectivo.

effeminate (iˈfeminət) *adj* afeminado.

effervesce (efəˈves) *vi* estar en efervescencia. **effervescence** *n* efervescencia *f*. **effervescent** *adj* efervescente.

efficient (iˈfiʃənt) *adj* **1** eficiente. **2** eficaz. **efficiency** *n* **1** eficiencia *f*. **2** eficacia *f*.

effigy (ˈefidʒi) *n* efigie *f*.

effort (ˈefət) *n* esfuerzo *m*. **effortless** *adj* fácil.

effusion *n* efusión *f*. **effusive** *adj* efusivo.

egg (eg) *n* huevo *m*. **eggbeater** *n* cul batidor *m*.

egg² (eg) *vt* **egg on** azuzar.

ego (ˈiːgou) *n* el yo, ego *m*. **egocentric** *adj* egocéntrico. **egoism** *n* egoísmo *m*. **egoist** *n* egoísta *m,f*. **egoistical** *adj* egoísta. **egotism** *n* egotismo *m*.

Egypt (ˈiːdʒipt) *n* Egipto *m*. **Egyptian** *adj,n* egipcio.

eiderdown (ˈaidədaun) *n* edredón *m*.

eight (eit) *adj,n* ocho *m*. **eighth** *adj* octavo.

eighteen (eiˈtiːn) *adj* dieciocho. **eighteenth** *adj* decimoctavo.

eighty (ˈeiti) *adj* ochenta. **eightieth** *adj* octogésimo.

either (ˈaiðə) *adj* **1** cualquier. **2** ambos. *pron* cualquiera *or* ninguno de los dos. *conj* **either...or** o...o. *adv* tampoco.

ejaculate (iˈdʒækjuleit) *vt* **1** exclamar. **2** *med* eyacular. **ejaculation** *n* **1** exclamación *f*. **2** *med* eyaculación *f*.

eject (iˈdʒekt) *vt* **1** expulsar, echar. **2** *law* desahuciar. **ejection** *n* **1** expulsión *f*. **2** *law* desahucio *m*. **ejector** *n* expulsor *m*.

elaborate (*adj* iˈlæbrət; *v* iˈlæbəreit) *adj* **1** complicado. **2** detallado. *vt* elaborar. **elaborate on** ampliar. **elaboration** *n* elaboración *f*.

elapse (iˈlæps) *vi* transcurrir.

elastic (iˈlæstik) *adj,n* elástico *m*. **elasticity** *n* elasticidad *f*.

elated (iˈleitid) *adj* **1** jubiloso. **2** exaltado. **elation** *n* **1** júbilo, regocijo *m*. **2** exaltación *f*.

elbow (ˈelbou) *n* codo *m*. *vt* empujar a codazos.

elder¹ (ˈeldə) *adj* mayor. *n* anciano *m*. **elderly** *adj* mayor, de edad.

elder² (ˈeldə) *n* saúco *m*. **elderberry** *n* baya del saúco *f*.

elect (iˈlekt) *vt* elegir. **elect to** optar por. ~*adj* electo. **election** *n* elección *f*. **elector** *n* elector *m*. **electoral** *adj* electoral. **electorate** *n* electorado *m*.

electric (iˈlektrik) *adj also* **electrical** eléctrico.

electrician (ilekˈtriʃən) *n* electricista *m,f*.

electricity (ilekˈtrisiti) *n* electricidad *f*.

electrify (iˈlektrifai) *vt* **1** electrificar. **2** electrizar. **electrification** *n* electrificación *f*.

electrocute (iˈlektrəkjuːt) *vt* electrocutar.

electrode (iˈlektroud) *n* electrodo *m*.

electron (iˈlektrɔn) *n* electrón *m*.

electronic (ilekˈtrɔnik) *adj* electrónico. **electronics** *n* electrónica *f*.

elegant ('eligənt) *adj* elegante. **elegance** *n* elegancia *f.*

element ('eləmənt) *n* elemento *m.* **elemental** *adj* elemental. **elementary** *adj* elemental.

elephant ('eləfənt) *n* elefante *m.*

elevate ('eləveit) *vt* elevar. **elevation** *n* elevación *f.*

elevator ('eləveitə) *n* 1 montacargas *m invar.* 2 elevador *m.*

eleven (i'levən) *adj,n* once *m.* **eleventh** *adj* undécimo.

elf (elf) *n, pl* **elves** duende, enanito *m.*

eligible ('elidʒibəl) *adj* elegible. **eligibility** *n* elegibilidad *f.*

eliminate (i'limineit) *vt* eliminar. **elimination** *n* eliminación *f.*

elite (ei'li:t) *n* minoría selecta, élite *f.*

ellipse (i'lips) *n* elipse *f.* **elliptical** *adj* elíptico.

elm (elm) *n* olmo *m.*

elocution (elə'kju:ʃən) *n* elocución *f.*

elope (i'loup) *vi* fugarse. **elopement** *n* fuga *f.*

eloquent ('eləkwənt) *adj* elocuente. **eloquence** *n* elocuencia *f.*

else (els) *adv* 1 más. 2 de otra manera. **elsewhere** *adv* en or a otra parte.

elucidate (i'lu:sideit) *vt* dilucidar, elucidar. **elucidation** *n* elucidación *f.*

elude (i'lu:d) *vt* eludir, esquivar. **elusive** *adj* difícil de encontrar, esquivo.

emaciated (i'meisieitid) *adj* demacrado.

emanate ('eməneit) *vi* emanar. **emanation** *n* emanación *f.*

emancipate (i'mænsipeit) *vt* emancipar. **emancipation** *n* emancipación *f.*

embalm (im'ba:m) *vt* embalsamar.

embankment (im'bæŋkmənt) *n* 1 terraplén *m.* 2 dique *m.*

embargo (im'ba:gou) *n, pl* **embargoes** 1 embargo *m.* 2 prohibición, suspensión *f.*

embark (im'ba:k) *vi* embarcarse. **embarkation** *n* 1 embarco *m.* 2 embarque *m.*

embarrass (im'bærəs) *vt* 1 turbar, azorar. 2 avergonzar. **embarrassing** *adj* 1 embarazoso. 2 violento. **embarrassment** *n* turbación *f.*

embassy ('embəsi) *n* embajada *f.*

embellish (im'beliʃ) *vt* embellecer. **embellishment** *n* embellecimiento *m.*

embers ('embəz) *n pl* rescoldo *m.* ascua *f*

embezzle (im'bezəl) *vt* malversar. **embezzlement** *n* malversación *f.* **embezzler** *n* malversador *m.*

embitter (im'bitə) *vt* amargar.

emblem ('embləm) *n* emblema *m.*

embody (im'bɔdi) *vt* encarnar. **embodiment** *n* encarnación *f.*

emboss (im'bɔs) *vt* estampar en relieve.

embrace (im'breis) *vt,vi* 1 abrazar. 2 abarcar. *n* abrazo *m.*

embroider (im'brɔidə) *vt* 1 bordar. 2 adornar. **embroidery** *n* bordado *m.*

embryo ('embriou) *n* embrión *m.* **embryonic** *adj* embrionario.

emerald ('emrəld) *n* esmeralda *f.*

emerge (i'mə:dʒ) *vi* emerger. **emergence** *n* emergencia *f.*

emergency (i'mə:dʒənsi) *n* emergencia *f.*

emigrate ('emigreit) *vi* emigrar. **emigrant** *n,adj* emigrante. **emigration** *n* emigración *f.*

eminent ('eminənt) *adj* eminente. **eminence** *n* eminencia *f.*

emit (i'mit) *vt* 1 emitir. 2 arrojar. 3 despedir. **emission** *n* emisión *f.*

emotion (i'mouʃən) *n* emoción. *f.* **emotional** *adj* 1 emocional. 2 emocionante.

empathy ('empəθi) *n* empatía *f.*

emperor ('empərə) *n* emperador *m.*

emphasis ('emfəsis) *n* énfasis *m.* **emphasize** *vt* 1 acentuar. 2 subrayar, recalcar. **emphatic** *adj* enfático.

empire ('empaiə) *n* imperio *m.*

empirical (im'pirikəl) *adj* empírico. **empiricism** *n* empirismo *m.*

employ (im'plɔi) *vt* emplear. **employee** *n* empleado *m.* **employer** *n* patrono, empresario *m.* **employment** *n* empleo *m.*

empower (im'pauə) *vt* 1 autorizar. 2 habilitar.

empress ('emprəs) *n* emperatriz *f.*

empty ('empti) *adj* 1 vacío. 2 vano. *vt* vaciar. *vi* vaciarse. **emptiness** *n* vacío *m.* **empty-handed** *adj* con las manos vacías. **empty-headed** *adj* tonto.

emu ('i:mju:) *n* emú *m.*

emulate ('emjuleit) *vt* emular. **emulation** *n* emulación *f.*

emulsion (i'mʌlʃən) *n* emulsión *f.*

enable (i'neibəl) *vt* permitir, poner en condiciones.

enact (i'nækt) *vt* 1 decretar. 2 *law* promulgar. 3 representar.

enamel (i'næməl) *n* esmalte *m.* *vt* esmaltar.

enchant (in'tʃa:nt) *vt* encantar. **enchanting** *adj* encantador.

encircle (in'sə:kəl) *vt* cercar, rodear.

enclose (in'klouz) *vt* 1 cercar. 2 encerrar. 3 incluir, adjuntar. **enclosure** *n* 1 cercado, recinto *m.* 2 inclusión *f*

encore ('ɔŋkɔ:) *interj* ¡bis! ¡que se repita! *n* repetición *f*.

encounter (in'kauntə) *n* encuentro *m*. *vt* encontrar, tropezar.

encourage (in'kʌridʒ) *vt* 1 animar, alentar. 2 fomentar, estimular. **encouragement** *n* 1 aliento, estímulo *m*. 2 fomento *m*.

encroach (in'krautʃ) *vi* 1 invadir. 2 usurpar.

encumber (in'kʌmbə) *vt* 1 gravar, cargar. 2 estorbar.

encyclopedia (insaiklə'pi:diə) *n* enciclopedia *f*.

end (end) *n* 1 fin *m*. 2 final *m*. 3 extremo, cabo *m*. punta *f*. *vt,vi* terminar, acabar. **endless** *adj* interminable. **ending** *n* conclusión *f*. fin *m*.

endanger (in'deindʒə) *vt* poner en peligro.

endeavour (in'devə) *n* esfuerzo, empeño *m*. *vt,vi* esforzar, procurar.

endemic (en'demik) *adj* endémico.

endive ('endaiv) *n* escarola endibia *f*.

endorse (in'dɔ:s) *vt* endosar. **endorsement** *n* 1 endoso *m*. 2 *mot* nota de inhabilitación *f*. **endorser** *n* endosante *m,f*.

endow (in'dau) *vt* dotar. **endowment** *n* 1 dotación *f*. 2 dote *f*.

endure (in'djuə) *vt* 1 aguantar, soportar. 2 resistir. *vi* durar, perdurar. **endurable** *adj* soportable. **endurance** *n* resistencia *f*. aguante *m*.

enemy ('enəmi) *n,adj* enemigo *m*.

energy ('enədʒi) *n* energía *f*. **energetic** *adj* enérgico.

enfold (in'fould) *vt* 1 envolver. 2 abrazar, estrechar.

enforce (in'fɔ:s) *vt* 1 hacer cumplir, imponer. 2 poner en vigor. 3 hacer valer. **enforcement** *n* 1 imposición *f*. 2 ejecución *f*.

engage (in'geidʒ) *vt* 1 alquilar, apalabrar. 2 ocupar. 3 trabar. **be engaged** 1 estar ocupado. 2 estar prometido para casarse. **engagement** *n* 1 compromiso *m*. 2 contrato *m*. **engaging** *adj* simpático, agraciado.

engine ('endʒin) *n* 1 motor *m*. 2 máquina, locomotora *f*. **engine-driver** *n* maquinista *m*.

engineer (endʒi'niə) *n* 1 ingeniero *m*. 2 mecánico *m*. *vt* maquinar, agenciar. **engineering** *n* ingeniería *f*.

England ('ingland) *n* Inglaterra *f*. **English** *adj* inglés. **English** (language) *n* inglés *m*. **Englishman** *n* inglés *m*.

engrave (in'greiv) *vt* grabar. **engraver** *n* grabador *m*. **engraving** *n* grabado *m*.

engross (in'grous) *vt* absorber, acaparar.

engulf (in'gʌlf) *vt* 1 sumergir, hundir. 2 tragar.

enhance (in'hɑ:ns) *vt* realzar.

enigma (i'nigmə) *n* enigma *m*. **enigmatic** *adj* enigmático.

enjoy (in'dʒɔi) *vt* 1 disfrutar de, gozar de. 2 gustar. **enjoyable** *adj* 1 agradable. 2 divertido. **enjoyment** *n* 1 disfrute, goce *m*. 2 gozo, gusto *m*.

enlarge (in'lɑ:dʒ) *vt,vi* 1 extender, ensanchar. 2 aumentar. 3 ampliar. 4 *med* dilatar. **enlargement** *n* 1 extensión *f*. ensanche *m*. 2 aumento *m*. 3 ampliación *f*. 4 *med* dilatación *f*.

enlighten (in'laitn) *vt* 1 instruir, informar. 2 ilustrar, iluminar. **enlightening** *adj* instructivo, informativo. **enlightenment** *n* ilustración *f*.

enlist (in'list) *vt* 1 alistar. 2 granjear, procurar.

enormous (i'nɔ:məs) *adj* enorme. **enormity** *n* enormidad *f*.

enough (i'nʌf) *adj,adv* bastante.

enquire (in'kwaiə) *vt* 1 averiguar. 2 preguntar. 3 informarse de. **enquirer** *n* 1 el que pregunta *m*. 2 investigador *m*. **enquiring** *adj* 1 curioso, investigador. 2 interrogativo. **enquiry** *n* 1 indagación, pesquisa *f*. 2 pregunta, petición de informes *f*. 3 encuesta *f*.

enrage (in'reidʒ) *vt* enfurecer.

enrich (in'ritʃ) *vt* enriquecer. **enrichment** *n* enriquecimiento *m*.

enrol (in'roul) *vt* 1 inscribir. 2 matricular. 3 *mil* alistar. **enrolment** *n* 1 inscripción *f*. 2 matrícula *f*. 3 alistamiento *m*.

ensign ('ensain) *n* 1 insignia *f*. 2 abanderado *m*.

enslave (in'sleiv) *vt* esclavizar. **enslavement** *n* esclavitud *f*.

ensure (in'ʃuə) *vt* asegurar.

entail (in'teil) *vt* 1 ocasionar, acarrear. 2 suponer. 3 *law* vincular.

entangle (in'tæŋgəl) *vt* enredar, embrollar. **entanglement** *n* enredo, embrollo *m*.

enter ('entə) *vi,vt* 1 entrar. 2 ingresar. 3 registrar, asentar. 4 matricular.

enterprise ('entəpraiz) *n* 1 empresa *f*. 2 iniciativa *f*. **enterprising** *adj* emprendedor.

entertain (entə'tein) *vt* 1 entretener. 2 recibir. 3 divertir. **entertainment** *n* 1 entretenimiento *m*. 2 espectáculo *m*.

enthral (in'θrɔ:l) *vt* encantar, embelesar.

enthusiasm (in'θju:ziæzəm) *n* entusiasmo *m*. **enthusiast** *n* entusiasta *m,f*. **enthusiastic** *adj* 1 entusiasta. 2 entusiástico.

entice (in'tais) *vt* tentar, seducir. **enticement** *n* tentación, seducción *f*.

entire (in'taiə) adj entero, completo. **entirety** n totalidad f.

entitle (in'tait) vt 1 titular. 2 dar derecho a. **be entitled** tener derecho.

entity ('entiti) n entidad f. ente m.

entrails ('entreilz) n pl entrañas f pl.

entrance[1] ('entrəns) n 1 entrada f. 2 ingreso m. **entrance hall** vestíbulo m.

entrance[2] (in'trɑːns) vt extasiar, hechizar.

entreat (in'triːt) vt suplicar, implorar. **entreaty** n súplica, imploración f.

entrench (in'trentʃ) vt atrincherar. **entrenchment** n atrincheramiento m.

entrepreneur (ɔntrəprə'nəː) n 1 empresario m. 2 socio capitalista m.

entrust (in'trʌst) vt confiar.

entry ('entri) n 1 entrada f. 2 ingreso m. 3 comm partida f. 4 artículo m. 5 participante m,f. 6 participación f.

entwine (in'twain) vt entrelazar, entretejer.

enunciate (i'nʌnsieit) vt enunciar. **enunciation** n enunciación f.

envelop (in'veləp) vt envolver. **enveloping** adj envolvente.

envelope ('envəloup) n 1 sobre m. 2 envoltura f.

environment (in'vairənmənt) n medio ambiente m. **environmental** adj ambiental.

envisage (in'vizidʒ) vt 1 prever. 2 concebir.

envoy ('envoi) n enviado m.

envy ('envi) vt envidiar. n envidia f.

enzyme ('enzaim) n enzima f.

epaulet ('epəlet) n charretera f.

ephemeral (i'femərəl) adj efímero.

epic ('epik) adj épico. n 1 épica f. 2 epopeya f.

epidemic (epi'demik) adj epidémico. n epidemia f.

epilepsy ('epilepsi) n epilepsia f. **epileptic** adj,n epiléptico m.

epilogue ('epilɔg) n epílogo m.

episcopal (i'piskəpəl) adj episcopal. **episcopate** n episcopado m.

episode ('episoud) n episodio m. **episodic** adj episódico m.

epitaph ('epitaːf) n epitafio m.

epitome (i'pitəmi) n epítome m. **epitomize** vt epitomar.

epoch ('iːpɔk) n época f.

equable ('ekwəbəl) adj 1 uniforme, igual. 2 ecuánime.

equal ('iːkwəl) adj igual. **be equal to** 1 tener fuerzas para. 2 estar a la altura de. ~n igual m,f. vt igualar. **equality** n igualdad f. **equalize** vt igualar. vi empatar.

equate (i'kweit) vt 1 igualar, considerar equivalente. 2 poner en ecuación. **equation** n ecuación f.

equator (i'kweitə) n ecuador m. **equatorial** adj ecuatorial.

equestrian (i'kwestriən) adj ecuestre. n jinete m.

equilateral (iːkwi'lætərəl) adj equilátero.

equilibrium (iːkwi'libriəm) n equilibrio m.

equinox ('iːkwinɔks) n equinoccio m.

equip (i'kwip) vt 1 equipar. 2 dotar, proveer. **equipment** n 1 equipo m. 2 material m. 3 dotes f pl.

equity ('ekwiti) n equidad f. **equitable** adj equitativo.

equivalent (i'kwivələnt) adj equivalente. **equivalence** n equivalencia f.

era ('iərə) n era f.

eradicate (i'rædikeit) vt erradicar. **eradication** n erradicación f.

erase (i'reiz) vt borrar. **eraser** n goma de borrar f.

erect (i'rekt) vt erigir. adj erguido. **erection** n erección f.

ermine ('əːmin) n armiño m.

erode (i'roud) vt 1 erosionar, desgastar. 2 corroer. 3 mermar. **erosion** n 1 erosión f. 2 desgaste m.

erotic (i'rɔtik) adj erótico. **eroticism** n erotismo m.

err (əː) vi 1 errar. 2 pecar.

errand ('erənd) n 1 recado m. 2 misión f. **run an errand** llevar un recado.

erratic (i'rætik) adj 1 desigual. 2 med errático.

error ('erə) n error m. **erroneous** adj erróneo.

erupt (i'rʌpt) vi 1 hacer erupción. 2 estallar. 3 irrumpir. **eruption** n erupción f.

escalate ('eskəleit) vt,vi extender, intensificar. **escalation** n extensión, intensificación f. **escalator** n escalera móvil f.

escalope (i'skæləp) n escalope m.

escape (i'skeip) vt,vi escapar. **escape notice** pasar inadvertido. ~n 1 escape m. 2 fuga f.

escort ('eskɔːt) vt 1 acompañar. 2 mil escoltar. n 1 acompañante m,f. 2 mil escolta f.

Eskimo ('eskimou) adj,n esquimal.

esoteric (esə'terik) adj esotérico.

especial (i'speʃəl) adj 1 especial. 2 particular. **especially** adv especialmente, sobre todo.

espionage ('espiənɑːʒ) n espionaje m.

esplanade ('espləneid) n paseo m.

essay ('esei) n ensayo m. **essayist** n ensayista m,f.

essence ('esəns) n esencia f. **essential** adj 1 esencial. 2 imprescindible.

establish (i'stæbliʃ) vt establecer. **establishment** n establecimiento m. **the Establishment** las clases directoras f pl.

estate (i'steit) n 1 finca, propiedad f. 2 bienes m pl. 3 herencia f. 4 estado m. **estate agent** n corredor de fincas m. **estate car** n rubia f.

esteem (i'sti:m) n estima, estimación f. vt estimar, apreciar.

estimate (n 'estimət; v 'estimeit) n 1 estimación f. 2 cálculo m. 3 tasación f. 4 presupuesto m. vt 1 estimar, calcular. 2 tasar. 3 presupuestar, hacer un presupuesto.

estuary ('estʃuəri) n estuario m.

etching ('etʃiŋ) n aguafuerte, grabado m.

eternal (i'tə:nl) adj eterno.

eternity (i'tə:niti) n eternidad f.

ether ('i:θə) n éter m.

ethereal (i'θiəriəl) adj etéreo.

ethics ('eθiks) n pl ética f. **ethical** adj ético.

Ethiopia (i:θi'oupiə) n Etiopía f. **Ethiopian** adj,n etíope.

ethnic ('eθnik) adj étnico.

etiquette ('etikit) n 1 etiqueta f. 2 honor profesional f.

etymology (eti'mɔlədʒi) n etimología f. **etymological** adj etimológico.

eucalyptus (ju:kə'liptəs) n eucalipto m.

Eucharist ('ju:kərist) n Eucaristía f.

eunuch ('ju:nək) n eunuco m.

euphemism ('ju:fəmizəm) n eufemismo m. **euphemistic** adj eufemístico.

euphoria (ju:'fɔ:riə) n euforia f.

Europe ('juərəp) n Europa f. **European** adj,n europeo.

European Economic Community n Comunidad Económica Europea f.

euthanasia (ju:θə'neiziə) n eutanasia f.

evacuate (i'vækjueit) vt evacuar. **evacuation** n evacuación f. evacuado m.

evade (i'veid) vt evadir, eludir. **evasion** n evasión m. **evasive** adj evasivo.

evaluate (i'væljueit) vt evaluar. **evaluation** n evaluación f.

evangelical (i:væn'dʒelikəl) adj evangélico. **evangelist** n evangelizador m.

evaporate (i'væpəreit) vt,vi evaporar. **evaporation** n evaporación f.

evasive adj evasivo.

eve (i:v) n víspera f.

even ('i:vən) adj 1 llano, liso. 2 constante, invariable, igual. 3 par. **break even** inf salir sin ganar ni perder. ~adv 1 hasta, incluso. 2 aun, todavía. **even if** or **though** aunque, aun cuando. **not even** ni siquiera. ~vt allanar, nivelar.

evening ('i:vniŋ) n 1 atardecer m. 2 noche f. 3 velada f. **good evening!** ¡buenas tardes! ¡buenas noches! ~adj vespertino. **evening class** n clase nocturna f. **evening dress** n traje de etiqueta, traje de noche m.

event (i'vent) n 1 acontecimiento m. 2 caso, evento m. 3 resultado m. **in the event of** en caso de. **eventful** adj accidentado, azaroso. **eventual** adj 1 final. 2 consiguiente. **eventuality** n eventualidad f. **eventually** adv con el tiempo.

ever ('evə) adv 1 siempre. 2 alguna vez. 3 nunca, jamás. **everlasting** adj 1 eterno, perdurable. 2 interminable.

every ('evri) adj 1 cada. 2 todo. **every now and then** de vez en cuando. **every so often** cada cierto tiempo. **everybody** pron todo el mundo. **everyday** adj 1 diario. 2 cotidiano, acostumbrado. 3 corriente, rutinario. **everyone** pron 1 todo el mundo. 2 cada uno. **everything** pron todo. **everywhere** adv 1 en todas partes. 2 dondequiera.

evict (i'vikt) vt desahuciar. **eviction** n desahucio m.

evidence ('evidəns) n 1 evidencia f. 2 prueba f. 3 law testimonio m. declaración f. **give evidence** 1 prestar declaración. 2 dar testimonio. **evident** adj evidente.

evil ('i:vəl) adj 1 malo, pernicioso. 2 malvado. n mal m. maldad f.

evoke (i'vouk) vt evocar.

evolve (i'vɔlv) vt 1 desarrollar. vi evolucionar. **evolution** n 1 evolución f. 2 desarrollo m.

ewe (ju:) n oveja f.

exact (ig'zækt) adj exacto. vt exigir. **exacting** adj 1 exigente. 2 arduo. **exaction** n exacción f. **exactitude** n exactitud f.

exaggerate (ig'zædʒəreit) vt exagerar. **exaggeration** n exageración f.

exalt (ig'zɔ:lt) vt exaltar. **exaltation** n exaltación f.

examine (ig'zæmin) vt 1 examinar. 2 med hacer un reconocimiento. 3 law interrogar. **examination** n 1 examen m. 2 med reconocimiento m. 3 law interrogación f.

example (ig'zɑ:mpəl) n ejemplo m. **make an**

example of castigar de modo ejemplar. **set an example** dar ejemplo.

exasperate (ig'za:spəreit) *vt* exasperar, sacar de quicio. **exasperation** *n* exasperación *f*.

excavate ('ekskəveit) *vt* excavar. **excavation** *n* excavación *f*. **excavator** *n* 1 excavador *m*. 2 *tech* excavadora *f*.

exceed (ik'si:d) *vt* exceder. **exceedingly** *adv* sumamente.

excel (ik'sel) *vi* sobresalir. *vt* aventajar, superar.

excellent ('eksələnt) *adj* excelente. **excellence** *n* excelencia *f*.

except (ik'sept) *vt* exceptuar. *prep* excepto, menos, salvo. **exception** *n* excepción *f*. **exceptional** *adj* excepcional.

excerpt (*n* 'eksə:pt; *v* ek'sə:pt) *n* extracto *m*. *vt* extractar.

excess (*n* ik'ses; *adj* 'ekses) *n* exceso *m*. *adj* excedente. **excessive** *adj* excesivo.

exchange (iks'tʃeindʒ) *vt* 1 cambiar. 2 canjear. 3 intercambiar. *n* 1 cambio *m*. 2 intercambio *m*. **exchangeable** *adj* cambiable, canjeable.

exchequer (iks'tʃekə) *n* hacienda *f*. tesoro público *m*.

excise ('eksaiz) *n* impuestos *m pl*.

excite (ik'sait) *vt* 1 entusiasmar. 2 excitar. provocar. 3 poner nervioso. **exciting** *adj* emocionante, excitante.

exclaim (ik'skleim) *vi,vt* exclamar. **exclamation** *n* exclamación *f*. **exclamation mark** *n* punto de admiración *m*.

exclude (ik'sklu:d) *vt* excluir. **exclusion** *n* exclusión *f*. **exclusive** *adj* 1 exclusivo. 2 selecto. **exclusive of** sin contar, excluyendo.

excommunicate (ekskə'mju:nikeit) *vt* excomulgar. **excommunication** *n* excomunión *f*.

excruciating (ik'skru:ʃieitiŋ) *adj* agudísimo, atroz.

excursion (ik'skə:ʒən) *n* excursión *f*.

excuse (*v* ik'skju:z; *n* ik'skju:s) *vt* 1 excusar, dispensar. 2 disculpar. **excuse me!** ¡perdón! ~*n* 1 excusa *f*. 2 disculpa *f*.

execute ('eksikju:t) *vt* 1 ejecutar. 2 *law* legalizar, otorgar. **execution** *n* 1 ejecución *f*. 2 *law* legalización *f*. otorgamiento *m*. **executioner** *n* verdugo *m*. **executive** *adj* ejecutivo. *n* 1 ejecutivo *m*. 2 director, gerente *m*. **executor** *n* 1 ejecutor *m*. 2 albacea, ejecutor testamentario *m*.

exempt (ig'zempt) *adj* exento. *vt* exentar, eximir, dispensar. **exemption** *n* exención *f*.

exercise ('eksəsaiz) *n* ejercicio *m*. *vt,vi* 1 ejercer. 2 ejercitar.

exert (ig'zə:t) *vt* ejercer, emplear. **exertion** *n* esfuerzo *m*.

exhale (eks'heil) *vt* 1 exhalar. 2 espirar. **exhalation** *n* 1 exhalación *f*. 2 espiración *f*.

exhaust (ig'zɔ:st) *vt* agotar. *n* escape *m*. **exhausting** *adj* agotador. **exhaustion** *n* agotamiento *m*. **exhaustive** *adj* exhaustivo.

exhibit (ig'zibit) *n* 1 objeto expuesto *m*. 2 *law* documento *m*. prueba *f*. *vt* 1 exhibir. 2 exponer. **exhibition** *n* 1 exhibición *f*. 2 exposición *f*. 3 beca *f*. **exhibitionism** *n* exhibicionismo *m*. **exhibitionist** *n,adj* exhibicionista *m,f*. **exhibitor** *n* expositor *m*.

exhilarate (ig'ziləreit) *vt* 1 regocijar. 2 estimular, levantar el ánimo. **exhilarating** *adj* estimulante. **exhilaration** *n* 1 regocijo *m*. 2 excitación *f*.

exile ('egzail) *n* 1 exilio, destierro *m*. 2 exiliado, desterrado *m*. *vt* exiliar, desterrar.

exist (ig'zist) *vi* existir. **existence** *n* existencia *f*. **existent** *adj* existente. **existentialism** *n* existencialismo *m*.

exit ('eksit) *n* 1 salida *f*. 2 mutis *m*. *vi* hacer mutis.

exorbitant (ig'zɔ:bitənt) *adj* exorbitante.

exorcize ('eksɔ:saiz) *vt* exorcizar. **exorcism** *n* exorcismo *m*. **exorcist** *n* exorcista *m,f*.

exotic (ig'zɔtik) *adj* exótico. **exoticism** *n* exotismo *m*.

expand (ik'spænd) *vt,vi* 1 extender, ampliar. 2 dilatar. 3 desarrollar. 4 expansionar.

expanse (ik'spæns) *n* extensión *f*. **expansion** *n* 1 expansión *f*. 2 dilatación *f*. **expansive** *adj* expansivo.

expatriate (eks'pætriit) *n* expatriado *m adj* expatriado.

expect (ik'spekt) *vt* 1 esperar, contar con. 2 figurarse. **expectancy** *n* expectación *f*. **expectant** *adj* expectante. **expectant mother** futura mamá *f*. **expectation** *n* 1 expectación *f*. 2 esperanza, expectativa *f*.

expedient (ik'spi:diənt) *adj* expeditivo, oportuno. *n* expediente *m*. **expedience** *also* **expediency** *n* conveniencia *f*.

expedition (ekspi'diʃən) *n* expedición *f*.

expel (ik'spel) *vt* 1 expulsar. 2 arrojar.

expenditure (ik'spenditʃə) *n* gasto *m*. desembolso *m*. **expendable** *adj* prescindible.

expense (ik'spens) *n* 1 gasto *m*. 2 expensas *f pl*. **expensive** *adj* caro, costoso.

experience (ik'spiəriəns) *n* experiencia *f*. *vt* experimentar, sentir.

experiment (ik'sperimənt) *n* experimento *m*. *vi*

experimentar, hacer experimentos. **experimental** *adj* experimental.

expert ('ekspə:t) *adj* 1 experto. 2 pericial. *n* experto, perito *m*. **expertise** *n* pericia *f*.

expire (ik'spaiə) *vi* 1 expirar. 2 vencer. 3 caducar. **expiration** *n* 1 expiración *f*. 2 vencimiento *m*.

explain (ik'splein) *vt* explicar. **explanation** *n* explicación *f*. **explanatory** *adj* explicativo.

expletive (ik'spli:tiv) *n* 1 expletivo *m*. 2 palabrota *f*.

explicit (ik'splisit) *adj* explícito.

explode (ik'sploud) *vt* 1 volar, hacer saltar. 2 reventar, hacer explotar. 3 *inf* desmentir, refutar. *vi* estallar, hacer explosión.

exploit[1] ('eksploit) *n* hazaña *f*.

exploit[2] (ik'sploit) *vt* explotar. **exploitation** *n* explotación *f*.

explore (ik'splo:) *vt* explorar. **exploration** *n* exploración *f*. **exploratory** *adj* exploratorio, preparatorio. **explorer** *n* explorador *m*.

explosive (ik'splousiv) *n,adj* explosivo *m*. **explosion** *n* explosión *f*.

exponent (ik'spounənt) *n* exponente *m,f*.

export (*v* ik'spo:t; *n* 'ekspo:t) *vt* exportar. *n* exportación *f*. **exporter** *n* exportador *m*.

expose (ik'spouz) *vt* 1 exponer. 2 desenmascarar. **exposition** *n* exposición *f*. **exposure** *n* 1 exposición *f*. 2 desenmascaramiento *m*.

express (ik'spres) *adj* 1 expreso. 2 rápido. **express letter** *n* carta urgente *f*. **express train** *n* rápido *m*. ~*vt* 1 expresar. 2 exprimir. **expression** *n* expresión *f*. **expressive** *adj* expresivo.

expulsion (ik'spʌlʃən) *n* expulsión *f*.

exquisite ('ek'skwizit) *adj* 1 exquisito. 2 intenso.

extend (ik'stend) *vt,vi* 1 extender. 2 ampliar. 3 prolongar. 4 exigir el máximo. **extension** *n* 1 extensión *f*. 2 ampliación *f*. 3 prolongación *f*. 4 prórroga *f*. **extensive** *adj* 1 extenso. 2 dilatado. 3 frecuente.

extent (ik'stent) *n* 1 extensión *f*. 2 alcance *m*. **to a large extent** en gran parte. **to what extent?** ¿hasta qué punto?

exterior (ek'stiəriə) *adj,n* exterior *m*.

exterminate (ik'stə:mineit) *vt* exterminar. **extermination** *n* exterminio *m*.

external (ek'stə:nl) *adj* externo.

extinct (ik'stiŋkt) *adj* extinto. **extinction** *n* extinción *f*.

extinguish (ik'stiŋgwiʃ) *vt* extinguir. **extinguisher** *n* extintor *m*.

extra ('ekstrə) *adj* 1 adicional. 2 de más, de sobra. 3 extraordinario, extra. *adv* 1 especialmente. 2 más. *n* extra *m*.

extract (*n* 'ekstrækt; *v* ik'strækt) *n* 1 extracto *m*. 2 trozo *m*. *vt* extraer. **extraction** *n* extracción *f*.

extramural (ekstrə'mjuərəl) *adj* de extramuros.

extraordinary (ik'stro:dənri) *adj* extraordinario.

extravagant (ik'strævəgənt) *adj* 1 derrochador, despilfarrador. 2 excesivo. 3 extravagante, estrafalario. **extravagance** *n* 1 derroche, despilfarro *m*. 2 exceso *m*. 3 extravagancia *f*.

extreme (ik'stri:m) *adj* extremo, extremado. *n* extremo *m*. **go to extremes** 1 tomar medidas extremas. 2 propasarse. **extremely** *adv* sumamente. **extremism** extremismo *m*. **extremist** *n* extremista *m,f*. **extremity** *n* 1 extremidad *f*. 2 apuro *m*.

extricate ('ekstrikeit) *vt* 1 desenredar, desembrollar. 2 sacar, librar.

extrovert ('ekstrəvə:t) *adj,n* extrovertido *m*.

exuberant (ig'zju:bərənt) *adj* 1 exuberante. 2 eufórico. **exuberance** *n* 1 exuberancia *f*. 2 euforia *f*.

exult (ig'zʌlt) *vi* exultar.

eye (ai) *n* 1 ojo *m*. 2 bot yema *f*. **black eye** ojo amoratado. ~*vt* mirar detenidamente.

eyeball ('aibo:l) *n* globo del ojo *m*.

eyebrow ('aibrau) *n* ceja *f*.

eyelash ('ailæʃ) *n* pestaña *f*.

eyelid ('ailid) *n* párpado *m*.

eye shadow *n* sombreador de ojos *m*.

eyesight ('aisait) *n* vista *f*.

eyesore ('aiso:) *n* cosa que ofende la vista *f*.

eyestrain ('aistrein) *n* vista cansada *f*.

eye-witness *n* testigo ocular *or* presencial *m*.

F

fable ('feibəl) *n* fábula *f*.

fabric ('fæbrik) *n* 1 tejido, género *m*. 2 estructura *f*. **fabricate** *vt* 1 fabricar. 2 inventar. 3 falsificar. **fabrication** *n* 1 fabricación *f*. 2 invención *f*. 3 falsificación *f*.

fabulous ('fæbjuləs) *adj* fabuloso.

facade (fə'sɑ:d) *n* 1 fachada *f*. 2 apariencia *f*.

face (feis) *n* 1 cara *f*. rostro *m*. 2 mueca *f*. 3 esfera *f*. 4 superficie *f*. 5 apariencias *f pl*. **lose face** desprestigiarse. **save one's face** salvar las apariencias. **show one's face** dejarse ver. ~*vt* 1 encarar. 2 estar enfrente de. 3 arrostrar, hacer frente a. 4 reconocer, aceptar. **be**

faced with presentársele a. **facecloth** n paño m.

facet ('fæsit) n faceta f.

facetious (fə'si:ʃəs) adj chistoso, gracioso.

facile ('fæsail) adj fácil, superficial, ligero. **facilitate** vt facilitar. **facility** n facilidad f.

facing ('feisiŋ) prep frente a.

facsimile (fæk'siməli) n, adj facsímil m.

fact (fækt) n 1 hecho m. 2 pl datos m pl. **as a matter of fact** en realidad. **factual** adj basado en hechos, objetivo.

faction ('fækʃən) n facción f.

factor ('fæktə) n factor m.

factory ('fæktəri) n fábrica f.

faculty ('fækəlti) n facultad f.

fad (fæd) n 1 manía f. 2 novedad, moda f.

fade (feid) vi,vt 1 descolorar, desteñir. 2 marchitar. 3 apagar, desvanecer.

fag (fæg) n 1 faena f. trabajo penoso m. 2 sl pitillo m.

Fahrenheit ('færənhait) adj referente al termómetro de Fahrenheit.

fail (feil) vi 1 fallar. 2 fracasar. 3 desfallecer. 4 dejar de. vt 1 faltar a. 2 educ suspender. **failure** n 1 fracaso m. 2 fallo m.

faint (feint) adj 1 débil. 2 tenue. **feel faint** estar mareado. ~vi desmayarse, desfallecer. n desmayo m. **faint-hearted** adj pusilánime, medroso.

fair[1] (fɛə) adj 1 justo. 2 imparcial. 3 razonable. 4 hermoso, bello. 5 rubio. **fair-minded** adj imparcial. **fairly** adv 1 justamente, imparcialmente, limpiamente. 2 bastante, medianamente. **fairness** n 1 justicia, imparcialidad f. 2 hermosura f.

fair[2] (fɛə) n feria f. **fairground** n parque de atracciones m.

fairy ('fɛəri) n hada f. adj de hadas, mágico. **fairytale** n cuento de hadas m.

faith (feiθ) n fe f. **faithful** adj fiel. **faithfulness** n fidelidad f.

fake (feik) n 1 falsificación f. imitación f. 2 impostor m. adj 1 falso. 2 fingido. vt 1 falsificar. 2 fingir.

falcon ('fɔ:lkən) n halcón m.

fall[*] (fɔ:l) n 1 caída f. 2 baja f. 3 desnivel m. vi 1 caer. 2 bajar. 3 recaer, tocar. 4 amainar. **fall down** 1 caerse. 2 derrumbarse. **fall in love** enamorarse.

fallacy ('fæləsi) n 1 error m. 2 sofisma m. 3 falacia f. 4 mentira f.

fallible ('fæləbəl) adj falible.

fallow ('fælou) adj barbechado.

false (fɔ:ls) adj 1 falso. 2 postizo. **falsehood** n falsedad f. **false teeth** n dentadura postiza f. **falsify** vt falsificar.

falter ('fɔ:ltə) vi 1 titubear, vacilar. 2 desfallecer.

fame (feim) n fama f. **famed** adj famoso.

familiar (fə'miliə) adj familiar. **be familiar with** estar familiarizado con. **familiarity** n familiaridad f. **familiarize** vt familiarizar.

family ('fæmili) n familia f.

famine ('fæmin) n 1 hambre f. 2 escasez f. **famished** adj hambriento, famélico.

famous ('feiməs) adj famoso, célebre.

fan[1] (fæn) n 1 abanico m. 2 ventilador. m. 3 aventadora f. vt 1 abanicar. 2 ventilar. **fan-belt** n correa de ventilador f.

fan[2] (fæn) n (inf) 1 admirador m. 2 entusiasta, hincha m,f. **fan club** n club de admiradores m.

fanatic (fə'nætik) adj fanático.

fancy ('fænsi) n 1 quimera f. 2 fantasía f. 3 capricho, antojo m. 4 afición f. adj 1 de fantasía. 2 caprichoso. 3 estrafalario. vt 1 imaginar, figurar. 2 antojar. 3 encaprichar. **fancy dress** n disfraz m. **fanciful** adj 1 caprichoso. 2 fantástico.

fanfare ('fænfɛə) n 1 toque de trompetas m. 2 charanga f.

fang (fæŋ) n colmillo m.

fantastic (fæn'tæstik) adj fantástico.

fantasy ('fæntəsi) n fantasía f.

far (fɑ:) adj lejano. adv lejos. **by far** con mucho. **so far** 1 hasta aquí. 2 hasta ahora. **far-away** adj remoto. **far-fetched** adj inverosímil. **far-off** adj lejano, remoto. **far-reaching** adj 1 trascendental. 2 de mucho alcance.

farce (fɑ:s) n farsa f. **farcical** adj ridículo, absurdo.

fare (fɛə) n 1 precio m. 2 billete m. 3 naut pasaje m. 4 comida f.

farewell (fɛə'wel) interj ¡adiós! n adiós m.

farm (fɑ:m) n 1 hacienda f. 2 granja f. 3 criadero m. vt cultivar, labrar. vi ser agricultor. **farmer** n agricultor, granjero m. **farmhouse** n casa de campo, granja f. **farming** n 1 cultivo m. 2 agricultura f. **farmland** n tierras de labor f pl. **farmyard** n corral m.

farther ('fɑ:ðə) adj más alejado. adv más lejos.

farthest ('fɑ:ðist) adj el más alejado. adv a lo más lejos.

fascinate ('fæsineit) vt fascinar. **fascinating** adj fascinador. **fascination** n fascinación f.

fascism ('fæʃizəm) n fascismo m. **fascist** adj,n fascista.

fashion ('fæʃən) n 1 manera f. modo m. 2 moda f. **after a fashion** en cierto modo. **in fashion** de moda. **out of fashion** pasado de moda. ~vt formar, modelar. **fashionable** adj de moda, elegante.

fast[1] (fɑːst) adj 1 rápido, veloz. 2 sólido, inalterable. adv 1 rápidamente, de prisa. 2 firmemente.

fast[2] (fɑːst) n ayuno m. vi ayunar.

fasten ('fɑːsən) vt 1 fijar, sujetar. 2 abrochar. **fastener** n 1 pestillo m. 2 corchete m. 3 grapa f.

fastidious (fə'stidiəs) adj 1 quisquilloso. 2 exigente.

fat (fæt) adj 1 gordo, grueso. 2 graso. **get fat** engordar. ~n grasa f. **fatten** vt engordar.

fatal ('feitl) adj fatal, mortal. **fatality** n fatalidad f.

fate (feit) n 1 destino m. 2 suerte f. **fateful** adj fatídico.

father ('fɑːðə) n padre m. vt engendrar. **fatherhood** n paternidad f. **father-in-law** n suegro m. **fatherland** n patria f. **fatherly** adj paternal.

fathom ('fæðəm) n 1 braza f. vt 1 sondear. 2 desentrañar. **fathomless** adj insondable.

fatigue (fə'tiːg) n fatiga f. vt fatigar.

fatuous ('fætjuəs) adj fatuo, necio.

fault (fɔːlt) n 1 falta f. 2 defecto m. 3 culpa f. 4 tech avería f. **be at fault** tener la culpa. **find fault with** criticar, censurar. ~vt tachar, encontrar defectos en.

favour ('feivə) n favor m. **be in favour of** estar a favor de. **be in favour with** gozar del favor de. **fall out of favour** caer en desgracia. ~vt favorecer. **favourable** adj favorable. **favourite** adj,n favorito m.

fawn[1] (fɔːn) n cervato m.

fawn[2] (fɔːn) vi adular, lisonjear. **fawning** adj servil, lisonjero.

fear (fiə) n miedo, temor m. vt temer. **fearful** adj 1 temeroso. 2 tímido. 3 espantoso, pavoroso. **fearless** adj intrépido, audaz.

feasible ('fiːzəbəl) adj factible.

feast (fiːst) n 1 fiesta f. 2 festín m. vt 1 festejar. 2 agasajar. **feast-day** n fiesta f.

feat (fiːt) n hazaña f.

feather ('feðə) n pluma f. vt emplumar. **featherbed** n colchón de pluma m.

feature ('fiːtʃə) n 1 rasgo m. característica f. 2 facción f. 3 artículo m. crónica f. 4 número m. **feature film** n película de largo metraje f. ~vt presentar, destacar.

February ('februəri) n febrero m.

feckless ('feklas) adj descuidado, atolondrado.

fed (fed) v see **feed.**

federal ('fedərəl) adj federal. **federalism** n federalismo m. **federalist** n federalista m, f. **federate** vt federar. **federation** n federación f.

fee (fiː) n 1 honorarios m pl. 2 cuota f.

feeble ('fiːbəl) adj débil. **feeble-minded** adj imbécil.

feed (fiːd) vt alimentar, dar de comer. vi comer. **be fed up** estar harto. **feedback** n 1 tech realimentación f. 2 reacción f. **feeding** n alimentación f. **feeding-bottle** n biberón m.

feel[•] (fiːl) vt,vi sentirse. vt 1 sentir. 2 tocar, tantear. 3 parecer. **feeler** n 1 zool antena f. 2 zool tentáculo m. 3 sondeo m. **feeling** n 1 sensación f. sentimiento m. 2 sensibilidad f. 3 parecer m. 4 presentimiento m. adj sensible.

feign (fein) vt 1 fingir. 2 inventar.

feint[1] (feint) n 1 treta f. 2 sport finta f. vi hacer una finta.

feint[2] (feint) adj tenue.

feline ('fiːlain) adj felino.

fell[1] (fel) vt 1 talar, cortar. 2 derribar.

fell[2] (fel) v see **fall.**

fellow ('feləu) n 1 compañero m. 2 miembro, socio m. 3 tipo, sujeto m. **fellowship** n 1 compañerismo m. 2 asociación f.

felony ('feləni) n delito grave m.

felt[1] (felt) n fieltro m.

felt[2] (felt) v see **feel.**

female ('fiːmeil) adj,n hembra f.

feminine ('feminin) adj femenino. **femininity** n feminidad f.

feminism ('feminizəm) n feminismo m. **feminist** n feminista m,f.

fence (fens) n valla, cerca f. vt cercar. vi esgrimir. **fencing** n esgrima f.

fend (fend) vi 1 defenderse. 2 apañarse.

fennel ('fenl) n hinojo m.

ferment (n 'fəːment; v fə'ment) n fermento m. vi fermentar.

fern (fəːn) n helecho m.

ferocious (fə'rəuʃəs) adj feroz. **ferocity** n ferocidad f.

ferret ('ferit) n hurón m.

ferry ('feri) vt pasar a través del río. n transbordador m. **ferryboat** n transbordador m.

fertile ('fəːtail) adj fértil. **fertility** n fertilidad

f. **fertilize** vt fecundar, fertilizar. **fertilizer** n fertilizante, abono m.

fervent ('fɜːvənt) adj ferviente.

fervour ('fɜːvə) n fervor m.

fester ('festə) vi enconarse, emponzoñarse.

festival ('festivəl) n 1 festival m. 2 fiesta f. **festive** adj festivo. **festivity** n festividad f.

festoon (fes'tuːn) n festón m. vt festonear.

fetch (fetʃ) vt 1 ir a buscar, ir por, traer. 2 hacer venir. 3 venderse por, alcanzar. **fetching** adj atractivo.

fete (feit) n fiesta f.

fetid ('fetid) adj fétido.

fetish ('fetiʃ) n fetiche m.

fetlock ('fetlɔk) n cerneja f.

fetter ('fetə) n grillete m. vt encadenar.

feud (fjuːd) n 1 enemistad heredada f. 2 disputa f. vi reñir, pelear.

feudal ('fjuːdl) adj feudal. **feudalism** n feudalismo m.

fever ('fiːvə) n fiebre f. **feverish** adj febril.

few (fjuː) adj 1 pocos. 2 algunos, unos. **a few** unos cuantos. **fewer** adj menos.

fiancé (fi'ɔnsei) n prometido, novio m.

fiasco (fi'æskou) n fiasco m.

fib (fib) n inf mentirijilla f. vi decir mentirijillas.

fibre ('faibə) n fibra f. **fibreglass** n fibra de vidrio f. **fibrous** adj fibroso.

fickle ('fikəl) adj veleidoso, mudable, inconstante.

fiction ('fikʃən) n ficción f. **fictional** adj novelesco. **fictitious** adj ficticio.

fiddle ('fidl) n 1 violín m. 2 inf trampa, estafa f. vt inf 1 hacer trampa. 2 agenciar. vi tocar el violín. **fiddler** n inf violinista m,f.

fidelity (fi'deliti) n fidelidad f.

fidget ('fidʒit) vi agitar nerviosamente. **fidgety** adj nervioso, azogado.

field (fiːld) n 1 campo m. 2 prado m. 3 esfera, especialidad f. vt parar, recoger.

fiend (fiːnd) n 1 demonio, diablo m. 2 fanático m. **fiendish** adj diabólico.

fierce (fiəs) adj 1 feroz, fiero. 2 intenso. **fierceness** n ferocidad, furia f.

fiery ('faiəri) adj ardiente, fogoso.

fifteen (fif'tiːn) adj,n quince m. **fifteenth** adj decimoquinto.

fifth (fifθ) adj quinto.

fifty ('fifti) adj,n cincuenta m. **go fifty-fifty** ir a medias. **fiftieth** adj quincuagésimo.

fig (fig) n higo m.

fight* (fait) vt luchar contra, combatir. **fight back** resistir. **fight off** rechazar. ~n lucha, pelea f.

figment ('figmənt) n invención f.

figure ('figə) n 1 figura f. 2 tipo m. vt figurar. **figurative** adj 1 figurado. 2 figurativo.

filament ('filəmənt) n filamento m.

file¹ (fail) n 1 ficha f. 2 carpeta f. 3 fichero, archivo m. 4 fila, hilera f. vt archivar. **filing cabinet** n fichero, archivador m.

file² (fail) n lima f. vt limar.

filial ('filiəl) adj filial.

fill (fil) vt 1 llenar. 2 rellenar. 3 ocupar, cubrir. 4 completar. **fill in** llenar, rellenar. **fill up** llenar hasta el tope. ~n 1 hartazgo m. 2 lleno m. **filling** n 1 relleno m. 2 med empaste m.

fillet ('filit) n filete m. vt cortar en filetes.

filly ('fili) n potra f.

film (film) n película f. vt filmar. vi hacer una película. **filmstar** n astro m. estrella f.

filter ('filtə) n filtro m. vt filtrar.

filth (filθ) n inmundicia, porquería f. **filthy** adj sucio, cochino.

fin (fin) n aleta f.

final ('fainl) adj 1 final. 2 decisivo. 3 terminante. n final f. **finalist** n finalista m,f. **finalize** vt ultimar, finalizar.

finance ('fainæns) n finanzas f pl. vt financiar. **financial** adj financiero. **financier** n financiero m.

find* (faind) vt encontrar, hallar. **find out** 1 averiguar. 2 descubrir. ~n hallazgo m. **finding** n 1 descubrimiento m. 2 pl recomendaciones f pl.

fine¹ (fain) adj 1 fino. 2 hermoso. 3 bueno, magnífico, excelente. adv muy bien. **feel fine** sentirse estupendamente. **that's fine!** ¡estupendo! **fine arts** n pl bellas artes f pl. **finery** n 1 galas f pl. 2 adornos m pl.

fine² (fain) n multa f. vt multar.

finger ('fiŋgə) n dedo m. **little finger** meñique m. **put one's finger on it** poner el dedo en la llaga. **twist someone round one's little finger** hacer con uno lo que le da la gana. ~vt 1 tocar. 2 manosear. **fingernail** n uña f. **fingerprint** n huella dactilar f. **fingertip** n punta del dedo f. **have at one's fingertips** saberse al dedillo.

finish ('finiʃ) vt,vi terminar, acabar. **finish off** rematar. ~n 1 fin, final m. 2 remate m. 3 sport meta f. 4 tech acabado m.

finite ('fainait) adj finito. **finite verb** n verbo conjugado m.

fir (fɜː) n abeto m.

fire (faiə) n 1 fuego m. 2 incendio m. **be on fire** estar ardiendo. **catch fire** encenderse. **set on fire, set fire to** pegar fuego, incendiar. ~vt 1 incendiar. 2 disparar. 3 inf despedir.

fire alarm n alarma de incendios f.

firearm ('faiərɑ:m) n arma de fuego f.

fire brigade n cuerpo de bomberos m.

fire engine n bomba de incendios f.

fire-escape n escalera de incendios f.

fire extinguisher n extintor m.

fireguard ('faiəgɑ:d) n guardafuego m.

fireman ('faiəmən) n bombero m.

fireplace ('faiəpleis) n chimenea f.

fireside ('faiəsaid) n hogar m.

fire station n parque de bomberos m.

firework ('faiəwə:k) n fuegos artificiales m pl.

firing ('faiəriŋ) n 1 mil disparo m. 2 mil tiroteo m. 3 tech encendido m. **firing squad** n pelotón de ejecución m.

firm [1] (fə:m) adj firme.

firm [2] (fə:m) n empresa, firma comercial f.

first (fə:st) adj,adv primero. **at first** al principio. **first of all** ante todo. ~n primero m. **first aid** n primeros auxilios m pl. **first-born** n primogénito m. **first-class** adj de primera clase. **first-hand** adj de primera mano. **first-name** n nombre de pila m. **first person** n primera persona f. **first-rate** adj de primera.

fiscal ('fiskəl) adj fiscal.

fish (fiʃ) n 1 pez m. 2 pescado m. vt,vi pescar. **fishbowl** n pecera f. **fisherman** n pescador m. **fish finger** n croqueta de pescado f. **fishing** n pesca f. **fishing rod** n caña de pescar f. **fishmonger** n pescadero m. **fishmonger's shop** pescadería f. **fishy** adj 1 de pescado. 2 inf sospechoso.

fission ('fiʃən) n 1 escisión f. 2 fisión f.

fist (fist) n puño m. **fistful** n puñado m.

fit [1] (fit) vt ajustar, encajar. vi sentar bien, ir bien. adj 1 idóneo, apropiado. 2 digno. 3 med bien de salud. 4 sport en forma. n 1 ajuste m. 2 corte m. **fitness** n 1 idoneidad f. 2 med buena salud f. 3 sport buena forma f. **fitting** adj apropiado, conveniente. n 1 prueba f. 2 talla f. 3 pl accesorios m pl. **fitted** adj 1 hecho a medida. 2 empotrado.

fit [2] (fit) n acceso, ataque m. **fitful** adj espasmódico.

five (faiv) adj,n cinco m.

fix (fiks) vt 1 fijar. 2 arreglar. **fixation** n fijación f. **fixed** adj fijo. **fixture** n 1 cosa fija f. 2 instalación fija f. 3 sport encuentro m.

fizz (fiz) vi estar en efervescencia. n efervescencia f. **fizzy** adj gaseoso, espumoso, efervescente. **fizzle** vi apagarse.

flabbergast ('flæbəgɑ:st) vt pasmar.

flabby ('flæbi) adj 1 flojo. 2 fofo.

flag [1] (flæg) n bandera f. vt hacer señales con una bandera. **flagpole** n asta de bandera f. **flagship** n buque insignia m.

flag [2] (flæg) vi flaquear, languidecer, decaer.

flagon ('flægən) n 1 jarra f. 2 comm garrafa f.

flagrant ('fleigrənt) adj flagrante, notorio.

flair (flɛə) n instinto, don especial m.

flake (fleik) n 1 copo m. 2 escama f. vi descascararse, desconcharse. vt separar en escamas. **flaky** adj 1 en copos. 2 escamoso. 3 desmenuzable.

flamboyant (flæm'bɔiənt) adj 1 extravagante. 2 llamativo.

flame (fleim) n llama, llamarada f. vi llamear. **flame up** enflamarse.

flamingo (flə'miŋgou) n flamenco m.

flan (flæn) n tarta f.

flank (flæŋk) n 1 costado m. 2 flanco m. vt flanquear.

flannel ('flænl) n franela f. **face-flannel** paño de la cara m.

flap (flæp) vt batir, sacudir. n 1 hoja plegadiza f. 2 aleteo m.

flare (flɛə) vi resplandecer, llamear. vt acampanar. **flare up** encenderse. ~n 1 llamarada f. 2 mil bengala f. 3 acampanado m.

flash (flæʃ) n 1 destello m. 2 llamarada f. 3 relámpago m. vi destellar, relampaguear. **flashback** n escena retrospectiva f. **flashbulb** n bombilla de flash f. **flashlight** n 1 flash m. 2 linterna de señales f.

flask (flɑ:sk) n 1 frasco m. 2 termo m.

flat [1] (flæt) adj 1 llano. 2 plano. 3 soso. 4 terminante. 5 mus bemol. adv de plano. **flatfish** n pez plano m. **flat-footed** adj 1 pies planos. 2 torpe. **flatten** vt allanar, aplanar.

flat [2] (flæt) n piso m.

flatter ('flætə) vt 1 halagar, adular. 2 favorecer. **flatterer** n adulador m. **flattery** n 1 halagos m pl. 2 adulación f.

flaunt (flɔ:nt) vt ostentar, hacer gala de. **flaunt oneself** pavonearse.

flautist ('flɔ:tist) n flautista m,f.

flavour ('fleivə) n 1 sabor m. 2 gustillo m. vt sazonar. **flavouring** n condimento m.

flaw (flɔ:) n 1 grieta f. 2 defecto m. **flawless** adj impecable, perfecto.

flax (flæks) n lino m.

flea (fli:) n pulga f.

fleck (flek) n mota f. punto m. vt motear.

fled (fled) v see **flee.**

flee* (fli:) vi,vt huir.

fleece (fli:s) n vellón m. vt esquilar. **fleecy** adj lanudo.

fleet (fli:t) n flota f.

fleeting ('fli:tiŋ) adj fugaz.

flesh (fleʃ) n carne f. **fleshy** adj carnoso.

flew (flu:) v see **fly .**

flex (fleks) vt flexionar. n cordón eléctrico m. **flexible** adj flexible. **flexibility** n flexibilidad f

flick (flik) n 1 golpecito m. 2 chasquido m. vt 1 dar un golpecito. 2 chasquear.

flicker ('flikə) vi 1 parpadear. 2 vibrar. n parpadeo m.

flight[1] (flait) n vuelo m.

flight[2] (flait) n huida f. **put to flight** ahuyentar.

flimsy ('flimzi) adj 1 endeble. 2 delgado. 3 baladí. **flimsiness** n 1 endeblez f. 2 delgadez f.

flinch (flintʃ) vi arredrarse, acobardarse.

fling* (fliŋ) vt arrojar, echar. n tiro m. bravata f.

flint (flint) n pedernal m.

flip (flip) n 1 capirotazo m. vt echar de un capirotazo. **flipper** n aleta f.

flippant ('flipənt) adj frívolo. **flippancy** n falta de seriedad f.

flirt (flə:t) vi coquetear, flirtear. **flirt with** jugar con. ~n coqueta f.

flit (flit) vi 1 revolotear. 2 escurrirse.

float (flout) vi flotar. vt 1 hacer flotar. 2 lanzar, emitir. n 1 flotador m. 2 carroza f.

flock[1] (flɔk) n 1 rebaño m. 2 bandada f. 3 manada f. vi congregarse, juntarse.

flock[2] (flɔk) n borra f.

flog (flɔg) vt azotar

flood (flʌd) n 1 inundación f. 2 diluvio m. vt inundar. vi desbordar. **floodgate** n compuerta m. **floodlight** n foco m. vt iluminar con focos.

floor (flɔ:) n 1 suelo m. 2 fondo m. 3 piso f. **have the floor** tener la palabra. **take the floor** salir a la palestra. ~vt 1 poner el piso a. 2 derribar. 3 confundir. **floorboard** n tabla f.

flop (flɔp) vi 1 desplomarse. 2 inf venirse abajo, fracasar. n inf fracaso m. **floppy** adj suelto, colgante.

floral ('flɔ:rəl) adj 1 floral. 2 de flores. **florist** n florista m,f. **florist's shop** n floristería f.

flounce[1] (flauns) vi brincar de enojo.

flounce[2] (flauns) n (of a dress) volante m.

flounder[1] ('flaundə) vi perder el hilo. **flounder about** forcejear.

flounder[2] ('flaundə) n zool platija f.

flour ('flauə) n harina f. vt enharinar.

flourish ('flʌriʃ) vi prosperar, florecer. n 1 rúbrica f. 2 toque de trompeta m. 3 floreo m. **flourishing** adj floreciente.

flout (flaut) vt mofarse de.

flow (flou) vi 1 fluir, correr. 2 ondear.

flower ('flauə) n flor f. vi florecer. **flowerbed** n macizo m. **flower pot** n maceta f.

fluctuate ('flʌktʃueit) vi fluctuar.

flue (flu:) n cañón de chimenea m.

fluent ('flu:ənt) adj fluido, fácil. **be fluent in a language** dominar un idioma. **fluency** n 1 fluidez, soltura f. 2 dominio m. **fluently** adv con fluidez or soltura.

fluff (flʌf) n pelusa f. **fluffy** adj ahuecado.

fluid ('flu:id) adj,n fluido m. **fluidity** n fluidez f.

flung (flʌŋ) v see **fling.**

fluorescent (fluə'resənt) adj fluorescente. **fluorescence** n fluorescencia f.

fluoride ('fluəraid) n fluoruro m.

flush[1] (flʌʃ) vi sofocarse. n rubor m.

flush[2] (flʌʃ) adj nivelado, parejo. vt tirar un chorro de agua. vi (of a toilet) funcionar.

fluster ('flʌstə) vt aturdir. n aturdimiento m.

flute (flu:t) n flauta f.

flutter ('flʌtə) vi 1 aletear. 2 palpitar. vt agitar. n 1 aleteo m. 2 palpitación f. 3 agitación f.

flux (flʌks) n flujo m.

fly*[1] (flai) vi 1 volar. 2 ir en avión. vt 1 hacer volar. 2 pilotear. 3 transportar en avión. **flyover** n puente de tráfico m.

fly[2] (flai) n 1 mosca f. 2 bragueta f.

foal (foul) n potro m.

foam (foum) n espuma f. vi echar espuma.

focus ('foukəs) n, pl **foci** foco m. **in focus** enfocado. **out of focus** desenfocado. ~vt enfocar. **focal** adj focal.

fodder ('fɔdə) n forraje m.

foe (fou) n enemigo m.

foetus ('fi:təs) n feto m.

fog (fɔg) n niebla f. **foghorn** n sirena de niebla f. **foggy** adj 1 brumoso. 2 velado.

foible ('fɔibəl) n debilidad f.

foil[1] (fɔil) vt desbaratar, frustrar.

foil[2] (fɔil) n papel de plata m.

foil[3] (fɔil) n florete m.

foist (fɔist) vt encajar con engaño.

fold[1] (fould) vt 1 plegar. 2 envolver. n pliegue m. **folder** n carpeta f. **folding** adj plegable.

fold[2] (fould) *n* redil *m*.

foliage ('fouliidʒ) *n* follaje *m*.

folk (fouk) *n* gente *f.* **folk dance** *n* danza folklórica *f.* **folklore** *n* folklore *m*. **folk song** *n* canción popular *f.* **folktale** *n* cuento popular *m*.

follicle ('fɔlikəl) *n* folículo *m*.

follow ('fɔlou) *vt,vi* seguir. **follow up 1** llevar hasta el fin. **2** proseguir. **3** investigar. **follower** *n* seguidor *m*. **following** *adj* siguiente. *n* seguidores *m pl*.

folly ('fɔli) *n* locura, insensatez *f*.

fond (fɔnd) *adj* cariñoso, indulgente. **be fond of 1** ser aficionado a. **2** estar encariñado con. **fondness** *n* **1** cariño *m*. **2** afición *f*.

fondle ('fɔndl) *vt* acariciar.

font (fɔnt) *n* pila *f*.

food (fu:d) *n* **1** comida *f*. **2** alimento *m*.

fool (fu:l) *n* **1** tonto, insensato *m*. **2** bufón *m*. **make a fool of** poner en ridículo. **play the fool** hacer el tonto. ~*vt* engañar, embaucar. **foolish** *adj* tonto, insensato. **foolishness** *n* tontería, insensatez *f.* **foolproof** *adj* **1** a prueba de impericia. **2** infalible.

foolscap ('fu:lzkæp) *n* papel tamaño folio *m*.

foot (fut) *n*, *pl* **feet** pie *m*. *vt inf* pagar. **football** *n* **1** fútbol *m*. **2** balón *m*. **football pools** *n* quinielas *f pl*. **footbridge** *n* puente de peatones *m*. **foothold** *n* pie firme *m*. base segura *f.* **footing** *n* **1** pie *m*. **2** posición *f.* **footlights** *n pl* candilejas *f pl*. **footnote** *n* nota *f.* **footprint** *n* huella *f.* **footstep** *n* paso *m*. pisada *f*.

for (fə; *stressed* fɔ:) *prep* **1** para. **2** por. **as for** en cuanto a. **be for** estar a favor de. **but for** a no ser por. **for all that** con todo. **for good** definitivamente. ~*conj* ya que, pues.

forage ('fɔridʒ) *n* forraje *m*. *vi* forrajear. **forage for** rebuscar.

forbear[*] (fɔ'bɛə) *vi* contenerse, reprimirse. **forbearance** *n* **1** paciencia *f.* **2** dominio propio *m*.

forbid[*] (fə'bid) *vi* prohibir. **forbidding** *adj* imponente.

force (fɔ:s) *n* **1** fuerza *f.* **2** personal *m*. **3** *mil* cuerpo *m*. **by force** a la fuerza. ~*vt* forzar. **forced** *adj* forzado. **forcefeed** *vt* alimentar a la fuerza. **forceful** *adj* fuerte, vigoroso, enérgico. **forcible** *adj* **1** forzoso. **2** vigoroso. **3** convincente.

forceps ('fɔ:seps) *n* fórceps *m*.

ford (fɔ:d) *n* vado *m*. *vt* vadear.

fore (fɔ:) *n* frente *m*. delantera *f.* *adj* delantero, anterior.

forearm[1] ('fɔ:rɑ:m) *n* antebrazo *m*.

forearm[2] (fɔ:'rɑ:m) *vt* armar previamente.

forebear ('fɔ:bɛə) *n* antepasado *m*.

forecast ('fɔ:kɑ:st) *vt* pronosticar. *n* pronóstico *m*.

forecourt ('fɔ:kɔ:t) *n* atrio *m*.

forefather ('fɔ:fɑ:ðə) *n* antepasado *m*.

forefinger ('fɔ:fiŋgə) *n* dedo índice *m*.

forefront ('fɔ:frʌnt) *n* vanguardia *f*.

foreground ('fɔ:graund) *n* primer plano *m*.

forehand ('fɔ:hænd) *n* directo *m*.

forehead ('fɔrid) *n* frente *f*.

foreign ('fɔrin) *adj* **1** extranjero. **2** extraño, ajeno. **foreigner** *n* extranjero *m*.

foreleg ('fɔ:leg) *n* pata delantera *f*.

forelock ('fɔ:lɔk) *n* guedeja *f*.

foreman ('fɔ:mən) *n* **1** capataz *m*. **2** *law* presidente del jurado *m*.

foremost ('fɔ:moust) *adj* **1** primero. **2** delantero.

forensic (fə'rensik) *adj* forénsico.

forerunner ('fɔ:rʌnə) *n* precursor *m*.

foresee[*] (fɔ:'si:) *vt* prever. **foreseeable** *adj* previsible.

foresight ('fɔ:sait) *n* previsión, perspicacia *f*.

forest ('fɔrist) *n* **1** bosque *m*. **2** selva *f.* *adj* forestal.

forestall (fɔ:'stɔ:l) *vt* **1** prevenir. **2** anticipar.

foretaste ('fɔ:teist) *n* anticipo *m*.

foretell[*] (fɔ:'tel) *vt* **1** predecir. **2** presagiar.

forethought ('fɔ:θɔ:t) *n* **1** prevención *f.* **2** premeditación *f*.

forfeit ('fɔ:fit) *n* **1** pena *f.* **2** prenda *f.* *vt* perder el derecho a.

forge[1] (fɔ:dʒ) *vt* **1** forjar, fraguar. **2** falsificar. falsear. *n* **1** fragua *f.* **2** fundición *f.* **forger** *n* falsificador *m*. **forgery** *n* falsificación *f*.

forge[2] (fɔ:dʒ) *vi* ir avanzando.

forget[*] (fə'get) *vt* olvidar. **forgetful** *adj* olvidadizo, descuidado. **forgetfulness** *n* **1** olvido *m*. **2** descuido *m*.

forgive[*] (fə'giv) *vt* perdonar. **forgiveness** *n* **1** perdón *m*. **2** misericordia *f*.

forgo[*] (fɔ:'gou) *vt* privarse de.

fork (fɔ:k) *n* **1** tenedor *m*. **2** horquilla *f.* **3** bifurcación *f.* *vi* bifurcarse. **fork out** *inf* desembolsar.

forlorn (fə'lɔ:n) *adj* abandonado, desamparado.

form (fɔ:m) *n* **1** forma *f.* **2** bulto *m*. **3** impreso *m*. **4** *educ* clase *f.* *vt* formar. **formal** *adj* **1** formal. **2** ceremonioso. **3** protocolario. **4** de etiqueta. **formality** *n* **1** formalidad *f.* **2** ceremonia f. **formalize** vt formalizar. **formation** n formación f. **formative** adj formativo.

former ('fɔ:mə) adj 1 pasado. 2 anterior. **the former** aquél m.

formidable ('fɔ:midəbəl) adj formidable.

formula ('fɔ:mjulə) n fórmula f. **formulate** vt formular.

forsake* (fə'seik) vt abandonar.

fort (fɔ:t) n fuerte m.

forte ('fɔ:tei) n fuerte m.

forth (fɔ:θ) adv 1 adelante. 2 afuera. **and so forth** y así sucesivamente. **forthcoming** adj 1 venidero. 2 en preparación. 3 disponible. 4 comunicativo. **forthright** adj franco, rotundo.

fortify ('fɔ:tifai) vt 1 fortalecer. 2 mil fortificar. **fortification** n fortificación f.

fortnight ('fɔ:tnait) n quincena f. **fortnightly** adj quincenal. adv cada quince días.

fortress ('fɔ:trəs) n fortaleza f.

fortune ('fɔ:tʃən) n fortuna f. **tell one's fortune** decir la buenaventura. **fortune-teller** n adivina f. **fortunate** adj afortunado.

forty ('fɔ:ti) adj,n cuarenta m. **fortieth** adj cuadragésimo.

forum ('fɔ:rəm) n foro m.

forward ('fɔ:wəd) adj 1 delantero. 2 adelantado. 3 de avance. 4 desenvuelto, fresco. n sport delantero m. vt 1 enviar. 2 (of a letter) hacer seguir. 3 entregar. **forwards** adv hacia adelante.

fossil ('fɔsəl) adj,n fósil m.

foster ('fɔstə) vt 1 nutrir, favorecer. 2 criar. 3 fomentar. **fostermother** n madre adoptiva f.

fought (fɔ:t) v see **fight**.

foul (faul) adj 1 sucio, inmundo. 2 viciado. 3 asqueroso. n sport falta f. vt ensuciar. vi sport cometer una falta. **foulmouthed** adj deslenguado. **foul play** n juego sucio m. **foul-smelling** adj hediondo.

found[1] (faund) v see **find**.

found[2] (faund) vt fundar. **foundation** n 1 fundación f. 2 fundamento m. 3 pl arch cimientos m pl. **founder** n fundador m.

foundry ('faundri) n fundición f.

fountain ('fauntin) n fuente f. **fountain pen** n estilográfica f.

four (fɔ:) adj,n cuatro m. **on all fours** a cuatro patas. **fourth** adj cuarto. n 1 cuarta parte f. 2 mus cuarta f. **fourthly** adv en cuarto lugar. **four-poster** n cama de columnas f. **foursome** n grupo de cuatro m.

fourteen (fɔ:'ti:n) adj,n catorce m. **fourteenth** adj decimocuarto.

fowl (faul) n ave de corral f.

fox (fɔks) n zorra f. vt despistar. **foxglove** n dedalera f. **foxhound** n perro raposero m. **foxhunting** n caza de la zorra f. **foxy** adj astuto.

foyer ('fɔiei) n vestíbulo, hall m.

fraction ('frækʃən) n fracción f. **fractional** adj fraccionario.

fracture ('fræktʃə) n fractura f. vt fracturar.

fragile ('frædʒail) adj frágil. **fragility** n fragilidad f.

fragment ('frægmənt) n fragmento m. **fragmentary** adj fragmentario.

fragrant ('freigrənt) adj fragante. **fragrance** n fragancia f.

frail (freil) adj 1 frágil. 2 débil. **frailty** n debilidad f.

frame (freim) n 1 marco m. 2 montura f. 3 estructura f. esqueleto m. vt 1 enmarcar. 2 construir, modelar. 3 formular. 4 incriminar por medio de una estratagema. **framework** n 1 marco, sistema m. 2 armazón f.

franc (fræŋk) n franco m.

France (frɑ:ns) n Francia f. **French** adj francés. **French** (language) n francés m. **French bean** n judía verde f. **French dressing** n aliño a la francesa m. **French horn** n trompa f. **French window** n puerta ventana f.

franchise ('fræntʃaiz) n 1 derecho al voto m. 2 franquicia f. 3 concesión f.

frank (fræŋk) adj franco. **frankness** n franqueza f.

frankfurter ('fræŋkfə:tə) n salchicha de Frankfurt f.

frantic ('fræntik) adj frenético m.

fraternal (frə'tə:nl) adj fraternal. **fraternity** n fraternidad, hermandad f. **fraternize** vi fraternizar.

fraud (frɔ:d) n 1 fraude m. 2 impostor m. **fraudulent** adj fraudulento.

fraught (frɔ:t) adj cargado, lleno.

fray[1] (frei) n combate m. lucha f.

fray[2] (frei) vt raer, desgastar. vi deshilacharse.

freak (fri:k) n 1 monstruo m. 2 fenómeno m. 3 capricho m.

freckle ('frekəl) n peca f. vt motear.

free (fri:) adj 1 libre. 2 gratuito. 3 liberal. adv gratis. vt libertar. **freedom** n libertad f. **freehand** adj hecho a pulso. **freehold** n dominio absoluto m. **freelance** adj independiente. n periodista independiente m,f. **free will** n libre albedrío m.

freeze* (fri:z) vt 1 helar. 2 congelar. vi helarse.

n helada *f*. **freezing point** *n* punto de congelación *m*.

freight (freit) *n* **1** flete *m*. **2** carga *f*. **3** mercancías *f pl*. **freight train** *n* tren de mercancías *m*.

frenzy ('frenzi) *n* frenesí *m*.

frequency ('fri:kwənsi) *n* frecuencia *f*. **frequent** *adj* frecuente. *vt* frecuentar.

fresco ('freskou) *n* fresco *m*.

fresh (freʃ) *adj* **1** fresco. **2** nuevo. **3** puro. **4** atrevido. **freshness** *n* pureza *f*. **freshwater** *adj* de agua dulce.

fret¹ (fret) *vt* irritar, molestar.

fret² (fret) *n* calado *m*. **fretwork** *n* calado *m*.

friar ('fraiə) *n* fraile *m*.

friction ('frikʃən) *n* **1** fricción *f*. **2** rozamiento *m*.

Friday ('fraidi) *n* viernes *m*.

fridge (fridʒ) *n inf* nevera *f*. frigorífico *m*.

friend (frend) *n* amigo *m*. **friendly** *adj* **1** simpático. **2** amistoso. **friendship** *n* amistad *f*.

frieze (fri:z) *n* friso *m*.

fright (frait) *n* susto *m*. **frighten** *vt* **1** asustar. **2** espantar. **be frightened** tener miedo. **frightful** *adj* espantoso.

frigid ('fridʒid) *adj* **1** frío. **2** frígido.

frill (fril) *n* lechuga *f*.

fringe ('frindʒ) *n* **1** franja *f*. **2** flequillo *m*. **3** margen *m*.

frisk (frisk) *vt* cachear. *vi* retozar.

fritter¹ ('fritə) *vt* desperdiciar.

fritter² ('fritə) *cul n* buñuelo, churro *m*. fruta de sartén *f*.

frivolity (fri'vɔliti) *n* frivolidad *f*. **frivolous** *adj* frívolo.

frizz (friz) *n* rizos pequeños *m pl*. frisado *m*.

frizzle¹ ('frizəl) *n* rizar, frisar.

frizzle² ('frizəl) *vi* chisporrotear.

fro (fro) *adv* **to and fro** de un lado a otro.

frock (frɔk) *n* vestido *m*. **frock coat** *n* levita *f*.

frog (frɔg) *n* rana *f*. **have a frog in the throat** tener carraspera.

frolic ('frɔlik) *n* travesura *f*. *vi* juguetear.

from (frəm; *stressed* frɔm) *prep* **1** de. **2** desde. **3** por. **4** de parte de.

front (frʌnt) *n* delantero. **front door** *n* puerta principal. ~ *n* **1** frente *m*. **2** fachada *f*.

frontier ('frʌntiə) *n* frontera *f*. *adj* fronterizo.

frost (frɔst) *n* **1** helada *f*. **2** escarcha *f*. *vt* cubrir de escarcha. **frostbite** *n* congelación *f*.

froth (frɔθ) *n* espuma *f*. *vi* espumar.

frown (fraun) *n* ceño *m*. *vi* fruncir el entrecejo.

froze (trouz) *v* see **freeze.**

frozen ('frouzən) *v* see **freeze.**

frugal ('fru:gəl) *adj* frugal.

fruit (fru:t) *n* fruta *f*. **fruitful** *adj* fructuoso, provechoso. **fruitless** *adj* infructuoso. **fruit machine** *n* máquina tragaperras *f*. **fruit salad** *n* ensalada de frutas *f*.

fruition (fru:'iʃən) *n* **1** fruición *f*. **2** cumplimiento *m*.

frustrate (frʌs'treit) *vt* frustrar. **frustration** *n* frustración *f*.

fry (frai) *vt* freír. **frying pan** *n* sartén *f*.

fuchsia ('fju:ʃə) *n* fucsia *f*.

fuel ('fju:əl) *n* combustible *m*. *vt* proveer de combustible.

fugitive ('fju:dʒitiv) *adj,n* fugitivo *m*.

fulcrum ('fʌlkrəm) *n* fulcro *m*.

fulfil (ful'fil) *vt* **1** cumplir con. **2** realizar. **3** llenar. **fulfilment** *n* cumplimiento *m*. realización *f*.

full (ful) *adj* **1** lleno. **2** completo. **3** pleno. **in full** sin abreviar. **full-length** *adj* **1** de tamaño natural. **2** de cuerpo entero. **full moon** *n* luna llena *f*. **full stop** *n* punto *m*. **fully** *adv* completamente.

fumble ('fʌmbəl) *vt* manosear. *vi* **1** titubear. **2** buscar con las manos.

fume (fju:m) *vi* **1** humear. **2** rabiar. *n* **1** vaho *m*. **2** tufo *m*. **3** emanación *f*.

fun (fʌn) *n* **1** diversión *f*. **2** broma *f*. **have fun** divertirse. **make fun of** burlarse de. **funfair** *n* parque de atracciones *m*.

function ('fʌŋkʃən) *n* función *f*. *vi* funcionar.

fund (fʌnd) *n* fondo *m*. *vt* consolidar.

fundamental (fʌndə'mentl) *adj* fundamental.

funeral ('fju:nərəl) *n* entierro, funeral *m*. *adj* fúnebre.

fungus ('fʌŋgəs) *n, pl* **fungi** *bot* hongo *m*.

funnel ('fʌnl) *n* **1** embudo *m*. **2** *naut* chimenea *f*.

funny ('fʌni) *adj* **1** divertido, gracioso. **2** raro.

fur (fə:) *n* piel *f*. **fur coat** *n* abrigo de pieles *m*.

furious ('fjuəriəs) *adj* furioso.

furnace ('fə:nis) *n* horno *m*.

furnish ('fə:niʃ) *vt* **1** amueblar. **2** proporcionar.

furniture ('fə:nitʃə) *n* mobiliario, mueblaje *m*.

furrow ('fʌrou) *n* surco *m*. *vt* **1** surcar. **2** arrugar.

further ('fə:ðə) *adj* **1** adicional. **2** más lejano. *adv* **1** más lejos. **2** además. *vt* promover. **furthest** *adv* más lejos. *adj* más lejano.

furtive ('fə:tiv) *adj* furtivo.

fury ('fjuəri) *n* furia *f*.

fuse¹ (fju:z) *n* **1** plomo, fusible *m*. **2** mecha *f*.

fuse² (fju:z) *vt* fundir. **fusion** *n* fusión *f*.

fuselage ('fju:zəlɑ:ʒ) *n* fuselaje *m*.

fuss (fʌs) *n* **1** bulla *f*. **2** lío *m*. **3** aspaviento *m*. *vi* agitarse.

futile ('fju:tail) *adj* **1** inútil. **2** fútil.

future ('fju:tʃə) *adj* **1** futuro. **2** venidero. *n* futuro, porvenir *m*.

fuzz (fʌz) *n* **1** pelusa *f*. **2** vello *m*. **3** *inf* policía *f*.

G

gabble ('gæbəl) *n* cotorreo *m*. *vi* **1** cotorrear. **2** hablar atropelladamente.

gable ('geibəl) *n* faldón, gablete *m*.

gadget ('gædʒit) *n* artilugio, chisme *m*.

gag[1] (gæg) *n* mordaza *f*. *vt* amordazar.

gag[2] (gæg) *n* **1** broma *f*. **2** chiste *m*.

gaiety ('geiəti) *n* alegría, jovialidad *f*.

gain (gein) *n* **1** ganancia *f*. **2** provecho *m*. **3** aumento *m*. *vt* ganar. *vi* avanzar.

gait (geit) *n* modo de andar *m*.

gala ('gɑ:lə) *n* fiesta, gala *f*.

galaxy ('gæləksi) *n* **1** galaxia *f*. **2** grupo brillante *m*.

gale (geil) *n* **1** ventarrón *m*. vendaval *f*. **2** tempestad; galerna *f*.

gallant ('gælənt) *adj* **1** valiente. **2** galante. *n* galán *m*.

galleon ('gæliən) *n* galeón *m*.

gallery ('gæləri) *n* **1** galería *f*. **2** pasadizo *m*.

galley ('gæli) *n* **1** galera *f*. **2** cocina *f*.

gallon ('gælən) *n* galón *m*.

gallop ('gæləp) *n* galope *m*. *vi* galopar.

gallows ('gæləuz) *n pl* horca *f*.

galore (gə'lɔ:) *adv* en abundancia.

galvanize ('gælvənaiz) *vt* galvanizar.

gamble ('gæmbəl) *n* **1** jugada *f*. **2** riesgo *m*. *vt,vi* jugar. *vi* especular.

game (geim) *n* **1** juego *m*. **2** partido *m*. **3** (hunting) caza *f*. *adj* animoso. **gamekeeper** *n* guardabosque *m*.

gammon ('gæmən) *n* jamón *m*.

gander ('gændə) *n* ganso *m*.

gang (gæg) *n* **1** pandilla *f*. grupo *m*. **2** brigada *f*. *vi* agrupar. **gang up** conspirar. **gangster** *n* pistolero, gángster *m*.

gangrene ('gæŋgri:n) *n* gangrena *f*.

gangway ('gæŋwei) *n* **1** pasillo *m*. pasarela *f*.

gap (gæp) *n* **1** hueco *m*. **2** desfiladero *m*. **3** intervalo *m*. **4** brecha *f*.

gape (geip) *vi* **1** abrirse mucho. **2** embobarse, estar boquiabierto.

garage ('gærɑ:ʒ) *n* garaje *m*. *vt* poner en el garaje.

garbage ('gɑ:bidʒ) *n* basura *f*. desperdicio *m*.

garble ('gɑ:bəl) *vt* mutilar, falsear.

garden ('gɑ:dn) *n* jardín *m*. *vi* cultivar. **gardener** *n* jardinero *m*. **gardening** *n* jardinería *f*.

gargle ('gɑ:gəl) *n* gárgaras *f pl*. *vi* hacer gárgaras.

garlic ('gɑ:lik) *n* ajo *m*.

garment ('gɑ:mənt) *n* prenda de vestir *f*.

garnish ('gɑ:niʃ) *vt* **1** adornar. **2** aderezar. *n* aderezo *m*.

garrison ('gærisən) *n* guarnición *f*. *vt* guarnecer.

garter ('gɑ:tə) *n* **1** ligas *f pl*. **2** jarretera *f*.

gas (gæs) *n* gas *m*. *vt* asfixiar con gas. **gas cooker** *n* cocina de gas *f*.

gash (gæʃ) *n* **1** hendedura, raja *f*. **2** cuchillada *f*. *vt* **1** acuchillar. **2** rajar.

gasket ('gæskit) *n tech* junta *f*.

gasp (gɑ:sp) *n* **1** boqueada *f*. jadeo *m*. **2** grito sofocado *m*. *vi* **1** boquear, jadear. **2** sofocarse.

gastric ('gæstrik) *adj* gástrico. **gastronomic** *adj* gastronómico.

gate (geit) *n* **1** puerta *f*. **2** verja *f*. **3** entrada *f*. **gatecrash** *vi* asistir sin ser invitado.

gather ('gæðə) *vt* **1** reunir. **2** coger. **3** recolectar. **4** fruncir. *vi* **1** reunirse. **2** acumularse.

gauche (gəuʃ) *adj* desmañado.

gaudy ('gɔ:di) *adj* **1** chillón. **2** cursi.

gauge (geidʒ) *n* **1** norma de medida *f*. **2** calibre *m*. **3** indicador *m*. *vt* **1** medir. **2** calibrar.

gaunt (gɔ:nt) *adj* **1** flaco, desvaído. **2** severo.

gauze (gɔ:z) *n* gasa *f*.

gave (geiv) *v see* **give**.

gay (gei) *adj* **1** alegre. **2** vistoso. **3** ligero.

gaze (geiz) *n* mirada fija *f*. *vi* mirar con fijeza.

gazelle (gə'zel) *n* gacela *f*.

gear (giə) *n* **1** engranaje *m*. **2** marcha *f*. **3** aparato *m*. **4** aparejos *m pl*. *vt* engranar. **gearbox** *n* caja de cambio *f*. **gear lever** *n* palanca de cambio *f*.

gelatine ('dʒeləti:n) *n* gelatina *f*.

gem (dʒem) *n* **1** joya *f*. **2** piedra preciosa *f*.

Gemini ('dʒeminai) *n* Géminis *m*.

gender ('dʒendə) *n* género *m*.

gene (dʒi:n) *n* gen *m*.

genealogy (dʒi:ni'ælədʒi) *n* genealogía *f*.

general ('dʒenərəl) *adj,n* general *m*. **general election** *n* elecciones generales *f*. **general practitioner** *n* médico general, médico de cabecera *m*. **generalize** *vi* generalizar.

generate ('dʒenəreit) vt 1 generar. 2 producir. **generation** n generación f.

generic (dʒi'nerik) adj genérico.

generous ('dʒenərəs) adj 1 generoso. 2 amplio. **generosity** n generosidad f.

genetic (dʒi'netik) adj genético. **genetics** n genética f.

genial ('dʒi:niəl) adj simpático, afable.

genital ('dʒenitl) adj,n genital. n pl órganos genitales m pl.

genitive ('dʒenitiv) n genitivo m.

genius ('dʒi:niəs) n 1 genio m. 2 genialidad f.

genteel (dʒen'ti:l) adj fino, elegante, gentil.

gentian ('dʒenʃən) n genciana f.

gentile ('dʒentail) adj,n 1 gentil ni. 2 pagano m.

gentle ('dʒentl) adj 1 benévolo. 2 suave. 3 ligero. **gentleman** n caballero m.

genuflect ('dʒenjuflekt) vi doblar la rodilla.

genuine ('dʒenjuin) adj 1 genuino. 2 sincero.

genus ('dʒi:nəs) n, pl **genera** género m.

geography (dʒi'ɔgrəfi) n geografía f. **geographical** adj geográfico. **geographer** n geógrafo m.

geology (dʒi'ɔlədʒi) n geología f.

geometry (dʒi'ɔmətri) n geometría f.

geranium (dʒə'reiniəm) n geranio m.

geriatrics (dʒeri'ætriks) n geriatría f.

germ (dʒə:m) n 1 germen m. 2 bacteria f.

Germany ('dʒə:məni) n Alemania f. **German** adj,n alemán m. **German** (language) n alemán m. **Germanic** adj germánico. **German measles** n rubéola f.

germinate ('dʒə:mineit) vi germinar.

gerund ('dʒerənd) n gerundio m.

gesticulate (dʒis'tikjuleit) vi accionar, gesticular.

gesture ('dʒestʃə) n 1 gesto, ademán m. 2 muestra f.

get* (get) vt 1 obtener. 2 coger. 3 comprender. vi ponerse. **get by** lograr pasar.

geyser ('gi:zə) n 1 géiser m. 2 calentador de agua m.

ghastly ('ga:stli) adj 1 horrible. 2 pálido, cadavérico.

gherkin ('gə:kin) n pepinillo m.

ghetto ('getou) n judería f.

ghost (goust) n fantasma m. **Holy Ghost** Espíritu Santo m.

giant ('dʒaiənt) n gigante m. adj gigantesco.

giddy ('gidi) adj 1 vertiginoso. 2 casquivano.

gift (gift) n 1 regalo m. 2 prenda f.

gigantic (dʒai'gæntik) adj gigantesco.

giggle ('gigəl) n risilla tonta f. vi reírse tontamente.

gild (gild) vt dorar.

gill [1] (gil) n agalla f.

gill [2] (dʒil) n cuarta parte de una pinta f.

gilt (gilt) adj,n dorado m.

gimmick ('gimik) n 1 truco publicitario m. 2 artimaña f.

gin (dʒin) n ginebra f.

ginger ('dʒindʒə) n jengibre m. **ginger up** animar. **gingerbread** n pan de jengibre m.

gingham ('giŋəm) n guinga, tela de algodón fino f.

Gipsy ('dʒipsi) adj,n gitano m.

giraffe (dʒi'ra:f) n jirafa f.

girder ('gə:də) n viga f.

girdle ('gə:dl) n 1 ceñidor m. 2 faja f. vt ceñir.

girl (gə:l) n 1 chica f. 2 niña f. **girlfriend** n 1 amiga f. 2 novia f.

girth (gə:θ) n 1 cincha f. 2 circunferencia f. 3 gordura f.

give* (giv) vt 1 dar. 2 entregar. 3 ofrecer. **give away** regalar. **give back** devolver. **give in** rendirse. **give up** 1 dejar. 2 renunciar. 3 sacrificar.

glacier ('glæsiə) n glaciar m.

glad (glæd) adj alegre, contento.

glamour ('glæmə) n encanto, atractivo m. **glamorous** adj encantador.

glance (gla:ns) n ojeada f. vistazo m. vi 1 mirar. 2 echar un vistazo.

gland (glænd) n glándula f.

glare (glɛə) n 1 brillo m. 2 deslumbramiento m. vi 1 relumbrar. 2 mirar ferozmente.

glass (gla:s) n 1 vaso m. 2 vidrio m. 3 artículos de vidrio m pl. 4 espejo m.

glaze (gleiz) n barniz, lustre m. vt 1 vidriar. 2 esmaltar.

gleam (gli:m) n destello m. vi brillar, relucir.

glean (gli:n) vt espigar.

glee (gli:) n 1 alegría f. 2 júbilo m.

glib (glib) adj 1 voluble. 2 engañoso.

glide (glaid) n 1 deslizamiento m. 2 planeo, vuelo sin motor m. vi 1 deslizarse. 2 volar sin motor. **glider** n planeador m.

glimmer ('glimə) n 1 vislumbre f. 2 luz tenue f. vi brillar tenuemente.

glimpse (glimps) n 1 vislumbre m. 2 vista momentánea f. vt vislumbrar.

glint (glint) vi destellar. n destello m.

glisten ('glisən) vi relucir, brillar.

glitter ('glitə) n resplandor m. vi relucir, centellear.

gloat (glout) vi relamerse, deleitarse.

globe (gloub) n globo m.

gloom[1] (glu:m) n oscuridad f.

gloom[2] (glu:m) n melancolía, tristeza f.

glory ('glɔ:ri) n gloria f. vi gloriarse. **glorify** vt glorificar. **glorious** adj glorioso.

gloss[1] (glɔs) n lustre m. vt lustrar.

gloss[2] (glɔs) n glosa f. vt glosar. **gloss over 1** encubrir. **2** paliar.

glossary ('glɔsəri) n glosario m.

glove (glʌv) n guante m.

glow (glou) n 1 resplandor m. 2 color vivo m. vi brillar, relucir.

glower ('glauə) vi mirar con ceño.

glucose ('glu:kous) n glucosa f.

glue (glu:) n cola f. vt encolar, pegar.

glum (glʌm) adj 1 taciturno. 2 triste. 3 sombrío.

glut (glʌt) n exceso m.

glutton ('glʌtn) n glotón m.

gnarled (nɑ:ld) adj nudoso, retorcido.

gnash (næʃ) vt,vi crujir los dientes.

gnat (næt) n mosquito m.

gnaw (nɔ:) vt roer.

gnome (noum) n gnomo m.

go* (gou) vi 1 ir. 2 marchar. 3 pasar. 4 partir. **go by** pasar. **go on** continuar. ~n 1 energía f. 2 jugada f.

goad (goud) n 1 aguijón m. 2 estímulo m. vt 1 aguijonear. 2 incitar, provocar.

goal (goul) n 1 meta f. 2 ambición f. 3 portería f. 4 gol m. **goalkeeper** n guardameta m.

goat (gout) n cabra, macho cabrío m.

gobble ('gɔbəl) vi (of a turkey) gluglutear. vt engullir.

goblin ('gɔblin) n duende m.

god (gɔd) n dios m. **for God's sake!** ¡por Dios! **goddaughter** n ahijada f. **godfather** n padrino m. **godmother** n madrina f. **godson** n ahijado m.

goddess ('gɔdis) n diosa f.

goggles ('gɔgəlz) n pl 1 anteojos m. 2 gafas submarinas f.

gold (gould) n oro m. **golden** adj de oro, dorado. **goldfish** n carpa dorada f. **goldmine** n mina de oro f. **goldsmith** n orfebre m.

golf (gɔlf) n golf m. **golfball** n pelota de golf f. **golf club** n palo de golf m. **golfcourse** n campo de golf m.

gondola ('gɔndələ) n góndola f. **gondolier** n gondolero m.

gone (gɔn) v see **go**.

gong (gɔŋ) n gong, gongo m.

good (gud) adj bueno. **as good as** tanto como. **feel good** estar satisfecho. ~n 1 bien, provecho m. 2 pl bienes, efectos m pl. **good afternoon** interj buenas tardes f pl. **goodbye** interj,n adiós m. **good evening** interj buenas tardes f pl. **Good Friday** n Viernes Santo m. **good-looking** adj bien parecido, guapo. **good morning** interj buenos días m pl. **good night** interj buenas noches f pl. **good-will** n buena voluntad f.

goose (gu:s) n, pl **geese** ganso m. **gooseberry** n uva espina, grosella f.

gore[1] (gɔ:) n sangre f.

gore[2] (gɔ:) vt cornear.

gorge (gɔ:dʒ) n 1 garganta f. 2 barranco m. vt engullir. vi hartarse.

gorgeous ('gɔ:dʒəs) adj magnífico, brillante.

gorilla (gə'rilə) n gorila m.

gorse (gɔ:s) n aulaga f. tojo m.

gory ('gɔ:ri) adj 1 ensangrentado. 2 inf desagradable.

gosh (gɔʃ) interj sl ¡caray!

gosling ('gɔzliŋ) n ganso pequeño m.

gospel ('gɔspəl) n evangelio m.

gossip ('gɔsip) n 1 chismoso m. 2 chismes m. 3 comadreo m. vi cotillear.

got (gɔt) v see **get**.

Gothic ('gɔθik) adj,n gótico m.

goulash ('gu:læʃ) n guiso húngaro m.

gourd (guəd) n calabaza f.

gourmet (guə'mei) n gastrónomo m.

govern ('gʌvən) vt,vi 1 gobernar. 2 gram regir. **government** n gobierno m. **governor** n gobernador m.

gown (gaun) n 1 toga f. 2 vestido m.

grab (græb) n agarro m. vt arrebatar.

grace (greis) n 1 gracia f. 2 elegancia f. 3 talante m. vt adornar. **say grace** bendecir la mesa. **graceful** adj elegante, gracioso.

gracious ('greiʃəs) adj 1 cortés. 2 benigno.

grade (greid) n 1 grado m. 2 clase f. vt clasificar, graduar. **gradient** n pendiente f. **gradual** adj 1 gradual. 2 graduado. **graduate** n graduado m.

graffiti (grə'fi:ti) n obras esgrafiadas f.

graft (grɑ:ft) n 1 injerto m. 2 corrupción f.

grain (grein) n 1 grano m. 2 cereal m. 3 fibra f. vt granular.

gram (græm) n gramo m.

grammar ('græmə) n gramática f. **grammar school** n centro de segunda enseñanza m. **grammatical** adj gramatical.

gramophone ('græməfoun) n gramófono m

209

granary ('grænəri) n granero m.

grand (grænd) adj grandioso, magnífico. **grandeur** n grandeza f. esplendor m.

grandad ('grændæd) n inf also **grandpa** abuelito m.

grandchild ('græntʃaild) n nieto m.

granddaughter ('grændɔːtə) n nieta f.

grandfather ('grænfɑːðə) n abuelo m.

grandma ('grænmɑː) n inf also **granny** abuelita f.

grandmother ('grænmʌðə) n abuela f.

grandparent ('grænpɛərənt) n abuelo m.

grand piano n piano de cola m.

grandson ('grænsʌn) n nieto m.

grandstand ('grændstænd) n tribuna f.

granite ('grænit) n granito m.

grant (grɑːnt) n 1 concesión f. 2 subvención f. 3 beca f. vt conceder. **take for granted** dar por supuesto.

grape (greip) n uva f. **grapefruit** n toronja f. pomelo m. **grapevine** n 1 vid f. 2 parra f.

graph (græf) n gráfica f. **graphic** adj gráfico.

grapple ('græpəl) vt agarrar. vi agarrarse.

grasp (grɑːsp) n 1 agarro m. 2 apretón m. 3 comprensión f. vt 1 agarrar. 2 comprender.

grass (grɑːs) n 1 hierba f. 2 césped m. **grassroots** adj 1 básico. 2 popular.

grate[1] (greit) n parrilla de hogar f.

grate[2] (greit) vt rallar. vi molestar.

grateful ('greitfəl) adj agradecido.

gratify ('grætifai) vt 1 satisfacer. 2 complacer.

gratitude ('grætitjuːd) n agradecimiento m.

grave[1] (greiv) n sepultura f. sepulcro m. **gravestone** n lápida sepulcral f. **graveyard** n cementerio m.

grave[2] (greiv) adj 1 serio. 2 grave.

gravel ('grævəl) n grava f. cascajo m.

gravity ('græviti) n 1 gravedad f. 2 gravitación f.

gravy ('greivi) n salsa f. jugo m.

graze[1] (greiz) vt 1 pacer. 2 apacentar.

graze[2] (greiz) n roce m. vt raspar, raer.

grease (griːs) n grasa f. vt engrasar. **greaseproof** adj impermeable a la grasa.

great (greit) adj 1 grande. 2 importante.

Great Britain n Gran Bretaña f.

Greece (griːs) n Grecia f. **Grecian** adj griego. **Greek** adj,n griego m. **Greek** (language) n griego m.

greed (griːd) n 1 codicia, avaricia f. 2 gula, glotonería f.

green (griːn) adj 1 verde. 2 novato. n 1 verde m. 2 pl verduras f pl. **greengrocer** n verdulero m. **greenhouse** n invernadero m.

greet (griːt) vt 1 saludar. 2 presentarse a. **greeting** n salutación f.

gregarious (griˈgɛəriəs) adj gregario.

grenade (griˈneid) n granada f.

grew (gruː) v see **grow**.

grey (grei) adj,n gris m. vi encanecer. **greyhound** n galgo m.

grid (grid) n 1 reja f. 2 parrilla f.

grief (griːf) n dolor, pesar m.

grieve (griːv) vt dar pena a. vi afligirse. **grievance** n 1 pesar m. 2 agravio m.

grill (gril) n 1 parrilla f. 2 asado a la parrilla m. vt 1 asar en parrilla. 2 interrogar.

grille (gril) n rejilla f.

grim (grim) adj 1 severo. 2 ceñudo. 3 fiero.

grimace (griˈmis) n mueca f. vi hacer muecas.

grime (graim) n mugre f.

grin (grin) n 1 sonrisa burlona f. 2 mueca f. vi sonreír mostrando los dientes.

grind* (graind) vt 1 moler. 2 afilar. vi rechinar. n trabajo pesado m.

grip (grip) n 1 apretón m. 2 asidero m. 3 bolso de mano m. vt agarrar, asir.

gripe (graip) n retorcijón de tripas m. vi inf quejarse.

gristle ('grisəl) n cartílago m. ternilla f.

grit (grit) n 1 arena f. 2 polvo m. 3 tesón m. vt apretar los dientes.

groan (groun) n gemido m. vi 1 gemir. 2 crujir.

grocer ('grousə) n verdulero, tendero m.

groin (grɔin) n ingle f.

groom (gruːm) n 1 novio m. 2 caballerizo m. vt almohazar.

groove (gruːv) n 1 ranura f. 2 surco m. vt estriar.

grope (group) vi ir a tientas.

gross (grous) adj 1 grueso. 2 craso. 3 grosero.

grotesque (grouˈtesk) adj grotesco.

grotto ('grotou) n gruta f.

ground[1] (graund) n 1 tierra f. 2 suelo m. 3 terreno m. 4 fundamento m. 5 pl parque, jardín m. **ground floor** n entresuelo m. **groundsheet** n tela impermeable f. **groundsman** n guarda encargado de recinto deportivo m. **groundwork** n trabajo preliminar m.

ground[2] (graund) v see **grind**.

group (gruːp) n grupo m. vt agrupar.

grouse[1] (graus) n invar lagópedo m.

grouse[2] (graus) n rezongo m. vt rezongar.

grove (grouv) n arboleda f.

grovel ('grɔvəl) *vi* arrastrarse.

grow* (grou) *vt* **1** cultivar. **2** dejar, crecer. *vi* **1** crecer. **2** aumentarse. **grown-up** *adj* adulto. *n* persona mayor *f*. **growth** *n* crecimiento, aumento *m*.

growl (graul) *n* gruñido *m*. *vi* gruñir.

grub (grʌb) *n* **1** gusano *m*. **2** *inf* comida *f*. *vi* escarbar.

grubby ('grʌbi) *adj* sucio, mugriento.

grudge (grʌdʒ) *n* rencor *m*. *vt* escatimar.

gruelling ('gruːəliŋ) *adj* duro, penoso.

gruesome ('gruːsəm) *adj* horrible, horripilante.

gruff (grʌf) *adj* **1** brusco. **2** bronco.

grumble ('grʌmbəl) *n* queja *f*. *vi* refunfuñar.

grumpy ('grʌmpi) *adj* gruñón, malhumorado.

grunt (grʌnt) *n* gruñido *m*. *vi* gruñir.

guarantee (gærən'tiː) *n* garantía *f*. *vt* garantizar. **guarantor** *n* fiador *m*.

guard (gɑːd) *n* guardia *f*. *vt* guardar, proteger. **guardian** *n* **1** guardián *m*. **2** tutor *m*.

guerrilla (gə'rilə) *n* guerrillero *m*.

guess (ges) *n* conjetura *f*. *vt,vi* **1** adivinar. **2** suponer. **guesswork** *n* conjeturas *f pl*.

guest (gest) *n* **1** convidado *m*. **2** huésped *m/f*. **guesthouse** *n* casa de huéspedes *f*.

guide (gaid) *n* guía *f*. *vt* **1** guiar. **2** dirigir. **guidance** *n* **1** guía *f*. **2** consejo *m*. **guidebook** *n* guía del viajero *f*.

guild (gild) *n* gremio *m*.

guillotine (gilə'tiːn) *n* guillotina *f*. *vt* guillotinar.

guilt (gilt) *n* culpabilidad *f*. **guilty** *adj* culpable.

guinea ('gini) *n* guinea *f*. **guinea pig** *n* cobayo, conejillo de Indias *m*.

guitar (gi'tɑː) *n* guitarra *f*.

gulf (gʌlf) *n* golfo *m*.

gull (gʌl) *n* gaviota *f*. *vt* estafar.

gullet ('gʌlit) *n* gaznate *m*.

gulp (gʌlp) *n* trago *m*. *vt* tragarse. *vi* tragar saliva.

gum¹ (gʌm) *n* goma *f*. *vt* engomar.

gum² (gʌm) *n* encía *f*.

gun (gʌn) *n* **1** fusil *m*. **2** cañón *m*. **3** pistola *f*. *vt* disparar sobre. **gunman** *n* pistolero *m*. **gunpowder** *n* pólvora *f*. **gunshot** *n* escopetazo *m*.

gurgle ('gɔːgəl) *n* gorgoteo *m*. *vi* gorgotear.

gush (gʌʃ) *n* chorro *m*. *vi* brotar, chorrear.

gust (gʌst) *n* ráfaga *f*.

gut (gʌt) *n* tripa *f*. **guts** *n* *inf* valor *m*. valentía *f*.

gutter ('gʌtə) *n* **1** arroyo *m*. **2** gotera *f*. **3** canal, canalera *f*.

guy¹ (gai) *n* mamarracho *m*.

guy² (gai) *n* *naut* cuerda *f*.

gymnasium (dʒim'neiziəm) *n* gimnasio *m*. **gymnast** *n* gimnasta *m,f*. **gymnastic** *adj* gimnástico.

gynaecology (gaini'kɔlədʒi) *n* ginecología *f*.

gypsum ('dʒipsəm) *n* yeso *m*.

H

haberdasher ('hæbədæʃə) *n* mercero *m*. **haberdashery** *n* mercería *f*.

habit ('hæbit) *n* **1** costumbre *f*. **2** hábito *m*. **habitable** *adj* habitable. **habitual** *adj* habitual.

hack¹ (hæk) *vt* tajar. *n* hachazo *m*.

hack² (hæk) *n* rocín *m*.

hackneyed ('hæknid) *adj* trillado.

had (hæd) *v see* **have.**

haddock ('hædək) *n* eglefino *m*.

haemorrhage ('heməridʒ) *n* hemorragia *f*.

hag (hæg) *n* **1** bruja *f*. **2** vejarrona *f*.

haggard ('hægəd) *adj* ojeroso.

haggle ('hægl) *vi* **1** discutir. **2** regatear.

hail¹ (heil) *vt* **1** llamar. **2** saludar.

hail² (heil) *n* granizo *m*. *vi* granizar. **hailstone** *n* pedrisco *m*. **hailstorm** *n* granizada *f*.

hair (hɛə) *n* pelo, cabello *m*. **grey hair** canas *f pl*. **hairbrush** *n* cepillo para el pelo *m*. **haircut** *n* corte de pelo *m*. **hairdo** *n* peinado *m*. **hairdresser** *n* peluquero *m*. **hairgrip** or **hairpin** *n* horquilla *f*.

half (hɑːf) *n,pl* **halves** mitad *f*. *adj* medio. *adv* a medias, semi.

half-back *sport n* medio *m*.

half-breed *adj* mestizo.

half-brother *n* medio hermano *m*.

half-hour *n* media hora *f*.

half-mast *n* **at half-mast** a media asta.

halfpenny ('heipəni) *n* medio penique *m*.

half-pint *n* media pinta *f*.

half-sister *n* media hermana, hermanastra *f*.

half-time *n* descanso *m*.

halftone ('hɑːftoun) *n* media tinta *f*.

halfway (hɑːf'wei) *adj* intermedio *adv* a medio camino.

halfwit ('hɑːfwit) *n* imbécil *m,f*.

hall (hɔːl) *n* **1** vestíbulo *m*. **2** comedor *m*. **3** sala *f*. **town hall** *n* ayuntamiento *m*.

hallmark ('hɔːlmɑːk) *n* **1** marca de ley *f*. **2** sello *m*.

Halloween (hælou'iːn) *n* víspera de todos los Santos *f*.

hallucination (həluːsi'neiʃən) *n* alucinación *f*.

halo ('heilou) *n pl* **-os** *or* **-oes 1** halo *m.* **2** aureola *f.*

halt (ho:lt) *n* alto *m.* parada *f.* *vt* parar. *vi* hacer alto.

halter ('ho:ltə) *n* cabestro, ronzal *m.*

halve (ha:v) *vt* partir por mitad.

ham (hæm) *n* **1** jamón *m.* **2** *Th inf* comicastro *m.*

hamburger ('hæmbə:gə) *n* hamburguesa *f.*

hammer ('hæmə) *n* martillo *m.* *vt* martillar.

hammock ('hæmək) *n* hamaca *f.*

hamper[1] ('hæmpə) *vt* impedir.

hamper[2] ('hæmpə) *n* cesto *m.* canasta *f.*

hand (hænd) *n* **1** mano *f.* **2** manecilla *f.* **3** palmo *m.* *vt* entregar.

handbag ('hændbæg) *n* bolso *m.*

handbook ('hændbuk) *n* **1** manual *m.* **2** guía *f.*

handbrake ('hændbreik) *n* freno de mano *m.*

handcart ('hændka:t) *n* carretilla *f.*

handcuffs ('hændkʌf) *n pl* esposas *f pl.*

handful ('hændful) *n* puñado *m.*

hand grenade *n* granada *f.*

handicap ('hændikæp) *n* desventaja *f.* obstáculo *m.* *vt* **1** impedir. **2** perjudicar.

handicraft ('hændikra:ft) *n* artesanía *f.*

handiwork ('hændiwə:k) *n* obra manual *f.*

handkerchief ('hæŋkətʃif) *n* pañuelo *m.*

handle ('hændl) *n* **1** mango *m.* **2** manivela *f.* **3** asa *m.* *vt* **1** tocar. **2** manipular. **3** manejar. **handlebars** *n pl* manillar *m.*

handmade (hænd'meid) *adj* hecho a mano.

hand-out *n* **1** distribución *f.* **2** limosna *f.*

hand-pick *vt* escoger a mano.

handrail ('hændreil) *n* pasamano *m.*

handshake ('hændʃeik) *n* apretón de manos *m.*

handsome ('hænsəm) *adj* **1** hermoso, guapo. **2** generoso.

handwriting ('hændraitiŋ) *n* escritura *f.*

handy ('hændi) *adj* **1** a mano. **3** hábil. **3** útil.

hang[*] (hæŋ) *vt* **1** colgar. **2** tender. **3** ahorcar. **hangman** *n* verdugo *m.* **hangover** *n* resaca *f.*

hanker ('hæŋkə) *vi* añorar, anhelar.

haphazard (hæp'hæzəd) *adj* fortuito.

happen ('hæpən) *vi* pasar, suceder, ocurrir. **happening** *n* suceso, acontecimiento *m.*

happy ('hæpi) *adj* **1** feliz. **2** contento. **3** alegre. **happiness** *n* felicidad *f.*

harass ('hærəs) *vt* acosar, hostigar.

harbour ('ha:bə) *n* puerto *m.* *vt* **1** abrigar. **2** hospedar.

hard (ha:d) *adj* **1** duro. **2** penoso. **3** severo. *adv* **1** fuerte. **2** duro. **hardback** *n* libro de tapas

duras *m.* **hardboard** *n* chapa de madera dura *f.* **hardship** *n* **1** trabajos *m pl.* penas *f pl.* **2** apuro económico *m.* **hardware** *n* ferretería, quincalla *f.*

harden ('ha:dn) *vt* endurecer.

hardly ('ha:dli) *adv* **1** duramente. **2** apenas.

hardy ('ha:di) *adj* **1** fuerte. **2** resistente.

hare ('hɛə) *n* liebre *f.*

haricot ('hærikou) *n* alubia *f.*

harm (ha:m) *n* daño, perjuicio. *m.* *vt* dañar. **harmful** *adj* perjudicial.

harmonic (ha:'mɔnik) *adj* armónico. **harmonize** *vt,vi* armonizar. **harmony** *n* armonía *f.*

harness ('ha:nis) *n* guarniciones *f pl.* *vt* **1** enjaezar. **2** utilizar.

harp (ha:p) *n* arpa *m.*

harpoon (ha:'pu:n) *n* arpón *m.* *vt* arponear.

harpsichord ('ha:psikɔ:d) *n* arpicordio *m.*

harsh (ha:ʃ) *adj* **1** áspero. **2** cruel.

harvest ('ha:vist) *n* cosecha *f.* *vt* cosechar.

has (hæz) *v see* **have.**

hashish ('hæʃiʃ) *n* hachís *m.*

haste (heist) *n* prisa *f.* **hasten** *vt* acelerar. *vi* apresurarse.

hat (hæt) *n* sombrero *m.*

hatch[1] (hætʃ) *vt* empollar. *vi* salir del huevo.

hatch[2] (hætʃ) *n naut* escotilla *f.*

hatchet ('hætʃit) *n* hacha *f.*

hate (heit) *n* odio *m.* *vt* odiar, aborrecer.

haughty ('hɔ:ti) *adj* altanero, arrogante.

haul (hɔ:l) *n* tirón *m.* **2** trayecto *m.* **3** redada *f.* *vt* arrastrar.

haunch (hɔ:ntʃ) *n* **1** anca *f.* **2** pierna *f.*

haunt (hɔ:nt) *n* guarida *f.* *vt* **1** frecuentar. **2** aparecer en. **3** obsesionar.

have[*] (hæv) *vt* **1** tener. **2** tomar. **3** llevar. *v aux* haber. **have to** tener que.

haven ('heivən) *n* **1** puerto *m.* **2** refugio *m.*

haversack ('hævəsæk) *n* mochila *f.*

havoc ('hævək) *n* estragos *m pl.*

hawk[1] (hɔ:k) *n* halcón *m.*

hawk[2] (hɔ:k) *vt* pregonar.

hawthorn ('hɔ:θɔ:n) *n* espino *m.*

hay (hei) *n* heno *m.* **haywire** *adj inf* **1** en desorden. **2** loco.

hazard ('hæzəd) *n* riesgo *m.* *vt* **1** arriesgar. **2** aventurar.

haze (heiz) *n* bruma, neblina *f.*

hazel ('heizəl) *n* avellano *m.*

he (hi:) *pron 3rd pers s* él.

head (hed) *n* **1** cabeza *f.* **2** cabecera *f.* **3** jefe *m.* *vt* encabezar. *vi* dirigirse. *adj* principal.

headache ('hedeik) *n* dolor de cabeza *m.*

heading ('hedɪŋ) n encabezamiento, título m.

headlamp or **headlight** ('hedlaɪt) n faro m.

headline ('hedlaɪn) n titular m.

headlong ('hedlɔŋ) adj precipitado. adv de cabeza.

headmaster (hed'maːstə) n director m.

headquarters ('hedkwɔːtəz) n cuartel general m.

headstrong ('hedstrɔŋ) adj terco, testarudo.

headway ('hedweɪ) n progreso, avance m.

heal (hiːl) vt curar, sanar. vi cicatrizarse.

health (helθ) n 1 salud f. 2 sanidad f. **healthy** adj sano, saludable.

heap (hiːp) n montón m. vt 1 amontonar. 2 colmar.

hear* (hɪə) vt 1 oír. 2 law ver. **hear of** oír hablar de. **hear that** oír decir que. **hearing** n 1 oído m. 2 audición f. **hearing aid** n audífono m.

hearse (həːs) n coche fúnebre m.

heart (haːt) n corazón m. **by heart** de memoria. **heart attack** n ataque cardíaco m. **heartbeat** n latido del corazón m. **heart-broken** adj angustiado, acongojado.

hearty ('haːtɪ) adj 1 cordial. 2 fuerte. 3 campechano. 4 (of a meal) copioso.

hearth (haːθ) n 1 hogar m. 2 chimenea f.

heat (hiːt) n 1 calor m. 2 ardor. 3 zool celo m. vt calentar. vi calentarse. **heater** n calentador m. **heatwave** n ola de calor f.

heath (hiːθ) n brezal m.

heathen ('hiːðən) adj,n pagano m.

heather ('heðə) n brezo m.

heave* (hiːv) n 1 esfuerzo m. 2 tirón m. 3 empujón m. vt 1 alzar. 2 exhalar.

heaven ('hevən) n 1 cielo m. 2 paraíso m.

heavy ('hevɪ) adj 1 pesado. 2 denso. 3 grueso.

Hebrew ('hiːbruː) adj,n hebreo m.

heckle ('hekəl) vt,vi interrumpir, importunar.

hectare ('hektɛə) n hectárea f.

hectic ('hektɪk) adj febril.

hedge (hedʒ) n 1 seto vivo m. vt 1 cercar. 2 rodear. vi contestar con evasivas. **hedgehog** n erizo m.

heed (hiːd) vt hacer caso de. n atención f.

heel (hiːl) n 1 talón m. 2 tacón m.

hefty ('heftɪ) adj 1 pesado. 2 fuerte.

height (haɪt) n 1 altura f. 2 estatura f. **heighten** vt 1 elevar. 2 realizar.

heir (ɛə) n heredero m. **heirloom** n herencia, reliquia f.

held (held) v see **hold.**

helicopter ('helɪkɔptə) n helicóptero m.

hell (hel) n infierno m.

hello (həˈlou) interj 1 ¡hola! 2 (in calling on telephone) ¡oiga! 3 (in answering telephone) ¡diga!

helm (helm) n timón m.

helmet ('helmɪt) n casco, yelmo m.

help (help) n 1 ayuda f. 2 socorro m. vt ayudar. **help yourself** sírvase. **helpless** adj 1 desvalido. 2 desamparado.

hem (hem) n dobladillo m.

hemisphere ('hemɪsfɪə) n hemisferio m.

hemp (hemp) n cáñamo m.

hen (hen) n 1 gallina f. 2 hembra f.

hence (hens) adv 1 de aquí. 2 desde ahora. 3 por lo tanto.

her (həː) pron 3rd pers s 1 la. 2 ella. poss adj 3rd pers s su, de ella. **herself** pron 3rd pers s 1 ella misma. 2 se. 3 sí misma.

herald ('herəld) n heraldo m. vt anunciar.

herb (həːb) n hierba f.

herd (həːd) n 1 rebaño m. 2 multitud f. vt guardar. vi reunirse. **herdsman** n 1 vaquero m. 2 pastor m.

here (hɪə) adv 1 aquí. 2 acá.

hereditary (hɪˈredɪtrɪ) adj hereditario.

heredity (hɪˈredɪtɪ) n herencia f.

heresy ('herəsɪ) n herejía f.

heritage ('herɪtɪdʒ) n 1 herencia f. 2 patrimonio m.

hermit ('həːmɪt) n ermitaño m.

hero ('hɪərou) n, pl **heroes** 1 héroe m. 2 protagonista m.

heroin ('herouɪn) n heroína f.

heron ('herən) n garza real f.

herring ('herɪŋ) n arenque m.

hers (həːz) pron poss 3rd pers s de ella, (el) suyo, (la) suya, (los) suyos, (las) suyas f.

hesitate ('hezɪteɪt) vi 1 vacilar. 2 titubear. **hesitation** n vacilación f.

hexagon ('heksəgən) n hexágono m.

hibernate ('haɪbəneɪt) vi 1 invernar. 2 hibernar.

hiccup ('hɪkʌp) n also **hiccough** hipo m. vi hipar.

hide* [1] (haɪd) vt esconder, ocultar.

hide [2] (haɪd) n 1 piel f. 2 cuero m.

hideous ('hɪdɪəs) adj horrible, horrendo.

hiding [1] ('haɪdɪŋ) n **be in hiding** estar escondido.

hiding [2] ('haɪdɪŋ) n paliza f.

hierarchy ('haɪərɑːkɪ) n jerarquía f.

high (haɪ) adj 1 alto. 2 mayor. 3 elevado.

highbrow ('haɪbrau) adj,n intelectual m,f.

high-fidelity adj alta fidelidad.

high frequency adj alta frecuencia.

highlands (ˈhailəndz) n pl montañas f pl. meseta montaña f.

highlight (ˈhailait) n punto más notable m. vt destacar.

Highness (ˈhainis) n alteza f.

highpitched (ˈhaipitʃt) adj de tono alto.

high tide n pleamar f.

highway (ˈhaiwei) n carretera f.

hijack (ˈhaidʒæk) vt atracar.

hike (haik) n caminata f. vi caminar por el campo.

hilarious (hiˈlɛəriəs) adj divertido.

hill (hil) n 1 colina f. cerro m. 2 cuesta f. **hillside** n ladera f. **hilltop** n cumbre f.

him (him) pron 3rd pers s 1 le, lo. 2 él. **himself** pron 3rd pers s 1 él mismo. 2 se. 3 sí mismo.

hind (haind) n 1 cierva f. 2 trasero m. **hindleg** n pata trasera f.

hinder (ˈhində) vt 1 estorbar. 2 dificultar. **hindrance** n estorbo.

Hindu (ˈhindu:) adj,n hindú.

hinge (hindʒ) n bisagra f. gozne m. vt engoznar.

hint (hint) n 1 indirecta f. 2 consejo m. 3 señal f. vt insinuar. vi aludir.

hip (hip) n cadera f.

hippopotamus (hipəˈpotəməs) n hipopótamo m.

hire (haiə) n 1 alquiler m. 2 salario, jornal m. vt 1 alquilar. 2 contratar.

his (hiz) poss adj 3rd pers s su, sus. poss pron 3rd pers s de él. (el) suyo. (la) suya, (los) suyos, (las) suyas.

hiss (his) n silbido, siseo m. vt,vi silbar, sisear.

history (ˈhistri) n historia f. **historian** n historiador m. **historic** adj histórico m.

hit* (hit) n 1 golpe m. 2 tiro m. 3 éxito m. vt 1 golpear. 2 dar en, atinar. vi chocar.

hitch (hitʃ) n 1 tirón m. 2 dificultad f. vt 1 atar. 2 mover de un tirón. **hitch-hike** vi hacer autostop.

hive (haiv) n colmena f.

hoard (hɔ:d) n 1 acumulación f. 2 tesoro escondido m. vt amontonar, atesorar, acaparar.

hoarding (ˈhɔ:diŋ) n cartelera f.

hoarse (hɔ:s) adj ronco.

hoax (houks) n trampa f. truco m. vt engañar, mistificar.

hobble (ˈhɔbəl) n 1 cojera f. 2 maniota, traba f. vi cojear. vt manear.

hobby (ˈhɔbi) n 1 pasatiempo m. 2 afición f.

hock¹ (hɔk) n anat corvejón m.

hock² (hɔk) n vino del Rin m.

hoe (hou) n azadón, sacho m. vt azadonar, sachar.

hog (hɔg) n cerdo m. vt acaparar.

hoist (hɔist) n 1 montacargas m invar. 2 grúa f. vt 1 alzar, levantar. 2 izar.

hold¹ (hould) n 1 agarro m. 2 influencia f. dominio m. vt agarrar, coger. vi 1 mantenerse firme. 2 valer. **holdall** n funda f. neceser m. **holder** n 1 poseedor, tenedor m. 2 inquilino m. 3 titular m. 4 asidero m.

hold² (hould) n naut bodega f.

hole (houl) n agujero, hoyo m.

holiday (ˈhɔlidi) n 1 día de fiesta m. 2 vacación f. vi pasar las vacaciones. **holiday camp** n colonia veraniega f.

Holland (ˈhɔlənd) n Holanda f.

hollow (ˈhɔlou) adj hueco, ahuecado. n hueco m. concavidad f. vt ahuecar, excavar.

holly (ˈhɔli) n acebo m. **hollyhock** n malva loca f.

holster (ˈhoulstə) n pistolera f.

holy (ˈhouli) adj santo, sagrado. **holiness** n santidad f.

homage (ˈhɔmidʒ) n homenaje m.

home (houm) n 1 casa f. hogar m. adj doméstico. **at home** en casa. **homecoming** n regreso al hogar m. **home-made** adj casero. **homesick** adj nostálgico.

homosexual (houməˈsekʃuəl) adj,n homosexual m,f.

honest (ˈɔnist) adj 1 honrado. 2 sincero. **honesty** n 1 honradez f. 2 franqueza f.

honey (ˈhʌni) n miel f. **honeycomb** n panal m. **honeymoon** n luna de miel f. vi pasar la luna de miel. **honeysuckle** n madreselva f.

honour (ˈɔnə) n 1 honor m. 2 honradez f. vt honrar. **honorary** adj honorario.

hood (hud) n 1 capucha f. 2 capirote m. 3 mot capota f.

hoof (hu:f) n, pl **hooves** casco m. pezuña f.

hook (huk) n 1 gancho m. 2 anzuelo m. vt 1 enganchar. 2 pescar. vi encorvar.

hooligan (ˈhu:ligən) n gamberro m.

hoop (hu:p) n aro m. argolla f. vt enarcar.

hoot (hu:t) n 1 grito m. 2 bocinazo m. vt abuchear. vi ulular, gritar.

Hoover (ˈhu:və) n Tdmk aspirador m.

hop¹ (hɔp) n salto, brinco m. vi 1 brincar. 2 cojear.

hop² (hɔp) n bot lúpulo m.

hope (houp) n esperanza f. vi esperar. **hopeful** adj esperanzador. **hopefully** adv con optimismo. **hopeless** adj 1 desesperado, sin esperanza. 2 sin remedio.

horde (hɔːd) n horda f.

horizon (hə'raizən) n horizonte m. **horizontal** adj horizontal.

hormone ('hɔːmoun) n hormona f.

horn (hɔːn) n 1 cuerno m. 2 mus trompa f. 3 bocina f.

hornet ('hɔːnit) n avispón, moscardón m.

horoscope ('hɔrəskoup) n horóscopo m.

horrible ('hɔrəbl) adj horrible.

horrid ('hɔrid) adj horroroso.

horrify ('hɔrifai) vt 1 horrorizar. 2 escandalizar.

horror ('hɔrə) n horror m.

hors d'oeuvre (ɔː 'dəːv) n entremeses m pl.

horse (hɔːs) n caballo m. **horse chestnut** n castaña de Indias f. **horsefly** n tábano m. **horsehair** n crin m. **horseman** n jinete m. **horsepower** n caballo de fuerza m. **horseradish** n rábano picante m. **horseshoe** n herradura f. **on horseback** a caballo.

horticulture ('hɔːtikʌltʃə) n horticultura f. **horticulturalist** n horticultor m.

hose (houz) n invar 1 medias, calzas f pl. 2 calceta f. 3 manga f manguera f. vt regar con manga.

hosiery ('houziəri) n calceta, calcetería f.

hospitable ('hɔspitəbəl) adj hospitalario.

hospital ('hɔspitl) n hospital m.

hospitality (hɔspi'tæliti) n hospitalidad f.

host[1] (houst) n 1 huésped m. 2 anfitrión m.

host[2] (houst) n multitud f.

hostage ('hɔstidʒ) n rehén m.

hostel ('hɔstl) n parador m. **youth hostel** albergue para jóvenes m.

hostess ('houstis) n 1 huéspeda f. 2 anfitriona f. 3 aviat azafata f. 4 camaretera f.

hostile ('hɔstail) adj enemigo, hostil. **hostility** n hostilidad f.

hot (hɔt) adj 1 caliente. 2 caluroso. 3 picante. **be hot** hacer or tener calor. **hot-blooded** adj apasionado. **hothouse** n invernadero m. **hotplate** n calientaplatos m invar. **hot-water bottle** n bolsa de agua caliente f.

hotel (hou'tel) n hotel m.

hound (haund) n podenco, sabueso m. vt acosar, perseguir.

hour (auə) n hora f.

house (haus) n casa f. vt alojar, hospedar.

houseboat ('hausbout) n casa flotante f.

household ('haushould) n 1 casa f. 2 familia f.

housekeeper ('hauskiːpə) n ama de casa, ama

de llaves f. **housekeeping** n gobierno doméstico m.

housemaid ('hausmeid) n criada f.

houseman (hausmən) n médico interno m.

House of Commons n Cámara de los Comunes f.

House of Lords n Cámara de los Lores f.

housewife ('hauswaif) n, pl **housewives** 1 ama de casa f. 2 madre de familia f.

housework ('hauswəːk) n quehacer doméstico m.

housing (hauziŋ) n alojamiento m.

hover ('hɔvə) vi 1 cernerse. 2 rondar. **hovercraft** n hidroala m.

how (hau) adv como, de que modo. **however** adv como, de cualquier modo. conj sin embargo.

howl (haul) n alarido, aullido m. vi 1 gritar. 2 reirse a carcajadas.

hub (hʌb) n cubo, centro m.

huddle ('hʌdl) n montón, grupo m. vi acurrucarse, amontonarse.

huff (hʌf) n rabieta f. enojo m. vt enojar.

hug (hʌg) n abrazo m. vt abrazar, apretar.

huge (hjuːdʒ) adj enorme, inmenso, vasto.

hulk (hʌlk) n 1 barco viejo, casco m. 2 carraca f. 3 bulto m.

hull[1] (hʌl) n vaina, cáscara f.

hull[2] (hʌl) n naut casco m.

hullo (hə'lou) interj ¡hola!

hum (hʌm) n 1 zumbido m. 2 tarareo m. vt canturrear. vi zumbar.

human ('hjuːmən) adj,n humano m. **human nature** n naturaleza humana f. **humane** adj humano, humanitario. **humanism** n humanismo m. **humanitarian** adj,n humanitario m,f. **humanity** n humanidad f.

humble ('hʌmbəl) adj humilde. vt humillar.

humdrum ('hʌmdrʌm) adj 1 monótono, aburrido. 2 rutinario.

humid ('hjuːmid) adj húmedo. **humidity** n humedad f.

humiliate (hjuː'milieit) vt humillar.

humility (hjuː'militi) n humildad f.

humour ('hjuːmə) n humor m. vt complacer, seguir el humor a. **humorist** n humorista m,f. **humorous** adj chistoso, divertido.

hump (hʌmp) n joroba, corcova, giba f. vt llevar.

hunch (hʌntʃ) n presentimiento m. **hunchback** adj,n jorobado, corcovado.

hundred ('hʌndrəd) adj ciento, cien. n centenar m. centena f. **hundredth** adj centésimo. **hundredweight** n quintal m.

hung (hʌŋ) v see **hang**.

Hungary ('hʌŋgəri) n Hungría f. **Hungarian** adj,n húngaro m. **Hungarian** (language) n húngaro m.

hunger ('hʌŋgə) n hambre m. vi tener hambre. **hungry** adj hambriento. **be hungry** tener hambre. **go hungry** pasar hambre.

hunt (hʌnt) n 1 caza, cacería f. 2 búsqueda f. vt 1 cazar. 2 perseguir. **hunting** n cacería, montería f. **huntsman** n cazador, montero m.

hurdle ('hə:dl) n 1 zarzo m. 2 obstáculo m.

hurl (hə:l) vt lanzar, arrojar.

hurrah (hu'ra:) interj ¡viva!

hurricane ('hʌrikein) n huracán m.

hurry ('hʌri) n prisa f. **be in a hurry** tener prisa. vt apresurar, dar prisa a. vi darse prisa.

hurt (hə:t) n 1 herida f. 2 daño m. vt 1 lastimar. 2 herir. vi doler.

husband ('hʌzbənd) n marido, esposo m. vt economizar.

hush (hʌʃ) n silencio m. vt hacer callar. vi callarse. **hush!** ¡chitón!

husk (hʌsk) n cáscara, vaina f.

husky ('hʌski) adj 1 ronco. 2 fornido. n perro esquimal m.

hustle ('hʌsəl) n bullicio m. vt empujar, dar prisa a. vi darse prisa.

hut (hʌt) n 1 cabaña f. 2 cobertizo m. 3 choza f.

hutch (hʌtʃ) n 1 conejera f. 2 cabaña f.

hyacinth ('haiəsinθ) n jacinto m.

hybrid ('haibrid) n,adj híbrido m.

hydraulic (hai'drɔ:lik) adj hidráulico.

hydro-electric adj hidroeléctrico.

hydrogen ('haidrədʒən) n hidrógeno m.

hyena (hai'i:nə) n hiena f.

hygiene ('haidʒi:n) n higiene f. **hygienic** adj higiénico.

hymn (him) n himno m. **hymnbook** n himnario m.

hyphen ('haifən) n guión m.

hypnosis (hip'nousis) n hipnosis f. **hypnotic** adj hipnótico. **hypnotism** n hipnotismo m.

hypochondria (haipə'kɔndriə) n hipocondría f.

hypocrisy (hi'pɔkrəsi) n hipocresía f. **hypocrite** n hipócrita m,f.

hypodermic (haipə'də:mik) n aguja hipodérmica f.

hypothesis (hai'pɔθəsis) n, pl **hypotheses** hipótesis f.

hysterectomy (histə'rektəmi) n histerectomía f.

hysteria (his'tiəriə) n histerismo m. histeria f.

I

I (ai) pron 1st pers s yo.

Iberia (ai'biəriə) n Iberia f. **Iberian** adj,n íbero.

ice (ais) n hielo m. vt helar. **iceberg** n témpano de hielo m. **ice-cream** n helado m. **ice hockey** n hockey sobre hielo m. **ice rink** n pista de hielo f. **ice-skate** vi patinar sobre hielo. **icicle** n carámbano m. **icing** n cul garapiña f. **icy** adj helado, glacial.

icon ('aikɔn) n icono m.

idea (ai'diə) n 1 idea f. 2 concepto m. 3 ocurrencia f.

ideal (ai'diəl) adj,n ideal m. **idealist** n idealista m,f. **idealize** vt idealizar.

identify (ai'dentifai) vt identificar.

identity (ai'dentiti) n identidad f. **identity card** n carnet de identidad m. **identical** adj idéntico.

ideology (aidi'ɔlədʒi) n ideología f.

idiom ('idiəm) n 1 modismo m. locución f. 2 lenguaje m.

idiosyncrasy (idiə'siŋkrəsi) n idiosincrasia f.

idiot ('idiət) n idiota m,f. tonto m.

idle ('aidl) adj 1 ocioso. 2 perezoso. 3 frívolo. v mot marchar en vacío.

idol ('aidl) n ídolo m. **idolatry** n idolatría f. **idolize** vt idolatrar.

idyllic (i'dilik) adj idílico.

if (if) conj si.

ignite (ig'nait) vt encender, incendiar. vi encenderse. **ignition** n ignición f.

ignore (ig'nɔ:) vt no hacer caso de, desconocer. **ignorant** adj ignorante. **be ignorant of** ignorar, desconocer.

ill (il) adj enfermo, malo. adv mal. **ill-bred** adj mal educado. **illness** n emfermedad f. **ill-treat** vt maltratar. **ill will** n 1 mala voluntad f. 2 rencor m.

illegal (i'li:gəl) adj ilegal.

illegible (i'ledʒəbl) adj ilegible.

illegitimate (ili'dʒitimət) adj ilegítimo.

illicit (i'lisit) adj ilícito.

illiterate (i'litərət) adj,n analfabeto m.

illogical (i'lɔdʒikəl) adj ilógico.

illuminate (i'lu:mineit) vt iluminar.

illusion (i'lu:ʒən) n ilusión f.

illustrate ('iləstreit) vt ilustrar.

illustrious (i'lʌstriəs) adj ilustre.

image ('imidʒ) n 1 imagen f. 2 reputación f. **imagery** n 1 imagen f. 2 metáfora f.

imagine (i'mædʒin) vt imaginar. **imaginary** adj imaginario. **imagination** n imaginación f. **imaginative** adj imaginativo.

imitate ('imiteit) vt 1 imitar. 2 remedar. **imitation** n imitación f.

immaculate (i'mækjulət) adj inmaculado.

immature (imə'tjuə) adj 1 inmaturo. 2 juvenil.

immediate (i'mi:diət) adj 1 inmediato. 2 urgente.

immense (i'mens) adj enorme, inmenso.

immerse (i'mə:s) vt sumergir, hundir.

immigrate ('imigreit) vi inmigrar. **immigrant** adj,n inmigrante m,f.

imminent ('iminənt) adj inminente.

immobile (i'moubail) adj inmóvil. **immobilize** vt inmovilizar.

immoral (i'mɔrəl) adj inmoral.

immortal (i'mɔ:tl) adj,n inmortal m,f.

immovable (i'mu:vəbəl) adj 1 inmóvil, inmoble. 2 inconmovible, inmovible.

immune (i'mju:n) adj inmune. **immunize** vt inmunizar.

imp (imp) n diablillo, duende m.

impact ('impækt) n choque, impacto m.

impair (im'pɛə) vt 1 perjudicar, dañar 2 empeorar, deteriorar.

impart (im'pɑ:t) vt comunicar.

impartial (im'pɑ:ʃəl) adj imparcial.

impatient (im'peiʃənt) adj 1 impaciente. 2 intolerante.

impeach (im'pi:tʃ) vt 1 acusar. 2 procesar.

impeccable (im'pekəbəl) adj impecable.

impediment (im'pedimənt) n 1 obstáculo m. 2 impedimento m. 3 defecto del habla m.

impel (im'pel) vt impulsar, impeler.

imperative (im'perətiv) adj,n imperativo m.

imperfect (im'pə:fikt) adj imperfecto, defectuoso.

imperial (im'piəriəl) adj imperial.

impersonal (im'pə:sənl) adj impersonal.

impersonate (im'pə:səneit) vt 1 hacerse pasar por. 2 imitar.

impertinent (im'pə:tinənt) adj impertinente.

impetuous (im'petʃuəs) adj impetuoso.

impetus ('impitəs) n ímpetu m.

impinge (im'pindʒ) vi **impinge on** afectar a.

implement ('impləmənt) n 1 herramienta f. apero m. vt poner en obra.

implicit (im'plisit) adj 1 implícito. 2 absoluto.

implore (im'plɔ:) vt implorar, suplicar.

imply (im'plai) vt 1 implicar. 2 querer decir. 3 insinuar.

import (n 'impɔ:t; v im'pɔ:t) n 1 importación m. 2 sentido m. 3 importancia f. vt importar.

importance (im'pɔ:tns) n importancia f.

impose (im'pouz) vt imponer. vi 1 embaucar. 2 abusar. **imposing** adj imponente.

impossible (im'posəbəl) adj imposible.

impostor (im'postə) n impostor m.

impotent ('impətənt) adj impotente.

impound (im'paund) vt embargar.

impoverish (im'povəriʃ) vt empobrecer.

impress (im'pres) vt 1 estampar. 2 impresionar. vi hacer buena impresión. **impression** n impresión f.

imprint (n 'imprint; v im'print) n 1 impresión, huella f. 2 pie de imprenta m. vt imprimir, grabar.

imprison (im'prizən) vt encarcelar.

improbable (im'probabəl) adj improbable.

impromptu (im'promptju:) adj 1 improvisado. 2 impremeditado. adv de improviso.

improper (im'propə) adj 1 impropio. 2 indecoroso.

improve (im'pru:v) vt 1 mejorar. 2 perfeccionar. **improvement** n mejoramiento m.

improvise ('imprəvaiz) vt,vi improvisar.

impudent ('impjudənt) adj impudente, descarado.

impulse ('impʌls) n impulso m.

impure (im'pjuə) adj impuro.

in (in) prep 1 en. 2 dentro de. 3 de. adv dentro, adentro.

inability (inə'biliti) n 1 inhabilidad f. 2 incapacidad f.

inaccurate (in'ækjurət) adj inexacto, incorrecto. **inaccuracy** n inexactitud f.

inadequate (in'ædikwit) adj inadecuado, insuficiente.

inadvertent (inəd'və:tnt) adj inadvertido.

inane (i'nein) adj necio, fatuo.

inanimate (in'ænimət) adj inanimado.

inarticulate (inɑ:'tikjulət) adj incapaz de expresarse.

inasmuch (inəz'mʌtʃ) conj puesto que.

inaudible (in'ɔ:dəbəl) adj inaudible.

inaugurate (i'nɔ:gjureit) vt inaugurar.

incapable (in'keipəbəl) adj incapaz.

incense[1] ('insens) n incienso m.

incense[2] (in'sens) vt indignar.

incessant (in'sesənt) adj incesante.

incest ('insest) n incesto m.

inch (intʃ) n pulgada f. **inch by inch** palmo a palmo. vi moverse poco a poco.

incident ('insidənt) n incidente m. **incidental** adj incidental.

incite (in'sait) vt incitar.

incline (in'klain) n declive m. vt inclinar.

include (in'klu:d) vt incluir. **inclusion** n inclusión f.

incoherent (inkou'hiərənt) adj incoherente.

income ('inkʌm) n 1 renta f. 2 rédito m.

incompatible (inkəm'pætibəl) adj incompatible.

incompetent (in'kɔmpətənt) adj incompetente. **incompetence** n incompetencia f.

incomplete (inkəm'pli:t) adj incompleto.

incomprehensible (inkɔmpri'hensəbəl) adj incomprensible.

inconceivable (inkən'si:vəbəl) adj inconcebible.

inconclusive (inkən'klu:siv) adj inconcluso.

incongruous (in'kɔŋgruəs) adj incongruo.

inconsiderate (inkən'sidərit) adj desconsiderado.

inconsistent (inkən'sistənt) adj inconsistente.

inconvenient (inkən'vi:niənt) adj 1 incómodo, molesto. 2 inoportuno. **inconvenience** n incomodidad f.

incorporate (in'kɔ:pəreit) vt 1 incorporar. 2 agregar.

incorrect (inkə'rekt) adj incorrecto.

increase (v in'kri:s; n 'inkri:s) n aumento, incremento m. vt aumentar.

incredible (in'kredəbəl) adj increíble.

incubate ('inkjubeit) vt incubar, empollar. **incubator** n incubadora f.

incur (in'kə:) vt 1 incurrir en. 2 contraer.

indecent (in'di:sənt) adj indecente.

indeed (in'di:d) adv de veras. **yes indeed!** ¡claro que sí!

indefinite (in'defənit) adj indefinido.

independent (indi'pendənt) adj independiente. **independence** n independencia f.

index ('indeks) n, pl **indices** índice m. **index finger** n dedo índice m.

India ('indiə) n la India f. **Indian** adj,n indio m.

indicate ('indikeit) vt indicar. **indicator** n indicador m.

indifferent (in'difrənt) adj indiferente.

indigestion (indi'dʒestʃən) n indigestión f.

indignant (in'dignənt) adj indignado.

indirect (indi'rekt) adj indirecto.

indiscreet (indi'skri:t) adj indiscreto.

indiscriminate (indi'skriminit) adj 1 indistinto. 2 que no hace distinción.

indispensable (indi'spensəbəl) adj indispensable, imprescindible.

individual (indi'vidʒuəl) adj individual. n individuo m.

indoctrinate (in'dɔktrineit) vt adoctrinar.

indolent ('indələnt) adj indolente.

indoor ('indɔ:) adj 1 de puerta adentro. 2 interior. **indoors** adv 1 en casa. 2 dentro.

induce (in'dju:s) vt 1 inducir. 2 ocasionar.

indulge (in'dʌldʒ) vt 1 satisfacer. 2 complacer. vi abandonarse a

industry ('indəstri) n industria f. **industrial** adj industrial. **industrious** adj trabajador, industrioso.

inefficient (ini'fiʃənt) adj ineficaz. **inefficiency** n ineficacia f.

inept (i'nept) adj inepto.

inequality (ini'kwɔliti) n desigualdad f.

inert (i'nə:t) adj inerte. **inertia** n 1 inercia f. 2 pereza f.

inevitable (in'evitəbəl) adj inevitable, ineludible.

infallible (in'fæləbəl) adj infalible.

infamous ('infəməs) adj infame.

infant ('infənt) n 1 niño m. 2 educ párvulo m. **infancy** n infancia f.

infantry ('infəntri) n infantería f.

infatuate (in'fætʃueit) vt 1 apasionar. 2 engreír.

infect (in'fekt) vt infectar, contagiar. **infection** n infección f.

infer (in'fə:) vt inferir, deducir.

inferior (in'fiəriə) adj,n inferior m,f.

infernal (in'fə:nl) adj infernal.

infest (in'fest) vt infestar.

infidelity (infi'deliti) n infidelidad f.

infiltrate ('infiltreit) vt infiltrarse en.

infinite ('infinit) adj,n infinito m. **infinity** n 1 infinidad f. 2 math infinito m.

infinitive (in'finitiv) adj,n infinitivo m.

infirm (in'fə:m) adj enfermizo, débil.

inflame (in'fleim) vt inflamar, encender.

inflammable (in'flæməbəl) adj inflamable.

inflate (in'fleit) vt hinchar, inflar. **inflation** n inflación f.

inflection (in'flekʃən) n inflexión f.

inflict (in'flikt) vt 1 infligir, inferir. 2 imponer.

influence ('influəns) n influencia f. vt influenciar. **influential** adj influyente.

influenza (influ'enzə) n gripe f.

inform (in'fɔ:m) vt informar, avisar. **information** n 1 información f. 2 conocimientos m pl.

informal (in'fɔ:məl) adj familiar, poco ceremonioso.

infringe (in'frindʒ) vt infringir, violar.

infuriate (in'fjuərieit) vt enfurecer

ingenious (inˈdʒiːnɪəs) *adj* ingenioso, genial.

ingredient (inˈgriːdɪənt) *n* ingrediente *m*.

inhabit (inˈhæbit) *vt* habitar.

inhale (inˈheil) *vt* aspirar, inhalar.

inherent (inˈhiərənt) *adj* 1 inherente. 2 innato.

inherit (inˈherit) *vt* heredar. **inheritance** *n* herrencia *f*.

inhibit (inˈhibit) *vt* inhibir, impedir. **inhibition** *n* inhibición *f*.

inhuman (inˈhjuːmən) *adj* inhumano.

initial (iˈniʃəl) *adj,n* inicial. *vt* marcar, rubricar.

initiate (iˈniʃieit) *vt* iniciar

initiative (iˈniʃiətiv) *n* iniciativa *f*.

inject (inˈdʒekt) *vt* inyectar. **injection** *n* inyección *f*

injure (ˈindʒə) *vt* 1 herir, lastimar. 2 perjudicar. **injury** *n* 1 herida, lesión *f*. 2 daño *m*.

injustice (inˈdʒʌstis) *n* injusticia *f*.

ink (iŋk) *n* tinta *f*. *vt* entintar

inkling (ˈiŋkliŋ) *n* 1 indicio *m*. 2 sospecha *f*

inland (*adj* ˈinlənd; *adv* inˈlænd) *adj* interior. *adv* tierra adentro. **Inland Revenue** *n* Delegación de Contribuciones *f*.

inmate (ˈinmeit) *n* 1 residente *m,f.* 2 asilado *m*. 3 preso *m*.

inn (in) *n* posada *f*. mesón *m*. taberna *f*.

innate (iˈneit) *adj* innato.

inner (ˈinə) *adj* interior.

innocent (ˈinəsənt) *adj,n* inocente.

innocuous (iˈnɔkjuəs) *adj* innocuo.

innovation (inəˈveiʃən) *n* innovación *f*.

innuendo (injuˈendou) *n* insinuación *f*

inoculate (iˈnɔkjuleit) *vt* inocular

inquest (ˈinkwest) *n* indagación judicial *f*.

inquire (inˈkwaiə) *vt* preguntar, informarse de. **inquire into** investigar. **inquiry** *n* 1 pregunta *f*. 2 pesquisa *f*. 3 investigación *f*

inquisition (inkwiˈziʃən) *n* inquisición *f*

inquisitive (inˈkwizitiv) *adj* inquiridor, curioso.

insane (inˈsein) *adj* loco, demente.

insatiable (inˈseiʃəbəl) *adj* insaciable.

inscribe (inˈskraib) *vt* 1 inscribir 2 dedicar **inscription** *n* inscripción *f*.

insect (ˈinsekt) *n* insecto *m*. **insecticide** *n* insecticida *f*

insecure (insiˈkjuə) *adj* inseguro.

inseminate (inˈsemineit) *vt* inseminar.

insert (inˈsəːt) *vt* insertar.

inside (inˈsaid) *adv* dentro *prep* dentro de. *adj,n* interior *m*.

insidious (inˈsidiəs) *adj* 1 insidioso. 2 maligno.

insight (ˈinsait) *n* perspicacia *f*

insignificant (insigˈnifikənt) *adj* insignificante

insinuate (inˈsinjueit) *vt* insinuar.

insist (inˈsist) *vi* insistir.

insolent (ˈinsələnt) *adj* insolente, descarado. **insolence** *n* insolencia *f*.

insomnia (inˈsɔmniə) *n* insomnio *m*.

inspect (inˈspekt) *vt* inspeccionar. **inspector** *n* inspector *m*.

inspire (inˈspaiə) *vt* inspirar, infundir. **inspiration** *n* inspiración *f*

instability (instəˈbiliti) *n* instabilidad *f*.

install (inˈstɔːl) *vt* instalar. **installation** *n* instalación *f*.

instalment (inˈstɔːlmənt) *n* 1 entrega *f*. 2 *comm* plazo *m*.

instance (ˈinstəns) *n* ejemplo *m*. *vt* poner por caso. **instant** *adj* inmediato, instantáneo. *n* instante *m*. **instantaneous** *adj* instantáneo.

instead (inˈsted) *adv* en lugar de. **instead of** en vez de.

instep (ˈinstep) *n* empeine *m*

instigate (ˈinstigeit) *vt* instigar.

instil (inˈstil) *vt* infundir, inculcar

instinct (ˈinstiŋkt) *n* instinto *m*. **instinctive** *adj* instintivo.

institute (ˈinstitjuːt) *n* instituto *m*. *vt* instituir. **institution** *n* 1 institución *f*. 2 tradición *f*. 3 asilo *m*. 4 manicomio *m*.

instruct (inˈstrʌkt) *vt* 1 instruir. 2 mandar. **instruction** *n* 1 instrucción *f*. 2 indicación *f*.

instrument (ˈinstrəmənt) *n* instrumento *m*. **instrumental** *adj* instrumental.

insubordinate (insəˈbɔːdinət) *adj* insubordinado.

insular (ˈinsjulə) *adj* insular.

inoulate (ˈinsjuleit) *vt* aislar

insulin (ˈinsjulin) *n* insulina *f*.

insult (*v* inˈsʌlt; *n* ˈinsʌlt) *n* insulto *m*. *vt* insultar

insure (inˈʃuə) *vt* asegurar. **insurance** *n* seguro *m*.

intact (inˈtækt) *adj* 1 intacto. 2 ileso.

integral (ˈintigrəl) *adj* integro. *n* *math* integral *f*.

integrate (ˈintigreit) *vt* integrar.

integrity (inˈtegriti) *n* integridad *f*.

intellect (ˈintəlekt) *n* intelecto *m*. **intellectual** *adj,n* intelectual

intelligent (inˈtelidʒənt) *adj* inteligente. **intelligence** *n* 1 inteligencia *f*. 2 información *f*. **intelligible** *adj* inteligible

intend (inˈtend) *vt* proponerse, pensar.

intense (inˈtens) *adj* intenso. **intensify** *vt* intensificar. **intensity** *n* intensidad *f*. **intensive** *adj* intensivo.

219

intent

intent¹ (in'tent) n intento, propósito m.
intent² (in'tent) adj 1 absorto. 2 resuelto.
intention (in'tenʃən) n 1 intención f. 2 propósito m.
inter (in'tə:) vt enterrar.
interact (intə'rækt) vi obrar recíprocamente.
intercept (intə'sept) vt interceptar.
interchange (intə'tʃeindʒ) vt intercambiar.
intercourse (ˈintəkɔ:s) n 1 trato m. 2 comercio m. 3 coito m.
interest (ˈintrəst) n 1 interés m. 2 beneficio m. vt interesar.
interfere (intə'fiə) vi 1 intervenir. 2 interferir.
interim (ˈintərim) adj interino, provisional.
interior (in'tiəriə) adj,n interior m.
interjection (intə'dʒekʃn) n interjección f.
interlude (ˈintəlu:d) n intervalo m.
intermediate (intə'mi:diət) adj intermedio, intermediario. intermediary adj,n intermediario m.
intermission (intə'miʃən) n intermisión f. intervalo m.
intermittent (intə'mitnt) adj intermitente.
intern (in'tə:n) vt internar, recluir.
internal (in'tə:nl) adj interno, interior.
international (intə'næʃnl) adj internacional.
interpose (intə'pouz) vt interponer.
interpret (in'tə:prit) vt interpretar. interpretation n interpretación f. interpreter n intérprete m,f.
interrogate (in'terəgeit) vt interrogar. interrogative adj interrogativo.
interrupt (intə'rʌpt) vt,vi interrumpir. interruption n interrupción f.
intersect (intə'sekt) vt cruzar.
interval (ˈintəvəl) n 1 intervalo m. 2 descanso m.
intervene (intə'vi:n) vi intervenir.
interview (ˈintəvju:) n entrevista f. vt entrevistarse con.
intestine (in'testin) n intestino m.
intimate¹ (ˈintimit) adj íntimo.
intimate² (ˈintimeit) vt dar a entender, intimar.
intimidate (in'timideit) vt intimidar.
into (ˈintə; stressed ˈintu:) prep 1 en. 2 dentro de. 3 hacia el interior de.
intolerable (in'tɔlərəbəl) adj intolerable. intolerant adj intolerante.
intonation (intə'neiʃən) n entonación f.
intoxicate (in'tɔksikeit) vt embriagar.
intransitive (in'trænsitiv) adj intransitivo.
intrepid (in'trepid) adj intrépido.
intricate (ˈintrikət) adj intrincado.

intrigue (in'tri:g) n intriga f. vt fascinar. vi intrigar.
intrinsic (in'trinsik) adj intrínseco.
introduce (intrə'dju:s) vt 1 introducir. 2 presentar. introduction n 1 introducción f. 2 presentación f.
introspective (intrə'spektiv) adj introspectivo.
introvert (in'trəvə:t) adj,n introvertido m.
intrude (in'tru:d) vi 1 estorbar. 2 entrometerse.
intuition (intju'iʃən) n intuición f. intuitive adj intuitivo.
inundate (ˈinʌndeit) vt inundar.
invade (in'veid) vt invadir. invasion n invasión f.
invalid¹ (ˈinvəli:d) adj,n inválido m.
invalid² (in'vælid) adj inválido, nulo.
invaluable (in'væljubəl) adj inestimable.
invariable (in'vɛəriəbəl) adj invariable.
invent (in'vent) vt inventar. invention n 1 invención f. 2 inventiva f.
inventory (ˈinvəntəri) n inventario m.
invert (in'və:t) vt invertir, trastocar.
invertebrate (in'və:təbreit) adj,n invertebrado m.
invest (in'vest) vt vi invertir. investment n comm inversión f.
investigate (in'vestigeit) vt investigar.
invincible (in'vinsəbəl) adj invencible.
invisible (in'vizəbəl) adj invisible.
invite (in'vait) vt invitar. invitation n invitación f. convite m.
invoice (ˈinvɔis) n factura f. vt facturar.
invoke (in'vouk) vt invocar.
involve (in'vɔlv) vt 1 implicar. 2 enredar. 3 suponer, implicar.
inward (ˈinwəd) adj interior.
inwards (ˈinwədz) adv hacia dentro.
iodine (ˈaiədi:n) n yodo m.
Ireland (ˈaiələnd) n Irlanda f. Irish adj,n irlandés m. Irish (language) n irlandés m.
iris (ˈairis) n 1 anat iris m. 2 bot lirio m.
iron (ˈaiən) n 1 hierro m. 2 plancha f. vt 1 planchar. 2 allanar. Iron Curtain n telón de acero m. ironmonger n ferretero m.
irony (ˈairəni) n ironía f. ironic adj irónico.
irrational (iˈræʃənl) adj irracional.
irregular (iˈregjulə) adj irregular.
irrelevant (iˈreləvənt) adj inaplicable, fuera de lugar.
irresistible (iri'zistəbəl) adj irresistible.
irrespective (iri'spektiv) adj aparte, sin hacer caso de.
irresponsible (iri'spɔnsəbəl) adj irresponsable

irrevocable (i'revəkəbəl) *adj* irrevocable.

irrigate ('irigeit) *vt* regar.

irritate ('iriteit) *vt* irritar.

is (iz) *v see* **be.**

Islam ('izla:m) *n* Islam *m.* **Islamic** *adj* islámico.

island ('ailənd) *n* isla *f.*

isolate ('aisəleit) *vt* aislar. **isolation** *n* aislamiento *m.*

issue ('ifu:) *n* 1 resultado *m.* 2 cuestión *f.* 3 emisión *f.* 4 edición *f.* 5 descendencia *f. vt* 1 emitir. 2 distribuir. 3 expedir. *vi* salir.

italic (i'tælik) *adj* 1 en bastardilla. 2 itálico.

Italy ('itəli) *n* Italia *f.* **Italian** *adj,n* italiano *m.* **Italian** (language) *n* italiano *m.*

itch (itf) *n* picazón *m. vi* picar, sentir comezón.

item ('aitəm) *n* 1 artículo *m.* 2 detalle, punto *m.*

itinerary (ai'tinərəri) *n* itinerario *m.*

its (its) *poss adj* 3rd *pers* s su, sus. *poss pron* 3rd *pers* s (el', suyo, (la) suya, (los) suyos, (las) suyas.

ivory ('aivəri) *n* marfil *m.*

ivy ('aivi) *n* hiedra, yedra *f.*

J

jab (dʒæb) *n* pinchazo *m. vt* pinchar.

jack (dʒæk) *n* 1 *mot* gato *m.* 2 *game* valet *m.*

jackal ('dʒækəl) *n* chacal *m.*

jackdaw ('dʒækdɔ:) *n* chova *f.*

jacket ('dʒækit) *n* 1 chaqueta *f.* 2 cazadora *f.* 3 forro de un libro *m.* cubierta *f.*

jackpot ('dʒækpɔt) *n* premio gordo *m.*

jade (dʒeid) *n* min jade *m.*

jaded ('dʒeidid) *adj* cansado, agotado.

jagged ('dʒægid) *adj* dentado.

jaguar ('dʒægjuə) *n* jaguar *m.*

jail (dʒeil) *n* cárcel *f.* calabozo *m. vt* encarcelar.

jam¹ (dʒæm) *n* 1 aprieto, atasco, apiñamiento *m.* 2 *mot* embotellamiento *m.* congestión *f. vt* apretar, obstruir, atascar.

jam² (dʒæm) *n* mermelada *f.*

January ('dʒænjuəri) *n* enero *m.*

Japan (dʒə'pæn) *n* Japón *m.* **Japanese** *adj,n* japonés. **Japanese** (language) *n* japonés *m.*

jar¹ (dʒɑ:) *n* 1 jarra *f.* 2 tarro *m.*

jar² (dʒɑ:) *n* 1 choque *m.* 2 sacudida *f.* 3 vibración *f. vt* 1 sacudir. 2 tocar. *vi* 1 vibrar. 2 chirriar.

jargon ('dʒɑ:gən) *n* jerga *f.*

jasmine ('dʒæzmin) *n* jazmín *m.*

jaundice ('dʒɔ:ndis) *n med* ictericia *f.*

jaunt (dʒɔ:nt) *n* paseo *m.* caminata *f.* **jaunty** *adj* garboso.

javelin ('dʒævlin) *n* jabalina *f.*

jaw (dʒɔ:) *n* 1 mandíbula, quijada *f.* 2 garras *f pl.* 3 boca *f.* **jawbone** *n* mandíbula *f.*

jazz (dʒæz) *n* jazz *m.*

jealous ('dʒeləs) *adj* envidioso, celoso. **jealousy** *n* envidia *f.* celos *m pl.*

jeans (dʒi:nz) *n* pantalones vaqueros *m pl.*

jeep (dʒi:p) *n* jeep *m.*

jeer (dʒiə) *n* 1 insulto *m.* 2 abucheo *m. vt* abuchear. *vi* mofarse.

jelly ('dʒeli) *n* gelatina, jalea *f.* **jellyfish** *n* medusa *f.*

jeopardize ('dʒepədaiz) *vt* arriesgar.

jerk (dʒə:k) *n* sacudida *f.* tirón *m. vt* sacudir, dar sacudidas a.

jersey ('dʒə:zi) *n* jersey *m.*

jest (dʒest) *n* burla, broma, chanza *f. vi* burlarse, bromear.

Jesus ('dʒi:zəs) *n* Jesús *m.*

jet¹ (dʒet) *n* 1 *aviat* avión a reacción *m.* 2 chorro, surtidor *m. vi inf* salir a chorro.

jet² (dʒet) *n min* azabache *m.*

jetty ('dʒeti) *n* muelle, malecón *m.*

Jew (dʒu:) *n,adj* judío *m.*

jewel ('dʒu:əl) *n* 1 joya *f.* 2 rubí *m.* **jeweller** *n* joyero *m.* **jeweller's** *n* joyería *f.*

jig¹ (dʒig) *n tech* plantilla de guía *f.* **jigsaw** *n* 1 rompecabezas *m invar.* 2 sierra de vaivén *f.*

jig² (dʒig) *n* jiga *f. vi* bailar la jiga.

jiggle ('dʒigəl) *vt* zarandear. *n* zarandeo *m.*

jilt (dʒilt) *vt* plantar, dejar.

jingle ('dʒiŋgəl) *n* 1 cascabeleo, tintineo *m.* 2 verso popular *m. vi* cascabelear, tintinear.

job (dʒɔb) *n* 1 trabajo *m.* 2 tarea, obra *f.* 3 empleo *m.*

jockey ('dʒɔki) *n* jockey *m.*

jodhpurs ('dʒɔdpəz) *n* pantalones de montar *m pl.*

jog (dʒɔg) *n* 1 golpecito, codazo *m.* 2 estímulo *m.* 3 trote *m. vt* 1 empujar. 2 estimular. *vi* trotar.

join (dʒɔin) *vt* juntar, unir. *vi* asociarse. **joint** *n* 1 juntura *f.* empalme *m.* 2 articulación *f.* nudillo *m. adj* común, colectivo.

joist (dʒɔist) *n* viga *f.*

joke (dʒouk) *n* chiste *m.* broma *f. vi* bromear.

jolly ('dʒɔli) *adj* alegre, divertido. *adv inf* muy, extremadamente.

jolt (dʒoult) *n* sacudida *f*. traqueteo *m*. *vt* dar sacudidas a. *vi* traquetear.

jostle ('dʒɔsəl) *n* empellón, empujón *m*. *vt* empujar.

journal ('dʒəːnl) *n* **1** periódico *m*. **2** revista *f*. **3** diario *m*. **journalism** *n* periodismo *m*. **journalist** *n* periodista *m*.

journey ('dʒəːni) *n* viaje *m*. *vi* viajar.

jovial ('dʒouviəl) *adj* jovial, alegre.

joy (dʒɔi) *n* alegría, felicidad *f*.

jubilee ('dʒuːbiliː) *n* jubileo *m*.

Judaism ('dʒuːdeiizəm) *n* judaísmo *m*.

judge (dʒʌdʒ) *n* juez *m*. *vt,vi* juzgar, estimar. **judgment** *n* juicio *m*.

judicial (dʒuː'diʃəl) *adj* judicial.

judicious (dʒuː'diʃəs) *adj* juicioso, sensato, prudente.

judo ('dʒuːdou) *n* sport judo *m*.

jug (dʒʌg) *n* jarro *m*.

juggle ('dʒʌgəl) *vi* hacer juego de manos. **juggler** *n* malabarista *m,f*.

juice (dʒuːs) *n* jugo, zumo *m*. **juicy** *adj* jugoso, suculento.

jukebox ('dʒuːkbɔks) *n* tocadiscos automático *m* invar.

July (dʒu'lai) *n* julio *m*.

jumble ('dʒʌmbəl) *n* confusión, mezcla, desorden *m*. *vt* mezclar, amontonar. **jumble sale** *n* venta de objetos usados *f*.

jump (dʒʌmp) *n* salto, brinco *m*. *vi* saltar, dar saltos, brincar.

jumper ('dʒʌmpə) *n* **1** saltador *m*. **2** jersey *m*.

junction ('dʒʌŋkʃən) *n* **1** cruce *m*. **2** unión *f*. **3** empalme *m*.

June (dʒuːn) *n* junio *m*.

jungle ('dʒʌŋgəl) *n* selva *f*.

junior ('dʒuːniə) *adj* **1** menor. **2** subalterno

juniper ('dʒuːnipə) *n* junipero *m*.

junk (dʒʌŋk) *n* **1** chatarra *f*. **2** baratijas *f pl*.

junta ('dʒʌntə) *n* junta *f*.

Jupiter ('dʒuːpitə) *n* Júpiter *m*.

jurisdiction (dʒuəris'dikʃən) *n* jurisdicción *f*.

jury ('dʒuəri) *n* jurado *m*. **juror** *n* jurado *m*.

just (dʒʌst) *adj* **1** justo. **2** imparcial. *adv* **1** justamente, precisamente. **2** recién. **3** sólo **4** poco más o menos, casi.

justice ('dʒʌstis) *n* **1** justicia *f*. **2** juez *m*.

justify ('dʒʌstifai) *vt* justificar.

jut (dʒʌt) *vi* sobresalir, proyectarse.

jute (dʒuːt) *n* yute *m*.

juvenile ('dʒuːvənail) *adj* juvenil, joven. *n* joven *m,f*. **juvenile delinquency** *n* delincuencia juvenil *f*.

juxtapose (dʒʌkstə'pouz) *vt* yuxtaponer.

K

kaleidoscope (kə'laidəskoup) *n* calidoscopio *m*.

kangaroo (kæŋgə'ruː) *n* canguro *m*.

keel (kiːl) *n* quilla *f*. *v* **keel over 1** *naut* zozobrar. **2** *inf* desplomarse.

keen (kiːn) *adj* **1** agudo, afilado. **2** penetrante, intenso. **3** deseoso, ansioso. **4** entusiasta.

keep (kiːp) *vt* **1** tener. **2** mantener. **3** observar **4** guardar. **5** detener. *vi* continuar, seguir. **keepsake** *n* recuerdo, regalo *m*.

keg (keg) *n* barril, barrilete *m*.

kennel ('kenl) *n* perrera *f*.

kept (kept) *v* see **keep.**

kerb (kəːb) *n* bordillo de la acera *m*.

kernel ('kəːnl) *n* **1** grano *m*. **2** almendra *f*. piñón *m*. **3** meollo *m*.

kettle ('ketl) *n* **1** olla, marmita, caldera *f*. **2** pava *f*. **kettledrum** *n* timbal *m*.

key (kiː) *n* **1** llave *f*. **2** tecla *f*. **3** *tech* chaveta *f*. **4** *mus* tono *m*. **keyboard** *n* teclado *m*. **keyhole** *n* ojo de la cerradura *m*. **keyring** *n* llavero *m*.

khaki ('kɑːki) *n* caqui *m*.

kick (kik) *n* **1** patada *f*. **2** puntapié *m*. **3** coz *f*. **4** culatazo *m*. *vt* **1** dar un puntapié a. **2** dar una patada a. *vi* dar coces. **kick-off** *n* sport saque *m*.

kid[1] (kid) *n* **1** *zool* cabrito *m*. **2** carne de cabrito *f*. **3** niño, muchacho *m*.

kid[2] (kid) *vt* tomar el pelo a, embromar.

kidnap ('kidnæp) *vt* raptar, secuestrar **kidnapping** *n* rapto, secuestro *m*.

kidney ('kidni) *n* riñón *m*. **kidney bean** *n* alubia *f*. frijol *m*.

kill (kil) *vt* matar, destruir. **kill time** pasar el tiempo, matar el tiempo.

kiln (kiln) *n* horno *m*.

kilo ('kiːlou) *n* kilo *m*.

kilogram ('kiləgræm) *n* kilogramo *m*.

kilometre (ki'lɔmitə) *n* kilómetro *m*.

kilowatt ('kiləwɔt) *n* kilovatio *m*.

kilt (kilt) *n* falda escocesa *f*.

kimono (ki'mounou) *n* kimono *m*.

kin (kin) *n* parientes *m pl*.

kind[1] (kaind) *adj* bueno, benévolo, bondadoso, amable.

kind[2] (kaind) *n* clase, especie, suerte *f*. género, tipo *m*.

kindergarten ('kindəgɑ:tṇ) n jardín de infancia m.

kindle ('kindḷ) vt encender.

kinetic (ki'netik) adj cinético.

king (kiŋ) n rey m. **kingdom** n reino m. **kingfisher** n martin pescador m.

kink (kiŋk) n 1 enroscadura f. 2 rizo m. **kinky** adj 1 rizado. 2 arrugado. 3 inf pervertido.

kiosk ('kiɔsk) n quiosco m.

kipper ('kipə) n arenque ahumado m.

kiss (kis) n beso m. vt besar.

kit (kit) n 1 equipo m. 2 caja para herramientas f. 3 med botiquín m.

kitchen ('kitʃin) n cocina f.

kite (kait) n 1 cometa m. 2 zool milano m.

kitten ('kitṇ) n gatito m.

kitty ('kiti) n 1 gatito m. 2 game polla, puesta f. bote m.

kleptomania (kleptə'meiniə) n cleptomanía f.

knack (næk) n 1 habilidad, maña f. 2 truco, artificio m.

knapsack ('næpsæk) n mochila f.

knave (neiv) n 1 bellaco m. 2 game sota f.

knead (ni:d) vt amasar.

knee (ni:) n rodilla f. **kneecap** n rótula f.

kneel* (ni:l) vi arrodillarse, hincar la rodilla.

knew (nu:) v see **know**.

knickers ('nikəz) n bragas f pl.

knife (naif) n, pl **knives** 1 cuchillo m. 2 navaja f. vt acuchillar.

knight (nait) n 1 caballero m. 2 game caballo m. **knighthood** n orden de caballería m.

knit* (nit) vt hacer a punto de aguja. vi hacer punto.

knob (nɔb) n 1 tirador m. 2 bulto m. 3 protuberancia f. **knobbly** adj nudoso.

knock (nɔk) n 1 golpe m. 2 llamada a la puerta f. vt 1 golpear. 2 inf denigrar. vi llamar a la puerta.

knot (nɔt) n 1 nudo, lazo m. 2 enredo m. vt 1 anudar. 2 atar, enlazar.

know* (nou) vt,vi 1 conocer. 2 saber.

knowledge ('nɔlidʒ) n 1 conocimiento m. 2 saber m. erudición, ciencia f.

knuckle ('nʌkəl) n 1 nudillo m. 2 cul jarrete m.

L

label ('leibəl) n etiqueta, marca f. rótulo, marbete m. vt 1 poner etiqueta. 2 clasificar, designar.

laboratory (lə'bɔrətri) n laboratorio m.

labour ('leibə) n 1 trabajo m. 2 labor f. 3 esfuerzo m. 4 parto m. **be in labour** estar de parto. ~vi trabajar. **Labour Party** n Partido Laborista m. **labour-saving** adj que ahorra trabajo. **laborious** adj penoso, pesado.

labyrinth ('læbərinθ) n laberinto m. **labyrinthine** adj laberíntico, intrincado.

lace (leis) n 1 cordón m. 2 encaje m. puntilla f. vt atar.

lack (læk) n falta, carencia f. vi faltar. vt carecer de.

lacquer ('lækə) n laca f. barniz m. vt laquear, barnizar.

lad (læd) n muchacho, mozalbete, chico m.

ladder ('lædə) n 1 escalera, escala f. 2 (of stockings) carrera f.

laden ('leidṇ) adj cargado.

ladle ('leidḷ) n cazo, cucharón m.

lady ('leidi) n señora f. **ladybird** n mariquita f.

lag[1] (læg) vi rezagarse, retrasarse.

lag[2] (læg) vt tech forrar, revestir.

lager ('lɑ:gə) n cerveza f.

laid (leid) v see **lay**[1].

lain (lein) v see **lie**[2].

laity ('leiəti) n laicado m.

lake (leik) n lago m.

lamb (læm) n cordero m.

lame (leim) adj 1 cojo, lisiado. 2 inf débil.

lament (lə'ment) n lamento m. queja f. vt lamentar.

lamp (læmp) n 1 lámpara f. 2 mot faro m. 3 bombilla f.

lance (lɑ:ns) n lanza f. vt med abrir con lanceta.

land (lænd) n 1 tierra f. 2 país m. 3 terreno m. vt,vi desembarcar. **landing** n 1 desembarco m. 2 desembarque m. 3 aviat aterrizaje m. 4 (of stairs) descanso m. **landlady** n 1 patrona f. 2 dueña f. **landlord** n 1 patrón m. 2 dueño m.

lane (lein) n 1 camino m. vereda f. 2 mot carril m.

language ('læŋgwidʒ) n 1 lenguaje m. 2 lengua, habla, idioma f.

lanky ('læŋki) adj larguirucho.

lantern ('læntən) n 1 linterna f. 2 farol m.

lap[1] (læp) n anat regazo m.

lap[2] (læp) vt envolver, plegar. n 1 sport etapa f. 2 traslapo m.

lap[3] (læp) vt lamer. vi chapalear. n 1 lamedura f. 2 chapaleteo m.

lapel (lə'pel) n solapa f. lapón m.

lapse (læps) n 1 lapso, error, desliz m. 2 periodo m. vi 1 pasar, transcurrir. 2 caer en error.

larceny (ˈlɑːsəni) n latrocinio m.

lard (lɑːd) n manteca de cerdo f.

larder (ˈlɑːdə) n despensa f.

large (lɑːdʒ) adj 1 grande. 2 amplio. 3 extenso. **largely** adv en gran parte.

lark[1] (lɑːk) n alondra f.

lark[2] (lɑːk) n broma f. vi divertirse.

larva (ˈlɑːvə) n, pl **larvae** larva f.

larynx (ˈlærɪŋks) n laringe f. **laryngitis** n laringitis f.

laser (ˈleizə) n láser m.

lash (læʃ) n 1 látigo, azote m. 2 latigazo m. 3 anat pestaña f. vt 1 azotar, dar latigazos a, flagelar. 2 atar.

lass (læs) n chica, joven, moza, muchacha f.

lasso (læˈsuː) n lazo m.

last[1] (lɑːst) adj 1 último, final. 2 pasado. n último m. adv por último.

last[2] (lɑːst) vi durar, permanecer, conservarse.

latch (lætʃ) n picaporte, pestillo m. aldaba f. vt cerrar con picaporte.

late (leit) adj 1 tarde. 2 difunto. adv tarde. **latecomer** n recién llegado, retrasado m. **later** adv 1 más tarde. 2 después. adj 1 más tardío. 2 más reciente. 3 ulterior. **latest** adj,adv último, más reciente, más tarde.

latent (ˈleitnt) adj latente, oculto.

lateral (ˈlætərəl) adj lateral.

lathe (leið) n torno m.

lather (ˈlɑːðə) n espuma f. vt 1 espumar. 2 enjabonar.

Latin (ˈlætin) adj latino. n latín m. **Latin America** América Latina. **Latin American** adj,n latinoamericano.

latitude (ˈlætitjuːd) n latitud f.

latter (ˈlætə) adj más reciente. n éste, este último, el segundo.

laugh (lɑːf) n risa f. vi reir, reirse.

launch[1] (lɔːntʃ) n 1 botadura f. 2 lancha, chalupa f.

launch[2] (lɔːntʃ) vt 1 botar. 2 lanzar. 3 emprender.

launder (ˈlɔːndə) vt lavar. **laundry** n 1 lavandería f. lavadero m. 2 ropa por lavar f.

laurel (ˈlɔrəl) n laurel m.

lavatory (ˈlævətri) n lavabo m.

lavender (ˈlævində) n espliego m. lavanda f.

lavish (ˈlæviʃ) adj pródigo, profuso, copioso. vt prodigar, dar con profusión.

law (lɔː) n 1 ley f. 2 derecho m. 3 jurisprudencia f. 4 justicia f. **lawsuit** n proceso, pleito, litigio m. **lawyer** n abogado m.

lawn (lɔːn) n césped m. **lawn-mower** n cortadora de césped f.

lax (læks) adj 1 decuidado, negligente. 2 (of morals) laxo.

laxative (ˈlæksətiv) adj,n laxativo m.

lay[1] (lei) vt poner, dejar. **layer** n 1 capa f. 2 estrato. 3 acodo m. vt acodar.

lay[2] (lei) v see **lie**[2].

lay[3] (lei) adj lego, seglar. **layman** n lego, seglar, laico m.

laze (leiz) vi holgazanear. **lazy** adj perezoso, holgazán, gandul, ocioso.

lead[1] (liːd) n 1 mando m. guía f. 2 primer lugar m. 3 tech conductor m. vt llevar, conducir, guiar, inducir. **leader** n 1 jefe, líder m. 2 guía, conductor m. **leadership** n dirección, jefatura f.

lead[2] (led) n min plomo m.

leaf (liːf) n, pl **leaves** bot hoja f. **leaflet** n prospecto, folleto m.

league (liːg) n liga, alianza, confederación f.

leak (liːk) n 1 fuga f. escape m. 2 gotera f. 3 pérdida f. vt dejar perderse. vi 1 tener fugas, escaparse. 2 naut hacer agua.

lean[1] vi inclinarse, ladearse. **leaning** n inclinación, tendencia f.

lean[2] (liːn) adj 1 delgado, enjuto. 2 magro.

leap (liːp) n salto, brinco m. vi saltar, brincar. **leapfrog** n pídola f. vi saltar a la rana. **leap year** n año bisiesto m.

learn (ləːn) vt,vi 1 aprender. 2 enterarse de, oir decir. **learned** adj erudito, docto, versado.

lease (liːs) n arriendo, arrendamiento m. vt arrendar. **leasehold** n tenencia en arriendo f.

leash (liːʃ) n cuerda f.

least (liːst) adj mínimo, menor. n lo menos. lo más pequeño. **at least** al menos, por lo menos.

leather (ˈleðə) n cuero m.

leave[1] (liːv) vt 1 partir, salir, marcharse. vt dejar.

leave[2] (liːv) n permiso m.

Lebanon (ˈlebənən) n Líbano m. **Lebanese** n,adj libanés m.

lecherous (ˈletʃərəs) adj lascivo. **lechery** n lascivia, lujuria f.

lectern (ˈlektən) n atril, facistol m.

lecture (ˈlektʃə) n conferencia, lección f. **lecturer** n conferenciante m.

led (led) v see **lead**[1].

ledge (ledʒ) n 1 repisa f. 2 saliente m. 3 antepecho, alféizar m. 4 anaquel m.

ledger (ˈledʒə) n comm libro mayor m.

leech (li:tʃ) n sanguijuela f.

leek (li:k) n puerro m.

leer (liə) n mirada impúdica f. vi mirar impúdicamente.

leeward (li:wəd) adj,adv naut sotavento m.

left[1] (left) n izquierda f. adj izquierdo. **left-handed** adj zurdo. **left-wing** adj pol izquierdista.

left[2] (left) v see **leave**[1]. **left-luggage office** n consigna f.

leg (leg) n 1 pierna f. 2 pata f. 3 pernera f.

legacy ('legəsi) n legado m. herencia f.

legal ('li:gəl) adj 1 legal. 2 de derecho. 3 legítimo, lícito. **legalize** vt 1 legalizar. 2 autorizar.

legend ('ledʒənd) n leyenda f.

legible ('ledʒibl) adj legible.

legion ('li:dʒən) n legión f.

legislate ('ledʒisleit) vi legislar. **legislation** n legislación f.

legitimate (li'dʒitimət) adj legítimo. vt also **legitimize** legitimar.

leisure ('leʒə) n tiempo libre, ocio m.

lemon ('lemən) n limón m. **lemonade** n limonada f.

lend* (lend) vt prestar, proporcionar. **lend a hand** echar una mano. **lend oneself to** prestarse a, entregarse a.

length (leŋθ) n 1 longitud, largura f. largo m. 2 espacio m. **at length** por extenso. **lengthen** vt prolongar, extender.

lenient ('li:niənt) adj indulgente, clemente.

lens (lenz) n 1 lente m. 2 anat cristalino m. 3 phot objetivo m.

lent (lent) v see **lend.**

Lent (lent) n Cuaresma f.

lentil ('lentl) n lenteja f.

Leo ('li:ou) n Leo m.

leopard ('lepəd) n leopardo m.

leper ('lepə) n leproso m. **leprosy** n lepra f.

lesbian ('lezbiən) n 1 lesbiana f. 2 inf tortillera f. adj lesbiano, lesbico.

less (les) adj menor, menos, inferior. adv menos. prep menos. **lessen** vt disminuir, achicar, mermar, quitar importancia.

lesson ('lesən) n lección f.

lest (lest) conj para que no.

let* (let) vt 1 dejar, permitir. 2 arrendar, alquilar. **let on** inf revelar.

lethal ('li:θəl) adj letal, mortífero.

lethargy ('leθədʒi) n letargo m.

letter ('letə) n 1 letra f. 2 carta f. vt inscribir, rotular. **letterbox** n buzón m.

lettuce ('letis) n lechuga f.

leukaemia (lu:'ki:miə) n med leucemia f.

level ('levəl) adj 1 llano, plano. 2 uniforme. **3 a nivel.** adv a nivel. n nivel m. vt 1 nivelar, allanar, aplanar. 2 derribar. **level crossing** n paso a nivel m. **level-headed** adj sensato, juicioso.

lever ('li:və) n palanca, barra f.

levy ('levi) n 1 exacción f. 2 impuesto m. 3 mil leva f. vt 1 recaudar, imponer. 2 mil reclutar.

lewd (lu:d) adj lúbrico, obsceno.

liable ('laiəbl) adj 1 propenso, expuesto. 2 responsable, obligado. **liability** n 1 riesgo m. exposición f. 2 responsabilidad f.

liaison (li'eizon) n enlace m.

liar ('laiə) n mentiroso, embustero m.

libel ('laibl) n libelo m. difamación f.

liberal ('libərəl) adj liberal. n pol liberal m,f.

liberate ('libəreit) vt librar, liberar, libertar. **liberator** n libertador m.

liberty ('libəti) n libertad f. **take liberties** tomarse libertades.

Libra ('li:brə) n Libra f.

library ('laibrəri) n biblioteca f. **librarian** n bibliotecario m.

libretto (li'bretou) n libreto m.

licence ('laisəns) n 1 licencia f. 2 permiso m. 3 libertinaje m. **license** vt autorizar. **licensee** n titular de una licencia f.

lichen ('laikən) n liquen m.

lick (lik) n lamedura, lengüetada f. vt lamer.

lid (lid) n tapa f.

lie[1] (lai) n mentira, falsedad f. embuste m. vi mentir.

lie*[2] (lai) vi acostarse, tenderse, echarse, tumbarse.

lieutenant (lef'tenənt) n teniente, lugarteniente m.

life (laif) n, pl **lives** vida f. **lifebelt** n cinturón salvavidas m. **lifeboat** n bote salvavidas m. **lifebuoy** n boya salvavidas f. **lifeguard** n vigilante m.

lift (lift) n 1 ascensor m. montacargas m invar. 2 elevación f. alzamiento m. 3 fuerza elevadora f. 4 inf viaje gratuito m. 5 estímulo m. vt alzar, levantar, izar.

light*[1] (lait) n 1 luz, lumbre f. 2 lámpara f. adj claro, con mucha luz. vt 1 iluminar, alumbrar. 2 encender. **lighthouse** n faro m. **lighting** n alumbrado m. iluminación f.

light[2] (lait) adj 1 ligero, ágil. 2 leve. 3 liviano. 4 alegre. **light-headed** adj aturdido, delirante, mareado. **light-hearted** adj alegre, despreocupado. **lightweight** *adj* ligero, de poco peso.

light[3] (lait) *vi* descender, posarse, caer.

lighten[1] ('laitn) *vt* 1 iluminar, alumbrar. 2 aclarar.

lighten[2] ('laitn) *vt* 1 aligerar, aliviar. 2 descargar.

lightning ('laitniŋ) *n* relámpago *m*.

like[1] (laik) *adj* igual, similar, semejante. **be like** parecerse a. ~*prep* como, igual que. *conj* como. **like-minded** *adj* de la misma mentalidad. **likeness** *n* parecido *m*. semejanza *f*. **likewise** *adv* 1 asimismo, también. 2 lo mismo, parecidamente.

like[2] (laik) *vt* 1 querer. 2 gustar.

likely ('laikli) *adj* 1 probable. 2 apropiado, adecuado. 3 creíble, verosímil.

lilac ('lailək) *n* lila *f*.

lily ('lili) *n* lirio *m*. azucena *f*. **lily-of-the-valley** *n* lirio de los valles, muguete *m*.

limb (lim) *n* 1 *anat* miembro *m*. 2 *bot* rama *f*.

limbo ('limbou) *n* limbo *m*.

lime[1] (laim) *n* *min* cal *f*. **limelight** *n* luz de calcio *m*. **be in the limelight** estar a la vista del público. **limestone** *n* piedra caliza *f*.

lime[2] (laim) *n* *bot* 1 lima *f*. 2 limero *m*.

limerick ('limərik) *n* quintilla jocosa *f*.

limit ('limit) *n* límite *m*. *vt* limitar. **limitation** *n* limitación *f*.

limp[1] (limp) *n* cojera *f*. *vi* cojear.

limp[2] (limp) *adj* fláccido, blando, lacio.

limpet ('limpit) *n* lapa *f*.

linden ('lindən) *n* tilo *m*.

line[1] (lain) *n* 1 línea *f*. 2 cuerda, cinta *f*. cable *m*. 3 raya *f*. 4 linaje *m*. *vt* 1 linear. 2 rayar. 3 alinear. **lineage** *n* linaje, abolengo *m*. **linear** *adj* lineal.

line[2] (lain) *vt* forrar, revestir, guarnecer.

linen ('linin) *n* 1 lino, lienzo *m*. 2 ropa blanca *f*. 3 mantelería *f*.

liner ('lainə) *n* *naut* vapor, trasatlántico *m*.

linger ('liŋgə) *vi* 1 entretenerse, demorar, vacilar. 2 prolongarse, durar.

lingerie ('lɔnʒəri:) *n* ropa interior de mujer *f*.

linguist ('liŋgwist) *n* lingüista *m,f*. **linguistic** *adj* lingüístico. **linguistics** *n* lingüística *f*.

lining ('lainiŋ) *n* 1 forro *m*. 2 revestimiento *m*.

link (liŋk) *n* 1 enlace, vínculo *m*. 2 eslabón *m*. *vt* unir, enlazar.

linoleum (li'nouliəm) *n* linóleo *m*.

linseed ('linsi:d) *n* linaza *f*.

lion ('laiən) *n* león *m*.

lip (lip) *n* labio *m*. **lip-read** *vi* leer el movemiento de los labios. **lipstick** *n* barra de labios *f*.

liqueur (li'kjuə) *n* licor *m*.

liquid ('likwid) *adj,n* líquido *m*. **liquidate** *vt* 1 liquidar. 2 matar. **liquidize** *vt* liquidar, hacer líquido.

liquor ('likə) *n* 1 licor *m*. 2 bebida *f*.

liquorice ('likəris) *n* regaliz *m*.

lira ('liərə) *n* lira *f*.

lisp (lisp) *n* ceceo *m*. *vt,vi* cecear.

list[1] (list) *n* 1 lista *f*. catálogo *m*. *vt* 1 registrar, catalogar. 2 alistar.

list[2] (list) *naut* escora *f*. *vi* escorar.

listen ('lisən) *vt,vi* escuchar, oír, prestar atención.

listless ('listləs) *adj* apático, sin interés.

lit (lit) *v* see **light**[1].

litany ('litəni) *n* letanía *f*.

literal ('litərəl) *adj* literal.

literary ('litərəri) *adj* literario.

literate ('litərət) *adj* que sabe leer y escribir.

literature ('litrətʃə) *n* literatura *f*.

litre ('li:tə) *n* litro *m*.

litter ('litə) *n* 1 basura *f*. escombros *m pl*. 2 cama para animales *f*. 3 litera *f*. 4 *zool* camada, cría *f*. *vt* esparcir papeles por. **litter-bin** *n* papelera *f*.

little ('litļ) *adj* 1 pequeño, chico, menor. 2 poco, escaso, corto. *adv* poco. *n* poco *m*. **little finger** *n* dedo meñique *m*. **little toe** *n* dedo meñique del pie *m*.

liturgy ('litədʒi) *n* liturgia *f*.

live[1] (liv) *vi* vivir, existir.

live[2] (laiv) *adj* 1 vivo. 2 ardiente, encendido. 3 cargado con corriente eléctrica.

livelihood ('laivlihud) *n* mantenimiento *m*.

lively ('laivli) *adj* 1 vivo. 2 vigoroso, fogoso. 3 alegre, animado.

liver ('livə) *n* *anat* hígado *m*.

livestock ('laivstɔk) *n* ganado *m*.

livid ('livid) *adj* lívido, pálido.

living ('liviŋ) *adj* vivo, viviente. *n* sustento *m*. vida *f*. **earn** or **make a living** ganarse la vida. **living room** *n* sala de estar *f*.

lizard ('lizəd) *n* lagarto *m*.

llama ('lɑ:mə) *n* llama *f*.

load (loud) *n* 1 carga *f*. 2 peso, fardo *m*. 3 *tech* resistencia *f*. *vt* 1 cargar. 2 oprimir, agobiar.

loaf[1] (louf) *n*, *pl* **loaves** pan *m*. hogaza *f*.

loaf[2] (louf) *vi* pasearse, holgazanear.

loan (loun) *n* préstamo, empréstito *m*.

loathe (louð) *vt* detestar, abominar. **loathsome** *adj* aborrecible, detestable, odioso.

lob (lɔb) n sport voleo alto m. vt,vi volear por alto.

lobby ('lɔbi) n 1 antecámara f. 2 pasillo m. 3 vestíbulo m. 4 grupo de presión m. vt ejercer influencia sobre.

lobe (loub) n lóbulo m.

lobster ('lɔbstə) n langosta f.

local ('loukəl) adj 1 local. 2 regional. **locality** n localidad f. **localize** vt localizar. **locate** vt situar, colocar. **location** n 1 posición f. 2 localización f.

lock[1] (lɔk) n 1 cerradura, cerraja f. 2 esclusa f. 3 tech chaveta f. vt cerrar con llave. **locker** n armario, cajón que se cierra con llave m.

lock[2] (lɔk) n rizo, mechón m.

locket ('lɔkit) n medallón, relicario m.

locomotive (loukə'moutiv) n locomotora f. adj locomotor.

locust ('loukəst) n langosta f.

lodge (lɔdʒ) n 1 portería f. 2 logia masónica f. vt alojar, hospedar. vi 1 alojarse, hospedarse. 2 quedarse. **lodgings** n pl alojamiento, hospedaje m.

loft (lɔft) n desván m.

log (lɔg) n 1 leño, tronco m. 2 naut diario de navegación m. vt registrar.

logarithm ('lɔgəriðəm) n logaritmo m.

logic ('lɔdʒik) n lógica f. **logical** adj lógico.

loin (lɔin) n 1 ijada f. 2 lomo m.

loiter ('lɔitə) vi ir despacio, vagar.

lollipop ('lɔlipɔp) n pirulí m.

London ('lʌndən) n Londres m. **Londoner** adj,n londinense m,f.

lonely ('lounli) adj 1 solo, solitario. 2 triste, desolado.

long[1] (lɔŋ) vi anhelar. **longing** n ansia f. anhelo m.

long[2] (lɔŋ) adj 1 largo. 2 prolongado. adv largo or mucho tiempo. **long-distance** adj de larga distancia. **long-distance call** n conferencia interurbana f. **long jump** n salto de longitud m. **long-playing** adj de larga duración. **long-range** adj de largo alcance. **long-sighted** adj 1 présbita. 2 sagaz, precavido. **longstanding** adj de mucho tiempo. **long wave** n onda larga f. **longwinded** adj latoso, pesado, fastidioso.

longevity (lɔn'dʒeviti) n longevidad f.

longitude ('lɔndʒitju:d) n longitud f.

look (luk) n 1 mirada f. vistazo m. 2 apariencia f. aspecto m. vi 1 mirar. 2 parecer. **look after** encargarse de.

loom[1] (lu:m) n telar m.

loom[2] (lu:m) vi asomar, aparecer confusamente.

loop (lu:p) n vuelta, curva f. lazo m. vt 1 formar curva. 2 asegurar con presilla. **loophole** n inf escapatoria, salida f.

loose (lu:s) adj 1 suelto. 2 flojo. 3 ancho, holgado. 4 vago, indeterminado. 5 libre, relajado. **loosen** vt soltar, desatar, aflojar.

loot (lu:t) n botín m. presa f. vt saquear.

lop (lɔp) vt 1 podar. 2 desmochar.

lopsided (lɔp'saidid) adj inclinado, mal equilibrado, asimétrico.

lord (lɔ:d) n señor m.

lorry ('lɔri) n camión m.

lose* (lu:z) vt perder.

loss (lɔs) n 1 pérdida f. 2 perdición f.

lost (lɔst) v see **lose.**

lot (lɔt) n 1 lote m. 2 parte, cuota f. 3 solar m. porción f.

lotion ('louʃən) n loción f.

lottery ('lɔtəri) n lotería f.

lotus ('loutəs) n loto m.

loud (laud) adj fuerte, ruidoso. **loud-mouthed** adj gritón. **loudspeaker** n altavoz m.

lounge (laundʒ) n salón m. vi pasar el tiempo holgazaneando.

louse (laus) n, pl **lice** piojo m. **lousy** adj 1 piojoso. 2 inf miserable, asqueroso.

love (lʌv) n amor, cariño m. devoción f. **be in love** estar enamorado. **fall in love** enamorarse. **make love** 1 hacer amor. 2 cortejar. ~vt amar, querer. **lovesick** adj enfermo de amor. **lovely** adj 1 bello, hermoso. 2 encantador.

low[1] (lou) adj 1 bajo. 2 grave. 3 ruin, vil. **lowbrow** n persona poco intelectual f. **low frequency** adj de baja frecuencia. **lowland** n tierra baja f. **low-necked** adj escotado. **low-pitched** adj sonido grave. **low tide** n marea baja f.

low[2] (lou) n mugido m. vi mugir.

lower ('louə) adj,adv más bajo. vt 1 bajar, inclinar hacia abajo. 2 naut arriar. 3 reducir, abatir, disminuir, rebajar.

loyal ('lɔiəl) adj leal, fiel.

lozenge ('lɔzindʒ) n 1 rombo m. 2 pastilla f.

lubricate ('lu:brikeit) vt lubricar.

lucid ('lu:sid) adj lúcido.

luck (lʌk) n suerte, fortuna f. **lucky** adj de suerte, afortunado.

lucrative ('lu:krətiv) adj lucrativo.

ludicrous ('lu:dikrəs) adj absurdo, ridículo.

lug (lʌg) n 1 asa f. 2 arrastre, tirón m. vt tirar de, arrastrar.

luggage ('lʌgidʒ) n equipaje m.
lukewarm (lu:k'wɔ:m) adj templado, tibio.
lull (lʌl) n momento de calma m. vt 1 arrullar. 2 sosegar, calmar. lullaby n canción de cuna f.
lumbago (lʌm'beigou) n lumbago m.
lumber¹ ('lʌmbə) n madera f. tablas f pl. tablones m pl. lumberjack n leñador m.
lumber² ('lʌmbə) vi moverse pesadamente.
luminous ('lu:minəs) adj luminoso.
lump (lʌmp) n 1 pedazo, trozo, terrón m. 2 nudo m. 3 bulto, chinchón m. vt amontonar, apelotonar.
lunacy ('lu:nəsi) n locura, demencia f.
lunar ('lu:nə) adj lunar.
lunatic ('lu:nətik) adj,n lunático m.
lunch (lʌntʃ) n almuerzo m.vi almorzar.
lung (lʌŋ) n pulmón m.
lunge ('lʌndʒ) n 1 estocada f. 2 salto hacia adelante m. embestida f. vi abalanzarse, arremeter.
lurch¹ (lə:tʃ) n leave in the lurch dejar plantado.
lurch² (lə:tʃ) n sacudida f. tumbo m. vi 1 dar sacudidas. 2 tambalearse.
lure (luə) n 1 reclamo m. 2 cebo m. 3 engaño m. tentación f. vt atraer, inducir, tentar.
lurid ('luərid) adj 1 sensacional. 2 espeluznante.
lurk (lə:k) vi ocultarse, esconderse, estar en acecho.
luscious ('lʌʃəs) adj 1 dulce, sabroso. 2 delicioso, meloso.
lush (lʌʃ) adj exuberante, rico.
lust (lʌst) n 1 sensualidad, lujuria f. 2 deseo vehemente m. vt anhelar, desear con lujuria.
lustre ('lʌstə) n lustre, brillo m.
lute (lu:t) n mus laúd m.
Luxembourg ('lʌksəmbə:g) n Luxemburgo m.
luxury ('lʌkʃəri) n lujo m. luxurious adj lujoso.
lynch (lintʃ) vt linchar. lynching n linchamiento m.
lynx (liŋks) n lince m.
lyre ('laiə) n lira f.
lyrical ('lirikəl) adj 1 lírico. 2 elocuente, entusiasmado.
lyrics ('liriks) n pl letras de una canción f pl. lyricism n lirismo m.

M

mac (mæk) n impermeable m.
macabre (mə'kɑ:b) adj macabro.
macaroni (mækə'rouni) n macarrones m pl.

mace¹ (meis) n maza f.
mace² (meis) n bot macis f.
machine (mə'ʃi:n) n 1 máquina f. 2 aparato m. 3 pol organización f. vt 1 trabajar a máquina. 2 coser a máquina. machine-made adj hecho a máquina. machine-gun n ametralladora f. vt ametrallar. machinery n 1 maquinaria f. 2 mecanismo m. 3 organización f. sistema m. machinist n operario de máquina, mecánico m.
mackerel ('mækrəl) n caballa f.
mackintosh ('mækintəʃ) n impermeable m.
mad (mæd) adj 1 loco, demente. 2 rabioso. 3 furioso. maddening adj desesperante.
madam ('mædəm) n señora f.
made (meid) v see make.
Madonna (mə'dɔnə) n Virgen, Madona f.
Madrid (mə'drid) n Madrid.
magazine (mægə'zi:n) n 1 revista f. 2 depósito de cartuchos m. recámara f. 3 almacén m.
maggot ('mægət) n cresa f. gusano m.
magic ('mædʒik) adj mágico. n magia f. magical adj mágico. magician n 1 mago, mágico, brujo m. 2 prestidigitador m.
magistrate ('mædʒistreit) n 1 magistrado m. 2 juez municipal m.
magnanimous (mæg'næniməs) adj magnánimo.
magnate ('mægneit) n magnate, potentado m.
magnet ('mægnit) n imán m. magnetic adj magnético. magnetism n magnetismo m. magnetize vt magnetizar, imantar.
magnificent (mæg'nifisənt) adj magnífico. magnificence n magnificencia f.
magnify ('mægnifai) vt 1 aumentar, magnificar. 2 agrandar, exagerar. magnifying glass n lupa, lente de aumento f.
magnitude ('mægnitju:d) n magnitud f.
magnolia (mæg'noulia) n magnolia f.
magpie ('mægpai) n urraca f.
mahogany (mə'hɔgəni) n caoba f.
maid (meid) n 1 criada, doncella f. 2 camarera f. 3 muchacha f. old maid n solterona f. maiden n 1 doncella f. 2 muchacha f. maiden name n apellido de soltera m.
mail (meil) n 1 malla f. 2 correo m. cartas f pl. correspondencia f. vt echar al correo. mailbag n saca de correos f. mail order n pedido postal m.
maim (meim) vt mutilar.
main (mein) adj 1 principal. 2 mayor. n cañería principal f. in the main en general. mainland n tierra firme f. continente m. mainsail

marathon

n vela mayor f. **mainspring** *n* muelle real *m*. *n* corriente principal f.

maintain (mein'tein) *vt* 1 mantener. 2 guardar. **maintenance** *n* 1 mantenimiento *m*. 2 conservación f.

maize (meiz) *n* maíz *m*.

majesty ('mædʒisti) *n* majestad f. **majestic** *adj* majestuoso.

major ('meidʒə) *adj* mayor, principal. *n mil* comandante *m*. **major general** general de división *m*. **majority** *adj* mayoritario. *n* 1 mayoría f. 2 mayor edad f.

Majorca (mə'dʒɔːkə) *n* Mallorca f.

make (meik) *vt* 1 hacer. 2 crear, formar, construir. 3 creer, deducir, calcular. 4 ganar, obtener. 5 forzar, obligar. **make away or off** largarse, huir, escaparse. **make off with** llevarse, escaparse con. **make out** salir bien. ~*n* 1 marca f. 2 tipo, modelo *m*. **making** *n* fabricación f. **make-believe** *adj* fingido, simulado. *vi* fingir. **makeshift** *adj* 1 improvisado. 2 provisional. *n* improvisación f. **make-up** *n* 1 composición f. 2 estructura f. 3 maquillaje *m*.

maladjusted (mælə'dʒʌstid) *adj* inadaptado.

malaria (mə'lɛəriə) *n* malaria f.

male (meil) *adj* 1 macho. 2 masculino. 3 viril. *n* 1 macho *m*. 2 varón *m*.

malfunction (mæl'fʌŋkʃən) *n* funcionamiento defectuoso *m*.

malice ('mælis) *n* malicia, mala voluntad f.

malignant (mə'lignənt) *adj* maligno. **malign** *adj* maligno. *vt* difamar.

mallet ('mælət) *n* mazo *m*.

malnutrition (mælnju'triʃən) *n* desnutrición f.

malt (mɔːlt) *n* malta f.

Malta ('mɔːltə) *n* Malta f. **Maltese** *adj,n* maltés *m*.

maltreat (mæl'triːt) *vt* tratar mal. **maltreatment** *n* maltrato *m*.

mammal ('mæməl) *n* mamífero *m*.

mammoth ('mæməθ) *adj* gigantesco. *n* mamut *m*.

man (mæn) *n, pl* **men** 1 hombre *m*. 2 el género humano *m*. *vt* tripular. **manly** *adj* varonil. **man-handle** *vt* maltratar. **manhole** *n* abertura de inspección f. **man-made** *adj* artificial. **manpower** *n* mano de obra f. **manslaughter** *n* homicidio sin premeditación *m*.

Man, Isle of (mæn) *n* Isla de Man f.

manage ('mænidʒ) *vt* 1 manejar. 2 dirigir, administrar, llevar. **management** *n* 1 manejo *m*. dirección, gerencia f. 2 junta de directores

f. **manager** *n* 1 *comm* director, gerente *m*. 2 administrador *m*. 3 empresario *m*.

mandarin ('mændərin) *n* mandarín *m*.

mandate ('mændeit) *n* 1 mandato *m*. 2 territorio bajo mandato *m*. *vt* asignar por mandato.

mane (mein) *n* 1 melena f. 2 crin f.

mange (meindʒ) *n* roña sarna f.

mangle[1] ('mæŋgəl) *n* rodillo, exprimidor *m*.

mangle[2] ('mæŋgəl) *vt* magullar, mutilar, estropear.

mango ('mæŋgou) *n, pl* **-oes** *or* **-os** mango *m*.

mania ('meiniə) *n* manía f. **maniac** *adj,n* maníaco *m*. **manic** *adj* maníaco.

manicure ('mænikjuə) *n* manicura f. *vt* hacer la manicura a.

manifest ('mænifest) *adj* manifiesto, evidente. *vt* mostrar, manifestar. **manifestation** *n* manifestación f.

manifesto (mæni'festou) *n* manifiesto *m*.

manifold ('mænifould) *adj* múltiple, numeroso.

manipulate (mə'nipjuleit) *vt* manipular. **manipulation** *n* manipulación f.

mankind (mæn'kaind) *n* género humano *m*.

manner ('mænə) *n* 1 manera f. modo *m*. 2 conducta f. 3 clase, especie f. **manners** *n pl* 1 costumbres f pl. 2 modales *m pl*. 3 educación f. **mannerism** *n* 1 amaneramiento *m*. 2 manerismo *m*. 3 hábito *m*. peculiaridad f.

manoeuvre (mə'nuːvə) *n* maniobra f. *vt* hacer maniobrar. *vi* maniobrar.

manor ('mænə) *n* 1 finca f. 2 señorío *m*. **manor house** *n* casa señorial f.

mansion ('mænʃən) *n* 1 casa grande f. 2 casa solariega f.

mantelpiece ('mæntəlpiːs) *n* repisa de chimenea f.

mantilla (mæn'tilə) *n* mantilla f.

mantle ('mæntl) *n* manto *m*. capa f.

manual ('mænjuəl) *adj,n* manual *m*.

manufacture (mænju'fæktʃə) *n* 1 fabricación f. 2 manufactura f. producto *m*. *vt* fabricar. **manufacturer** *n* fabricante *m*.

manure (mə'njuə) *n* estiércol, abono *m*. *vt* estercolar, abonar.

manuscript ('mænjuskript) *n* manuscrito *m*.

many ('meni) *adj* muchos *pl*. **how many?** ¿cuántos? **so** *or* **as many** tanto. **many-sided** *adj* 1 multilátero. 2 polifacético.

map (mæp) *n* 1 mapa *m*. 2 plano *m*. *vt* trazar el mapa de. **map out** proyectar.

maple ('meipəl) *n* arce *m*.

mar (mɑː) *vt* 1 desfigurar. 2 aguar.

marathon ('mærəθən) *n* carrera de maratón f

229

marble ('ma:bəl) *adj* marmóreo, de mármol. *n* 1 mármol *m*. 2 canica *f*.

march (ma:tʃ) *n* 1 marcha *f*. *vt* hacer marchar, llevar. *vi* 1 marchar. 2 ir a pie.

March (ma:tʃ) *n* marzo *m*.

marchioness ('ma:ʃənis) *n* marquesa *f*.

mare (mɛə) *n* yegua *f*.

margarine (ma:dʒə'ri:n) *n* margarina *f*.

margin ('ma:dʒin) *n* 1 margen *m*. 2 *comm* reserva *f*. 3 borde *m*. **marginal** *adj* marginal.

marguerite (ma:gə'ri:t) *n* margarita *f*.

marigold ('mærigould) *n* caléndula *f*.

marinade (mæri'neid) *n* escabeche *m*. **marinate** *vt* escabechar.

marine (mə'ri:n) *adj* marino. *n* soldado de marina *m*. **maritime** *adj* marítimo.

marital ('mæritl) *adj* marital.

marjoram ('ma:dʒərəm) *n* mejorana *f*. orégano *m*.

mark[1] (ma:k) *n* 1 señal, marca *f*. 2 mancha. 3 huella. 4 etiqueta *f*. 5 blanco *m*. 6 calificación, nota. *f*. *vt* 1 señalar, marcar. 2 manchar. **marked** *adj* 1 fuerte. 2 notable. **marksman** *n* tirador *m*. **marksmanship** *n* buena puntería *f*.

mark[2] (ma:k) *n* marco *m*.

market ('ma:kit) *n* 1 mercado *m*. **stock market** *n* bolsa *f*. *vt* llevar al mercado. **market garden** *n* huerto *m*. **market research** *n* análisis de mercados *f*.

marmalade ('ma:məleid) *n* mermelada *f*.

maroon[1] (mə'ru:n) *adj,n* marrón *m*.

maroon[2] (mə'ru:n) *vt* abandonar.

marquee (ma:'ki:) *n* entoldado *m*.

marquess ('ma:kwis) *n* marqués *m*.

marriage ('mæridʒ) *n* 1 matrimonio *m*. 2 casamiento *m*. 3 boda *f*. **marriage certificate** *n* partida de casamiento *f*.

marrow ('mærou) *n* 1 *anat* médula *f*. tuétano *m*. 2 *inf* meollo *m*. 3 *bot* calabacín *m*. **marrowbone** *n* hueso medular *m*.

marry ('mæri) *vt* casar.

Mars (ma:z) *n* Marte *m*.

marsh (ma:ʃ) *n* 1 pantano *m*. ciénaga *f*. 2 marisma *f*. **marshy** *adj* pantanoso.

marshal ('ma:ʃəl) *n* 1 mariscal *m*. *vt* 1 ordenar. 2 formar.

martial ('ma:ʃəl) *adj* marcial.

martin ('ma:tin) *n* *zool* avión, vencejo *m*.

martyr ('ma:tə) *n* mártir *m,f*. *vt* martirizar. **martyrdom** *n* martirio *m*.

marvel ('ma:vəl) *n* maravilla *f*. *vi* maravillarse.

marvellous ('ma:vələs) *adj* maravilloso.

Marxism ('ma:ksizəm) *n* marxismo *m*. **Marxist** *adj,n* marxista *m,f*.

mascara (mæ'ska:rə) *n* rimel *m*.

mascot ('mæskɔt) *n* mascota *f*.

masculine ('mæskjulin) *adj,n* masculino *m*. **masculinity** *n* masculinidad *f*.

mash (mæʃ) *n* 1 mezcla *f*. 2 amasijo *m*. **mashed potatoes** puré de patatas. ~*vt* 1 mezclar. 2 amasar. 3 hacer un puré de.

mask (ma:sk) *n* 1 máscara *f*. 2 disfraz *m*. 3 careta *f*. antifaz *m*. *vt* enmascarar.

mason ('meisən) *n* 1 albañil, cantero *m*. 2 masón, francmasón *m*. **masonry** *n* 1 albañilería *f*. 2 masonería *f*.

masquerade (mæskə'reid) *n* baile de máscaras *m*. mascarada *f*.

mass[1] (mæs) *n* 1 masa *f*. 2 bulto *m*. 3 macizo *m*. **the masses** las masas *f pl*. **mass media** *n pl* medios de comunicación con las masas *m pl*. **mass-produce** *vt* producir en serie. **mass-production** producción en serie *f*.

mass[2] (mæs) *n* rel misa *f*. **high mass** misa mayor. **low mass** misa rezada.

massacre ('mæsəkə) *n* carnicería, matanza *f*. *vt* hacer una carnicería de, masacrar.

massage ('mæsa:ʒ) *n* masaje *m*. *vt* dar masaje a. **masseur** *n* masajista *m*.

massive ('mæsiv) *adj* 1 macizo, sólido, abultado. 2 impresionante.

mast (ma:st) *n* palo, mástil *m*. **masthead** *n* tope *m*.

master ('ma:stə) *n* 1 amo *m*. 2 señor *m*. 3 dueño *m*. 4 maestro, profesor *m*. **master of ceremonies** maestro de ceremonias *m*. ~*vt* 1 dominar. 2 vencer, derrotar. **masterful** *adj* imperioso, dominante. **masterpiece** *n* obra maestra *f*.

masturbate ('mæstəbeit) *vi* masturbarse. **masturbation** *n* masturbación *f*.

mat (mæt) *n* 1 estera, esterilla *f*. 2 felpudo *m*. salvamanteles *m*.

match[1] (mætʃ) *n* 1 cerilla *f*. fósforo *m*. 2 mecha *f*. **matchbox** *n* caja de cerillas *f*. **matchstick** *n* fósforo *m*.

match[2] (mætʃ) *n* 1 igual *m,f*. 2 compañero *m*. 3 casamiento *m*. 4 *sport* partido *m*. *vt* 1 emparejar. 2 igualar. 3 hacer juego con. *vi* armonizar.

mate (meit) *n* 1 compañero, camarada *m*. 2 cónyuge *m,f*. 3 ayudante *m,f*. 4 *naut* primer oficial *m*. *vt zool* parear.

material (mə'tiəriəl) *adj* material, importante. *n* 1 material *m*. materia *f*. 2 tejido *m*. tela *f*.

materialist *adj,n* materialista. **materialistic** *adj* materialista. **materialism** *n* materialismo *m*.

maternal (mə'tɜ:nl) *adj* 1 materno. 2 maternal. **maternity** *n* maternidad *f*.

mathematics (mæθə'mætiks) *n* matemáticas *f pl*. **mathematician** *n* matemático *m*.

matinee ('mætinei) *n* función de tarde, matiné *f*.

matins ('mætinz) *n pl* maitines *m pl*.

matrimony ('mætriməni) *n* matrimonio *m*.

matrix ('meitriks) *n, pl* **matrices** matriz *f*.

matron ('meitrən) *n* matrona *f*.

matter ('mætə) *n* 1 materia *f*. material *m*. 2 tema *m*. 3 asunto *m*. cuestión *f*. 4 cosa *f*. **a matter of** cosa de. **as a matter of course** por rutina. **it doesn't matter** no importa, el caso es que. **no matter** no importa. **what's the matter?** ¿qué hay? ¿qué pasa? ~*vi* importar. **it doesn't matter** no importa, da lo mismo, es igual. **matter-of-fact** *adj* prosaico, práctico.

mattress ('mætrəs) *n* colchón *m*.

mature (mə'tjuə) *adj* 1 maduro. 2 *comm* vencido. *vt,vi* madurar. **maturity** *n* 1 madurez *f*. 2 *comm* vencimiento *m*.

maudlin ('mɔ:dlin) *adj* 1 sensiblero. 2 llorón

maul (mɔ:l) *vt* 1 magullar. 2 maltratar.

mausoleum (mɔ:sə'liəm) *n* mausoleo *m*.

mauve (mouv) *adj,n* color malva *m*.

maxim ('mæksim) *n* máxima *f*.

maximum ('mæksiməm) *adj* máximo. *n* máximo, máximum *m* **maximize** *vt* llevar al máximo, extremar.

may* (mei) *v mod aux* 1 poder. 2 ser posible. 3 tener permiso para. **maybe** *adv* quizá, tal vez.

May (mei) *n* mayo *m*. **May Day** *n* primero de mayo. **maypole** *n* mayo *m*.

mayonnaise (meiə'neiz) *n* mayonesa *f*.

mayor ('mɛə) *n* alcalde *m*.

maze (meiz) *n* 1 laberinto *m*. 2 enredo *m*.

me (mi:) *pron 1st pers s* 1 me. 2 mí. **with me** conmigo.

meadow ('medou) *n* prado *m*. pradera *f*.

meagre ('mi:gə) *adj* escaso, exiguo.

meal¹ (mi:l) *n* comida *f*.

meal² (mi:l) *n* harina *f*. **mealy** *adj* harinoso.

mean*¹ (mi:n) *vt* 1 querer decir. 2 significar. **mean well** tener buenas intenciones. **meaning** *n* 1 intención *f*. propósito *m*. 2 sentido, significado *m*.

mean² (mi:n) *adj* mezquino, tacaño.

meander (mi'ændə) *n* meandro *m*. *vi* 1 serpentear. 2 errar, vagar.

means (mi:nz) *n, pl* 1 medios, recursos *m pl*. 2 manera *f*. 3 dinero *m*. **by all means** ¡claro que sí! **by means of** por medio de.

meanwhile ('mi:nwail) *adv* entretanto, mientras tanto.

measles ('mi:zəlz) *n* sarampión *m*.

measure ('meʒə) *n* 1 medida *f*. 2 *mus* compás *m*. **made to measure** hecho a medida. ~*vt* 1 medir. 2 tallar. 3 tomar las medidas a. **measurement** *n* medida, medición *f*.

meat (mi:t) *n* carne *f*. **cold meat** fiambre *m*.

mechanic (mi'kænik) *n* mecánico *m*. **mechanical** *adj* 1 mecánico. 2 maquinal. **mechanical engineering** *n* ingeniería mecánica *f*. **mechanism** *n* mecanismo *m*. **mechanize** *vt* mecanizar.

medal ('medl) *n* medalla *f*. **medallion** *n* medallón *m*.

meddle ('medl) *vi* entrometerse. **meddler** *n* entrometido *m*. **meddlesome** *adj* entrometido.

media ('mi:diə) *n pl* medios *m pl*.

medial ('mi:diəl) *adj* medial.

median ('mi:diən) *adj* mediano. *n* número medio, punto medio *m*.

mediate ('mi:dieit) *vi* mediar. **mediation** *n* mediación *f*.

medical ('medikəl) *adj* 1 médico. 2 de medicina. *n* reconocimiento médico *m*. **medicine** *n* medicación *f*. n medicina *f*. medicamento *m*. **medicine chest** *n* botiquín *m*. **medicinal** *adj* medicinal.

medieval (medi'i:vəl) *adj* medieval.

mediocre (mi:di'oukə) *adj* mediocre, mediano.

meditate ('mediteit) *vi* meditar, reflexionar. **meditation** *n* meditación, reflexión *f*.

Mediterranean (meditə'reiniən) *adj* mediterráneo. **Mediterranean Sea** *n* Mar Mediterráneo *m. n* Mediterráneo *m*.

medium ('mi:diəm) *adj* mediano, regular, intermedio. *n* 1 medio *m*. 2 médium *m,f*.

meek (mi:k) *adj* dócil, humilde, manso.

meet* (mi:t) *vt* 1 encontrar. 2 encontrarse con. 3 tropezar con. 4 conocer. 5 pagar, satisfacer. *vi* 1 encontrarse, verse. 2 conocerse. **meeting** *n* 1 reunión *f*. 2 encuentro *m*. 3 mitin *m*. 4 *sport* concurso *m*.

megaphone ('megəfoun) *n* megáfono *m*.

melancholy ('melənkəli) *adj* melancólico *f*.

mellow ('melou) *adj* 1 maduro, sazonado. 2

blando, suave, meloso. *vt* madurar. *vi* madurarse, suavizarse.

melodrama ('meladra:ma) *n* melodrama *m*. **melodramatic** *adj* melodramático.

melody ('meladi) *n* melodía *f*.

melon ('melan) *n* melón *m*.

melt (melt) *vt* 1 fundir. 2 derretir. 3 disolver. 4 ablandar. **melting point** *n* punto de fusión *m*.

member ('memba) *n* 1 miembro *m*. 2 socio *m*. 3 *anat* miembro *m*. **member of parliament** diputado *m*. **membership** *n* calidad de miembro *f*.

membrane ('membrein) *n* membrana *f*.

memento (ma'mentou) *n* recuerdo *m*.

memo ('memou) *n inf* memorándum *m*.

memoir ('memwa:) *n* memoria *f*.

memorandum (mema'rændam) *n* 1 memorándum, memorando *m*. 2 apunte *m*. nota *f*. memo *m*.

memory ('memari) *n* 1 memoria *f*. 2 recuerdo *m*. **from memory** de memoria. **in memory of** en memoria de. **memorable** *adj* memorable. **memorial** *adj* conmemorativo. *n* 1 monumento *m*. 2 memorial *m*. **memorize** *vt* aprender de memoria.

menace ('menas) *n* 1 amenaza *f*. 2 *inf* persona peligrosa *f*. *vt* amenazar.

menagerie (ma'nædʒari) *n* casa de fieras, colección de fieras *f*.

mend (mend) *vt* 1 remendar. 2 zurcir. 3 reparar, componer. *vi* mejorar, reponerse.

menial ('mi:nial) *adj* 1 doméstico. 2 bajo, servil.

menopause ('menapɔ:z) *n* menopausia *f*.

menstrual ('menstrual) *adj* menstrual. **menstruate** *vi* menstruar. **menstruation** *n* menstruación *f*. periodo *m*.

mental ('mentl) *adj* mental. **mentality** *n* mentalidad *f*.

menthol ('menθɔl) *n* mentol *m*. **mentholated** *adj* mentolado.

mention ('menʃan) *n* mención *f*. *vt* mencionar, aludir a. **don't mention it!** ¡no hay de qué! **not to mention** sin contar, además de.

menu ('menju:) *n* lista *f*. menú *m*.

mercantile ('ma:kantail) *adj* mercantil, comercial.

mercenary ('ma:sanari) *adj,n* mercenario *m*.

merchant ('ma:tʃant) *adj* mercante, mercantil. *n* comerciante, negociante *m*. **merchant bank** *n* banco mercante *m*. **merchant navy** *n* marina mercante *f*. **merchandise** *n* mercancías *f pl*. géneros *m pl*.

mercury ('ma:kjuri) *n* mercurio *m*.

mercy ('ma:si) *n* misericordia, merced *f*.

mere (mia) *adj* mero, simple, solo, no más que.

merge (ma:dʒ) *vt* 1 unir, combinar. 2 fundir. 3 *comm* fusionar. **merger** *n* fusión, consolidación *f*.

meridian (ma'ridian) *n geog* meridiano *m*.

meringue (ma'ræŋ) *n* merengue *m*.

merit ('merit) *n* mérito *m*. *vt* merecer, ser digno de. **meritorious** *adj* meritorio.

merry ('meri) *adj* alegre, regocijado.

mesh (meʃ) *n* 1 malla *f*. 2 *tech* engrane, engranaje *m*. *vt* enredar. *vi* engranar.

mesmerize ('mezmaraiz) *vt* hipnotizar

mess (mes) *n* 1 confusión *f*. lío *m*. 2 asco *m*. suciedad *f*. 3 *mil* comedor, rancho *m*. **make a mess of** desordenar, ensuciar. *v* **mess about** perder el tiempo. **mess up** 1 desordenar. 2 ensuciar. **messy** *adj* 1 sucio. 2 en desorden.

message ('mesidʒ) *n* mensaje, recado *m*.

messenger ('mesindʒa) *n* mensajero *m*.

met (met) *v see* **meet**.

metabolism (mi'tæbalizam) *n* metabolismo *m*.

metal ('metl) *n* metal *m*. *adj* metálico. **metallurgy** *n* metalurgia *f*.

metamorphosis (meta'mɔ:fasis) *n* metamorfosis *f*.

metaphor ('metafa) *n* metáfora *f*. **metaphorical** *adj* metafórico.

metaphysics (meta'fiziks) *n* metafísica *f*. **metaphysical** *adj* metafísico.

meteor ('mi:tia) *n* meteorito, meteoro *m*. **meteorology** *n* meteorología *f*.

meter ('mi:ta) *n* contador *m*.

method ('meθad) *n* método *m*. **methodical** *adj* metódico. **methodology** *n* metodología *f*.

Methodist ('meθadist) *adj,n* metodista *m,f*. **Methodism** *n* metodismo *m*.

meticulous (mi'tikjulas) *adj* meticuloso.

metre ('mi:ta) *n* metro *m*. **metric** *adj* métrico. **metric system** *n* sistema métrico *m*.

metropolis (ma'trapalis) *n* metrópoli *f*. **metropolitan** *adj,n* metropolitano *m*.

Mexico ('meksikou) *n* Méjico, México *m*. **Mexican** *adj,n* mejicano, mexicano.

miaow (mi'au) *n* miau *m*. *vi* maullar.

microbe ('maikroub) *n* microbio *m*.

microphone ('maikrafoun) *n* micrófono *m*.

microscope ('maikraskoup) *n* microscopio *m*. **microscopic** *adj* microscópico.

mid (mid) *adj* medio. **midday** *n* mediodía *m*. **midland** *adj* del interior, del centro. **mid-morning** *n* media mañana *f*. **midnight** *n* medianoche *f*. **midsummer** *n* pleno verano

m. **midway** adj,adv a medio camino. **mid-week** adj de entre semana.

middle ('midl) adj 1 medio, central. 2 intermedio. 3 mediano, medio. n 1 medio, centro m. mitad f. 2 cintura f. **middle-aged** adj de edad madura. **Middle Ages** n pl Edad Media f. **middle class** n clase media f.

midget ('midʒit) n enano m.

midst (midst) n **in the midst of** entre, en medio de.

midwife ('midwaif) n partera, comadrona f.

might[1] (mait) n 1 fuerza f. poder, poderío m. **mighty** adj fuerte, poderoso, potente.

might[2] (mait) v see **may**.

migraine ('mi:grein) n jaqueca f.

migrate (mai'greit) vi emigrar. **migration** n migración f.

mike (maik) n inf micrófono m.

mild (maild) adj 1 manso. 2 blando. 3 suave, dulce. 4 leve, ligero.

mildew ('mildju:) n moho m.

mile (mail) n milla f. **mileage** n kilometraje m. **mileometer** n mot cuentakilómetros m invar.

militant ('militənt) adj,n militante.

military (militri) adj militar.

milk (milk) n leche f. vt 1 ordeñar. 2 chupar. **milky** adj lácteo. **milkman** n lechero m. **Milky Way** n Vía Láctea f.

mill (mil) n 1 molino m. 2 fábrica f. taller m. vt moler. **miller** n molinero m. **millstone** n 1 piedra de molino, muela f. 2 inf gran estorbo m.

millennium (mi'leniəm) n milenio, milenario m.

milligram ('miligræm) n miligramo m.

millilitre ('mili:li:tə) n mililitro m.

millimetre ('mili:mi:tə) n milímetro m.

million ('miliən) n millón m. **millionaire** n millonario m. **millionth** adj,n millonésimo m.

mime (maim) n 1 pantomima, mímica f. 2 mimo m. vt hacer en pantomima, representar con gestos. **mimic** adj n 1 mímico m. 2 fingido. n remedador m. vt remedar, imitar. **mimicry** n mímica, imitación f. remedo m.

minaret (minə'ret) n alminar m.

mince (mins) n carne picada f. **mincemeat** n conserva de picadillo de fruta f. ~vt picar, desmenuzar. vi 1 andar con pasos menudos. 2 hablar remilgadamente. **mincer** n molinillo de picar m. **mincing** adj 1 remilgado, afectado. 2 menudito.

mind (maind) n 1 mente f. 2 inteligencia, entendimiento m. 3 parecer m. 4 memoria f.

vt 1 sentir molestia por. 2 hacer caso de. 3 tener cuidado con.

mine[1] (main) pron 1st pers s el mío, la mía.

mine[2] (main) n mina f. vt extraer. vi extraer minerales. **miner** n minero m.

mineral ('minərəl) adj,n mineral m. **mineral water** n agua mineral f.

minestrone (mini'strouni) n sopa juliana f.

mingle ('miŋgəl) vt mezclar. vi 1 mezclarse. 2 confundirse.

miniature ('miniətʃə) n,adj miniatura f.

minim ('minim) n mus blanca f.

minimum ('miniməm) adj mínimo. n mínimo, minimum m. **minimal** adj mínimo. **minimize** vt minimizar.

mining ('mainiŋ) n 1 minería f. 2 extracción f. **mining engineer** n ingeniero de minas m.

minister ('ministə) n 1 ministro m. 2 rel pastor m. vi 1 ministrar. 2 atender. **ministerial** adj ministerial, de ministro. **ministry** n ministerio m.

mink (miŋk) n 1 zool visón m. 2 piel de visón f.

minor ('mainə) adj 1 menor. 2 secundario. 3 pequeño. n menor de edad m,f. **minority** n minoría f. adj minoritario.

Minorca (mi'nɔ:kə) n Menorca f.

minstrel ('minstrəl) n 1 juglar m. 2 cantor m.

mint[1] (mint) n 1 bot menta f. 2 pastilla de menta f.

mint[2] (mint) n casa de moneda f. adj nuevo, sin usar. **in mint condition** en perfecto estado. ~vt acuñar.

minuet (minju'et) n minué m.

minus ('mainəs) adj menos, negativo. n cantidad negativa f. **minus sign** n signo menos m. ~prep 1 menos. 2 sin.

minute[1] ('minit) n 1 minuto m. 2 minuta, nota f. 3 pl acta f. vt levantar acta de.

minute[2] (mai'nju:t) adj diminuto, menudo, pequeño. **minutely** adv minuciosamente.

miracle ('mirəkəl) n milagro m. **miraculous** adj milagroso.

mirage ('mira:ʒ) n espejismo m.

mirror ('mirə) n 1 espejo m. 2 mot retrovisor m. vt reflejar.

mirth (mə:θ) n alegría f. regocijo m.

misbehave (misbi'heiv) vi 1 portarse mal. 2 ser malo. **misbehaviour** n mala conducta f.

miscarriage (mis'kæridʒ) n med aborto, malparto m. **miscarry** vi 1 med abortar, malparir. 2 fracasar, salir mal.

miscellaneous (misə'leiniəs) adj misceláneo, vario, diverso. **miscellany** n miscelánea f.

mischance (mis'tʃɑ:ns) n desgracia, mala suerte f

mischief ('mistʃif) n 1 mal, daño m. 2 malicia f. **mischief-maker** n revoltoso m. **mischievous** adj 1 dañoso, malo. 2 malicioso. 3 travieso.

misconceive (miskən'si:v) vt entender mal. **misconception** n concepto erróneo m.

misconduct (mis'kɔndʌkt) n mala conducta f.

misdeed (mis'di:d) n delito, crimen m.

miser ('maizə) n avaro, tacaño m. **miserly** adj avariento, tacaño.

miserable ('mizərəbəl) adj 1 triste. 2 vil. 3 lastimoso. 4 despreciable. **miserably** adv tristemente. **misery** n 1 sufrimiento m. 2 miseria f.

misfire (mis'faiə) vi fallar.

misfit ('misfit) n persona inadaptada, persona mal ajustada f.

misfortune (mis'fɔ:tʃən) n desgracia, desventura f. infortunio m.

misgiving (mis'giviŋ) n recelo m. duda f.

misguided (mis'gaidid) adj equivocado.

mishap ('mishæp) n contratiempo, accidente m.

mislay (mis'lei) vt perder.

mislead (mis'li:d) vt 1 despistar. 2 engañar. **misleading** adj 1 erróneo. 2 engañoso.

misprint ('misprint) n errata f. error de imprenta m.

miss[1] (mis) n 1 tiro errado, tiro perdido m. 2 error, desacierto m. 3 fracaso m. vt 1 errar. 2 perder. 3 no acertar. 4 no entender. 5 omitir. 6 no encontrar. 7 echar de menos. vi 1 errar el blanco. 2 fallar, salir mal. **missing** adj 1 ausente. 2 perdido. 3 mil desaparecido.

miss[2] (mis) n señorita f.

missile ('misail) n proyectil m.

mission ('miʃən) n misión f. **missionary** n misionero m

mist (mist) n 1 niebla f. 2 neblina f. 3 bruma f. vt empañar, velar. **misty** adj nebuloso, brumoso.

mistake＊ (mis'teik) n equivocación, falta f. error m. **make a mistake** equivocarse. ～vt entender mal, equivocarse sobre. **mistake for** equivocar con, confundir por. **mistaken** adj 1 equivocado, erróneo. 2 incorrecto. **be mistaken** equivocarse, estar equivocado.

mister ('mistə) n señor m.

mistletoe ('misəltou) n muérdago m.

mistress ('mistrəs) n 1 señora, ama de casa f. 2 dueña f. 3 amante, querida f.

mistrust (mis'trʌst) n desconfianza f. recelo m.

vt desconfiar de. **mistrustful** adj desconfiado, receloso.

misunderstand＊ (misʌndə'stænd) vt entender mal, comprender mal. **misunderstanding** n equivocación f. error m.

misuse (n mis'ju:s; v mis'ju:z) n 1 abuso, mal uso m. 2 empleo erróneo. 3 maltratamiento m. vt 1 abusar de. 2 emplear de. 3 maltratar.

mitre ('maitə) n rel mitra f.

mitten ('mitn) n mitón m.

mix (miks) vt 1 mezclar. 2 combinar, unir. 3 confundir. 4 amasar. **mixture** n 1 mezcla f. 2 med medicina f. **mix-up** n 1 confusión f. 2 inf lío, enredo m.

moan (moun) n 1 gemido, quejido m. 2 queja, protesta f. vt lamentar. vi 1 gemir. 2 quejarse, protestar.

moat (mout) n foso m.

mob (mɔb) n 1 gentio m. muchedumbre, multitud f. 2 populacho m. vt acosar, atropellar.

mobile ('moubail) adj móvil, movible. **mobility** n movilidad f. **mobilize** vt movilizar.

mock (mɔk) adj fingido, simulado. vt 1 ridiculizar. 2 burlarse de, mofarse de. **mockery** n mofa, burla f. **make a mockery of** hacer ridículo. **mocking** adj burlón.

mode (moud) n 1 modo m. 2 manera f. 3 moda f.

model ('mɔdl) adj,n modelo m. vt modelar. vi 1 servir de modelo. 2 ejercer la profesión de modelo.

moderate ('mɔdərət) adj,n moderado m. vt 1 moderar. 2 mitigar. **moderation** n moderación f. **in moderation** con moderación.

modern ('mɔdən) adj moderno. **modernize** vt modernizar. **modernization** n modernización f

modest ('mɔdist) adj 1 modesto. 2 pudoroso. **modesty** n 1 modestia f. 2 pudor m.

modify ('mɔdifai) vt modificar. **modification** n modificación f

modulate ('mɔdjuleit) vt,vi modular.

module ('mɔdju:l) n módulo m.

moist (mɔist) adj húmedo, mojado. **moisten** vt humedecer, mojar. **moisture** n humedad f. **moisturize** vt humedecer, mojar.

mole[1] (moul) n anat lunar m.

mole[2] (moul) n zool topo m.

molecule ('mɔlikju:l) n molécula f. **molecular** adj molecular.

molest (mə'lest) vt importunar, meterse con.

mollusc ('mɔləsk) n molusco m.

molten ('moultən) adj fundido, líquido.

moment ('moumənt) n 1 momento, instante m.
2 importancia f. **momentary** adj momentáneo. **momentous** adj grave, de suma importancia. **momentum** n 1 momento m. 2 ímpetu m.

monarch ('monək) n monarca m. **monarchy** n monarquía f.

monastery ('monəstri) n monasterio m. **monastic** adj monástico.

Monday ('mʌndi) n lunes m.

money ('mʌni) n 1 dinero m. 2 moneda f. **moneybox** n hucha f. **money order** n giro postal m. **monetary** adj monetario.

mongrel ('mʌŋgrəl) n 1 perro mestizo, perro callejero m. 2 mestizo m. adj 1 mestizo. 2 cruzado, callejero.

monitor ('monitə) n monitor m. vt 1 escuchar. 2 controlar.

monk (mʌŋk) n monje m.

monkey ('mʌŋki) n mono m. **make a monkey out of** poner en ridículo. **monkey about with** manosear.

monogamy (mə'nogəmi) n monogamia f.

monologue ('monəlog) n monólogo m.

monopoly (mə'nopəli) n monopolio m. **monopolize** vt monopolizar.

monosyllable ('monəsiləbəl) n monosílabo m.

monotone ('monətoun) n monotonía f. **monotonous** adj monótono.

monsoon (mon'su:n) n monzón m,f.

monster ('monstə) n monstruo m. **monstrosity** n monstruosidad f. **monstrous** adj monstruoso, enorme.

month (mʌnθ) n mes m. **monthly** adj mensual. n revista mensual f.

monument ('monjumənt) n monumento m. **monumental** adj monumental.

moo (mu:) n mugido m. vi mugir.

mood¹ (mu:d) n 1 humor m. 2 capricho m. **moody** adj de mal humor.

mood² (mu:d) n gram modo m.

moon (mu:n) n luna f. **full moon** luna llena. **new moon** luna nueva. **once in a blue moon** de Pascuas a Ramos. **moonlight** n luz de la luna f.

moor¹ (muə) n páramo, brezal m. **moorhen** n polla de agua f.

moor² (muə) vt amarrar. vi echar las amarras.

Moor (muə) n moro m.

mop (mop) n 1 fregasuelos m invar. 2 mata, greña f. vt fregar, limpiar.

mope (moup) vi estar deprimido or abatido.

moped ('mouped) n ciclomotor m.

moral ('morəl) adj 1 moral, ético. 2 virtuoso. n 1 moraleja f. sentido moral m. 2 moral, ética, moralidad f. **morale** n moral f. **morality** n moralidad f. **moralize** vt,vi moralizar.

morbid ('mo:bid) adj 1 mórbido, morboso. 2 malsano. **morbidity** n morbosidad f.

more (mo:r) adj, adv más. **all the more** tanto más. **no more** ya no, no más. **once more** otra vez. **moreover** adv además, por otra parte.

morgue (mo:g) n depósito de cadáveres m. morgue f.

morning ('mo:niŋ) n 1 mañana f. 2 madrugada f. **good morning!** ¡buenos días! **in the morning** por la mañana. **tomorrow morning** mañana por la mañana...

Morocco (mə'rokou) n Marruecos m.

moron ('mo:ron) n imbécil m,f. **moronic** adj imbécil.

morose (mə'rous) adj malhumorado, hosco.

morphine ('mo:fi:n) n morfina f.

Morse Code (mo:s) n alfabeto Morse m.

mortal ('mo:tl) adj,n mortal. **mortality** n mortalidad f.

mortar¹ ('mo:tə) n mortero m.

mortar² ('mo:tə) n argamasa f.

mortgage ('mo:gidʒ) n hipoteca f. vt hipotecar.

mortify ('mo:tifai) vt 1 mortificar. 2 humillar.

mortuary ('mo:tjuəri) n depósito de cadáveres m.

mosaic (mou'zeiik) n mosaico m.

mosque (mosk) n mezquita f.

mosquito (mə'ski:tou) n mosquito m. **mosquito net** n mosquitero m.

moss (mos) n bot musgo m. **mossy** adj musgoso.

most (moust) adj 1 más. 2 la mayor parte de, los más, la mayoría de, casi todos. adv 1 más. 2 sumamente, de lo más. **most of all** sobre todo. ~n la mayor parte, el mayor número, los más. **at most** a lo más, a lo sumo, todo lo más. **make the most of** sacar el mejor partido de. **mostly** adv por la mayor parte, en general.

motel (mou'tel) n motel m.

moth (moθ) n 1 polilla f. 2 mariposa nocturna f. **mothball** n bola de naftalina f. **motheaten** adj apolillado.

mother ('mʌðə) n madre f. vt servir de madre a. **motherhood** n maternidad f. **mother-in-law** n suegra f. **mother superior** n madre superiora f.

motion ('mouʃən) n 1 movimiento m. 2 marcha

235

f. 3 moción, proposición f. **set in motion** poner en marcha.

motive ('moutiv) n motivo m. **ulterior motive** motivo oculto.

motor ('mouta) n 1 motor m. 2 coche, automóvil m. vi ir en coche or automóvil. **motor car** n coche, automóvil m. **motor cycle** n motocicleta f. **motorist** n automovilista m,f. **motorway** n autopista f.

motto ('mɔtou) n, pl **-os** or **-oes** 1 lema f. 2 divisa f.

mould[1] (mould) n 1 molde m. 2 cosa moldeada f. vt moldear.

mould[2] (mould) n moho m. **mouldy** adj mohoso, enmohecido.

moult (moult) n muda f. vi mudar.

mound (maund) n 1 montón m. 2 terraplén m.

mount[1] (maunt) vt montar, subir a. vi 1 subir. 2 montar. 3 aumentar.

mount[2] (maunt) n montón, montículo, monte m.

mountain ('mauntin) n 1 montaña f. 2 montón m. **mountain range** n sierra f. **mountainous** adj montañoso. **mountaineer** n 1 montañero m. 2 alpinista m. **mountaineering** adj,n montañismo, alpinismo m.

mourn (mɔ:n) vt llorar, lamentar. **mourner** n 1 doliente m,f. 2 plañidero m. **mournful** adj triste, afligido. **mourning** n 1 luto m. 2 lamentación f.

mouse (maus) n, pl **mice** ratón m. **mousetrap** n ratonera f. **mousy** adj 1 tímido. 2 pardusco.

mousse (mu:s) n postre de crema m.

moustache (mə'sta:ʃ) n bigote m. bigotes m pl. **wear a moustache** tener bigote.

mouth (mauθ) n boca f. **mouthful** n bocado m. **mouthpiece** n 1 mus boquilla f. 2 inf portavoz m. **mouth-watering** adj sumamente apetitoso.

move (mu:v) n 1 movimiento m. 2 game jugada, movida f. 3 paso m. acción f. 4 mudanza f. traslado m. vt 1 mover. 2 trasladar. 3 conmover. 4 proponer. **movable** adj movible. **movement** n 1 movimiento, juego m. 2 mus tiempo m. **moving** adj 1 movedor. 2 móvil. 3 conmovedor.

mow[*] (mou) vt 1 segar. 2 cortar. **lawn-mower** n cortacésped m.

Mr ('mistə) n señor, don m.

Mrs ('misiz) n señora, doña f.

much (mʌtʃ) adj,adv 1 mucho. 2 casi, más o menos. 3 con mucho. **as much, so much**

tanto. **how much?** ¿cuánto? **however much** por mucho que.

muck (mʌk) n 1 estiércol m. 2 suciedad f. **mucky** adj sucio.

mud (mʌd) n lodo, barro, fango m. **mudguard** n guardabarros m invar.

muddle ('mʌdl) n 1 desorden m. confusión f. 2 embrollo, lío m. **get into a muddle** embrollarse. ~vt 1 embrollar, confundir. 2 aturdir, confundir.

muff (mʌf) n manguito m.

muffle ('mʌfəl) vt 1 envolver. 2 embozar, tapar. 3 amortiguar, apagar. **muffled** adj sordo, apagado.

mug (mʌg) n 1 taza f. 2 jarra f.

mulberry ('mʌlbəri) n mora, morera f. adj morado.

mule[1] (mju:l) n zool mulo m.

mule[2] (mju:l) n babucha f.

multiple ('mʌltipəl) adj múltiple, múltiplo. n múltiplo m.

multiply ('mʌltiplai) vt multiplicar. **multiplication** n multiplicación f.

multitude ('mʌltitju:d) n multitud f.

mum[1] (mʌm) adj callado. **keep mum** callarse.

mum[2] (mʌm) n inf mamá f.

mumble ('mʌmbəl) vt decir entre dientes. vi musitar, refunfuñar. **speak in a mumble** hablar entre dientes.

mummy[1] ('mʌmi) n momia f.

mummy[2] ('mʌmi) n inf mamá f.

mumps (mʌmps) n paperas, parótidas f pl.

munch (mʌntʃ) vt mascar, ronzar.

mundane ('mʌndein) adj 1 mundano. 2 vulgar, trivial.

municipal (mju:'nisipəl) adj municipal. **municipality** n municipio m.

mural ('mjuərəl) n pintura mural f.

murder ('mə:də) n asesinato, homicidio m. vt 1 asesinar. 2 matar. **murderer** n asesino m.

murmur ('mə:mə) n 1 murmullo, murmurio m. 2 susurro. vt,vi murmurar.

muscle ('mʌsəl) n 1 músculo m. 2 inf fuerza muscular f. v **muscle in** entrar por fuerza. **muscular** adj 1 muscular. 2 musculoso. 3 fornido.

muse (mju:z) n musa f.

museum (mju:'ziəm) n museo m.

mushroom ('mʌʃrum) n 1 seta f. hongo m. 2 champiñón m. vi inf crecer como los hongos.

music ('mu:zik) n música f. **face the music** pagar el pato. **set to music** poner música a, musicar. **musical** adj musical, músico. n comedia musical f. **musician** n músico m.

musk (mʌsk) n 1 almizcle m. 2 bot almizcleña f.

musket ('mʌskit) n mosquete m.

Muslim ('muzlim) adj,n musulmán m.

muslin ('mʌzlln) n muselina f.

mussel ('mʌsəl) n mejillón m.

must* (mʌst) v aux deber, tener que, haber de.

mustard ('mʌstəd) n mostaza f.

mute (mju:t) adj mudo, silencioso. n 1 mudo m. 2 mus sordina f.

mutilate ('mju:tileit) vt mutilar.

mutiny ('mju:tini) n motín m. sublevación f. vi amotinarse, sublevarse.

mutter ('mʌtə) n murmullo m. vt,vi murmurar.

mutton ('mʌtn) n carne de carnero f.

mutual ('mju:tjuəl) adj 1 mútuo. 2 común.

muzzle ('mʌzəl) n 1 hocico m. 2 bozal m. 3 boca f. vt 1 abozalar. 2 amordazar.

my (mai) poss adj 1st pers s mi, mis. **myself** pron 1st pers s 1 yo mismo, yo misma. 2 me. 3 mí.

myopia (mai'oupiə) n miopía f.

myrrh (mə:) n mirra f.

myrtle ('mə:tl) n arrayán, mirto m.

mystery ('mistəri) n misterio m. **mysterious** adj misterioso.

mystic ('mistik) adj,n místico m. **mysticism** n misticismo m. mística f.

mystify ('mistifai) vt dejar perplejo, desconcertar.

mystique (mi'sti:k) n misterio m.

myth (miθ) n mito m. **mythical** adj mítico. **mythology** n mitología f.

N

nag[1] (næg) vt regañar, importunar, machacar. **nagging** adj 1 regañón. 2 persistente.

nag[2] (næg) n jaca f. rocín m.

nail (neil) n 1 anat uña f. 2 zool garra f. 3 clavo m. vt clavar, enclavar. **nailfile** n lima f. **nail varnish** n esmalte para las uñas m.

naive (nai'i:v) adj ingenuo.

naked ('neikid) adj desnudo. **nakedness** n desnudez f.

name (neim) n nombre m. **what is your name?** ¿cómo se llama? ~vt nombrar. **namely** adv a saber. **namesake** n tocayo, homónimo m.

nanny ('næni) n niñera f.

nap (næp) n sueño ligero m. **have** or **take a nap** descabezar un sueño. ~vi dormitar.

napkin ('næpkin) n 1 servilleta f. 2 pañal m.

nappy ('næpi) n inf pañal m.

narcotic adj,n narcótico m.

narrate (nə'reit) vt narrar. **narration** n narración f. **narrative** n narrativa f. adj narrativo. **narrator** n narrador m.

narrow ('nærou) adj 1 estrecho, angosto. 2 reducido, justo. vt 1 estrechar. 2 reducir. **narrowly** adv 1 estrechamente. 2 por poco. **narrow-minded** adj intolerante, estrecho de conciencia.

nasal ('neizəl) adj nasal.

nasty ('na:sti) adj 1 asqueroso. 2 horrible. 3 grosero. 4 odioso, malo. 5 desagradable.

nation ('neiʃən) n nación f. **national** adj nacional. **national anthem** n himno nacional m. **national insurance** n seguro obligatorio m. **national service** n servicio nacional m. **nationalism** n nacionalismo m. **nationalist** adj,n nacionalista m,f. **nationality** n nacionalidad f. **nationalize** vt nacionalizar.

native ('neitiv) n 1 natural m,f. 2 indígena m,f. adj 1 nativo. 2 natal.

nativity (nə'tiviti) n natividad f.

natural ('nætʃərəl) adj 1 natural. 2 innato. **natural history** n historia natural f. **naturalize** vt naturalizar.

nature ('neitʃə) n 1 naturaleza f. 2 natural, carácter m.

naughty ('nɔ:ti) adj 1 malo, travieso, pícaro. 2 picante.

nausea ('nɔ:siə, -ziə) n náusea f. **nauseate** vt dar náuseas. **nauseating** adj nauseabundo.

nautical ('nɔ:tikəl) adj 1 náutico. 2 marino.

naval ('neivəl) adj naval, de marina.

nave (neiv) n nave f.

navel ('neivəl) n ombligo m.

navigate ('nævigeit) vi navegar. vt guiar. **navigator** n 1 navegante m. 2 piloto m.

navy ('neivi) n marina f. **navy blue** adj azul marino.

near (niə) adv cerca. prep 1 cerca de. 2 hacia. adj 1 cercano, próximo. 2 aproximado. vi acercarse, aproximarse. **nearby** adv cerca. adj cercano, próximo. **nearly** adv 1 casi. 2 de cerca.

neat (ni:t) adj 1 pulcro. 2 hábil. 3 puro.

nebulous ('nebjuləs) adj nebuloso.

necessary ('nesəsəri) adj necesario **necessity** n necesidad f.

neck (nek) n cuello m. **neck and neck** al

mismo nivel. ~vi inf besuquearse. **necklace** n collar m. **neckline** n escote m.

need (ni:d) n necesidad f. **if need be** si fuera necesario. ~vt 1 necesitar. 2 tener que. **needless** adj innecesario, inútil.

needle ('ni:dl) n aguja f. vt provocar.

negate (ni'geit) vt anular. **negative** adj negativo. n 1 negativa f. 2 phot negativo m.

neglect (ni'glekt) vt 1 descuidar, desatender. 2 abandonar, arrinconar. n 1 abandono m. 2 desatención f. **negligence** n negligencia f. **negligent** adj negligente. **negligible** adj insignificante, despreciable.

negotiate (ni'gouʃieit) vt 1 negociar, gestionar. 2 salvar. **negotiation** n negociación, gestión f

Negro ('ni:grou) n, pl -**oes**, adj negro.

neigh (nei) vi relinchar. n relincho m.

neighbour ('neibə) n vecino m. **neighbourhood** n 1 vecindario m. 2 vecindad f. **neighbourly** adj de buen vecino.

neither ('naiðə) adv ni. **neither...nor** ni...ni. ~conj 1 ni. 2 tampoco. 3 ni tampoco. pron ninguno m.

nephew ('nevju:) n sobrino m.

nepotism ('nepətizəm) n nepotismo m.

Neptune ('neptju:n) n Neptuno m.

nerve (nə:v) n 1 nervio m. 2 inf caradura f. **get on one's nerves** crispar los nervios. **nervous** adj nervioso. **nervous breakdown** n crisis nerviosa f. **nervous system** n sistema nervioso m. **nervousness** n nerviosismo m. **nervy** adj nervioso.

nest (nest) n 1 nido m. 2 hogar m. vi 1 anidar. 2 buscar nidos.

nestle ('nesəl) vi 1 abrigarse, arrimarse. 2 anidarse.

net[1] (net) n 1 red f. 2 malla f. 3 tul m. vt 1 prender con red, cubrir con red. **netball** n balonvolea f. **network** n red f.

net[2] (net) adj neto. vt sacar un neto de.

nettle ('netl) n ortiga f. vt irritar.

neurosis (njuə'rousis) n neurosis f. **neurotic** adj,n neurótico.

neuter ('nju:tə) adj 1 neutro. 2 castrado. vt castrar

neutral ('nju:trəl) adj 1 neutral. 2 tech neutro. **in neutral** mot en punto muerto. **neutralize** vt neutralizar

never ('nevə) adv nunca, jamás. **never-ending** adj interminable. **nevertheless** adv no obstante.

new (nju:) adj nuevo. **newcomer** n recién

llegado m. **newly** adv 1 recién. 2 nuevamente.

New Testament n Nuevo Testamento m.

New Year n Año Nuevo m.

news (nju:z) n noticias f pl. **a piece of news** una noticia f. **what's the news?** ¿qué hay de nuevo? **newsagent** n vendedor de periódicos m. **newspaper** n periódico m. adj periodístico. **newsreel** n noticiario m.

New Zealand ('zi:lənd) n Nueva Zelanda f. **New Zealander** n neozelandés m.

next (nekst) adj 1 próximo, que viene. 2 siguiente. 3 contiguo, de al lado. adv 1 después, luego. 2 otra vez. **next to** 1 junto a, al lado de. 2 cerca. ~n próximo, siguiente m.

nib (nib) n punta f

nibble ('nibəl) vt mordisquear. n mordisco m.

nice (nais) adj 1 bueno, agradable. 2 bonito, mono. 3 simpático. 4 fino. **nicety** n 1 detalle m. exactitud f. 2 refinamiento m.

niche (nitʃ) n 1 nicho m. 2 hornacina f.

nick (nik) vt 1 mellar, hacer muescas en. 2 inf birlar. 3 inf trincar. n 1 mella, muesca f. 2 sl cárcel f. **in the nick of time** en el momento justo.

nickel ('nikəl) n níquel m.

nickname ('nikneim) n apodo m. vt apodar.

nicotine ('nikəti:n) n nicotina f.

niece (ni:s) n sobrina f.

nigger ('nigə) n derog negro m.

night (nait) n noche f. **good night!** ¡buenas noches! **last night** anoche. ~adj nocturno. **nightdress** n camisón m. **nightfall** n anochecer m. **nightly** adv todas las noches. **nightmare** n pesadilla f. **night-time** n noche f. **in the night-time** de noche.

nightingale ('naitiŋgeil) n ruiseñor m.

nil (nil) n cero m. nada f

nimble ('nimbəl) adj ágil, ligero.

nine (nain) adj,n nueve m. **ninth** adj noveno.

nineteen (nain'ti:n) adj,n diecinueve m. **nineteenth** adj decimonoveno, decimonono.

ninety ('nainti) adj,n noventa m. **ninetieth** adj nonagésimo.

nip[1] (nip) vt 1 dar un mordisco a. 2 pellizcar. 3 helar. n 1 mordisco m. 2 pellizco m. 3 frío m.

nip[2] (nip) n trago m.

nipple ('nipəl) n 1 pezón m. 2 tetilla f.

nit (nit) n 1 liendre m. 2 inf imbécil m.

nitrogen ('naitrədʒən) n nitrógeno m.

no[1] (nou) adv no.

no[2] (nou) adj 1 ninguno. 2 sin.

noble ('noubǝl) *adj* noble. **nobility** *n* nobleza f. **nobleman** *n* noble *m*.

nobody ('noubǝdi) *pron* nadie.

nocturnal (nɔk'tǝ:nl) *adj* nocturno.

nod (nɔd) *vi* 1 inclinar la cabeza. 2 asentir con la cabeza. 3 cabecear. *n* 1 inclinación de cabeza f. 2 cabezada f.

node (noud) *n* 1 *bot* nudo *m*. 2 *med,tech* nódulo, nodo *m*.

noise (nɔiz) *n* ruido *m*. **noisy** *adj* ruidoso, estrepitoso.

nomad ('noumæd) *n* nómada *m,f*. **nomadic** *adj* nómada.

nominal ('nominl) *adj* nominal.

nominate ('nomineit) *vt* nominar, nombrar. **nomination** *n* nominación f. nombramiento *m*. **nominee** *n* candidato *m*.

nominative ('nominǝtiv) *n* nominativo *m*.

non- *pref* no, des-, in-.

nonchalant ('nonʃǝlǝnt) *adj* 1 indiferente. 2 descuidado.

nondescript ('nondiskript) *adj* 1 indefinible. 2 indefinido. 3 mediocre.

none (nʌn) *pron* ninguno *m*. **none of that** nada de eso. ~*adv* de ningún modo. nada. **none the less** no obstante.

nonentity (non'entiti) *n* nulidad f.

nonsense ('nonsǝns) *n* disparate, desatino *m. interj* ¡tonterías! **nonsensical** *adj* disparatado, absurdo.

noon (nu:n) *n* mediodía *m*.

no-one *pron* nadie.

noose (nu:s) *n* lazo corredizo *m*. *vt* cazar con lazo.

nor (nɔ:) *conj* ni.

norm (nɔ:m) *n* norma, pauta f. **normal** *adj* normal. **normality** *n* normalidad f. **normalize** *vt* normalizar.

north (nɔ:θ) *n* norte *m*. *adj* del norte, septentrional. *adv* al norte. **northeast** *adj,n* nordeste *m*. **northeasterly** *adj* nordeste. **northeastern** *adj* nordeste. **northerly** *adj* del norte, septentrional. **northern** *adj* del norte, norteño, septentrional. **northwest** *adj,n* noroeste *m*. **northwesterly** *adj* del noroeste. **northwestern** *adj* noroeste.

Northern Ireland *n* Irlanda del Norte f.

Norway ('nɔ:wei) *n* Noruega f. **Norwegian** *adj,n* noruego *m*. **Norwegian** (language) *n* noruego *m*.

nose (nouz) *n* 1 nariz f. *inf* narices f pl. 2 hocico *m*. 3 olfato *m*. **nosy** *adj inf* fisgón, curioso.

nostalgia (nɔ'stældʒiǝ) *n* nostalgia f. **nostalgic** *adj* nostálgico.

nostril ('nostril) *n* nariz, ventana de la nariz f.

not (nɔt) *adv* no. **not at all** de ningún modo.

notch (nɔtʃ) *n* muesca f. corte *m*. *vt* cortar muescas en.

note (nout) *n* 1 nota f. 2 *comm* vale *m*. *vt* 1 notar. 2 anotar. **notebook** *n* cuaderno *m*. **notable** *adj* notable. **notation** *n* notación f. **noteworthy** *adj* digno de ser notado.

nothing ('nʌθiŋ) *n* nada f. **for nothing** de balde. **nothing much** poca cosa. ~*adv* en nada.

notice ('noutis) *n* 1 aviso *m*. 2 anuncio *m*. 3 letrero *m*. 4 plazo *m*. 5 atención *m*. **notice board** *n* tablero de anuncios *m*. ~*vt* notar, advertir, fijarse. **noticeable** *adj* 1 perceptible. 2 notable.

notify ('noutifai) *vt* notificar. **notification** *n* notificación f.

notion ('nouʃǝn) *n* noción, idea f.

notorious (nou'tɔ:riǝs) *adj* 1 notorio, muy conocido. 2 escandaloso. **notoriety** *n* 1 notoriedad f. 2 mala fama f.

notwithstanding (nɔtwiθ'stændiŋ) *adv* no obstante. *prep* a pesar de. *conj* a pesar de que.

nougat ('nu:ga:) *n* turrón *m*.

nought (nɔ:t) *n* 1 nada f. 2 cero *m*.

noun (naun) *n* nombre, sustantivo *m*.

nourish ('nʌriʃ) *vt* nutrir, alimentar, sustentar. **nourishing** *adj* nutritivo, alimenticio. **nourishment** *n* alimento, sustento *m*.

novel[1] ('novǝl) *n* novela f. **novelist** *n* novelista *m,f*.

novel[2] ('novǝl) *adj* 1 nuevo. 2 original. **novelty** *n* novedad f.

November (nou'vembǝ) *n* noviembre *m*.

novice ('novis) *n* novicio *m*.

now (nau) *adv* ahora. **from now on** de aquí en adelante. **just now** hace un momento. ~*conj* ahora bien. **nowadays** *adv* hoy día, hoy en día.

nowhere ('nouwɛǝ) *adv* en or a ninguna parte.

noxious ('nɔkʃǝs) *adj* nocivo.

nozzle ('nozǝl) *n* boquilla f.

nuance ('nju:ǝns) *n* matiz *m*.

nucleus ('nju:kliǝs) *n*, *pl* -clei *or* -cleuses núcleo *m*. **nuclear** *adj* nuclear.

nude (nju:d) *adj,n* desnudo *m*. **in the nude** desnudo. **nudism** *n* nudismo *m*. **nudist** *n* nudista *m,f*. **nudity** *n* desnudez f.

nudge (nʌdʒ) *vt* dar un codazo. *n* codazo *m*.

nugget

nugget ('nʌgit) n pepita de oro f.
nuisance ('njuːsəns) n 1 molestia, fastidio m. 2 pesado m.
null (nʌl) adj nulo. **nullify** vt anular. **nullity** n nulidad f.
numb (nʌm) adj 1 entumecido. 2 insensible. vt 1 entumecer. 2 paralizar. **numbness** n 1 entumecimiento m. 2 insensibilidad f.
number ('nʌmbə) n número m. vt 1 numerar. 2 contar. **number plate** n mot placa de matrícula f. **numeral** adj,n numeral. n cifra f. **numerical** adj numérico. **numerous** adj 1 numeroso. 2 muchos.
nun (nʌn) n monja f.
nurse (nəːs) n 1 enfermera f. 2 nodriza f. 3 niñera f. vt 1 cuidar. 2 fomentar. vi hacer de enfermera. **nursing home** n clínica privada f. **nursery** n 1 cuarto de los niños m. 2 vivero, plantel m. **nursery rhyme** n rima infantil f.
nurture ('nəːtʃə) vt 1 nutrir. 2 criar. 3 educar. n crianza f.
nut (nʌt) n 1 nuez f. 2 tech tuerca f. **be nuts** inf estar chiflado. **nutcrackers** n often pl cascanueces m invar. **nutmeg** n nuez moscada f.
nutrition (njuːˈtriʃən) n nutrición f. **nutritional** adj nutritivo.
nuzzle ('nʌzəl) vt 1 hociquear. 2 arrimar.
nylon ('nailən) n nilón, nylón m.

O

oak (ouk) n roble m.
oar (ɔː) n remo m. **oarsman** n remero m.
oasis (ouˈeisis) n, pl **oases** oasis m.
oath (ouθ) n juramento m. **take an oath** prestar juramento.
oatmeal ('outmiːl) n harina de avena f.
oats (outs) n pl avena f.
obedient (əˈbiːdiənt) adj obediente. **obedience** n obediencia f.
obese (ouˈbiːs) adj obeso. **obesity** n obesidad f.
obey (əˈbei) vt,vi obedecer.
obituary (əˈbitjuəri) n obituario m.
object (n 'ɔbdʒikt; v əbˈdʒekt) n 1 objeto m. 2 gram complemento m. vt objetar vi 1 hacer objeciones, oponerse. 2 protestar. **objection** n objeción f. **objectionable** adj 1 discutible. 2 desagradable. **objective** adj,n objetivo m. **objectivity** n objetividad f.

oblige (əˈblaidʒ) vt 1 obligar. 2 complacer. **be obliged (for)** estar agradecido (por). **obligation** n 1 obligación f. 2 compromiso m. **obligatory** adj obligatorio. **obliging** adj complaciente, servicial.
oblique (əˈbliːk) adj oblicuo.
obliterate (əˈblitəreit) vt 1 borrar. 2 aniquilar. **obliteration** n 1 borradura f. 2 aniquilación f.
oblivion (əˈbliviən) n olvido m. **oblivious** adj abstraído, inconsciente.
oblong ('ɔblɔŋ) adj rectangular.
obnoxious (əbˈnɔkʃəs) adj detestable, odioso.
oboe ('oubou) n oboe m.
obscene (əbˈsiːn) adj obsceno. **obscenity** n obscenidad f.
obscure (əbˈskjuə) adj oscuro. vt oscurecer. **obscurity** n oscuridad f.
observe (əbˈzəːv) vt observar. **observance** n observancia f. **observant** adj observador. **observation** n observación f. **observatory** n observatorio m. **observer** n observador m.
obsess (əbˈses) vt obsesionar. **obsession** n obsesión f.
obsolete ('ɔbsəliːt) adj obsoleto, en desuso.
obstacle ('ɔbstəkəl) n obstáculo m.
obstinate ('ɔbstinət) adj obstinado. **obstinacy** n obstinación, terquedad f.
obstruct (əbˈstrʌkt) vt obstruir. **obstruction** n obstrucción f. **obstructive** adj obstructivo.
obtain (əbˈtein) vt obtener. vi prevalecer. **obtainable** adj 1 asequible. 2 en venta.
obtrusive (əbˈtruːsiv) adj 1 importuno. 2 que salta a la vista. 3 penetrante. **obtrusion** n imposición, importunidad f.
obtuse (əbˈtjuːs) adj obtuso.
obvious ('ɔbviəs) adj obvio.
occasion (əˈkeiʒən) n 1 ocasión f. 2 acontecimiento m. vt ocasionar. **occasional** adj 1 ocasional. 2 poco frecuente. **occasionally** adv de vez en cuando.
Occident ('ɔksidənt) n occidente m. **occidental** adj occidental.
occult (ɔˈkʌlt) adj oculto. n lo sobrenatural, lo oculto neu.
occupy ('ɔkjupai) vt ocupar. **occupation** n 1 ocupación f. 2 profesión f. 3 inquilinato m. **occupant** n 1 ocupante m,f. 2 inquilino m.
occur (əˈkəː) vi 1 ocurrir. 2 encontrarse. **occurrence** n 1 acontecimiento m. 2 aparición f. 3 ocurrencia f.
ocean ('ouʃən) n océano m. **oceanic** adj oceánico.

240

ochre ('ouka) n ocre m.

octagon ('ɔktəgən) n octágono m. **octagonal** adj octagonal.

octane ('ɔktein) n octano m.

octave ('ɔktiv) n octava f.

October (ɔk'toubə) n octubre m.

octopus ('ɔktəpəs) n pulpo m.

oculist ('ɔkjulist) n oculista m,f.

odd (ɔd) adj 1 impar. 2 suelto. 3 sobrante. 4 raro, estrambótico. **oddity** n rareza, singularidad f. **oddment** n 1 artículo suelto m. 2 resto de serie m. 3 retal m. **odds** n pl 1 ventaja f. 2 probabilidades f pl. **odds and ends 1** retazos m pl. 2 chismes m pl.

ode (oud) n ode f.

odious ('oudiəs) adj odioso.

odour ('oudə) n olor m.

oesophagus ('i:sɔfəgəs) n esófago m.

oestrogen ('i:strədʒən) n ostrógeno m.

of (əv; stressed ɔv) prep de.

off (ɔf) adv 1 lejos, a distancia. 2 fuera. **be off 1** marcharse. 2 estar desconectado. 3 estar pasado. 4 quedar cancelado. ~prep 1 lejos de. 2 fuera de. 3 que sale de.

offal ('ɔfəl) n 1 asadura f. 2 despojos m pl.

offend (ə'fend) vt ofender. **offend against** pecar contra. **offence** n 1 ofensa f. 2 law delito m. **give offence** ofender. **take offence** ofenderse. **offender** n 1 ofensor m. 2 law delincuente m,f. **offensive** adj ofensivo. n ofensiva f.

offer ('ɔfə) n oferta f. vt ofrecer.

offhand (ɔf'hænd) adj 1 brusco. 2 informal. adv de improviso.

office ('ɔfis) n 1 oficina f. 2 cargo m. 3 oficio m. **officer** n 1 oficial m. 2 policía m. **office-worker** n oficinista m,f. **official** adj 1 oficial. 2 autorizado. n 1 oficial m. 2 funcionario m.

officious (ə'fiʃəs) adj oficioso.

offing ('ɔfiŋ) n **be in the offing** estar a la vista.

off-licence n tienda de bebidas alcohólicas f.

off-peak adj fuera de las horas punta.

off-putting adj 1 disuasivo. 2 distante, frío.

off-season adv fuera de temporada.

offset ('ɔfset) vt compensar.

offshore (ɔf'ɔ:) adj 1 poco distante de la costa. 2 de tierra.

offside (ɔf'said) adv fuera de juego.

offspring ('ɔfspriŋ) n vástago m.

offstage (ɔf'steidʒ) adv entre bastidores.

often ('ɔfən) adv a menudo. **how often?** ¿cuántas veces?

ogre ('ougə) n ogro m.

oil (ɔil) n 1 aceite m. 2 petróleo m. 3 óleo m. vt engrasar. **oilfield** n campo petrolífero m. **oil painting** n pintura al óleo f. **oilskin** n hule, impermeable m.

ointment ('ɔintmənt) n ungüento m.

old (ould) adj 1 viejo m. 2 antiguo. **how old is he?** ¿cuántos años tiene? ¿qué edad tiene? **old age** n vejez f. **old-fashioned** adj anticuado.

Old Testament n Antiguo Testamento m.

olive ('ɔliv) n aceituna, oliva f. adj aceitunado, oliváceo. **olive grove** n olivar m. **olive oil** n aceite de oliva m. **olive tree** n olivo m.

omelette ('ɔmlət) n tortilla f.

omen ('oumen) n agüero, presagio m.

ominous ('ɔminəs) adj amenazador.

omit (ə'mit) vt omitir. **omission** n omisión f.

omnibus ('ɔmnibəs) n ómnibus m.

omnipotent (ɔm'nipətənt) adj omnipotente. **omnipotence** n omnipotencia f.

on (ɔn) prep en, encima de, sobre. adv 1 adelante. 2 encima. 3 en marcha. **and so on** y así sucesivamente. **on and off** intermitentemente.

once (wʌns) adv 1 una vez. 2 antes, antiguamente. **at once** de una vez. **once in a while** de tarde en tarde. ~conj una vez que.

one (wʌn) adj 1 uno. 2 único. n uno m. pron uno, una. **oneself** pron 1 uno mismo, una misma. 2 se. 3 sí. **by oneself** solo. **one-way** adj de dirección única.

onion ('ʌniən) n cebolla f.

onlooker ('ɔnlukə) n espectador, mirón m.

only ('ounli) adj único. adv sólo, solamente, únicamente. conj sólo que.

onset ('ɔnset) n comienzo m.

onslaught ('ɔnslɔ:t) n arremetida f.

onus ('ounəs) n responsabilidad, carga f.

onward ('ɔnwəd) adj hacia adelante, progresivo. **onwards** adv adelante. **from now onwards** desde ahora en adelante.

ooze (u:z) vt rezumar.

opal ('oupəl) n ópalo m.

opaque (ou'peik) adj opaco.

open ('oupən) adj 1 abierto. 2 expuesto. 3 susceptible de. 4 público. vt 1 abrir. 2 inaugurar. 3 iniciar. **open air** n aire libre m. **opening** n 1 abertura f. 2 salida f. 3 apertura f. adj 1 primero. 2 de apertura. **open-minded** adj 1 imparcial. 2 receptivo. 3 sin decidir. **open-mouthed** adj boquiabierto.

opera ('ɔprə) n ópera f. **opera house** n teatro de la ópera m. **operetta** n opereta f.

operate ('opareit) vi operar vt 1 funcionar. 2 hacer funcionar. **operating** adj 1 operante. 2 de explotación. **operating theatre** n quirófano m. **operation** n 1 operación f. 2 funcionamiento m. 3 explotación m. **operator** n 1 maquinista m,f. 2 operador m. 3 telefonista m,f. 4 agente m,f.

opinion (a'pinian) n opinión f. **opinionated** adj 1 pertinaz. 2 dogmático. **opinion poll** n encuesta f.

opium ('oupiam) n opio m.

opponent (a'pounant) n contrincante m.

opportune (opa'tju:n) adj oportuno.

opportunity (opa'tju:niti) n oportunidad f.

oppose (a'pouz) vt oponer.

opposite ('opazit) adj 1 opuesto. 2 de enfrente. adv 1 en frente. 2 frente a frente. prep frente a, enfrente de. n lo contrario neu. **opposition** n 1 oposición f. 2 resistencia f.

oppress (a'pres) vt 1 oprimir. 2 agobiar. **oppression** n 1 opresión f. 2 agobio m. **oppressive** adj opresivo, agobiante. **oppressor** n opresor m.

opt (opt) vi optar.

optical ('optikal) adj óptico. **optician** n óptico m

optimism ('optimizam) n optimismo m. **optimist** n optimista m,f. **optimistic** adj optimista

option ('opʃan) n opción f. **optional** adj opcional.

opulent ('opjulant) adj opulento. **opulence** n opulencia f

or (ɔ:) conj 1 o. 2 u.

oral ('ɔ:ral) adj oral.

orange ('orindʒ) n naranja f. adj color naranja. **orange blossom** n azahar m. **orange grove** n naranjal m. **orange tree** n naranjo m.

oration (ɔ'reiʃan) n oración f. discurso m. **orator** n orador m.

orbit ('ɔ:bit) n órbita f. vt,vi órbitar.

orchard ('ɔ:tʃad) n huerta f.

orchestra ('ɔ:kistra) n 1 orquesta f. 2 Th platea f. **orchestral** adj orquestal. **orchestrate** vt orquestar. **orchestration** n orquestación f.

orchid ('ɔ:kid) n orquídea f.

ordain (ɔ:'dein) vt 1 ordenar. 2 disponer.

ordeal (ɔ:'di:l) n 1 prueba f. 2 sufrimiento m.

order ('ɔ:da) n 1 orden m. 2 orden f. 3 comm pedido m. in order en regla. in order that para que. **in order to** para. ~vt 1 ordenar. 2 mandar. 3 encargar. 4 comm pedir. **orderly** adj 1 ordenado. 2 pacífico. n ordenanza m.

ordinal ('ɔ:dinl) adj,n ordinal m.

ordinary ('ɔ:danri) adj ordinario.

ore (ɔ:) n mena f. mineral metalífero m.

oregano (ɔri'ga:nou) n orégano m.

organ ('ɔ:gan) n órgano m. **organist** n organista m,f. **organic** adj orgánico.

organism ('ɔ:ganizam) n organismo m.

organize ('ɔ:ganaiz) vt organizar. **organization** n organización f. organismo m. **organizer** n organizador m.

orgasm ('ɔ:gæzam) n orgasmo m.

orgy ('ɔ:dʒi) n orgia f

Orient ('ɔ:riant) n Oriente m. **oriental** adj,n oriental m,f.

orientate ('ɔ:rienteit) vt orientar. **orientation** n orientación f.

origin ('ɔridʒin) n origen m. **original** adj,n original m. **originality** n originalidad f. **originate** vt originar.

ornament ('ɔ:namant) n 1 adorno m. 2 ornamento m. vt adornar, ornamentar. **ornamental** adj ornamental.

ornate (ɔ:'neit) adj recargado, ornado.

ornithology (ɔ:ni'ɵɔladʒi) n ornitología f. **ornithologist** n ornitólogo m.

orphan ('ɔ:fan) n huérfano m. **orphanage** n orfanato m.

orthodox ('ɔ:ɵadɔks) adj ortodoxo. **orthodoxy** n ortodoxia f.

orthography (ɔ:'ɵɔgrafi) n ortografía f.

orthopaedic (ɔ:ɵa'pi:dik) adj ortopédico. **orthopaedics** n ortopedia f.

oscillate ('osaleit) vi oscilar.

ostensible (o'stensabal) adj pretendido.

ostentatious (osten'teiʃas) adj ostentoso.

osteopath ('ostiapaɵ) n osteópata m. **osteopathy** n osteoplastia f.

ostracize ('ostrasaiz) vt condenar al ostracismo.

ostrich ('ɔ:stritʃ) n avestruz m.

other ('ʌða) adj otro. pron 1 el otro m. 2 los demás m pl. las demás f pl. **otherwise** adv 1 de otro modo. 2 por lo demás.

otter ('ɔta) n nutria f.

ought (ɔ:t) v aux deber.

ounce (auns) n 1 onza f. 2 pizca f.

our (aua) poss adj 1st pers pl nuestro, nuestra, nuestros, nuestras. **ours** poss pron 1st pers pl el nuestro, la nuestra, los nuestros, las nuestras. **ourselves** pron 1st pers pl 1 nosotros mismos m pl. 2 nos.

oust (aust) vt desalojar, echar.

out (aut) adv fuera, a fuera, hacia fuera. **out**

of 1 fuera de. 2 entre, de entre. 3 de. 4 por. 5 sin.

outboard ('autbɔːd) adj fuera de borda.

outbreak ('autbreik) n 1 estallido m. 2 erupción f. 3 epidemia f. 4 ola f.

outburst ('autbɜːst) n 1 explosión f. 2 arranque m.

outcast ('autkaːst) n paria m,f.

outcome ('autkʌm) n resultado m.

outcry ('autkrai) n clamor m. protesta vehemente f.

outdo* (aut'duː) vt exceder, eclipsar.

outdoor ('autdɔː) adj al aire libre, exterior. **outdoors** adv also **out-of-doors** 1 fuera de casa. 2 al aire libre.

outer ('autə) adj exterior, externo.

outfit ('autfit) n 1 equipo m. 2 conjunto m.

outgoing ('autgouiŋ) adj saliente.

outgrow* (aut'grou) vt 1 crecer más que. 2 hacerse demasiado mayor para. 3 superar.

outhouse ('authaus) n dependencia f. cobertizo m.

outing ('autiŋ) n excursión, salida f. paseo m.

outlandish (aut'lændiʃ) adj disparatado, extravagante.

outlaw ('autlɔː) vt proscribir. n 1 proscrito m. 2 forajido m.

outlay ('autlei) n desembolso m. inversión f.

outlet ('autlet) n salida f.

outline ('autlain) n 1 contorno m. 2 esbozo m. **in outline** a grandes rasgos. ~vt 1 perfilar. 2 esbozar.

outlive (aut'liv) vt 1 sobrevivir a. 2 durar más que.

outlook ('autluk) n 1 perspectiva f. 2 actitud f. 3 punto de vista m.

outlying ('autlaiiŋ) adj 1 lejano, remoto. 2 exterior.

outnumber (aut'nʌmbə) vt exceder en número.

outpatient ('autpeiʃənt) n med paciente externo m,f.

outpost ('autpoust) n avanzada f.

output ('autput) n 1 producción f. 2 tech rendimiento m.

outrage (aut'reidʒ) n 1 atrocidad f. 2 ultraje, atropello m. vt ultrajar, atropellar. **outrageous** adj 1 inaudito. 2 escandaloso.

outright ('autrait) adj 1 completo. 2 cabal, acabado. adv 1 de un golpe. 2 de plano.

outside (aut'said) adv fuera. prep fuera de. adj 1 exterior. 2 extremo. n exterior m. **at the outside** a lo sumo. **outsider** n 1 desconocido m. 2 independiente m,f.

outsize ('autsaiz) adj de tamaño fuera de serie.

outskirts ('autskɜːts) n pl afueras f pl.

outspoken (aut'spoukən) adj franco, abierto.

outstanding (aut'stændiŋ) adj 1 destacado. 2 comm pendiente.

outstrip (aut'strip) vt dejar atrás. aventajar.

outward ('autwəd) adj exterior, externo. **outwards** adv hacia fuera.

outweigh (aut'wei) vt pesar más que.

outwit (aut'wit) vt 1 ser más listo que. 2 burlar.

outworn (aut'wɔːn) adj gastado.

oval ('ouvəl) adj ovalado. n óvalo m.

ovary ('ouvəri) n ovario m.

ovation (ou'veiʃən) n ovación f.

oven ('ʌvən) n horno m.

over ('ouvə) adv 1 encima, por encima. 2 al otro lado. 3 al revés, patas arriba. 4 demasiado. **be over** estar terminado. **over and over again** repetidas veces. ~prep 1 por encima de, sobre. 2 al otro lado de. 3 más allá de. 4 a través de.

overall ('ɔːvərɔːl) adj de conjunto. **overalls** n pl bata f.

overbalance (ouvə'bæləns) vt hacer perder el equilibrio.

overboard ('ouvəbɔːd) adv por la borda.

overcast ('ouvəkaːst) adj encapotado.

overcharge (ouvə'tʃaːdʒ) vt 1 sobrecargar. 2 comm cobrar más de la cuenta.

overcoat ('ouvəkout) n abrigo m.

overcome* (ouvə'kʌm) vt vencer, superar.

overdo* (ouvə'duː) vt 1 excederse. 2 exagerar. **overdone** adj 1 exagerado. 2 cul muy hecho, pasado.

overdose ('ouvədous) n dosis excesiva f.

overdraft ('ouvədraːft) n 1 giro en descubierto m. 2 saldo deudor m. 3 préstamo bancario m.

overdraw* (ouvə'drɔː) vt girar en descubierto.

overdue (ouvə'djuː) adj 1 atrasado. 2 comm vencido y por pagar.

overestimate (v ouvər'estimeit; n ouvər'estimit) vt sobreestimar. n 1 sobreestimación f. 2 comm presupuesto excesivo m.

overfill (ouvə'fil) vt hacer rebosar.

overflow (v ouvə'flou; n 'ouvəflou) vi 1 rebosar. 2 desbordarse. n 1 desbordamiento m. 2 desagüe m. **overflowing** adj rebosante.

overhang* ('ouvə'hæŋ) vi sobresalir. vt colgar sobre.

overhaul (ouvə'hɔːl) vt revisar, repasar. n revisión f. repaso general m.

overhead (adv ouvə'hed; adj,n 'ouvəhed) adv

por arriba, por lo alto. *adj* **1** de arriba. **2** aéreo. **3** suspendido. *n pl* gastos generales *m pl*.

overhear* (ouvə'hiə) *vt* oír por casualidad.

overheat (ouvə'hi:t) *vt* recalentar.

overjoyed (ouvə'dʒɔid) *adj* lleno de alegría.

overland (*adv* ouvə'lænd; *adj* 'ouvəlænd) *adv*, *adj* por vía terrestre.

overlap (*v* ouvə'læp; *n* 'ouvəlæp) *vt* traslapar, coincidir en parte, cubrir en parte. *n* traslapo *m*. coincidencia parcial *f*.

overlay* (*v* ouvə'lei; *n* 'ouvəlei) *vt* **1** cubrir con. **2** incrustar. *n* **1** capa *f*. **2** cobertura *f*. **3** incrustación *f*.

overleaf (ouvə'li:f) *adv* al dorso.

overload (*v* ouvə'loud; *n* 'ouvəloud) *vt* sobrecargar. *n* sobrecarga *f*.

overlook (ouvə'luk) *vt* **1** dominar. **2** dar a. **3** vigilar. **4** pasar por alto.

overnight (*adv* ouvə'nait; *adj* 'ouvənait) *adv* **1** durante la noche. **2** de la noche a la mañana. *adj* de (una) noche.

overpower (ouvə'pauə) *vt* **1** vencer. **2** dominar. **overpowering** *adj* abrumador, arrollador.

overrate (ouvə'reit) *vt* exagerar el valor de.

overreach (ouvə'ri:tʃ) *vt* **overreach oneself 1** excederse. **2** pasarse de listo.

overrule (ouvə'ru:l) *vt* **1** anular. **2** denegar.

overrun* (ouvə'rʌn) *vt* **1** arrollar. **2** infestar, invadir. **3** rebasar.

overseas (ouvə'si:z) *adv* en ultramar, allende el mar. *adj* de ultramar, extranjero.

overshadow (ouvə'ʃædou) *vt* **1** sombrear. **2** hacer sombra. **3** eclipsar.

overshoot* (ouvə'ʃu:t) *vt* **1** sobrepasar. **2** pasar de largo.

oversight ('ouvəsait) *n* **1** descuido *m*. **2** equivocación *f*.

oversleep* (ouvə'sli:p) *vi* dormir más de la cuenta.

overspill ('ouvəspil) *n* exceso *m*.

overt ('ouvə:t) *adj* **1** abierto. **2** patente.

overtake* (ouvə'teik) *vt* **1** alcanzar. **2** *mot* adelantar.

overthrow* (*v* ouvə'θrou; *n* 'ouvəθrou) *vt* derrocar. *n* derrocamiento *m*.

overtime ('ouvətaim) *n* horas extraordinarias *f pl*.

overtone ('ouvətoun) *n* **1** sugestión, implicación *f*. **2** *mus* armónico *m*.

overture ('ouvətʃə) *n* **1** *mus* obertura *f*. **2** proposición *f*.

overturn (ouvə'tə:n) *vt*, *vi* volcar. **2** trastornar. **3** derrocar.

overweight (ouvə'weit) *adj* que excede el peso reglamentario. **be overweight** estar demasiado gordo.

overwhelm (ouvə'welm) *vt* **1** abrumar. **2** aplastar. **3** inundar. **overwhelming** *adj* abrumador, aplastante.

overwork (*v* ouvə'wə:k; *n* 'ouvəwə:k) *vi* trabajar demasiado. *vt* hacer trabajar demasiado. *n* trabajo excesivo *m*.

overwrought (ouvə'rɔ:t) *adj* sobreexcitado.

ovulate ('ɔvjuleit) *vi* ovular. **ovulation** *n* ovulación *f*.

owe (ou) *vt* deber. *vi* estar en deuda. **owing** *adj* debido. **owing to** debido a.

owl (aul) *n* lechuza *f*. mochuelo, búho *m*.

own (oun) *adj* propio. *vt* **1** ser dueño de, poseer. **2** reconocer. **owner** *n* dueño, propietario *m*. **ownership** *n* propiedad *f*.

ox (ɔks) *n*, *pl* **oxen** buey *m*. **oxtail** *n* cola de buey *f*.

oxygen ('ɔksidʒən) *n* oxígeno *m*. **oxygenate** *vt* oxigenar.

oyster ('ɔistə) *n* ostra *f*.

P

pace (peis) *n* **1** paso *m*. **2** ritmo *m*. **keep pace with** mantenerse a la par con. *vi* pasearse. *vt* medir a pasos.

Pacific (pə'sifik) *n* (Océano) Pacífico *m*.

pacify ('pæsifai) *vt* **1** apaciguar. **2** pacificar. **pacifism** *n* pacifismo *m*. **pacifist** *n* pacifista *m*, *f*.

pack (pæk) *n* **1** fardo *m*. **2** paquete *m*. **3** manada *f*. **4** baraja *f*. *vt* **1** empaquetar. **2** envasar. **3** llenar. **4** atestar. *vi* hacer las maletas. **package** *n* paquete, bulto *m*. **packet** *n* paquete *m*.

pact (pækt) *n* pacto *m*.

pad[1] (pæd) *n* **1** almohadilla *f*. **2** bloc (of paper) *m*. *vt* **1** almohadillar. **2** rellenar. **padding** *n* relleno *m*.

pad[2] (pæd) *vi* pisar sin hacer ruido.

paddle[1] ('pædl) *n* paleta *f*. remo *m*. *vt* remar.

paddle[2] ('pædl) *vi* chapotear.

padlock ('pædlɔk) *n* candado *m*. *vt* cerrar con candado.

paediatric (pi:di'ætrik) *adj* pediátrico. **paediatrician** *n* pediatra *m*, *f*. **paediatrics** *n* pediatría *f*.

pagan ('peigən) *adj*, *n* pagano *m*.

page¹ (peidʒ) n 1 página f. 2 plana f. vt paginar.

page² (peidʒ) n paje m.

pageant ('pædʒənt) n 1 espectáculo brillante m. 2 desfile m. **pageantry** n pompa f.

paid (peid) v see **pay.**

pain (pein) n 1 dolor m. 2 pl esfuerzos m pl. cuidados m pl. vt 1 doler. 2 dar lástima a. **painful** adj 1 doloroso. 2 penoso. **painstaking** adj esmerado, cuidadoso.

paint (peint) n pintura f. vt,vi pintar. **paintbrush** n 1 pincel m. 2 brocha f. **painter** n pintor m. **painting** n pintura f.

pair (pɛə) n 1 par m. 2 pareja f. vt emparejar.

pal (pæl) n compañero, amigo m.

palace ('pælis) n palacio m.

palate ('pælət) n paladar m. **palatable** adj 1 apetitoso. 2 aceptable.

pale (peil) adj pálido. vi palidecer. **paleness** n palidez f.

palette ('pælit) n paleta f. **palette knife** n espátula f.

pall (pɔ:l) vi 1 perder su sabor. 2 empalagar.

palm¹ (pɑ:m) n anat palma f. **palmistry** n quiromancia f.

palm² (pɑ:m) n bot 1 palma f. 2 palmera f.

Palm Sunday n Domingo de Ramos m.

pamper ('pæmpə) vt 1 mimar. 2 regalar.

pamphlet ('pæmflət) n folleto m.

pan (pæn) n cazuela f. cazo m. **frying pan** sartén f. **pancake** n hojuela, tortita f.

Panama ('pænəmɑ:) n Panamá m. **Panamanian** adj,n panameño m.

pancreas ('pæŋkriəs) n páncreas m.

pane (pein) n cristal m.

panel ('pænl) n 1 panel m. 2 jurado m. 3 registro m.

pang (pæŋ) n punzada f.

panic* ('pænik) n pánico m. vi llenarse de pánico. vt aterrar.

panorama (pænə'rɑ:mə) n panorama m. **panoramic** adj panorámico.

pansy ('pænzi) n bot pensamiento m.

pant (pænt) vi jadear.

panther ('pænθə) n pantera f.

pantomime ('pæntəmaim) n pantomima f.

pantry ('pæntri) n despensa f.

pants (pænts) n pl calzoncillos m pl. **panties** n pl bragas f pl.

papal ('peipəl) adj papal.

paper ('peipə) n 1 papel m. 2 periódico m. 3 exámen escrito m. 4 artículo m. 5 ponencia f. 6 pl documentación f. vt empapelar. **paper-**

back n libro en rústica m. **paperclip** n sujetapapeles m invar. **paperweight** n pisapapeles m invar.

papier-mâché (pæpiei'mæʃei) n cartón piedra m. pasta f.

paprika ('pæprikə) n pimentón m.

par (pɑ:) n par f. **at par** a la par. ~adj nominal.

parable ('pærəbəl) n parábola f.

parachute ('pærəʃu:t) n paracaídas m invar. vi lanzarse en paracaídas.

parade (pə'reid) n 1 desfile m. 2 parada f. 3 alarde m. vi desfilar. vt lucir.

paradise ('pærədais) n paraíso m.

paradox ('pærədɔks) n paradoja f. **paradoxical** adj paradójico.

paraffin ('pærəfin) n 1 petróleo m. 2 (wax) parafina f.

paragraph ('pærəgrɑ:f) n párrafo m.

Paraguay ('pærəgwai) n Paraguay m. **Paraguayan** adj,n paraguayo m.

parallel ('pærəlel) adj,n paralelo m. vt ser paralelo a. **parallelism** n paralelismo m.

paralyse ('pærəlaiz) vt paralizar. **paralysis** n,pl **paralyses** parálisis f. **paralytic** adj,n paralítico m.

paramount ('pærəmaunt) adj supremo, primordial.

paranoia (pærə'nɔiə) n paranoia f.

parapet ('pærəpit) n parapeto m.

paraphernalia (pærəfə'neiliə) n inf avíos m pl.

paraphrase ('pærəfreiz) n paráfrasis f. vt parafrasear.

parasite ('pærəsait) n parásito m. **parasitic** adj parasítico.

parcel ('pɑ:səl) n 1 paquete m. 2 parcela f. vt parcelar, dividir.

parch (pɑ:tʃ) vt resecar.

parchment ('pɑ:tʃmənt) n pergamino m.

pardon ('pɑ:dṇ) n 1 perdón m. 2 law indulto m. **I beg your pardon** Vd perdone. **I beg your pardon?** ¿cómo? ~vt 1 perdonar. 2 law indultar.

pare (pɛə) vt 1 cortar. 2 mondar.

parent ('pɛərənt) n 1 padre m. 2 madre f. 3 pl padres m pl. adj madre, matriz. **parentage** n 1 familia f. linaje m. 2 nacimiento m. **parental** adj 1 de los padres. 2 paternal. 3 maternal.

parenthesis (pə'renθəsis) n, pl **parentheses** paréntesis m.

parish ('pæriʃ) n parroquia f. adj parroquial. **parishioner** n feligrés m.

parity ('pæriti) n paridad f.

park (pɑ:k) n parque m. **car park** aparcamiento, parking m. ~vt 1 estacionar. 2 aparcar. vi estacionarse. **parking** n estacionamiento, aparcamiento m. **parking meter** n parquímetro m.

parliament ('pɑ:ləmənt) n parlamento m. **parliamentarian** n parlamentario m. **parliamentary** adj parlamentario.

parlour ('pɑ:lə) n 1 salón m. 2 locutorio m.

parochial (pə'roukiəl) adj 1 parroquial. 2 de miras estrechas, limitado.

parody ('pærədi) n parodia f. vt parodiar.

parole (pə'roul) n 1 palabra de honor f. 2 law libertad bajo palabra f. vt poner en libertad bajo palabra.

parquet ('pɑ:kei) n entarimado, parquet m.

parrot ('pærət) n loro, papagayo m.

parsley ('pɑ:sli) n perejil m.

parsnip ('pɑ:snip) n chirivía f.

parson ('pɑ:sən) n 1 cura m. 2 párroco m. **parsonage** n casa parroquial f.

part (pɑ:t) n 1 parte f. 2 tech pieza f. 3 Th papel m. vt 1 separar. 2 dividir, partir. **part from** despedirse. **part with** 1 ceder. 2 desprenderse de. ~adj parcial. adv en parte. **parting** n 1 separación f. 2 despedida f. 3 (of hair) raya f. **part-time** adj,adv por horas.

partake* (pɑ:'teik) vi 1 participar en. 2 aceptar

partial ('pɑ:ʃəl) adj parcial. **be partial to** sentir inclinación por. **partiality** n 1 parcialidad f. 2 inclinación f.

participate (pɑ:'tisipeit) vi participar. **participant** n partícipe m,f. **participation** n participación f.

participle ('pɑ:tisəpəl) n participio m.

particle ('pɑ:tikəl) n 1 partícula f. 2 pizca f.

particular (pə'tikjulə) adj 1 particular. 2 exigente. n pl informe detallado m.

partisan (pɑ:ti'zæn) n 1 partidario m. 2 partisano, guerrillero m. adj 1 partidista. 2 de partisanos.

partition (pɑ:'tiʃən) n 1 partición f. 2 tabique m. vt repartir, dividir.

partner ('pɑ:tnə) n 1 comm socio m. 2 pareja f. 3 compañero m. vt acompañar. **partnership** n 1 comm sociedad f. 2 asociación f.

partridge ('pɑ:tridʒ) n perdiz f.

party ('pɑ:ti) n 1 partido m. 2 partida f. 3 reunión f. 4 fiesta f. 5 law parte f. **be a party to** 1 subscribir a. 2 ser cómplice de.

pass (pɑ:s) vt 1 pasar. 2 cruzarse con. 3 aprobar. n 1 pase m. 2 aprobado m. 3 educ paso m. 4 geog puerto m. 5 inf requiebro m.

passage ('pæsidʒ) n 1 paso m. 2 pasaje m. 3 pasillo m.

passenger ('pæsindʒə) n pasajero m.

passion ('pæʃən) n pasión f. **passionate** adj apasionado.

passive ('pæsiv) adj pasivo. **passivity** n pasividad f.

passport ('pɑ:spɔ:t) n pasaporte m.

past (pɑ:st) adj pasado. n 1 pasado m. 2 historia f. adv por delante. prep 1 más allá de. 2 más de. 3 por delante de.

pasta ('pæstə) n macarrones, fideos m pl.

paste (peist) n 1 pasta f. 2 engrudo m. vt 1 pegar. 2 empastar.

pastel ('pæstəl) adj,n pastel m.

pasteurize ('pæstəraiz) vt pasteurizar.

pastime ('pɑ:staim) n pasatiempo m.

pastoral ('pæstərəl) adj,n pastoral f.

pastry ('peistri) n 1 pasta f. 2 repostería f.

pasture ('pɑ:stʃə) n pasto m.

pasty[1] ('peisti) adj pastoso.

pasty[2] ('pæsti) n empanada f.

pat[1] (pæt) vt 1 dar una palmadita a. 2 pasar la mano por. n 1 palmadita, palmada f. 2 golpecito m.

pat[2] (pæt) adj oportuno, justo. adv al dedillo.

patch (pætʃ) n 1 remiendo m. 2 parche m. 3 retazo m. vt 1 remendar. 2 componer. **patchwork** n labor de retazos m. **patchy** adj 1 desigual. 2 manchado.

pate (peit) n inf mollera f.

patent ('peitnt) adj 1 patente. 2 comm patentado, de patente. n patente f. vt patentar. **patent leather** n charol m.

paternal (pə'tə:nl) adj 1 paternal. 2 paterno. **paternity** n paternidad f.

path (pɑ:θ) n 1 senda f. 2 camino m. 3 trayectoria f. 4 órbita f.

pathetic (pə'θetik) adj 1 patético, conmovedor. 2 que da pena.

pathology (pə'θɔlədʒi) n patología f. **pathological** adj patológico. **pathologist** n patólogo m.

patience ('peiʃəns) n paciencia f. **patient** adj,n paciente.

patio ('pætiou) n patio m.

patrician (pə'triʃən) adj,n patricio m.

patriot ('peitriət) n patriota m,f. **patriotic** adj patriótico. **patriotism** n patriotismo m.

patrol (pə'troul) n patrulla f. vt,vi patrullar.

patron ('peitrən) n 1 comm parroquiano m. 2 patrono m. 3 patrón m. **patronage** n 1 patrocinio m. 2 patronazgo m. **patronize** n patrocinar. 2 tratar con aire condescendiente. **patronizing** adj condescendiente.

patter[1] ('pætə) vi andar con pasos ligeros. n pasos ligeros m pl.

patter[2] ('pætə) n 1 jerga f. 2 parloteo m.

pattern ('pætən) n 1 modelo m. 2 muestra f. 3 (for clothes) patrón m. 4 diseño m. vt modelar.

paunch (pɔ:ntʃ) n panza, barriga f. **paunchy** adj panzudo.

pauper ('pɔ:pə) n pobre m,f.

pause (pɔ:z) n pausa f. vi hacer una pausa.

pave (peiv) vt pavimentar. **pavement** n 1 acera f. 2 pavimento m.

pavilion (pə'viliən) n pabellón m.

paw (pɔ:) n 1 pata f. 2 garra f. vt 1 dar zarpazos a. 2 piafar.

pawn[1] (pɔ:n) n prenda f. vt empeñar, dejar en prenda. **pawnbroker** n prestamista m.

pawn[2] (pɔ:n) n game peón m.

pay* (pei) vt 1 pagar. 2 salir a cuenta. 3 prestar (attention). n paga f. **payroll** n nómina f.

pea (pi:) n guisante m.

peace (pi:s) n 1 paz f. 2 tranquilidad f. **make peace** hacer las paces. **peaceful** adj 1 tranquilo. 2 pacífico.

peach (pi:tʃ) n melocotón m.

peacock ('pi:kɔk) n pavo real m.

peak (pi:k) n 1 pico m. 2 cumbre f. 3 punta f. 4 visera f.

peal (pi:l) n repiqueteo m. vt,vi repicar.

peanut ('pi:nʌt) n cacahuete m.

pear (pɛə) n pera f.

pearl (pɔ:l) n perla f.

peasant ('pezənt) n,adj campesino m.

peat (pi:t) n turba f.

pebble ('pebəl) n guijarro m.

peck (pek) n picotazo m. vt picotear.

peculiar (pi'kju:liə) adj peculiar. **peculiarity** n peculiaridad f.

pedal ('pedl) n pedal m. vt,vi pedalear.

peddle ('pedl) vt andar vendiendo. **pedlar** n vendedor ambulante m.

pedestal ('pedistəl) n pedestal m.

pedestrian (pi'destriən) n peatón m. adj pedestre.

pedigree ('pedigri:) n árbol genealógico m. adj de raza.

peel (pi:l) n piel f. vt pelar.

peep (pi:p) vi 1 atisbar, espiar. 2 asomar. n atisbo m. mirada furtiva f. **peephole** m mirilla f.

peer[1] (piə) n par m. **peerage** n 1 dignidad de par f. 2 nobleza f.

peer[2] (piə) vi 1 escudriñar. 2 asomar.

peevish ('pi:viʃ) adj malhumorado, enojadizo.

peg (peg) n 1 colgador m. 2 pinza f. 3 clavija f. 4 estaca f. vt fijar con estacas.

pejorative (pi'dʒɔrətiv) adj peyorativo.

pelican ('pelikən) n pelícano m.

pellet ('pelit) n 1 bolita f. 2 perdigón m.

pelt[1] (pelt) vt 1 arrojar. 2 apedrear.

pelt[2] (pelt) n pellejo m.

pelvis ('pelvis) n pelvis m.

pen[1] (pen) n pluma f. **fountain pen** n estilográfica f. vt escribir, redactar. **penknife** n cortaplumas m invar. **pen-nib** n 1 plumilla f. 2 plumín m.

pen[2] (pen) n corral, redil m. vt acorralar.

penal ('pi:nl) adj 1 penal. 2 gravoso. **penalize** vt penalizar. **penalty** n 1 pena f. castigo m. 2 sport penalty m.

penance ('penəns) n penitencia f.

pencil ('pensəl) n lápiz m.

pendant ('pendənt) n medallón, pendiente m.

pending ('pendiŋ) adj pendiente. prep 1 durante. 2 hasta.

pendulum ('pendjuləm) n péndulo m.

penetrate ('penitreit) vt penetrar. **penetration** n penetración f.

penguin ('peŋgwin) n pingüino m.

penicillin (peni'silin) n penicilina f.

peninsula (pə'ninsjulə) n península f. **peninsular** adj peninsular.

penis ('pi:nis) n pene m.

penitent ('penitənt) adj,n penitente.

pennant ('penənt) n gallardete m.

penny ('peni) n, pl **pence** penique m. **penniless** adj sin un céntimo.

pension ('penʃən) n pensión f. vt pensionar. **pension off** jubilar.

pensive ('pensiv) adj pensativo, meditabundo.

pent (pent) adj **pent-up** 1 reprimido. 2 encerrado.

Pentecost ('pentikɔst) n Pentecostés m invar.

penthouse ('penthaus) n ático m.

people ('pi:pəl) n 1 gente f. 2 pueblo m. vt poblar.

pepper ('pepə) n 1 pimienta f. 2 pimiento m. vt 1 sazonar con pimienta. 2 salpicar. **peppercorn** n grano de pimienta m. **peppermill** n molinillo de pimienta m. **peppermint** n 1 menta f. 2 pastilla de menta f.

per (pə:) prep por. **per annum** al año.

perceive (pə'si:v) vt **1** percibir, notar. **2** apercibirse de.

per cent (pə 'sent) adv por ciento.

percentage (pə'sentidʒ) n porcentaje m.

perception (pə'sepʃən) n **1** percepción f. **2** perspicacia f. **perceptible** adj perceptible. **perceptive** adj **1** perspicaz, agudo. **2** perceptivo.

perch (pə:tʃ) vi **1** posarse. **2** encaramarse. n **1** percha f. **2** posición elevada f.

percolate ('pə:kəleit) vi filtrarse. **percolator** n cafetera de filtro f.

percussion (pə'kʌʃən) n percusión f.

perennial (pə'reniəl) adj perenne. n planta perenne f.

perfect (adj,n 'pə:fikt; v pə'fekt) adj,n perfecto m. vt perfeccionar. **perfection** n perfección f. **perfectionist** n perfeccionista m,f.

perforate ('pə:fəreit) vt perforar. **perforation** n perforación f.

perform (pə'fɔ:m) vt **1** realizar, cumplir. **2** desempeñar. **3** ejecutar. **4** *Th* representar. vi **1** actuar. **2** *tech* funcionar. **performance** n **1** ejecución f. **2** desempeño m. **3** representación f. **4** actuación f. **5** *tech* rendimiento m. **performer** n **1** actor m. **2** *mus* intérprete m,f.

perfume (n 'pə:fju:m; v pə'fju:m) n perfume m. vt perfumar.

perhaps (pə'hæps) adv tal vez.

peril ('peril) n peligro m.

perimeter (pə'rimitə) n perímetro m.

period ('piəriəd) n período m. adj de época. **periodic** adj periódico. **periodical** adj periódico. n publicación periódica, revista f.

peripheral (pə'rifərəl) adj periférico. **periphery** n periferia f.

periscope ('periskoup) n periscopio m.

perish ('periʃ) vi perecer. **perishable** adj **1** perecedero. **2** corruptible.

perjure ('pə:dʒə) vt perjurar. **perjurer** n perjuro m. **perjury** n perjurio m.

perk (pə:k) vi **perk up 1** erguir la cabeza. **2** reanimarse, cobrar ánimo. **perky** adj **1** despabilado. **2** alegre.

permanent ('pə:mənənt) adj permanente. **permanence** n permanencia f.

permeate ('pə:miənt) vt **1** penetrar. **2** impregnar. **permeability** n permeabilidad f. **permeable** adj permeable.

permit (v pə'mit; n 'pə:mit) vt permitir. n permiso m. licencia f. **permission** n permiso m. **permissible** adj permisible. **permissive** adj permisivo.

permutation (pə:mju'teiʃən) n permutación f.

peroxide (pə'rɔksaid) n peróxido m.

perpendicular (pə:pən'dikjulə) adj,n perpendicular f.

perpetual (pə'petʃuəl) adj perpetuo.

perpetuate (pə'petʃueit) vt perpetuar. **perpetuation** n perpetuación f. **perpetuity** n perpetuidad f.

perplex (pə'pleks) vt dejar perplejo, confundir. **perplexed** adj perplejo. **perplexing** adj desconcertante. **perplexity** n perplejidad f.

persecute ('pə:sikju:t) vt **1** perseguir. **2** importunar. **persecution** n persecución f. **persecutor** n perseguidor m.

persevere (pə:si'viə) vi perseverar. **perseverance** n perseverancia f. **persevering** adj perseverante.

persist (pə'sist) vi **1** persistir. **2** empeñarse. **persistence** n persistencia f. **persistent** adj persistente.

person ('pə:sən) n persona f. **personable** adj bien parecido. **personal** adj personal. **personality** n personalidad f.

personify (pə'sɔnifai) vt personificar. **personification** n personificación f.

personnel (pə:sə'nel) n personal m.

perspective (pə'spektiv) n perspectiva f.

perspire (pə'spaiə) vi transpirar, sudar. **perspiration** n sudor m.

persuade (pə'sweid) vt persuadir. **persuasion** n persuasión f. **persuasive** adj persuasivo.

pert (pə:t) adj **1** vivaracho. **2** descarado, fresco.

pertain (pə'tein) vi atañer.

pertinent ('pə:tinənt) adj pertinente. **pertinence** n pertinencia f.

perturb (pə'tə:b) vt perturbar. **perturbation** n perturbación f.

Peru (pə'ru:) n Perú m. **Peruvian** adj,n peruano.

pervade (pə'veid) vt **1** extenderse por. **2** impregnar. **pervasive** adj penetrante.

perverse (pə'və:s) adj **1** perverso. **2** contumaz. **3** díscolo. **perversion** n perversión f. **perversity** n **1** perversidad f. **2** contumacia f.

pervert ('pə:və:t) n pervertido m. vt pervertir.

pessimism ('pesimizəm) n pesimismo m. **pessimist** n pesimista m,f. **pessimistic** adj pesimista.

pest (pest) n **1** plaga f. **2** parásito m. **pesticide** n pesticida m.

pester ('pestə) vt importunar, molestar.

pet[1] (pet) n **1** animal domesticado m. **2** favorito m. **3** *inf* encanto m. adj **1** domesticado. **2** favorito. **3** (of a name) cariñoso. vt acariciar.

pile

pet[2] (pet) n malhumor m.

petal ('petl) n pétalo m.

peter out ('pi:tə) vi 1 agotarse. 2 desvanecerse.

petition (pi'tiʃən) n petición f. vt dirigir una instancia, solicitar.

petrify ('petrifai) vt petrificar.

petrol ('petrəl) n gasolina f. **petrol pump** n 1 surtidor de gasolina m. 2 tech bomba de gasolina f.

petroleum (pi'trouliəm) n petróleo m.

petticoat ('petikout) n enaguas f pl.

petty ('peti) adj 1 insignificante, nimio. 2 quisquilloso, intransigente. **petty cash** n dinero para gastos menores m.

petulant ('petjulənt) adj irritable, malhumorado. **petulance** n mal humor m.

pew (pju:) n banco de iglesia m.

pewter ('pju:tə) n peltre m. adj de peltre.

phantom ('fæntəm) n fantasma m. adj fantasmal.

pharmacy ('fɑ:məsi) n farmacia f. **pharmaceutical** adj farmacéutico. **pharmacist** n farmacéutico m.

pharynx ('færiŋks) n faringe f.

phase (feiz) n fase f. vt organizar por etapas.

pheasant ('fezənt) n faisán m.

phenomenon (fi'nɔminən) n, pl **phenomena** fenómeno m. **phenomenal** adj fenomenal.

philanthropy (fi'lænθrəpi) n filantropía f. **philanthropic** adj filantrópico. **philanthropist** n filántropo m.

philately (fi'lætəli) n filatelia f.

Philippines ('filipi:nz) n pl Islas Filipinas f pl.

Philistine ('filistain) adj,n filisteo m.

philosophy (fi'lɔsəfi) n filosofía f. **philosopher** n filósofo m. **philosophical** adj filosófico.

phlegm (flem) n flema f. **phlegmatic** adj flemático.

phobia ('foubiə) n fobia f.

phone (foun) n inf teléfono m. vt,vi telefonear.

phonetic (fə'netik) adj fonético.

phoney ('founi) adj inf 1 falso. 2 postizo.

phosphate ('fɔsfeit) n fosfato m.

phosphorescence (fɔsfə'resəns) n fosforescencia f.

phosphorus ('fɔsfərəs) n fósforo m. **phosphorous** adj fosforoso.

photo ('foutou) n foto f.

photocopy ('foutoukɔpi) n fotocopia f. vt fotocopiar.

photogenic (foutə'dʒenik) adj fotogénico.

photograph ('foutəgrɑ:f) n fotografía f. vt fotografiar. **photographer** n fotógrafo m.

photographic adj fotográfico. **photography** n fotografía f.

phrase (freiz) n frase f. vt expresar. **phrasebook** n manual de conversación m.

physical ('fizikəl) adj físico.

physician (fi'ziʃən) n médico m.

physics ('fiziks) n física f. **physicist** n físico m.

physiology (fizi'ɔlədʒi) n fisiología f. **physiologist** n fisiólogo m.

physiotherapy (fiziou'θerəpi) n fisioterapia f. **physiotherapist** n fisioterapeuta m,f.

physique (fi'zi:k) n físico m.

piano (pi'ænou) n piano m. **pianist** n pianista m,f.

picador ('pikədɔ:) n picador m.

pick[1] (pik) vt 1 escoger, seleccionar. 2 recoger. 3 coger. n 1 elección f. 2 selección f. 3 lo más selecto, lo mejor neu. **pickpocket** n carterista, ratero m.

pick[2] (pik) n pico m.

picket ('pikit) n 1 piquete m. 2 estaca f. vt,vi hacer guardia.

pickle ('pikəl) n escabeche m. vt escabechar.

picnic ('piknik) n excursión campestre f. vi 1 ir de picnic. 2 hacer un picnic.

pictorial (pik'tɔ:riəl) adj ilustrado.

picture ('piktʃə) n 1 cuadro m. 2 imagen f. 3 retrato m.

picturesque (piktʃə'resk) adj pintoresco.

pie (pai) n pastel m.

piece (pi:s) n 1 trozo, pedazo m. 2 pieza f. **piece together** 1 juntar. 2 atar cabos. **piecemeal** adv a trozos. adj fragmentario. **piecework** n trabajo a destajo m.

pier (piə) n embarcadero m.

pierce (piəs) vt,vi 1 penetrar. 2 atravesar. 3 perforar. **piercing** adj penetrante.

piety ('paiəti) n piedad, devoción f.

pig (pig) n cerdo m. **pig-headed** adj testarudo. **pig-iron** n hierro en lingotes m. **pigskin** n piel de cerdo f. **pigsty** n pocilga f. **pigtail** n coleta f.

pigeon ('pidʒən) n paloma f. **pigeonhole** n casilla f. vt archivar. **pigeon-toed** adj patituerto.

pigment ('pigmənt) n pigmento m.

pike (paik) n zool lucio m.

pilchard ('piltʃəd) n sardina arenque f.

pile[1] (pail) n montón m. pila f. vt amontonar, apilar. **pile-up** n accidente múltiple m.

pile[2] (pail) n arch pilote m. **piledriver** n martinete m.

pile[3] (pail) n pelo, pelillo m.

piles (pailz) *n pl* hemorroides, almorranas *f pl*.

pilfer ('pilfə) *vt, vi* sisar, ratear.

pilgrim ('pilgrim) *n* peregrino *m*. **pilgrimage** *n* peregrinación *f*.

pill (pil) *n* píldora *f*.

pillage ('pilidʒ) *n* pillaje *m*. *vt* pillar, saquear.

pillar ('pilə) *n* pilar *m*. **pillar-box** *n* buzón *m*.

pillion ('piliən) *n* asiento de atrás *m*.

pillow ('pilou) *n* almohada *f*. **pillowcase** *n* funda de almohada *f*.

pilot ('pailət) *n* piloto *m*. *vt* pilotar.

pimento (pi'mentou) *n* pimiento *m*.

pimple ('pimpəl) *n* grano *m*.

pin (pin) *n* 1 alfiler *m*. 2 clavija *f*. 3 *tech* perno *m*. *vt* 1 prender, sujetar. 2 clavar. **pinball** *n* billar automático *m*. **pincushion** *n* acerico *m*. **pin-money** *n* alfileres *m pl*. **pinpoint** *vt* precisar, determinar. **pinstripe** *adj* a rayas, rayado.

pinafore ('pinəfɔ:) *n* delantal *m*.

pincers ('pinsəz) *n pl* tenazas, pinzas *f pl*.

pinch (pintʃ) *n* 1 pellizco *m*. 2 pizca *f*. 3 aprieto *m*. *vt* 1 pellizcar. 2 apretar. 3 *inf* birlar. *vi* privarse, economizar.

pine[1] (pain) *n* pino *m*. **pinecone** *n* piña *f*. **pinewood** *n* pinar *m*.

pine[2] (pain) *vi* languidecer. **pine for** suspirar por.

pineapple ('painæpəl) *n* ananás *m*.

pinion ('piniən) *n* piñón *m*. *vt* atar los brazos a.

pink (piŋk) *n bot* clavellina *f*. *adj* rosa.

pinnacle ('pinəkəl) *n* pináculo *m*.

pint (paint) *n* pinta *f*.

pioneer (paiə'niə) *n* 1 explorador, pionero *m*. 2 zapador *m*. *vt* iniciar.

pious ('paiəs) *adj* piadoso, devoto.

pip[1] (pip) *n* 1 *game* punto *m*. 2 *mil* estrella *f*.

pip[2] (pip) *n bot* pepita *f*.

pipe (paip) *n* 1 tubo, caño *m*. 2 *mus* cañón *m*. 3 *mus* caramillo *m*. 4 pipa *f*. *vt* 1 conducir en cañerías. 2 *mus* tocar. **pipeline** *n* tubería, cañería *f*.

piquant ('pi:kənt) *adj* picante.

pirate ('pairət) *n* pirata *m*. *vt* pillar, robar. **piracy** *n* piratería *f*. **piratical** *adj* pirático.

Pisces ('pisi:z) *n* Piscis.

pistachio (pis'tæʃiou) *n* pistacho *m*.

pistol ('pistəl) *n* pistola *f*. revólver *m*.

piston ('pistən) *n* pistón, émbolo *m*.

pit (pit) *n* 1 hoyo, foso *m*. hoya *f*. 2 mina *f*. *vt* 1 marcar (con hoyas). 2 oponer (a). **pitfall** *n* escollo *m*. trampa *f*.

pitch[1] (pitʃ) *n* 1 lanzamiento *m*. 2 *sport* campo,

terreno *m*. 3 punto, extremo *m*. *vt* 1 arrojar, lanzar, tirar. 2 armar (a tent).

pitch[2] (pitʃ) *n* pez, brea *f*. *vt* embrear.

pith (piθ) *n* 1 *bot* médula *f*. 2 *inf* meollo, jugo *m*. esencia *f*.

pittance ('pitns) *n* miseria, renta miserable *f*.

pity ('piti) *n* 1 compasión, piedad *f*. 2 lástima *f*. *vt* compadecer, tener lástima a.

pivot ('pivət) *n* 1 pivote *m*. 2 *inf* eje, punto central *m*. *vt* montar sobre un pivote. *vi* girar.

placard ('plækɑ:d) *n* 1 cartel, letrero *m*. 2 pancarta *f*.

placate (plə'keit) *vt* aplacar.

place (pleis) *n* 1 sitio, lugar *m*. 2 local *m*. 3 puesto, empleo *m*. 4 lugar, puesto *m*. 5 plaza *f*. 6 (table) cubierto *m*. **take place** tener lugar. ~*vt* 1 colocar, poner. 2 acordarse bien de. 3 identificar. **placename** *n* topónimo *m*.

placenta (plə'sentə) *n* placenta *f*.

placid ('plæsid) *adj* plácido.

plagiarize ('pleidʒəraiz) *vt* plagiar. **plagiarism** *n* plagio *m*.

plague (pleig) *n med* peste, plaga *f*. *vt* 1 plagar, infestar. 2 *inf* acosar, atormentar.

plaice (pleis) *n invar* platija *f*.

plaid (plæd) *n* 1 tela a cuadros *f*. 2 manta escocesa *f*.

plain (plein) *adj* 1 claro, evidente. 2 sencillo, llano, sin adornos. 3 natural, puro. 4 sin atractivo, ordinario. *adv* claro, claramente. *n* llano *m*. llanura *f*. **plainly** *adv* 1 claramente, evidentemente. 2 francamente. **plain-clothes man** *n* policía vestido de paisano *m*. **plain sailing** coser y cantar.

plaintiff ('pleintif) *n* demandante *m,f*.

plaintive ('pleintiv) *adj* dolorido.

plait (plæt) *n* trenza *f*. *vt* trenzar.

plan (plæn) *n* 1 proyecto, plan *m*. 2 *arch* plano *m*. 3 programa *m*. *vt* 1 proyectar. 2 planear, planificar. *vi* hacer proyectos. **plan to** proponerse.

plane[1] (plein) *adj* plano. *n* 1 nivel *m*. esfera *f*. 2 avión *m*.

plane[2] (plein) *n* cepillo (de carpintero) *m*. *vt* acepillar.

planet ('plænit) *n* planeta *m*.

plank (plæŋk) *n* tablón *m*. tabla *f*. *vt* entablar, entarimar.

plankton ('plæŋktən) *n* plankton *m*.

plant (plɑ:nt) *n* 1 *bot* planta *f*. 2 *tech* instalación, maquinaria *f*. 3 fábrica *f*. *vt* 1 plantar, sembrar. 2 poner, colocar. **plantation** *n* 1 plantación *f*. 2 hacienda *f*.

plaque (pla:k) *n* placa *f.*

plasma ('plæzmə) *n* plasma *m.*

plaster ('pla:stə) *n* 1 yeso *m.* 2 argamasa *f.* 3 *med* parche *m.* escayola *f.* **adhesive plaster** esparadrapo *m.* ~*vt* 1 enyesar, enlucir. 2 *med* emplastar. **plaster cast** *n* vaciado *m.* **plaster of Paris** *n* yeso mate *m.*

plastic ('plæstik) *adj,n* plástico *m.* **plastic surgery** *n* cirugía estética *or* plástica *f.*

Plasticine ('plæstisi:n) *n Tdmk* plasticina *f*

plate (pleit) *n* 1 plato *m.* 2 placa *f.* 3 lámina, chapa, plancha *f.* 4 *phot* placa *f.* 5 vajilla de plata *f. vt* planchear, chapear. **plate glass** *n* vidrio cilindrado or en planchas *m.*

plateau ('plætou) *n* meseta *f.*

platform ('plætfɔ:m) *n* 1 plataforma *f.* 2 andén *m.* **platform ticket** *n* billete de andén *m.*

platinum ('plætnəm) *n* platino *m.*

platonic (plə'tɔnik) *adj* platónico *m.*

plausible ('plɔ:zəbəl) *adj* verosímil.

play (plei) *n* 1 juego, recreo *m.* 2 obra dramática *f.* **fair play** juego limpio *m.* ~*vt* 1 jugar a *or* contra. 2 *mus* tocar. 3 representar. *vi* 1 jugar, divertirse. 2 *mus* tocar. **player** *n* 1 actor *m.* actriz *f.* 2 músico *m.* 3 jugador *m.* **playground** *n* patio de recreo *m.* **playhouse** *n* teatro *m.* **playing card** *n* carta *f.* **playing field** *n* campo de deportes *m.* **playmate** *n* compañero de juego *m.* **playschool** *n* guardería *f.* **playwright** *n* dramaturgo *m.*

plea (pli:) *n* 1 pretexto *m.* disculpa *f.* 2 *law* alegato *m.* defensa *f.* 3 contestación a la demanda, declaración *f.*

plead (pli:d) *vi* 1 suplicar, rogar. 2 *law* abogar. 3 declarar. **plead guilty** declararse *or* confesarse culpable. **plead not guilty** negar la acusación.

please (pli:z) *vt* gustar. *vi* dar satisfacción. **please!** ¡por favor! **pleasing** *adj* grato. **be pleased** estar contento. **be pleased to** complacerse en. **pleasant** *adj* agradable, ameno, simpático. **pleasantry** *n* chiste *m.* agudeza *f.* **pleasure** *n* 1 placer, gusto *m.* 2 voluntad *f.* **with pleasure** con mucho gusto.

pleat (pli:t) *n* pliegue *m. vt* plegar, plisar.

pledge (pledʒ) *n* 1 prenda *f.* 2 promesa *f. vt* 1 empeñar, dejar en prenda. 2 prometer. 3 brindar por.

plenty ('plenti) *adv inf* bastante, muchísimo. *n* abundancia *f.* **plentiful** *adj* abundante, copioso.

pliable ('plaiəbəl) *adj* flexible, pegable.

pliers ('plaiəz) *n pl* tenazas *f pl.* alicates *m pl.*

plight (plait) *n* apuro, aprieto *m.* condición inquietante, situación difícil *f.*

plimsoll ('plimsəl) *n* zapatilla de goma *f.*

plod (plɔd) *vi* 1 avanzar laboriosamente, caminar despacio. 2 trabajar laboriosamente.

plonk (plɔŋk) *n* 1 golpe seco *m.* 2 *inf* vino barato *m.*

plot[1] (plɔt) *n* 1 complot *m.* conspiración *f.* 2 *Th* argumento *m.* trama, intriga *f. vt* 1 trazar. 2 tramar, maquinar. *vi* conspirar, intrigar.

plot[2] (plɔt) *n* parcela *f.* terreno *m.*

plough (plau) *n* arado *m. vt* arar.

pluck (plʌk) *n* valor, ánimo *m. vt* 1 coger, arrancar. 2 desplumar. 3 *mus* puntear. **plucky** *adj* valiente, animoso.

plug (plʌg) *n* 1 tapón, taco *m.* 2 *tech* enchufe *m.* 3 *inf* anuncio incidental *m.* publicidad incidental *f. vt* tapar, llenar, obturar. **plug in** enchufar.

plum (plʌm) *n* ciruela *f.* **plum tree** *n* ciruelo *m.*

plumage ('plu:midʒ) *n* plumaje *m.*

plumb (plʌm) *n* plomada *f. adj* vertical. *vt* sondar, sondear. **plumber** *n* fontanero *m.* **plumbing** *n* fontanería *f.*

plume (plu:m) *n* pluma *f.* **plumed** *adj* plumado.

plump[1] (plʌmp) *adj* rechoncho, rollizo, gordo.

plump[2] (plʌmp) *vi* caer pesadamente.

plunder ('plʌndə) *n* botín, pillaje *m. vt* 1 saquear, pillar. 2 robar. **plunderer** *n* saqueador *m.*

plunge (plʌndʒ) *n* salto *m.* zambullida *f. vt* sumergir, hundir. **plunger** *n* émbolo *m.*

pluperfect (plu:'pə:fikt) *n* pluscuamperfecto *m.*

plural ('pluərəl) *adj,n* plural *m.*

plus (plʌs) *adj* positivo. *n math* 1 signo más *m.* 2 cantidad positiva *f. prep inf* más, y, además de.

plush (plʌʃ) *adj* 1 de felpa. 2 lujoso, de buen tono.

Pluto ('plu:tou) *n* Plutón *m.*

ply[1] (plai) *vt* 1 manejar, menear. 2 ejercer. 3 emplear. **ply between** hacer el servico entre.

ply[2] (plai) *n* 1 cabo (of wool) *m.* 2 capa *f.* **plywood** *n* madera contrachapeada *f.*

pneumatic (nju:'mætik) *adj* neumático. **pneumatic drill** *n* perforadora *f.* martillo picador *m.*

pneumonia (nju:'mouniə) *n* pulmonía *f.*

poach[1] (poutʃ) *vt cul* escalfar.

poach[2] (poutʃ) *vt* 1 cazar en vedado. 2 robar. *vi* cazar en finca ajena.

pocket ('pɔkit) *n* 1 bolsillo *m.* 2 bolsa *f. vt* 1 meter en el bolsillo. 2 ganar. **pocket-knife** *n* navaja f. **pocket-money** n dinero para pequeños gastos personales m.

pod (pɔd) n vaina f.

poem ('pouim) n poesía f. poema m.

poet ('pouit) n poeta m. **poet laureate** poeta laureado. m. **poetic** adj poético. **poetry** n poesía f.

poignant ('pɔinjant) adj 1 conmovedor, patético. 2 intenso, agudo.

point (pɔint) n 1 punto m. 2 punta f. 3 lo significativo, lo importante neu. 4 fin, objeto m. 5 utilidad f. **point of view** punto de vista m. ~vt 1 afilar, aguzar. 2 apuntar. vt,vi señalar con el dedo, indicar. **pointed** adj 1 puntiagudo. 2 afilado, agudo. 3 lleno de intención, enfático. **pointless** adj 1 inútil. 2 sin motivo.

poise (pɔiz) n 1 equilibrio m. 2 porte m. 3 confianza en sí mismo f. vt equilibrar. **poised** adj confiado en sí mismo.

poison ('pɔizən) n veneno m. vt envenenar. **poisonous** adj venenoso, tóxico.

poke (pouk) n empuje, empujón, codazo, hurgonazo m. vt 1 empujar. 2 hurgar. **poke fun at** burlarse de. **poky** adj 1 estrecho, muy pequeño. 2 mezquino.

poker[1] ('poukə) n atizador m. badila f.

poker[2] ('poukə) n game póquer m.

Poland ('poulənd) n Polonia f. **Pole** n polaco m. **Polish** adj polaco. **Polish (language)** n polaco m.

polar ('poulə) adj polar. **polar bear** n oso blanco m. **polarize** vt polarizar.

pole[1] (poul) n 1 palo m. 2 mástil m. 3 poste m. 4 pértiga f. **pole-vault** n salto con pértiga m.

pole[2] (poul) n polo m. **Pole Star** n estrella polar f.

polemic (pə'lemik) adj polémico. n polémica f.

police (pə'li:s) n policía f. vt vigilar, patrullar. **policeman** n policía, guardia m. **police station** n comisaria f.

policy[1] ('pɔlisi) n política f.

policy[2] ('pɔlisi) n (insurance) póliza f.

polish ('pɔliʃ) n 1 lustre, brillo m. 2 betún m. 3 cera de lustrar. 4 pulimento m. 5 inf finura, cultura f. vt 1 limpiar. 2 encerar, sacar brillo a. 3 pulir. **polished** adj 1 pulido. 2 limado, elegante. 3 culto, distinguido.

polite (pə'lait) adj cortés, atento, fino.

politics ('pɔlitiks) n pl política f. **political** adj político. **politician** n político m.

polka ('pɔlkə) n polca f. **polka dot** n punto, lunar m.

poll (poul) n 1 votación, elección f. 2 votos m pl. vt recibir. **polling booth** n cabina de votar f. **polling station** n colegio electoral m. urnas electorales f pl.

pollen ('pɔlən) n polen m. **pollinate** vt fecundar. **pollination** n polinización f.

pollute (pə'lu:t) vt 1 contaminar. 2 corromper. **pollution** n contaminación f.

polygamy (pə'ligəmi) n poligamia f. **polygamist** n polígamo m.

polygon ('pɔligən) n polígono m.

polytechnic (pɔli'teknik) n escuela politécnica f.

polythene ('pɔliθi:n) n politene m.

pomegranate ('pɔmigrænət) n granada f. **pomegranate tree** n granado m.

pomp (pɔmp) n pompa f. **pompous** adj pomposo.

pond (pɔnd) n 1 charca f. 2 estanque m.

ponder ('pɔndə) vt ponderar. vi reflexionar, pensar. **ponderous** adj pesado.

pony ('pouni) n caballito m. jaca f.

poodle ('pu:dl) n perro de lanas m.

pool[1] (pu:l) n 1 charca, balsa f. 2 estanque m. 3 piscina f.

pool[2] (pu:l) n 1 game trucos m pl. 2 mancomunidad f. 3 reserva f. **football pools** quinielas f pl. ~vt mancomunar.

poor (puə, pɔ:) adj 1 pobre. 2 malo. 3 mezquino.

pop[1] (pɔp) n taponazo m. vi estallar, reventar. **popcorn** n palomitas, rosetas f pl.

pop[2] (pɔp) adj popular. **pop music** n música moderna y popular f.

pope (poup) n papa m.

poplar ('pɔplə) n chopo m.

poppy ('pɔpi) n amapola f.

popular ('pɔpjulə) adj popular. **popularity** n popularidad f.

population (pɔpju'leiʃən) n población f.

porcelain ('pɔ:slin) n porcelana f.

porch (pɔ:tʃ) n pórtico m.

porcupine ('pɔ:kjupain) n puerco espín m.

pore[1] (pɔ:) vi **pore over** estudiar con atención.

pore[2] (pɔ:) n poro m.

pork (pɔ:k) n carne de cerdo f.

pornography (pɔ:'nɔgrafi) n pornografía f. **pornographic** adj pornográfico.

porous ('pɔ:rəs) adj poroso.

porpoise ('pɔ:pəs) n marsopa f.

porridge ('pɔridʒ) n gachas de avena f pl.

port[1] (pɔ:t) n puerto m. **port of call** n puerto de escala m.

port² (pɔːt) n naut babor m.

port³ (pɔːt) n oporto m.

portable ('pɔːtəbəl) adj portátil.

porter¹ ('pɔːtə) n mozo de estación, mozo de equipajes m.

porter² ('pɔːtə) n portero, conserje m.

portfolio (pɔːtˈfouliou) n cartera, carpeta f. **minister without portfolio** n ministro sin cartera m.

porthole ('pɔːthoul) n portilla f.

portion ('pɔːʃən) n porción, parte f.

portrait ('pɔːtrit) n retrato m.

portray (pɔːˈtrei) vt 1 art retratar. 2 describir. **portrayal** n descripción f.

Portugal ('pɔːtjugəl) n Portugal m. **Portuguese** adj,n portugués m. **Portuguese** (language) n portugués m.

pose (pouz) n 1 postura, actitud f. 2 afectación f. vt 1 colocar. 2 plantear. 3 formular. vi 1 posar. 2 darse tono.

posh (pɔʃ) adj inf elegante, lujoso.

position (pəˈziʃən) n 1 posición f. 2 categoría f. 3 puesto m.

positive ('pɔzitiv) adj 1 positivo. 2 enfático, categórico. 3 enérgico. 4 afirmativo. n phot positiva f. **positively** adv 1 absolutamente. 2 con énfasis.

possess (pəˈzes) vt poseer. **possessed** adj poseso. **possession** n 1 posesión f. 2 pl bienes m pl. **take possession of** tomar posesión de. **possessive** adj 1 gram posesivo. 2 dominante. n gram posesivo m.

possible ('pɔsəbəl) adj posible. **possibility** n posibilidad f.

post¹ (poust) n poste m.

post² (poust) n puesto, empleo m. vt 1 apostar, situar. 2 destinar.

post³ (poust) n correo m. **by post** por correo. **by return post** a vuelta de correo. **registered post** correo certificado. ~vt mandar por correos, despachar. **postage** n franqueo, porte m. **postage stamp** n sello de correo m. **postal order** n giro postal m. **postbox** n buzón m. **postcard** n tarjeta postal f. **postman** n cartero m. **postmark** n matasellos m invar. **post office** n (casa de) correos f.

poster ('poustə) n cartel m.

posterior (pɔsˈtiəriə) adj,n posterior. n inf culo m.

posterity (pɔsˈteriti) n posteridad f.

postgraduate (poustˈgrædjuət) adj,n postgraduado m.

posthumous ('pɔstjuməs) adj póstumo. **posthumously** adv después de la muerte.

post-mortem (poustˈmɔːtəm) n autopsia f.

postpone (pəˈspoun) vt aplazar. **postponement** n aplazamiento m.

postscript ('pousskript) n posdata f.

postulate (v 'pɔstjuleit; n 'pɔstjulət) vt postular. n postulado m.

posture ('pɔstʃə) n postura f. vi adoptar una actitud.

pot (pɔt) n 1 cul olla, marmita f. puchero m. 2 pote m. 3 tiesto m. **go to pot** echarse a perder, arruinarse. ~vt 1 cul conservar. 2 plantar en tiesto. **pothole** n bache m.

potassium (pəˈtæsiəm) n potasio m.

potato (pəˈteitou) n, pl **potatoes** patata f.

potent ('poutnt) adj 1 potente. 2 fuerte.

potential (pəˈtenʃəl) adj,n potencial m,f.

potion ('pouʃən) n poción f.

potter ('pɔtə) vi hacer bagatelas.

pottery ('pɔtəri) n 1 alfarería f. 2 art cerámica f. 3 cacharros m pl. 4 cerámicas f pl. **potter** n alfarero m.

pouch (pautʃ) n bolsa f.

poultice ('poultis) n cataplasma f. emplasto m.

poultry ('poultri) n aves de corral f pl.

pounce (pauns) n salto m. vi atacar súbitamente. **pounce on** saltar sobre.

pound¹ (paund) vt 1 golpear repetidamente, machacar. vi dar golpes.

pound² (paund) n 1 libra f. 2 libra esterlina f.

pour (pɔː) vt 1 echar, derramar. 2 servir. vi 1 llover mucho, llover a cántaros. 2 correr a raudales, fluir.

pout (paut) n puchero m. vi hacer pucheros.

poverty ('pɔvəti) n pobreza f. **poverty-stricken** adj menesteroso.

powder ('paudə) n 1 polvo, m. 2 polvos m pl. 3 pólvora f. vt reducir a polvo. **powdery** adj polvoriento. **powder room** n aseos m pl. tocador m.

power ('pauə) n 1 poder m. 2 empuje m. vt accionar, impulsar. **powerful** adj poderoso, potente. **powerless** adj impotente, ineficaz.

practicable ('præktikəbəl) adj factible, practicable.

practical ('præktikəl) adj práctico. **practicality** n factibilidad f.

practice ('præktis) n 1 costumbre, uso m. 2 práctica f. 3 ejercicio m. 4 med clientela f. 5 law bufete m. **be out of practice** haber perdido la costumbre.

practise ('præktis) vt 1 practicar. 2 ejercitar, ejercer. 3 sport entrenarse en. 4 hacer prác-

ticas de. *vi* **1** *mus* tocar, estudiar. **2** *sport*
entrenarse. **practised** *adj* experto.
practitioner (præk'tiʃənə) *n* **1** practicante *m,f*.
2 *med* médico *m*. **general practitioner** *n*
médico general *m*.
pragmatic (præg'mætik) *adj* pragmático.
prairie ('preəri) *n* pradera, llanura *f*.
praise (preiz) *n* alabanza *f*. elogio *m*. *vt* alabar,
elogiar. **praiseworthy** *adj* digno de alabanza
or elogio.
pram (præm) *n* *inf* cochecito de niño *m*.
prance (prɑːns) *vi* saltar, hacer cabriolas.
prank (præŋk) *n* broma *f*.
prattle ('prætl) *n* **1** parloteo *m*. **2** balbuceo *m*. *vi*
1 parlotear. **2** balbucear.
prawn (prɔːn) *n* gamba *f*.
pray (prei) *vt* suplicar. *vi* orar. **prayer** *n* **1** rel
oración *f*. rezo *m*. **2** ruego *m*. súplica *f*. **say
one's prayers** rezar. **prayerbook** *n* misal *m*.
preach (priːtʃ) *vi* predicar. **preacher** *n* predica-
dor *m*.
precarious (pri'kɛəriəs) *adj* precario.
precaution (pri'kɔːʃən) *n* precaución *f*. **pre-
cautionary** *adj* de precaución, preventivo.
precede (pri'siːd) *vt,vi* preceder. **preceding** *adj*
precedente. **precedence** *n* precedencia *f*.
precedent *n* precedente *m*. **without precedent** sin precedentes.
precinct ('priːsiŋkt) *n* recinto *m*.
precious ('preʃəs) *adj* **1** precioso. **2** amado,
querido. **3** afectado. *adv inf* muy.
precipice ('presipis) *n* precipicio *m*.
precipitate (prə'sipiteit) *vt* **1** precipitar. **2** acelerar. *n sci* precipitado *m*.
precis ('preisi) *n* resumen *m*.
precise (pri'sais) *adj* preciso, exacto. **precisely**
adv precisamente, con precisión. **precisely!**
¡perfectamente!, ¡eso es! **precision** *n* precisión *f*.
precocious (pri'kouʃəs) *adj* precoz. **precocity**
n precocidad *f*.
preconceive (priːkən'siːv) *vt* preconcebir. **pre-
conception** *n* preconcepción *f*.
predatory ('predətəri) *adj* rapaz, de rapiña.
predator *n* predador *m*.
predecessor ('priːdisesə) *n* predecesor *m*.
predestine (pri'destin) *vt* predestinar. **pre-
destination** *n* predestinación *f*.
predicament (pri'dikəmənt) *n* apuro *m*.
predicate (*n* 'predikit; *v* 'predikeit) *n* predicado
m. *vt* predicar.
predict (pri'dikt) *vt* pronosticar, predecir.
prediction *n* pronóstico *m*. predicción *f*.

predominate (pri'dɔmineit) *vi* predominar.
predominant *adj* predominante. **predomi-
nantly** *adv* por la mayor parte.
pre-eminent *adj* preeminente.
preen (priːn) *vt* arreglar con el pico. **preen
oneself** *inf* pavonearse. **preen oneself on**
jactarse de.
prefabricate (pri'fæbrikeit) *vt* prefabricar.
preface ('prefis) *n* prefacio *m*. *vt* prologar,
introducir.
prefect ('priːfekt) *n* prefecto *m*.
prefer (pri'fəː) *vt* **1** preferir. **2** promover. **prefer
a charge against** acusar a. **preferable** *adj*
preferible. **preferably** *adv* más bien. **preference** *n* preferencia *f*. **preferential** *adj* pre-
ferente.
prefix ('priːfiks) *n* prefijo *m*. *vt* prefijar.
pregnant ('pregnənt) *adj* embarazada, encinta.
pregnancy *n* embarazo *m*.
prehistoric (priːhis'tɔrik) *adj* prehistórico.
prejudice ('predʒədis) *n* prejuicio *m*. **have a
prejudice against** estar predispuesto contra.
without prejudice to sin perjuicio de. ~*vt* **1**
predisponer. **2** perjudicar. **prejudiced** *adj* **1**
parcial, interesado. **2** lleno de prejuicios. **pre-
judicial** *adj* perjudicial.
preliminary (pri'liminəri) *adj,n* preliminar *m*.
prelude ('preljuːd) *n* preludio *m*.
premarital (pri'mæritl) *adj* premarital.
premature ('premətʃə) *adj* prematuro.
premeditate (priː'mediteit) *vt* premeditar. **premeditation** *n* premeditación *f*.
premier ('premiə) *adj* primero, principal. *n*
primer ministro *m*.
premiere ('premiə) *n* estreno *m*.
premise ('premis) *n* premisa *f*. **on the
premises** en el local.
premium ('priːmiəm) *n* **1** *comm* prima *f*. **2**
premio *m*. **be at a premium** tener mucha
demanda.
preoccupied (priː'ɔkjupaid) *adj* preocupado.
preoccupation *n* preocupación *f*.
prepare (pri'pɛə) *vt* preparar. **be prepared to**
disponerse a. **preparation** *n*. preparación
f. **preparations** preparativos *m pl*.
preposition (prepə'ziʃən) *n* preposición *f*.
preposterous (pri'pɔstərəs) *adj* absurdo, pre-
póstero.
prerogative (pri'rɔgətiv) *n* prerrogativa *f*.
Presbyterian (prezbi'tiəriən) *adj,n* presbite-
riano.
prescribe (pri'skraib) *vt,vi* **1** prescribir. **2** *med*

recetar. **prescription** n 1 prescripción f. 2 med receta f.

presence ('prezəns) n presencia f. **in the presence of** ante, en presencia de.

present[1] ('prezənt) adj presente, actual. **be present** asistir. ~n 1 presente m. actualidad f. 2 gram tiempo presente m. **at present** actualmente. **for the present** por ahora. **present participle** n participio de presente m.

present[2] (v pri'zent; n 'prezənt) n regalo, presente m. vt 1 presentar. 2 exponer. **presentable** adj presentable. **presentation** n presentación f. **presently** adv dentro de poco, luego.

preserve (pri'zə:v) n 1 cul conserva, confitura f. 2 coto m. vt 1 conservar. 2 cul hacer una conserva de. **preservation** n conservación, preservación f. **preservative** adj,n preservativo m.

preside (pri'zaid) vi presidir.

president ('prezidənt) n presidente m. **presidency** n presidencia f. **presidential** adj presidencial.

press (pres) n 1 prensa f. 2 imprenta f. 3 presión f. apretón m. 4 apiñamiento m. vt 1 apretar, pulsar. 2 planchar. 3 insistir en. vi 1 apretar, hacer presión. 2 urgir, apremiar. **pressing** adj urgente. **press conference** n conferencia de prensa f. **press-gang** n ronda de enganche f. **press-up** n flexión f.

pressure ('preʃə) n 1 presión f. 2 urgencia f. 3 med tensión nerviosa f. **pressure cooker** n olla a presión f. **pressurize** vt presionar.

prestige (pres'ti:ʒ) n prestigio m.

presume (pri'zju:m) vt,vi presumir, suponer. **presume to** atreverse a. **presumably** adv según cabe presumir. **presumption** n 1 presunción f. 2 atrevimiento m.

pretend (pri'tend) vt 1 fingir. 2 pretender. **pretence** n 1 pretensión f. 2 afectación f. **false pretences** fraude m. **pretension** n 1 pretensión f. 2 afectación f. **pretentious** adj pretencioso, presumido.

pretext ('pri:tekst) n pretexto m.

pretty ('priti) adj 1 bonito, guapo, lindo. 2 considerable. adv con gracia.

prevail (pri'veil) vi 1 prevalecer. 2 predominar. **prevail upon** persuadir. **prevailing** adj reinante, imperante, predominante. **prevalent** adj corriente, frecuente, predominante. **prevalence** n uso corriente m. costumbre f.

prevent (pri'vent) vt 1 impedir, estorbar. 2

evitar. **prevention** n prevención f. el impedir m.

preview ('pri:vju:) n 1 pre-estreno m. 2 vista anticipada f.

previous ('pri:viəs) adj previo, anterior. **previous to** antes de.

prey (prei) n 1 presa, víctima f. **bird of prey** ave de rapiña f. **prey on 1** atacar, alimentarse de, pillar. 2 preocupar, remorder.

price (prais) n precio m. **at any price** a toda costa. **not at any price** de ningún modo. ~vt estimar, valuar, fijar el precio de. **priceless** adj 1 inapreciable. 2 inf divertidísimo.

prick (prik) n 1 pinchazo, alfilerazo m. punzada f. vt pinchar, picar. **prick up one's ears** aguzar el oído. **prickle** n 1 espina, púa f. 2 picazón m. **prickly** adj 1 espinoso, lleno de espinas. 2 malhumorado, difícil.

pride (praid) n orgullo m. **pride oneself on** enorgullecerse de.

priest (pri:st) n sacerdote, cura m. **parish priest** n párroco m. **priesthood** n sacerdocio, clero m. **priestly** adj sacerdotal.

prim (prim) adj 1 remilgado. 2 etiquetero.

primary ('praiməri) adj primario, principal. **primary school** n escuela primaria f.

primate n 1 ('praimit) rel primado m. 2 ('praimeit) zool primate m.

prime (praim) adj 1 primero, principal, fundamental. 2 selecto, de primera clase. n flor f. vt 1 cebar. 2 preparar. **prime minister** n primer ministro m.

primitive ('primitiv) adj 1 primitivo. 2 rudimentario.

primrose ('primrouz) n primavera f.

prince (prins) n príncipe m. **princely** adj principesco, magnífico.

princess (prin'ses) n princesa f.

principal ('prinsəpəl) adj principal, mayor. n 1 principal, jefe m. 2 educ director m.

principality (prinsi'pæliti) n principado m.

principle ('prinsəpəl) n principio m.

print (print) n 1 marca f. 2 tipo m. 3 art estampa f. grabado m. 4 phot positiva f. **be in print** estar impreso. **printer** n impresor m. **printing** n 1 imprenta, tipografía f. 2 impresión f. 3 tirada f.

prior ('praiə) adj anterior, previo. adv **prior to** antes de. **priority** n prioridad f.

prise (praiz) vt **prise open** abrir por fuerza.

prism ('prizəm) n prisma m.

prison ('prizən) n cárcel, prisión f. **prisoner** n detenido, prisionero m.

private

private (`praivit) *adj* 1 privado, particular. 2
confidencial. 3 íntimo. *n mil* soldado raso
m. **in private** confidencialmente. **privacy** *n*
soledad *f*. retiro, aislamiento *m*.
privet (`privit) *n* ligustro *m*.
privilege (`prividʒ) *n* privilegio *m*. prerrogativa
f. **privileged** *adj* privilegiado.
prize[1] (praiz) *n* premio *m*. *adj* premiado.
prize[2] (praiz) *vt* apreciar, estimar.
probable (`prɔbabəl) *adj* probable. **probability**
n probabilidad *f*.
probation (prə`beiʃən) *n law* libertad condicio-
nal *f*.
probe (proub) *n* 1 *med* sonda *f*. 2 *inf* investigación, encuesta *f*. *vt* 1 *med* sondar, tentar.
2 investigar. **probing** *n* 1 sondeo *m*. 2 investigación *f*.
problem (`prɔbləm) *n* problema *m*.
proceed (prə`si:d) *vi* 1 proceder. 2 continuar.
proceed against procesar. **proceed with**
proseguir. **proceeds** *n pl* ganancias *f pl*.
procedure *n* procedimiento *m*. **proceeding** *n*
procedimiento *m*. **proceedings** *n pl* 1 actos
m pl. 2 medidas *f pl*.
process (`prouses) *n* procedimiento, proceso *m*.
vt preparar, tratar.
procession (prə`seʃən) *n* 1 desfile *m*. 2 *rel*
procesión *f*.
proclaim (prə`kleim) *vt* proclamar. **proclama-
tion** *n* proclamación *f*.
procreate (`proukrieit) *vt* procrear. **procreation**
n procreación *f*.
procure (prə`kjuə) *vt* 1 obtener, conseguir. 2
lograr. **procurement** *n* obtención *f*.
prod (prɔd) *n* 1 empuje *m*. 2 codazo *m*. *vt* 1
empujar. 2 codear.
prodigy (`prɔdidʒi) *n* prodigio *m*. **prodigal**
adj,n pródigo *m*.
produce (v prə`dju:s; *n* `prɔdju:s) *n* producto. *vt*
1 producir, presentar, mostrar. 2 fabricar. 3
causar. 4 *Th* poner en escena. **producer** *n* 1
productor *m*. 2 *Th* director de escena *m*.
product *n* 1 producto *m*. 2 resultado *m*.
consecuencia *f*. **waste products** desperdicios
n pl. **production** *n* 1 producción *f*. 2 *Th*
presentación *f*. **production line** línea de montaje *f*. **productive** *adj* productivo. **productivity** *n* productividad *f*.
profane (prə`fein) *adj* profano. *vt* profanar.
profanity *n* 1 profanidad *f*. 2 lenguaje indecente *m*.
profess (prə`fes) *vt* 1 profesar. 2 manifestar.
profession *n* profesión *f*. **professional** *adj* 1

profesional. 2 experto. *n* profesional *m,f*.
professor *n* profesor *m*.
proficient (prə`fiʃənt) *adj* perito, hábil. **pro-
ficiency** *n* pericia, habilidad *f*.
profile (`proufail) *n* perfil *m*.
profit (`prɔfit) *n comm* ganancia *f*. **gross profit**
ganancia bruta *f*. **net profit** ganancia neta
f. **profit and loss** ganancias y pérdidas *f pl*.
~*vt* servir a, aprovechar. *vi* ganar, sacar
ganancia. **profitable** *adj* 1 provechoso, útil. 2
lucrativo. **profitably** *adv* 1 con provecho. 2
comm lucrativamente.
profound (prə`faund) *adj* profundo.
profuse (prə`fju:s) *adj* 1 profuso. 2 pródigo.
profusion *n* profusión *f*.
programme (`prougræm) *n* programa *m*. *vt*
programar. **program** (in computers) *n* programa *f*. *vt* programar.
progress (n `prougres; v prə`gres) *n* 1 progreso
m. 2 marcha *f*. desarrollo *m*. *vi* 1 hacer
progresos, progresar. 2 avanzar. **progression**
n progresión *f*.
progressive (prə`gresiv) *adj* 1 progresivo. 2 *pol*
progresista. *n pol* progresista *m,f*.
prohibit (prə`hibit) *vt* prohibir. **prohibition** *n*
prohibición *f*. **prohibitive** *adj* prohibitivo.
project (n `prɔdʒekt; v prə`dʒekt) *n* proyecto *m*.
vt proyectar. *vi* salir, resaltar. **projectile** *n*
proyectil *m*. **projecting** *adj* saliente. **projection** *n* 1 proyección *f*. 2 saliente, resalto
m. **projector** *n* proyector *m*.
proletariat (prouli`tɛəriət) *n* proletariado *m*.
proliferate (prə`lifəreit) *vt* multiplicar, extender.
vi proliferar, extenderse.
prolific (prə`lifik) *adj* prolífico.
prologue (`proulɔg) *n* prólogo *m*.
prolong (prə`lɔŋ) *vt* prolongar. **prolongation** *n*
prolongación *f*.
promenade (prɔmə`nɑ:d) *n* paseo *m*. *vi* pasear.
prominent (`prɔminənt) *adj* 1 saliente, promi-
nente. 2 (of eyes) saltón. 3 eminente, importante. **prominence** *n* 1 prominencia *f*. 2
eminencia, importancia *f*.
promiscuous (prə`miskjuəs) *adj* promiscuo.
promiscuity *n* libertinaje *m*. promiscuidad *f*.
promise (`prɔmis) *n* 1 promesa *f*. 2 esperanza *f*.
porvenir *m*. **keep one's promise** cumplir su
promesa. ~*vt* 1 prometer. 2 augurar. **promis-
ing** *adj* prometedor, que promete.
promote (prə`mout) *vt* 1 promover, fomentar. 2
estimular. 3 dar publicidad a. 4 apoyar. **promotion** *n* 1 promoción *f*. fomento *m*. 2
facilitación *f*. 3 ascenso *m*.

256

prompt (prɔmpt) *adj* pronto, puntual. *adv* puntualmente. *vt* 1 mover, incitar. 2 *Th* apuntar. **prompter** *n Th* apuntador *m*.

prone (proun) *adj* postrado. **be prone to** ser propenso a.

prong (prɔŋ) *n* punta, púa *f*.

pronoun ('prounaun) *n* pronombre *m*. **personal pronoun** pronombre personal. **possessive pronoun** pronombre posesivo.

pronounce (prə'nauns) *vt* pronunciar. **pronounce on** expresar una opinión sobre. **pronounced** *adj* fuerte. **pronouncement** *n* declaración, opinión *f*. **pronunciation** *n* pronunciación *f*.

proof (pru:f) *n* 1 prueba *f*. 2 (of alcohol) graduación normal *f*. **give proof** dar prueba de. **proofread** *vt* corregir las pruebas de.

prop¹ (prɔp) *n* apoyo *m*. *vt* apoyar. **prop up** apuntalar, sostener.

prop² (prɔp) *n Th* accesorio *m*.

propaganda (prɔpə'gændə) *n* propaganda *f*.

propagate ('prɔpəgeit) *vt* propagar.

propel (prə'pel) *vt* impulsar, propulsar. **propeller** *n* hélice *f*.

proper ('prɔpə) *adj* 1 propio. 2 apropiado, conveniente. 3 decente, correcto. 4 etiquetero. 5 *inf* verdadero. **properly** *adv* correctamente, debidamente. **proper noun** *n* nombre propio *m*.

property ('prɔpəti) *n* propiedad *f*.

prophecy ('prɔfisi) *n* profecía *f*. **prophesy** *vt* 1 profetizar. 2 *inf* predecir, prever.

prophet ('prɔfit) *n* profeta *m*.

proportion (prə'pɔ:ʃən) *n* proporción *f*.

propose (prə'pouz) *vt* proponer, ofrecer. *vi* **propose to** proponerse. **proposal** *n* propuesta, proposición, oferta *f*. **proposition** *n* proposición, propuesta *f*.

proprietor (prə'praiətə) *n* proprietario, dueño *m*.

propriety (prə'praiəti) *n* decoro *m*. corrección *f*. **proprieties** convenciones *f pl*.

propulsion (prə'pʌlʃən) *n* propulsión *f*.

prose (prouz) *n* prosa *f*.

prosecute ('prɔsikju:t) *vt law* procesar, llevar a juicio. **prosecution** 1 *law* proceso, juicio *m*. 2 prosecución *f*. cumplimiento *m*.

prospect *n* ('prɔspekt) 1 perspectiva *f*. 2 vista *f*. 3 probabilidad *f*. *vt* explorar. **prospect for** buscar. **prospective** *adj* anticipado, esperado. **prospectus** *n* prospecto *m*.

prosper ('prɔspə) *vi* prosperar. **prosperity** *n* prosperidad *f*. **prosperous** *adj* próspero.

prostitute ('prɔstitju:t) *n* prostituta *f*. **prostitution** *n* prostitución *f*.

prostrate (*v* prɔs'treit; *adj* 'prɔstreit) *adj* postrado. *vt* postrar. **prostration** *n* postración *f*.

protagonist (prə'tægənist) *n* protagonista *m,f*.

protect (prə'tekt) *vt* proteger. **protection** *n* protección *f*. **protective** *adj* protector.

protégé ('prɔtiʒei) *n* protegido *m*.

protein ('prouti:n) *n* proteína *f*.

protest (*n* 'proutest; *v* prə'test) *n* protesta *f*. **under protest** bajo protesta. ~*vt,vi* protestar.

Protestant ('prɔtistənt) *adj,n* protestante.

protocol ('proutəkɔl) *n* protocolo *m*.

proton ('prouton) *n* protón *m*.

prototype ('proutətaip) *n* prototipo *m*.

protrude (prə'tru:d) *vt* sacar fuera. *vi* sobresalir, salir fuera. **protruding** *adj* saliente. **protrusion** *n* protuberancia *f*.

proud (praud) *adj* 1 orgulloso. 2 soberbio, engreido. **be proud of** enorgullecerse de. **be proud to** tener el honor de.

prove (pru:v) *vt* 1 probar, demostrar. 2 confirmar. 3 verificar. *vi* resultar.

proverb ('prɔvə:b) *n* refrán, proverbio *m*. **proverbial** *adj* proverbial.

provide (prə'vaid) *vt* 1 surtir. 2 proporcionar. **provide for** proveer. **provide that** disponer que. **provided that** con tal que. **provision** *n* 1 provisión *f*. abastecimiento *m*. 2 disposición, estipulación *f*. *vt* abastecer. **provisional** *adj* provisional.

province ('prɔvins) *n* 1 provincia *f*. 2 jurisdicción *f*.

proviso (prə'vaizou) *n* condición, estipulación *f*.

provoke (prə'vouk) *vt* 1 provocar, irritar. 2 mover, incitar. **provocation** *n* provocación *f*. **provocative** *adj* provocador, provocativo.

prow (prau) *n* proa *f*.

prowess ('prauis) *n* 1 valor *m*. 2 destreza *f*.

prowl (praul) *vi* rondar. *n* ronda *f*.

proximity (prɔk'simiti) *n* proximidad *f*.

prude (pru:d) *n* remilgado, gazmoño *m*. **prudery** *n* remilgo *m*. gazmoñería *f*. **prudish** *adj* remilgado, gazmoño.

prudent ('pru:dnt) *adj* prudente. **prudence** *n* prudencia *f*.

prune¹ (pru:n) *n* ciruela pasa *f*.

prune² (pru:n) *vt* 1 podar. 2 reducir, escamondar. **pruning** *n* poda *f*.

pry (prai) *vi* 1 fisgonear. 2 entrometerse. **prying** *adj* 1 fisgón, curioso. 2 entrometido.

psalm (sɑ:m) *n* salmo *m*.

pseudonym ('sju:dənim) n seudónimo m.
psychedelic (saiki'delik) adj psiquedélico.
psychiatry (sai'kaiətri) n psiquiatría f.
psychiatrist n psiquiatra m,f.
psychic ('saikik) adj psíquico.
psychoanalysis (saikouə'nælisis) n psicoanálisis m. **psychoanalyse** vt psicoanalizar.
psychoanalyst n psicoanalista m,f.
psychology (sai'kolədʒi) n psicología f. **psychologist** n psicólogo m. **psychological** adj psicológico.
psychopathic (saikə'pæθik) adj psicopático.
psychopath n psicópata m,f.
psychosomatic (saikousə'mætik) adj psicosomático.
pub (pʌb) n taberna f. **publican** n inf tabernero m.
puberty ('pju:bəti) n pubertad f.
public ('pʌblik) adj,n público m. **public house** n taberna f. **public relations** n pl relaciones públicas f pl. **public school** n internado privado m.
publication (pʌbli'keiʃən) n publicación f.
publicity (pʌb'lisiti) n publicidad f.
publicize ('pʌblisaiz) vt publicar, dar publicidad a.
publish ('pʌbliʃ) vt publicar. **publisher** n editor m. **publishing** n publicación f. **publishing firm** or **house** n casa editorial f.
pucker ('pʌkə) vt arrugar. n arruga f.
pudding ('pudiŋ) n pudín m.
puddle ('pʌdl) n charco m.
puff (pʌf) n 1 soplo m. 2 borla (for powder) f. vt,vi soplar. **puffy** adj hinchado. **puff pastry** n hojaldre m.
pull (pul) n 1 tirón, estirón m. 2 inf influencia f. 3 cuerda f. vt 1 tirar de. 2 arrastrar. 3 torcerse, dislocarse. vi tirar, dar un tirón. **pullover** n jersey m.
pulley ('puli) n polea f.
pulp (pʌlp) n pulpa, pasta f. vt hacer pulpa. **pulpy** adj pulposo.
pulpit ('pulpit) n púlpito m.
pulsate (pʌl'seit) vi pulsar, latir. **pulsation** n pulsación f. latido m.
pulse (pʌls) n 1 anat pulso m. 2 pulsación f. **take someone's pulse** tomar el pulso a uno. ~vi pulsar, latir.
pulverize ('pʌlvəraiz) vt 1 pulverizar. 2 cascar. **pulverization** n pulverización f.
pummel ('pʌml) vt apuñear, cascar.
pump (pʌmp) n 1 bomba f. 2 pompa f. vt 1

sacar con bomba. 2 sonsacar. **pump up** inflar.
pumpkin ('pʌmpkin) n calabaza f.
pun (pʌn) n juego de palabras m. vi hacer un juego de palabras.
punch[1] (pʌntʃ) n puñetazo, golpe m. vt dar un puñetazo a, golpear.
punch[2] (pʌntʃ) n 1 punzón m. 2 taladro m. vt 1 punzar, taladrar. 2 picar.
punch[3] (pʌntʃ) n ponche m.
punctual ('pʌŋktʃuəl) adj punctual. **punctuality** n puntualidad f.
punctuate ('pʌŋktʃueit) vt puntuar.
punctuation (pʌŋktʃu'eiʃən) n puntuación f.
puncture ('pʌŋktʃə) n 1 perforación, puntura f. 2 pinchazo m. vt 1 perforar. 2 pinchar.
pungent ('pʌndʒənt) adj 1 acre. 2 picante. 3 mordaz, acerbo. **pungency** 1 lo acre neu. 2 picante m. 3 mordacidad, acerbidad f.
punish ('pʌniʃ) vt 1 castigar. 2 maltratar. **punishment** n 1 castigo m. 2 tratamiento severo m. **capital punishment** pena de muerte f. **corporal punishment** castigo corporal m.
punt[1] (pʌnt) n batea f. vt sport dar un puntapié a.
punt[2] (pʌnt) vi jugar, hacer apuestas.
pupil[1] ('pju:pəl) n alumno m.
pupil[2] ('pju:pəl) n anat pupila f.
puppet ('pʌpit) n títere m. marioneta m,f.
puppy ('pʌpi) n perrito, cachorro m.
purchase ('pə:tʃis) n 1 compra f. 2 adquisición f. vt comprar.
pure (pjuə) adj puro. **purity** n pureza f.
purgatory ('pə:gətri) n purgatorio m.
purge (pə:dʒ) n purga f. purgante m. vt purgar, purificar.
purify ('pjuərifai) vt purificar, depurar. **purification** n purificación, depuración f.
Puritan ('pjuəritən) adj,n puritano m.
purple ('pə:pəl) adj purpúreo. n púrpura f. **purplish** adj purpurino.
purpose ('pə:pəs) n propósito, objeto m. intención f. vt proponerse, proyectar. **purposeful** adj resuelto, determinado. **purposely** adv adrede, a propósito.
purr (pə:) n ronroneo m. vi ronronear.
purse (pə:s) n bolsa f. **purse one's lips** fruncir los labios.
pursue (pə'sju:) vt 1 seguir, perseguir, cazar. 2 dedicarse a. 3 proceder de acuerdo con. 4 ejercer. **pursuit** n 1 caza, busca f. 2 ocupación f. 3 pasatiempo m.

pus (pʌs) *n* pus *m*.

push (puʃ) *n* empuje, empujón *m*. **get the push** ser despedido. ~*vt* 1 empujar. 2 proseguir. **pushchair** *n* sillita de ruedas *f*.

pussy ('pusi) *n* minino, micho *m*.

put (put) *vt* 1 poner, colocar, meter. 2 hacer, proponer. **put in for** presentarse a, solicitar. **put on** 1 (clothes) ponerse. 2 afectar. **put up with** aguantar, resignarse a.

putrid ('pjuːtrid) *adj* podrido.

putty ('pʌti) *n* masilla *f*.

puzzle ('pʌzəl) *n* 1 *game* rompecabezas *m*. 2 problema, enigma *m*. **crossword puzzle** crucigrama *m*. ~*vt* confundir, dejar perplejo. **puzzled** *adj* perplejo. **puzzling** 1 extraño. 2 enigmático.

PVC *n* (una especie de) impermeable plástico *m*.

pyjamas (pə'dʒɑːməz) *n pl* pijama *m*.

pylon ('pailən) *n* pilón *m*.

pyramid ('pirəmid) *n* pirámide *f*.

Pyrenees (pirə'niːz) *n pl* Pirineos *m pl*.

python ('paiθən) *n* pitón *m*.

Q

quack[1] (kwæk) *n* (of a duck) graznido *m*. *vi* graznar.

quack[2] (kwæk) *n inf* curandero *m*.

quadrangle ('kwɔdræŋgəl) *n* 1 cuadrángulo *m*. 2 patio *m*.

quadrant ('kwɔdrənt) *n* cuadrante *m*.

quadrilateral (kwɔdri'lætərəl) *adj,n* cuadrilátero *m*.

quadruped ('kwɔdrupɛd) *n* cuadrúpedo *m*.

quadruple ('kwɔdrupəl) *vt* cuadruplicar **quadruplet** *n* cuatrillizo *m*.

quail[1] (kweil) *n* codorniz *f*.

quail[2] (kweil) *vi* acobardarse, descorazonarse.

quaint (kweint) *adj* singular, típico.

quake (kweik) *vi* temblar, estremecerse.

qualify ('kwɔlifai) *vt* 1 calificar. 2 habilitar. 3 modificar. *vi* 1 habilitarse, capacitarse. 2 obtener el título, graduarse. **qualification** *n* 1 calificación *f*. 2 requisito *m*. 3 reserva, modificación *f*. 4 *pl* aptitud, capacidad *f*. títulos *m pl*. **qualified** *adj* 1 calificado, competente. 2 modificado, limitado.

quality ('kwɔliti) *n* calidad *f*.

qualm (kwɑːm) *n* escrúpulo *m*. **have no qualms about doing** hacer sin escrúpulos.

quandary ('kwɔndəri) *n* apuro, dilema *m*.

quantity ('kwɔntiti) *n* cantidad *f*.

quarantine ('kwɔrəntiːn) *n* cuarentena *f*.

quarrel ('kwɔrəl) *n* 1 riña *f*. 2 reyerta, pelea *f*. **pick a quarrel** buscar camorra. ~*vi* 1 reñir. 2 pelear.

quarry[1] ('kwɔri) *n* cantera *f*. *vt* extraer.

quarry[2] ('kwɔri) *n* presa *f*.

quart (kwɔːt) *n* cuarto de galón *m*.

quarter ('kwɔːtə) *n* 1 cuarto *m,f*. 2 trimestre *m*. 3 barrio *m*. 4 *pl mil* alojamiento, cuartel *m*. **at close quarters** de cerca. ~*vt* 1 cuartear. 2 descuartizar. 3 *mil* acuartelar, alojar. **quarterly** *adj* trimestral. *n* publicación trimestral *f*.

quartet (kwɔː'tɛt) *n* cuarteto *m*.

quash[1] (kwɔʃ) *vt* reprimir.

quash[2] (kwɔʃ) *vt* anular, invalidar.

quaver ('kweivə) *n* 1 temblor *m*. 2 *mus* corchea *f*. *vi* temblar, vibrar.

quay (kiː) *n* muelle *m*.

queasy ('kwiːzi) *adj* 1 bascoso. 2 escrupuloso.

queen (kwiːn) *n* 1 reina *f*. 2 *game* dama, reina *f*. caballo *m*. **queen mother** reina madre.

queer (kwiə) *adj* 1 raro, extraño, excéntrico. 2 *inf med* enfermo. 3 *sl* maricón. *n sl* maricón, marica *m*. *vt* estropear.

quell (kwel) *vt* reprimir, aquietar.

quench (kwentʃ) *vt* apagar.

query ('kwiəri) *n* 1 pregunta *f*. 2 duda *f*. 3 interrogante *m*. *vt,vi* preguntar.

quest (kwest) *n* busca, búsqueda *f*.

question ('kwestʃən) *n* 1 pregunta *f*. 2 asunto, problema *m*. cuestión *f*. **be a question of** tratarse de. **question mark** *n* signo de interrogación *m*. ~*vt* 1 hacer preguntas a, interrogar. 2 poner en duda. **questionable** *adj* cuestionable. **questionnaire** *n* cuestionario *m*.

queue (kjuː) *n* cola *f*. **jump the queue** salirse de su turno. ~*vi* hacer cola.

quibble ('kwibəl) *n* sofistería, sutileza *f*. *vi* sutilizar, argüir.

quick (kwik) *adj* rápido, veloz, pronto, vivo, ágil, inteligente. **quicken** *vt* acelerar, apresurar. *vi* acelerarse, apresurarse. **quicksand** *n* arena movediza *f*. **quickstep** *n* paso doble *m*. **quick-tempered** *adj* de genio vivo. **quick-witted** *adj* agudo, perspicaz.

quiet[1] ('kwaiət) *n* silencio, reposo *m*. paz, tranquilidad *f*. **on the quiet** a hurtadillas.

quiet[2] ('kwaiət) *adj* silencioso, callado, quieto, inactivo. **quiet** or **quieten** *vt* calmar, hacer callar.

quill (kwil) *n* 1 *zool* pluma de ave *f*. 2 cañón de pluma *m*. 3 pluma de ganso *f*.

quilt (kwilt) n edredón m. vt acolchar.
quince (kwins) n membrillo m.
quinine (kwiˈniːn) n quinina f.
quintessence (kwinˈtesəns) n quinta esencia f.
quintet (kwinˈtet) n quinteto m.
quirk (kwəːk) n 1 capricho m. 2 peculiaridad f.
quit* (kwit) vt 1 dejar, renunciar. 2 salir de. vi 1 irse, marcharse. 2 retirarse. 3 dimitir. **quits** adj inf en paz.
quite (kwait) adv completamente.
quiver[1] (ˈkwivə) n temblor m. vi temblar.
quiver[2] (ˈkwivə) n carcaj m. aljaba f.
quiz (kwiz) n, pl **-zes,** acertijo m. encuesta f. vt interrogar.
quizzical (ˈkwizikəl) adj burlón.
quota (ˈkwoutə) n cuota f.
quote (kwout) vt 1 citar. 2 comm cotizar. **quotation** n 1 citación. 2 comm cotización f. **quotation marks** n pl comillas f pl.

R

rabbi (ˈræbai) n rabino, rabí m.
rabbit (ˈræbit) n conejo m.
rabble (ˈræbəl) n canalla, gentualla f.
rabies (ˈreibiːz) n rabia f. **rabid** adj 1 med rabioso. 2 inf fanático.
race[1] (reis) n sport carrera, regata f. vt hacer correr, presentar. vi 1 correr de prisa. 2 competir, presentarse. **racecourse** n hipódromo m.
race[2] (reis) n raza, casta, estirpe, familia f. **human race** género humano m. **racial** adj racial, racista. **racialism** n racismo m.
rack (ræk) n 1 estante, anaquel m. 2 percha f. 3 potro m. vt atormentar.
racket[1] (ˈrækit) n 1 ruido, estrépito m. 2 barahunda f. 3 inf trampa, estafa f.
racket[2] (ˈrækit) n sport raqueta f.
radar (ˈreidɑː) n radar m.
radial (ˈreidiəl) adj radial.
radiant (ˈreidiənt) adj radiante. **radiance** n brillantez f.
radiate (ˈreidieit) vt irradiar. **radiation** n radiación f. **radiator** n radiador m.
radical (ˈrædikəl) adj,n radical m.
radio (ˈreidiou) n radio f. **radio station** n emisora f. ~vt radiar, transmitir por radio.
radioactivity (reidiouæk'tiviti) n radiactividad f.
radish (ˈrædiʃ) n rábano m.
radium (ˈreidiəm) n radio m.
radius (ˈreidiəs) n, pl **-dii** or **-diuses** radio m.

raffle (ˈræfəl) n rifa f. sorteo m. vt rifar, sortear.
raft (rɑːft) n balsa f.
rafter (ˈrɑːftə) n cabrio m.
rag[1] (ræg) n 1 trapo m. 2 sl periodicucho m. **ragged** adj harapiento, andrajoso.
rag[2] (ræg) vt tomar el pelo a. n broma pesada f.
rage (reidʒ) n 1 rabia f. furor m. 2 manía f. vi rabiar.
raid (reid) n 1 correría, incursión f. 2 aviat bombardeo m. vt 1 invadir, atacar. 2 bombardear.
rail (reil) n 1 barandilla f. 2 carril m. **railway** n ferrocarril m. **railway station** n estación de ferrocarril f.
rain (rein) n lluvia f. vi llover. **rainbow** n arco iris m. **raindrop** n gota de lluvia f.
raise (reiz) vt 1 levantar, alzar. 2 criar. 3 aumentar. 4 reunir.
raisin (ˈreizən) n pasa f.
rake (reik) n 1 rastrillo, rastro m. 2 libertino m. vt rastillar.
rally (ˈræli) n 1 reunión, manifestación f. 2 comm recuperación f. vt reunir.
ram (ræm) n 1 zool carnero m. 2 mil ariete m. vt 1 apisonar, apretar. 2 dar contra.
ramble (ˈræmbəl) n paseo m. excursión f. vi 1 salir de excursión a pie. 2 divagar. **rambling** adj divagador, errante.
ramp (ræmp) n rampa f.
rampage (ˈræmpeidʒ) n alboroto m. vi alborotar, desbocarse.
rampant (ˈræmpənt) adj prevaleciente, desenfrenado.
rampart (ˈræmpɑːt) n muralla f. terraplén m.
ramshackle (ˈræmˌʃækəl) adj destartalado.
ran (ræn) v see **run.**
ranch (rɑːntʃ) n rancho m.
rancid (ˈrænsid) adj rancio.
rancour (ˈræŋkə) n rencor m.
random (ˈrændəm) adj casual, fortuito. **at random** al azar.
rang (ræŋ) v see **ring**[2].
range (reindʒ) n 1 alcance m. 2 gama f. 3 línea, sierra f. vt ordenar, clasificar. vi extenderse.
rank[1] (ræŋk) n 1 rango, grado m. 2 fila, línea f. vt clasificar, ordenar. vi clasificarse. **rank and file** n masas f pl.
rank[2] (ræŋk) adj 1 lozano. 2 rancio.
rankle (ˈræŋkəl) vi roer.
ransack (ˈrænsæk) vt 1 saquear. 2 rebuscar, registrar.
ransom (ˈrænsəm) n rescate m. vt rescatar.
rap (ræp) n golpecito m. vt golpear, tocar.

rape (reip) n violación f. vt violar, forzar.

rapid ('ræpid) adj rápido. **rapids** n pl rápidos m pl.

rapier ('reipiə) n estoque m.

rapture ('ræptʃə) n rapto, éxtasis m.

rare[1] (rɛə) adj raro, poco común. **rarity** n rareza f.

rare[2] (rɛə) adj cul poco hecho.

rascal ('rɑːskəl) n pícaro m.

rash[1] (ræʃ) adj precipitado, inconsiderado.

rash[2] (ræʃ) n med erupción f.

raspberry ('rɑːzbri) n frambuesa f.

rat (ræt) n rata f.

rate (reit) n 1 proporción, razón f. 2 precio m. tarifa, tasa f. 3 clase f. orden m. **at any rate** de todos modos. **first-rate** de primer orden. ~vt 1 valuar, apreciar. 2 clasificar.

rather ('rɑːðə) adv 1 más bien. 2 bastante.

ratio ('reiʃiou) n 1 relación f. 2 math razón f.

ration ('ræʃən) n ración f. vt racionar.

rational ('ræʃənəl) adj racional. **rationalize** vt racionalizar.

rattle ('rætl) n ruido, golpeteo m. vt 1 sacudir. 2 hacer sonar. 3 desconcertar. vi hacer ruido.

raucous ('rɔːkəs) adj ronco.

ravage ('rævidʒ) n 1 estrago, destrozo m. 2 saqueo m. vt asolar, arruinar, saquear.

rave (reiv) vi 1 delirar, desvariar. 2 declamar con violencia.

raven ('reivən) n cuervo m. **ravenous** adj 1 voraz. 2 famélico, hambriento.

ravine (rə'viːn) n barranco m.

ravioli (rævi'ouli) n canalones m pl.

ravish ('ræviʃ) vt 1 forzar, violar. 2 raptar.

raw (rɔː) adj crudo.

ray (rei) n 1 rayo m. 2 zool raya f.

rayon ('reiɔn) n rayón m.

razor ('reizə) n navaja de afeitar f. **razor blade** n hoja de afeitar f.

reach (riːtʃ) n 1 alcance, poder m. 2 distancia. extensión f. vt 1 alargar. 2 alcanzar, llegar a. vi llegar, extenderse.

react (ri'ækt) vi reaccionar. **reaction** n reacción f. **reactionary** adj,n reaccionario m.

read[*] (riːd) vt 1 leer. 2 descifrar, interpretar. 3 estudiar, aprender. **reader** n 1 lector m. 2 libro de lectura m.

readjust (riːə'dʒʌst) vt reajustar. **readjustment** n reajuste m.

ready ('redi) adj 1 preparado, listo, dispuesto. 2 disponible, a la mano. vt preparar, aprestar.

real (riəl) adj real. **realism** n realismo

m. **realize** vt 1 comprender, darse cuenta de. 2 realizar, llevar a cabo. **reality** n realidad f.

realm (relm) n 1 reino m. 2 esfera f.

reap (riːp) vt 1 segar. 2 cosechar, recoger. 3 obtener, sacar fruto.

reappear (riːə'piə) vi reaparecer.

rear[1] (riə) adj trasero, de atrás, de cola, posterior. n 1 trasera, espalda, parte de atrás f. 2 mil retaguardia f. **rear admiral** n contralmirante m. **rearguard** n retaguardia f.

rear[2] (riə) vt 1 criar, educar. 2 levantar, erguir. 3 erigir.

rearrange (riə'reindʒ) vt volver a arreglar, volver a ordenar.

reason ('riːzən) n 1 razón f. 2 causa f. motivo m. 3 cordura f. buen sentido m. vi razonar, raciocinar. **reasonable** adj 1 racional. 2 razonable.

reassure (riːə'ʃuə) vt tranquilizar, devolver la confianza.

rebate ('riːbeit) n rebaja f.

rebel (n,adj 'rebəl; v ri'bel) adj,n rebelde m. vi rebelarse, insurreccionarse.

rebound (n 'riːbaund; v ri'baund) n rebote, resalto m. vi rebotar.

rebuff (ri'bʌf) n desaire m. repulsa f. vt desairar.

rebuild (riː'bild) vt reedificar.

rebuke (ri'bjuːk) n reproche m. reprimenda f. vt reñir, reprender.

recall (ri'kɔːl) vt 1 llamar, hacer volver. 2 hacer revivir, rememorar. n 1 llamada para hacer volver f. 2 recordación f. 3 revocación f.

recede (ri'siːd) vi retroceder.

receipt (ri'siːt) n 1 recibo m. 2 quitanza f. **receipts** n pl ingresos m pl.

receive (ri'siːv) vt 1 recibir. 2 aceptar, tomar. 3 cobrar. **receiver** n 1 receptor m. 2 law liquidador m. 3 tech auricular m.

recent ('riːsənt) adj reciente, moderno.

receptacle (ri'septəkəl) n receptáculo, recipiente m.

reception (ri'sepʃən) n 1 recepción f. 2 recibimiento m. acogida f. **receptive** adj receptivo.

recess (ri'ses) n 1 vacación f. recreo m. 2 lugar apartado, retiro m. 3 hueco m. alcoba f. **recession** n retroceso m. recesión f.

recipe ('resipi) n récipe m. receta f.

recipient (ri'sipiənt) n recibidor m.

reciprocate (ri'siprəkeit) vt reciprocar, devolver. **reciprocal** adj recíproco.

recite (ri'sait) vt,vi 1 recitar. 2 narrar, contar. 3 declamar.

reckless ('reklǝs) *adj* **1** descuidado. **2** atrevido, atolondrado.

reckon ('rekǝn) *vt* **1** contar, calcular. **2** suponer, creer. **reckoning** *n* **1** cuenta *f.* cálculo *m.* **2** ajuste de cuentas *m.*

reclaim (ri'kleim) *vt* **1** reclamar. **2** reformar, civilizar. **3** recuperar, volver a hacer útil.

recline (ri'klain) *vt* reclinar. *vi* rechinarse, recostarse.

recluse (ri'klu:s) *n* solitario, recluso *m.*

recognize ('rekǝgnaiz) *vt* **1** reconocer. **2** admitir, aceptar. **recognition** *n* reconocimiento *m.*

recoil (ri'kɔil) *n* retroceso *m.* *vi* retroceder, retirarse.

recollect (rekǝ'lekt) *vt* recordar, acordarse de. **recollection** *n* recuerdo *m.*

recommence (ri:kǝ'mens) *vt,vi* volver a comenzar.

recommend (rekǝ'mend) *vt* recomendar. **recommendation** *n* recomendación *f.*

recompense ('rekǝmpens) *n* recompensa *f.* *vt* recompensar.

reconcile ('rekǝnsail) *vt* reconciliar. **reconciliation** *n* reconciliación *f.*

reconstruct (ri:kǝn'strʌkt) *vt* reconstruir. **reconstruction** *n* reconstrucción *f.*

record (*n* 'rekɔ:d; *v* ri'kɔ:d) *n* **1** anotación *f.* registro *m.* **2** acta, crónica *f.* anales *m pl.* **3** *mus* disco *m.* **4** récord *m.* marca *f.* *vt* **1** registrar. **2** apuntar. **3** marcar. **record-player** *n* tocadiscos *m invar.*

recount (ri'kaunt) *vt* referir, narrar, detallar.

recover (ri'kʌvǝ) *vt* recobrar, recuperar. *vi* recobrar la salud. **recovery** *n* recobro *m.* recuperación *f.*

recreation (rekri'eiʃǝn) *n* recreación *f.* recreo *m.*

recruit (ri'kru:t) *n* recluta *m.* *vt* reclutar, alistar.

rectangle ('rektæŋgǝl) *n* rectángulo *m.* **rectangular** *adj* rectangular.

rectify ('rektifai) *vt* rectificar.

recuperate (ri'kju:pǝreit) *vt* recuperar. *vi* reponerse, convalecer.

recur (ri'kǝ:) *vi* repetirse.

red (red) *adj* **1** rojo. **2** colorado. **redcurrant** *n* grosella roja *f.*

redeem (ri'di:m) *vt* **1** redimir. **2** rescatar. **3** desempeñar. **redemption** *n* **1** redención *f.* rescate *m.* **2** desempeño *m.*

redevelop (ri:di'velǝp) *vt* volver a desarrollar.

red-handed *adj* con las manos en la masa.

redress (ri'dres) *n* **1** reparación *f.* desagravio *m.* **2** satisfacción *f.* *vt* **1** enderezar. **2** compensar. **3** corregir.

reduce (ri'dju:s) *vt* reducir.

redundant (ri'dʌndǝnt) *adj* redundante, de más. **be made redundant** quedar sin trabajo.

reed (ri:d) *n* caña *f.* junco *m.*

reef (ri:f) *n* arrecife, escollo *m.*

reek (ri:k) *n* humo, tufo, vaho *m.* *vi* humear, oler mal.

reel¹ (ri:l) *n* **1** carrete de pesca *m.* **2** *phot* rollo, carrete *m.* **3** broca, bobina *f.*

reel² (ri:l) *vi* tambalearse, andar haciendo eses, vacilar

refectory (ri'fektǝri) *n* refectorio *m.*

refer (ri'fǝ:) *vt* referir, remitir, aludir. **referee** *n* árbitro *m.* *vt* arbitrar. **reference** *n* **1** referencia, relación *f.* **2** remisión, alusión *f.* **referendum** *n* referéndum *m.*

refill (*v* ri:'fil; *n* 'ri:fil) *vt* rellenar. *n* repuesto *m.*

refine (ri'fain) *vt* refinar, purificar. **refinement** *n* refinamiento *m.* **refinery** *n* refinería *f.*

reflect (ri'flekt) *vt* reflejar. *vi* reflexionar, pensar. **reflection** *n* **1** reflexión *f.* **2** reflejo *m.* **reflector** *n* reflector *m.*

reflex ('ri:fleks) *adj,n* reflejo *m.* **reflexive** *adj* reflexivo.

reform (ri'fɔ:m) *n* reforma *f.* *vt* reformar. *vi* reformarse. **reformation** *n* reforma, reformación *f.*

refract (ri'frækt) *vt* refractar.

refrain¹ (ri'frein) *vi* abstenerse.

refrain² (ri'frein) *n* estribillo *m.*

refresh (ri'freʃ) *vt* refrescar. **refreshment** *n* refresco *m.*

refrigerator (ri'fridʒǝreitǝ) *n* refrigerador, frigorífico *m.* nevera *f.*

refuge ('refju:dʒ) *n* refugio, asilo *m.* **refugee** *n* refugiado *m.*

refund (*n* 'rifʌnd; *v* ri'fʌnd) *n* reembolso *m.* *vt* reintegrar, reembolsar.

refuse¹ (ri'fju:z) *vt* **1** rehusar, rechazar. **2** negarse a. **refusal** *n* **1** repulsa *f.* **2** denegación *f.*

refuse² ('refju:s) *n* basura *f.*

refute (ri'fju:t) *vt* refutar.

regain (ri'gein) *vt* recobrar, recuperar.

regal ('ri:gǝl) *adj* real, regio.

regard (ri'ga:d) *n* **1** miramiento *m.* consideración *f.* **2** relación *f.* respecto *m.* **with regard to** con respecto a. ~*vt* **1** mirar. **2** considerar, tener en cuenta. **3** estimar, apreciar. **4** concernir. **regardless** *adj* indiferente, que no hace caso. *adv* a pesar de todo.

regatta (ri'ga:tǝ) *n* regata *f.*

regent ('ri:dʒǝnt) *adj,n* regente *m.*

regime (rei'ʒi:m) n régimen m.

regiment ('redʒimənt) n regimiento m.

region ('ri:dʒən) n región f.

register ('redʒistə) n registro m. vt 1 registrar, inscribir, matricular. 2 (of a letter) certificar. 3 indicar. **registrar** n 1 registrador, archivero m. 2 secretario m. 3 (in a hospital) doctor m.

regress (ri'gres) vi retroceder. **regression** n regresión f. **regressive** adj regresivo.

regret (ri'gret) n 1 pesar, sentimiento m. pena f. 2 pl excusa f. vt lamentar, sentir. **regretful** adj pesaroso.

regular ('regjulə) adj 1 regular. 2 metódico, ordenado. 3 normal, corriente. n parroquiano m.

regulate ('regjuleit) vt regular, regularizar, ajustar. **regulation** n 1 regulación f. 2 reglamentación f. **regulations** n pl ordenanzas f pl.

rehabilitate (ri:ə'biliteit) vt rehabilitar. **rehabilitation** n rehabilitación f.

rehearse (ri'hə:s) vt ensayar, repasar. **rehearsal** n ensayo m. repetición f.

reheat (ri:'hi:t) vt volver a calentar.

reign (rein) n reino, reinado m. vi reinar.

reimburse (ri:im'bə:s) vt reembolsar, indemnizar.

rein (rein) n rienda f.

reincarnation (ri:inka:'neiʃən) n reencarnación f.

reindeer ('reindiə) n reno m.

reinforce (ri:in'fɔ:s) vt reforzar. **reinforcement** n refuerzo m.

reinstate (ri:in'steit) vt reinstalar, rehabilitar.

reinvest (ri:in'vest) vt reinvertir.

reissue (ri:'iʃu:) vt 1 reimprimir. 2 emitir de nuevo. n reimpresión f. nueva emisión f.

reject (v ri'dʒekt; n ri:dʒekt) vt rechazar, desechar, expeler. n desecho m.

rejoice (ri'dʒɔis) vi regocijarse, alegrarse.

rejuvenate (ri'dʒu:vəneit) vt rejuvenecer.

relapse (ri'læps) n recaída, reincidencia f. vi recaer, reincidir.

relate (ri'leit) vt 1 relatar, contar. 2 relacionar. **relation** n 1 relato m. narración f. 2 relación f. 3 parentesco m. afinidad f. **in relation to** en relación con. **relations** n pl parientes m pl. **relationship** n relación, afinidad f. parentesco m. **relative** adj,n relativo m. **relativity** n relatividad f.

relax (ri'læks) vt 1 relajar. 2 aliviar, mitigar. vi 1 relajarse. 2 descansar, esparcirse, calmarse.

relaxation n 1 relajación f. 2 descanso, esparcimiento m. 3 mitigación f.

relay (n 'ri:lei; v ri'lei) n tanda f. vt 1 tech retransmitir. 2 pasar.

release (ri'li:s) n 1 liberación f. 2 emisión f. lanzamiento, descargo, disparo m. vt 1 emitir. 2 libertar. 3 lanzar, disparar. 4 estrenar, publicar. 5 aflojar.

relent (ri'lent) vi 1 ablandarse, aplacarse. 2 enternecerse.

relevant ('reləvənt) adj pertinente, a propósito, al caso.

reliable (ri'laiəbəl) adj 1 digno de confianza. 2 fidedigno.

relic ('relik) n reliquia f.

relief (ri'li:f) n 1 ayuda f. socorro m. 2 consuelo, alivio m. 3 relevo m. 4 relieve m.

relieve (ri'li:v) vt 1 aliviar. 2 relevar, socorrer. 3 realzar, dar relieve.

religion (ri'lidʒən) n religión f. **religious** adj religioso.

relinquish (ri'liŋkwiʃ) vt 1 abandonar, desistir de. 2 ceder.

relish ('reliʃ) n 1 buen sabor m. 2 gusto, goce m. 3 condimento m. vt 1 saborear. 2 apreciar con gusto.

reluctant (ri'lʌktənt) adj reluctante, reacio.

rely (ri'lai) vi confiar. **rely on** contar con.

remain (ri'mein) vi 1 quedar. 2 restar. 3 permanecer. **remainder** n 1 resto, sobrante, restante m. 2 math residuo m.

remand (ri'ma:nd) vt mandar de nuevo a la cárcel.

remark (ri'ma:k) n 1 observación f. 2 nota f. comentario m. vt 1 advertir. 2 hacer notar, observar. **remarkable** adj 1 considerable, señalado. 2 observable, notable.

remedy ('remədi) n remedio m. vt remediar.

remember (ri'membə) vt acordarse de, recordar. **remembrance** n recuerdo m. memoria, conmemoración f.

remind (ri'maind) vt recordar, hacer presente. **reminder** n 1 recordatorio m. 2 advertencia f.

reminiscence (remi'nisəns) n reminiscencia f. **reminiscent** adj 1 recordativo, evocador. 2 lleno de recuerdos.

remiss (ri'mis) adj remiso, descuidado. **remission** n remisión f. perdón m.

remit (ri'mit) vt 1 remitir. 2 perdonar. **remittance** n giro m. remesa f.

remnant ('remnənt) n 1 remanente m. 2 resto m. 3 retazo m.

remorse (ri'mɔ:s) n remordimiento m.

remote (ri'mout) *adj* remoto.

remove (ri'mu:v) *vt* **1** quitar. **2** eliminar. **3** extirpar. **4** deponer, destituir. **removal** *n* **1** remoción *f.* **2** extirpación *f.* **3** mudanza *f.* **4** destitución *f.*

remunerate (ri'mju:nəreit) *vt* renumerar.

renaissance (ri'neisəns) *n* renacimiento *m.*

render ('rendə) *vt* **1** dar, rendir. **2** pagar, devolver. **3** hacer. **4** entregar.

rendezvous ('rondivu:) *n invar* cita *f.* *vi* acudir a una cita.

renew (ri'nju:) *vt* **1** renovar. **2** reanudar. **3** *comm* extender. **renewal** *n* **1** renovación *f.* **2** reanudación *f.* **3** prórroga *f.*

renounce (ri'nauns) *vt* renunciar.

renovate ('renəveit) *vt* renovar.

renown (ri'naun) *n* renombre *m.*

rent[1] (rent) *vt* **1** alquilar, arrendar. **2** hacer pagar la renta. *n* alquiler *m.* arrendamiento *f.* renta *f.* **rental** *n* renta *f.* alquiler *m.*

rent[2] (rent) *n* rasgadura *f.*

reorganize (ri:'ɔ:gənaiz) *vt* reorganizar.

rep (rep) *n comm inf* agente, viajante *m.*

repair (ri'pɛə) *n* reparación *f.* arreglo, reparo *m.* *vt* reparar.

repartee (repə'ti:) *n* agudeza *f.*

repatriate (ri'pætrieit) *vt* repatriar.

repay (ri'pei) *vt* volver a pagar, recompensar.

repeal (ri'pi:l) *n* abrogación, anulación *f.* *vt* abrogar, anular.

repeat (ri'pi:t) *vt* repetir.

repel (ri'pel) *vt* repeler, rechazar. **repellent** *adj* repelente.

repent (ri'pent) *vt* arrepentirse de.

repercussion (ri:pə'kʌʃən) *n* repercusión *f.*

repertory ('repətri) *n also* **repertoire** repertorio *m.*

repetition (repə'tiʃən) *n* repetición *f.*

replace (ri'pleis) *vt* reemplazar, substituir. **replacement** *n* reemplazo *m.*

replay (ri:'plei) *vt,vi* **1** volver a jugar. **2** volver a tocar.

replenish (ri'pleniʃ) *vt* rellenar.

replica ('replikə) *n* reproducción, copia, réplica *f.*

reply (ri'plai) *n* respuesta *f.* *vt* responder, contestar.

report (re'pɔ:t) *n* **1** relato *m.* **2** informe *m.* memoria *f.* **3** reportaje *m.* noticia, información *f.* **4** detonación *f.* *vt* **1** relatar, dar cuenta. **2** denunciar. **3** rumorear, propalar. **4** hacer reportaje. **reporter** *n* periodista, reportero *m.*

repose (ri'pouz) *n* reposo, descanso *m.* *vi* reclinarse, tenderse, descansar, reposar.

reposition (ri:pə'ziʃən) *n* reposición *f.*

represent (repri'zent) *vt* representar. **representation** *n* representación *f.* **representative** *adj* representativo. *n* representante, delegado *m.*

repress (ri'pres) *vt* reprimir.

reprieve (ri'pri:v) *n* **1** *law* indulto *m.* **2** alivio *m.* *vt* **1** indultar. **2** aliviar.

reprimand ('reprimɑ:nd) *n* reprimenda *f.* *vt* reprender.

reprint (*v* ri:'print; *n* 'ri:print) *n* reimpresión *f.* *vt* reimprimir.

reprisal (ri'praizəl) *n* represalia *f.*

reproach (ri'proutʃ) *n* **1** reproche *m.* **2** tacha *f.* *vt* reprochar, reprender.

reproduce (ri:prə'dju:s) *vt* reproducir. **reproduction** *n* reproducción *f.*

reptile ('reptail) *n* reptil *m.*

republic (ri'pʌblik) *n* república *f.* **republican** *adj,n* republicano *m.*

repudiate (ri'pju:dieit) *vt* repudiar.

repugnant (ri'pʌgnənt) *adj* repugnante.

repulsion (ri'pʌlʃən) *n* repulsión *f.* **repulsive** *adj* repelente, repulsivo, repugnante.

repute (ri'pju:t) *n* **1** reputación, fama *f.* **2** opinión *f.* **reputable** *adj* de buena reputación. **reputation** *n* reputación, fama *f.*

request (ri'kwest) *n* **1** petición, súplica *f.* **2** demanda *f.* *vt* pedir, solicitar, rogar.

requiem ('rekwiəm) *n* réquiem *m.*

require (ri'kwaiə) *vt* requerir, demandar, necesitar. **requirement** *n* requisito *m.* demanda, exigencia *f.*

rescue ('reskju:) *n* rescate, socorro *m.* *vt* rescatar, socorrer, librar.

research (ri'sə:tʃ) *n* investigación, indagación *f.* *vt* investigar, indagar.

resemble (ri'zembəl) *vt* parecerse a. **resemblance** *n* parecido *m.* semejanza *f.*

resent (ri'zent) *vt* resentirse de, ofenderse por.

reserve (ri'zə:v) *vt* **1** reservar. **2** preservar, conservar. **3** retener. *n* reserva *f.* **reservation** *n* reserva, reservación *f.* **reserved** *adj* **1** reservado. **2** frío, poco efusivo.

reservoir ('rezəvwɑ:) *n* **1** depósito *m.* **2** embalse *m.* presa *f.*

reside (ri'zaid) *vi* residir. **residence** *n* residencia, morada *f.* **resident** *adj,n* residente *m.*

residue ('rezidju:) *n* residuo *m.*

resign (ri'zain) *vt,vi* dimitir, resignar. **resignation** *n* dimisión, renuncia *f.*

resilient (ri'ziliənt) *adj* **1** elástico. **2** resistente. **3**

con poder de adaptarse. **resilience** n 1 elasticidad f. 2 resistencia f.

resin ('rezin) n resina f.

resist (ri'zist) vt resistir. **resistance** n resistencia f.

resolute ('rezəlu:t) adj resuelto, determinado.

resolution (rezə'lu:ʃən) n 1 resolución f. 2 propósito m. 3 decisión f. acuerdo m.

resolve (ri'zɔlv) vt resolver. n 1 resolución f. 2 propósito m.

resonant ('rezənənt) adj resonante.

resort (ri'zɔ:t) n 1 recurso, medio m. 2 lugar de recreo m. vi 1 acudir, frecuentar. 2 acudir, recurrir.

resound (ri'zaund) vi resonar, repercutir.

resource (ri'zɔ:s) n recurso, remedio, medio m. **resourceful** adj ingenioso.

respect (ri'spekt) n respeto m. estima f. vt respetar. **respectable** adj respetable. **respective** adj respectivo.

respite ('respit) n respiro, descanso m. tregua f. prórroga f.

respond (ri'spɔnd) vi responder. **response** n respuesta f. **responsive** adj sensible, que responde.

responsibility (rispɔnsə'biliti) n responsabilidad f. **responsible** adj responsable.

rest[1] (rest) n 1 descanso, reposo m. 2 pausa f. 3 tranquilidad, paz f. **at rest** en reposo. ~vi descansar, reposar.

rest[2] (rest) n resto, restante m.

restaurant ('restərɔnt) n restaurante m.

restless ('restləs) adj 1 inquieto, intranquilo. 2 revoltoso, bullicioso.

restore (ri'stɔ:) vt 1 restaurar. 2 reconstruir. 3 instaurar. 4 restituir, devolver. **restoration** n 1 restauración f. 2 restitución, devolución f. 3 renovación f.

restrain (ri'strein) vt 1 refrenar, cohibir, contener. 2 privar, encerrar. 3 limitar, restringir. **restraint** n 1 freno m. restricción, limitación f. 2 moderación f. dominio m.

restrict (ri'strikt) vt restringir, limitar, contener.

result (ri'zʌlt) n resultado m. consecuencia f. **as a result** por consiguiente, debido a. **result in** terminar en, producir.

resume (ri'zju:m) vt 1 continuar, reasumir. 2 resumir.

résumé ('rezumei) n resumen m.

resurrect (rezə'rekt) vt resucitar.

retail ('ri:teil) n venta al por menor f. vt vender al por menor.

retain (ri'tein) vt retener.

retaliate (ri'tælieit) vi vengarse de.

retard (ri'tɑ:d) vt retardar, retrasar.

reticent ('retisənt) adj reticente.

retina ('retinə) n retina f.

retire (ri'taiə) vi 1 jubilarse. 2 mil retirarse. **retirement** n retiro m.

retort[1] (ri'tɔ:t) n réplica, respuesta aguda f. vi replicar.

retort[2] (ri'tɔ:t) n sci retorta f.

retrace (ri'treis) vt 1 retroceder sobre los pasos. 2 volver a trazar.

retract (ri'trækt) vt 1 revocar, retractar. 2 retraer.

retreat (ri'tri:t) n 1 rel retiro m. 2 refugio m. 3 mil retirada f. vi retirarse.

retrieve (ri'tri:v) vt recobrar, recuperar, salvar.

retrograde ('retrəgreid) adj retrógrado.

retrogress (retrə'gres) vi retroceder. **retrogressive** adj retrógrado.

retrospect ('retrəspekt) n retrospección f. **in retrospect** retrospectivamente.

return (ri'tə:n) n 1 vuelta f. regreso m. 2 comm ganancia f. **in return for** a cambio de. **many happy returns** feliz cumpleaños m invar. **return ticket** billete de ida y vuelta m. ~vt 1 volver, regresar. 2 devolver.

reunite (ri:ju:'nait) vt reunir.

reveal (ri'vi:l) vt revelar. **revelation** n revelación f.

revel ('revəl) vi jaranear. **revel in** deleitarse en or con.

revenge (ri'vendʒ) n venganza f. vt vengar.

revenue ('revənju:) n rentas f pl.

reverberate (ri'və:bəreit) vi reverberar, resonar.

reverence ('revərəns) n reverencia f. vt reverenciar. **reverent** adj reverente.

reverse (ri'və:s) adj opuesto, inverso. n 1 revés m. 2 mot marcha atrás f. 3 contrario m. vt 1 mot poner en marcha atrás. 2 revocar. 3 invertir.

revert (ri'və:t) vi volver a, revertir.

review (ri'vju:) n 1 lit,mil revista f. 2 reseña f. vt 1 repasar, examinar, analizar. 2 (journalism) reseñar. 3 mil pasar revista.

revise (ri'vaiz) vt 1 revisar, volver a mirar. 2 (correct) corregir, modificar.

revive (ri'vaiv) vt reponerse, revivir, resucitar. vi 1 resucitar. 2 reanimar.

revoke (ri'vouk) vt revocar, anular.

revolt (ri'voult) n rebelión f. vi rebelarse. vt dar asco, repugnar. **revolting** adj repugnante, asqueroso, repelente. **revolution** n 1 revolución, sublevación f. 2 vuelta f. giro m.

revolve (ri'vɔlv) vt girar, revolver. **revolver** n revólver m.

revue (ri'vju:) n Th revista f.

revulsion (ri'vʌlʃən) n asco m. repugnancia f.

reward (ri'wɔ:d) n premio, pago m. recompensa f. vt premiar, pagar, recompensar.

rhetoric ('retərik) n retórica f. **rhetorical** adj retórico.

rheumatism ('ru:mətizəm) n reumatismo m.

rhinoceros (rai'nɔsərəs) n rinoceronte m.

rhyme (raim) n rima, poesía f. verso m. vt,vi rimar.

rhythm ('riðəm) n ritmo m.

rib (rib) n 1 anat costilla f. 2 varilla f. vt inf tomar el pelo.

ribbon ('ribən) n cinta f.

rice (rais) n arroz m.

rich (ritʃ) adj 1 rico. 2 lujoso, suntuoso. 3 sabroso, delicioso. 4 fértil.

rickety ('rikiti) adj inseguro, inestable, peligroso.

rid* (rid) vt librar, desembarazar. **get rid of** desembarazarse de.

riddance ('ridns) n libramiento m. **good riddance!** ¡menos mal!

riddle[1] ('ridl) n problema, misterio, acertijo m.

riddle[2] ('ridl) vt cribar.

ride* (raid) n 1 excursión f. paseo a caballo, paseo en coche m. 2 recorrido m. vi 1 montar. 2 viajar, ir.

ridge (ridʒ) n 1 (of mountains) sierra f. 2 arruga f.

ridicule ('ridikju:l) n ridículo m. burla f. vt ridiculizar. **ridiculous** adj ridículo, absurdo, grotesco.

rife (raif) adj muy común.

rifle[1] ('raifəl) n fusil m.

rifle[2] ('raifəl) vt robar, saquear.

rift (rift) n grieta, rendija f.

rig (rig) n naut aparejo m. vt 1 naut aparejar. 2 construir. **rigging** n naut cordaje, aparejo m.

right (rait) adj 1 justo. 2 exacto, preciso. 3 debido. 4 verdadero. 5 ideal. adv 1 bien. 2 exactamente. 3 a la derecha. n 1 derecha f. 2 law derecho m. 3 bien m. n pl derechos m pl. **all right** ¡conforme! ¡está bien! **be right** tener razón. **right angle** n ángulo recto m. **right-hand** adj a la derecha, por la derecha. **right-handed** adj que usa la mano derecha. **right now** ahora mismo. **right of way** n derecho de paso m. **right-wing** adj derechista.

righteous ('raitʃəs) adj honrado, virtuoso, justo.

rigid ('ridʒid) adj rígido, firme.

rigour ('rigə) n rigor m.

rim (rim) n borde, extremo, canto m.

rind (raind) n piel, corteza, cáscara f.

ring[1] (riŋ) n 1 círculo m. anillo m. vt 1 rodear. 2 anillar. **ringleader** n cabecilla f. **ring-road** n carretera de circunvalación f.

ring*[2] (riŋ) n 1 resonancia f. 2 repique, campaneo m. 3 llamada f. vt 1 hacer sonar. 2 repicar.

rink (riŋk) n pista f. patinadero m.

rinse (rins) n 1 aclarado m. 2 reflejos m pl. vt enjuagar, aclarar.

riot ('raiət) n alboroto, tumulto, disturbio m. vi alborotar, rebelarse.

rip (rip) n rasgadura f. rasgón m. vt rasgar.

ripe (raip) adj 1 maduro. 2 listo, dispuesto, preparado. **ripen** vt,vi madurar.

ripple ('ripəl) n onda, ola f. rizo m. vi rizarse.

rise* (raiz) n 1 subida, elevación f. 2 aumento m. 3 salida f. vi 1 levantarse. 2 subir, elevar. 3 aumentar.

risk (risk) n riesgo m. vt arriesgar.

rite (rait) n rito m. **last rites** exequias f pl.

ritual ('ritjuəl) adj,n ritual m.

rival ('raivəl) adj,n rival m. vt competir con, rivalizar con.

river ('rivə) n río m. **riverside** adj ribereño. n orilla, margen, ribera f.

rivet ('rivit) n remache, roblón m. vt remachar, clavar.

road (roud) n camino m. carretera, calle, calzada f.

roam (roum) vt vagar por, errar por. vi vagar, errar.

roar (rɔ:) n rugido, bramido m. vi rugir, bramar.

roast (roust) n carne asada f. adj asado. vt asar.

rob (rɔb) vt robar, hurtar.

robe (roub) n 1 manto m. vestidura, túnica f. 2 rel hábito m. sotana f.

robin ('rɔbin) n petirrojo m.

robot ('roubɔt) n autómata, robot m.

robust (rou'bʌst) adj robusto.

rock[1] (rɔk) n roca, piedra, peña f.

rock[2] (rɔk) vi 1 bambolear, tambalear. 2 mecerse, balancearse. **rocker** n 1 tech balancín m. 2 mecedora f. **rocking-chair** n mecedora f. **rocking-horse** n caballo mecedor, caballo de balancín m.

rocket ('rɔkit) n cohete m.

rod (rɔd) n 1 palo m. vara, varilla f. 2 tech barra f. **fishing rod** n caña f.

rode (roud) v see **ride.**

rodent ('roudņt) n roedor m.

roe (rou) n 1 (hard) hueva f. 2 (soft) lecha f.

roe deer n corzo m.

rogue (roug) n pillo, gamberro, bribón, pícaro m.

role (roul) n papel m.

roll (roul) n 1 panecillo, bollo m. 2 lista f. catálogo m. 3 bamboleo m. 4 redoble m. vt 1 hacer rodar, dar vueltas. 2 liar. 3 tambalear. **roller** n 1 tech rodillo m. 2 rueda, ruedecilla f. 3 naut ola grande. **roller-skate** n patín de ruedas m. **rolling pin** n rodillo m.

Roman Catholic adj,n católico romano m.

romance (rə'mæns) adj romance. n 1 lit novela sentimental f. 2 amores m pl. **romantic** adj romántico, sentimental. n romántico m.

Rome (roum) n Roma f. **Roman** adj,n romano m.

romp (romp) n juego, retozo m. vi 1 retozar, hacer cabriolas. 2 jugar, juguetear.

roof (ru:f) n 1 techa, tejado m. techumbre f. 2 anat paladar m. 3 hogar m. morada f. vt techar.

rook (ruk) n 1 zool grajo m. 2 game torre f. vt engañar, defraudar.

room (ru:m) n 1 cuarto m. habitación, pieza f. 2 lugar, sitio m. n pl alojamiento m. vi alojarse. **roomy** adj espacioso, amplio.

roost (ru:st) n percha f. gallinero m. vi descansar en la percha.

root[1] (ru:t) n 1 bot,math raíz f. 2 origen m. base f. **root out** vt arrancar, desarraigar. **take root** vi bot echar raíces.

root[2] (ru:t) vi hocicar.

rope (roup) n cuerda, soga f. cordel m.

rosary ('rouzəri) n rosario m.

rose[1] (rouz) n bot rosa f. **rosebush** n rosal m. **rose garden** n rosaleda f. **rosy** adj 1 rosado, color de rosa. 2 inf prometedor, alegre.

rose[2] (rouz) v see **rise**.

rosemary ('rouzməri) n romero m.

rot (rot) n 1 podredumbre f. 2 decadencia, ruina f. 3 inf disparate m. tontería f. vt pudrir, descomponer. **rotten** adj 1 podrido, descompuesto, fétido, corrompido. 2 vil, desagradable, fatal.

rota ('routə) n lista f. **rotary** adj rotativo. **rotate** vt 1 hacer girar, dar vueltas a.

rouge (ru:ʒ) n carmín m.

rough (rʌf) adj 1 aspéro, escabroso. 2 brutal, abrupto. 3 tempestuoso, violento. 4 borroso,

aproximado. n 1 bruto m. 2 aspereza, dureza f.

round (raund) adj 1 redondo, circular. 2 rotundo. adv alrededor. n 1 esfera f. círculo m. 2 circuito m. vuelta f. 3 rodaja f. 4 tiro m. 5 ronda f. prep alrededor de. vt doblar, circundar, rodear. **roundabout** adj indirecto. n 1 tiovivo m. 2 mot redondel m.

rouse (rauz) vt 1 despertar. 2 excitar, estimular, provocar. 3 animar.

route (ru:t) n ruta, vía f.

routine (ru:'ti:n) adj rutinario, acostumbrado. n rutina, costumbre f.

rove (rouv) vt errar por, vagar por.

row[1] (rou) n fila, línea, hilera f. **in a row** seguido.

row[2] (rou) vt,vi remar.

row[3] (rau) n 1 alboroto, ruido, tumulto, estrépito m. 2 disputa, querella, riña f. vi reñir, querellar, pelear.

rowdy ('raudi) adj ruidoso, alborotador, estrepitoso.

royal ('rɔiəl) adj 1 real. 2 espléndido, magnífico. **royalty** n 1 realeza f. 2 familia real f. 3 pl derechos m pl.

rub (rʌb) n frotamiento, roce m. vt frotar, estregar, rozar, raer.

rubber ('rʌbə) n 1 goma f. caucho m. 2 goma de borrar. f. 3 game partida f. adj de goma, de caucho. **rubber band** n liga de goma, gomita f.

rubbish ('rʌbiʃ) n 1 basura, suciedad f. 2 inf tontería, necedad f. disparate m.

rubble ('rʌbəl) n escombros m pl.

ruby ('ru:bi) n rubí m.

rucksack ('rʌksæk) n mochila f. morral m.

rudder ('rʌdə) n naut timón, gobernalle m.

rude (ru:d) adj 1 grosero, descortés, insolente. 2 rudo, inculto.

rudiment ('ru:dimənt) n rudimento m.

rueful ('ru:fəl) adj triste, afligido, melancólico.

ruff (rʌf) n gorguera f.

ruffian ('rʌfiən) n gamberro, pícaro, pillo m.

ruffle ('rʌfəl) n volante m. vt 1 arrugar. 2 perturbar, agitar.

rug (rʌg) n alfombra f.

rugby ('rʌgbi) n rugby m.

rugged ('rʌgid) adj 1 robusto, vigoroso. 2 duro, tosco. 3 fuerte. 4 áspero, escabroso.

ruin ('ru:in) n ruina f. vt arruinar, destrozar.

rule (ru:l) n 1 gobierno, mando m. 2 regla, ley f. 3 costumbre f. hábito m. vt 1 gobernar, mandar, regir. 2 math reglar, rayar. **ruler** n 1 monarca, soberano, gobernante m. 2 *math* regla f.

rum (rʌm) n ron m.

Rumania (ruːˈmeiniə) n Rumania f. **Rumanian** *adj,n* rumano. **Rumanian** (language) n rumano m.

rumble (ˈrʌmbəl) n retumbo, rumor, trueno m. *vi* retumbar, tronar.

rummage (ˈrʌmidʒ) *vi* **rummage in** revolver en. **rummage sale** n venta de prendas usadas f.

rumour (ˈruːmə) n rumor m.

rump (rʌmp) n 1 *anat* trasero, culo m. nalgas f pl. 2 *cul* cuarto trasero m. 3 anca f.

run* (rʌn) n 1 carrera f. 2 serie, sucesión f. *vt* 1 correr. 2 dirigir, gobernar. **run away** corretear. **runner** n 1 corredor, competidor m. 2 patín m. 3 corredera f. **runner bean** n judía f. frijol m. **runner-up** n subcampeón m. **running** *adj* 1 corriente, corredor. 2 *med* supurante. n 1 funcionamiento m. marcha f. 2 carrera, corrida f. 3 dirección f. gobierno m. **runway** n *aviat* pista de aterrizaje f.

rung[1] (rʌŋ) v see **ring**[2].

rung[2] (rʌŋ) n escalón, peldaño m.

rupture (ˈrʌptʃə) n ruptura f. *vt* causar una hernia en, quebrar, romper.

rural (ˈruərəl) *adj* rural, campestre, rústico.

rush[1] (rʌʃ) *adj* urgente, apremiante. n prisa f. apuro m. *vi* darse prisa, apresurarse, precipitarse, apurar. *vt* *mil* asaltar, atacar de repente.

rush[2] (rʌʃ) n *bot* junco m.

Russia (ˈrʌʃə) n Rusia f. **Russian** *adj,n* ruso. **Russian** (language) n ruso m.

rust (rʌst) n herrumbre, oxidación f. *vi* oxidarse. **rusty** *adj* herrumbroso, oxidado.

rustic (ˈrʌstik) *adj* 1 rústico, campesino, campestre, pastoral. 2 palurdo, toso, rudo. n rústico, palurdo m.

rustle (ˈrʌsəl) n murmullo, susurro m. *vi* murmurar, susurrar.

rut (rʌt) n 1 bache, carril, surco m. rodera f. 2 rutina f. 3 *zool* celo m. **be in a rut** de esclavo ser la rutina.

ruthless (ˈruːθləs) *adj* despiadado, desalmado.

rye (rai) n centeno m.

S

Sabbath (ˈsæbəθ) n 1 sábado m. 2 domingo m.
sable (ˈseibəl) n *zool* cebellina.
sabotage (ˈsæbətɑːʒ) n sabotaje m. *vt* sabotear.

sabre (ˈseibə) n sable m.
saccharin (ˈsækərin) n sacarina f. *adj* sacarino.
sachet (ˈsæʃei) n bolsita f. saquito m.
sack[1] (sæk) n 1 costal, saco, zurrón m. 2 *inf* despedida f. *vt* *inf* despedir.
sack[2] (sæk) n saqueo m. *vt* saquear.
sacrament (ˈsækrəmənt) n sacramento m.
sacred (ˈseikrid) *adj* sagrado, santo.
sacrifice (ˈsækrifais) n sacrificio m. *vt,vi* sacrificar.
sacrilege (ˈsækrilidʒ) n sacrilegio m.
sad (sæd) *adj* triste, sombrío, melancólico. **sadden** *vt* entristecer.
saddle (ˈsædl) n 1 silla de montar f. 2 sillín m. 3 (of meat) cuarto trasero m. *vt* ensillar.
sadism (ˈseidizəm) n sadismo m.
safari (səˈfɑːri) n safari m.
safe (seif) *adj* 1 seguro. 2 salvo. 3 cierto. n caja fuerte f. **safely** *adv* con seguridad. **safeguard** n salvaguardia f. *vt* salvaguardar. **safety** n seguridad f. **safety belt** n cinturón de seguridad m. **safety pin** n imperdible m.
saffron (ˈsæfrən) n *bot* azafrán m.
sag (sæg) *vi* 1 ceder. 2 combarse. n comba f.
saga (ˈsɑːgə) n saga f.
sage[1] (seidʒ) *adj,n* sabio.
sage[2] (seidʒ) n *bot* salvia f.
Sagittarius (sædʒiˈtɛəriəs) n Sagitario m.
sago (ˈseigou) n sagú m.
said (sed) v see **say**.
sail (seil) n 1 *naut* vela f. 2 aspa f. *vt* *naut* gobernar. *vi* *naut* 1 navegar. 2 flotar, volar. **sailor** n marinero, marino m.
saint (seint) n santo m.
sake (seik) n causa f. motivo m. **for the sake of** por motivo de, por.
salad (ˈsæləd) n ensalada f. **salad dressing** n 1 aliño m. 2 mayonesa f.
salami (səˈlɑːmi) n salchichón m.
salary (ˈsæləri) n salario, sueldo m.
sale (seil) n 1 venta f. 2 liquidación f. saldo m. **for sale** se vende. **on sale** de venta. **salesman** n vendedor m. **salesmanship** n arte de vender m. **travelling salesman** n viajante m.
saliva (səˈlaivə) n saliva f. **salivate** *vi* salivar.
sallow (ˈsælou) *adj* amarillento, cetrino.
salmon (ˈsæmən) n *invar* salmón m.
salon (ˈsælɔn) n salón m.
saloon (səˈluːn) n 1 salón m. 2 *mot* turismo m.
salt (sɔːlt) n 1 sal f. **salt-cellar** n salero m. **salty** *adj* salado.
salute (səˈluːt) n saludo m. *vt* saludar.

salvage ('sælvidʒ) n salvamento m. vt salvar.
salvation (sæl'veiʃən) n salvación f.
salve (sælv) n ungüento m.
same (seim) adj 1 mismo, idéntico, igual. 2 monótono. **all the same** a pesar de todo.
sample ('sɑːmpəl) n muestra f. vt probar, ensayar.
sanatorium (sænə'tɔːriəm) n sanatorio m.
sanction ('sæŋkʃən) n 1 sanción f. 2 autorización f. vt 1 sancionar. 2 autorizar.
sanctity ('sæŋktiti) n santidad f.
sanctuary ('sæŋktʃuəri) n santuario m.
sand (sænd) n arena f. **sandpaper** n papel de lija m. vt lijar. **sandpit** n arenal, hoyo de arena m.
sandal ('sændl) n sandalia, alpargata f.
sandwich ('sænwidʒ) n bocadillo, sándwich m. vt intercalar.
sane (sein) adj 1 cuerdo, juicioso. 2 prudente. **sanity** n cordura, sensatez f.
sang (sæŋ) v see **sing.**
sanitary ('sænitri) adj higiénico, sanitario. **sanitary towel** n compresa higiénica f. **sanitation** n sanidad f.
sank (sæŋk) v see **sink.**
sap (sæp) n bot savia f. vt agotar, desgastar.
sapphire ('sæfaiə) n zafiro m.
sarcasm ('sɑːkæzəm) n sarcasmo m. **sarcastic** adj sarcástico.
sardine (sɑː'diːn) n sardina f.
sardonic (sɑː'dɔnik) adj sardónico.
sash[1] (sæʃ) n banda, faja f.
sash[2] (sæʃ) n marco corredizo de ventana m.
sat (sæt) v see **sit.**
Satan (seitn) n Satán m. **satanic** adj satánico.
satchel ('sætʃəl) n cartera f. cartapacio m.
satellite ('sætəlait) n satélite m.
satin ('sætin) n raso m.
satire ('sætaiə) n sátira f. **satirical** adj satírico. **satirize** vt satirizar.
satisfy ('sætisfai) vt satisfacer. **satisfactory** adj satisfactorio. **satisfaction** n satisfacción f.
saturate ('sætʃəreit) vt saturar.
Saturday ('sætədi) n sábado m.
Saturn ('sætən) n Saturno m.
sauce (sɔːs) n salsa f. **saucepan** n cacerola f. **saucer** n platillo m. **saucy** adj impertinente, fresco.
Saudi Arabia ('saudi) n Arabia Saudita, Arabia Saudí f.
sauerkraut ('sauəkraut) n chucruta f.
sauna ('sɔːnə) n sauna f.

saunter ('sɔːntə) vi pasearse lentamente. n paseo lento m.
sausage ('sɔsidʒ) n salchicha f. embutido m.
savage ('sævidʒ) adj,n salvaje. vt atacar, embestir.
save[1] (seiv) vt 1 salvar. 2 ahorrar, economizar. 3 guardar.
save[2] (seiv) prep, conj salvo, excepto.
saviour ('seiviə) n salvador m.
savoury ('seivəri) adj 1 sabroso. 2 no dulce, salado.
saw[*1] (sɔː) n sierra f. vt 1 serrar, aserrar. 2 talar. **sawdust** n serrín m.
saw[2] (sɔː) v see **see**[1].
Saxon ('sæksən) n,adj sajón m.
saxophone ('sæksəfoun) n saxofón m.
say[*] (sei) vt decir, afirmar. **saying** n dicho, refrán m.
scab (skæb) n costra f.
scaffold ('skæfəld) n cadalso m. **scaffolding** n andamio m.
scald (skɔːld) vt escaldar.
scale[1] (skeil) n escama f.
scale[2] (skeil) n 1 escala f. 2 mus pentagrama m. vt escalar.
scale[3] (skeil) n balanza f.
scallop ('skɔləp) n 1 zool venera f. 2 festón m.
scalp (skælp) n cuero cabelludo m.
scalpel ('skælpəl) n 1 escalpelo m. 2 bisturí m.
scampi ('skæmpi) n gamba grande f.
scan (skæn) vt examinar, medir.
scandal ('skændl) n escándalo m. **scandalous** adj escandaloso, vergonzoso.
Scandinavia (skændi'neivia) n Escandinavia f. **Scandinavian** adj,n escandinavo.
scant (skænt) adj escaso.
scapegoat ('skeipgout) n víctima f.
scar (skɑː) n cicatriz, señal f. vt señalar, marcar.
scarce (skɛəs) adj escaso. **scarcity** n escasez f. **scarcely** adv escasamente, apenas.
scare (skɛə) vt 1 asustar, atemorizar. 2 ahuyentar. n susto m. **scarecrow** n espantapájaros m invar.
scarf (skɑːf) n, pl **scarfs** or **scarves** 1 bufanda f. 2 pañuelo de cabeza m.
scarlet ('skɑːlit) n escarlata, grana f. adj de color escarlata, grana. **scarlet fever** n escarlatina f.
scathing ('skeiðiŋ) adj mordaz.
scatter ('skætə) vt dispersar, esparcir. **scatterbrain** n cabeza loca f.
scavenge ('skævindʒ) vi recoger la basura.
scene (siːn) n 1 Th escena f. 2 paisaje m

scenery ('si:nəri) n 1 paisaje m. 2 Th decorado m.

scent (sent) n 1 perfume m. 2 rastro m.

sceptic ('skeptik) adj,n escéptico m. **scepticism** n escepticismo m.

sceptre ('septə) n cetro m.

schedule ('ʃedju:l) n 1 lista f. 2 horario m. vt fijar la hora.

scheme (ski:m) n esquema, plan m. vt planear, proyectar.

schizophrenia (skitsou'fri:niə) n esquizofrenia f. **schizophrenic** n esquizofrénico m.

scholar ('skɔlə) n 1 colegial, escolar m. 2 sabio m. **scholarship** n 1 beca f. 2 erudición f.

scholastic (skə'læstik) adj escolástico.

school[1] (sku:l) n colegio m. escuela f. **schoolboy** n colegial m. **schoolmaster** n profesor, maestro m.

school[2] (sku:l) n escuela f. grupo m.

schooner ('sku:nə) n goleta f.

science ('saiəns) n ciencia f. **scientist** n científico m. **science fiction** n ciencia ficción f. **scientific** adj científico.

scissors ('sizəz) n pl tijeras f pl.

scoff[1] (skɔf) vi mofarse de.

scoff[2] (skɔf) inf vt engullir. n comida f.

scold (skould) vt reñir, regañar.

scoop (sku:p) vt 1 recoger. 2 sacar, excavar. n pala, cuchara f.

scooter ('sku:tə) n 1 escuter, moto m. 2 patinete m.

scope (skoup) n extensión f. alcance m.

scorch (skɔ:tʃ) vt chamuscar, abrasar.

score (skɔ:) vt 1 sport marcar. 2 rayar. n 1 mus partitura f. 2 sport tanteo m. 3 veintena f. **scoreboard** n tanteador m.

scorn (skɔ:n) vt desdeñar. n desdén, desprecio m.

Scorpio ('skɔ:piou) n Escorpión m.

scorpion ('skɔ:piən) n escorpión, alacrán m.

Scotland ('skɔtlənd) n Escocia f. **Scot** n escocés m. **Scotch** adj escocés. n wisky m. **Scottish** adj escocés.

scoundrel ('skaundrəl) n canalla m. sinvergüenza m.

scour[1] ('skauə) vt limpiar, fregar.

scour[2] ('skauə) vt buscar, registrar.

scout (skaut) n explorador, adelantado m. vt explorar, reconocer.

scowl (skaul) vi fruncir el ceño. n mueca f. ceño m.

scramble ('skræmbəl) vt revolver. **scrambled eggs** n pl huevos revueltos m pl.

scrap[1] (skræp) n 1 resto m. 2 pizca f. vt desechar. **scrap iron** n hierro viejo m. chatarra f.

scrap[2] (skræp) inf n riña. vi riñar.

scrape (skreip) vt 1 raspar. 2 rebañar.

scratch (skrætʃ) vt rascar, arañar. n rasguño, arañazo m.

scrawl (skrɔ:l) vt garabatear. n garabato m.

scream (skri:m) vi chillar. n chillido m.

screech (skri:tʃ) vi 1 chillar. 2 chirriar.

screen (skri:n) n 1 biombo m. 2 pantalla f. vt 1 ocultar. 2 examinar. 3 proyectar.

screw (skru:) n tornillo m. vt atornillar, fijar. **screwdriver** n destornillador m.

scribble ('skribəl) vt garabatear, emborronar. n garabato m.

script (skript) n 1 letra f. 2 guión m.

Scripture ('skriptʃə) n Sagrada Escritura f.

scroll (skroul) n rollo de pergamino m.

scrounge (skraundʒ) vt gorronear.

scrub[1] (skrʌb) vt fregar, estregar. **scrubbing brush** n estregadera f.

scrub[2] (skrʌb) n matorral m.

scruffy ('skrʌfi) adj desaliñado.

scruple ('skru:pəl) n escrúpulo m. **scrupulous** adj escrupuloso.

scrutinize ('skru:tinaiz) vt escudriñar. **scrutiny** n escrutinio, examen m.

scuffle ('skʌfəl) n riña, pelea f. vi reñir, pelearse.

scullery ('skʌləri) n fregadero, office m.

sculpt (skʌlpt) vt esculpir. **sculptor** n escultor m. **sculpture** n escultura f.

scum (skʌm) n 1 espuma f. 2 canalla f. 3 heces m pl.

scythe (saið) n guadaña f. vt guadañar.

sea (si:) n mar m,f.

seabed ('si:bed) n fondo del mar m.

seafaring ('si:fɛəriŋ) adj marinero.

seafront ('si:frʌnt) n paseo marítimo m.

seagull ('si:gʌl) n gaviota f.

seahorse ('si:hɔ:s) n caballito de mar m.

seal[1] (si:l) n sello m. vt 1 sellar. 2 cerrar. 3 lacrar. **sealing-wax** n lacre m.

seal[2] (si:l) n zool foca f. **sealskin** n piel de foca f.

sea-level n nivel del mar m.

sea-lion n león marino m.

seam (si:m) n 1 dom costura f. 2 junta f. 3 veta, vena f. vt coser.

seaman ('si:mən) n marinero m. **seamanship** n náutica, marinería f.

search (sə:tʃ) vt 1 buscar. 2 registrar. 3 examinar. n 1 búsqueda f. 2 registro m. **searchlight** n proyector m.

seashore ('si:ʃɔ:) n costa del mar, orilla del mar f.

seasick ('si:sik) adj mareado. **become seasick** marearse.

seaside ('si:said) n playa del mar, orilla del mar f.

season ('si:zən) n 1 estación f. 2 temporada f. vt 1 cul sazonar. 2 curar. **seasonable** adj propio de la estación. **seasoning** n condimento m. **season ticket** n abono m.

seat (si:t) n 1 asiento m. 2 pol escaño m. 3 Th localidad f. **seat-belt** n cinturón de seguridad m.

sea water n agua de mar f.

seaweed ('si:wi:d) n alga marina f.

secluded (si'klu:did) adj aislado, retirado.

second[1] ('sekənd) adj,n segundo m. **second best** n sustituto m. adj de segunda categoría. **second class** n segunda clase f. **secondhand** adj de segunda mano. **second-rate** adj de baja calidad. ~vt apoyar. **secondary** adj secundario. **secondary school** n instituto de enseñanza media m.

second[2] ('sekənd) n segundo m.

secret ('si:krət) adj,n secreto m. **secret agent** n agente secreto m. **secrecy** n secreto. **secretive** adj reservado.

secretary ('sekrətri) n secretario m.

secrete (si'kri:t) vt 1 esconder. 2 secretar.

sect (sekt) n secta f. **sectarian** adj sectario.

section ('sekʃən) n sección f.

sector ('sektə) n sector m.

secular ('sekjulə) adj invar secular.

secure (si'kjuə) vt 1 conseguir. 2 asegurar. adj seguro. **security** n 1 seguridad f. 2 comm fianza f. 3 pl comm valores m pl.

sedate (si'deit) adj sosegado. **sedation** n sedación f. tratamiento con calmantes m. **sedative** n,adj calmante, sedante m.

sediment ('sedimənt) n sedimento m. **sedimentary** adj sedimentario.

seduce (si'dju:s) vt seducir. **seduction** n seducción f. **seductive** adj seductor.

see[*][1] (si:) vt ver, percibir. **see about** encargarse de. **see to** atender a.

see[2] (si:) n rel sede f.

seed (si:d) n semilla f. **seedling** n planta de semillero f. **seedy** adj inf 1 ojeroso. 2 asqueroso.

seek[*] (si:k) vt buscar. **seek to** intentar.

seem (si:m) vi parecer.

seen (si:n) v see **see**[1].

seep (si:p) vi filtrarse.

seesaw ('si:sɔ:) n columpio de balancín m. vi columpiarse.

seethe (si:ð) vi hervir.

segment ('segmənt) n segmento m.

segregate ('segrigeit) vt segregar. **segregation** n segregación f.

seize (si:z) vt 1 coger. 2 apoderarse de.

seldom ('seldəm) adv raramente.

select (si'lekt) vt seleccionar. adj selecto. **selection** n selección f. **selective** adj selectivo.

self (self) n, pl **selves** uno mismo, una misma. pron 1 se. 2 sí mismo.

self-assured adj seguro de sí mismo.

self-aware adj consciente de sí mismo.

self-centred adj egocéntrico.

self-confident adj seguro de sí mismo.

self-conscious adj cohibido.

self-contained adj independiente.

self-defence n defensa propia f.

self-discipline n autodisciplina f.

self-employed adj que trabaja por cuenta propia.

self-expression n autoexpresión f.

self-indulgent adj inmoderado.

self-interest n egoísmo m.

selfish ('selfiʃ) adj egoísta.

self-pity n compasión de sí mismo f.

self-portrait n autorretrato m.

self-respect n dignidad f.

self-righteous adj santurrón.

self-sacrifice n abnegación f.

selfsame ('selfseim) adj mismísimo.

self-satisfied adj pagado de sí mismo.

self-service n autoservicio m.

self-sufficient adj independiente.

self-will n obstinación f.

sell[*] (sel) vt vender.

Sellotape ('seləteip) n Tdmk cinta adhesiva f.

semantic (si'mæntik) adj semántico. **semantics** n semántica f.

semaphore ('seməfɔ:) n semáforo m.

semibreve ('semibri:v) n semibreve f.

semicircle ('semisə:kəl) n semicírculo m.

semicolon (semi'koulən) n punto y coma m.

semidetached (semidi'tætʃt) adj semiseparado. **semidetached house** n casa parcialmente separada f.

semifinal (semi'fainl) n semifinal f.

seminar ('seminɑ:) n seminario m. **seminary** n seminario m.

271

semiprecious (semi'preʃəs) adj semiprecioso.

semiquaver (semi'kweivə) n semicorchea f.

semivowel ('semivauəl) n semivocal f.

semolina (semə'li:nə) n sémola f.

senate ('senət) n senado m.

send* (send) vt 1 enviar. 2 despachar. 3 lanzar.

senile ('si:nail) adj senil. **senility** n debilidad senil f.

senior ('si:niə) adj mayor, más antiguo.

sensation (sen'seiʃən) n sensación f. **sensational** adj sensacional.

sense (sens) n 1 sentido m. 2 juicio m.

sensible ('sensəbəl) adj sensato. **sensibility** n sensibilidad f.

sensitive ('sensitiv) adj sensible, impresionable. **sensitivity** n lo impresionable. *neu.* delicadeza f.

sensual ('senʃuəl) adj sensual. **sensuality** n sensualidad f.

sensuous ('senʃuəs) adj sensual.

sentence ('sentəns) n 1 *gram* oración f. 2 *law* sentencia, condena f. vt sentenciar.

sentiment ('sentimənt) n sentimiento m. **sentimental** adj sentimental.

sentry ('sentri) n centinela m.

separate (adj 'seprit; v 'sepəreit) adj separado. vt separar. **separation** n separación f.

September (sep'tembə) n septiembre m.

septet (sep'tet) n septeto m.

septic ('septik) adj séptico.

sequel ('si:kwəl) n 1 *lit* continuación f. 2 resultado m.

sequence ('si:kwəns) n 1 orden m. 2 secuencia f.

sequin ('si:kwin) n lentejuela f.

serenade (serə'neid) n serenata f.

serene (si'ri:n) adj sereno. **serenity** n serenidad f.

serf (sə:f) n siervo m.

sergeant ('sɑ:dʒənt) n sargento m. **sergeant major** n sargento major m.

serial ('siəriəl) adj consecutivo. n serial m. **serial number** n número de serie m. **serialize** vt convertir en serial.

series ('siəri:z) n invar serie f.

serious ('siəriəs) adj serio. **seriousness** n seriedad f.

sermon ('sə:mən) n sermón m.

serpent ('sə:pənt) n sierpe, serpiente f.

serve (sə:v) vt servir. vi *sport* sacar. **servant** n sirviente, criado m.

service ('sə:vis) n servicio m. **service station** n estación de servicio f.

serviette (sə:vi'et) n servilleta f.

servile ('sə:vail) adj servil.

session ('seʃən) n sesión f.

set* (set) n 1 juego m. 2 grupo m. 3 colección f. vt colocar, poner. adj 1 resuelto. 2 rígido. **setback** n contratiempo m. **setting** n 1 alrededores m pl. 2 puesta f.

settee (se'ti·) n sofá m.

settle ('setl) vt 1 arreglar. 2 ajustar. 3 calmar. **settlement** n 1 colonia f. 2 convenio m.

seven ('sevən) n,adj siete m. **seventh** n,adj séptimo m.

seventeen (sevən'ti:n) n,adj diecisiete m. **seventeenth** adj decimoséptimo.

seventy ('sevənti) n,adj setenta m. **seventieth** adj septuagésimo.

several ('sevrəl) adj varios pl.

severe (si'viə) adj severo. **severity** n severidad f.

Seville (sə'vil) n Sevilla f.

sew* (sou) vt coser. **sewing machine** n máquina de coser f.

sewage ('su:idʒ) n aguas residuales f pl.

sewer ('su:ə) n alcantarilla f. **sewerage** n alcantarillado m.

sex (seks) n sexo m. **sexual** adj sexual. **sexuality** n sexualidad f. **sexy** adj sensual.

sextet (seks'tet) n sexteto m.

shabby ('ʃæbi) adj raído, gastado.

shack (ʃæk) n choza, chabola f.

shade (ʃeid) n 1 sombra f. 2 tonalidad f. vt dar sombra a.

shadow ('ʃædou) n sombra f. vt seguir. **shadow cabinet** n gabinete de oposición m.

shaft (ʃɑ:ft) n 1 rayo m. 2 *mot* eje m. 3 pozo m.

shaggy ('ʃægi) adj velludo, peludo.

shake* (ʃeik) vt sacudir, agitar. n sacudida f. meneo m. **shake hands** estrecharse la mano.

shall* (ʃəl; *stressed* ʃæl) v aux used in forming the future.

shallot (ʃə'lɔt) n chalote m.

shallow ('ʃælou) adj poco profundo, vadoso.

sham (ʃæm) n,vi fingir. n engaño m. adj falso.

shame (ʃeim) n vergüenza f. vt avergonzar. **shameless** adj descarado. **shamefaced** adj avergonzado.

shampoo (ʃæm'pu:) n champú m. vi lavarse la cabeza.

shamrock ('ʃæmrɔk) n trébol m.

shandy ('ʃændi) n bebida de cerveza mezclada con limonada f.

shanty[1] ('ʃænti) n choza f.

shanty[2] ('ʃænti) n *naut* saloma f.

shape (ʃeip) vt formar. n forma f. **take shape** tomar forma.

share (ʃɛə) vt compartir. **share out** repartir. ~n 1 parte f. 2 comm acción f. **shareholder** n accionista f.

shark (ʃɑ:k) n 1 tiburón m. 2 inf estafador m.

sharp (ʃɑ:p) adj 1 agudo. 2 afilado. 3 definido. 4 mus sostenido. **sharp-sighted** adj de vista aguda or penetrante. **sharpen** vt afilar.

shatter ('ʃætə) vt estrellar, romper.

shave (ʃeiv) vt afeitar. n afeitado m. **shavings** n pl virutas f pl.

shawl (ʃɔ:l) n mantón m.

she (ʃi:) pron 3rd pers s ella f.

sheaf (ʃi:f) n, pl **sheaves** 1 bot gavilla f. 2 haz m.

shear (ʃiə) vt 1 cortar. 2 esquilar.

sheath (ʃi:θ) n vaina, funda f. **sheathe** vt envainar, enfundar.

shed[1] (ʃed) n 1 cobertizo m. 2 nave f.

shed[2] (ʃed) vt 1 verter. 2 mudarse de.

sheen (ʃi:n) n brillo m.

sheep (ʃi:p) n invar oveja f. **sheepish** adj tímido. **sheepdog** n perro pastor m. **sheepskin** n zamarra f.

sheer[1] (ʃiə) adj diáfano, fino.

sheer[2] (ʃiə) vi desviarse. adv completamente.

sheet (ʃi:t) n 1 dom sábana f. 2 lámina f.

sheikh (ʃeik) n jeque m.

shelf (ʃelf) n, pl **shelves** 1 estante m. 2 geog banco m.

shell (ʃel) n 1 zool concha f. 2 mil granada f. projectil m. 3 bot cáscara f. vt 1 desvainar, descascarar. 2 mil bombardear. **shellfish** n mariscos m pl.

shelter ('ʃeltə) n refugio m. vt proteger, abrigar.

shelve (ʃelv) vt aplazar.

shepherd ('ʃepəd) n pastor m.

sherbet ('ʃə:bət) n sorbete m.

sheriff ('ʃerif) n sheriff m.

sherry ('ʃeri) n jerez m.

shield (ʃi:ld) n escudo m. vt proteger, escudar.

shift (ʃift) vt cambiar. n 1 cambio m. 2 turno m. **shifty** adj furtivo, sospecho.

shilling ('ʃiliŋ) n chelín m.

shimmer ('ʃimə) vi rielar. n resplandor, reflejo m.

shin (ʃin) n anat espinilla f.

shine (ʃain) vi brillar. n brillo m.

ship (ʃip) n buque, barco m. vt transportar. **shipbuilding** n construcción naval f. **shipment** n 1 envío m. 2 transporte m. **shipshape** adj en buen orden, en buena forma. **shipwreck** n naufragio m. **shipyard** n astillero m.

shirk (ʃə:k) vt eludir. **shirker** n gandul m.

shirt (ʃə:t) n camisa f.

shiver ('ʃivə) vi 1 tiritar. 2 temblar. n 1 tiritón m. 2 temblor m.

shock[1] (ʃɔk) n choque, sobresalto m. vt chocar, sobresaltar. **shocking** adj chocante. **shock absorber** n amortiguador m.

shock[2] (ʃɔk) n (of hair) greña f.

shoddy ('ʃɔdi) adj de pésima calidad.

shoe[*] (ʃu:) n 1 zapato m. 2 herradura f. vt 1 calzar. 2 herrar. **shoe-shop** n zapatería f. **shoelace** n cordón m.

shone (ʃɔn) v see **shine.**

shook (ʃuk) v see **shake.**

shoot (ʃu:t) n 1 bot brote, renuevo m. 2 sport partida de caza f. vi 1 tirar, disparar. 2 fusilar. vi lanzarse.

shop (ʃɔp) n 1 tienda f. 2 taller m. vi ir de compras. **shop assistant** n dependiente m. dependienta f. **shop floor** n taller m. **shopkeeper** n tendero m. **shoplifter** n mechera f. ratero m. **shopping** n compras f pl. **shopwindow** n escaparate m.

shore[1] (ʃɔ:) n orilla, ribesa f.

shore[2] (ʃɔ:) vt apuntalar. **shore up** sostener.

shorn (ʃɔ:n) v see **shear.**

short (ʃɔ:t) adj 1 corto. 2 brusco. **shorten** vt acortar.

shortage ('ʃɔ:tidʒ) n escasez f.

shortcoming ('ʃɔ:tkʌmiŋ) n defecto m.

shorthand ('ʃɔ:thænd) n taquigrafía f.

short-handed adv falto de personal.

shortlived ('ʃɔ:tlivd) adj efímero.

short-sighted adj miope.

short-tempered adj enojadizo.

short-term adj a corto plazo.

short-wave n onda corta f.

shot[1] (ʃɔt) n 1 disparo m. 2 sport tiro m. **shotgun** n escopeta f.

shot[2] (ʃɔt) v see **shoot.**

should (ʃəd; stressed ʃud) v aux see **shall.**

shoulder ('ʃouldə) n 1 hombro m. 2 geog lomo m. vt 1 llevar al hombro. 2 cargar con. **shoulder-blade** n omóplato m. paletilla f.

shout (ʃaut) n grito m. vt, vi gritar.

shove (ʃʌv) vt empujar. n empujón m.

shovel ('ʃʌvəl) n pala f. vt traspalar.

show[*] (ʃou) n 1 exhibición f. 2 Th función f. vt exhibir. **show off** hacer gala de. **show business** n negocio del espectáculo m. **showcase** n vitrina f. **showdown** n momento decisivo, momento de la verdad m. **showjumping** n concurso hípico m. **showmanship** n teatralidad f. **showroom** n sala de exposiciones f

shower ('ʃauə) n 1 ducha f. 2 chubasco m. vi 1 ducharse. 2 llover. **showerproof** adj impermeable

shrank (ʃræŋk) v see **shrink**.

shred (ʃred) n triza f. vt hacer trizas.

shrewd (ʃru:d) adj astuto. **shrewdness** n astucia f

shriek (ʃri:k) vt chillar. n chillido m.

shrill (ʃril) adj agudo, chillón.

shrimp (ʃrimp) n camarón m.

shrine (ʃrain) n 1 capilla f. 2 santuario m.

shrink* (ʃriŋk) vt encoger. **shrinkage** n encogimiento m.

shrivel ('ʃrival) vt arrugar.

shroud (ʃraud) n mortaja f. vt amortajar.

Shrove Tuesday (ʃrouv) n martes de carnaval m

shrub (ʃrʌb) n arbusto m. **shrubbery** n plantío de arbustos m.

shrug (ʃrʌg) vi encogerse de hombros. n encogimiento de hombros m.

shrunk (ʃrʌŋk) v see **shrink**.

shudder ('ʃʌdə) vi estremecerse. n estremecimiento m.

shuffle ('ʃʌfəl) vi arrastrar los pies. vt game barajar. n game barajadura f.

shun (ʃʌn) vt evitar, esquivar.

shunt (ʃʌnt) vt maniobrar.

shut* (ʃʌt) vt cerrar, obstruir. **shut up!** ¡cállate!

shutter ('ʃʌtə) n 1 contraventana f. 2 phot obturador m

shuttlecock ('ʃʌtəlkɔk) n volante m.

shy (ʃai) adj tímido. vi espantarse. **shyness** n timidez f.

Sicily ('sisəli) n Sicilia f.

sick (sik) adj enfermo. **be sick** vomitar, estar enfermo. **be sick of** inf estar harto de. **sicken** vt dar asco a. vi enfermar. **sickness** n enfermedad f, náusea f.

side (said) n lado, costado m. **sideboard** n aparador m. **side effect** n efecto secundario m. **sidelight** n luz de costado f. **sideline** n 1 sport línea lateral f. 2 comm empleo secundario m. **sideshow** n caseta de feria f. **sidestep** vt esquivar. **sidetrack** vt apartar, desviar. **sideways** adv de lado, hacia un lado. **siding** n mot apartadero m.

sidle ('saidl) vi acercarse cautelosamente.

siege (si:dʒ) n sitio m. **lay seige to** sitiar.

sieve (siv) n colador, tamiz m. vt colar.

sift (sift) vt tamizar, colar.

sigh (sai) n suspiro m. vi suspirar.

sight (sait) n 1 vista f. 2 mira f. 3 espectáculo m. vt 1 divisar. 2 apuntar. **catch sight of** alcanzar a ver. **sightread** vt ejecutar a la primera lectura. **sightseeing** n excursionismo m.

sign (sain) n 1 señal f. indicio m. 2 signo m vt firmar. **signpost** n poste indicador m.

signal ('signl) n señal. f. vt señalar, comunicar por señales. adj insigne, señalado.

signature ('signətʃə) n firma f. **signatory** n firmante m.

signify ('signifai) vt significar. **significant** adj significante, significativo. **significance** n significación f.

silence ('sailəns) n silencio m. vt imponer silencio. **silencer** n tech silenciador m. **silent** adj silencioso.

silhouette (silu:'et) n silueta f.

silk (silk) n seda f. **silky** adj sedoso. **silkworm** n gusano de seda m.

sill (sil) n 1 umbral m. 2 alféizar m.

silly ('sili) adj tonto. **silliness** n tontería f.

silt (silt) n sedimento m.

silver ('silvə) n plata f. adj de plata.

similar ('similə) adj semejante, parecido. **similarity** n parecido m.

simile ('simili) n símil m.

simmer ('simə) vt cocer a fuego lento. vi hervir a fuego lento.

simple ('simpəl) adj sencillo. **simple-minded** adj inocente. **simplify** vt simplificar.

simultaneous (siməl'teiniəs) adj simultáneo.

sin (sin) n pecado m. vi pecar. **sinful** adj pecador.

since (sins) prep desde. conj 1 desde que. 2 puesto que. adv desde entonces, después.

sincere (sin'siə) adj sincero. **sincerity** n sinceridad f.

sinew ('sinju:) n tendón m.

sing* (siŋ) vt 1 cantar. 2 (of birds) trinar.

singe (sindʒ) vt chamuscar.

single ('siŋgəl) adj único, solo. v **single out** señalar, escoger. **single person** n soltero m. **single-handed** adj sin ayuda.

singular ('siŋgjulə) adj singular, extraordinario. adj,n gram singular m.

sinister ('sinistə) adj siniestro.

sink* (siŋk) vt hundir. vi 1 hundirse. 2 sumergirse. 3 declinar. **sink in** penetrar. ~n pila f. fregadero m.

slip

sinner ('sinə) n pecador m.

sinus ('sainəs) n seno m.

sip (sip) n sorbo m. vt sorber.

siphon ('saifən) n sifón. vt sacar con sifón.

sir (sə:) n señor m. dear sir muy señor mío.

siren ('sairən) n sirena f.

sirloin ('sə:lɔin) n solomillo m.

sister ('sistə) n hermana f. sisterhood n hermandad f. sister-in-law n cuñada f.

sit* (sit) vi sentarse. sit-in n huelga de brazos caídos f. sitting n sesión f. sitting room n sala de estar f.

site (sait) n sitio, solar m. vt situar.

situation (sitju'eiʃən) n 1 situación f. 2 colocación f.

six (siks) n,adj seis m. sixth adj sexto.

sixteen (siks'ti:n) n,adj dieciseis m. sixteenth adj decimosexto.

sixty ('siksti) n,adj sesenta m. sixtieth adj sexagésimo.

size (saiz) n tamaño m. sizeable adj considerable.

sizzle ('sizəl) vi chisporrotear.

skate¹ (skeit) n patín m. vi patinar. skating-rink n pista de patinaje f.

skate² (skeit) n zool raya f.

skeleton ('skelətn) n 1 anat esqueleto m. 2 esquema m.

sketch (sketʃ) n 1 boceto m. 2 Th pieza corta f. vt bosquejar. sketchy adj incompleto.

skewer ('skjuə) n broqueta f. pincho m. vt espetar.

ski (ski:) vi esquiar. ski-lift n teleski m.

skid (skid) vi mot patinar. n mot patinazo m.

skill (skil) n destreza f. skillful adj diestro. skilled adj hábil, experto.

skim (skim) vt espumar. vi pasar rasando. skim through a book hojear. skimmed milk n leche descremada f.

skimp (skimp) vt escatimar. vi economizar. skimpy adj escaso.

skin (skin) n 1 piel f. 2 cuero m. 3 cutis m. vt 1 zool despellejar. 2 bot peler. skin-diving n natación submarina f. skinny adj flaco. skin-tight adj ajustado.

skip (skip) vi saltar. n salto m.

skipper ('skipə) n naut capitán m.

skirmish ('skə:miʃ) n escaramuza f.

skirt (skə:t) n falda f. vt bordear.

skittle ('skitl) n bolo m.

skull (skʌl) n 1 calavera f. 2 anat cráneo m.

skunk (skʌŋk) n 1 zool mofeta f. 2 canella m.

sky (skai) n cielo m. sky-high adj por las nubes. skylark n alondra f. skyline n línea del horizonte f. skyscraper n rascacielos m invar.

slab (slæb) n 1 plancha f. 2 losa f.

slack (slæk) adj flojo. slacken vt aflojar.

slacks (slæks) n pl pantalones m pl.

slam (slæm) vt 1 cerrar de golpe. 2 golpear. n 1 golpe m. 2 game slam m.

slander ('slændə) vt calumniar, difamar. n calumnia, difamación f.

slang (slæŋ) n argot m. jerga f.

slant (sla:nt) n inclinación f. vt inclinar.

slap (slæp) n 1 palmada f. 2 bofetada f. vt dar una palmada o bofetada a. slapdash adj descuidado. slapstick adj payaso.

slash (slæʃ) vt 1 azotar. 2 acuchillar. n 1 latigazo m. 2 cuchillada f.

slat (slæt) n tablilla f.

slate (sleit) n pizarra f. vt 1 cubrir de pizarra. 2 inf criticar.

slaughter ('slɔ:tə) n matanza f. vt matar. slaughterhouse n matadero m.

slave (sleiv) n esclavo m. vi trabajar duro. slavery n esclavitud f.

sledge (sledʒ) n trineo m.

sledgehammer ('sledʒhæmə) n mazo m.

sleek (sli:k) adj liso, pulido. vt alisar.

sleep* (sli:p) vi dormir. n sueño m. sleeper n 1 durmiente m,f. 2 (railway) traviesa f. sleeping-bag n saco de dormir m. sleeping-car n coche-cama m. sleeping-pill n somnífero m. sleepwalk vi sonambulear. sleepwalker n sonámbulo m.

sleet (sli:t) n aguanieve m. vi caer aguanieve.

sleeve (sli:v) n manga f.

sleigh (slei) n see sledge.

slender ('slendə) adj delgado.

slept (slept) v see sleep.

slice (slais) n 1 tajada f. 2 rebanada f. vt tajar, rebanar.

slick (slik) adj listo, hábil.

slide* (slaid) vt deslizar. n 1 resbaladero m. 2 corredera f. 3 phot diapositiva f. slide-rule n regla de cálculo f.

slight (slait) adj leve, ligero. n desaire m. vt desairar. slightly adv un poco.

slim (slim) adj delgado. vi adelgazar.

slime (slaim) n 1 limo, légamo m. 2 (of a snail) baba f. slimy adj limoso, legamoso.

sling* (sliŋ) n 1 honda f. 2 med cabestrillo m. vt lanzar, tirar.

slink (sliŋk) vi andar furtivamente.

slip* (slip) vt resbalar. n 1 resbalón m. 2 desliz

275

m. 3 falta, equivocación *f.* 4 (garment) combinación *f.* **slippery** *adj* resbaladizo.

slip² (slip) *n* (cutting) tira *f.*

slipper ('slipə) *n* zapatilla *f.*

slit* (slit) *vt* rajar. *n* raja *f.*

slobber ('slɔbə) *n* baba *f. vi* babear.

slog (slɔg) *vi* 1 afanarse. 2 andar penosamente.

slogan ('slougən) *n* slogan *m.*

slop (slɔp) *n* gachas *f pl.* **sloppy** *adj* 1 desaliñado. 2 poco sólido. 3 descuidado.

slope (sloup) *n* 1 inclinación *f.* 2 cuesta *f.* 3 pendiente *f.* 4 ladera *f. vi* inclinarse.

slot (slɔt) *n* ranura *f.*

slovenly ('slʌvənli) *adj* descuidado.

slow (slou) *adj* lento. *vi* atrasarse. **slow down** reducir la marcha de, retardar.

slug¹ ('slʌg) *n* babosa *f.* **sluggish** *adj* lento, inactivo.

slug² (slʌg) *vt inf* aporrear.

sluice (slu:s) *n* compuerta *f.*

slum (slʌm) *n* barrio bajo, barrio pobre *m.*

slump (slʌmp) *n comm* depresión *f. vi* hundirse, desplomarse.

slung (slʌŋ) *v* see **sling.**

slur (slə:) *n* 1 calumnia *f.* 2 *mus* ligado *m. vt* 1 omitir. 2 pronunciar con poca claridad.

slush (slʌʃ) *n* fango *m.*

sly (slai) *adj* astuto.

smack¹ (smæk) *vi* **smack of** saber a.

smack² (smæk) *vt* pegar. *n* golpe *m.*

small (smɔ:l) *adj* pequeño, chico. **smallholding** *n* minifundio *m.* **small-minded** *adj* de miras estrechas. **smallpox** *n* viruela *f.*

smart (smɑ:t) *adj* 1 pulcro, elegante. 2 *inf* listo. 3 rápido. *vi* escocer. **smarten up** *vt* arreglar.

smash (smæʃ) *vt* 1 romper. 2 hacer pedazos. *n* 1 colisión *f.* 2 rotura *f.*

smear (smiə) *vt* 1 untar. 2 difamar. *n* mancha *f.*

smell* (smel) *n* 1 olor *m.* 2 olfato *m. vt* oler. **smelly** *adj* maloliente.

smile (smail) *n* sonrisa *f. vi* sonreír.

smirk (smə:k) *n* sonrisa afectada *f. vi* sonreír afectadamente.

smock (smɔk) *n* 1 blusa *f.* 2 bata corta *f.*

smog (smɔg) *n* niebla y humo *f.*

smoke (smouk) *n* 1 humo *m.* 2 pitillo *m. vi* humear. *vt* 1 fumar. 2 ahumar. **smoker** *n* fumador *m.*

smooth (smu:ð) *adj* 1 liso. 2 zalamero. *vt* 1 alisar. 2 allanar. 3 suavizar.

smother ('smʌðə) *vt,vi* ahogar, sofocar.

smoulder ('smouldə) *vi* arder sin llama.

smudge (smʌdʒ) *vt* manchar, tiznar. *n* mancha *f.* tiznón *m.*

smug (smʌg) *adj* pagado de sí mismo.

smuggle ('smʌgəl) *vt* pasar de contrabando. **smuggler** *n* contrabandista *m,f.* **smuggling** *n* contrabando *m.*

snack (snæk) *n* bocado, tentempié *m.* **snackbar** *n* cafetería *f.*

snag (snæg) *n* 1 dificultad, pega *f.* 2 muñón *m.* 3 raigón *m.*

snail (sneil) *n* caracol *m.*

snake (sneik) *n* serpiente *f.*

snap (snæp) *vt,vi* 1 romper. 2 hacer saltar. 3 chasquear. *n* 1 chasquido *m.* 2 cierre *m.* 3 *inf* foto *f. adj* repentino. **snapshot** *n* instantánea *f.* foto *m.*

snarl (snɑ:l) *vi* gruñir. *n* gruñido *m.*

snatch (snætʃ) *vt* 1 arrebatar. 2 coger al vuelo. *n* 1 arrebatamiento *m.* 2 fragmento *m.*

sneak (sni:k) *n* soplón *m. vi* andar a hurtadillas. **sneak away** escabullirse.

sneer (sniə) *vi* mofarse. *n* sonrisa despreciativa *f.*

sneeze (sni:z) *vi* estornudar. *n* estornudo *m.*

sniff (snif) *vt* husmear, olfatear. *n* husmeo, olfateo *m.*

snip (snip) *vt* tijeretear. *n* tijeretazo *m.*

snipe (snaip) *vi* disparar desde un escondite. *n zool* agachadiza *f.* **sniper** *n* tirador escondido *m.*

snivel ('snivəl) *vi* lloriquear.

snob (snɔb) *n* esnob *m,f.* **snobbery** *n* esnobismo *m.*

snooker ('snu:kə) *n* billar *m.*

snoop (snu:p) *vi* fisgonear.

snooty ('snu:ti) *adj* arrogante, engreído.

snooze (snu:z) *vi* dormitar. *n* siestecita *f.*

snore (snɔ:) *vi* roncar. *n* ronquido *m.*

snort (snɔ:t) *vi* bufar, resoplar. *n* bufido, resoplido *m.*

snout (snaut) *n* hocico, morro *m.*

snow (snou) *n* nieve *f. vi* nevar. **snowball** *n* bola de nieve *f.* **snowdrift** *n* amontonamiento de nieve, ventisquero *m.* **snowdrop** *n* campanilla de invierno *f.* **snowfall** *n* nevada *f.* **snowflake** *n* copo de nieve *m.* **snowman** *n* muñeco de nieve *m.* **snowplough** *n* quitanieves *m invar.* **snowstorm** *n* ventisca *f.* temporal de nieve *m.*

snub (snʌb) *vt* desairar. *n* desaire *m.* **snubnosed** *adj* chato.

snuff (snʌf) *n* rapé *m. vt* 1 aspirar. 2 extinguir.

snug (snʌg) *adj* **1** abrigado. **2** cómodo. **3** ajustado.

snuggle ('snʌgəl) *vi* acurrucarse.

so (sou) *adv* **1** tan. **2** así, de este modo. **so that** de modo que. ~*conj* **1** por consiguiente. **2** conque. **so-and-so** *n* fulano de tal *m*. **so-called** *adj* llamado. **so-so** *adv* así así, regular.

soak (souk) *vt* empapar, remojar, chupar.

soap (soup) *n* jabón. *vt* enjabonar. **soap powder** *n* jabón en polvo *m*. **soapy** *adj* jabonoso.

soar (sɔ:) *vi* remontarse, elevarse.

sob (sɔb) *vi* sollozar. *n* sollozo *m*.

sober ('soubə) *adj* **1** sobrio, serio. **2** sereno.

social ('souʃəl) *adj* social. **sociable** *adj* sociable. **socialism** *n* socialismo *m*. **socialist** *adj,n* socialista.

society (sə'saiəti) *n* **1** sociedad *f*. **2** asociación *f*.

sociology (sousi'ɔlədʒi) *n* sociología *f*. **sociological** *adj* sociológico. **sociologist** *n* sociólogo *m*.

sock[1] (sɔk) *n* calcetín *m*.

sock[2] (sɔk) *inf vt* pegar, cascar. *n* castaña *f*.

socket ('sɔkit) *n* **1** cavidad *f*. **2** *tech* enchufe *m*.

soda ('soudə) *n* **1** soda *f*. **2** sosa *f*. **soda-water** *n* sifón *m*.

sofa ('soufə) *n* sofá *m*.

soft (sɔft) *adj* **1** blando. **2** muelle. **3** suave. **4** *inf* tonto. **soften** *vt* **1** ablandar. **2** suavizar. **soft-hearted** *adj* bondadoso, compasivo.

soggy ('sɔgi) *adj* empapado, mojado.

soil[1] (sɔil) *n* suelo *m*.

soil[2] (sɔil) *vt* ensuciar.

solar ('soulə) *adj* solar.

sold (sould) *v see* **sell.**

solder ('sɔldə) *vt* soldar. *n* soldadura *f*.

soldier ('souldʒə) *n* soldado *m*. *vi* ser soldado, servir.

sole[1] (soul) *adj* único, exclusivo.

sole[2] (soul) *n* **1** *anat* planta *f*. **2** suela *f*.

sole[3] (soul) *n* *zool* lenguado *m*.

solemn ('sɔləm) *adj* solemne.

solicitor (sə'lisitə) *n* **1** abogado *m*. **2** notario *m*.

solid ('sɔlid) *adj* **1** sólido. **2** macizo. *n* sólido *m*. **solidarity** *n* solidaridad *f*. **solidify** *vt* solidificar. **solidity** *n* solidez *f*.

solitary ('sɔlitri) *adj* solitario, solo.

solitude ('sɔlitju:d) *n* soledad *f*.

solo ('soulou) *n* solo *m*. *adj* **1** a solas. **2** para solo. **soloist** *n* solista *m,f*.

solstice ('sɔlstis) *n* solsticio *m*.

soluble ('sɔljubəl) *adj* soluble.

solution (sə'lu:ʃən) *n* solución *f*.

solve (sɔlv) *vt* resolver, solucionar. **solvent** *adj,n* solvente *m*. **solvency** *n* solvencia *f*.

sombre ('sɔmbə) *adj* sombrio.

some (sʌm) *adj* **1** alguno, algún. **2** unos. **3** un poco de, algo de. *pron* **1** algunos *m pl*. algunas *f pl*. **2** algo *neut*. *adv* aproximadamente. **somebody** *pron* alguien. **somebody else** algún otro, otra persona. **somehow** *adv* de algún modo. **someone** *pron* alguien. **something** *pron* algo. **something else** otra cosa. **sometime** *adv* algún día, alguna vez. *adj* antiguo. **sometimes** *adv* algunas veces, a veces. **somewhat** *adv* algo, un tanto. **somewhere** *adv* en *or* a alguna parte. **somewhere else** en *or* a otra parte.

somersault ('sʌməsɔ:lt) *n* salto mortal *m*. *vi* dar un salto mortal.

son (sʌn) *n* hijo *m*. **son-in-law** *n* yerno, hijo político *m*.

song (sɔŋ) *n* **1** canción *f*. **2** canto *m*. **3** cantar *m*.

sonic ('sɔnik) *adj* sónico.

sonnet ('sɔnit) *n* soneto *m*.

soon (su:n) *adv* **1** pronto. **2** temprano. **as soon as possible** cuanto antes, lo antes possible. **how soon?** ¿para cuándo? **soon after** poco después. **sooner** *adv* más temprano, antes. **no sooner...than** apenas. **the sooner the better** cuanto antes mejor.

soot (sut) *n* hollín *m*.

soothe (su:ð) *vt* calmar. **soothing** *adj* calmante.

sophisticated (sə'fistikeitid) *adj* sofisticado.

soprano (sə'prɑ:nou) *n* soprano, tiple *f*.

sorbet ('sɔ:bit) *n* sorbete *m*.

sordid ('sɔ:did) *adj* sórdido.

sore (sɔ:) *adj* inflamado. **be sore** doler. ~*n* llaga *f*.

sorrow ('sɔrou) *n* dolor *m*. pena *f*. *vi* apenarse.

sorry ('sɔri) *adj* **1** arrepentido. **2** apenado. **3** lastimoso, triste. **be sorry 1** sentirlo. **2** saber mal. ~*interj* ¡perdón!

sort (sɔ:t) *n* clase, especie *f*. tipo *m*. *vt,vi* clasificar. **sort out 1** arreglar. **2** solucionar.

soufflé ('su:flei) *n* suflé *m*.

sought (sɔ:t) *v see* **seek.**

soul (soul) *n* alma *f*.

sound[1] (saund) *n* **1** sonido *m*. **2** son *m*. **3** ruido *m*. **4** tech sonda *f*. *vt* **1** sonar. **2** tocar. **3** entonar. **soundproof** *adj* insonorizado.

sound[2] (saund) *adj* **1** sano, robusto. **2** firme, sólido. **3** razonable. **4** profundo. **5** *comm* solvente. **safe and sound** sano y salvo.

soup (su:p) *n* sopa *f*.

sour (sauə) adj 1 agrio. 2 acre.

source (sɔ:s) n fuente f.

south (sauθ) n sur, mediodía m. adj del sur, meridional. adv hacia el sur. **south-east** adj,n sudeste m. **southerly** adj sudeste, del sudeste. **southern** adj del sur, meridional. **southward** adv hacia el sur. **south-west** adj,n sudoeste m.

South Africa n Africa del Sur f. **South African** adj,n sudafricano.

South America n América del Sur, Sudamérica f. **South American** adj,n sudamericano.

South Pole n Polo Sur m.

souvenir (su:və'niə) n recuerdo m.

sovereign ('sɔvrin) adj,n soberano m. **sovereignty** n soberanía f.

Soviet Union ('souviət) n Unión Soviética f. **Soviet** adj soviético. n soviet m.

sow[1] (sou) vt sembrar. **sowing** n siembra f.

sow[2] (sau) n cerda f.

soya bean ('sɔiə) n semilla de soja f.

spa (spa:) n balneario m.

space (speis) n espacio m. adj espacial. vt espaciar. **spacious** adj espacioso.

spade[1] (speid) n pala f. **call a spade a spade** llamar al pan pan y al vino vino. **spade-work** n desbaste m.

spade[2] (speid) n game 1 picos m pl. 2 espadas f pl.

Spain (spein) n España f. **Spaniard** n español m. **Spanish** adj español. **Spanish** (language) n español m.

span (spæn) n 1 envergadura f. 2 arco m. 3 extensión, duración f. vt 1 extenderse sobre. 2 abarcar

spaniel ('spæniəl) n perro de aguas, pachón m.

spank (spæŋk) vt azotar, zurrar. n azote m. nalgada f.

spanner ('spænə) n llave inglesa f.

spare (spɛə) adj 1 sobrante, de sobra. 2 disponible. 3 tech de recambio, de repuesto. n pieza de recambio f. vt 1 escatimar. 2 ahorrar. 3 perdonar. **sparing** adj 1 escaso. 2 económico.

spark (spa:k) n chispa f. chispazo m. vi echar chispas, chispear.

sparkle ('spa:kəl) n 1 destello, centelleo m. 2 vivacidad f. vi centellear. **sparkling** adj centelleante.

sparrow ('spærou) n gorrión m.

sparse (spa:s) adj 1 disperso. 2 escaso.

spasm ('spæzəm) n espasmo m. **spasmodic** adj espasmódico. **spastic** adj,n espástico.

spat (spæt) v see **spit**.

spatial ('speiʃəl) adj espacial.

spatula ('spætjulə) n espátula f.

spawn (spɔ:n) vi 1 desovar. 2 engendrar, procrear. n 1 huevas f pl. 2 semillas f pl.

speak[*] (spi:k) vt,vi hablar. **so to speak** por así decirlo. **speak up** hablar alto. **speaker** n 1 el que habla. 2 orador m.

spear (spiə) n 1 lanza f. 2 arpón m. vt 1 dar una lanzada a. 2 arponear

special ('speʃəl) adj especial, particular. **specialist** n especialista m,f. **speciality** n especialidad f. **specialize** vi especializarse.

species ('spi:ʃi:z) n especie f.

specify ('spesifai) vt especificar. **specific** adj específico.

specimen ('spesimən) n ejemplar, espécimen m.

speck (spek) n 1 mota f. 2 partícula f.

spectacle ('spektəkəl) n 1 espectáculo m. 2 pl gafas f pl. **spectacular** adj espectacular.

spectator (spek'teitə) n espectador m.

spectrum ('spektrəm) n, pl **-tra** or **-trums** espectro m.

speculate ('spekjuleit) vi especular. **speculation** n especulación f. **speculative** adj especulativo. **speculator** n especulador m.

speech (spi:tʃ) n 1 discurso m. 2 habla f. 3 palabra f. 4 lenguaje m. **speechless** adj mudo, cortado.

speed[*] (spi:d) n 1 velocidad f. 2 rapidez f. vi mot exceder la velocidad permitida. **speedboat** n lancha rápida f

spell[*][1] (spel) vt,vi escribir correctamente. **spelling** n ortografía f.

spell[2] (spel) n hechizo m. **cast a spell** hechizar. **spellbound** adj hechizado.

spell[3] (spel) n 1 rato m. 2 temporada f. 3 período m.

spend[*] (spend) vt,vi 1 gastar. 2 pasar. **spendthrift** adj,n derrochador.

sperm (spə:m) n esperma m.

sphere (sfiə) n esfera f. **spherical** adj esférico.

spice (spais) n 1 especia f. 2 picante m. 3 aliciente m. vt especiar, condimentar. **spicy** adj 1 especiado. 2 picante. 3 sabroso.

spider ('spaidə) n araña f.

spike (spaik) n 1 pincho m. púa f. 2 clavo m. 3 bot espiga f. vt sujetar con un pincho, clavar. **spiked** adj claveteado.

spill[*] (spil) vt 1 derramar, verter. 2 desarzonar. **spill over** desbordarse. ~n caída f.

spin[*] (spin) vt 1 hacer girar. 2 tech hilar. n

vuelta f. **spin-dry** vt secar con centrífuga. **spin-drier** n secadora centrífuga f.

spinach ('spinidʒ) n espinaca f.

spindle ('spindl) n 1 huso m. 2 tech eje m.

spine (spain) n 1 anat espinazo m. 2 zool espina f. **spineless** adj flojo, débil.

spinster ('spinstə) n solterona f.

spire [1] (spaiə) n arch aguja f. chapitel m.

spire [2] (spaiə) n espiral f. spiral adj,n espiral f. vi dar vueltas en espiral.

spirit ('spirit) n 1 espíritu m. 2 ánimo m. 3 pl alcohol m. licores m pl. **spirited** adj animoso, fogoso. **spiritual** adj espiritual. **spiritualism** n espiritismo m.

spit [1] (spit) vt,vi 1 escupir. 2 bufar. n saliva f.

spit [2] (spit) n cul asador m.

spite (spait) n rencor, despecho m. **in spite of** a pesar de, a despecho de. ~vt mortificar. **spiteful** adj rencoroso.

splash (splæʃ) vt salpicar. vi chapotear. n 1 salpicadura, rociada f. 2 chapoteo m.

splendid ('splendid) adj espléndido. **splendour** n esplendor m.

splint (splint) n tablilla f. **splinter** n astilla f. vt astillar.

split [*] (split) vt 1 partir, hender. 2 dividir. 3 separar. n 1 hendedura f. 2 división f. adj 1 partido, hendido. 2 dividido.

splutter ('splʌtə) vi 1 chisporrotear. 2 balbucear. n 1 chisporroteo m. 2 balbuceo m.

spoil (spɔil) vt 1 echar a perder, estropear. 2 malograr. 3 mimar. **spoilt** adj 1 estropeado. 2 mimado. **spoilsport** n aguafiestas m,f invar.

spoke [1] (spouk) v see **speak.**

spoke [2] (spouk) n rayo m.

spoken ('spoukən) v see **speak.**

spokesman ('spouksmən) n portavoz m.

sponge (spʌndʒ) n esponja f. vt pasar la esponja por. **sponge on** inf gorrear.

sponsor ('spɔnsə) n 1 patrocinador m. 2 comm fiador m. vt patrocinar. **sponsorship** n patrocinio m.

spontaneous (spɔn'teiniəs) adj espontáneo.

spool (spu:l) n carrete m.

spoon (spu:n) n cuchara f. vt coger a cucharadas. **spoonful** n cucharada f.

sport (spɔːt) n 1 deporte m. 2 juego m. diversión f. **sporting** adj 1 deportivo. 2 arriesgado. **sportsman** n deportista m. **sportsmanship** n deportividad f.

spot (spɔt) n 1 punto m. 2 mancha f. 3 grano, lunar m. vt 1 manchar, salpicar. 2 notar. 3

encontrar, descubrir. **spotless** adj nítido, inmaculado. **spotlight** n foco, reflector m.

spouse (spaus) n cónyuge m,f.

spout (spaut) n 1 pitón m. 2 caño m. 3 canalón m. 4 chorro m. vt 1 arrojar en chorro. 2 recitar.

sprain (sprein) vt torcer. n torcedura f.

sprang (spræŋ) v see **spring.**

sprawl (sprɔːl) vi desparramarse.

spray [1] (sprei) vt 1 rociar. 2 regar. 3 aplicar con pulverizador. n 1 rociada f. 2 (of the sea) espuma f. 3 atomizador m.

spray [2] (sprei) n ramita con hojas y flores f.

spread [*] (spred) vt 1 extender. 2 esparcir, diseminar. 3 difundir. n 1 extensión f. 2 envergadura f. 3 difusión f.

spree (spri:) n parranda, juerga f.

sprig (sprig) n ramita f.

sprightly ('spraitli) adj animado.

spring [*] (spriŋ) n 1 primavera f. 2 manantial m. 3 brinco m. vi 1 brotar, nacer. 2 saltar, brincar. **springboard** n trampolín m. **spring-clean** vt hacer limpieza general. **springtime** n primavera f.

sprinkle ('spriŋkəl) vt salpicar, rociar. n 1 rociada f. 2 salpicadura f.

sprint (sprint) n esprint m. vi esprintar.

sprout (spraut) vi brotar. vt echar. n brote m.

sprung (sprʌŋ) v see **spring.**

spun (spʌn) v see **spin.**

spur (spəː) n 1 espuela f. 2 estímulo, aguijón m. vt espolear. **spur on** estimular.

spurt (spəːt) n 1 esfuerzo supremo. 2 chorro m. vi 1 hacer un esfuerzo supremo. 2 surgir.

spy (spai) vt,vi 1 espiar. 2 divisar. n espía m,f.

squabble ('skwɔbəl) vi reñir. n riña.

squad (skwɔd) n pelotón m. brigada f.

squadron ('skwɔdrən) n 1 escuadrón m. 2 escuadrilla f.

squalid ('skwɔlid) adj escuálido.

squander ('skwɔndə) vt despilfarrar.

square (skweə) adj cuadrado. n 1 cuadrado m. 2 plaza f. vt 1 cuadrar. 2 ajustar.

squash (skwɔʃ) vt 1 aplastar. 2 apretar. n 1 zumo m. 2 inf apretujamiento m.

squat (skwɔt) vi 1 agacharse. 2 apropiarse de un edificio. adj 1 rechoncho. 2 achaparrado.

squawk (skwɔːk) vi graznar. n graznido m.

squeak (skwi:k) vi chirriar. n chirrido m.

squeal (skwi:l) vi chillar. n chillido m.

squeamish ('skwi:miʃ) adj 1 delicado. 2 aprensivo.

squeeze (skwi:z) *vt* 1 apretar, estrujar. 2 exprimir. 3 oprimir. *n* apretón, estrujón *m*.

squid (skwid) *n* calamar *m*.

squiggle ('skwigəl) *n* garabato *m*.

squint (skwint) *vi* bizquear, ser bizco. *n* estrabismo *m*.

squire ('skwaiə) *n* 1 hacendado *m*. 2 escudero *m*.

squirm (skwə:m) *vi* retorcerse.

squirrel ('skwirl) *n* ardilla *f*.

squirt (skwə:t) *vt* arrojar un chorro de. *vi* salir a chorro. *n* chorro *m*.

stab (stæb) *vt* apuñalar. *n* puñalada *f*.

stable[1] ('steibəl) *n* cuadra *f*.

stable[2] ('steibəl) *adj* estable. **stability** *n* estabilidad *f*. **stabilize** *vt* estabilizar. **stabilizer** *n* estabilizador *m*.

stack (stæk) *n* montón *m*. pila *f*. *vt*. amontonar, apilar.

stadium ('steidiəm) *n, pl* **-dia** or **-diums** estadio *m*.

staff (stɑ:f) *n* 1 bastón *m*. 2 palo *m*. 3 personal *m*.

stag (stæg) *n* ciervo, venado *m*.

stage (steidʒ) *n* 1 *Th* escena *f*. 2 estrado *m*. 3 etapa *f*. 4 tramo *m*. *vt* 1 *Th* representar. 2 efectuar. 3 organizar. **stage manager** *n* director de escena *m*.

stagger ('stægə) *vi* tambalearse. *vt* 1 asombrar. 2 hacer vacilar. *n* tambaleo *m*. **staggering** *adj* asombroso.

stagnate (stæg'neit) *vi* estancarse. **stagnant** *adj* estancado.

stain (stein) *n* mancha *f*. *vt* 1 manchar. 2 teñir.

stair (stɛə) *n* 1 escalón *m*. 2 *pl* escalera *f*. **staircase** *n* escalera *f*.

stake[1] (steik) *n* estaca *f*. poste *m*. *vt* estacar.

stake[2] (steik) *n* 1 *game* 1 apuesta *f*. 2 *pl* premio *m*. **at stake** en juego. ~*vt* 1 apostar. 2 aventurar, arriesgar.

stale (steil) *adj* 1 pasado, viejo. 2 viciado.

stalemate ('steilmeit) *n* 1 *game* tablas *f pl*. 2 estancamiento *m*.

stalk[1] (stɔ:k) *n bot* tallo *m*.

stalk[2] (stɔ:k) *vt* seguir los pasos de. *vi* andar con paso majestuoso.

stall[1] (stɔ:l) *n* 1 casilla de establo *f*. 2 puesto *m*. 3 *Th* butacas *f pl*.

stall[2] (stɔ:l) *vt* parar, atascar. *vi* 1 pararse. 2 andar con evasivas.

stallion ('stæliən) *n* semental *m*.

stamina ('stæminə) *n* vigor *m*.

stammer ('stæmə) *vt,vi* tartamudear. *n* tartamudeo *m*.

stamp (stæmp) *n* 1 sello *m*. 2 marca *f*. 3 cuño *m*. 4 pataleo *m*. *vt* 1 franquear. 2 sellar. 3 estampar. 4 marcar. *vi* patalear.

stampede (stæm'pi:d) *n* estampida *f*. *vi* salir de estampida.

stand (stænd) *vi* 1 estar de pie. 2 encontrarse. 4 mantenerse en vigor. *vt* 1 colocar, poner. 2 soportar. *n* 1 posición *f*. 2 soporte *m*. **standing** *adj* 1 en pie. 2 permanente. *n* 1 posición *f*. 2 importancia *f*. 3 categoría *f*. reputación *f*.

standard ('stændəd) *n* 1 modelo *m*. 2 nivel *m*. *adj* 1 corriente, standard. 2 patrón, tipo. **standardize** *vt* regularizar.

stanza ('stænzə) *n* estrofa *f*.

stank (stæŋk) *v see* **stink.**

staple[1] ('steipəl) *n* grapa *f*. *vt* sujetar con grapas.

staple[2] ('steipəl) *adj* principal. *n* 1 producto principal *m*. 2 elemento esencial *m*.

star (stɑ:) *n* estrella *f*. astro *m*. *adj* 1 estelar. 2 destacado, especial. *vi* ser la estrella or el astro. **stardom** *n* estrellato *m*. **starfish** *n* estrella de mar *f*.

starboard ('stɑ:bəd) *n* estribor *m*.

starch (stɑ:tʃ) *n* 1 almidón *m*. 2 fécula *f*. *vt* almidonar.

stare (stɛə) *vi* mirar fijamente. *n* mirada fija *f*.

stark (stɑ:k) *adj* 1 rígido. 2 severo.

starling ('stɑ:liŋ) *n* estornino *m*.

start (stɑ:t) *vt* 1 empezar, iniciar. 2 poner en marcha. *vi* sobresaltarse. *n* 1 principio *m*. 2 salida *f*. 3 sobresalto *m*.

startle ('stɑ:tl) *vt* asustar, dar un susto, sobresaltar. **startling** *adj* 1 asombroso. 2 sobrecogedor.

starve (stɑ:v) *vi* 1 morir de hambre. 2 pasar hambre. *vt* 1 hacer morir de hambre. 2 hacer pasar hambre. **starvation** *n* hambre *f*. **starving** *adj* hambriento.

state (steit) *n* estado *m*. *adj* 1 estatal. 2 de gala. *vt* 1 declarar. 2 exponer, formular. **stately** *adj* majestuoso, imponente. **statement** *n* 1 declaración *f*. 2 informe *m*. **statesman** *n* estadista *m*. **statesmanship** *n* arte de gobernar *m*.

static ('stætik) *adj* 1 estático. 2 estancado.

station ('steiʃən) *n* 1 estación *f*. 2 puesto *m*. 3 condición *f*. *vt* 1 estacionar. 2 situar. **stationmaster** *n* jefe de estación *m*.

stationary ('steiʃənri) *adj* estacionario.

stationer ('steiʃənə) *n* papelero *m*. **stationer's**

shop *n* papelería *f*. **stationery** *n* papel de escribir *m*.

statistics (stə'tistiks) *n* estadística *f*.

statue ('stætju:) *n* estatua *f*.

stature ('stætʃə) *n* estatura *f*.

status ('steitəs) *n* **1** estado *m*. condición *f*. **2** categoría, posición *f*. rango *m*.

statute ('stætju:t) *n* estatuto *m*. **statutory** *adj* estatutario, obligatorio.

stay [1] (stei) *vi* **1** quedar, quedarse, permanecer. **2** hospedarse. *n* estancia *f*.

stay [2] (stei) *n* (prop) sostén, puntal *m*. *vt* sostener, apuntalar.

steadfast ('stedfə:st) *adj* resuelto, firme.

steady ('stedi) *adj* **1** firme, fijo. **2** estable. **3** constante. **4** formal. *vt* **1** estabilizar. **2** calmar.

steak (steik) *n* **1** bistec, biftec *m*. **2** tajada *f*.

steal (sti:l) *vt* robar.

steam (sti:m) *n* vapor *m*. *vt* **1** empañar. **2** *cul* cocer al vapor. *vi* echar vapor. **steam-engine** *n* máquina de vapor *f*. **steamer** *n* vapor *m*. **steamroller** *n* apisonadora *f*.

steel (sti:l) *n* acero *m*.

steep [1] (sti:p) *adj* **1** empinado. **2** escarpado, abrupto.

steep [2] (sti:p) *vt* empapar, remojar.

steeple ('sti:pəl) *n* campanario *m*. torre *f*. **steeplechase** *n* carrera de obstáculos *f*.

steer (stiə) *vt* **1** conducir, dirigir, guiar. **2** *naut* gobernar. **steer clear of** evitar. **steering-wheel** *n* volante *m*.

stem [1] (stem) *n* tallo *m*.

stem [2] (stem) *vt* refrenar. **stem from** provenir de.

stencil ('stensəl) *n* **1** cliché *m*. **2** patrón picado *m*. *vt* estarcir.

step (step) *n* **1** paso *m*. **2** peldaño, escalón *m*. **3** medida *f*. *vi* **1** dar un paso. **2** pisar. **step aside** hacerse a un lado. **step down** **1** bajar. **2** renunciar. **stepladder** *n* escalera de mano *f*

stepbrother ('stepbrʌðə) *n* hermanastro *m*.

stepdaughter ('stepdɔ:tə) *n* hijastra *f*.

stepfather ('stepfɑ:ðə) *n* padrastro *m*.

stepmother ('stepmʌðə) *n* madrastra *f*.

stepsister ('stepsistə) *n* hermanastra *f*.

stepson ('stepsʌn) *n* hijastro *m*.

stereo ('steriou) *adj* estéreo.

stereophonic (steriə'fɔnik) *adj* estereofónico, estéreo.

stereotype ('steriətaip) *n* cliché, estereotipo *m*. *vt* estereotipar.

sterile ('sterail) *adj* estéril. **sterilize** *vt* esterilizar.

sterling ('stə:liŋ) *adj* genuino, de ley. **pound sterling** *n* libra esterlina *f*.

stern [1] (stə:n) *adj* severo, austero.

stern [2] (stə:n) *n* *naut* popa *f*.

stethoscope ('steθəskoup) *n* estetoscopio *m*.

stew (stju:) *vt,vi* estofar, guisar. *n* estofado, guiso *m*.

steward ('stju:əd) *n* **1** camarero, mozo *m*. **2** administrador *m*. **3** mayordomo *m*. **stewardess** *n* azafata *f*.

stick [1] (stik) *n* **1** bastón *m*. **2** palo *m*. **3** barra *f*.

stick [2] (stik) *vt* **1** pegar. **2** clavar. **3** meter. **4** *inf* aguantar. *vi* **1** atascarse. **2** quedarse, pararse. **stick to** **1** persistir. **2** ser fiel a. **sticker** *n* etiqueta engomada *f*.

sticky ('stiki) *adj* **1** pegajoso. **2** *inf* difícil.

stiff (stif) *adj* **1** tieso, rígido. **2** duro. **3** entumecido. **4** fuerte. **stiffness** *n* tiesura, rigidez, inflexibilidad *f*. **stiffen** *vt* **1** poner rígido. **2** endurecer. **3** entumecer.

stifle ('staifəl) *vt* ahogar, sofocar. **stifling** *adj* sofocante.

stigma ('stigmə) *n*, *pl* **-mas** *or* **-mata** estigma *m*. **stigmatize** *vt* estigmatizar.

stile (stail) *n* portillo con escalones *m*.

still [1] (stil) *adj* inmóvil, quieto. *adv* todavía, aún. *conj* con todo, a pesar de todo. *vt* calmar, aquietar. **stillborn** *adj* nacido muerto. **still life** *n* bodegón *m*.

still [2] (stil) *n* alambique *m*.

stilt (stilt) *n* zanco *m*. **stilted** *adj* afectado, amanerado.

stimulate ('stimjuleit) *vt* estimular. **stimulant** *n* estimulante *m*. **stimulating** *adj* **1** estimulador. **2** estimulante.

stimulus ('stimjuləs) *n*, *pl* **-li** *or* **-luses** estímulo *m*.

sting (stiŋ) *n* **1** *zool* aguijón *m*. **2** picadura *f*. **3** punzada *f*. **4** escozor *m*. *vi* **1** picar. **2** punzar. **3** escocer.

stink (stiŋk) *vi* oler mal. *n* mal olor *m*.

stint (stint) *vt* escatimar. *n* (of work) destajo *m*.

stipulate ('stipjuleit) *vt* estipular.

stir (stə:) *vt* **1** revolver. **2** agitar. **3** remover. **4** despertar. **stir up** excitar. ~*n* **1** agitación *f*. **2** conmoción *f*. **stirring** *adj* emocionante, conmovedor.

stirrup ('stirəp) *n* estribo *m*.

stitch (stitʃ) *n* **1** punto *m*. puntada *f*. **2** punzada *f*. *vt* **1** coser. **2** hilvanar.

stoat (stout) *n* *zool* armiño *m*.

stock (stɔk) n 1 provisión f. 2 comm existencias f pl. surtido m. 3 valores m pl. 4 cepa f. tronco m. 5 culata f. 6 estirpe f. 7 cul caldo m. **take stock** 1 comm hacer inventario. 2 asesorarse. ~adj 1 acostumbrado. 2 corriente, normal. vt 1 proveer. 2 comm tener en existencia. **stockbreeding** n ganadería f. **stockbreeder** n ganadero m. **stockbroker** n agente de bolsa m. **stock exchange** n bolsa f. **stockholder** n accionista m,f. **stockpile** vt acumular. **stocktaking** n inventario m.

stocking ('stɔkiŋ) n media f.

stodge (stɔdʒ) n inf comida pesada f. **stodgy** adj indigesto, pesado.

stoic ('stouik) n estoico m. **stoical** adj estoico. **stoicism** n estoicismo m.

stoke (stouk) vt cargar, echar carbón a, cebar.

stole¹ (stoul) n estola f.

stole² (stoul) v see **steal**.

stolen (stoulən) v see **steal**.

stomach ('stʌmək) n 1 estómago m. 2 vientre m. vt aguantar, tragar. **stomach-ache** n dolor de estómago m.

stone (stoun) n 1 piedra f. 2 hueso m. vt 1 apedrear. 2 deshuesar. **stony** adj pedregoso.

stood (stud) v see **stand**.

stool (stu:l) n taburete m.

stoop (stu:p) vi inclinarse, agacharse, encorvarse. **stoop to** rebajarse a. ~n inclinación f.

stop (stɔp) vt 1 parar, detener. 2 impedir. 3 tapar. vi alojarse. n 1 parada f. 2 alto m. **put a stop to** poner fin a. **stopgap** n recurso provisional f. **stoppage** n 1 parada, interrupción f. 2 paro m. 3 obstrucción f. **stopper** n tapón m. **stopwatch** n cronómetro m.

store (stɔ:) n 1 provisión f. 2 almacén m. reserva f. vt 1 almacenar. 2 abastecer. **store up** acumular. **storage** n almacenaje m.

storey ('stɔ:ri) n piso m.

stork (stɔ:k) n cigüeña f.

storm (stɔ:m) n tormenta, tempestad f. vi enfurecerse, rabiar. vt tomar por asalto. **stormy** adj tempestuoso.

story ('stɔ:ri) n 1 historia f. 2 cuento m.

stout (staut) adj 1 macizo, sólido, recio. 2 robusto, corpulento. n cerveza negra f.

stove (stouv) n 1 estufa f. 2 hornillo, fogón m.

stow (stou) vt colocar, meter. **stowaway** n polizón m.

straddle ('strædl) vt 1 montar a horcajadas. 2 caer a ambos lados de.

straggle ('strægəl) vi 1 desparramarse. 2 rezagarse. **straggler** n rezagado m.

straight (streit) adj 1 recto, derecho. 2 franco, honrado. 3 en órden. adv 1 en línea recta. 2 directamente. 3 francamente. **straight away** en seguida. **straight on** or **ahead** todo seguido. ~n recta f. **straighten** vt 1 enderezar. 2 arreglar. **straightforward** adj 1 franco, honrado. 2 sencillo.

strain¹ (strein) vt 1 estirar, tender. 2 torcer. 3 forzar. 4 cul colar. n 1 tensión, tirantez f. 2 torcedura f. 3 esfuerzo m.

strain² (strein) n 1 estirpe, raza f. 2 tendencia, vena f. 3 variedad f.

strand¹ (strænd) vt encallar. **be stranded** quedarse colgado.

strand² (strænd) n cabo, ramal m. hebra f.

strange (streindʒ) adj 1 extraño. 2 desconocido. **stranger** n 1 desconocido m. 2 forastero m.

strangle ('stræŋgəl) vt estrangular.

strap (stræp) n 1 correa f. 2 tira f. vt sujetar con una correa.

strategy ('strætidʒi) n estrategia f. **strategic** adj estratégico.

straw (strɔ:) n paja f. **strawberry** n fresa f. fresón m.

stray (strei) vi extraviarse. adj 1 extraviado, perdido. 2 aislado. 3 errante. n animal extraviado m.

streak (stri:k) n 1 veta, vena f. 2 racha f. vt listar, rayar. vi pasar como un rayo. **streaky** adj 1 listado. 2 entreverado.

stream (stri:m) n 1 arroyo m. 2 corriente f. 3 raudal m. vi 1 correr, fluir. 2 brotar, manar. 3 ondear. **streamer** n serpentina f. **streamline** vt 1 aerodinamizar. 2 hacer más eficiente, coordinar.

street (stri:t) n calle f.

strength (streŋθ) n 1 fuerza f. resistencia f. **strengthen** vt fortalecer, reforzar, fortificar.

strenuous ('strenjuəs) adj 1 enérgico. 2 tenaz. 3 arduo.

stress (stres) n 1 presión f. 2 tensión f. 3 acento m. 4 énfasis m. vt 1 insistir en. 2 acentuar.

stretch (stretʃ) vt 1 extender, estirar. 2 ensanchar. 3 tender. n 1 extensión f. 2 trecho m. **stretcher** n camilla f.

strict (strikt) adj 1 estricto. 2 severo.

stride* (straid) vi andar a trancos, por zancadas. vt cruzar de un tranco. n zancada f. tranco m.

strike* (straik) vt 1 golpear, pegar. 2 asestar. 3 alcanzar. 4 dar con. 5 tocar. 6 naut arriar. 1 hacer impresión. 2 hacer huelga. 3 dar la hora. 4 atacar. n huelga f. **go on strike**

declararse en huelga. **striker** n huelguista m,f.

string (striŋ) n 1 cordel m. 2 cuerda f. 3 sarta f. 4 hilera f. **pull strings** inf mover palancas. ~vt 1 ensartar. 2 mus encordar.

stringent ('strindʒənt) adj riguroso, severo. **stringency** n rigor m. severidad f.

strip[1] (strip) vt 1 despojar. 2 desnudar. 3 tech desmontar. **striptease** n strip-tease, estriptis m.

strip[2] (strip) n 1 tira f. 2 faja f. 3 franja f.

stripe (straip) n 1 raya, lista f. 2 banda f. 3 mil galón m. vt rayar, listar.

strive* (straiv) vi esforzarse.

strode (stroud) v see **stride.**

stroke[1] (strouk) n 1 golpe m. 2 med apoplejía f.

stroke[2] (strouk) vt acariciar. n caricia f.

stroll (stroul) vi pasear. n paseo m.

strong (strɔŋ) adj fuerte. **stronghold** n 1 plaza fuerte f. 2 baluarte m. **strong-minded** adj resuelto.

strove (strouv) v see **strive.**

struck (strʌk) v see **strike.**

structure ('strʌktʃə) n estructura f.

struggle ('strʌgəl) vi luchar. n lucha f.

strum (strʌm) vt rasguear.

strung (strʌŋ) v see **string.**

strut[1] (strʌt) vi pavonearse. n contoneo m.

strut[2] (strʌt) n puntal m.

stub (stʌb) n 1 cabo m. 2 talón m. 3 colilla f. vt 1 desarraigar. 2 apagar.

stubborn ('stʌbən) adj tenaz. **stubbornness** n tenacidad f.

stud[1] (stʌd) n 1 botón de pasador m. 2 tachón m. tachuela f.

stud[2] (stʌd) n caballeriza f.

student ('stju:dnt) n estudiante m,f.

studio ('stju:diou) n estudio m.

study ('stʌdi) n estudio m. vt,vi estudiar. **studious** adj estudioso.

stuff (stʌf) n 1 materia f. 2 tela f. 3 inf cosa f. vt 1 llenar. 2 tapar. 3 cul rellenar. **stuffing** n relleno m. **stuffy** adj 1 sofocante. 2 inf remilgado, estirado. 3 inf de miras estrechas.

stumble ('stʌmbəl) vi tropezar. n tropezón, traspié m. **stumbling block** n obstáculo m.

stump (stʌmp) n 1 tocón m. 2 muñón m. 3 raigón m. vi pisar fuerte, cojear. vt inf confundir.

stun (stʌn) vt 1 aturdir. 2 pasmar.

stung (stʌŋ) v see **sting.**

stunk (stʌŋk) v see **stink.**

stunt[1] (stʌnt) vt atrofiar.

stunt[2] (stʌnt) n 1 acrobacia f. 2 truco m.

stupid ('stju:pid) adj estúpido. **stupidity** n estupidez f.

sturdy ('stə:di) adj 1 robusto, fuerte. 2 vigoroso.

sturgeon ('stə:dʒən) n esturión m.

stutter ('stʌtə) vi tartamudear. n tartamudeo m. **stutterer** n tartamudo m.

sty (stai) n pocilga f.

style (stail) n estilo m. vt cortar a la moda. **stylish** adj elegante, a la moda. **stylist** n estilista m,f. **stylized** adj estilizado.

stylus ('stailəs) n 1 aguja f. 2 estilo m.

subconscious (sʌb'kɔnʃəs) adj,n subconsciente m.

subcontract (sʌbkɔn'trækt) vt subcontratar.

subdue (səb'dju:) vt 1 dominar. 2 suavizar. 3 amansar.

subject (n,adj 'sʌbdʒikt; v səb'dʒekt) n 1 gram sujeto m. 2 tema, asunto m. 3 educ asignatura f. adj 1 sujeto. 2 sometido, supeditado. vt someter. **subjective** adj subjetivo.

subjunctive (səb'dʒʌŋktiv) adj,n subjuntivo m.

sublime (sə'blaim) adj sublime.

submachine gun (sʌbmə'ʃi:ngʌn) n metralleta f.

submarine (sʌbmə'ri:n) adj,n submarino m.

submerge (səb'mə:dʒ) vt sumergir.

submit (səb'mit) vt 1 someter. 2 presentar 3 proponer. vi someterse, rendirse. **submission** n sumisión f. **submissive** adj sumiso.

subnormal (sʌb'nɔ:məl) adj subnormal.

subordinate (adj,n sə'bɔ:dinət; v sə'bɔ:dineit) adj,n subordinado m. vt subordinar.

subscribe (səb'skraib) vi suscribirse. **subscriber** n suscriptor, abonado m. **subscription** n 1 suscripción m. 2 cuota f.

subsequent ('sʌbsikwint) adj subsiguiente.

subservient (səb'sə:viənt) adj 1 subordinado. 2 servil.

subside (səb'said) vi 1 bajar. 2 amainar. 3 hundirse.

subsidiary (səb'sidiəri) adj 1 subsidiario, auxiliar. 2 comm filial. n filial, sucursal f.

subsidize ('sʌbsidaiz) vt subvencionar. **subsidy** n subvención f. subsidio m.

subsist (səb'sist) vi subsistir. **subsistence** n subsistencia f.

substance ('sʌbstəns) n sustancia f. **substantial** adj 1 sustancial. 2 considerable. 3 sólido. **substantive** adj,n sustantivo m.

substitute ('sʌbstitju:t) vt 1 sustituir. 2 reemplazar. n sustituto m. adj 1 sucedáneo. 2 suplente.

subtitle ('sʌbtaitļ) n subtítulo m.

subtle ('sʌtļ) adj 1 sutil. 2 fino. **subtlety** n 1 sutileza f. 2 astucia f.

subtract (səb'trækt) vt sustraer. **subtraction** n sustracción f.

suburb ('sʌbə:b) n barrio de las afueras, extrarradio m. **suburban** adj suburbano.

subvert (sʌb'və:t) vt subvertir. **subversion** n subversión f. **subversive** adj subversivo.

subway ('sʌbwei) n paso subterráneo m.

succeed (sək'si:d) vi lograr, conseguir. vt 1 suceder. 2 seguir. **success** n éxito m. **successful** adj 1 afortunado. 2 próspero. 3 feliz. **be successful** vi tener éxito. 2 prosperar. **succession** n sucesión f. **successive** adj sucesivo. **successor** n sucesor m.

succulent ('sʌkjulənt) adj suculento.

succumb (sə'kʌm) vi sucumbir.

such (sʌtʃ) adj tal, semejante. adv tan. pron tal. **suchlike** adj tal. pron otros tales m pl. otras tales f pl.

suck (sʌk) vt 1 chupar. 2 mamar. 3 sorber.

sucker ('sʌkə) n 1 zool ventosa f. 2 bot serpollo m. 3 sl primo m.

suction ('sʌkʃən) n succión f.

Sudan (su:'dæn) n Sudán m. **Sudanese** adj,n sudanés.

sudden ('sʌdn) adj repentino, súbito. **all of a sudden** de repente. **suddenly** adv de repente, pronto.

suds (sʌdz) n pl jabonaduras f pl.

sue (su:) vt,vi demandar, poner pleito.

suede (sweid) n ante m. gamuza f.

suet ('su:it) n sebo m.

suffer ('sʌfə) vt,vi 1 sufrir. 2 padecer. 3 aguantar. 4 adolecer de. **sufferer** n 1 enfermo m. 2 víctima f. **suffering** n sufrimiento, dolor m.

suffice (sə'fais) vi bastar, ser suficiente. **sufficient** adj suficiente.

suffix ('sʌfiks) n sufijo m.

suffocate ('sʌfəkeit) vt ahogar, asfixiar. **suffocating** adj sofocante, asfixiante. **suffocation** n sofocación, asfixia f.

sugar ('ʃugə) n azúcar m. vt azucarar. **sugar cane** n caña de azúcar f. **sugary** adj 1 azucarado. 2 almibarado.

suggest (sə'dʒest) vt sugerir. **suggestion** n 1 sugerencia f. 2 sugestión f. 3 indicación f. **suggestive** adj 1 sugestivo. 2 sugerente.

suicide ('su:isaid) n 1 suicidio m. 2 suicida m,f. **commit suicide** suicidarse. **suicidal** adj suicida.

suit (sju:t) n 1 traje m. 2 pleito m. 3 petición f. 4 game palo m. **follow suit** 1 jugar el mismo palo. 2 hacer lo mismo. ~vt 1 adaptar, ajustar. 2 convenir, ir bien. **suitable** adj conveniente, apropiado, adecuado. **suitcase** n maleta f.

suite (swi:t) n 1 juego m. 2 séquito m. 3 suite f.

sulk (sʌlk) vi estar mohino. **sulky** adj mohino, malhumorado.

sullen ('sʌlən) adj hosco, malhumorado.

sulphur ('sʌlfə) n azufre m.

sultan ('sʌltən) n sultán m. **sultana** (sʌl'ta:nə) n pasa de Esmirna f.

sultry ('sʌltri) adj bochornoso.

sum (sʌm) n 1 suma f. 2 problema m. 3 cantidad f. vt sumar. **sum up** resumir.

summarize ('sʌməraiz) vt resumir, compendiar.

summer ('sʌmə) n verano, estío m. adj de verano. **summertime** n verano m.

summit ('sʌmit) n cima, cumbre f.

summon ('sʌmən) vt 1 llamar. 2 convocar. 3 citar. **summon up** 1 evocar. 2 (courage, energy, etc.) colorar. **summons** n 1 citación f. 2 requerimiento m.

sun (sʌn) n sol m.

sunbathe ('sʌnbeið) vi tomar el sol.

sunburn ('sʌnbə:n) n quemadura del sol f.

Sunday ('sʌndi) n domingo m. adj dominical.

sundial ('sʌndaiəl) n reloj de sol m.

sundry ('sʌndri) adj varios. **sundries** n pl géneros diversos m pl.

sunflower ('sʌnflauə) n girasol m.

sung (sʌŋ) v see **sing**.

sunglasses ('sʌnglɑ:siz) n pl gafas de sol f pl.

sunk (sʌŋk) v see **sink**.

sunlight ('sʌnlait) n luz del sol f.

sunny ('sʌni) adj soleado.

sunrise ('sʌnraiz) n salida del sol f.

sunset ('sʌnset) n puesta del sol f.

sunshine ('sʌnʃain) n sol m. luz del sol f.

sunstroke ('sʌnstrouk) n insolación f.

suntan ('sʌntæn) n bronceado m.

super ('su:pə) adj inf estupendo. interj ¡qué bien!

superannuation (su:pərænju'eiʃən) n jubilación f.

superb (su:'pə:b) adj magnífico, espléndido.

superficial (su:pə'fiʃəl) adj superficial.

superfluous (su:'pə:fluəs) adj 1 superfluo. 2 sobrante.

superhuman (su:pə'hju:mən) adj sobrehumano.

superimpose (su:pərim'pouz) vt sobreponer.

superintendent (su:pərin'tendənt) n superintendente m,f.

sweet

superior (su'piəriə) adj,n superior m.

superlative (su'pə:lətiv) adj,n superlativo m.

supermarket ('su:pəmɑ:kit) n supermercado m.

supernatural (su:pə'nætʃrəl) adj sobrenatural.

supersonic (su:pə'sɔnik) adj supersónico.

superstition (su:pə'stiʃən) n superstición f.

supervise ('su:pəvaiz) vt supervisar.

supper ('sʌpə) n cena f. have supper cenar.

supple ('sʌpəl) adj 1 flexible. 2 dócil. 3 servil.

supplement ('sʌplimənt) n 1 suplemento m. 2 apéndice m.

supply (sə'plai) n 1 suministro m. 2 pl provisiones f pl. supply and demand oferta y demanda. ~vt 1 proveer. 2 suplir.

support (sə'pɔ:t) n 1 soporte m. 2 apoyo m. vt 1 sostener. 2 aguantar. support oneself ganarse la vida.

suppose (sə'pouz) vt,vi 1 suponer. 2 imaginarse.

suppress (sə'pres) vt 1 suprimir. 2 contener. 3 reprimir.

supreme (sə'pri:m) adj 1 supremo. 2 sumo.

surcharge ('sə:tʃɑ:dʒ) n sobrecarga f.

sure (ʃuə) adj 1 seguro. 2 cierto. make sure comprobar. ~adv ciertamente. surely adj 1 seguramente. 2 por supuesto. surety n 1 garantía f. 2 fianza f. 3 fiador m.

surf (sə:f) n 1 espuma f. 2 rompiente m. 3 oleaje m.

surface ('sə:fis) n superficie f. adj de la superficie. vt recubrir. vi emerger.

surfeit ('sə:fit) n 1 hartura f. 2 empacho m. 3 exceso m. vt hartar. vi saciarse.

surge (sə:dʒ) n oleada f. vi agitarse, hervir.

surgeon ('sə:dʒən) n cirujano m. surgery n 1 cirugía f. 2 consultorio m.

surly ('sə:li) adj malhumorado, hosco.

surmise (sə'maiz) n conjetura, suposición f. vt conjeturar.

surmount (sə'maunt) vt 1 superar, vencer. 2 coronar.

surname ('sə:neim) n apellido m. vt apellidar.

surpass (sə'pɑ:s) vt 1 superar. 2 exceder.

surplus ('sə:pləs) n 1 excedente m. 2 superávit m. adj sobrante, de sobra.

surprise (sə'praiz) n sorpresa f. asombro m. vt asombrar, sorprender.

surrealism (sə'riəlizəm) n surrealismo m.

surrender (sə'rendə) n 1 rendición f. 2 entrega f. vt rendir. vi entregarse.

surreptitious (sʌrəp'tiʃəs) adj subrepticio, clandestino.

surround (sə'raund) n borde m. vt 1 rodear. 2 sitiar.

survey (v sə'vei; n 'sə:vei) vt 1 mirar. 2 inspeccionar. n vista, inspección f. surveyor n 1 agrimensor m. 2 inspector m.

survive (sə'vaiv) vt,vi 1 sobrevivir. 2 subsistir. survival n supervivencia f.

susceptible (sə'septəbəl) adj 1 susceptible. 2 impresionable. 3 enamoradizo.

suspect (v sə'spekt; n,adj 'sʌspekt) vt 1 sospechar. 2 recelar. adj,n sospechoso m.

suspend (sə'spend) vt suspender. suspense n incertidumbre f. suspense m. suspension n suspensión f.

suspicion (sə'spiʃən) n 1 sospecha f. 2 recelo m. 3 dejo m. suspicious adj 1 sospechoso. 2 receloso.

sustain (sə'stein) vt 1 sostener. 2 sustentar. 3 sufrir. 4 confirmar.

swab (swɔb) n med algodón m. vt med limpiar con algodón.

swagger ('swægə) n contoneo m. vi contonearse.

swallow¹ ('swɔlou) n trago m. vt 1 tragar. 2 engullir.

swallow² ('swɔlou) n golondrina f.

swam (swæm) v see swim.

swamp (swɔmp) n pantano m. vt 1 sumergir. 2 hundir. 3 abrumar.

swan (swɔn) n cisne m.

swank (swæŋk) n 1 fachenda f. 2 ostentación f. fachendón m. vi darse humos.

swap (swɔp) n intercambio m. vt intercambiar, canjear.

swarm (swɔ:m) n 1 enjambre m. 2 multitud f. vi 1 enjambrar. 2 pulular.

swastika ('swɔstikə) n esvástica, cruz gamada f.

swat (swɔt) vt aplastar, matar.

sway (swei) n 1 balanceo m. 2 dominio m. 3 influencia f. vt 1 balancear. 2 influir. vi oscilar.

swear* (swɛə) vt 1 jurar. 2 declarar bajo juramento. vi 1 jurar. 2 decir tacos. 3 blasfemar.

sweat (swet) n 1 sudor m. 2 trabajo duro m. vt,vi sudar. sweater n suéter m.

swede (swi:d) n nabo sueco m.

Sweden ('swi:dn) n Suecia f. Swede n sueco m. Swedish adj sueco. Swedish (language) n sueco m.

sweep* (swi:p) n 1 barredura f. 2 redada f vt barrer. sweep along arrastrar. sweep by pasar rápidamente.

sweet (swi:t) adj 1 dulce. 2 melodioso. 3 amable. n 1 dulce m. 2 postre m. sweet-

285

bread n lechecilla f. **sweet corn** n maíz tierno m. **sweeten** vt 1 endulzar. 2 azucarar. **sweetheart** n novio m. **sweet pea** n guisante de olor m.

swell' (swel) n mar de fondo m. vt hinchar. vi abultarse.

swept (swept) v see **sweep.**

swerve (swə:v) n desvío brusco m. vt,vi desviar bruscamente.

swift (swift) adj 1 rápido. 2 repentino. n vencejo m.

swig (swig) n trago m. vt beber a grandes tragos.

swill (swil) n bazofia f. vt limpiar con agua.

swim' (swim) n nadadura f. vt pasar a nado. vi nadar. **swimming** n natación f. **swimming costume** n traje de baño m. **swimming pool** n piscina f.

swindle ('swindl) n estafa f. vt estafar, timar.

swine (swain) n puerco, cerdo m.

swing' (swiŋ) n 1 balanceo m. 2 columpio m. vt balancear. vi 1 columpiarse. 2 cambiar de dirección.

swipe (swaip) n golpe fuerte m. vt pegar, golpear.

swirl (swə:l) vi arremolinarse. n remolino m.

swish (swiʃ) vi silbar, crujir.

switch (switʃ) n 1 varilla f. 2 látigo m. 3 interruptor m. vt desviar. vi cambiar. **switch on** encender. **switchboard** n cuadro de mandos m.

Switzerland ('switsələnd) n Suiza f. **Swiss** adj,n suizo m.

swivel ('swivəl) n pivote m. vt girar sobre un eje.

swollen ('swoulən) v see **swell.**

swoop (swu:p) n 1 calada f. 2 redada f. vi precipitarse.

swop (swɔp) n intercambio m. vt intercambiar.

sword (sɔ:d) n espada f. **swordfish** n pez espada m. **swordsman** n espadachín m.

swore (swɔ:) v see **swear.**

sworn (swɔ:n) v see **swear.**

swot (swɔt) n inf empollón m. vt inf empollar.

swum (swʌm) v see **swim.**

swung (swʌŋ) v see **swing.**

sycamore ('sikəmɔ:) n sicomoro m.

syllable ('siləbəl) n sílaba f.

syllabus ('siləbəs) n programa f.

symbol ('simbəl) n símbolo m. **symbolism** n simbolismo m. **symbolize** vt simbolizar.

symmetry ('simitri) n simetría f.

sympathy ('simpəθi) n 1 simpatía f. 2 com-

pasión f. **sympathize** vi 1 simpatizar. 2 compadecerse. 3 comprender.

symphony ('simfəni) n sinfonía f.

symposium (sim'pouziəm) n, pl **symposia** simposio m.

symptom ('simptəm) n 1 síntoma m. 2 indicio m.

synagogue ('sinəgɔg) n sinagoga f.

synchronize ('siŋkrənaiz) vt sincronizar.

syndicate (n 'sindikit; v 'sindikeit) n sindicato m. vt sindicar.

syndrome ('sindroum) n síndrome m.

synonym ('sinənim) n sinónimo m.

synopsis (si'nɔpsis) n, pl **synopses** sinopsis f.

syntax ('sintæks) n sintaxis f.

synthesis ('sinθəsis) n, pl **syntheses** síntesis f. **synthetic** adj sintético.

syphilis ('sifəlis) n sífilis f.

Syria ('siriə) n Siria f. **Syrian** adj,n sirio.

syringe (si'rindʒ) n jeringa f. vt jeringar.

syrup ('sirəp) n 1 jarabe m. 2 almíbar m.

system ('sistəm) n 1 sistema m. 2 método m. **systematic** adj sistemático, metódico.

T

tab (tæb) n 1 oreja f. 2 etiqueta f. **keep tabs on** irgilar a.

tabby ('tæbi) n gato atigrado m.

table ('teibəl) n 1 mesa f. 2 math tabla f. vt presentar. **tablecloth** n mantel m. **tablemat** n salvamanteles m invar. **tablespoon** n cuchara grande f. **table tennis** n tenis de mesa m

tablet ('tæblət) n 1 tableta f. 2 píldora f. 3 pastilla f.

taboo (tə'bu:) n adj,n tabú m.

tack (tæk) n 1 tachuela f. 2 hilván m. vt clavar con tachuelas. vi naut virar.

tackle ('tækəl) n 1 aparejo m. 2 equipo m. vt 1 agarrar. 2 emprender.

tact (tækt) n tacto m. discreción f. **tactful** adj discreto.

tactic ('tæktik) n 1 táctica f. 2 maniobra f.

tadpole ('tædpoul) n renacuajo m.

taffeta ('tæfitə) n tafetán m.

tag (tæg) n 1 etiqueta f. 2 cabo m. 3 herrete m. vt pegar una etiqueta a. **tag along** ir también.

tail (teil) n 1 cola f. 2 faldón m. vt inf seguir de cerca a. **tail off** disminuir.

tailor ('teilə) n sastre m. **tailor's shop** n sastrería f. vt confeccionar.

taint (teint) n 1 infección f. 2 mancha f. vt corromper, viciar.

take* (teik) vt 1 tomar. 2 coger. **take aback** desconcertar. vi 1 pegar. 2 tener éxito. **take after** parecerse a. **take-off** n 1 despegue m. 2 caricatura f. **take-over** n tomar posesión f.

talcum powder ('tælkəm) n polvos de talco m pl.

tale (teil) n 1 cuento m. 2 patraña f. **tell tales** chismear, contar cuentos.

talent ('tælənt) n talento m.

talk (tɔ:k) n 1 conversación f. 2 charla f. vi,vt hablar. **talk into** persuadir. **talk over** discutir. **talkative** adj locuaz, hablador.

tall (tɔ:l) adj alto.

tally ('tæli) n 1 tarja f. 2 cuenta f. vi concordar.

talon ('tælən) n garra, uña f.

tambourine (tæmbə'ri:n) n pandereta f.

tame (teim) adj 1 domesticado. 2 manso. 3 soso. vt 1 amansar. 2 reprimir.

tamper ('tæmpə) vi **tamper with** 1 estropear. 2 falsificar. 3 entrometerse.

tampon ('tæmpɔn) n 1 tapón m. 2 tampón m.

tan (tæn) n bronceado m. vt 1 broncear. 2 curtir.

tangent ('tændʒənt) n tangente f.

tangerine (tændʒə'ri:n) n mandarina f.

tangible ('tændʒəbəl) adj 1 tangible. 2 palpable.

tangle ('tæŋgəl) n enredo m. maraña f. vt enredar.

tango ('tæŋgou) n tango m. vi bailar el tango.

tank (tæŋk) n 1 tanque m. 2 cisterna f. 3 carro de combate m. **tanker** n 1 petrolero m. 2 camión-tanque m.

tankard ('tæŋkəd) n pichel m.

tantalize ('tæntəlaiz) vt,vi atormentar, tentar.

tantrum ('tæntrəm) n rabieta f.

tap¹ (tæp) n 1 palmadita f. 2 golpecito m. vt golpear ligeramente.

tap² (tæp) n grifo m. **on tap** de tonel. ~vt 1 espitar. 2 sangrar.

tape (teip) n cinta f. vt grabar en cinta. **tape-measure** n cinta métrica f. **tape-recorder** n magnetófon m.

taper ('teipə) n 1 bujía f. 2 cirio m. vt afilar. vi rematar en punta.

tapestry ('tæpistri) n 1 tapiz m. 2 tapicería f.

tar (tɑ:) n alquitrán m. brea f. vt alquitranar. **tarmac** n alquitranado m.

tarantula (tə'ræntjulə) n tarántula f.

target ('tɑ:git) n 1 blanco m. 2 objetivo m.

tariff ('tærif) n tarifa f.

tarnish ('tɑ:niʃ) vt deslustrar.

tarragon ('tærəgən) n estragón m.

tart¹ (tɑ:t) adj ácido, agrio.

tart² (tɑ:t) n 1 tarta f. 2 pastelillo m. 3 inf fulana f.

tartan ('tɑ:tn) n tartán m.

task (tɑ:sk) n 1 tarea f. 2 empresa f. **take to task** reprender.

tassel ('tæsəl) n borla f.

taste (teist) n 1 sabor m. 2 gusto m. 3 afición f. vt probar. vi saber.

tattoo¹ (tə'tu:) n 1 retreta f. 2 espectáculo militar m.

tattoo² (tə'tu:) n tatuaje m. vt tatuar.

taught (tɔ:t) v see **teach.**

taunt (tɔ:nt) n 1 mofa f. 2 sarcasmo m. vt 1 mofarse de. 2 reprochar.

Taurus ('tɔ:rəs) n Tauro m.

taut (tɔ:t) adj tieso, tirante.

tautology (tɔ:'tɔlədʒi) n tautología f.

tavern ('tævən) n taberna f.

tax (tæks) n 1 impuesto m. 2 carga f. vt 1 imponer contribuciones a. 2 tasar. 3 acusar.

taxi ('tæksi) n taxi m. vi aviat rodar de suelo.

tea (ti:) n 1 té m. 2 merienda f. **high tea** merienda-cena f. **tea-bag** n sobre de té m. **tea-break** n descanso para té m. **tea-cloth** n paño de cocina m. **teacup** n taza para té f. **teapot** n tetera f. **teaspoon** n cucharilla f.

teach* (ti:tʃ) vt enseñar. vi ser profesor.

teak (ti:k) n teca f.

team (ti:m) n 1 equipo m. 2 yunta f. v **team up with** asociarse con.

tear¹ (tiə) n lágrima f. **shed tears** llorar. **teardrop** n lágrima f. **tear-gas** n gas lacrimógeno m.

tear*² (tɛə) n rasgón m. vt rasgar. vi arrancar. **tear up** romper.

tease (ti:z) vt 1 fastidiar. 2 tomar el pelo a. 3 cardar. n guasón m.

teat (ti:t) n 1 pezón m. 2 teta f.

technical ('teknikəl) adj 1 técnico. 2 laboral. **technician** n 1 técnico m. 2 ayudante de laboratorio m. **technique** n técnica f. **technology** n tecnología f.

tedious ('ti:diəs) adj aburrido, tedioso.

tee (ti:) n meta f.

teenage ('ti:neidʒ) adj,n adolescente.

teetotal (ti:'toutl) adj abstemio.

telegram ('teligræm) n telegrama m.

telegraph ('teligrɑ:f) n telégrafo m. vt,vi telegrafiar. **telegraph pole** n poste telegráfico m.

telepathy (ti'lepəθi) n telepatía f.

telephone ('telifoun) n teléfono m. vt,vi telefonear. **be on the telephone** tener teléfono.

telescope ('teliskoup) n telescopio m. vt 1 enchufar. 2 telescopar.

television ('teləviʒən) n televisión f. **televize** vt televisar.

telex ('teleks) n télex m.

tell* (tel) vt 1 decir. 2 contar. 3 anunciar. **tell off** regañar. vi 1 hablar. 2 distinguir. **telltale** adj revelador.

temper ('tempə) n 1 genio, humor m. 2 temple m. vt templar. **temperament** n temperamento m. **temperate** adj 1 templado. 2 moderado. **temperature** n 1 temperatura f. 2 fiebre f.

tempest ('tempist) n tempestad f.

tempestuous (tem'pestjuəs) adj tempestuoso.

temple[1] ('tempəl) n templo m.

temple[2] ('tempəl) n anat sien f.

tempo ('tempou) n, pl **tempi** 1 tempo m. 2 ritmo m.

temporal ('tempərəl) adj temporal. **temporary** adj 1 provisional. 2 interino.

tempt (tempt) vt 1 tentar. 2 atraer.

ten (ten) adj,n diez m. **tenth** adj,n décimo m.

tenacious (tə'neiʃəs) adj 1 tenaz. 2 porfiado. **tenacity** n tenacidad f.

tenant ('tenənt) n 1 inquilino m. 2 morador m. **tenancy** n 1 tenencia f. 2 arriendo m.

tend[1] (tend) vi 1 tender. 2 inclinarse a. **tendency** n tendencia, propensión f.

tend[2] (tend) vt cuidar, atender.

tender[1] ('tendə) adj 1 tierno. 2 delicado. 3 blando.

tender[2] ('tendə) n oferta f. **legal tender** moneda de curso legal f. vt 1 ofrecer. 2 presentar.

tendon ('tendən) n tendón m.

tendril ('tendril) n zarcillo m.

tenement ('tenəmənt) n 1 vivienda f. 2 casa de vecindad f.

tennis ('tenis) n tenis m. **tennis court** n pista de tenis f.

tenor ('tenə) n 1 tenor m. 2 curso m.

tense[1] (tens) adj 1 tirante. 2 tieso. 3 tenso. **tension** n 1 tirantez f. 2 tensión f.

tense[2] (tens) n gram tiempo m.

tent (tent) n tienda de campaña f.

tentacle ('tentəkəl) n tentáculo m.

tentative ('tentətiv) adj 1 provisional. 2 experimental.

tenuous ('tenjuəs) adj 1 tenue. 2 sutil.

tepid ('tepid) adj tibio.

term (tə:m) n 1 término m. 2 periodo m. 3 trimestre m. 4 pl condiciones f pl.

terminal ('tə:minl) adj terminal. n 1 término m. 2 borne m.

terminate ('tə:mineit) vt,vi terminar.

terminology (tə:mi'nolədʒi) n terminología f.

terminus ('tə:minəs) n, pl **termini** 1 término m. 2 estación terminal f.

terrace ('terəs) n 1 terraza f. 2 terraplén m. vt terraplenar.

terrestrial (tə'restriəl) adj terrestre.

terrible ('teribəl) adj terrible.

terrify ('terifai) vt aterrar, aterrorizar. **terrific** adj 1 tremendo. 2 inf fabuloso.

territory ('teritri) n territorio m.

terror ('terə) n terror, espanto m. **terrorist** adj,n terrorista m. **terrorize** vt aterrorizar.

Terylene ('terili:n) n Tdmk terylene m.

test (test) n 1 prueba f. 2 examen m. 3 ensayo m. vt probar, poner a prueba.

testament ('testəmənt) n testamento m.

testicle ('testikəl) n. esticulo m.

testify ('testifai) vi declarar. vt atestiguar.

testimony ('testiməni) n testimonio m. **testimonial** n 1 certificado m. 2 recomendación f

tether ('teðə) n atadura, cuerda f. vt atar.

Teutonic (tju:'tonik) adj teutónico.

text (tekst) n 1 texto m. 2 tema m. **textbook** n libro de texto m.

textile ('tekstail) adj textil. **textiles** n pl tejidos m pl.

texture ('tekstʃə) n textura f.

Thames (temz) n Támesis m.

than (ðən; stressed ðæn) conj 1 que. 2 de. 3 del que. 4 de lo que.

thank (θæŋk) vt dar las gracias a. **thank for** agradecer. **thanks** n pl gracias f pl.

that (ðæt) adj 1 ese, aquel. 2 esa, aquella. pron 1 ése, aquél. 2 ésa, aquélla. 3 que, el cual. conj que.

thatch (θætʃ) n 1 paja f. 2 barda f. vt bardar.

thaw (θɔ:) n deshielo m. vt deshelar, derretir. vi deshelarse.

the (ðə; stressed ði:) def art el, la, lo, los, las. adv cuanto.

theatre ('θiətə) n 1 teatro m. 2 quirófano m.

theft (θeft) n hurto, robo m.

their (ðeə) poss adj 3rd pers pl su, sus. **theirs** poss pron 3rd pers pl el suyo, la suya, los suyos, las suyas, de ellos, de ellas.

them (ðəm; stressed ðem) pron 3rd pers pl 1 los, las. 2 les. 3 ellos, ellas. **themselves** pron

3rd pers pl **1** ellos mismos, ellas mismas. **2** se. **3** sí mismos, ellas mismas.

theme (θi:m) *n* tema *m.*

then (ðən; *stressed* ðen) *adv* **1** entonces. **2** después. **now and then** de vez en cuando. *conj* **1** pues. **2** por tanto.

theology (θiˈɔlədʒi) *n* teología *f.* **theologian** *n* teólogo *m.*

theorem (ˈθiərəm) *n* teorema *m.*

theory (ˈθiəri) *n* teoría *f.* **theoretical** *adj* teórico. **theorize** *vi* teorizar.

therapy (ˈθerəpi) *n* terapia *f.* **therapeutic** *adj* terapéutico.

there (ðɛə) *adv* **1** ahí. **2** allí. **3** allá. **there** *is or* **are** hay. ~*interj* ¡vaya! ¡llévamos! **thereabouts** *adv* **1** por ahí. **2** aproximadamente. **thereafter** *adv* después de eso. **thereby** *adv* **1** por eso. **2** por esa razón. **therefore** *adv* por tanto, por consiguiente. **thereupon** *adv* **1** en eso. **2** en seguida. **3** por tanto. **therewith** *adv* con eso, con lo mismo.

thermal (ˈθəːməl) *adj* termal.

thermodynamics (θəːmoudaiˈnæmiks) *n* termodinámica *f.*

thermometer (θəˈmɔmitə) *n* termómetro *m.*

thermonuclear (θəːmouˈnjuːkliə) *adj* termonuclear.

Thermos (ˈθəːməs) *n Tdmk* termo *m.*

thermostat (ˈθəːməstæt) *n* termostato *m.*

these (ðiːz) *adj* estos, estas. *pron* éstos, éstas.

thesis (ˈθiːsis) *n, pl* **theses** tesis *f.*

they (ðei) *pron 3rd pers pl* ellos, ellas.

thick (θik) *adj* **1** espeso. **2** grueso. **3** denso. **4** turbio. **5** *inf* estúpido. **thicken** *vt* espesar. **thick-skinned** *adj* insensible, duro.

thief (θiːf) *n, pl* **thieves** ladrón *m.*

thigh (θai) *n* muslo *m.*

thimble (ˈθimbəl) *n* **1** dedal *m.* **2** guardacabo *m.*

thin (θin) *adj* **1** delgado. **2** escaso. **3** flaco. *vi* **1** adelgazar. **2** reducirse. **thin-skinned** *adj* **1** de piel fina. **2** sensible.

thing (θiŋ) *n* **1** cosa *f.* **2** asunto *m.*

think* (θiŋk) *vt* **1** pensar. **2** imaginar. **3** considerar. **4** creer. **think of 1** considerar. **2** pensar en. **think over** reflexionar.

third (θəːd) *adj* tercero. *n* tercio *m.* tercera parte *f.* **third party** *adj* tercera persona. **third-rate** *adj* de baja categoría.

thirst (θəːst) *n* **1** sed *f.* **2** ansia *m.* *vi* tener sed. **thirsty** *adj* **1** sediento. **2** árido. **be thirsty** tener sed.

thirteen (θəːˈtiːn) *adj,n* trece *m.* **thirteenth** *adj* decimotercio.

thirty (ˈθəːti) *adj,n* treinta *m.* **thirtieth** *adj* trigésimo.

this (ðis) *adj* este, esta. *pron* éste, ésta, esto.

thistle (ˈθisəl) *n* cardo *m.*

thorn (θɔːn) *n* espina *f.*

thorough (ˈθʌrə) *adj* **1** completo. **2** concienzudo. **thoroughbred** *adj* de pura sangre. **thoroughfare** *n* vía pública *f.*

those (ðouz) *adj* esos, aquellos, esas, aquellas. *pron* ésos, aquéllos, ésas, aquéllas.

though (ðou) *conj* aunque. *adv* sin embargo.

thought[1] (θɔːt) *n* **1** pensamiento *m.* **2** concepto *m.* **3** reflexión *f.* **on second thoughts** después de pensarlo bien. **thoughtful** *adj* **1** pensativo. **2** atento. **3** serio. **thoughtless** *adj* **1** irreflexivo. **2** inconsiderado.

thought[2] (θɔːt) *v see* **think**.

thousand (ˈθauzənd) *adj,n* mil *m.* **thousandth** *adj,n* milésimo *m.*

thrash (θræʃ) *vt* **1** golpear. **2** azotar. **3** derrotar. **thrash about** sacudirse.

thread (θred) *n* **1** hilo *m.* **2** hebra *f.* **3** rosca *f.* *vt* enhebrar. **threadbare** *adj* raído, gastado.

threat (θret) *n* amenaza *f.* **threaten** *vt,vi* amenazar.

three (θriː) *adj,n* tres *m.* **three-cornered** *adj* triangular. **three-dimensional** *adj* tridimensional.

thresh (θreʃ) *vt* trillar.

threshold (ˈθreʃhould) *n* umbral *m.*

threw (θruː) *v see* **throw**.

thrift (θrift) *n* economía, frugalidad *f.*

thrill (θril) *n* **1** emoción *f.* **2** estremecimiento *m.* *vt* emocionar. **thriller** *n* novela de misterio *f.*

thrive (θraiv) *vi* **1** prosperar. **2** crecer mucho.

throat (θrout) *n* garganta *f.* **clear the throat** aclarar la voz.

throb (θrɔb) *n* **1** latido *m.* **2** vibración *f.* *vi* **1** latir. **2** vibrar.

throne (θroun) *n* **1** trono *m.* **2** corona *f.*

throng (θrɔŋ) *n* multitud *f.* *vt* atestar. **throng together** reunirse en tropel.

throttle (ˈθrɔtl) *n* **1** gaznate *m.* **2** regulador *m.* *vt* ahogar.

through (θruː) *adj* **1** a través. **2** completamente. *prep* **1** por. **2** a través de. **3** hasta. **throughout** *adv* **1** en todas partes. **2** todo el tiempo. *prep* por todo.

throw* (θrou) *n* **1** tirada *f.* **2** lance *m.* *vt* echar, tirar. **throw up** vomitar.

thrush (θrʌʃ) *n zool* zorzal, tordo *m.*

thrust* (θrʌst) n 1 empuje m. 2 avance m. 3 puñalada f. vt empujar. vi 1 acometer. 2 meterse.

thud (θʌd) n ruido sordo m. vi hacer un ruido sordo.

thumb (θʌm) n pulgar m. vt manosear.

thump (θʌmp) n golpazo m. vt golpear.

thunder ('θʌndə) n 1 trueno m. 2 estruendo m. vi tronar. **thunderstorm** n tormenta, tronada f.

Thursday ('θəːzdi) n jueves m.

thus (ðʌs) adv 1 así. 2 de este modo. **thus far** hasta aquí.

thwart (θwɔːt) n bancada f. vt frusrar.

thyme (taim) n tomillo m.

thyroid ('θairɔid) n tiroides m. adj tiroideo.

tiara (ti'ɑːrə) n diadema f.

tick¹ (tik) n 1 tictac m. 2 momento m. 3 señal f.

tick² (tik) n zool garrapata f.

ticket ('tikit) n 1 billete m. 2 entrada f. 3 etiqueta f. **ticket-collector** n revisor m. **ticket-office** n 1 despacho de billetes m. 2 Th taquilla f.

tickle ('tikəl) vt 1 hacer cosquillas a. 2 divertir. n cosquillas f pl. **ticklish** adj 1 cosquilloso. 2 delicado.

tide (taid) n 1 marea f. 2 corriente f. **tidemark** n lengua del agua f.

tidy ('taidi) adj 1 ordenado. 2 aseado. 3 considerable. vt asear, limpiar.

tie (tai) n 1 lazo m. 2 corbata f. 3 empate m. vt 1 atar. 2 anudar. **tie up** atracar.

tier (tiə) n grada, fila f.

tiger ('taigə) n tigre m.

tight (tait) adj 1 tieso. 2 apretado. 3 escaso. 4 inf borracho. **tighten** vt 1 apretar. 2 estirar. **tight-fisted** adj agarrado, tacaño. **tightrope** n cuerda de volatinero f. **tights** n pl mallas f pl. leotardos m pl.

tilde ('tildə) n tilde f.

tile (tail) n 1 teja f. 2 baldosa f. 3 azulejo m. vt tejar.

till¹ (til) prep hasta. conj hasta que.

till² (til) vt cultivar, labrar.

till³ (til) n caja registradora f.

tiller ('tilə) n naut caña del timón f.

tilt (tilt) n 1 inclinación f. 2 ladeo m. 3 torneo m. vt inclinar.

timber ('timbə) n 1 madera f. 2 bosque m. 3 madero m.

time (taim) n 1 tiempo m. 2 período m. 3 época f. 4 hora f. **from time to time** de vez en cuando. **time bomb** n bomba de relojería f. **timetable** n 1 horario m. 2 programa m.

timid ('timid) adj tímido.

timpani ('timpəni) n pl tímpanos m pl.

tin (tin) n 1 estaño m. 2 lata f. 3 hojalata f. vt 1 estañar. 2 envasar en lata. **tin-opener** n abrelatas m invar.

tinge (tindʒ) n 1 tinte m. 2 matiz m. vt 1 teñir. 2 matizar.

tingle ('tiŋgəl) n 1 picazón f. 2 hormigueo m. vi sentir hormigueo.

tinker ('tiŋkə) n calderero m. vt remendar. vi tratar de reparar.

tinkle ('tiŋkəl) n 1 retintín m. 2 campanilleo m. vi campanillear.

tinsel ('tinsəl) n oropel m.

tint (tint) n tinte m. vt teñir, matizar.

tiny ('taini) adj pequeñito, diminuto.

tip¹ (tip) n punta f. cabo m. **from tip to toe** de pies a cabeza. **tiptoe** vi ir de puntillas. **on tiptoe** de puntillas f.

tip² (tip) vt inclinar, ladear.

tip³ (tip) n propina f.

tipsy ('tipsi) adj achispado.

tire ('taiə) vt 1 cansar. 2 aburrir. **tired** adj cansado.

tissue ('tiʃuː) n 1 tejido m. 2 tisú m. 3 pañuelo de papel m.

title ('taitl) n 1 título m. 2 derecho m. vt titular.

to (tə; stressed tuː) prep 1 a. 2 hacia. 3 hasta. 4 para. **to-do** n inf lío, follón m.

toad (toud) n sapo m. **toadstool** n hongo venenoso m.

toast¹ (toust) n pan tostado m. vt tostar.

toast² (toust) n brindis m. vt brindar por.

tobacco (tə'bækou) n tabaco m.

toboggan (tə'bɔgən) n tobogán m.

today (tə'dei) adv 1 hoy. 2 hoy en día.

toddler ('tɔdlə) n niño aprendiendo a andar m.

toe (tou) n dedo del pie m. **toenail** n uña del dedo del pie f.

toffee ('tɔfi) n caramelo m.

together (tə'geðə) adv 1 junto. 2 juntamente. 3 a la vez.

toil (tɔil) n 1 labor f. 2 fatiga f. 3 esfuerzo m. vi 1 trabajar. 2 fatigarse.

toilet ('tɔilət) n 1 tocado m. 2 lavabo m. 3 tocador m. 4 wáter m. **toilet paper** n papel higiénico m. **toilet water** n agua de colonia m.

token ('toukən) n 1 signo m. 2 prenda f. 3 recuerdo m.

told (tould) v see **tell.**

tolerate ('tɔləreit) vt tolerar. **tolerance** n tolerancia f.

toll[1] (toul) vt tañer, doblar.

toll[2] (toul) n 1 peaje m. 2 portazgo m. **tollgate** n barrera de peaje f.

tomato (tə'mɑːtou) n, pl **-oes** tomate m.

tomb (tuːm) n tumba f. sepulcro m. **tombstone** n lápida sepulcral f.

tomorrow (tə'mɔrou) adv mañana f. **the day after tomorrow** pasado mañana.

ton (tʌn) n tonelada f.

tone (toun) n 1 tono m. 2 acento. 3 matiz m. vt entonar. vi armonizar.

tongs (tɔŋz) n pl tenacillas, tenazas f pl.

tongue (tʌŋ) n 1 lengua f. 2 badajo m. **hold one's tongue** callarse. **tongue-tied** adj premioso. **tongue-twister** n trabalenguas m invar.

tonic ('tɔnik) adj,n tónico m. n mus tónica f. **tonic water** n agua tónica f.

tonight (tə'nait) adv esta noche.

tonsil ('tɔnsəl) n amígdala f. **tonsilitis** n amigdalitis f.

too (tuː) adv 1 demasiado. 2 también. 3 además.

took (tuk) v see **take**.

tool (tuːl) n herramienta f. 2 instrumento m.

tooth (tuːθ) n, pl **teeth** 1 diente m. 2 muela f. **have a sweet tooth** ser goloso. **toothache** n dolor de muelas m. **toothbrush** n cepillo de dientes m. **toothpaste** n pasta dentífrica f. **toothpick** n mondadientes m invar.

top[1] (tɔp) n 1 cumbre f. 2 parte superior f. adj 1 más alto. 2 superior. vt encabezar. **top hat** n chistera f. **top-heavy** adj mal equilibrado.

top[2] (tɔp) n peonza f.

topaz ('toupæz) n topacio m.

topic ('tɔpik) n asunto, tema m. **topical** adj actual.

topography (tə'pɔgrəfi) n topografía f.

topple ('tɔpəl) vt 1 derribar. 2 hacer caer. vi caerse.

topsoil ('tɔpsɔil) n capa superficial del suelo f.

topsy-turvy (tɔpsi'təːvi) adj confuso, desordenado. adv en desorden.

torch (tɔːtʃ) n 1 antorcha f. 2 linterna f.

tore (tɔː) v see **tear**[2].

toreador ('tɔriədɔ) n torero m.

torment (v tɔː'ment, n 'tɔːment) vt atormentar. n tormento m. tortura f.

torn (tɔːn) v see **tear**[2].

tornado (tɔː'neidou) n, pl **-dos** or **-does** tornado m.

torpedo (tɔː'piːdou) n, pl **-does** torpedo m. vt torpedear.

torrent ('tɔrənt) n torrente m.

torso ('tɔːsou) n torso m.

tortilla (tɔː'tiːjə) n tortilla f.

tortoise ('tɔːtəs) n tortuga f.

tortuous ('tɔːtʃuəs) adj tortuoso.

torture ('tɔːtʃə) n 1 tortura f. 2 tormento m. vt torturar.

Tory ('tɔːri) adj,n conservador m.

toss (tɔs) vt 1 sacudir. 2 echar. **toss up** echar a cara or cruz. ~n 1 sacudida f. 2 echada f.

tot[1] (tɔt) n nene m.

tot[2] (tɔt) vt **tot up** sumar.

total ('toutl) adj 1 total. 2 completo. n total m. vt sumar. **totalitarian** adj totalitario.

totem ('toutəm) n tótem m. **totem pole** n poste totémico f.

totter ('tɔtə) vi 1 bambolearse. 2 estar para caerse.

touch (tʌtʃ) n 1 tacto m. 2 contacto m. 3 pizca m. vt 1 tocar. 2 conmover. **touch off** estallar. **touchy** adj susceptible.

tough (tʌf) adj 1 duro. 2 resistente. 3 tenaz. **toughen** vt.endurecer.

toupee ('tuːpei) n peluca f. pelo postizo m.

tour (tuə) n 1 viaje m. 2 gira f. vt viajar por. vi viajar. **tourism** n turismo m. **tourist** n turista m,f.

tournament ('tuənəmənt) n 1 torneo m. 2 concurso m.

tow (tou) n remolque m. vt remolcar. **towrope** n cable de remolque m.

towards (tə'wɔːdz) prep also **toward** 1 hacia. 2 cerca de. 3 para con.

towel ('tauəl) n toalla f.

tower ('tauə) n torre f. **tower-block** n alto bloque de pisos m. v **tower above** destacarse sobre.

town (taun) n 1 ciudad f. 2 pueblo m. **town clerk** n secretario del ayuntamiento m. **town hall** n ayuntamiento m. **town-planning** n urbanismo m.

toxic ('tɔksik) adj tóxico.

toy (tɔi) n juguete m. v **toy with** jugar con.

trace (treis) n 1 rastro m. 2 vestigio m. 3 señal f. vt 1 trazar. 2 calcar.

track (træk) n 1 huella f. 2 sport pista f. 3 senda f. 4 vía f. vt rastrear. **tracksuit** n mono de entrenamiento m.

tract[1] (trækt) n zona, región f. **digestive tract** canal digestivo m.

tract[2] (trækt) n tratado, folleto m.

tractor ('træktə) n tractor m.
trade (treid) n comercio m. **trademark** n marca registrada f. **tradesman** n tendero, artesano m. **trade union** n sindicato, gremio m. **trade unionism** n sindicalismo m. **trade unionist** n sindicalista m.f.
tradition (trə'diʃən) n tradición f. **traditional** adj tradicional. **traditionalism** n tradicionalismo m.
traffic ('træfik) n 1 mot circulación f. 2 comm tráfico, comercio m. trata f. **traffic jam** n embotellamiento m. **traffic lights** n pl semáforo m. luces de tráfico f pl. **traffic warden** n guardián del tráfico m.
tragedy ('trædʒədi) n tragedia f. **tragic** adj trágico.
trail (treil) n 1 rastro m. pista f. 2 estela, cola f. 3 camino, sendero m. vt 1 arrastrar. 2 rastrear, seguir la pista de. **trailer** n 1 mot remolque m. 2 trailer, avance m.
train (trein) n 1 mot tren m. 2 serie f. **train of thought** hilo del pensamiento m. ~vt 1 adiestrar, preparar. 2 apuntar. **trained** adj capacitado, amaestrado. **trainee** n aprendiz m. **trainer** n entrenador m.
traitor ('treitə) n traidor m. **traitorous** adj traidor, traicionero.
tram (træm) n tranvía m.
tramp (træmp) n 1 marcha pesada f. 2 paseo largo m. 3 vagabundo m. vi marchar pesadamente.
trample ('træmpəl) vt pisar, pisotear.
trampoline ('træmpəli:n) n trampolín m.
trance (trɑ:ns) n 1 arrobamiento, éxtasis m. 2 trance m.
tranquil ('træŋkwil) adj tranquilo. **tranquillity** n tranquilidad f. **tranquillizer** n tranquilizante m.
transact (træn'zækt) vt tramitar, despachar. **transaction** n negocio m. transacción f.
transatlantic (trænzət'læntik) adj transatlántico.
transcend (træn'send) vt exceder, superar.
transcribe (træn'skraib) vt transcribir.
transfer (v træns'fə:; n 'trænsfə:) vt transferir, traspasar. vi trasladarse. n 1 transferencia f. 2 traspaso m. 3 traslado m.
transform (træns'fɔ:m) vt transformar. **transformation** n transformación f.
transfuse (træns'fju:z) vt transfundir. **transfusion** n transfusión f.
transistor (træn'zistə) n transistor m.
transit ('trænsit) n tránsito m. **in transit** de tránsito.

transition (træn'ziʃən) n transición f. **transitional** adj transicional.
transitive ('trænsitiv) adj transitivo.
translate (trænz'leit) vt 1 traducir. 2 interpretar. **translation** n traducción f. **translator** n traductor m.
translucent (trænz'lu:sənt) adj translúcido.
transmit (trænz'mit) vt transmitir. **transmission** n transmisión f. **transmitter** n 1 transmisor m. 2 transmisora, emisora f.
transparent (træns'pærənt) adj transparente.
transplant (v træns'plɑ:nt; n 'trænsplɑ:nt) vt trasplantar. n trasplante m.
transport (v træns'pɔ:t; n 'trænspɔ:t) vt transportar. n transporte m. **transportation** n transportación f.
transpose (træns'pouz) vt transponer.
trap (træp) n 1 trampa f. 2 coche m. vt entrampar, atrapar. **trapdoor** n 1 escotilla f. 2 Th escotillón m.
trapeze (trə'pi:z) n trapecio m.
trash (træʃ) n 1 hojarasca f. 2 trastos viejos m pl.
trauma ('trɔ:mə) n trauma m. **traumatic** adj traumático.
travel ('trævəl) vi 1 viajar. 2 ir. n turismo m. viajes m pl. **travel agency** n agencia de turismo f. **traveller** n 1 viajero m. 2 comm viajante m. **traveller's cheque** n cheque de viajeros m.
trawl (trɔ:l) vi pescar a la rastra. vt rastrear. **trawler** n barco rastreador m.
tray (trei) n bandeja f.
treachery ('tretʃəri) n traición f. **treacherous** adj 1 traidor. 2 engañoso.
treacle ('tri:kəl) n melado m. melaza f.
tread* (tred) n 1 paso m. 2 huella f. vt pisar.
treason ('tri:zən) n traición f. **high treason** alta traición f.
treasure ('treʒə) n 1 tesoro m. 2 inf joya f. **treasure trove** n tesoro hallado m. ~vt atesorar. **treasurer** n tesorero m. **treasury** n tesoro m. hacienda f.
treat (tri:t) vt 1 tratar. 2 invitar. n convite m. **treatment** n tratamiento m.
treatise ('tri:tiz) n tratado m. disertación f.
treatment ('tri:tmənt) n tratamiento m.
treaty ('tri:ti) n tratado m.
treble ('trebəl) adj 1 triple. 2 mus de tiple. **treble clef** n clave de sol f. tiple m, f. ~vt triplicar.
tree (tri:) n árbol m.

trek (trek) n 1 viaje m. 2 migración f. 3 jornada f. vi emigrar, viajar.

trellis ('trelis) n enrejado m.

tremble ('trembəl) vi temblar, estremecerse. n temblor m. **trembling** adj tembloroso. n temblar, temblor m.

tremendous (tri'mendəs) adj tremendo, imponente, formidable.

tremor ('tremə) n 1 temblor m. 2 vibración f.

trench (trentʃ) n zanja f. foso m.

trend (trend) n 1 tendencia, dirección f. 2 moda f. **trendy** adj elegante, modernísimo.

trespass ('trespəs) n 1 intrusión, entrada sin permiso f. 2 ofensa f. vi entrar sin derecho. **no trespassing** prohibida la entrada. **trespasser** n intruso m.

trestle ('tresəl) n caballete m.

trial ('traiəl) n 1 law proceso, juicio m. 2 prueba f. 3 adversidad f. **trial run** n viaje de ensayo m.

triangle ('traiæŋgəl) n triángulo m. **triangular** adj triangular.

tribe (traib) n tribu f. **tribal** adj tribal. **tribesman** n miembro de una tribu m.

tribunal (trai'bju:nl) n tribunal m.

tributary ('tribju:təri) n 1 tributario m. 2 geog afluente m.

tribute ('tribju:t) n 1 tributo m. 2 homenaje m.

trick (trik) n 1 truco m. trampa f. 2 burla f. 3 peculiaridad f. vt engañar, trampear, burlar. **trickery** n astucia f. fraude m. **tricky** adj 1 astuto. 2 delicado, difícil.

trickle ('trikəl) n chorro delgado, gotas m. vi gotear.

tricycle ('traisikəl) n triciclo m.

trifle ('traifəl) n 1 bagatela, fruslería f. 2 pizca f. 3 cul dulce de bizcocho, fruta y natillas o crema. vi trifle away malgastar. trifle with jugar con. **trifling** adj insignificante.

trigger ('trigə) n gatillo m. v **trigger off** 1 hacer estallar. 2 provocar.

trill (tril) n 1 trino m. 2 vibración f. vt pronunciar con vibración. vi trinar.

trim (trim) adj aseado. n recorte m. vt 1 cortar. 2 adornar. 3 ordenar.

trio ('triou) n trío m.

trip (trip) n 1 viaje m. 2 tropiezo m. vi 1 andar con paso ligero. 2 tropezar. **trip up** 1 hacer tropezar. 2 coger en la falta.

tripe (traip) n 1 cul callos m pl. 2 inf tonterías f pl.

triple ('tripəl) adj,n triple m. vt triplicar. **triplet**

n 1 mus tresillo m. 2 pl trillizos m pl. **triplicate** adj,n triplicado m.

tripod ('traipɔd) n trípode m.

trite (trait) adj vulgar, trivial.

triumph ('traiʌmf) n triunfo m. vi triunfar. **triumphant** adj triunfante. **triumphantly** adv triunfalmente.

trivial ('triviəl) adj trivial.

trod (trɔd) v see **tread**.

trodden ('trɔdn) v see **tread**.

trolley ('trɔli) n carretilla f. **tea trolley** mesita de ruedas f.

trombone (trɔm'boun) n trombón m.

troop (tru:p) n 1 mil tropa f. 2 grupo m. vi marchar.

trophy ('troufi) n trofeo m.

tropic ('trɔpik) n trópico m. **tropical** adj trópico.

trot (trɔt) n trote m. vi trotar. **trotter** n cul pata de cerdo f.

trouble ('trʌbəl) n 1 aflicción f. 2 dificultad f. 3 conflicto m. vt 1 afligir. 2 molestar. **troublemaker** n alborotador m.

trough (trɔf) n abrevadero, comedero m.

troupe (tru:p) n Th compañía f.

trousers ('trauzəz) n pl pantalones m pl.

trout (traut) n trucha f.

trowel ('trauəl) n 1 desplantador m. 2 paleta f.

truant ('truənt) n novillero m. **play truant** hacer novillos. **truancy** n ausencia sin permiso f.

truce (tru:s) n tregua f.

truck (trʌk) n 1 camión m. 2 carretilla f. **truck driver** n camionero m.

trudge (trʌdʒ) vi caminar con pena. n caminata f.

true (tru:) adj 1 verdadero. 2 auténtico. 3 fiel, leal. 4 conforme. **be true** ser verdad. **truly** adv verdaderamente. **yours truly** le saluda atentamente.

truffle ('trʌfəl) n trufa f.

trump (trʌmp) n triunfo m. vt game fallar, inventar. vi triunfar, poner un triunfo.

trumpet ('trʌmpit) n trompeta f. vt trompetear. vi barritar. **trumpet blast** n trompetazo m.

truncheon ('trʌntʃən) n porra f.

trunk (trʌŋk) n 1 anat tronco m. 2 baúl m. 3 zool trompa f.

trust (trʌst) n 1 confianza f. 2 comm crédito m. 3 cargo m. obligación f. **on trust** al fiado. ~vt 1 confiar. 2 comm dar al fiado. 3 esperar. vi esperar, confiar. **trusted** adj leal, de confianza. **trustee** n 1 síndico m. 2 depositario m. **trustworthy** adj 1 confiable, de confianza. 2 fidedigno.

truth (truːθ) n 1 verdad f. **truthful** adj verídico, veraz.

try (trai) n 1 tentativa f. 2 game ensayo m. vt 1 intentar, probar. 2 ensayar. 3 law procesar. vi probar. **try on** probarse. **try out** someter a prueba. **trying** adj molesto.

tsar (tsɑː) n zar m. **tsarina** n zarina f.

T-shirt n camiseta f.

tub (tʌb) n cubo m. tina, cuba f.

tuba ('tjuːbə) n tuba f.

tube (tjuːb) n 1 tubo m. 2 mot metro m. **tube station** n estación de metro f.

tuber ('tjuːbə) n tubérculo m.

tuberculosis (tjuːbəːkjuˈlousis) n tuberculosis f.

tuck (tʌk) n alforza f. pliegue m. vt alforzar, plegar.

Tuesday ('tjuːzdi) n martes m.

tuft (tʌft) n 1 copete, mechón m. 2 manojo m.

tug (tʌg) n 1 tirón, estirón m. 2 naut remolcador m. **tug of war** n lucha de cuerda f. ~vt tirar de, arrastrar.

tuition (tjuːˈiʃən) n enseñanza f.

tulip ('tjuːlip) n tulipán m.

tumble ('tʌmbəl) n caída, voltereta f. vi caer, tropezar. **tumbler** n vaso m.

tummy ('tʌmi) n estómago, vientre m.

tumour ('tjuːmə) n tumor m.

tumult ('tjuːmʌlt) n tumulto m.

tuna ('tjuːnə) n atún m.

tune (tjuːn) n 1 aire m. melodía f. 2 tono m. **change one's tune** mudar de tono. ~vt,vi afinar, acordar, templar. **tune in** sintonizar. **tuneful** adj melodioso.

tunic ('tjuːnik) n túnica f.

Tunisia (tjuːˈniziə) n Túnez m. **Tunisian** adj,n tunecino m.

tunnel ('tʌnəl) n túnel m. vi construir un túnel.

tunny ('tʌni) n atún m.

turban ('təːbən) n turbante m.

turbine ('təːbain) n turbina f.

turbot ('təːbət) n rodaballo m.

turbulent ('təːbjulənt) adj turbulento. **turbulence** n turbulencia f.

turf (təːf) n 1 césped m. 2 turba f. vt encespedar. **turf out** echar.

turkey ('təːki) n pavo m.

Turkey ('təːki) n Turquía f. **Turk** n turco m. **Turkish** adj turco.

turmeric ('təːmərik) n cúrcuma f.

turmoil ('təːmɔil) n desorden m. confusión f.

turn (təːn) n 1 vuelta f. 2 giro, cambio de dirección m. 3 vez f. turno m. **good turn** favor m. ~vt volver, girar. vi girar, dar vueltas. **turning** n vuelta f. **turnover** n 1 volumen de ventas m. 2 cul empanada de fruta f. **turnstile** n torniquete m. **turntable** n placa giratoria f.

turnip ('təːnip) n nabo m.

turpentine ('təːpəntain) n 1 aguarrás m invar. 2 trementina f.

turquoise ('təːkwɔiz) n turquesa f.

turret ('tʌrət) n 1 arch torreón m. 2 torre f.

turtle ('təːtl) n tortuga marina f.

tusk (tʌsk) n colmillo m.

tussle ('tʌsəl) n lucha, pelea f. vi luchar.

tutor ('tjuːtə) n preceptor, profesor particular m. vt enseñar. **tutorial** adj preceptoral. n clase particular f.

tweed (twiːd) n tela de lana escocesa f.

tweezers ('twiːzəz) n pl pinzas f pl.

twelve (twelv) adj,n doce m. **twelfth** adj duodécimo.

twenty ('twenti) adj,n veinte m. **twentieth** adj vigésimo.

twice (twais) adv dos veces.

twiddle ('twidl) n vuelta f. vt girar, hacer girar. **twiddle one's thumbs** voltear los pulgares.

twig (twig) n ramita f.

twilight ('twailait) n crepúsculo m. adj crepuscular.

twin (twin) n gemelo m.

twine (twain) n guita f. bramante m. vt 1 tejer. 2 ceñir. vi enroscarse, trepar.

twinge (twindʒ) n punzada f.

twinkle ('twiŋkəl) n centelleo m. vi centellear. **twinkling** adj centelleante, risueño.

twirl (twəːl) n vuelta f. giro m. vt volver rápidamente.

twist (twist) vt torcer, retorcer. n 1 torsión f. 2 torzal m. 3 vuelta f. 4 sesgo m.

twitch (twitʃ) n contracción nerviosa f. tic m. vt tirar ligeramente de. vi crisparse.

twitter ('twitə) vi gorjear. n gorjeo m.

two (tuː) adj,n dos m. **two-faced** adj doble, falso. **twosome** n pareja f. **two-way** adj de dos direcciones.

tycoon (taiˈkuːn) n magnate m.

type (taip) n tipo m. vt,vi escribir a máquina. **typewriter** n máquina de escribir f. **typist** n mecanógrafo m.

typhoid ('taifɔid) n fiebre tifoidea f.

typhoon (taiˈfuːn) n tifón m.

typical ('tipikəl) adj típico.

tyrant ('tairənt) n tirano m. **tyranny** n tiranía f.

tyre ('taiə) n neumático m. **spare tyre** neumático de recambio m.

U

ubiquitous (ju:'bikwitəs) adj omnipresente. **ubiquity** n omnipresencia f.

udder ('ʌdə) n ubre f.

ugly ('ʌgli) adj feo.

ulcer ('ʌlsə) n úlcera f.

ulterior (ʌl'tiəriə) adj ulterior. **ulterior motive** motivo oculto m.

ultimate ('ʌltimət) adj último, final. **ultimatum** n, pl -**tums** or -**ta** ultimátum m.

ultraviolet (ʌltrə'vaiələt) adj ultravioleta.

umbrella (ʌm'brelə) n paraguas m invar.

umpire ('ʌmpaiə) n árbitro m. vt,vi arbitrar.

unable (ʌn'eibəl) adj incapaz. **be unable** no poder.

unacceptable (ʌnək'septəbəl) adj inaceptable.

unaccompanied (ʌnə'kʌmpnid) adj sin acompañamiento.

unanimous (ju:'naniməs) adj unánime.

unarmed (ʌn'a:md) adj desarmado.

unattractive (ʌnə'træktiv) adj poco atractivo.

unavoidable (ʌnə'vɔidəbl) adj inevitable.

unaware (ʌnə'wɛə) adj ignorante. **be unaware** ignorar, no saber. **unawares** adv de improviso.

unbalanced (ʌn'bælənst) adj desequilibrado.

unbearable (ʌn'bɛərəbəl) adj inaguantable, insoportable.

unbelievable (ʌnbi'li:vəbəl) adj increíble.

unbend (ʌn'bend) vt endevezar. vi inf suavizarse.

unbreakable (ʌn'breikəbəl) adj irrompible.

unbutton (ʌn'bʌtn) vt desabotonar.

uncalled-for adj 1 gratuito. 2 impertinente.

uncanny (ʌn'kæni) adj misterioso.

uncertain (ʌn'sə:tn) adj incierto. **be uncertain of** no estar seguro de.

uncle ('ʌŋkəl) n tío m.

unclear (ʌn'kliə) adj oscuro.

uncomfortable (ʌn'kʌmftəbəl) adj incómodo.

unconscious (ʌn'kɔnʃəs) adj 1 inconsciente. 2 med sin sentido. n **the unconscious** lo inconsciente neu.

unconventional (ʌnkən'venʃnəl) adj poco convencional.

uncooked (ʌn'kukt) adj crudo.

uncouth (ʌn'ku:θ) adj grosero.

uncover (ʌn'kʌvə) vt descubrir, destapar.

undecided (ʌndi'saidid) adj indeciso.

undeniable (ʌndi'naiəbəl) adj innegable.

under ('ʌndə) adv debajo, abajo. prep 1 debajo de, bajo. 2 inferior a.

undercharge (ʌndə'tʃa:dʒ) vt cobrar menos del precio justo a.

undercoat ('ʌndəkout) n primera capa f.

undercover ('ʌndəkʌvə) adj secreto.

undercut (ʌndə'kʌt) vt competir con (rebajando los precios).

underdeveloped (ʌndədi'veləpd) adj subdesarrollado.

underdone (ʌndə'dʌn) adj poco hecho, medio asado.

underestimate (ʌndər'estimeit) vt menospreciar.

undergo (ʌndə'gou) vt sufrir, someterse a.

undergraduate (ʌndə'grædjuət) adj de licenciatura. n inf estudiante no graduado m,f.

underground (adv ʌndə'graund; adj,n 'ʌndəgraund) adv bajo tierra. adj 1 subterráneo. 2 clandestino. n metro m.

undergrowth ('ʌndəgrouθ) n maleza f.

underhand (ʌndə'hænd) adj secreto, clandestino.

underline (ʌndə'lain) vt subrayar.

undermine (ʌndə'main) vt socavar, minar.

underneath (ʌndə'ni:θ) adj inferior, de abajo. adv debajo. prep bajo, debajo de.

underpants ('ʌndəpænts) n pl calzoncillos m pl.

underpass ('ʌndəpa:s) n paso inferior m.

underrate (ʌndə'reit) vt menospreciar, subestimar.

understand (ʌndə'stænd) vt,vi 1 comprender, entender. 2 sobreentender. **understanding** n 1 entendimiento m. comprensión f. 2 acuerdo m. adj comprensivo, compasivo.

understate (ʌndə'steit) vt exponer incompletamente, subestimar.

understudy ('ʌndəstʌdi) n suplente m,f.

undertake (ʌndə'teik) vt emprender. **undertake to** comprometerse a. **undertaker** n director de pompas fúnebres m. **undertaker's** n funeraria f. **undertaking** n 1 empresa, tarea f. 2 compromiso m.

undertone ('ʌndətoun) n 1 voz baja. 2 trasfondo m.

underwater (ʌndə'wɔ:tə) adj submarino.

underwear ('ʌndəwɛə) n ropa interior f.

underwent (ʌndə'went) v see **undergo**.

underworld ('ʌndəwə:ld) n 1 infierno m. 2 hampa f.

underwrite ('ʌndərait) vt asegurar.

undesirable (ʌndi'zaiərəbəl) adj,n indeseable m,f.

undo (ʌn'du:) vt deshacer, desatar.

undoubted (ʌn'dautid) adj indudable.

undress (ʌn'dres) vt desnudar.

undue ('ʌndju:) adj indebido.

undulate ('ʌndʒəleit) vi ondular.

unearth (ʌn'ə:θ) vt 1 desenterrar. 2 inf descubrir. **unearthly** adj sobrenatural, misterioso.

uneasy (ʌn'i:zi) adj inquieto.

unemployed (ʌnim'plɔid) adj sin empleo. **unemployment** n paro, desempleo m. desocupación f.

unequal (ʌn'i:kwəl) adj desigual. **unequalled** adj sin par.

uneven (ʌn'i:vən) adj 1 desigual. 2 ondulado.

unfair (ʌn'fɛə) adj injusto.

unfaithful (ʌn'feiθfəl) adj infiel.

unfamiliar (ʌnfə'miliə) adj desconocido. **be unfamiliar with** desconocer.

unfit (ʌn'fit) adj incapaz.

unfold (ʌn'fould) vt 1 desplegar. 2 exponer.

unfortunate (ʌn'fɔ:tʃunət) adj,n desgraciado m.

unfurnished (ʌn'fə:niʃt) adj desamueblado.

ungrateful (ʌn'greitfəl) adj ingrato.

unhappy (ʌn'hæpi) adj infeliz, desdichado.

unhealthy (ʌn'helθi) adj enfermizo.

unicorn ('ju:nikɔ:n) n unicornio m.

uniform ('ju:nifɔ:m) adj,n uniforme m.

unify ('ju:nifai) vt unificar, unir.

unilateral (ju:ni'lætərəl) adj unilateral.

uninterested (ʌn'intrəstid) adj sin interés. **uninteresting** adj poco interesante.

union ('ju:niən) n 1 unión f. 2 enlace m. 3 pol sindicato m.

unique (ju:'ni:k) adj único.

unison ('ju:nizən) n armonía f. **in unison** mus al unísono. **in unison with** de acuerdo con.

unit ('ju:nit) n unidad f. grupo m.

unite (ju:'nait) vt unir, juntar. **united** adj unido. **unity** n unidad f.

United Kingdom n Reino Unido m.

United States of America n Estados Unidos de América m pl.

universe ('ju:nivə:s) n universo m. **universal** adj universal.

university (ju:ni'və:siti) n universidad f. adj universitario.

unkempt (ʌn'kempt) adj 1 desaseado. 2 despeinado.

unkind (ʌn'kaind) adj poco amable.

unlawful (ʌn'lɔ:fəl) adj ilegal.

unless (ən'les) conj a menos que, a no ser que.

unlike (ʌn'laik) adj desemejante, diferente. prep a diferencia de. **unlikely** adj improbable.

unload (ʌn'loud) vt,vi descargar.

unlucky (ʌn'lʌki) adj desgraciado, nefasto. **be unlucky** tener mala suerte.

unnatural (ʌn'nætʃərəl) adj innatural, anormal.

unnecessary (ʌn'nesəsri) adj innecesario.

unofficial (ʌnə'fiʃəl) adj extraoficial, no oficial.

unorthodox (ʌn'ɔ:θədɒks) adj 1 poco ortodoxo. 2 rel heterodoxo.

unpack (ʌn'pæk) vt 1 desembalar. 2 deshacer. vi deshacer las maletas.

unpleasant (ʌn'plezənt) adj desagradable. **unpleasantness** n lo desagradable neu.

unpopular (ʌn'pɒpjulə) adj impopular. **unpopularity** n impopularidad f.

unravel (ʌn'rævəl) vt desenmarañar.

unreasonable (ʌn'ri:zənəbəl) adj irrazonable. **unreasoning** adj irracional.

unreliable (ʌnri'laiəbəl) adj de poca confianza.

unrest (ʌn'rest) n 1 malestar m. inquietud f. 2 pol desorden m.

unruly (ʌn'ru:li) adj ingobernable.

unscrew (ʌn'skru:) vt destornillar.

unsettle (ʌn'setl) vt perturbar, agitar. **unsettled** 1 inquieto. 2 variable. 3 inhabitado. **unsettling** adj perturbador.

unsightly (ʌn'saitli) adj feo.

unsound (ʌn'saund) adj 1 falso. 2 defectuoso.

unsteady (ʌn'stedi) adj inestable.

unsuccessful (ʌnsək'sesfəl) adj fracasado. **be unsuccessful in** no lograr. **unsuccessfully** adv en vano.

untangle (ʌn'tæŋgəl) vt desenmarañar.

untidy (ʌn'taidi) adj desaliñado, en desorden.

untie (ʌn'tai) vt desatar.

until (ʌn'til) conj hasta que. prep hasta.

untrue (ʌn'tru:) adj falso, infiel.

unusual (ʌn'ju:ʒuəl) adj insólito.

unwanted (ʌn'wɒntid) adj no deseado.

unwell (ʌn'wel) adj indispuesto.

unwind (ʌn'waind) vt desenvolver. vi 1 desenvolverse. 2 inf esparcirse.

unwrap (ʌn'ræp) vt desenvolver.

up (ʌp) adv arriba, hacia arriba, de pie. prep en lo alto de. **be up to** ser capaz de.

upbringing ('ʌpbriŋiŋ) n educación f.

upheaval (ʌp'hi:vəl) n 1 solevantamiento m. 2 inf cataclismo, trastorno m.

uphill (ʌp'hil) adj arduo. adv cuesta arriba.

uphold (ʌp'hould) vt sostener, defender.

upholstery (ʌp'houlstəri) n tapicería f. **upholster** vt tapizar, entapizar.
upkeep ('ʌpki:p) n conservación f.
uplift (ʌp'lift) n 1 sustentación f. 2 inf edificación f. vt edificar.
upon (ə'pɔn) prep en, sobre.
upper ('ʌpə) adj superior, más alto, de arriba. **upper class** adj de la clase alta. n clase alta f. **uppermost** adj 1 más alto. 2 principal.
upright ('ʌprait) adj 1 vertical. 2 honrado. adv erguido. n montante m.
uprising ('ʌpraiziŋ) n alzamiento m.
uproar ('ʌprɔ:) n alboroto m. **uproarious** adj tumultuoso.
uproot (ʌp'ru:t) vt arrancar.
upset (v,adj ʌp'set; n 'ʌpset) adj perturbado. n 1 vuelco m. 2 contratiempo m. vt 1 volcar, trastornar. 2 perturbar.
upshot ('ʌpʃɔt) n resultado m.
upside down (ʌpsaid 'daun) adj al revés.
upstairs (ʌp'stɛəz) adv arriba. adj de arriba.
upstream (ʌp'stri:m) adv río arriba.
upward ('ʌpwəd) adj ascendente. **upwards** adv hacia arriba.
Uranus (juə'reinəs) n Urano m.
urban ('ə:bən) adj urbano.
urge (ə:dʒ) n impulso, instinto m. vt animar, impeler, incitar.
urgent ('ə:dʒənt) adj urgente. **urgency** n urgencia f.
urine ('juərin) n orina f. **urinate** vi orinar.
urn (ə:n) n urna f.
us (ʌs) pron 1st pers pl 1 nos. 2 nosotros.
use (v ju:z; n ju:s) n uso, empleo m. usage n uso, tratamiento m. costumbre f. ~t usar, emplear, utilizar. **use up** consumir. **be used to** estar acostumbrado a. **get used to** acostumbrarse a. **used** adj usado, gastado. **useful** adj útil, provechoso. **useless** adj inútil.
usher ('ʌʃə) n 1 ujier m. 2 Th acomodador m.
usual ('ju:ʒuəl) adj usual, acostumbrado, corriente. **as usual** como de costumbre.
usurp (ju'zə:p) vt usurpar.
utensil (ju:'tensəl) n utensilio m.
uterus ('ju:tərəs) n útero m.
utility (ju:'tiliti) adj utilitario. n utilidad f.
utmost ('ʌtmoust) adj mayor, supremo. **do one's utmost** hacer todo lo posible. **to the utmost** hasta más no poder.
utter[1] ('ʌtə) vt pronunciar, proferir.
utter[2] ('ʌtə) adj completo, total, absoluto. **utterly** adv completamente.

V

vacant ('veikənt) adj libre, desocupado. **vacancy** n 1 vacío m. vaciedad f. 2 cuarto vacante m. 3 vacante f.
vacate (və'keit) vt desocupar, dejar vacante.
vacation (və'keiʃən) n vacación f.
vaccine ('væksi:n) n vacuna f. **vaccinate** vt vacunar. **vaccination** n vacunación f.
vacillate ('væsəleit) vi 1 vacilar. 2 oscilar.
vacuum ('vækjuəm) n vacío m. **vacuum cleaner** n aspirador m. **vacuum flask** n termo or termos m.
vagina (və'dʒainə) n vagina f.
vagrant ('veigrənt) adj vagabundo, vagante. n vagabundo m.
vague (veig) adj vago. **vagueness** n vaguedad f.
vain (vein) adj vano. **in vain** en vano.
Valencia (və'lensiə) n Valencia f. **Valencian** adj,n valenciano m.
valiant ('væliənt) adj valiente.
valid ('vælid) adj válido, valedero. **validity** n validez f.
valley ('væli) n valle m.
value ('vælju:) n valor m. vt 1 valorar. 2 estimar, apreciar. **valuable** adj valioso, estimable. **valuables** n pl objetos de valor m pl.
valve ('vælv) n válvula f.
vampire ('væmpaiə) n vampiro m.
van (væn) n mot camioneta f.
vandal ('vændl) n vándalo m. **vandalism** n vandalismo m.
vanilla (və'nilə) n vainilla f.
vanish ('væniʃ) vi desaparecer.
vanity ('væniti) n vanidad f. **vanity case** n neceser de belleza m.
vapour ('veipə) n vapor m.
varnish ('vɑ:niʃ) n barniz m. vt 1 barnizar. 2 esmaltar.
variety (və'raiəti) n variedad f.
various ('vɛəriəs) adj vario, diverso.
vary ('vɛəri) vt,vi variar. **varying** adj diverso, cambiante. **variable** adj,n variable f. **variant** adj,n variante f. **variation** n variación f.
vase (vɑ:z) n jarrón m.
vasectomy (væ'sektəmi) n vasectomía f.
vast (vɑ:st) adj vasto. **vastly** adv sumamente.
vat (væt) n tina f.
Vatican ('vætikən) n Vaticano m.

vault¹ (vɔ:lt) n 1 bóveda f. 2 bodega f. 3 tumba f. vt abovedar.

vault² (vɔ:lt) n salto m. vt, vi saltar.

veal (vi:l) n ternera f.

veer (viə) vi virar, cambiar.

vegetable ('vedʒtəbəl) n 1 bot vegetal f. 2 legumbre, hortaliza f. 3 pl cul verduras f pl. ~adj vegetal. **vegetable garden** n huerto m. **vegetarian** adj,n vegetariano m. **vegetation** n vegetación f.

vehement ('viəmənt) adj vehemente. **vehemence** n vehemencia f.

vehicle ('vi:ikəl) n vehículo m.

veil (veil) n velo m. vt velar.

vein (vein) n vena f.

velocity (və'lɔsiti) n velocidad f.

velvet ('velvit) n terciopelo m.

vendetta (ven'detə) n disputa f.

veneer (vi'niə) n 1 chapa f. enchapado m. 2 apariencia f. vt chapear.

venerate ('venəreit) vt venerar. **venerable** adj venerable. **veneration** n veneración f.

venereal disease (vi'niəriəl) n enfermedad venérea f.

Venezuela (veni'zweilə) n Venezuela f. **Venezuelan** adj,n venezolano m.

vengeance ('vendʒəns) n venganza f. **with a vengeance** con creces. **vengeful** adj vengativo.

venison ('venisən) n carne de venado f.

venom ('venəm) n 1 veneno m. 2 virulencia, malignidad f. **venomous** adj 1 venenoso. 2 virulento, maligno.

vent¹ (vent) n abertura f. respiradero m.

vent² (vent) vt descargar, desahogar. **give vent to** dar salida a.

ventilate ('ventileit) vt ventilar. **ventilation** n ventilación f.

venture ('ventʃə) n aventura, empresa f. vt aventurar. **venture to** atreverse a.

Venus ('vi:nəs) n Venus f.

veranda (və'rændə) n veranda, terraza f.

verb (və:b) n verbo m. **verbal** adj verbal.

verdict ('və:dikt) n 1 law veredicto m. 2 juicio m. sentencia f. 3 opinión f.

verge (və:dʒ) n borde, margen m. **on the verge of** al borde de. v **verge on** acercarse a.

verify ('verifai) vt verificar.

vermicelli (və:mi'seli) n fideos m pl.

vermin ('və:min) n sabandija f.

vermouth ('və:məθ) n vermut m.

vernacular (və'nækjulə) adj vernáculo, vulgar. n 1 lengua vernácula f. 2 inf idioma corriente m.

versatile ('və:sətail) adj versátil. **versatility** n versatilidad f.

verse (və:s) n 1 estrofa f. 2 versículo m 3 poesías f pl. versos m pl. 4 verso m.

version ('və:ʃən) n versión f.

vertebrate ('və:tibreit) adj,n vertebrado m.

vertical ('və:tikəl) adj,n vertical f.

verve (və:v) n brio m. energía f.

very ('veri) adj mismo. adv muy, mucho. **very much** mucho, muchísimo.

vessel ('vesəl) n 1 anat vaso m. 2 vasija f. 3 barco m.

vest (vest) n camiseta f.

vestment ('vestmənt) n vestidura f.

vestry ('vestri) n sacristía f.

vet (vet) n veterinario m. vt examinar, investigar.

veteran ('vetərən) adj,n veterano m.

veterinary surgeon ('vetrinəri) n veterinario m.

veto ('vi:tou) n, pl **vetoes** veto m. vt vedar, vetar.

vex (veks) vt vejar, fastidiar, enojar. **vexation** n vejación f. **vexatious** adj vejatorio, fastidioso. **vexed** adj 1 vejado, enojado, enfadado. 2 debatido. **vexing** adj fastidioso, molesto.

via ('vaiə) prep por, por vía de.

viable ('vaiəbəl) adj viable. **viability** n viabilidad f.

viaduct ('vaiədʌkt) n viaducto m.

vibrate (vai'breit) vt, vi vibrar. **vibration** n vibración f.

vicar ('vikə) n 1 vicario m. 2 párroco, cura m.

vicarious (vi'kɛəriəs) adj experimentado por otro, vicario.

vice¹ (vais) n vicio m.

vice² (vais) n torno de banco m.

vice versa ('və:sə) adv viceversa.

vicinity (vi'siniti) n vecindad f. **in the vicinity** cerca.

vicious ('viʃəs) adj 1 vicioso. 2 virulento, rencoroso.

victim ('viktim) n víctima f. **victimize** vt hacer víctima de, escoger y castigar. **victimization** n persecución f.

victory ('viktri) n victoria f. **victorious** adj victorioso.

video-tape ('vidiouteip) n cinta de video f.

view (vju:) n 1 vista f. 2 opinión f. **in view of** en vista de. ~vt mirar, examinar, contemplar. **view-finder** n visor de imagen m.

wait

vigil ('vidʒil) n vigilia f. **keep vigil** velar. **vigilant** adj vigilante. **vigilance** n vigilancia f.

vigour ('vigə) n vigor m. **vigorous** adj vigoroso.

vile (vail) adj vil.

villa ('vilə) n 1 villa f. 2 chalet m. 3 casa de campo f.

village ('vilidʒ) n aldea f. pueblecito m. **villager** n aldeano m.

villain ('vilən) n 1 malvado m. 2 Th malo m. **villainous** adj malvado.

vindictive (vin'diktiv) adj vengativo. **vindictively** adv rencorosamente. **vindictiveness** n deseo de venganza m.

vine (vain) n 1 vid f. 2 parra f. **vineyard** n viña f.

vinegar ('vinigə) n vinagre m.

vintage ('vintidʒ) n 1 vendimia f. 2 cosecha f. adj clásico. **vintage wine** n vino añejo, vino de calidad m.

vinyl ('vainil) n vinilo m.

viola (vi'oulə) n viola f.

violate ('vaiəleit) vt volar. **violation** n violación f.

violence ('vaiələns) n violencia f. **violent** adj violento.

violet ('vaiələt) adj violado. n 1 bot violeta f. 2 violado m.

violin (vaiə'lin) n violín m.

viper ('vaipə) n víbora f.

virgin ('və:dʒin) adj,n virgen f. **virginal** adj virginal. **virginity** n virginidad f.

Virgo ('və:gou) n Virgo.

virile ('virail) adj viril. **virility** n virilidad f.

virtue ('və:tju:) n virtud f. **virtuous** adj virtuoso. **virtual** adj virtual.

virus ('vairəs) n virus m.

visa ('vi:zə) n visado m.

viscount ('vaikaunt) n vizconde m.

vision ('viʒən) n 1 visión f. 2 clarividencia f. **visible** adj visible. **visibility** n visibilidad f.

visit ('vizit) n visita f. vt visitar. vi hacer visitas.

visual ('viʒual) adj visual. **visualize** vt 1 imaginarse. 2 prever.

vital ('vaitl) adj 1 indispensable, esencial. 2 enérgico. 3 vital. **vitals** n pl partes vitales f pl. **vitality** n vitalidad f.

vitamin ('vitəmin) n vitamina f.

vivacious (vai'veiʃəs) adj vivaz.

vivid ('vivid) adj 1 intenso. 2 vivo.

vocabulary (və'kæbjuləri) n vocabulario m.

vocal ('voukəl) adj vocal. **vocal chords** n pl cuerdas vocales f pl.

vocation (vou'keiʃən) n vocación f.

vocative ('vokətiv) n vocativo m.

vodka ('vodkə) n vodka f.

voice (vois) n voz f. vt expresar.

void (void) adj 1 vacío. 2 law inválido. n vacío, hueco m. vt 1 evacuar, vaciar. 2 law anular.

volatile ('volətail) adj volátil.

volcano (vol'keinou) n volcán m. **volcanic** adj volcánico.

volley ('voli) n 1 descarga f. 2 sport voleo m. vt 1 dirigir. 2 sport volear.

volt (voult) n voltio m. **voltage** n voltaje m.

volume ('volju:m) n 1 volumen m. 2 tomo m.

voluntary ('volən'tiə) n voluntario m. vt ofrecer. **voluntary** adj voluntario.

voluptuous (və'lʌptʃuəs) adj voluptuoso.

vomit ('vomit) n vómito m. vt,vi vomitar.

voodoo ('vu:du:) n vudú m.

vote (vout) n voto m. votación f. vt,vi votar.

vouch (vautʃ) v **vouch for** responder de, responder, confirmar. **vouch that** asegurar que, afirmar que.

voucher ('vautʃə) n 1 documento justificativo m. 2 comm comprobante m. 3 vale m.

vow (vau) n voto m. vt jurar. vi hacer voto de.

vowel ('vauəl) n vocal f.

voyage ('voiidʒ) n viaje m. vi viajar.

vulgar ('vʌlgə) adj 1 vulgar. 2 grosero. **vulgarity** n vulgaridad f.

vulnerable ('vʌlnrəbl) adj vulnerable. **vulnerability** n vulnerabilidad f.

vulture ('vʌltʃə) n buitre m.

W

wad (wod) n 1 taco m. 2 lío m. vt rellenar. **wadding** n 1 taco m. 2 relleno m.

waddle ('wodl) n anadeo m. vi anadear.

wade (weid) vi vadear.

wafer ('weifə) n galleta f. barquillo m.

waft (woft) vt llevar por el aire. vi flotar. n soplo m.

wag (wæg) vt menear. n meneo m.

wage (weidʒ) n salario, jornal m.

waggle ('wægəl) vt menear. n meneo m.

wagon ('wægən) n carro, vagón m.

waif (weif) n niño abandonado m.

wail (weil) n lamento m. vi lamentarse, gemir.

waist (weist) n cintura f. talle m. **waistband** n cinturilla f. **waistcoat** n chaleco m.

wait (weit) vt,vi esperar. **wait on** servir. **waiter** n camarero m. **waiting list** n lista de

299

aspirantes f. **waiting room** n sala de espera f. **waitress** n camarera f.

waive (weiv) vt renunciar a.

wake (weik) vt,vi despertar. n vela f. **waken** vt,vi despertar.

Wales (weilz) n Gales f. **Welsh** adj,n galés. **Welsh** (language) n galés m.

walk (wɔːk) n 1 paseo, andar, paso m. 2 alameda f. 3 caminata f. **go for a walk** dar un paseo. ~vt llevar a paseo. vi andar, pasear, pasearse. **walking stick** n bastón m. **walkout** n 1 salida f. 2 huelga f. **walkover** n triunfo fácil m.

wall (wɔːl) n pared, tapia f. muro m. **wallflower** n alhelí m. **be a wallflower** comer pavo. **wallpaper** n papel de empapelar m. ~vt murar.

wallet ('wɔlit) n cartera f.

wallow ('wɔlou) vi revolcarse.

walnut ('wɔːlnʌt) n nuez f. **walnut tree** n nogal m.

walrus ('wɔːlrəs) n morsa f.

waltz (wɔːls) n vals m. vi valsar.

wand (wɔnd) n vara f.

wander ('wɔndə) vt vagar por. vi 1 vagar. 2 extraviarse.

wane (wein) vi 1 disminuir. 2 menguar. n disminución f.

wangle ('wæŋgəl) n chanchullo m. trampa f. vt agenciarse.

want (wɔnt) n 1 falta f. 2 miseria f. 3 necesidad f. vt 1 necesitar. 2 querer. vi carecer de.

war (wɔː) n guerra f. vi guerrear.

warble ('wɔːbəl) n trino, gorjeo m. vi trinar.

ward (wɔːd) n 1 tutela f. 2 pupilo m. 3 sala f. v **ward off** desviar. **warden** n 1 guardián m. 2 director m. 3 alcaide m. **warder** n guardián, vigilante m. **wardrobe** n 1 vestidos m pl. 2 vestuario m. 3 armario m.

warehouse ('wɛəhaus) n almacén, depósito m.

warm (wɔːm) adj 1 caliente. 2 cálido. 3 caluroso. **be warm** tener calor. ~vt 1 calentar. 2 alegrar. **warm-blooded** adj 1 de sangre caliente. 2 apasionado. **warm-hearted** adj bondadoso, afectuoso. **warm-up** n 1 sport ejercicios m pl. 2 preparativos m pl.

warn (wɔːn) vt 1 advertir. 2 amonestar. 3 prevenir. **warning** n 1 aviso m. 2 advertencia f.

warp (wɔːp) n 1 urdimbre f. 2 deformación f. vt 1 deformar. 2 pervertir. vi deformarse.

warrant ('wɔrənt) n 1 autorización f. 2 cédula f. 3 garantía f. vt 1 autorizar. 2 garantizar. f.

warrant officer n suboficial m. **warranty** n garantía f.

warren ('wɔrən) n 1 madriguera f. 2 conejera f.

warrior ('wɔriə) n guerrero m.

wart (wɔːt) n verruga f.

wary ('wɛəri) adj cauteloso, cauto.

was (wəz; stressed wɔz) v see **be**.

wash (wɔʃ) n 1 lavado m. 2 ropa sucia f. 3 remolino m. vt 1 lavar. 2 fregar. vi lavarse. **washbasin** n 1 palangana f. 2 lavabo m. **washer** n tech arandela f. **washing** n 1 lavado m. 2 colada f. 3 ropa sucia f. **washing machine** n lavadora f. **wash-out** n fracaso m. **washroom** n aseos m pl.

wasp (wɔsp) n avispa f.

waste (weist) adj 1 desechado. 2 inútil. 3 yermo. n 1 despilfarro m. 2 desperdicio m. 3 pérdida f. 4 desierto m. vt despilfarrar. **wastepaper bin** or **basket** n papelera f.

watch (wɔtʃ) n 1 vigilancia f. 2 guardia f. 3 reloj m. vt 1 guardar. 2 observar. vi mirar. **watchdog** n perro guardián m. **watchful** adj 1 vigilante. 2 desvelado.

water ('wɔːtə) n agua m. vt 1 regar. 2 mojar. **water-closet** n retrete m. **watercolour** n acuarela f. **watercress** n berro m. **waterfall** n cascada f. **waterlogged** adj 1 anegado. 2 empapado. **watermark** n filigrana f. **watermelon** n sandía f. **waterproof** adj,n impermeable m. vt impermeabilizar. **watertight** adj 1 impermeable. 2 inf irrefutable. **waterworks** n central depuradora f. **watery** adj 1 acuoso. 2 húmedo. 3 lloroso.

watt (wɔt) n vatio m.

wave (weiv) n 1 ola f. 2 onda f. 3 ademán m. vt 1 ondear. 2 agitar. vi hacer señales. **waveband** n banda de ondas f. **wavelength** n longitud de onda f. **wavy** adj ondulado.

waver ('weivə) vi 1 oscilar. 2 vacilar.

wax[1] (wæks) n cera. vt encerar.

wax[2] (wæks) vi crecer.

way (wei) n 1 camino m. 2 ruta f. 3 vía f. 4 modo m. **by the way** a propósito. **give way** ceder el paso.

waylay (wei'lei) vt acechar.

wayward ('weiwəd) adj 1 travieso. 2 caprichoso. 3 voluntarioso.

we (wiː) pron 1st pers pl nosotros, nosotras.

weak (wiːk) adj 1 débil. 2 flojo. 3 tenue. **weaken** vt 1 debilitar. 2 disminuir. **weakling** n 1 persona débil f. 2 cobarde m. **weakminded** adj 1 vacilante. 2 imbécil. **weakwilled** adj de voluntad débil.

wealth (welθ) n 1 riqueza f. 2 abundancia f. **wealthy** adj rico.

weapon ('wepən) n arma m.

wear* (wɛə) n 1 uso m. 2 deterioro m. vt 1 llevar. 2 usar. **wear away** desgastar. ~vi durar.

weary ('wiəri) adj 1 cansado. 2 aburrido. vt cansar.

weasel ('wi:zəl) n comadreja f.

weather ('weðə) n tiempo m. **under the weather** destemplado. ~vt 1 aguantar. 2 curtir. vi desgastarse.

weave* (wi:v) n 1 tejido m. 2 textura f. vt,vi tejer.

web (web) n 1 tela f. 2 telaraña f. 3 membrana f.

wedding ('wediŋ) n 1 boda f. 2 casamiento m. **wedding ring** n anillo de boda m.

wedge (wedʒ) n 1 cuña f. 2 calza f. vt 1 acuñar, calzar. 2 sujetar.

Wednesday ('wenzdi) n miércoles m.

weed (wi:d) n 1 hierba mala f. vt 1 escardar. 2 suprimir.

week (wi:k) n semana f. **weekday** n día laborable m. **weekend** n fin de semana m.

weep* (wi:p) vt,vi llorar.

weigh (wei) vt 1 pesar. 2 ponderar. 3 agobiar. vi pesar. **weighbridge** n báscula de puente f. **weight** n 1 peso m. 2 pesa f. 3 carga f. **put on weight** engordar. **weight-lifting** n levantamiento de pesos m.

weird ('wiəd) adj 1 misterioso. 2 raro.

welcome ('welkəm) adj 1 bienvenido. 2 grato. **you are welcome!** ¡de nada! ~n bienvenida f. vt dar la bienvenida a.

weld (weld) vt 1 soldar. 2 unir.

welfare ('welfɛə) n 1 bienestar m. 2 prosperidad f. 3 asistencia social f.

well¹ (wel) n 1 pozo m. 2 hueco m. vi brotar.

well² (wel) adv bien. **as well** también. **well!** ¡vaya! ~adj 1 bien. 2 sano.

well-bred adj 1 bien educado. 2 de pura raza.

well-built adj 1 de construcción sólida. 2 fornido.

well-known adj conocido.

well-off adj 1 acomodado. 2 adinerado.

well-paid adj bien pagado.

well-spoken adj bien hablado.

well-to-do adj pudiente.

well-worn adj 1 raído. 2 trillado.

went (went) v see **go**.

wept (wept) v see **weep**.

were (wə:) v see **be**.

west (west) n oeste, occidente m. adj occidental. **westerly** adj del oeste. **western** adj occidental, del oeste. n novela o película del oeste f. **westward** adj al oeste, occidental. adv hacia el oeste. **westwards** adv hacia el oeste.

West Indies ('indiz) n Antillas f.

wet (wet) adj 1 mojado. 2 húmedo. 3 lluvioso. n lluvia f. vt mojar.

whack (wæk) n 1 golpe m. 2 tentativa f. 3 inf porción f. vt golpear.

whale (weil) n ballena f.

wharf (wɔ:f) n, pl **wharves** or **wharfs** muelle m.

what (wɔt) adj 1 que. 2 qué, cuál de. pron 1 el que, la que, lo que. 2 ¿qué? ¿cómo? 3 ¡cómo! **whatever** pron 1 lo que. 2 todo lo que. adj cualquier.

wheat (wi:t) n trigo m.

wheedle ('wi:dl) vt engatusar.

wheel (wi:l) n 1 rueda f. 2 volante m. vt hacer girar. vi 1 girar. 2 dar vueltas. **wheelbarrow** n carretilla f. **wheelchair** n silla de ruedas f.

wheeze (wi:z) n respiración silbante f. vt,vi jadear, respirar con dificultad.

whelk (welk) n caracol de mar, buccino m.

when (wen) adv cuándo. conj cuando. **whenever** adv 1 siempre que. 2 cuando quiera que. 3 cuando.

where (wɛə) adv 1 ¿dónde? 2 donde. 3 adonde. **whereabouts** adv ¿dónde? n paradero m. **whereas** conj 1 visto que, mientras. 2 considerando que. **whereby** adv por lo cual, por donde. **whereupon** adv con lo cual, sobre lo cual. **wherever** adv dondequiera que.

whether ('weðə) conj 1 si. 2 que.

which (witʃ) adj ¿que? ¿cuál? pron 1 ¿cuál? 2 que, lo que. 3 el que, el cual, lo cual. **whichever** adj cualquier. pron 1 cualquiera. 2 el que, la que.

whiff (wif) n 1 soplo m. 2 olorcillo m. vt soplar.

while (wail) conj also **whilst** 1 mientras. 2 aunque. n tiempo, rato m.

whim (wim) n capricho, antojo m. **whimsical** adj 1 caprichoso. 2 fantástico.

whimper ('wimpə) n quejido, gemido m. vi 1 lloriquear. 2 gemir.

whine (wain) n quejido, gimoteo m. vi gimotear.

whip (wip) vt 1 azotar. 2 cul batir. **whip up** avivar. ~n 1 látigo m. 2 azote m. **whip-round** n colecta f.

whippet ('wipit) n perro lebrel m.

whir (wə:) vi zumbar, runrunear.

whirl (wə:l) n 1 giro m. 2 rotación f. 3 remolino m. vt hacer girar. vi girar. **whirlwind** n torbellino m.

whisk[1] (wisk) n movimiento brusco m. vi moverse rápidamente.

whisk[2] (wisk) n batidor m. vt batir.

whisker ('wiskə) n 1 pelo de la barba m. 2 pl barbas f pl. 3 pl bigotes m pl.

whisky ('wiski) n whisky m.

whisper ('wispə) n 1 cuchicheo m. 2 susurro m. 3 rumor m. vt susurrar. vi cuchichear.

whistle ('wisəl) n 1 silbido m. 2 silbato m. vt,vi silbar.

white (wait) adj,n blanco m. **whitewash** n 1 jalbegue m. 2 excusas f pl. vt 1 enjalbegar. 2 encubrir.

whiting ('waitiŋ) n pescadilla f.

Whitsun ('witsən) n Pentecostés m invar.

whiz (wiz) vi silbar, zumbar. n silbido, zumbido m.

who (hu:) pron 1 quién. 2 quiénes. 3 que. 4 el que, quien. **whoever** pron 1 quienquiera que, cualquiera que. 2 ¿quién?

whole (houl) adj 1 todo. 2 entero. 3 sano. n 1 todo m. 2 conjunto m. **on the whole** en general. **wholehearted** adj entusiasta. **wholemeal** adj íntegro. n harina integral f. **wholesale** n venta al por mayor f. adj 1 mayorista. 2 en masa. **wholesome** adj saludable, sano. **wholly** adv completamente, enteramente.

whom (hu:m) pron 1 a quién. 2 que, a quien, quienes.

whooping cough ('hu:piŋ) n tos ferina f.

whore (hɔ:) n puta f.

whose (hu:z) pron 1 ¿de quién? 2 cuyo, cuya, cuyos, cuyas.

why (wai) adv por qué. interj ¡como! ¡toma!

wick (wik) n mecha f.

wicked ('wikid) adj 1 malo. 2 perverso. 3 inicuo.

wicket ('wikit) n sport palos m pl. rastrillo m.

wide (waid) adj 1 ancho. 2 extenso. 3 amplio. adv lejos. **far and wide** por todas partes. **widen** vt ensanchar. **widespread** adj 1 extendido. 2 difuso. 3 general.

widow ('widou) n viuda f.

width (widθ) n 1 anchura f. 2 ancho m. 3 amplitud f.

wield (wi:ld) vt 1 manejar. 2 empuñar. 3 ejercer.

wife (waif) n, pl **wives** esposa, mujer f.

wig (wig) n peluca f.

wiggle ('wigəl) n meneo rápido m. vt menear rápidamente.

wild (waild) adj 1 salvaje. 2 silvestre. 3 feroz. 4 furioso. 5 loco. n yermo m. **wildlife** n fauna f.

wilderness ('wildənəs) n desierto, yermo m.

wilful ('wilfəl) adj 1 voluntarioso. 2 testarudo.

will[1] (wil) v aux 1 used in forming the future tense. 2 querer.

will[2] (wil) n 1 voluntad f. 2 albedrío m. 3 testamento m. vt ordenar. **willpower** n fuerza de voluntad f.

willing ('wiliŋ) adj 1 dispuesto. 2 servicial.

willow ('wilou) n sauce m.

wilt (wilt) vt marchitar.

win (win) vt ganar. vi 1 ganar. 2 triunfar. n triunfo m.

wince (wins) vi 1 hacer una mueca de dolor. 2 retroceder. n mueca de dolor f.

winch (wintʃ) n torno m.

wind[1] (wind) n 1 viento m. 2 flatulencia f. 3 aliento m. **windfall** n ganancia inesperada f. **windmill** n molino de viento m. **windpipe** n tráquea f. **windscreen** n parabrisas m invar. **windscreen wiper** n limpiaparabrisas m invar. **windswept** adj azotado por el viento. **windy** adj ventoso.

wind[2] (waind) vt 1 enrollar. 2 devanar. 3 dar vueltas a. **wind up** 1 liquidar. 2 serpentear.

windlass ('windləs) n 1 torno m. 2 cabestrante m.

window ('windou) n 1 ventana f. 2 ventanilla f. 3 escaparate m. **window-shop** vi mirar los escaparates.

wine (wain) n vino m. **wineglass** n copa para vino f.

wing (wiŋ) n 1 ala f. 2 Th bastidores m pl. vt herir en el ala. vi volar. **wing commander** n teniente coronel de aviación m. **wingspan** n envergadura f.

wink (wiŋk) n 1 pestañeo m. 2 guiño m. vt guiñar. vi pestañear.

winkle ('wiŋkəl) n 1 bigarro m. 2 zool caracolillo m.

winter ('wintə) n invierno m. vi invernar.

wipe (waip) vt 1 limpiar. 2 enjugar. **wipe out** borrar. ~n limpión m.

wire ('waiə) n 1 alambre m. 2 telegrama m. vt alambrar. vi poner un telegrama.

wise (waiz) adj 1 sabio. 2 prudente.

wish (wiʃ) n 1 deseo m. 2 ruego m. vt desear, querer. vi desear.

wisp (wisp) n 1 mechón m. 2 vestigio m.

wisteria (wis'tiəriə) n vistaria f.

wistful ('wistfəl) adj 1 triste. 2 pensativo. 3 ansioso.

wit (wit) n 1 inteligencia f. entendimiento m. 2 talento m. 3 ingenio m. 4 gracia f.

witch (witʃ) n bruja f. **witchcraft** n brujería f.

with (wið) prep 1 con. 2 según. 3 de.

withdraw* (wið'drɔ:) vt retirar, sacar.

wither ('wiðə) vi marchitarse. vt 1 marchitar. 2 aplastar.

withhold* (wið'hould) vt 1 retener. 2 ocultar. 3 negar.

within (wið'in) adv dentro. prep 1 dentro de. 2 al alcance de.

without (wið'aut) adv 1 fuera. 2 por fuera. prep 1 sin. 2 a falta de.

withstand* (wið'stænd) vt 1 resistir a. 2 oponerse. 3 aguantar.

witness ('witnəs) n 1 testimonio m. 2 testigo m. **bear witness** atestiguar. vt 1 asistir a, presenciar. 2 ver.

witty ('witi) adj 1 ingenioso. 2 gracioso.

wizard ('wizəd) n 1 hechicero, brujo m. 2 genio m.

wobble ('wɔbəl) vi 1 bambolear. 2 vacilar. n bamboleo m.

woke (wouk) v see **wake.**

woken ('woukən) v see **wake.**

wolf (wulf) n, pl **wolves** 1 lobo m. 2 inf tenorio m.

woman ('wumən) n, pl **women** mujer f. **womanhood** n 1 feminidad f. 2 sexo femenino m.

womb (wu:m) n 1 matriz f. utero m. 2 seno m.

won (wʌn) v see **win.**

wonder ('wʌndə) n 1 maravilla f. 2 admiración f. 3 prodigio m. vt,vi 1 preguntarse. 2 admirarse. **wonderful** adj 1 maravilloso. 2 estupendo.

wonky ('wɔŋki) adj poco firme, poco seguro.

wood (wud) n 1 bosque m. 2 madera f. 3 leña f. **woodcock** n chochaperdiz f. **wooden** adj 1 de madera. 2 inexpresivo. **woodland** n bosque, arbolado m. **woodpecker** n pájaro carpintero m. **woodpigeon** n paloma torcaz f. **woodwind** n mus instrumento de viento de madera m. **woodwork** n 1 maderaje m. 2 carpintería f. **woodworm** n carcoma f.

wool (wul) n lana f. adj lanar. **woollen** adj 1 de lana. 2 lanar. **woolly** adj 1 lanudo, lanoso. 2 borroso.

word (wə:d) n 1 palabra f. 2 vocablo m. 3 aviso m. 4 orden f. vt redactar.

wore (wɔ:) v see **wear.**

work (wə:k) n 1 trabajo m. 2 labor f. 3 obra f. vt 1 trabajar. 2 bordar. vi funcionar. **worker** n trabajador, obrero m. **working class** adj clase obrera. **workman** n 1 obrero m. 2 trabajador m. **workmanship** n habilidad f. **workshop** n taller m.

world (wə:ld) n mundo m. **worldly** adj mundano. **worldwide** adj mundial, universal.

worm (wə:m) n 1 gusano m. 2 lombriz f. 3 inf canalla m.

wormwood ('wə:mwud) n ajenjo m.

worn (wɔ:n) v see **wear.** adj 1 gastado. 2 estropeado. 3 inservible.

worry ('wʌri) n 1 preocupación f. 2 cuidado m. vt 1 preocupar. 2 molestar. vi preocuparse.

worse ('wə:s) adj 1 peor. 2 inferior. **so much the worse** tanto peor. ~adv peor. **worsen** vt agravar, hacer peor. vi empeorar.

worship ('wə:ʃip) n 1 adoración f. 2 veneración f. 3 culto m. vt adorar. vi 1 adorar. 2 dar culto.

worst (wə:st) adj 1 peor. n lo peor neu. **get the worst of it** salir perdiendo.

worsted ('wustid) n estambre m.

worth (wə:θ) adj 1 digno de. 2 que vale. **be worth** valer. ~n 1 valor m. 2 mérito m. **worthwhile** adj 1 valioso. 2 que vale la pena. **worthy** adj 1 meritorio. 2 honesto. **worthy of** digno de.

would* (wəd; stressed wud) v see **will**[1].

wound[1] (wu:nd) n herida f. vt herir.

wound[2] (waund) v see **wind**[2].

wove (wouv) v see **weave.**

woven ('wouvn) v see **weave.**

wrangle ('ræŋgəl) n altercado m. riña f. vi 1 reñir. 2 regatear.

wrap (ræp) n bata f. abrigo m. vt 1 envolver. 2 arropar.

wrath (rɔθ) n ira f.

wreath (ri:θ) n 1 guirnalda f. 2 corona f. 3 (of smoke) espiral f.

wreathe (ri:ð) vt 1 ceñir. 2 trenzar. 3 enguirnaldar.

wreck (rek) n 1 naufragio m. 2 buque naufragado m. 3 destrucción f. 4 ruina f. vt hundir, naufragar. **wreckage** n 1 naufragio m. 2 restos m pl.

wren (ren) n chochín m.

wrench (rentʃ) n **1** torcedura f. **2** tirón m. **3** llave inglesa f. vt **1** arrancar. **2** torcer.

wrestle ('resəl) n lucha f. vi luchar.

wretch (retʃ) n desgraciado, infeliz m. **wretched** adj **1** desgraciado. **2** miserable. **3** horrible.

wriggle ('rigəl) n **1** meneo m. **2** serpenteo m. vt menear. vi culebrear.

wring (riŋ) vt **1** torcer. **2** exprimir. **3** acongojar.

wrinkle ('riŋkəl) n **1** arruga f. **2** pliegue m. vt arrugar. vi plegarse.

wrist (rist) n muñeca f.

writ (rit) n **1** escritura f. **2** mandato m. **3** autoridad f.

write* (rait) vt,vi escribir. **write down** apuntar. **write out** copiar. **write up** redactar. **writing paper** n papel de escribir m.

writhe (raið) vi **1** retorcerse. **2** debatirse.

wrong (rɔŋ) adj **1** malo. **2** injusto. **3** erróneo. **4** impropio. n **1** mal m. **2** injusticia f. vt agraviar.

wrote (rout) v see **write.**

wrought iron (rɔːt) n hierro forjado m.

wrung (rʌŋ) v see **wring.**

wry (rai) adj **1** torcido. **2** irónico. **wry face** mueca.

X

xenophobia (zenə'foubiə) n xenofobia f.

Xerox ('ziərɔks) n Tdmk xérox m.

X-ray n radiografía f. **x-rays** rayos x m pl. vt radiografiar.

xylophone ('zailəfoun) n xilófono m.

Y

yacht (jɔt) n yate m. vi navegar en yate. **yachtsman** n deportista náutico m.

yank (jæŋk) n tirón m. vt tirar de.

yap (jæp) n ladrido agudo m. vi **1** ladrar. **2** inf charlar.

yard[1] (jɑːd) n yarda f. **yardstick** n criterio m. norma f.

yard[2] (jɑːd) n **1** patio m. **2** corral m.

yarn (jɑːn) n **1** hilo m. **2** cuento m. vi contar historias.

yawn (jɔːn) n bostezo m. vi bostezar.

year (jiə) n año m.

yearn (jɔːn) vi suspirar. **yearn for** anhelar.

yeast (jiːst) n levadura f.

yell (jel) n grito, alarido m. vt gritar, vociferar. vi gritar.

yellow ('jelou) adj **1** amarillo. **2** inf cobarde. n amarillo m.

yelp (jelp) n gañido m. vi **1** gañir. **2** gritar.

yes (jes) adv sí.

yesterday ('jestədi) adv,n ayer m. **the day before yesterday** anteayer.

yet (jet) adv todavía, aún. **as yet** hasta ahora. ~conj con todo, sin embargo.

yew (juː) n tejo m.

Yiddish ('jidiʃ) adj judío. n lengua alemánhebreo usado por algunos judíos f.

yield (jiːld) n **1** producción f. **2** cosecha f. **3** rédito m. vt **1** producir. **2** rendir. vi rendirse.

yoghurt ('jɔgət) n yogur m.

yoke (jouk) n **1** yunta f. **2** canesú m. **3** yugo m. vt uncir.

yolk (jouk) n yema f.

yonder ('jɔndə) adj aquel. adv allá, a lo lejos.

you (juː) pron 2nd pers s **1** fam tú, te, ti. **with you** contigo. **2** s fml usted, le, la. **with you** consigo. **3** pl fam vosotros, vosotras, os. **4** pl fml ustedes, los, las, les.

young (jʌŋ) adj **1** joven. **2** nuevo. **3** menor. n cría f. **youngster** n joven, jovencito m.

your (jɔː, juə) poss adj 2nd pers s **1** fam tu, tus. **2** pl fam vuestro, vuestra, vuestros, vuestras. **3** fml su, sus. **yours** poss pron 2nd pers s **1** fam (el) tuyo, (la) tuya, (los) tuyos, (las) tuyas. **2** fam pl (el) vuestro, (la) vuestra, (los) vuestros, (las) vuestras. **3** fml (el) suyo, (la) suya, (los) suyos, (las) suyas. **yours faithfully** le saluda atentamente. **yourself** pron **1** s fam tu mismo, tu misma. **2** s fml usted mismo. **yourselves 1** pl fam vosotros mismos. **2** pl fml ustedes mismos.

youth (juːθ) n **1** juventud f. **2** joven m.

Yugoslavia (ju:gou'sla:viə) n Yugoslavia f. **Yugoslav** adj,n yugoslavo m.

Z

zeal (ziːl) n celo, entusiasmo m.

zebra ('zebrə) n cebra f. **zebra crossing** n paso de peatones m.

zenith ('zeniθ) n cenit m.

zero ('ziərou) adj,n cero m.

zest (zest) n gusto, entusiasmo m.

zigzag ('zigzæg) n zigzag m. vi zigzaguear.

zinc (ziŋk) n cinc m.

Zionism ('zaiənizəm) n sionismo m.

The Newnes Pocket Reference Series includes:

Foreign Language Dictionaries and Phrasebooks:

Newnes French Dictionary
Newnes German Dictionary
Newnes Italian Dictionary
Newnes Spanish Dictionary
Newnes Arabic Phrase Book
Newnes French Phrase Book
Newnes German Phrase Book
Newnes Greek Phrase Book
Newnes Italian Phrase Book
Newnes Portuguese Phrase Book
Newnes Russian Phrase Book
Newnes Spanish Phrase Book

English Language:

Newnes Pocket English Dictionary
Newnes Pocket Thesaurus of English Words
Newnes Guide to English Usage
Newnes Pocket Dictionary of Quotations
Newnes Pocket Crossword Dictionary

Other subjects:

Newnes Concise Dictionary of Greek and Roman Mythology
Newnes Pocket Dictionary of Business Terms
Newnes Pocket Dictionary of Wines
Newnes Pocket Gazetteer of the World
Newnes Pocket Medical Dictionary

zip (zip) n 1 cremallera f. 2 energía f. 3 silbido m. v **zip up** cerrar la cremallera de.
zither ('ziðə) n cítara f.
zodiac ('zoudiæk) n zodíaco m.
zone (zoun) n zona f.
zoo (zu:) n zoo m.
zoology (zou'ɔlədʒi) n zoología f.
zoom (zu:m) n zumbido. vi 1 zumbar. 2 empinarse.